P9-CFD-909

Sports Illustrated
FOR **KiDS**

YEAR IN 2004
SPORTS

from the Editors of SPORTS ILLUSTRATED FOR KIDS

SCHOLASTIC REFERENCE

Copyright © 2003 by Time Inc.

All rights reserved. Published by Scholastic Inc.
SCHOLASTIC, SCHOLASTIC REFERENCE, and associated logos are trademarks and/or registered trademarks of Scholastic Inc.

SPORTS ILLUSTRATED FOR KIDS and  are registered trademarks of Time Inc.

No part of this publication may be reproduced or stored in a retrieval system or transmitted in any form or by any means, electronic, mechanical, photocopying, recording, or otherwise, without written permission of the publisher. For information regarding permission, write to Scholastic Inc., Attention: Permissions Department, 557 Broadway, New York, N.Y. 10012.

Some material included in this publication is from the SPORTS ILLUSTRATED 2003 Almanac and is used with permission.

Library of Congress Cataloging-in-Publication Data Available

Cover photography credits
Michael Vick: Al Tielemans/Sports Illustrated
Barry Bonds: Julie Jacobson/AP
Serena Williams: Bob Martin/Sports Illustrated
Sarah Hughes: Heinz Kluetmeier/Sports Illustrated
Annika Sorenstam: Darren Carroll
Mario Lemieux: David E. Klutho/Sports Illustrated
Yao Ming: John W. McDonough/Sports Illustrated

Back-cover photography credits
Maurice Clarett: Heinz Kluetmeier/Sports Illustrated
Lisa Leslie: John W. McDonough/Sports Illustrated
Landon Donovan: Simon Bruty/Sports Illustrated

SPORTS ILLUSTRATED FOR KIDS Year in Sports 2004 is a production of SPORTS ILLUSTRATED FOR KIDS and SPORTS ILLUSTRATED FOR KIDS Books: Erin Egan, Senior Editor/Editorial Projects; Beth Bugler, Art Director; Mark Rosenthal, Designer; Andrew Erbelding, Photo Editor; Nick Friedman, John Rolfe, Senior Editors; Ellen Cosgrove, Justin Tejada, Andrea Whittaker, Associate Editors; Sachin Shenolikar, Chief of Reporters; Josh Blumkin, André Carter, Ted Keith, Shawn Nicholls, Michelle Yu, Reporters; Robert J. Rohr (Manager), Copy Desk; Howard Gotfryd (Manager), Steve Chanin (Deputy), Page Makeup; Marc Bertucco, Eric Ramos, Data Entry.

Scholastic Reference staff: Kenneth Wright, Editorial Director; Mary Varilla Jones, Editor; Danielle Denega, Assistant Editor; Manuela Soares, Managing Editor; Karen Capria, Production Editor; Nancy Sabato, Art Director; Kristen Ekeland, Assistant Designer; Kirk Howle, Manufacturing Coordinator

0-439-52027-4

10 9 8 7 6 5 4 3 2 1   03 04 05 06 07

Printed in U.S.A. 23
First printing, December 2003

CONTENTS

FOOTBALL

An explosion of offense and record-breaking feats, most famously by running back Emmitt Smith of the Dallas Cowboys, were the big stories of 2002. But it was the NFL's most dominating defense that stole the show.

Smith became the NFL's all-time leading rusher in week 8. In the fourth quarter against the Seattle Seahawks, he rumbled 11 yards to break Walter Payton's all-time record of 16,726 rushing yards. Smith finished the game with 109 yards and 1 touchdown. He finished the season with 17,162 career rushing yards but was released by the Cowboys on February 27, 2003.

Wide receiver Marvin Harrison of the Indianapolis Colts set the NFL record for most catches in a season (143). He was nearly unstoppable on his way to a league-leading 1,722 yards and 11 touchdowns.

The Oakland Raiders were the most productive team on offense, scoring at least 30 points in their first four games. Overall, 26 NFL teams topped the 300-point mark during the season. Only six teams fell below that mark, the fewest teams under 300 points since the NFL-AFL merger, in 1970.

But it was the NFL's stingiest defense, not its most explosive offense, that won the Super Bowl. The Tampa Bay Buccaneers gave

Defensive tackle Warren Sapp of the Tampa Bay Buccaneers celebrated his team's first Super Bowl victory.

JOHN W. McDONOUGH/SPORTS ILLUSTRATED

AFC TEAMS

Baltimore Ravens
Buffalo Bills
Cincinnati Bengals
Cleveland Browns
Denver Broncos
Houston Texans
Indianapolis Colts
Jacksonville Jaguars
Kansas City Chiefs
Miami Dolphins
New England Patriots
New York Jets
Oakland Raiders
Pittsburgh Steelers
San Diego Chargers
Tennessee Titans

up just 12.3 points per game during the season. In Super Bowl XXXVII, they held the Raiders to 269 total yards and only 19 on the ground. They picked off a Super Bowl-record five passes and sacked Raider quarterback Rich Gannon five times. The Bucs won, 48–21, and safety Dexter Jackson, who had two interceptions, was named the game's MVP.

HEINZ KLUETMEIER/SPORTS ILLUSTRATED

NFC TEAMS

Arizona Cardinals
Atlanta Falcons
Carolina Panthers
Chicago Bears
Dallas Cowboys
Detroit Lions
Green Bay Packers
Minnesota Vikings
New Orleans Saints
New York Giants
Philadelphia Eagles
San Francisco 49ers
Seattle Seahawks
St. Louis Rams
Tampa Bay Buccaneers
Washington Redskins

Super Bowl MVP Dexter Jackson picked off two passes in the first half — a Super Bowl record.

2002 NFL Final Standings

AFC East

Team	W	L	T	PCT	PF	PA
y-Jets	9	7	0	.562	359	336
Patriots	9	7	0	.562	381	346
Dolphins	9	7	0	.562	378	301
Bills	8	8	0	.500	379	397

AFC North

Team	W	L	T	PCT	PF	PA
y-Steelers	10	5	1	.656	390	345
x-Browns	9	7	0	.562	344	320
Ravens	7	9	0	.438	316	354
Bengals	2	14	0	.125	279	456

AFC South

Team	W	L	T	PCT	PF	PA
yz-Titans	11	5	0	.688	367	324
x-Colts	10	6	0	.625	349	313
Jaguars	6	10	0	.375	328	315
Texans	4	12	0	.250	213	356

AFC West

Team	W	L	T	PCT	PF	PA
*yz-Raiders	11	5	0	.688	450	304
Broncos	9	7	0	.562	392	344
Chargers	8	8	0	.500	333	367
Chiefs	8	8	0	.500	467	399

NFC East

Team	W	L	T	PCT	PF	PA
*yz-Eagles	12	4	0	.750	415	241
x-Giants	10	6	0	.625	320	279
Redskins	7	9	0	.438	307	365
Cowboys	5	11	0	.312	217	329

NFC North

Team	W	L	T	PCT	PF	PA
y-Packers	12	4	0	.750	398	328
Vikings	6	10	0	.375	390	442
Bears	4	12	0	.250	281	379
Lions	3	13	0	.188	306	451

NFC South

Team	W	L	T	PCT	PF	PA
yz-Buccaneers	12	4	0	.750	346	196
x-Falcons	9	6	1	.594	402	314
Saints	9	7	0	.562	432	388
Panthers	7	9	0	.438	258	302

NFC West

Team	W	L	T	PCT	PF	PA
y-49ers	10	6	0	.625	367	351
Rams	7	9	0	.438	316	369
Seahawks	7	9	0	.438	355	369
Cardinals	5	11	0	.312	262	417

x-clinched playoff berth y-clinched division title z-clinched first-round bye *clinched homefield advantage

KEY — W=win; L=loss; T=tie; PCT=winning percentage; PF=points for; PA=points against

2002 NFL Playoffs

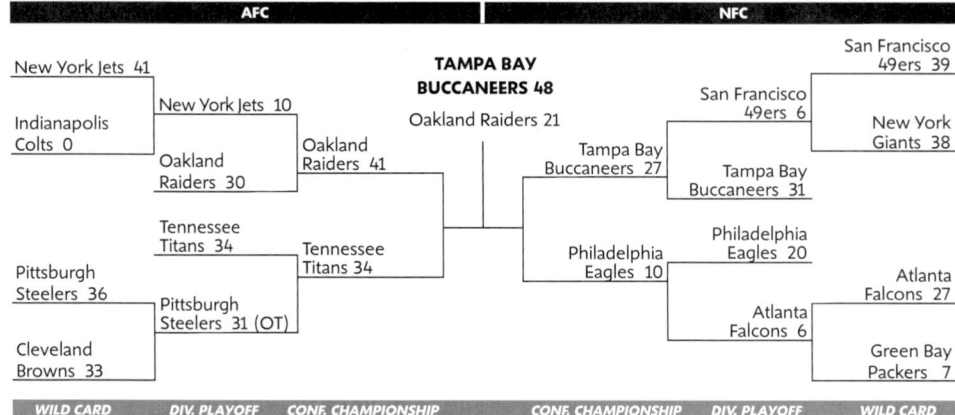

AFC		NFC

AFC ... **NFC**

San Francisco 49ers 39

New York Jets 41

New York Jets 10

TAMPA BAY BUCCANEERS 48

Indianapolis Colts 0

San Francisco 49ers 6

Oakland Raiders 30

Oakland Raiders 41

Oakland Raiders 21

New York Giants 38

Tennessee Titans 34

Tampa Bay Buccaneers 27

Tampa Bay Buccaneers 31

Pittsburgh Steelers 36

Tennessee Titans 34

Philadelphia Eagles 20

Pittsburgh Steelers 31 (OT)

Philadelphia Eagles 10

Atlanta Falcons 27

Cleveland Browns 33

Atlanta Falcons 6

Green Bay Packers 7

WILD CARD   DIV. PLAYOFF   CONF. CHAMPIONSHIP   CONF. CHAMPIONSHIP   DIV. PLAYOFF   WILD CARD

AFC Wild-Card Games

New York Jets 41
Indianapolis Colts 0

SCORING SUMMARY

	1Q	2Q	3Q	4Q	OT	T
COLTS	0	0	0	0		0
JETS	7	17	10	7		41

1ST QUARTER
TD Richie Anderson, 56-yard pass from Chad Pennington (John Hall, extra point), 10:50. Drive: 5 plays, 77 yards in 2:27.

2ND QUARTER
FG John Hall, 41 yards, 14:08. Drive: 9 plays, 46 yards in 5:34.
TD LaMont Jordan, 1-yard run (John Hall, extra point), 9:41. Drive: 7 plays, 39 yards in 4:18.
TD Santana Moss, 4-yard pass from Chad Pennington (John Hall, extra point), 0:37. Drive: 6 plays, 42 yards in 1:02.

3RD QUARTER
FG John Hall, 39 yards, 13:28.
TD Chris Baker, 3-yard pass from Chad Pennington (John Hall, extra point), 1:44. Drive: 11 plays, 74 yards in 6:30.

4TH QUARTER
TD LaMont Jordan, 1-yard run (John Hall, extra point), 4:59. Drive: 13 plays, 64 yards in 9:17.

Pittsburgh Steelers 36
Cleveland Browns 33

SCORING SUMMARY

	1Q	2Q	3Q	4Q	OT	T
BROWNS	7	10	7	9		33
STEELERS	0	7	7	22		36

1ST QUARTER
TD William Green, 1-yard run (Phil Dawson, extra point), 13:44. Drive: 4 plays, 80 yards in 1:16.

2ND QUARTER
TD Dennis Northcutt, 32-yard pass from Kelly Holcomb (Phil Dawson, extra point), 14:38. Drive: 1 play, 32 yards in 0:06.
TD Antwaan Randle El, 66-yard punt return (Jeff Reed, extra point), 9:35.
FG Phil Dawson, 31 yards, 0:49. Drive: 10 plays, 45 yards in 4:24.

3RD QUARTER
TD Dennis Northcutt, 15-yard pass from Kelly Holcomb (Phil Dawson, extra point), 12:11. Drive: 3 plays, 14 yards in 0:49.
TD Plaxico Burress, 6-yard pass from Tommy Maddox (Jeff Reed, extra point), 3:50. Drive: 10 plays, 71 yards in 3:45.

4TH QUARTER
FG Phil Dawson, 24 yards, 14:52. Drive: 8 plays, 64 yards in 3:58.
TD Jerame Tuman, 3-yard pass from Tommy Maddox (Jeff Reed, extra point), 12:28. Drive: 6 plays, 65 yards in 2:24.
TD Andre Davis, 22-yard pass from Kelly Holcomb (Kelly Holcomb 2-point conversion pass to Quincy Morgan failed), 10:17. Drive: 5 plays, 61 yards in 2:11.
TD Hines Ward, 5-yard pass from Tommy Maddox (Jeff Reed, extra point), 3:06. Drive: 10 plays, 77 yards in 2:24.
TD Chris Fuamatu-Ma'afala, 3-yard run (Antwaan Randle El pass to Jerame Tuman for 2-point conversion), 0:54. Drive: 6 plays, 61 yards in 1:41.

NFC Wild-Card Games

San Francisco 49ers 39
New York Giants 38

SCORING SUMMARY

	1Q	2Q	3Q	4Q	OT	T
GIANTS	7	21	10	0		38
49ERS	7	7	8	17		39

1ST QUARTER
TD Terrell Owens, 76-yard pass from Jeff Garcia (Jeff Chandler, extra point), 9:59. Drive: 1 play, 76 yards in 0:11.

NFC Wild-Card Games (cont.)

TD Amani Toomer, 12-yard pass from Kerry Collins (Matt Bryant, extra point), 0:18. Drive: 11 plays, 65 yards in 4:15.

2ND QUARTER

TD Jeremy Shockey, 2-yard pass from Kerry Collins (Matt Bryant, extra point), 12:19. Drive: 5 plays, 61 yards in 2:24.

TD Kevan Barlow, 1-yard run (Jeff Chandler, extra point), 6:05. Drive: 10 plays, 69 yards in 6:14.

TD Amani Toomer, 8-yard pass from Kerry Collins (Matt Bryant, extra point), 2:49. Drive: 1 play, 8 yards in 0:05.

TD Amani Toomer, 24-yard pass from Kerry Collins (Matt Bryant, extra point), 0:10. Drive: 5 plays, 56 yards in 1:43.

3RD QUARTER

TD Tiki Barber, 6-yard run (Matt Bryant, extra point), 9:53. Drive: 6 plays, 54 yards in 2:16.

FG Matt Bryant, 21 yards, 4:27. Drive: 9 plays, 63 yards in 4:20.

TD Terrell Owens, 26-yard pass from Jeff Garcia (Jeff Garcia pass to Terrell Owens for 2-point conversion), 2:03. Drive: 7 plays, 70 yards in 2:24.

4TH QUARTER

TD Jeff Garcia, 14-yard run (Jeff Garcia pass to Terrell Owens for 2-point conversion), 14:55. Drive: 3 plays, 27 yards in 0:41.

FG Jeff Chandler, 25 yards, 7:49. Drive: 15 plays, 74 yards in 5:26.

TD Tai Streets, 13-yard pass from Jeff Garcia (Jeff Garcia 2-point-conversion pass to Terrell Owens failed), 1:00. Drive: 9 plays, 68 yards in 2:01.

Atlanta Falcons 27
Green Bay Packers 7

SCORING SUMMARY

	1Q	2Q	3Q	4Q	OT	T
FALCONS	14	10	3	0		27
PACKERS	0	0	7	0		7

1ST QUARTER

TD Shawn Jefferson, 10-yard pass from Michael Vick (Jay Feely, extra point), 9:17. Drive: 10 plays, 76 yards in 5:43.

TD Artie Ulmer, 1 yard blocked punt return (Jay Feely, extra point), 6:38.

2ND QUARTER

TD T.J. Duckett, 6-yard run (Jay Feely, extra point), 12:06. Drive: 4 plays, 21 yards in 2:30.

FG Jay Feely, 22 yards, 0:00. Drive: 16 plays, 90 yards in 6:34.

3RD QUARTER

TD Donald Driver, 14-yard pass from Brett Favre (Ryan Longwell, extra point), 10:26. Drive: 10 plays, 73 yards in 4:34.

FG Jay Feely, 23 yards, 3:43. Drive: 12 plays, 73 yards in 6:43.

4TH QUARTER

None

AFC Divisional Games
Tennessee Titans 34
Pittsburgh Steelers 31 (OT)

SCORING SUMMARY

	1Q	2Q	3Q	4Q	OT	T
STEELERS	0	13	7	11	0	31
TITANS	14	0	14	3	3	34

1ST QUARTER

TD Steve McNair, 8-yard run (Joe Nedney, extra point), 11:01. Drive: 7 plays, 52 yards in 3:19.

TD Eddie George, 1-yard run (Joe Nedney, extra point), 0:17. Drive: 16 plays, 76 yards in 9:03.

2ND QUARTER

TD Hines Ward, 8-yard pass from Tommy Maddox (Jeff Reed, extra point), 9:29. Drive: 2 plays, 8 yards in 0:38.

FG Jeff Reed, 30 yards, 6:47. Drive: 5 plays, 47 yards in 1:53.

FG Jeff Reed, 39 yards, 0:00. Drive: 8 plays, 61 yards in 1:35.

3RD QUARTER

TD Amos Zereoue, 31-yard run (Jeff Reed, extra point), 14:37. Drive: 1 play, 31 yards in 0:08.

TD Frank Wycheck, 7-yard pass from Steve McNair (Joe Nedney, extra point), 9:37. Drive: 8 plays, 63 yards in 5:00.

TD Erron Kinney, 2-yard pass from Steve McNair (Joe Nedney, extra point), 4:38. Drive: 8 plays, 58 yards in 4:04.

4TH QUARTER

TD Hines Ward, 21-yard pass from Tommy Maddox (Hines Ward pass to Plaxico Burress for 2-point conversion), 10:09. Drive: 6 plays, 65 yards in 2:07.

FG Jeff Reed, 40 yards, 8:30. Drive: 5 plays, 35 yards in 1:24.

FG Joe Nedney, 42 yards, 5:40. Drive: 7 plays, 34 yards in 2:50.

OVERTIME

FG Joe Nedney, 26 yards, 12:45. Drive: 5 plays, 61 yards in 2:15.

Oakland Raiders 30
New York Jets 10

SCORING SUMMARY

	1Q	2Q	3Q	4Q	OT	T
JETS	3	7	0	0		10
RAIDERS	3	7	7	13		30

1ST QUARTER

FG John Hall, 38 yards, 10:58. Drive: 8 plays, 45 yards in 4:02.

FG Sebastian Janikowski, 29 yards, 5:48. Drive: 9 plays, 53 yards in 5:10.

2ND QUARTER

TD Zack Crockett, 1-yard run (Sebastian Janikowski, extra point), 13:44. Drive: 6 plays, 27 yards in 2:41.

TD Jerald Sowell, 1-yard pass from Chad Pennington (John Hall, extra point), 0:22. Drive: 16 plays, 81 yards in 7:46.

3RD QUARTER

TD Jerry Porter, 29-yard pass from Rich Gannon (Sebastian Janikowski, extra point), 4:24. Drive: 2 plays, 45 yards in 0:30.

4TH QUARTER

TD Jerry Rice, 9-yard pass from Rich Gannon (Sebastian Janikowski, extra point), 14:15. Drive: 4 plays, 65 yards in 2:03.

FG Sebastian Janikowski, 34 yards, 7:55. Drive: 7 plays, 46 yards in 3:27.

FG Sebastian Janikowski, 31 yards, 2:42. Drive: 8 plays, 37 yards in 4:28.

NFC Divisional Games
Philadelphia Eagles 20
Atlanta Falcons 6

SCORING SUMMARY

	1Q	2Q	3Q	4Q	OT	T
FALCONS	0	6	0	0		6
EAGLES	10	3	0	7		20

1ST QUARTER

TD Bobby Taylor, 39-yard interception return (David Akers, extra point), 7:58.

NFC Divisional Games (cont.)

FG David Akers, 34 yards, 3:47. Drive: 6 plays, 47 yards in 2:27.

2ND QUARTER
FG David Akers, 39 yards, 10:05. Drive: 9 plays, 65 yards in 5:05.
FG Jay Feely, 34 yards, 4:10. Drive: 13 plays, 61 yards in 5:55.
FG Jay Feely, 52 yards, 0:00. Drive: 10 plays, 45 yards in 1:49.

3RD QUARTER
None

4TH QUARTER
TD James Thrash, 35-yard pass from Donovan McNabb (David Akers, extra point), 6:26. Drive: 10 plays, 75 yards in 5:42.

Tampa Bay Buccaneers 31
San Francisco 49ers 6

SCORING SUMMARY

	1Q	2Q	3Q	4Q	OT	T
49ERS	3	3	0	0		6
BUCCANEERS	7	21	3	0		31

1ST QUARTER
TD Mike Alstott, 2-yard run (Martin Gramatica, extra point), 6:34. Drive: 12 plays, 74 yards in 5:16.
FG Jeff Chandler, 24-yards, 0:17. Drive: 12 plays, 63 yards in 6:17.

2ND QUARTER
TD Joe Jurevicius, 20-yard pass from Brad Johnson (Martin Gramatica, extra point), 9:27. Drive: 11 plays, 77 yards in 5:50.
FG Jeff Chandler, 40 yards, 8:31. Drive: 5 plays, 24 yards in 0:56.
TD Rickey Dudley, 12-yard pass from Brad Johnson (Martin Gramatica, extra point), 7:24. Drive: 2 plays, 52 yards in 1:07.
TD Mike Alstott, 2-yard run (Martin Gramatica, extra point), 0:50. Drive: 4 plays, 26 yards in 1:10.

3RD QUARTER
FG Martin Gramatica, 19 yards, 8:28. Drive: 10 plays, 36 yards in 6:16.

4TH QUARTER
None

AFC Conference Championship
Oakland Raiders 41
Tennessee Titans 24

SCORING SUMMARY

	1Q	2Q	3Q	4Q	OT	T
TITANS	7	10	7	0		24
RAIDERS	14	10	3	14		41

1ST QUARTER
TD Jerry Porter, 3-yard pass from Rich Gannon (Sebastian Janikowski, extra point), 10:59. Drive: 7 plays, 69 yards in 4:01.

TD Drew Bennett, 33-yard pass from Steve McNair (Joe Nedney, extra point), 5:59. Drive: 9 plays, 74 yards in 5:00.
TD Charlie Garner, 12-yard pass from Rich Gannon (Sebastian Janikowski, extra point), 2:47. Drive: 7 plays, 85 yards in 3:12.

2ND QUARTER
FG Joe Nedney, 29 yards, 12:39. Drive: 10 plays, 62 yards in 5:08.
TD Steve McNair, 9-yard run (Joe Nedney, extra point), 2:47. Drive: 11 plays, 55 yards in 6:07.
TD Doug Jolley, 1-yard pass from Rich Gannon (Sebastian Janikowski, extra point), 1:00. Drive: 2 plays, 16 yards in 0:28.
FG Sebastian Janikowski, 43 yards, 0:00. Drive: 5 plays, 14 yards in 0:49.

3RD QUARTER
FG Sebastian Janikowski, 32 yards, 4:29. Drive: 4 plays, 5 yards in 1:00.
TD Steve McNair, 13-yard run (Craig Hentrich, extra point), 0:31. Drive: 8 plays, 67 yards in 3:58.

4TH QUARTER
TD Rich Gannon, 2-yard run (Sebastian Janikowski, extra point), 11:27. Drive: 9 plays, 66 yards in 4:04.
TD Zack Crockett, 7-yard run (Sebastian Janikowski, extra point), 3:25. Drive: 10 plays, 69 yards in 6:29.

NFC Conference Championship
Tampa Bay Buccaneers 27
Philadelphia Eagles 10

SCORING SUMMARY

	1Q	2Q	3Q	4Q	OT	T
BUCCANEERS	10	7	3	7		27
EAGLES	7	3	0	0		10

1ST QUARTER
TD Duce Staley, 20-yard run (David Akers, extra point), 14:08. Drive: 2 plays, 26 yards in 0:52.
FG Martin Gramatica, 48 yards, 9:58. Drive: 9 plays, 37 yards in 4:10.
TD Mike Alstott, 1-yard run (Martin Gramatica, extra point), 0:40. Drive: 7 plays, 96 yards in 3:15.

2ND QUARTER
FG David Akers, 30 yards, 8:04. Drive: 8 plays, 26 yards in 3:53.
TD Keyshawn Johnson, 9-yard pass from Brad Johnson (Martin Gramatica, extra point), 2:28. Drive: 12 plays, 80 yards in 5:36.

3RD QUARTER
FG Martin Gramatica, 27 yards, 1:02. Drive: 8 plays, 43 yards in 3:35.

4TH QUARTER
TD Ronde Barber, 92-yard interception return (Martin Gramatica, extra point), 3:12.

Trivia Challenge

Emmitt Smith became the NFL's career rushing leader in 2002. Which active rusher has the next-highest career rushing total?

Jerome Bettis of the Pittsburgh Steelers began the 2003 season with 11,542 yards.

SUPER BOWL XXXVII

Tampa Bay Buccaneers 48
Oakland Raiders 21

JANUARY 26, 2003
QUALCOMM STADIUM, SAN DIEGO, CALIFORNIA

SCORING SUMMARY

	1Q	2Q	3Q	4Q	OT	T
RAIDERS	3	0	6	12		21
BUCCANEERS	3	17	14	14		48

1ST QUARTER
FG Sebastian Janikowski, 40 yards, 10:40. Drive: 7 plays, 14 yards in 2:55.
FG Martin Gramatica, 31 yards, 7:51. Drive: 9 plays, 58 yards in 2:49.

2ND QUARTER
FG Martin Gramatica, 43 yards, 11:16. Drive: 9 plays, 26 yards in 3:53.
TD Mike Alstott, 2-yard run (Martin Gramatica, extra point), 6:24. Drive: 4 plays, 27 yards in 2:02.

TD Keenan McCardell, 5-yard pass from Brad Johnson (Martin Gramatica, extra point), 0:30. Drive: 10 plays, 77 yards in 3:15.

3RD QUARTER
TD Keenan McCardell, 8-yard pass from Brad Johnson (Martin Gramatica, extra point), 5:30. Drive: 14 plays, 89 yards in 7:52.
TD Dwight Smith, 44-yard interception return (Martin Gramatica, extra point), 4:47.
TD Jerry Porter, 39-yard pass from Rich Gannon (Rich Gannon 2-point conversion attempt failed), 2:14. Drive: 8 plays, 82 yards in 2:33.

4TH QUARTER
TD Eric Johnson, 13-yard blocked punt return (Rich Gannon 2-point conversion pass to Tim Brown failed), 14:16.
TD Jerry Rice, 48-yard pass from Rich Gannon (Rich Gannon 2-point conversion pass to Jerry Porter failed), 6:06. Drive: 8 plays, 78 yards in 2:56.
TD Derrick Brooks, 44-yard interception return (Martin Gramatica, extra point), 1:18.
TD Dwight Smith, 50-yard interception return (Martin Gramatica, extra point), 0:02.

Legends

Joe Montana was an eight-time Pro Bowl player and was elected to the Football Hall of Fame in 2000.

Joe Montana, quarterback, b. June 11, 1956, Monongahela, Pennsylvania. Playing for the San Francisco 49ers and Kansas City Chiefs, Montana was one of the most accurate quarterbacks the game has ever seen. His career passing rating of 92.3 is second in NFL history. He holds the NFL record for consecutive passes completed (22). "Joe Cool" was at his best when the pressure was on. He engineered 31 fourth-quarter game-winning comebacks. Most important, he won four Super Bowls (1982, 1985, 1989, 1990) and was named the game's MVP a record three times.

Walter Payton, running back, b. July 25, 1954, Columbia, Missouri; d. November 1, 1999. "Sweetness" was one of the most complete backs in the NFL. This Chicago Bear could block, catch, pass, and run. He rushed for 100 yards or more in 77 games, tops in the NFL. He won two regular-season MVP awards (1977, 1985) and led the Bears to a Super Bowl victory in 1986. When he retired, in 1987, Payton held NFL records for career rushing yards (16,726), most rushing yards in a game (275), and most seasons with at least 1,000 rushing yards (10).

Johnny Unitas, quarterback, b. May 7, 1933, Pittsburgh, Pennsylvania; d. September 11, 2002. Unitas was almost as well known for his black high-tops and crew cut as he was for his touchdown passes. Playing for the Baltimore Colts (he later played for the San Diego Chargers), Unitas led the NFL in touchdown passes for four straight seasons and threw at least one touchdown pass in a league-record 47 straight games. Unitas was the first player to pass for more than 40,000 yards. He led the Colts to three NFL championships (1958, 1959, 1971) and was a two-time NFL MVP (1964, 1967).

PETER READ MILLER/SPORTS ILLUSTRATED

SUPER BOWL XXXVII (cont.)

Team Stats

	RAIDERS	BUCCANEERS
First Downs	11	24
Rushing	1	6
Passing	9	15
Penalty	1	3
3rd-Down Conversions	7-16	6-15
4th-Down Conversions	0-0	0-1
Total Net Yards	269	365
Total Plays	60	76
Average Gain	4.5	4.8
Net Yards Rushing	19	150
Rushes	11	42
Avg. Per Rush	1.7	3.6

	RAIDERS	BUCCANEERS
Net Yards Passing	250	215
Comp.-Att.	24-44	18-34
Yards Per Pass	5.1	6.3
Sacked-Yards Lost	5-22	0-0
Had Intercepted	5	1
Punts-Average	5-39.0	5-31.0
Return Yards	190	287
Punts-Returns	3-29	1-25
Kickoffs-Returns	9-149	4-90
Int.-Returns	1-12	5-172
Penalties-Yards	7-51	5-41
Fumbles-Lost	1-0	1-0
Time of Pos.	22:46	37:14

Raiders Player Statistics

OFFENSE

PASSING	COMP-ATT	YDS	TD	INT
R. Gannon	24-44	272	2	5

RUSHING	ATT	YDS	TD	LG
C. Garner	7	10	0	4
Z. Crockett	2	6	0	4
R. Gannon	2	3	0	2

RECEIVING	REC	YDS	TD	LG
J. Rice	5	77	1	48
J. Porter	4	62	1	39
D. Jolley	5	59	0	25
C. Garner	7	51	0	9
T. Brown	1	9	0	9
J. Ritchie	1	7	0	7
T. Wheatley	1	7	0	7

DEFENSE

DEFENSE	T-A	SCK	INT	FF
E. Barton	8-5	0	0	0
C. Woodson	8-0	0	1	0
B. Romanowski	7-3	0	0	0
T. Smith	7-4	0	0	0
R. Woodson	7-1	0	0	0
A. Dorsett	6-2	0	0	0
R. Coleman	4-1	0	0	0
T. James	4-0	0	0	0
J. Parrella	3-1	0	0	0
C. Cooper	2-1	0	0	0
N. Harris	2-1	0	0	0
T. Johnson	2-0	0	0	0
T. Brown	1-0	0	0	0
Z. Crockett	1-0	0	0	0
J. Ioane	1-0	0	0	0
A. Treu	1-0	0	0	0

Buccaneers Player Statistics

OFFENSE

PASSING	COMP-ATT	YDS	TD	INT
B. Johnson	18-34	215	2	1

RUSHING	ATT	YDS	TD	LG
M. Pittman	29	124	0	24
M. Alstott	10	15	1	5
B. Johnson	1	10	0	10
A. Stecker	1	1	0	1
T. Tupa	1	0	0	0

RECEIVING	REC	YDS	TD	LG
J. Jurevicius	4	78	0	33
K. Johnson	6	69	0	18
M. Alstott	5	43	0	16
K. McCardell	2	13	2	8
K. Dilger	1	12	0	12

DEFENSE

DEFENSE	T-A	SCK	INT	FF
S. Quarles	7-0	0	0	0
B. Kelly	5-3	0	0	0
S. Rice	5-0	2	0	0
D. Smith	5-0	0	2	0
C. Ivy	4-0	0	0	0
G. Spires	3-0	1	0	0
E. Wyms	3-0	1	0	0
R. Barber	2-2	0	0	0
D. Barnes	2-0	0	0	0
D. Brooks	2-1	0	1	0
J. Howell	2-0	0	0	0
D. Jackson	2-0	0	2	0
W. Sapp	2-0	1	0	1
N. Webster	2-1	0	0	0
J. Golden	1-0	0	0	0
J. Jurevicius	1-0	0	0	0
J. Phillips	1-0	0	0	0
A. Singleton	1-0	0	0	0

▷ **Random Fact:** Buffalo Bill signal-caller Drew Bledsoe holds the NFL record for touchdown passes in overtime (4).

KEY COMP-ATT: completions-attempts; YDS: yards; TD: touchdowns; INT: interceptions; ATT: attempts; LG: long; REC: receptions; T-A: tackles-assists; SCK: sacks; FF: forced fumbles

2002 A.P. All-Pro Team

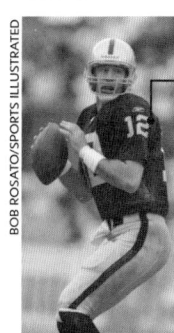

BOB ROSATO/SPORTS ILLUSTRATED

**Rich Gannon,
Oakland Raiders**

Offense

QUARTERBACK
Rich Gannon, Oakland Raiders
RUNNING BACKS
Ricky Williams, Miami Dolphins
Priest Holmes, Kansas City Chiefs
TIGHT END
Jeremy Shockey, New York Giants
WIDE RECEIVERS
Terrell Owens, San Francisco 49ers
Marvin Harrison, Indianapolis Colts
TACKLES
Lincoln Kennedy, Oakland Raiders
Jon Ogden, Baltimore Ravens
GUARDS
Alan Faneca, Pittsburgh Steelers
Will Shields, Kansas City Chiefs
CENTER
Barret Robbins, Oakland Raiders
KICKER
Adam Vinatieri, New England Patriots
KICK RETURNER
Michael Lewis, New Orleans Saints

Defense

ENDS
Jason Taylor, Miami
Simeon Rice, Tampa Bay Buccaneers
TACKLES
Kris Jenkins, Carolina Panthers
Warren Sapp, Tampa Bay Buccaneers
OUTSIDE LINEBACKERS
Joey Porter, Pittsburgh Steelers
Derrick Brooks, Tampa Bay Buccaneers
INSIDE LINEBACKERS
Zach Thomas, Miami Dolphins
Brian Urlacher, Chicago Bears
CORNERBACKS
Patrick Surtain, Miami Dolphins
Troy Vincent, Philadelphia Eagles
SAFETIES
Brian Dawkins, Philadelphia Eagles
Rod Woodson, Oakland Raiders
PUNTER
Todd Sauerbrun, Carolina Panthers

2002 Regular-Season Results—AFC

Baltimore Ravens

Week	Opponent	Score	W/L/T
1	at Panthers	7–10	L
2	BUCCANEERS	0–25	L
3	BYE WEEK		
4	BRONCOS	34–23	W
5	at Browns	26–21	W
6	at Colts	20–22	L
7	JAGUARS	17–10	W
8	STEELERS	18–31	L
9	at Falcons	17–20	L
10	BENGALS	38–27	W
11	at Dolphins	7–26	L
12	TITANS	13–12	W
13	at Bengals	27–23	W
14	SAINTS	25–37	L
15	at Texans	23–19	W
16	BROWNS	13–14	L
17	at Steelers	31–34	L

Buffalo Bills

Week	Opponent	Score	W/L/T
1	JETS	31–37	L
2	at Vikings	45–39	W
3	at Broncos	23–28	L
4	BEARS	33–27	W
5	RAIDERS	31–49	L
6	at Texans	31–24	W
7	at Dolphins	23–10	W
8	LIONS	24–17	W
9	PATRIOTS	7–38	L
10	BYE WEEK		
11	at Chiefs	16–17	L
12	at Jets	13–31	L
13	DOLPHINS	38–21	W
14	at Patriots	17–27	L
15	CHARGERS	20–13	W
16	at Packers	0–10	L
17	BENGALS	27–9	W

Cincinnati Bengals

Week	Opponent	Score	W/L/T
1	CHARGERS	6–34	L
2	at Browns	7–20	L
3	at Falcons	3–30	L
4	BUCCANEERS	7–35	L
5	at Colts	21–28	L
6	STEELERS	7–34	L
7	BYE WEEK		
8	TITANS	24–30	L
9	at Texans	38–3	W
10	at Ravens	27–38	L
11	BROWNS	20–27	L
12	at Steelers	21–29	L
13	RAVENS	23–27	L
14	at Panthers	31–52	L
15	JAGUARS	15–29	L
16	SAINTS	20–13	W
17	at Bills	9–27	L

Cleveland Browns

Week	Opponent	Score	W/L/T
1	CHIEFS	39–40	L
2	BENGALS	20–7	W
3	at Titans	31–28	W
4	at Steelers	13–16	L
5	RAVENS	21–26	L
6	at Buccaneers	3–17	L
7	TEXANS	34–17	W
8	at Jets	24–21	W
9	STEELERS	20–23	L
10	BYE WEEK		
11	at Bengals	27–20	W
12	at Saints	24–15	W
13	PANTHERS	6–13	L
14	at Jaguars	21–20	W
15	COLTS	23–28	L
16	at Ravens	14–13	W
17	FALCONS	24–16	W

Note: Home games are capitalized.

2002 Regular-Season Results—AFC (cont.)

Denver Broncos

Week	Opponent	Score	W/L/T
1	RAMS	23–16	W
2	at 49ers	24–14	W
3	BILLS	28–23	W
4	at Ravens	23–24	L
5	CHARGERS	26–9	W
6	DOLPHINS	22–24	L
7	at Chiefs	37–34	W
8	at Patriots	24–16	W
9	BYE WEEK		
10	RAIDERS	10–34	L
11	at Seahawks	31–9	W
12	COLTS	20–23	L
13	at Chargers	27–30	L
14	at Jets	13–19	L
15	CHIEFS	31–24	W
16	at Raiders	16–28	L
17	CARDINALS	37–7	W

Houston Texans

Week	Opponent	Score	W/L/T
1	COWBOYS	19–10	W
2	at Chargers	3–24	L
3	COLTS	3–23	L
4	at Eagles	17–35	L
5	BYE WEEK		
6	BILLS	24–31	L
7	at Browns	17–34	L
8	at Jaguars	21–19	W
9	BENGALS	3–38	L
10	at Titans	10–17	L
11	JAGUARS	21–24	L
12	GIANTS	16–14	W
13	at Colts	3–19	L
14	at Steelers	24–6	W
15	RAVENS	19–23	L
16	at Redskins	10–26	L
17	TITANS	3–13	L

Indianapolis Colts

Week	Opponent	Score	W/L/T
1	at Jaguars	28–25	W
2	DOLPHINS	13–21	L
3	at Texans	23–3	W
4	BYE WEEK		
5	BENGALS	28–21	W
6	RAVENS	22–20	W
7	at Steelers	10–28	L
8	at Redskins	21–26	L
9	TITANS	15–23	L
10	at Eagles	35–13	W
11	COWBOYS	20–3	W
12	at Broncos	23–20	W
13	TEXANS	19–3	W
14	at Titans	17–27	L
15	at Browns	28–23	W
16	GIANTS	27–44	L
17	JAGUARS	20–13	W

Jacksonville Jaguars

Week	Opponent	Score	W/L/T
1	COLTS	25–28	L
2	at Chiefs	23–16	W
3	BYE WEEK		
4	JETS	28–3	W
5	EAGLES	28–25	W
6	at Titans	14–23	L
7	at Ravens	10–17	L
8	TEXANS	19–21	L
9	at Giants	17–24	L
10	REDSKINS	26–7	W
11	at Texans	24–21	W
12	at Cowboys	19–21	L
13	STEELERS	23–25	L
14	BROWNS	20–21	L
15	at Bengals	29–15	W
16	TITANS	10–28	L
17	at Colts	13–20	L

Kansas City Chiefs

Week	Opponent	Score	W/L/T
1	at Browns	40–39	W
2	JAGUARS	16–23	L
3	at Patriots	38–41	L
4	DOLPHINS	48–30	W
5	at Jets	29–25	W
6	at Chargers	34–35	L
7	BRONCOS	34–37	L
8	RAIDERS	20–10	W
9	BYE WEEK		
10	at 49ers	13–17	L
11	BILLS	17–16	W
12	at Seahawks	32–39	L
13	CARDINALS	49–0	W
14	RAMS	49–10	W
15	at Broncos	24–31	L
16	CHARGERS	24–22	W
17	at Raiders	0–24	L

Miami Dolphins

Week	Opponent	Score	W/L/T
1	LIONS	49–21	W
2	at Colts	21–13	W
3	JETS	30–3	W
4	at Chiefs	30–48	L
5	PATRIOTS	26–13	W
6	at Broncos	24–22	W
7	BILLS	10–23	L
8	BYE WEEK		
9	at Packers	10–24	L
10	at Jets	10–13	L
11	RAVENS	26–7	W
12	CHARGERS	30–3	W
13	at Bills	21–38	L
14	BEARS	27–9	W
15	Raiders	23–17	W
16	at Vikings	17–20	L
17	at Patriots	24–27	L

New England Patriots

Week	Opponent	Score	W/L/T
1	STEELERS	30–14	W
2	at Jets	44–7	W
3	CHIEFS	41–38	W
4	at Chargers	14–21	L
5	at Dolphins	13–26	L
6	PACKERS	10–28	L
7	BYE WEEK		
8	BRONCOS	16–24	L
9	at Bills	38–7	W
10	at Bears	33–30	W
11	at Raiders	20–27	L
12	VIKINGS	24–17	W
13	at Lions	20–12	W
14	BILLS	27–17	W
15	at Titans	7–24	L
16	JETS	17–30	L
17	DOLPHINS	27–24	W

New York Jets

Week	Opponent	Score	W/L/T
1	at Bills	37–31	W
2	PATRIOTS	7–44	L
3	at Dolphins	3–30	L
4	at Jaguars	3–28	L
5	CHIEFS	25–29	L
6	BYE WEEK		
7	VIKINGS	20–7	W
8	BROWNS	21–24	L
9	at Chargers	44–13	W
10	DOLPHINS	13–10	W
11	at Lions	31–14	W
12	BILLS	31–13	W
13	at Raiders	20–26	L
14	BRONCOS	19–13	W
15	at Bears	13–20	L
16	at Patriots	30–17	W
17	PACKERS	42–17	W

Oakland Raiders

Week	Opponent	Score	W/L/T
1	SEAHAWKS	31–17	W
2	at Steelers	30–17	W
3	BYE WEEK		
4	TITANS	52–25	W
5	at Bills	49–31	W
6	at Rams	13–28	L
7	CHARGERS	21–27	L
8	at Chiefs	10–20	L
9	49ers	20–23	L
10	at Broncos	34–10	W
11	PATRIOTS	27–20	W
12	at Cardinals	41–20	W
13	JETS	26–20	W
14	at Chargers	27–7	W
15	at Dolphins	17–23	L
16	BRONCOS	28–16	W
17	CHIEFS	24–0	W

Pittsburgh Steelers

Week	Opponent	Score	W/L/T
1	at Patriots	14–30	L
2	RAIDERS	17–30	L
3	BYE WEEK		
4	BROWNS	16–13	W
5	at Saints	29–32	L
6	at Bengals	34–7	W
7	COLTS	28–10	W
8	at Ravens	31–18	W
9	at Browns	23–20	W
10	FALCONS	34–34	T
11	at Titans	23–31	L
12	BENGALS	29–21	W
13	at Jaguars	25–23	W
14	TEXANS	6–24	L
15	PANTHERS	30–14	W
16	at Buccaneers	17–7	W
17	RAVENS	34–31	W

San Diego Chargers

Week	Opponent	Score	W/L/T
1	at Bengals	34–6	W
2	TEXANS	24–3	W
3	at Cardinals	23–15	W
4	PATRIOTS	21–14	W
5	at Broncos	9–26	L
6	CHIEFS	35–34	W
7	at Raiders	27–21	W
8	BYE WEEK		
9	JETS	13–44	L
10	at Rams	24–28	L
11	49ERS	20–17	W
12	at Dolphins	3–30	L
13	BRONCOS	30–27	W
14	RAIDERS	7–27	L
15	at Bills	13–20	L
16	at Chiefs	22–24	L
17	SEAHAWKS	28–31	L

Tennessee Titans

Week	Opponent	Score	W/L/T
1	EAGLES	27–24	W
2	at Cowboys	13–21	L
3	BROWNS	28–31	L
4	at Raiders	25–52	L
5	REDSKINS	14–31	L
6	JAGUARS	23–14	W
7	BYE WEEK		
8	at Bengals	30–24	W
9	at Colts	23–15	W
10	TEXANS	17–10	W
11	STEELERS	31–23	W
12	at Ravens	12–13	L
13	at Giants	32–29	W
14	COLTS	27–17	W
15	PATRIOTS	24–7	W
16	at Jaguars	28–10	W
17	at Texans	13–3	W

2002 Regular-Season Results—NFC

Arizona Cardinals

Week	Opponent	Score	W/L/T
1	at Redskins	23 – 31	L
2	at Seahawks	24 – 13	W
3	CHARGERS	15 – 23	L
4	GIANTS	21 – 7	W
5	at Panthers	16 – 13	W
6	BYE WEEK		
7	COWBOYS	9 – 6	W
8	at 49ers	28 – 38	L
9	RAMS	14 – 27	L
10	SEAHAWKS	6 – 27	L
11	at Eagles	14 – 38	L
12	RAIDERS	20 – 41	L
13	at Chiefs	0 – 49	L
14	LIONS	23 – 20	W
15	at Rams	28 – 30	L
16	49ERS	14 – 17	L
17	at Broncos	7 – 37	L

Note: Home games are capitalized.

Did You Know?

Tampa Bay Buccaneer defensive end Simeon Rice recorded at least two sacks in an NFL-record five straight games in 2002.

▷**Random Fact**: There were 25 overtime games in the 2002 regular season, breaking the NFL record of 21 set in 1995.

Today's Stars

Brian Urlacher, linebacker, b. May 25, 1978, Pasco, Washington. Urlacher's combination of strength and speed make him a dominator on defense. In 2002, the Chicago Bear led the NFL with 115 tackles and was second with 96 solo takedowns. He also had one interception and was named to his third straight Pro Bowl.

Michael Vick, quarterback, b. June 26, 1980, Newport News, Virginia. In 2002, the Atlanta Falcons' second-year quarterback shocked everyone with his blazing speed and cannon arm. Vick passed for 2,936 yards and 16 touchdowns with only 8 interceptions. He led the Falcons to the playoffs for the first time since 1999. Vick also made plays with his feet, rushing for 777 yards and 8 touchdowns. On December 1, 2002, he set the NFL single-game rushing record for a quarterback when he ran for 173 yards against the Minnesota Vikings.

Ricky Williams, running back, b. May 21, 1977, San Diego, California. Williams led the NFL in rushing in 2002 with 1,853 yards, 170 yards more than the second-best rusher. The Miami Dolphins' bruising back ran away from the field with back-to-back 200-yard rushing games on December 1st and 9th. For the season, Williams rushed for 16 touchdowns, tying for second in the NFL.

Brian Urlacher has become one of the NFL's elite linebackers in just three seasons.

BOB ROSATO/SPORTS ILLUSTRATED

Atlanta Falcons

Week	Opponent	Score	W/L/T
1	at Packers	34–37	L
2	BEARS	13–14	L
3	BENGALS	30–3	W
4	BYE WEEK		
5	BUCCANEERS	6–20	L
6	at Giants	17–10	W
7	PANTHERS	30–0	W
8	at Saints	37–35	W
9	RAVENS	20–17	W
10	at Steelers	34–34	T
11	SAINTS	24–17	W
12	at Panthers	41–0	W
13	at Vikings	30–24	W
14	at Buccaneers	10-34	L
15	SEAHAWKS	24–30	L
16	LIONS	36–15	W
17	at Browns	16–24	L

Carolina Panthers

Week	Opponent	Score	W/L/T
1	RAVENS	10–7	W
2	LIONS	31–7	W
3	at Vikings	21–14	W
4	at Packers	14–17	L
5	CARDINALS	13–16	L
6	at Cowboys	13–14	L
7	at Falcons	0–30	L
8	BUCCANEERS	9–12	L
9	BYE WEEK		
10	SAINTS	24–34	L
11	at Buccaneers	10–23	L
12	FALCONS	0–41	L
13	at Browns	13–6	W
14	BENGALS	52–31	W
15	at Steelers	14–30	L
16	BEARS	24–14	W
17	at Saints	10–6	W

Chicago Bears

Week	Opponent	Score	W/L/T
1	VIKINGS	27–23	W
2	at Falcons	14–13	W
3	SAINTS	23–29	L
4	at Bills	27–33	L
5	PACKERS	21–34	L
6	BYE WEEK		
7	at Lions	20–23	L
8	at Vikings	7–25	L
9	EAGLES	13–19	L
10	PATRIOTS	30–33	L
11	at Rams	16–21	L
12	LIONS	20–17	W
13	at Packers	20–30	L
14	at Dolphins	9–27	L
15	JETS	20–13	W
16	at Panthers	14–24	L
17	BUCCANEERS	0–15	L

Dallas Cowboys

Week	Opponent	Score	W/L/T
1	at Texans	10–19	L
2	TITANS	21–13	W
3	at Eagles	13–44	L
4	at Rams	13–10	W
5	GIANTS	17–21	L
6	PANTHERS	14–13	W
7	at Cardinals	6–9	L
8	SEAHAWKS	14–17	L
9	at Lions	7–9	L
10	BYE WEEK		
11	at Colts	3–20	L
12	JAGUARS	21–19	W
13	REDSKINS	27–20	W
14	49ERS	27–31	L
15	at Giants	7–37	L
16	EAGLES	3–27	L
17	at Redskins	14–20	L

Detroit Lions

Week	Opponent	Score	W/L/T
1	at Dolphins	21–49	L
2	at Panthers	7–31	L
3	PACKERS	31–37	L
4	SAINTS	26–21	W
5	BYE WEEK		
6	at Vikings	24–31	L
7	BEARS	23–20	W
8	at Bills	17–24	L
9	COWBOYS	9–7	W
10	at Packers	14–40	L
11	JETS	14–31	L
12	at Bears	17–20	L
13	PATRIOTS	12–20	L
14	at Cardinals	20–23	L
15	BUCCANEERS	20–23	L
16	at Falcons	15–36	L
17	VIKINGS	36–38	L

Green Bay Packers

Week	Opponent	Score	W/L/T
1	FALCONS	37–34	W
2	at Saints	20–35	L
3	at Lions	37–31	W
4	PANTHERS	17–14	W
5	at Bears	34–21	W
6	at Patriots	28–10	W
7	REDSKINS	30–9	W
8	BYE WEEK		
9	DOLPHINS	24–10	W
10	LIONS	40–14	W
11	at Vikings	21–31	L
12	at Buccaneers	7–21	L
13	BEARS	30–20	W
14	VIKINGS	26–22	W
15	at 49ers	20–14	W
16	BILLS	10–0	W
17	at Jets	17–42	L

Note: Home games are capitalized.

2002 Regular-Season Results—NFC (cont.)

Minnesota Vikings

Week	Opponent	Score	W/L/T
1	at Bears	23–27	L
2	BILLS	39–45	L
3	PANTHERS	14–21	L
4	at Seahawks	23–48	L
5	BYE WEEK		
6	LIONS	31–24	W
7	at Jets	7–20	L
8	BEARS	25–7	W
9	at Buccaneers	24–38	L
10	GIANTS	20–27	L
11	PACKERS	31–21	W
12	at Patriots	17–24	L
13	FALCONS	24–30	L
14	at Packers	22–26	L
15	at Saints	32–31	W
16	DOLPHINS	20–17	W
17	at Lions	38–36	W

New Orleans Saints

Week	Opponent	Score	W/L/T
1	at Buccaneers	26–20	W
2	PACKERS	35–20	W
3	at Bears	29–23	W
4	at Lions	21–26	L
5	STEELERS	32–29	W
6	at Redskins	43–27	W
7	49ers	35–27	W
8	FALCONS	35–37	L
9	BYE WEEK		
10	at Panthers	34–24	W
11	at Falcons	17–24	L
12	BROWNS	15–24	L
13	BUCCANEERS	23–20	W
14	at Ravens	37–25	W
15	VIKINGS	31–32	L
16	at Bengals	13–20	L
17	PANTHERS	6–10	L

New York Giants

Week	Opponent	Score	W/L/T
1	49ERS	13–16	L
2	at Rams	26–21	W
3	SEAHAWKS	9–6	W
4	at Cardinals	7–21	L
5	at Cowboys	21–17	W
6	FALCONS	10–17	L
7	BYE WEEK		
8	at Eagles	3–17	L
9	JAGUARS	24–17	W
10	at Vikings	27–20	W
11	REDSKINS	19–17	W
12	at Texans	14–16	L
13	TITANS	29–32	L
14	at Redskins	27–21	W
15	COWBOYS	37–7	W
16	at Colts	44–27	W
17	EAGLES	10–7	W

Philadelphia Eagles

Week	Opponent	Score	W/L/T
1	at Titans	24–27	L
2	at Redskins	37–7	W
3	COWBOYS	44–13	W
4	TEXANS	35–17	W
5	at Jaguars	25–28	L
6	BYE WEEK		
7	BUCCANEERS	20–10	W
8	GIANTS	17–3	W
9	at Bears	19–13	W
10	COLTS	13–35	L
11	CARDINALS	38–14	W
12	at 49ers	38–17	W
13	RAMS	10–3	W
14	at Seahawks	27–20	W
15	REDSKINS	34–21	W
16	at Cowboys	27–3	W
17	at Giants	7–10	L

San Francisco 49ers

Week	Opponent	Score	W/L/T
1	at Giants	16–13	W
2	BRONCOS	14–24	L
3	REDSKINS	20–10	W
4	BYE WEEK		
5	RAMS	37–13	W
6	at Seahawks	28–21	W
7	at Saints	27–35	L
8	CARDINALS	38–28	W
9	at Raiders	23–20	W
10	CHIEFS	17–13	W
11	at Chargers	17–20	L
12	EAGLES	17–38	L
13	SEAHAWKS	31–24	W
14	at Cowboys	31–27	W
15	PACKERS	14–20	L
16	at Cardinals	17–14	W
17	at Rams	20–31	L

Seattle Seahawks

Week	Opponent	Score	W/L/T
1	at Raiders	17–31	L
2	CARDINALS	13–24	L
3	at Giants	6–9	L
4	VIKINGS	48–23	W
5	BYE WEEK		
6	49ers	21–28	L
7	at Rams	20–37	L
8	at Cowboys	17–14	W
9	REDSKINS	3–14	L
10	at Cardinals	27–6	W
11	BRONCOS	9–31	L
12	CHIEFS	39–32	W
13	at 49ers	24–31	L
14	EAGLES	20–27	L
15	at Falcons	30–24	W
16	RAMS	30–10	W
17	at Chargers	31–28	W

St. Louis Rams

Week	Opponent	Score	W/L/T
1	at Broncos	16–23	L
2	GIANTS	21–26	L
3	at Buccaneers	14–26	L
4	COWBOYS	10–13	L
5	at 49ers	13–37	L
6	RAIDERS	28–13	W
7	SEAHAWKS	37–20	W
8	BYE WEEK		
9	at Cardinals	27–14	W
10	CHARGERS	28–24	W
11	BEARS	21–16	W
12	at Redskins	17–20	L
13	at Eagles	3–10	L
14	at Chiefs	10–49	L
15	CARDINALS	30–28	W
16	at Seahawks	10–30	L
17	49ERS	31–20	W

Tampa Bay Buccaneers

Week	Opponent	Score	W/L/T
1	SAINTS	20–26	L
2	at Ravens	25–0	W
3	RAMS	26–14	W
4	at Bengals	35–7	W
5	at Falcons	20–6	W
6	BROWNS	17–3	W
7	at Eagles	10–20	L
8	at Panthers	12–9	W
9	VIKINGS	38–24	W
10	BYE WEEK		
11	PANTHERS	23–10	W
12	PACKERS	21–7	W
13	at Saints	20–23	L
14	FALCONS	34–10	W
15	at Lions	23–20	W
16	STEELERS	7–17	L
17	at Bears	15–0	W

Washington Redskins

Week	Opponent	Score	W/L/T
1	CARDINALS	31–23	W
2	EAGLES	7–37	L
3	at 49ers	10–20	L
4	BYE WEEK		
5	at Titans	31–14	W
6	SAINTS	27–43	L
7	at Packers	9–30	L
8	COLTS	26–21	W
9	at Seahawks	14–3	W
10	at Jaguars	7–26	L
11	at Giants	17–19	L
12	RAMS	20-17	W
13	at Cowboys	20–27	L
14	GIANTS	21–27	L
15	at Eagles	21–34	L
16	TEXANS	26–10	W
17	COWBOYS	20–14	W

Did You Know?

Oakland Raider quarterback Rich Gannon passed for at least 300 yards in an NFL-record 10 games in 2002. The previous record of nine games of at least 300 yards passing was shared by Dan Marino, Warren Moon, and Kurt Warner.

2002 Individual Leaders—AFC

TOUCHDOWNS	TEAM	TD	RSH	REC	RET	PTS
Priest Holmes	KC	24	21	3	0	144
Ricky Williams	MIA	17	16	1	0	102
Clinton Portis	DEN	17	15	2	0	102
LaDainian Tomlinson	SD	15	14	1	0	90
Travis Henry	BUF	14	13	1	0	84
Eddie George	TEN	14	12	2	0	84
Hines Ward	PIT	12	0	12	0	72
Marvin Harrison	IND	11	0	11	0	66
Charlie Garner	OAK	11	7	4	0	66
Eric Moulds	BUF	10	0	10	0	60

KEY TD=touchdowns; RSH=rushing touchdowns; REC=receiving touchdowns; RET=returns; PTS=points

2002 Individual Leaders—AFC (cont.)

KICKING	TEAM	FGM	FGA	LONG	XPA	XPM	PTS
Sebastian Janikowski	OAK	26	33	51	50	50	128
Jason Elam	DEN	26	36	55	43	42	120
Adam Vinatieri	NE	27	30	57	36	36	117
Morten Andersen	KC	22	26	50	51	51	117
Mike Hollis	BUF	25	33	54	40	40	115
Olindo Mare	MIA	24	31	53	43	42	114
Joe Nedney	TEN	25	31	53	36	36	111
John Hall	NYJ	24	31	46	37	35	107
Mike Vanderjagt	IND	23	31	54	34	34	103
Phil Dawson	CLE	22	28	52	35	34	100

PASSING	TEAM	YDS	ATT	COMP	TD	INT	LONG	RATING
Chad Pennington	NYJ	3,120	399	275	22	6	47	104.2
Rich Gannon	OAK	4,689	618	418	26	10	75	97.3
Trent Green	KC	3,690	470	287	26	13	99	92.6
Peyton Manning	IND	4,200	591	392	27	19	69	88.8
Drew Bledsoe	BUF	4,359	610	375	24	15	73	86.0
Tom Brady	NE	3,764	601	373	28	14	49	85.7
Mark Brunell	JAC	2,788	416	245	17	7	79	85.7
Brian Griese	DEN	3,214	436	291	15	15	82	85.6
Jay Fiedler	MIA	2,024	292	179	14	9	59	85.2
Tommy Maddox	PIT	2,836	377	234	20	16	72	85.2

RECEPTIONS	TEAM	REC	YDS	AVG	TD	LONG
Marvin Harrison	IND	143	1,722	12.0	11	69
Hines Ward	PIT	112	1,329	11.9	12	72
Eric Moulds	BUF	100	1,292	12.9	10	70
Troy Brown	NE	97	890	9.2	3	38
Peerless Price	BUF	94	1,252	13.3	9	73
Jerry Rice	OAK	92	1,211	13.2	7	75
Charlie Garner	OAK	91	941	10.3	4	69
Laveranues Coles	NYJ	89	1,264	14.2	5	43
Rod Smith	DEN	89	1,027	11.5	5	46
Tim Brown	OAK	81	930	11.5	2	45

Marvin Harrison, Indianapolis Colts

JOHN BIEVER/SPORTS ILLUSTRATED

RECEIVING YARDS	TEAM	REC	YDS	AVG	TD	LONG
Marvin Harrison	IND	143	1,722	12.0	11	69
Hines Ward	PIT	112	1,329	11.9	12	72
Plaxico Burress	PIT	78	1,325	17.0	7	62
Eric Moulds	BUF	100	1,292	12.9	10	70
Laveranues Coles	NYJ	89	1,264	14.2	5	43
Peerless Price	BUF	94	1,252	13.3	9	73
Jerry Rice	OAK	92	1,211	13.2	7	75
Chad Johnson	CIN	69	1,166	16.9	5	72
Jimmy Smith	JAC	80	1,027	12.8	7	47
Rod Smith	DEN	89	1,027	11.0	5	46

KEY FGM=field goals made; FGA=field goals attempted; XPA=extra points attempted; XPM=extra points made; PTS=points; YDS=yards; ATT=attempts; COMP=completions; TD=touchdowns; INT=interceptions; REC=receptions; AVG=average

2002 Individual Leaders—AFC (cont.)

RUSHING	TEAM	YDS	ATT	AVG	TD	LONG
Ricky Williams	MIA	1,853	383	4.8	16	63
LaDainian Tomlinson	SD	1,683	372	4.5	14	76
Priest Holmes	KC	1,615	313	5.2	21	56
Clinton Portis	DEN	1,508	273	5.5	15	59
Travis Henry	BUF	1,438	325	4.4	13	34
Jamal Lewis	BAL	1,327	308	4.3	6	75
Fred Taylor	JAC	1,314	287	4.6	8	63
Corey Dillon	CIN	1,311	314	4.2	7	67
Eddie George	TEN	1,165	343	3.4	12	35
Curtis Martin	NYJ	1,094	261	4.2	7	35

Ricky Williams, Miami Dolphins

BOB ROSATO/SPORTS ILLUSTRATED

INTERCEPTIONS	TEAM	INTS	YDS	TD	LONG
Rod Woodson	OAK	8	225	2	98
Nate Clements	BUF	6	82	1	42
Patrick Surtain	MIA	6	79	1	40
Marion McCree	JAC	6	129	0	53
Lance Schulters	TEN	6	56	0	28
Greg Wesley	KC	6	170	0	50
Brock Marion	MIA	5	99	0	62
Ed Reed	BAL	5	167	0	59
Deltha O'Neal	DEN	5	70	2	28
Donnie Edwards	SD	5	95	1	46
Aaron Glenn	HOU	5	181	2	70

SACKS	TEAM	SACKS	TACKLE
Jason Taylor	MIA	18.5	45
Dwight Feeney	IND	13.0	40
Roderick Coleman	OAK	11.0	32
John Abraham	NYJ	10.0	48
Kevin Carter	TEN	10.0	27
Adewale Ogunleye	MIA	9.5	32
Jason Gildon	PIT	9.0	45
Joey Porter	PIT	9.0	60
Trevor Pryce	DEN	9.0	40
Eric Hicks	KC	9.0	40
Aaron Schobel	BUF	8.5	34

PUNTING	TEAM	NO.	YDS	AVG	NAVG	LG	TB	BLK	IN 20	RET	RET AVG	RET TD
Chris Hanson	JAC	81	3,583	44.2	37.6	64	10	0	27	39	8.7	0
Brian Moorman	BUF	66	2,844	43.1	36.0	84	7	0	18	29	10.1	0
Shane Lechler	OAK	53	2,251	42.5	32.7	70	12	0	18	18	15.3	0
Craig Hentrich	TEN	65	2,725	41.9	33.9	56	5	0	28	28	13.9	3
Chris Gardocki	CLE	81	3,388	41.8	35.3	59	6	0	27	42	9.7	1
Dave Zastudil	BAL	81	3,368	41.6	33.7	61	5	0	31	40	11.8	2
Josh Miller	PIT	55	2,267	41.2	32.5	62	5	0	14	28	12.4	1
Darren Bennett	SD	87	3,540	40.7	34.3	63	6	0	31	36	10.2	1
Hunter Smith	IND	66	2,672	40.5	34.9	69	9	0	26	27	5.8	0
Mark Royals	MIA	69	2,772	40.2	34.5	56	6	0	15	39	7.0	0

2002 Individual Leaders—NFC

TOUCHDOWNS	TEAM	TD	RSH	REC	RET	PTS
Shaun Alexander	SEA	18	16	2	0	108
Deuce McAllister	NO	16	13	3	0	96
Terrell Owens	SF	14	1	13	0	84
Tiki Barber	NYG	11	11	0	0	66
Moe Williams	MIN	11	11	0	0	66
Daunte Culpepper	MIN	10	10	0	0	60
Marshall Faulk	STL	10	8	2	0	60
Marcel Shipp	ARI	9	6	3	0	54
Donald Driver	GB	9	0	9	0	54
Ahman Green	GB	9	7	2	0	54
Warrick Dunn	ATL	9	7	2	0	54

KEY NO.=number; NAVG=net average; LG=long; TB=touchback; BLK=blocked; IN 20=inside 20-yard line; RET=returned; RET AVG=return average; RET TD=returned for a touchdown

2002 Individual Leaders—NFC (cont.)

KICKING	TEAM	FGM	FGA	LONG	XPA	XPM	PTS
Jay Feely	ATL	32	40	52	43	42	138
David Akers	PHI	30	34	51	43	43	133
John Carney	NO	31	35	48	37	37	130
Martin Gramatica	TB	32	39	53	32	32	128
Ryan Longwell	GB	28	34	49	44	44	128
Matt Bryant	NYG	26	32	47	32	30	108
Rian Lindell	SEA	23	29	52	38	38	107
Jason Hanson	DET	23	28	49	31	31	100
Paul Edinger	CHI	22	28	53	29	29	95
Jeff Wilkins	STL	19	25	47	37	37	94

PASSING	TEAM	YDS	ATT	COMP	TD	INT	LONG	RATING
Marc Bulger	STL	1,826	214	138	14	6	58	101.5
Brad Johnson	TB	3,049	451	281	22	6	76	92.9
Matt Hasselbeck	SEA	3,075	419	267	15	10	49	87.8
Donovan McNabb	PHI	2,289	361	211	17	6	59	86.0
Jeff Garcia	SF	3,344	528	328	21	10	76	85.6
Brett Favre	GB	3,658	551	341	27	16	85	85.6
Kerry Collins	NYG	4,073	545	335	19	14	82	85.4
Michael Vick	ATL	2,936	421	231	16	8	74	81.6
Aaron Brooks	NO	3,572	528	283	27	15	64	80.1
Chris Chandler	CHI	1,023	161	103	4	4	76	79.8

RECEPTIONS	TEAM	REC	YDS	AVG	TD	LONG
Randy Moss	MIN	106	1,347	12.7	7	60
Terrell Owens	SF	100	1,300	13.0	13	76
Marty Booker	CHI	97	1,189	12.3	6	54
Torry Holt	STL	91	1,302	14.3	4	58
Joe Horn	NO	88	1,312	14.9	7	63
Amani Toomer	NYG	82	1,343	16.4	8	82
Marshall Faulk	STL	80	537	6.7	2	40
Isaac Bruce	STL	79	1,075	13.6	7	34
Koren Robinson	SEA	78	1,240	15.9	5	83
Keyshawn Johnson	TB	76	1,088	14.3	5	76

RECEIVING YARDS	TEAM	REC	YDS	AVG	TD	LONG
Randy Moss	MIN	106	1,347	12.7	7	60
Amani Toomer	NYG	82	1,343	16.4	8	82
Joe Horn	NO	88	1,312	14.9	7	63
Torry Holt	STL	91	1,302	14.3	4	58
Terrell Owens	SF	100	1,300	13.0	13	76
Koren Robinson	SEA	78	1,240	15.9	5	83
Marty Booker	CHI	97	1,189	12.3	6	54
Keyshawn Johnson	TB	76	1,088	14.3	5	76
Isaac Bruce	STL	79	1,075	13.6	7	34
Donald Driver	GB	70	1,064	15.2	9	85

RUSHING	TEAM	YDS	ATT	AVG	TD	LONG
Deuce McAllister	NO	1,388	325	4.3	13	62
Tiki Barber	NYG	1,387	304	4.6	11	70
Michael Bennett	MIN	1,296	255	5.1	5	85
Ahman Green	GB	1,240	286	4.3	7	43
Shaun Alexander	SEA	1,175	295	4.0	16	58
Duce Staley	PHI	1,029	269	3.8	5	57
James Stewart	DET	1,021	231	4.4	4	56
Emmitt Smith	DAL	975	254	3.8	5	30
Garrison Hearst	SF	972	215	4.5	8	40
Marshall Faulk	STL	953	212	4.5	8	44

JOHN BIEVER/SPORTS ILLUSTRATED

INTERCEPTIONS	TEAM	INT	YDS	TD	LONG
Brian Kelly	TB	8	68	0	31
Darren Sharper	GB	7	233	1	89
Tony Parrish	SF	7	204	0	60
Reggie Tongue	SEA	5	118	1	46
Derek Ross	DAL	5	17	0	12
Roy Williams	DAL	5	90	2	85
Bobby Taylor	PHI	5	43	1	23
Derrick Brooks	TB	5	218	3	97
Sammy Knight	NO	5	36	0	17
Fred Thomas	NO	5	80	0	43

Darren Sharper, Green Bay Packers

SACKS	TEAM	SACKS	TACKLES
Simeon Rice	TB	15.5	41.0
Hugh Douglas	PHI	12.5	44.0
Andre Carter	SF	12.5	45.0
Kabeer Gbaja-Biamila	GB	12	35.0
Julius Peppers	CAR	12	28.0
Leonard Little	STL	12	37.0
Michael Strahan	NYG	11	55.0
LaVar Arrington	WAS	11	67.0
Rosevelt Colvin	CHI	10.5	55.0
Patrick Kerney	ATL	10.5	45.0

Trivia Challenge

Who holds the NFL record for most 100-yard-receiving games in a single season?

Michael Irvin of the Dallas Cowboys. Irvin reached 100 yards in 11 games during the 1995 season.

PUNTING	TEAM	NO.	YDS	AVG	NAVG	LG	TB	BLK	IN 20	RET	RET AVG	RET TD
Todd Sauerbrun	CAR	104	4,735	45.5	37.5	67	12	0	31	63	8.8	0
Scott Player	ARI	88	3,864	43.9	35.0	58	10	0	28	42	13.0	3
Sean Landeta	PHI	52	2,229	42.9	34.6	63	7	0	19	20	14.4	2
Tom Tupa	TB	90	3,856	42.8	35.4	71	12	0	30	42	10.3	0
Brad Maynard	CHI	87	3,679	42.3	37.4	75	2	0	26	46	8.4	0
John Jett	DET	91	3,838	42.2	38.0	57	7	0	29	53	4.5	0
Toby Gowin	NO	61	2,553	41.9	36.9	59	6	0	15	33	5.5	0
Chris Mohr	ATL	67	2,804	41.9	38.7	59	5	0	21	23	4.7	0
Mitch Berger	STL	72	3,020	41.9	32.7	64	10	0	26	34	13.6	1
Jeff Feagles	SEA	61	2,542	41.7	37.0	58	4	0	22	17	11.9	1
Josh Bidwell	GB	79	3,296	41.7	35.7	57	6	0	26	41	8.7	1

FOOTBALL *PRO*

TEAM-BY-TEAM STATS—AFC

BALTIMORE RAVENS

Passing

Player	ATT	COMP	YDS	PCT. COMP	YDS/ATT	TD	INT	Rating
Jeff Blake	295	165	2,084	55.9	7.1	13	11	77.3
Chris Redman	182	97	1,034	53.3	5.7	7	3	76.1

Rushing

Player	NO.	YDS	AVG	LG	TD
Jamal Lewis	308	1,327	4.3	75	6
Chester Taylor	33	122	3.7	17	0
Jeff Blake	39	106	2.7	17	1
Travis Taylor	11	105	9.5	39	0

Receiving

Player	NO.	YDS	AVG	LG	TD
Travis Taylor	61	869	14.2	64	6
Todd Heap	68	836	12.3	43	6
Jamal Lewis	47	442	9.4	77	1
Brandon Stokley	24	357	14.9	35	2
Chester Taylor	14	129	9.2	20	2
Ron Johnson	10	114	11.4	33	1

Punting

Player	NO.	AVG	NET AVG	TB	IN 20	LG	BLK
Dave Zastudil	81	41.6	33.7	5	31	61	0

Interceptions Ed Reed, 5   **Sacks** Peter Boulware, 7

BUFFALO BILLS

Passing

Player	ATT	COMP	YDS	PCT. COMP	YDS/ATT	TD	INT	Rating
Drew Bledsoe	610	375	4,359	61.5	7.1	24	15	86.0

Rushing

Player	NO.	YDS	AVG	LG	TD
Travis Henry	325	1,438	4.4	34	13
Drew Bledsoe	27	67	2.5	11	2
Larry Centers	11	56	5.1	13	2

Receiving

Player	NO.	YDS	AVG	LG	TD
Eric Moulds	100	1,292	12.9	70	10
Peerless Price	94	1,252	13.3	73	9
Josh Reed	37	509	13.8	42	2
Larry Centers	43	388	9.0	25	0
Jay Riemersma	32	350	10.9	29	0
Travis Henry	43	309	7.2	26	1
Dave Moore	16	141	8.8	19	2

Punting

Player	NO.	AVG	NET AVG	TB	IN 20	LG	BLK
Brian Moorman	66	43.1	36.0	7	18	84	0

Interceptions Nate Clements, 6   **Sacks** Aaron Schobel, 8.5

KEY ATT=attempts; COMP=completions; YDS=yards; PCT COMP=completion percentage; YDS/ATT=yards per attempt; TD=touchdowns; INT=interceptions; NO.=number; AVG=average; LG=long; NET AVG=net average; TB=touchbacks; IN 20=inside 20 yard line; BLK=blocked

CINCINNATI BENGALS

Passing

Player	ATT	COMP	YDS	PCT. COMP	YDS/ATT	TD	INT	Rating
Jon Kitna	473	294	3,178	62.2	6.7	16	16	79.1
Gus Frerotte	85	44	437	51.8	5.1	1	5	46.1

Rushing

Player	NO.	YDS	AVG	LG	TD
Corey Dillon	314	1,311	4.2	67	7
Brandon Bennett	33	155	4.7	29	0
Rudi Johnson	17	67	3.9	13	0
Nicolas Luchey	12	59	4.9	10	2
Jon Kitna	24	57	2.4	12	4

Receiving

Player	NO.	YDS	AVG	LG	TD
Chad Johnson	69	1,166	16.9	72	5
Peter Warrick	53	606	11.4	37	6
T.J. Houshmandzadeh	41	492	12.0	31	1
Ron Dugans	47	421	9.0	31	0
Corey Dillon	43	298	6.9	19	0
Matt Schobel	27	212	7.9	20	2
Lorenzo Neal	21	133	6.3	15	1

Punting

Player	NO.	AVG	NET AVG	TB	IN 20	LG	BLK
Nick Harris	65	40.1	31.4	4	11	57	0

Interceptions Kevin Kaesviharn, Artrell Hawkins, 2 **Sacks** Justin Smith, 6.5

CLEVELAND BROWNS

Passing

Player	ATT	COMP	YDS	PCT. COMP	YDS/ATT	TD	INT	Rating
Tim Couch	443	273	2,842	61.6	6.4	18	18	76.8
Kelly Holcomb	106	64	790	60.4	7.5	8	4	92.9

Rushing

Player	NO.	YDS	AVG	LG	TD
William Green	243	887	3.7	64	6
Jamel White	106	470	4.4	54	3
Dennis Northcutt	8	104	13.0	36	1

Receiving

Player	NO.	YDS	AVG	LG	TD
Quincy Morgan	56	964	17.2	78	7
Kevin Johnson	67	703	10.5	30	4
Dennis Northcutt	38	601	15.8	43	5
Jamel White	63	452	7.2	33	0
Andre Davis	37	420	11.4	31	6
Mark Campbell	25	179	7.2	26	3
William Green	16	113	7.1	18	0
Steve Heiden	17	105	6.2	12	1

Punting

Player	NO.	AVG	NET AVG	TB	IN 20	LG	BLK
Chris Gardocki	81	41.8	35.3	6	27	59	0

Interceptions Earl Little, 4 **Sacks** Mark Word, 8

FOOTBALL PRO

DENVER BRONCOS

Passing

Player	ATT	COMP	YDS	PCT. COMP	YDS/ATT	TD	INT	Rating
Brian Griese	436	291	3,214	66.7	7.4	15	15	85.6
Steve Beuerlein	117	68	925	58.1	7.9	6	5	82.7

Rushing

Player	NO.	YDS	AVG	LG	TD
Clinton Portis	273	1,508	5.5	59	15
Mike Anderson	84	386	4.6	32	2
Olandis Gary	37	147	4.0	26	1
Brian Griese	37	107	2.9	13	1

Receiving

Player	NO.	YDS	AVG	LG	TD
Rod Smith	89	1,027	11.5	46	5
Ed McCaffrey	69	903	13.1	69	2
Shannon Sharpe	61	686	11.2	82	3
Ashley Lelie	35	525	15.0	48	2
Clinton Portis	33	364	11.0	66	2
Dwayne Carswell	21	189	9.0	19	1
Mike Anderson	18	167	9.3	52	2
Olandis Gary	18	148	8.2	19	0

Punting

Player	NO.	AVG	NET AVG	TB	IN 20	LG	BLK
Tom Rouen*	44	42.9	34.5	7	8	63	2
Micah Knorr**	24	37.8	34.1	2	8	59	0

Interceptions Deltha O'Neal, 5   **Sacks** Trevor Pryce, 9

HOUSTON TEXANS

Passing

Player	ATT	COMP	YDS	PCT. COMP	YDS/ATT	TD	INT	Rating
David Carr	444	233	2,592	52.5	5.8	9	15	62.8

Rushing

Player	NO.	YDS	AVG	LG	TD
Jonathan Wells	197	529	2.7	37	3
James Allen	155	519	3.3	32	0
David Carr	59	282	4.8	20	3

Receiving

Player	NO.	YDS	AVG	LG	TD
Corey Bradford	45	697	15.5	81	6
Billy Miller	51	613	12.0	42	3
Jabar Gaffney	41	483	11.8	27	1
James Allen	47	302	6.4	21	0
JaJuan Dawson	21	286	13.6	28	0

Punting

Player	NO.	AVG	NET AVG	TB	IN 20	LG	BLK
Chad Stanley	114	41.4	36.8	6	36	62	1

Interceptions Aaron Glenn, 5   **Sacks** Gary Walker, 6.5

*Played for Denver, New York Giants, and Pittsburgh in 2002. Totals for all three teams included here. **Played for Denver and Dallas in 2002.

INDIANAPOLIS COLTS

Passing

Player	ATT	COMP	YDS	PCT. COMP	YDS/ATT	TD	INT	Rating
Peyton Manning	591	392	4,200	66.3	7.1	27	19	88.8

Rushing

Player	NO.	YDS	AVG	LG	TD
Edgerrin James	277	989	3.6	20	2
James Mungro	97	336	3.5	49	8
Peyton Manning	38	148	3.9	13	2

Receiving

Player	NO.	YDS	AVG	LG	TD
Marvin Harrison	143	1,722	12.0	69	11
Reggie Wayne	49	716	14.6	49	4
Marcus Pollard	43	478	11.1	41	6
Qadry Ismail	44	462	10.5	42	3
Edgerrin James	61	354	5.8	23	1
Troy Walters	18	207	11.5	27	0
James Mungro	13	81	6.2	11	0

Punting

Player	NO.	AVG	NET AVG	TB	IN 20	LG	BLK
Hunter Smith	66	40.5	34.9	9	26	69	0

Interceptions Mike Peterson, 3   **Sacks** Dwight Freeney, 13

JACKSONVILLE JAGUARS

Passing

Player	ATT	COMP	YDS	PCT. COMP	YDS/ATT	TD	INT	Rating
Mark Brunell	416	245	2,788	58.9	6.7	17	7	85.7
David Garrard	46	23	231	50.0	5.0	1	2	53.8

Rushing

Player	NO.	YDS	AVG	LG	TD
Fred Taylor	287	1,314	4.6	63	8
Stacey Mack	98	436	4.4	23	9
Mark Brunell	43	207	4.8	27	0
David Garrard	25	139	5.6	41	2

Receiving

Player	NO.	YDS	AVG	LG	TD
Jimmy Smith	80	1,027	12.8	47	7
Bobby Shaw	44	525	11.9	48	1
Kyle Brady	43	461	10.7	42	4
Fred Taylor	49	408	8.3	72	0
Pete Mitchell	25	246	9.8	45	2
Patrick Johnson	9	187	20.8	79	2

Punting

Player	NO.	AVG	NET AVG	TB	IN 20	LG	BLK
Chris Hanson	81	44.2	37.6	10	27	64	0

Interceptions Marlon McCree, 6   **Sacks** John Henderson, Marcus Stroud, 6.5

KANSAS CITY CHIEFS

Passing

Player	ATT	COMP	YDS	PCT. COMP	YDS/ATT	TD	INT	Rating
Trent Green	470	287	3,690	61.1	7.9	26	13	92.6

Rushing

Player	NO.	YDS	AVG	LG	TD
Priest Holmes	313	1,615	5.2	56	21
Trent Green	31	225	7.3	24	1
Johnnie Morton	10	124	12.4	36	0
Mike Cloud	49	115	2.3	9	2
Tony Richardson	22	81	3.7	14	2

Receiving

Player	NO.	YDS	AVG	LG	TD
Eddie Kennison	53	906	17.1	64	2
Tony Gonzalez	63	773	12.3	42	7
Priest Holmes	70	672	9.6	64	3
Marc Boerigter	20	420	21.0	99	8
Johnnie Morton	29	397	13.7	30	1
Tony Richardson	18	125	6.9	23	1

Punting

Player	NO.	AVG	NET AVG	TB	IN 20	LG	BLK
Dan Stryzinski	64	37.8	31.2	6	15	56	0

Interceptions Greg Wesley, 6   **Sacks** Erik Hicks, 9

MIAMI DOLPHINS

Passing

Player	ATT	COMP	YDS	PCT. COMP	YDS/ATT	TD	INT	Rating
Jay Fiedler	292	179	2,024	61.3	6.9	14	9	85.2
Ray Lucas	160	92	1,045	57.5	6.5	4	6	69.9

Rushing

Player	NO.	YDS	AVG	LG	TD
Ricky Williams	383	1,853	4.8	63	16
Travis Minor	44	180	4.1	23	2
Ray Lucas	36	126	3.5	17	2
Robert Edwards	20	107	5.4	19	1
Jay Fiedler	28	99	3.5	12	3

Receiving

Player	NO.	YDS	AVG	LG	TD
Chris Chambers	52	734	14.1	59	3
James McKnight	29	528	18.2	77	2
Randy McMichael	39	485	12.4	45	4
Ricky Williams	47	363	7.7	52	1
Rob Konrad	34	233	6.9	19	3
Oronde Gadsden	16	228	14.3	29	0

Punting

Player	NO.	AVG	NET AVG	TB	IN 20	LG	BLK
Mark Royals	69	40.2	34.5	6	15	56	0

Interceptions Patrick Surtain, 6   **Sacks** Jason Taylor, 18.5

NEW ENGLAND PATRIOTS

Passing

Player	ATT	COMP	YDS	PCT. COMP	YDS/ATT	TD	INT	Rating
Tom Brady	601	373	3,764	62.1	6.3	28	14	85.7

Rushing

Player	NO.	YDS	AVG	LG	TD
Antowain Smith	252	982	3.9	42	6
Kevin Faulk	52	271	5.2	45	2
Tom Brady	42	110	2.6	15	1

Receiving

Player	NO.	YDS	AVG	LG	TD
Troy Brown	97	890	9.2	38	3
David Patten	61	824	13.5	39	5
Deion Branch	43	489	11.4	49	2
Kevin Faulk	37	379	10.2	36	3
Christian Fauria	27	253	9.4	33	7
Antowain Smith	31	243	7.8	35	2
Marc Edwards	23	196	8.5	27	0
Daniel Graham	15	150	10.0	31	1
Donald Hayes	12	133	11.1	40	2
Cameron Cleeland	16	112	7.0	22	1

Punting

Player	NO.	AVG	NET AVG	TB	IN 20	LG	BLK
Ken Walter	70	38.9	33.3	9	19	55	0

Interceptions Ty Law, Terrell Buckley, 4   **Sacks** Willie McGinest, Richard Seymour, 5.5

NEW YORK JETS

Passing

Player	ATT	COMP	YDS	PCT. COMP	YDS/ATT	TD	INT	Rating
Chad Pennington	399	275	3,120	68.9	7.8	22	6	104.2
Vinny Testaverde	83	54	499	65.1	6.0	3	3	78.3

Rushing

Player	NO.	YDS	AVG	LG	TD
Curtis Martin	261	1,094	4.2	35	7
LaMont Jordan	84	316	3.8	61	3
Chad Pennington	29	49	1.7	14	2

Receiving

Player	NO.	YDS	AVG	LG	TD
Laveranues Coles	89	1,264	14.2	43	5
Wayne Chrebet	51	691	13.5	37	9
Santana Moss	30	433	14.4	47	4
Curtis Martin	49	362	7.4	28	0
Richie Anderson	45	257	5.7	15	1
Anthony Becht	28	243	8.7	21	5

Punting

Player	NO.	AVG	NET AVG	TB	IN 20	LG	BLK
Matt Turk	63	41.0	34.9	9	13	65	0

Interceptions Donnie Abraham, 4   **Sacks** John Abraham, 10

OAKLAND RAIDERS

Passing

Player	ATT	COMP	YDS	PCT. COMP	YDS/ATT	TD	INT	Rating
Rich Gannon	618	418	4,689	67.6	7.6	26	10	97.3

Rushing

Player	NO.	YDS	AVG	LG	TD
Charlie Garner	182	962	5.3	36	7
Tyrone Wheatley	108	419	3.9	36	2
Rich Gannon	50	156	3.1	24	3
Zack Crockett	40	118	3.0	33	8

Receiving

Player	NO.	YDS	AVG	LG	TD
Jerry Rice	92	1,211	13.2	75	7
Charlie Garner	91	941	10.3	69	4
Tim Brown	81	930	11.5	45	2
Jerry Porter	51	688	13.5	36	9
Doug Jolley	32	409	12.8	33	2
Roland Williams	27	213	7.9	19	0
Terry Kirby	17	115	6.8	24	1

Punting

Player	NO.	AVG	NET AVG	TB	IN 20	LG	BLK
Shane Lechler	53	42.5	32.7	12	18	70	0

Interceptions Rod Woodson, 8   **Sacks** Roderick Coleman, 11

PITTSBURGH STEELERS

Passing

Player	ATT	COMP	YDS	PCT. COMP	YDS/ATT	TD	INT	Rating
Tommy Maddox	377	234	2,836	62.1	7.5	20	16	85.2
Kordell Stewart	166	109	1,155	65.7	7.0	6	6	82.8

Rushing

Player	NO.	YDS	AVG	LG	TD
Amos Zereoue	193	762	3.9	42	4
Jerome Bettis	187	666	3.6	41	9
Kordell Stewart	43	191	4.4	28	2
Hines Ward	12	142	11.8	39	0
Antwaan Randle El	19	134	7.1	24	0

Receiving

Player	NO.	YDS	AVG	LG	TD
Hines Ward	112	1,329	11.9	72	12
Plaxico Burress	78	1,325	17.0	62	7
Antwaan Randle El	47	489	10.4	36	2
Amos Zereoue	42	341	8.1	54	0
Terance Mathis	23	218	9.5	22	2
Dan Kreider	18	122	6.8	15	1

Punting

Player	NO.	AVG	NET AVG	TB	IN 20	LG	BLK
Josh Miller	55	41.2	32.5	5	14	62	0

Interceptions Joey Porter, Brent Alexander, 4   **Sacks** Joey Porter, Jason Gildon, 9

SAN DIEGO CHARGERS

Passing

Player	ATT	COMP	YDS	PCT. COMP	YDS/ATT	TD	INT	Rating
Drew Brees	526	320	3,284	60.8	6.2	17	16	76.9

Rushing

Player	NO.	YDS	AVG	LG	TD
LaDainian Tomlinson	372	1,683	4.5	76	14
Drew Brees	38	130	3.4	15	1
Terrell Fletcher	26	128	4.9	15	1
Tim Dwight	12	108	9.0	20	1
Fred McCrary	22	96	4.4	25	3

Receiving

Player	NO.	YDS	AVG	LG	TD
Curtis Conway	57	852	14.9	52	5
Tim Dwight	50	623	12.5	42	2
Stephen Alexander	45	510	11.3	32	1
LaDainian Tomlinson	79	489	6.2	30	1
Eric Parker	17	268	15.8	31	1
Reche Caldwell	22	208	9.5	26	3
Josh Norman	16	201	12.6	29	1

Punting

Player	NO.	AVG	NET AVG	TB	IN 20	LG	BLK
Darren Bennett	87	40.7	34.3	6	31	63	0

TENNESSEE TITANS

Passing

Player	ATT	COMP	YDS	PCT. COMP	YDS/ATT	TD	INT	Rating
Steve McNair	492	301	3,387	61.2	6.9	22	15	84.0

Rushing

Player	NO.	YDS	AVG	LG	TD
Eddie George	343	1,165	3.4	35	12
Steve McNair	82	440	5.4	26	3
Robert Holcombe	47	242	5.1	39	0

Receiving

Player	NO.	YDS	AVG	LG	TD
Derrick Mason	79	1,012	12.8	40	5
Drew Bennett	33	478	14.5	53	2
Kevin Dyson	41	460	11.2	40	4
Frank Wycheck	40	346	8.7	19	2
Justin McCareins	19	301	15.8	55	2
Eddie George	36	255	7.1	14	2
Erron Kinney	13	173	13.3	31	0
John Simon	16	167	10.4	42	3

Punting

Player	NO.	AVG	NET AVG	TB	IN 20	LG	BLK
Craig Hentrich	65	41.9	33.9	5	28	56	0

Interceptions Lance Schulters, 6

Sacks Kevin Carter, 10

 **F**OOTBALL *PRO*

TEAM-BY-TEAM STATS—NFC

ARIZONA CARDINALS

Passing

Player	ATT	COMP	YDS	PCT. COMP	YDS/ATT	TD	INT	Rating
Jake Plummer	530	284	2,972	53.6	5.6	18	20	65.7

Rushing

Player	NO.	YDS	AVG	LG	TD
Marcel Shipp	188	834	4.4	56	6
Thomas Jones	138	511	3.7	58	2
Jake Plummer	46	283	6.2	34	2

Receiving

Player	NO.	YDS	AVG	LG	TD
David Boston	32	512	16.0	34	1
Marcel Shipp	38	413	10.9	80	3
Frank Sanders	34	400	11.8	37	2
Jason McAddley	25	362	14.5	42	1
Freddie Jones	44	358	8.1	24	1
MarTay Jenkins	21	250	11.9	65	1
Kevin Kasper	15	180	12.0	24	3
Steve Bush	19	121	6.4	13	1
Thomas Jones	20	113	5.7	17	0

Punting

Player	NO.	AVG	NET AVG	TB	IN 20	LG	BLK
Scott Player	88	43.9	35.0	10	28	58	0

Interceptions Adrian Wilson, 4   **Sacks** Kyle Vanden Bosch, 3.5

ATLANTA FALCONS

Passing

Player	ATT	COMP	YDS	PCT. COMP	YDS/ATT	TD	INT	Rating
Michael Vick	421	231	2,936	54.9	7.0	16	8	81.6
Doug Johnson	57	37	448	64.9	7.9	2	3	78.7

Rushing

Player	NO.	YDS	AVG	LG	TD
Warrick Dunn	230	927	4.0	59	7
Michael Vick	113	777	6.9	46	8
T.J. Duckett	130	507	3.9	33	4
Bob Christian	31	119	3.8	16	3

Receiving

Player	NO.	YDS	AVG	LG	TD
Brian Finneran	56	838	15.0	47	6
Alge Crumpler	36	455	12.6	33	5
Shawn Jefferson	27	394	14.6	63	1
Trevor Gaylor	25	385	15.4	74	3
Warrick Dunn	50	377	7.5	31	2
Willie Jackson	18	199	11.1	29	0
Bob Christian	13	174	13.4	55	0
Reggie Kelly	14	162	11.6	33	0

Punting

Player	NO.	AVG	NET AVG	TB	IN 20	LG	BLK
Chris Mohr	67	41.9	38.7	5	21	59	0

Interceptions Keion Carpenter, 4   **Sacks** Patrick Kerney, 10.5

CAROLINA PANTHERS

Passing

Player	ATT	COMP	YDS	PCT. COMP	YDS/ATT	TD	INT	Rating
Rodney Peete	381	223	2,630	58.5	6.9	15	14	77.4

Rushing

Player	NO.	YDS	AVG	LG	TD
Lamar Smith	209	737	3.5	59	7
Dee Brown	102	360	3.5	24	4
Nick Goings	50	188	3.8	20	0
Brad Hoover	31	129	4.2	11	0

Receiving

Player	NO.	YDS	AVG	LG	TD
Steve Smith	54	872	16.1	69	3
Muhsin Muhammad	63	823	13.1	42	3
Wesley Walls	19	241	12.7	27	4
Brad Hoover	17	187	11.0	33	2
Lamar Smith	20	167	8.4	58	0
Isaac Byrd	14	164	11.7	31	1

Punting

Player	NO.	AVG	NET AVG	TB	IN 20	LG	BLK
Todd Sauerbrun	104	45.5	37.5	12	31	67	0

Interceptions Mike Minter, 4 **Sacks** Julius Peppers, 12

CHICAGO BEARS

Passing

Player	ATT	COMP	YDS	PCT. COMP	YDS/ATT	TD	INT	Rating
Jim Miller	314	180	1,944	57.3	6.2	13	9	77.5
Chris Chandler	161	103	1,023	64.0	6.4	4	4	79.8

Rushing

Player	NO.	YDS	AVG	LG	TD
Anthony Thomas	214	721	3.4	34	6
Leon Johnson	103	329	3.2	23	1
Henry Burris	15	104	6.9	17	0
Adrian Peterson	19	101	5.3	14	1

Receiving

Player	NO.	YDS	AVG	LG	TD
Marty Booker	97	1,189	12.3	54	6
Dez White	51	656	12.9	76	4
Marcus Robinson	21	244	11.6	45	3
John Davis	20	193	9.7	37	3
Stanley Pritchett	19	165	8.7	24	1
Anthony Thomas	24	163	6.8	19	0
David Terrell	9	127	14.1	52	3

Punting

Player	NO.	AVG	NET AVG	TB	IN 20	LG	BLK
Brad Maynard	87	42.3	37.4	2	26	75	0

Interceptions Mike Brown, 3 **Sacks** Rosevelt Colvin, 10.5

DALLAS COWBOYS

Passing

Player	ATT	COMP	YDS	PCT. COMP	YDS/ATT	TD	INT	Rating
Chad Hutchinson	250	127	1,555	50.8	6.2	7	8	66.3
Quincy Carter	221	125	1,465	56.6	6.6	7	8	72.3

Rushing

Player	NO.	YDS	AVG	LG	TD
Emmitt Smith	254	975	3.8	30	5
Troy Hambrick	79	317	4.0	18	1
Michael Wiley	22	168	7.6	46	1
Quincy Carter	27	91	3.4	16	0

Receiving

Player	NO.	YDS	AVG	LG	TD
Joey Galloway	61	908	14.9	80	6
Antonio Bryant	44	733	16.7	78	6
Tony McGee	23	294	12.8	58	1
Darnay Scott	2	218	9.9	17	1
Ken-Yon Rambo	14	211	15.1	47	0
James Whalen	17	152	8.9	33	0
Michael Wiley	13	144	11.1	31	0

Punting

Player	NO.	AVG	NET AVG	TB	IN 20	LG	BLK
Filip Filipovic	65	40.6	31.5	6	14	60	0
Micah Knorr*	47	41.0	35.1	4	11	56	0

Interceptions Derek Ross, Roy Williams, 5

Sacks Greg Ellis, 7.5

DETROIT LIONS

Passing

Player	ATT	COMP	YDS	PCT. COMP	YDS/ATT	TD	INT	Rating
Joey Harrington	429	215	2,294	50.1	5.3	12	16	59.9
Mike McMahon	147	62	874	42.2	5.9	7	9	52.4

Rushing

Player	NO.	YDS	AVG	LG	TD
James Stewart	231	1,021	4.4	56	4
Cory Schlesinger	49	139	2.8	17	2
Aveion Cason	26	107	4.1	40	0
Mike McMahon	14	96	6.9	22	3

Receiving

Player	NO.	YDS	AVG	LG	TD
Bill Schroeder	36	595	16.5	46	5
Az-Zahir Hakim	37	541	14.6	64	3
Mikhael Ricks	27	339	12.6	49	3
James Stewart	46	333	7.2	52	2
Scotty Anderson	25	322	12.9	34	1
Aveion Cason	19	288	15.2	37	2
Cory Schlesinger	35	263	7.5	43	0
Larry Foster	14	152	10.9	22	0

Punting

Player	NO.	AVG	NET AVG	TB	IN 20	LG	BLK
John Jett	91	42.2	38.0	7	29	57	0

Interceptions Chris Claiborne, 3

Sacks Kalimba Edwards, 6.5

*Played for Dallas and Denver in 2002.

GREEN BAY PACKERS

Passing

Player	ATT	COMP	YDS	PCT. COMP	YDS/ATT	TD	INT	Rating
Brett Favre	551	341	3,658	61.9	6.6	27	16	85.6

Rushing

Player	NO.	YDS	AVG	LG	TD
Ahman Green	286	1,240	4.3	43	7
Tony Fisher	70	283	4.0	28	2
Najeh Davenport	39	184	4.7	43	1

Receiving

Player	NO.	YDS	AVG	LG	TD
Donald Driver	70	1,064	15.2	85	9
Terry Glenn	56	817	14.6	49	2
Bubba Franks	54	442	8.2	20	7
Ahman Green	57	393	6.9	23	2
Javon Walker	23	319	13.9	30	1
Robert Ferguson	22	293	13.3	40	3
William Henderson	26	168	6.5	17	3
Tyrone Davis	9	107	11.9	24	1

Punting

Player	NO.	AVG	NET AVG	TB	IN 20	LG	BLK
Josh Bidwell	79	41.7	35.7	6	26	57	0

Interceptions Darren Sharper, 7   **Sacks** Kabeer Gbaja-Biamila, 12

MINNESOTA VIKINGS

Passing

Player	ATT	COMP	YDS	PCT. COMP	YDS/ATT	TD	INT	Rating
Daunte Culpepper	549	333	3,853	60.7	7.0	18	23	75.3

Rushing

Player	NO.	YDS	AVG	LG	TD
Michael Bennett	255	1,296	5.1	85	5
Daunte Culpepper	106	609	5.7	38	10
Moe Williams	84	414	4.9	44	11

Receiving

Player	NO.	YDS	AVG	LG	TD
Randy Moss	106	1,347	12.7	60	7
D'Wayne Bates	50	689	13.8	59	4
Jimmy Kleinsasser	37	393	10.6	39	1
Byron Chamberlain	34	389	11.4	61	0
Michael Bennett	37	351	9.5	45	1
Moe Williams	27	251	9.3	36	0
Kelly Campbell	13	176	13.5	32	3
Chris Walsh	14	172	12.3	28	1
Derrick Alexander	14	134	9.6	18	1

Punting

Player	NO.	AVG	NET AVG	TB	IN 20	LG	BLK
Kyle Richardson	62	39.9	35.3	6	21	59	0

Interceptions Greg Biekert, 4   **Sacks** Lance Johnstone, 7

NEW ORLEANS SAINTS

Passing

Player	ATT	COMP	YDS	PCT. COMP	YDS/ATT	TD	INT	Rating
Aaron Brooks	528	283	3,572	53.6	6.8	27	15	80.1

Rushing

Player	NO.	YDS	AVG	LG	TD
Deuce McAllister	325	1,388	4.3	62	13
Aaron Brooks	62	253	4.1	21	2
James Fenderson	13	65	5.0	17	1

Receiving

Player	NO.	YDS	AVG	LG	TD
Joe Horn	88	1,312	14.9	63	7
Donte' Stallworth	42	594	14.1	57	8
Jerome Pathon	43	523	12.2	64	4
Jake Reed	21	360	17.1	54	3
Deuce McAllister	47	352	7.5	30	3
Michael Lewis	8	200	25.0	59	0
Boo Williams	13	143	11.0	32	2

Punting

Player	NO.	AVG	NET AVG	TB	IN 20	LG	BLK
Toby Gowin	61	41.9	36.9	6	15	59	0

Interceptions Fred Thomas, Sammy Knight, 5   **Sacks** Darren Howard, 8

NEW YORK GIANTS

Passing

Player	ATT	COMP	YDS	PCT. COMP	YDS/ATT	TD	INT	Rating
Kerry Collins	545	335	4,073	61.5	7.5	19	14	85.4

Rushing

Player	NO.	YDS	AVG	LG	TD
Tiki Barber	304	1,387	4.6	70	11
Ron Dayne	125	428	3.4	30	3

Receiving

Player	NO.	YDS	AVG	LG	TD
Amani Toomer	82	1,343	16.4	82	8
Jeremy Shockey	74	894	12.1	30	2
Tiki Barber	69	597	8.7	38	0
Ike Hilliard	27	386	14.3	38	2
Ron Dixon	22	377	17.1	33	2
Dan Campbell	22	175	8.0	27	1

Punting

Player	NO.	AVG	NET AVG	TB	IN 20	LG	BLK
Matt Allen	63	36.9	32.5	4	20	65	0

Interceptions Shaun Williams, Will Peterson, 2   **Sacks** Michael Strahan, 11

PHILADELPHIA EAGLES

Passing

Player	ATT	COMP	YDS	PCT. Comp	YDS/ATT	TD	INT	Rating
Donovan McNabb	361	211	2,289	58.4	6.3	17	6	86.0
A.J. Feeley	154	86	1,011	55.8	6.6	6	5	75.4

Rushing

Player	NO.	YDS	AVG	LG	TD
Duce Staley	269	1,029	3.8	57	5
Donovan McNabb	63	460	7.3	40	6
Dorsey Levens	75	411	5.5	47	1
Brian Westbrook	46	193	4.2	18	0
James Thrash	18	126	7.0	32	2

Receiving

Player	NO.	YDS	AVG	LG	TD
Todd Pinkston	60	798	13.3	42	7
James Thrash	52	635	12.2	39	6
Antonio Freeman	46	600	13.0	59	4
Duce Staley	51	541	10.6	45	3
Chad Lewis	42	398	9.5	30	3
Jeff Thomason	10	128	12.8	24	2
Cecil Martin	15	126	8.4	53	0
Dorsey Levens	19	124	6.5	24	1

Punting

Player	NO.	AVG	NET AVG	TB	IN 20	LG	BLK
Sean Landeta	52	42.9	34.6	7	19	63	0
Jason Baker*	13	34.2	29.8	1	2	44	0

Interceptions Bobby Taylor, 5   **Sacks** Hugh Douglas, 12.5

SAN FRANCISCO 49ERS

Passing

Player	ATT	COMP	YDS	PCT. COMP	YDS/ATT	TD	INT	Rating
Jeff Garcia	528	328	3,344	62.1	6.3	21	10	85.6

Rushing

Player	NO.	YDS	AVG	LG	TD
Garrison Hearst	215	972	4.5	40	8
Kevan Barlow	145	675	4.7	35	4
Jeff Garcia	73	353	4.8	21	3
Paul Smith	18	90	5.0	16	0
Terrell Owens	7	79	11.3	38	1

Receiving

Player	NO.	YDS	AVG	LG	TD
Terrell Owens	100	1,300	13.0	76	13
Tai Streets	72	756	10.5	47	5
J.J. Stokes	32	332	10.4	51	1
Eric Johnson	36	321	8.9	38	0
Garrison Hearst	48	317	6.6	16	1
Cedrick Wilson	15	166	11.1	22	1
Fred Beasley	22	152	6.9	25	1
Kevan Barlow	14	136	9.7	29	1

Punting

Player	No.	AVG	NET AVG	TB	IN 20	LG	BLK
Jason Baker*	42	40.2	32.0	3	12	51	0
Bill LaFleur	22	36.6	30.8	1	5	60	0

Interceptions Tony Parrish, 7   **Sacks** Andre Carter, 12.5

*Played for Philadelphia and San Francisco in 2002.

SEATTLE SEAHAWKS

Passing

Player	ATT	COMP	YDS	PCT. COMP	YDS/ATT	TD	INT	Rating
Matt Hasselbeck	419	267	3,075	63.7	7.3	15	10	87.8
Trent Dilfer	168	94	1,182	56.0	7.0	4	6	71.1

Rushing

Player	NO.	YDS	AVG	LG	TD
Shaun Alexander	295	1,175	4.0	58	16
Matt Hasselbeck	40	202	5.1	21	1
Maurice Morris	32	153	4.8	24	0
Mack Strong	22	120	5.5	12	2

Receiving

Player	NO.	YDS	AVG	LG	TD
Koren Robinson	78	1,240	15.9	83	5
Darrell Jackson	62	877	14.1	48	4
Bobby Engram	50	619	12.4	38	0
Itula Mili	43	508	11.8	49	2
Shaun Alexander	59	460	7.8	80	2
Jerramy Stevens	26	252	9.7	29	3

Punting

Player	NO.	AVG	NET AVG	TB	IN 20	LG	BLK
Jeff Feagles	61	41.7	37.0	4	22	58	0

Interceptions Reggie Tongue, 5   **Sacks** John Randle, 7

ST. LOUIS RAMS

Passing

Player	ATT	COMP	YDS	PCT. COMP	YDS/ATT	TD	INT	Rating
Marc Bulger	214	138	1,826	64.5	8.5	14	6	101.5
Kurt Warner	220	144	1,431	65.5	6.5	3	11	67.4
Jamie Martin	195	124	1,216	63.6	6.2	7	10	71.7

Rushing

Player	NO.	YDS	AVG	LG	TD
Marshall Faulk	212	953	4.5	44	8
Lamar Gordon	65	228	3.5	29	1

Receiving

Player	NO.	YDS	AVG	LG	TD
Torry Holt	91	1,302	14.3	58	4
Isaac Bruce	79	1,075	13.6	34	7
Marshall Faulk	80	537	6.7	40	2
Ricky Proehl	43	466	10.8	33	4
Ernie Conwell	34	419	12.3	52	2
Lamar Gordon	30	278	9.3	25	2
Troy Edwards	18	157	8.7	48	2
Brandon Manumaleuna	8	106	13.3	27	1

Punting

Player	NO.	AVG	NET AVG	TB	IN 20	LG	BLK
Mitch Berger	72	41.9	32.7	10	26	64	0

Interceptions Kim Herring, 3   **Sacks** Leonard Little, 12

TAMPA BAY BUCCANEERS

Passing

Player	ATT	COMP	YDS	PCT. COMP	YDS/ATT	TD	INT	Rating
Brad Johnson	451	281	3,049	62.3	6.8	22	6	92.9

Rushing

Player	NO.	YDS	AVG	LG	TD
Michael Pittman	204	718	3.5	21	1
Mike Alstott	146	548	3.8	32	5
Aaron Stecker	28	174	6.2	59	0

Receiving

Player	NO.	YDS	AVG	LG	TD
Keyshawn Johnson	76	1,088	14.3	76	5
Keenan McCardell	61	670	11.0	65	6
Michael Pittman	59	477	8.1	64	0
Joe Jurevicius	37	423	11.4	26	4
Ken Dilger	34	329	9.7	40	2
Mike Alstott	35	242	6.9	44	2
Rickey Dudley	16	192	12.0	35	3

Punting

Player	NO.	AVG	NET AVG	TB	IN 20	LG	BLK
Tom Tupa	90	42.8	35.4	12	30	71	0

Interceptions Brian Kelly, 8

Sacks Simeon Rice, 15.5

WASHINGTON REDSKINS

Passing

Player	ATT	COMP	YDS	PCT. COMP	YDS/ATT	TD	INT	Rating
Patrick Ramsey	227	117	1,539	51.5	6.8	9	8	71.8
Shane Matthews	237	124	1,251	52.3	5.3	11	6	72.6
Danny Wuerffel	92	58	719	63.0	7.8	3	6	70.9

Rushing

Player	NO.	YDS	AVG	LG	TD
Stephen Davis	207	820	4.0	33	7
Kenny Watson	116	534	4.6	24	1
Ladell Betts	65	307	4.7	27	1

Receiving

Player	NO.	YDS	AVG	LG	TD
Rod Gardner	71	1,006	14.2	43	8
Derrius Thompson	53	773	14.6	47	4
Darnerien McCants	21	256	12.2	32	2
Kenny Watson	32	253	7.9	62	1
Chris Doering	18	192	10.7	33	2
Ladell Betts	12	154	12.8	40	0
Zeron Flemister	10	146	14.6	25	2
Stephen Davis	23	142	6.2	14	1
Kevin Lockett	11	129	11.7	26	2
Rock Cartwright	11	121	11.0	22	1
Bryan Johnson	15	114	7.6	23	0

Punting

Player	NO.	AVG	NET AVG	TB	IN 20	LG	BLK
Bryan Barker	48	40.1	30.0	5	13	63	0

Interceptions Fred Smoot, 4

Sacks LaVar Arrington, 11

Super Bowl Results

	Date	Winner	Loser	Score	Site	Attendance
XXXVII	1-26-03	Buccaneers	Raiders	48-21	San Diego, CA	67,603
XXXVI	2-3-02	Patriots	Rams	20-17	New Orleans, LA	72,922
XXXV	1-28-01	Ravens	Giants	34-7	Tampa, FL	71,921
XXXIV	1-30-00	Rams	Titans	23-16	Atlanta, GA	72,625
XXXIII	1-31-99	Broncos	Falcons	34-19	Miami, FL	74,803
XXXII	1-25-98	Broncos	Packers	31-24	San Diego, CA	68,912
XXXI	1-26-97	Packers	Patriots	35-21	New Orleans, LA	72,301
XXX	1-28-96	Cowboys	Steelers	27-17	Tempe, AZ	76,347
XXIX	1-29-95	49ers	Chargers	49-26	Miami, FL	74,107
XXVIII	1-30-94	Cowboys	Bills	30-13	Atlanta, GA	72,817
XXVII	1-31-93	Cowboys	Bills	52-17	Pasadena, CA	98,374
XXVI	1-26-92	Redskins	Bills	37-24	Minneapolis, MN	63,130
XXV	1-27-91	Giants	Bills	20-19	Tampa, FL	73,813
XXIV	1-28-90	49ers	Broncos	55-10	New Orleans, LA	72,919
XXIII	1-22-89	49ers	Bengals	20-16	Miami, FL	75,129
XXII	1-31-88	Redskins	Broncos	42-10	San Diego, CA	73,302
XXI	1-25-87	Giants	Broncos	39-20	Pasadena, CA	101,063
XX	1-26-86	Bears	Patriots	46-10	New Orleans, LA	73,818
XIX	1-20-85	49ers	Dolphins	38-16	Stanford, CA	84,059
XVIII	1-22-84	Raiders	Redskins	38-9	Tampa, FL	72,920
XVII	1-30-83	Redskins	Dolphins	27-17	Pasadena, CA	103,667
XVI	1-24-82	49ers	Bengals	26-21	Pontiac, MI	81,270
XV	1-25-81	Raiders	Eagles	27-10	New Orleans, LA	76,135
XIV	1-20-80	Steelers	Rams	31-19	Pasadena, CA	103,985
XIII	1-21-79	Steelers	Cowboys	35-31	Miami, FL	79,484
XII	1-15-78	Cowboys	Broncos	27-10	New Orleans, LA	75,583
XI	1-9-77	Raiders	Vikings	32-14	Pasadena, CA	103,438
X	1-18-76	Steelers	Cowboys	21-17	Miami, FL	80,187
IX	1-12-75	Steelers	Vikings	16-6	New Orleans, LA	80,997
VIII	1-13-74	Dolphins	Vikings	24-7	Houston, TX	71,882
VII	1-14-73	Dolphins	Redskins	14-7	Los Angeles, CA	90,182
VI	1-16-72	Cowboys	Dolphins	24-3	New Orleans, LA	81,023
V	1-17-71	Colts	Cowboys	16-13	Miami, FL	79,204
IV	1-11-70	Chiefs	Vikings	23-7	New Orleans, LA	80,562
III	1-12-69	Jets	Colts	16-7	Miami, FL	75,389
II	1-14-68	Packers	Raiders	33-14	Miami, FL	75,546
I	1-15-67	Packers	Chiefs	35-10	Los Angeles, CA	61,946

Super Bowl Most Valuable Players

Super Bowl	Player/Team	Position	Super Bowl	Player/Team	Position
XXXVII	Dexter Jackson, Buccaneers	S	XVIII	Marcus Allen, Raiders	RB
XXXVI	Tom Brady, Patriots	QB	XVII	John Riggins, Redskins	RB
XXXV	Ray Lewis, Ravens	LB	XVI	Joe Montana, 49ers	QB
XXXIV	Kurt Warner, Rams	QB	XV	Jim Plunkett, Raiders	QB
XXXIII	John Elway, Broncos	QB	XIV	Terry Bradshaw, Steelers	QB
XXXII	Terrell Davis, Broncos	RB	XIII	Terry Bradshaw, Steelers	QB
XXXI	Desmond Howard, Packers	KR	XII	Randy White, Cowboys	DT
XXX	Larry Brown, Cowboys	DB		Harvey Martin, Cowboys	DE
XXIX	Steve Young, 49ers	QB	XI	Fred Biletnikoff, Raiders	WR
XXVIII	Emmitt Smith, Cowboys	RB	X	Lynn Swann, Steelers	WR
XXVII	Troy Aikman, Cowboys	QB	IX	Franco Harris, Steelers	RB
XXVI	Mark Rypien, Redskins	QB	VIII	Larry Csonka, Dolphins	RB
XXV	Ottis Anderson, Giants	RB	VII	Jake Scott, Dolphins	S
XXIV	Joe Montana, 49ers	QB	VI	Roger Staubach, Cowboys	QB
XXIII	Jerry Rice, 49ers	WR	V	Chuck Howley, Cowboys	LB
XXII	Doug Williams, Redskins	QB	IV	Len Dawson, Chiefs	QB
XXI	Phil Simms, Giants	QB	III	Joe Namath, Jets	QB
XX	Richard Dent, Bears	DE	II	Bart Starr, Packers	QB
XIX	Joe Montana, 49ers	QB	I	Bart Starr, Packers	QB

KEY S=safety; QB=quarterback; LB=linebacker; RB=running back; KR=kick returner; DB=defensive back; WR=wide receiver; DE=defensive end; DT=defensive tackle

2002-03 TIMELINE --

September 5, 2002: The San Francisco 49ers topple the New York Giants, 16–13, as the NFL season opens. The game is the first mid-week season opener in NFL history.

September 8, 2002: The Houston Texans become the first NFL expansion team to win their season opener since the NFL-AFL merger in 1970. The Texans beat the Dallas Cowboys, 19–10, in the "Texas Super Bowl."

September 29, 2002: Seattle running back Shaun Alexander sets an NFL record for most touchdowns in a half. He scores five TDs in the first half of a 48–23 romp over the Minnesota Vikings.

October 20, 2002: Denver Bronco tight end Shannon Sharpe gallops for 214 receiving yards and two touchdowns, setting an NFL record for receiving yards in a single game by a tight end.

October 27, 2002: Running back Emmitt Smith of the Dallas Cowboys becomes the NFL's all-time leading rusher with a season-high 109 yards against the Seattle Seahawks. Smith finishes the game with 16,743 career rushing yards, surpassing Chicago Bear legend Walter Payton by 17 yards. He finishes the season with a total of 17,162 career rushing yards.

November 11, 2002: Oakland Raider quarterback Rich Gannon completes 21 consecutive passes, an NFL single-game record, as the Raiders rout the Denver Broncos, 34–10. Gannon's teammate, wide receiver Jerry Rice, catches a pair of touchdowns to become the first NFL player with 200 career touchdowns.

December 1, 2002: Michael Vick of the Atlanta Falcons sets an NFL single-game record for quarterbacks with 173 rushing yards. His 46-yard touchdown dash through the entire Minnesota Viking defense gives the Falcons a 30–24 overtime win.

December 15, 2002: Indianapolis Colt receiver Marvin Harrison catches nine passes for 172 yards and two touchdowns in a 28–23 win over the Cleveland Browns. The nine catches give Harrison an NFL single-season record 127. He finishes the season with 143 grabs, shattering the previous record by 20.

December 22, 2002: Rich Gannon sets another NFL record with his 405th completion of the season. He finishes the season with 418.

January 4, 2003: The Atlanta Falcons shock the Green Bay Packers, 27–7, in an NFC wild-card game at Lambeau Field, in Green Bay. The win snaps the Packers' perfect 13–0 record at home in the playoffs.

January 11, 2003: The Tennessee Titans sneak past the Pittsburgh Steelers in overtime, 34–31, in a wild AFC divisional playoff game. Titan kicker Joe Nedney misses a field goal from 31 yards, but a penalty is called on Steelers cornerback Dewayne Washington for running into the kicker. Given a second chance, Nedney boots the 26-yard game-winner.

January 26, 2003: The Tampa Bay Buccaneers set a Super Bowl record with five interceptions — returning three for touchdowns — to win the franchise's first championship, over the Oakland Raiders, 48–21.

February 27, 2003: Emmitt Smith, the leading rusher in NFL history, is released by the Dallas Cowboys after 13 seasons. A three-time Super Bowl winner, Smith won rushing titles in 1991, 1992, 1993, and 1995. He was the league's MVP in 1993. Smith signs with the Arizona Cardinals on March 27.

Visit **www.sikids.com** for the latest sports stats and info. Site code: slamdunk AOL keyword: sikids

Emmitt Smith

PETER READ MILLER/SPORTS ILLUSTRATED

All-time NFL Individual Statistical Leaders— Career Leaders

Scoring

Player	YRS	TD	FG	PAT	PTS
†Gary Anderson	21	0	494	741	2,223
†Morten Andersen	21	0	486	695	2,153
George Blanda	26	9	335	943	2,002
Norm Johnson	18	0	366	638	1,736
Nick Lowery	18	0	383	562	1,711
Jan Stenerud	19	0	373	580	1,699
Eddie Murray	19	0	352	539	1,595
Al Del Greco	17	0	347	543	1,584
Pat Leahy	18	0	304	558	1,470
Jim Turner	16	1	304	521	1,439
Matt Bahr	17	0	300	522	1,422
Mark Moseley	16	0	300	482	1,382
Jim Bakken	17	0	282	534	1,380
Fred Cox	15	0	282	519	1,365
Lou Groza	17	1	234	641	1,349
†Steve Christie	13	0	299	399	1,296
Jim Breech	14	0	243	517	1,246
Pete Stoyanovich	12	0	272	420	1,236
Chris Bahr	14	0	241	490	1,213
Kevin Butler	13	0	265	426	1,208

Rushing

Player	YRS	ATT	YDS	AVG	LG	TD
†Emmitt Smith	13	4,052	17,162	4.2	75	153
Walter Payton	13	3,838	16,726	4.4	76	110
Barry Sanders	10	3,062	15,269	5.0	85	99
Eric Dickerson	11	2,996	13,259	4.4	85	90
Tony Dorsett	12	2,936	12,739	4.3	99	77
Jim Brown	9	2,359	12,312	5.2	80	106
Marcus Allen	16	3,022	12,243	4.1	61	123
Franco Harris	13	2,949	12,120	4.1	75	91
Thurman Thomas	13	2,877	12,074	4.2	80	66
†Jerome Bettis	10	2,873	11,542	4.0	71	62
John Riggins	14	2,916	11,352	3.9	66	104
O.J. Simpson	11	2,404	11,236	4.7	94	61
Ricky Watters	11	2,622	10,643	4.1	57	78
†Marshall Faulk	9	2,367	10,395	4.4	71	87
Ottis Anderson	14	2,562	10,273	4.0	76	81
Earl Campbell	8	2,187	9,407	4.3	81	74
Curtis Martin	7	2,343	9,267	4.0	70	64
Terry Allen	11	2,152	8,614	4.0	55	73
Jim Taylor	10	1,941	8,597	4.4	84	83
Joe Perry	14	1,737	8,378	4.8	78	53

Touchdowns

Player	YRS	RUSH	REC	RET	TD
†Jerry Rice	18	10	192	0	202
†Emmitt Smith	13	153	11	0	164
Marcus Allen	16	123	21	1	145
†Cris Carter	16	0	130	0	130
Jim Brown	9	106	20	0	126
Walter Payton	13	110	15	0	125
†Marshall Faulk	9	87	33	0	120
John Riggins	14	104	12	0	116
Lenny Moore	12	63	48	2	113
Barry Sanders	10	99	10	0	109

Player	YRS	RUSH	REC	RET	TD
Don Hutson	11	3	99	3	105
Steve Largent	14	1	100	0	101
†Tim Brown	15	1	97	3	101
Franco Harris	13	91	9	0	100
Eric Dickerson	11	90	6	0	96
Jim Taylor	10	83	10	0	93
Tony Dorsett	12	77	13	1	91
Bobby Mitchell	11	18	65	8	91
Ricky Watters	11	78	13	0	91

Two tied with 90.

Passing—Efficiency*

Player	YRS	ATT	COMP	PCT COMP	YDS	AVG GAIN	TD	INT	Rating
Steve Young	15	4,149	2,667	64.3	33,124	7.98	232	107	96.8
Joe Montana	15	5,391	3,409	63.2	40,551	7.52	273	139	92.3
†Brett Favre	12	5,993	3,652	60.9	42,285	7.10	314	188	86.7
Dan Marino	17	8,358	4,967	59.4	61,361	7.34	420	252	86.4
†Peyton Manning	5	2,817	1,749	62.1	20,618	7.30	138	100	85.9
†Rich Gannon	15	3,913	2,367	60.5	26,945	6.90	171	98	85.3
†Mark Brunell	10	3,561	2,142	60.2	25,309	7.10	142	86	85.1
†Brad Johnson	11	2,831	1,747	61.7	19,428	6.90	114	74	84.6
Jim Kelly	11	4,779	2,874	60.1	35,467	7.42	237	175	84.4
Roger Staubach	11	2,958	1,685	57.0	22,700	7.67	153	109	83.4

Passing—Yards

Player	YRS	ATT	COMP	PCT COMP	YDS
Dan Marino	17	8,358	4,967	59.4	61,361
John Elway	16	7,250	4,123	56.9	51,475
Warren Moon	17	6,823	3,988	58.5	49,325
Fran Tarkenton	18	6,467	3,686	57.0	47,003
Dan Fouts	15	5,604	3,297	58.8	43,040
†Brett Favre	12	5,993	3,652	60.9	42,285

Player	YRS	ATT	COMP	PCT COMP	YDS
Joe Montana	15	5,391	3,409	63.2	40,551
Johnny Unitas	18	5,186	2,830	54.6	40,239
†Vinny Testaverde	16	5,727	3,211	56.1	39,558
Dave Krieg	19	5,311	3,105	58.5	38,147
Boomer Esiason	14	5,205	2,969	57.0	37,920
Jim Kelly	11	4,779	2,874	60.1	35,467

KEY YRS=years; TD=touchdowns; FG=field goals; PAT=extra points; PTS=points; ATT=attempts; AVG=average; LG=long; RUSH=rushing; RET=returns; Comp=completions; PCT COMP=completion percentage; AVG GAIN=average gain; INT=interceptions; COMP YDS=completion yards

*1,500 or more attempts. The passer ratings are based on performance standards established for completion percentage, interception percentage, touchdown percentage, and average gain. Passers are allocated points according to how their marks compare with those standards.
† Active in 2002

All-time NFL Individual Statistical Leaders (cont.)

Passing—Touchdowns

Player	TD
Dan Marino	420
Fran Tarkenton	342
†Brett Favre	314
John Elway	300
Warren Moon	291
Johnny Unitas	290
Joe Montana	273
Dave Krieg	261
Sonny Jurgensen	255
Dan Fouts	254
Boomer Esiason	247
John Hadl	244
†Vinny Testaverde	244
Len Dawson	239
Jim Kelly	237
George Blanda	236
Steve Young	232

Sacks

Player	Sacks
Reggie White	198.0
†Bruce Smith	195.0
Kevin Greene	160.0
Chris Doleman	150.5
Richard Dent	137.5

Note: Officially compiled since 1982

Interceptions

Player	YRS	NO.	YDS	AVG	LG	TD
Paul Krause	16	81	1,185	14.6	81	3
Emlen Tunnell	14	79	1,282	16.2	55	4
Dick "Night Train" Lane	14	68	1,207	17.8	80	5
Ken Riley	15	65	596	9.2	66	5
Ronnie Lott	14	63	730	11.6	83	5

PETER READ MILLER/SPORTS ILLUSTRATED

Jerry Rice, Oakland Raiders

Receiving—Receptions

Player	YRS	NO.	YDS	AVG	LG	TD
†Jerry Rice	18	1,456	21,597	14.8	96	192
†Cris Carter	16	1,101	13,899	12.6	80	130
†Tim Brown	15	1,018	14,167	13.9	80	97
Andre Reed	16	951	13,198	13.9	83	87
Art Monk	16	940	12,721	13.5	79	68
Irving Fryar	17	851	12,785	15.0	80	84
Steve Largent	14	819	13,089	16.0	74	100
Henry Ellard	16	814	13,777	16.9	81	65
†Larry Centers	13	808	6,691	8.3	54	27
James Lofton	16	764	14,004	18.3	80	75
†Shannon Sharpe	13	753	9,290	12.3	82	54
Michael Irvin	12	750	11,904	15.9	87	65
Charlie Joiner	18	750	12,146	16.2	87	65

Receiving—Yards

Player	YDS
†Jerry Rice	21,597
†Tim Brown	14,167
James Lofton	14,004
†Cris Carter	13,899
Henry Ellard	13,777
Andre Reed	13,198
Steve Largent	13,089
Irving Fryar	12,785
Art Monk	12,721
Charlie Joiner	12,146

† Active in 2002

Single-Season Leaders

Scoring—Points

Player	YEAR	TD	PAT	FG	PTS
Paul Hornung, Packers	1960	15	41	15	176
Gary Anderson, Vikings	1998	0	59	35	164
Mark Moseley, Redskins	1983	0	62	33	161
Marshall Faulk, Rams	2000	26	0	0	156
Gino Cappelletti, Patriots	1964	7	38	25	155
Emmitt Smith, Cowboys	1995	25	0	0	150
Chip Lohmiller, Redskins	1991	0	56	31	149
Gino Cappelletti, Patriots	1961	8	48	17	147
Paul Hornung, Packers	1961	10	41	15	146

Note: Cappelletti's 1964 total includes a 2-point conversion.

Field Goals

Player	YEAR	ATT	NO.
Olindo Mare, Dolphins	1999	46	39
John Kasay, Panthers	1996	45	37
Cary Blanchard, Colts	1996	40	36
Al Del Greco, Titans	1998	39	36
Gary Anderson, Vikings	1998	35	35
Jeff Jaeger, Raiders	1993	44	35
Ali Haji-Sheikh, Giants	1983	42	35
Matt Stover, Ravens	2000	39	35

Six tied with 34.

Touchdowns

Player	YEAR	RUSH	REC	RET	TOTAL
Marshall Faulk, Rams	2000	18	8	0	26
Emmitt Smith, Cowboys	1995	25	0	0	25
John Riggins, Redskins	1983	24	0	0	24
Priest Holmes, Chiefs	2002	21	3	0	24
O.J. Simpson, Bills	1975	16	7	0	23
Jerry Rice, 49ers	1987	1	22	0	23
Terrell Davis, Broncos	1998	21	2	0	23
Gale Sayers, Bears	1965	14	6	2	22
Emmitt Smith, Cowboys	1994	21	1	0	22

Rushing—Yards Gained

Player	YEAR	ATT	YDS	AVG
Eric Dickerson, Rams	1984	379	2,105	5.6
Barry Sanders, Lions	1997	335	2,053	6.1
Terrell Davis, Broncos	1998	392	2,008	5.1
O.J. Simpson, Bills	1973	332	2,003	6.0
Earl Campbell, Oilers	1980	373	1,934	5.2
Jim Brown, Browns	1963	291	1,883	6.4
Barry Sanders, Lions	1994	331	1,883	5.7
Ricky Williams, Dolphins	2002	383	1,853	4.8
Walter Payton, Bears	1977	339	1,852	5.5

Single-Season Leaders (cont.)

Rushing—Average Gain

Player	YEAR	AVG
Beattie Feathers, Bears	1934	8.44
Randall Cunningham, Eagles	1990	7.98
Michael Vick, Falcons	2002	6.88
Bobby Douglass, Bears	1972	6.87

Minimum 100 attempts.

Rushing—Touchdowns

Player	YEAR	NO.
Emmitt Smith, Cowboys	1995	25
John Riggins, Redskins	1983	24

Five tied with 21.

Passing—Yards Gained

Player	YEAR	ATT	COMP	PCT	YDS
Dan Marino, Dolphins	1984	564	362	64.2	5,084
Kurt Warner, Rams	2001	546	375	68.7	4,830
Dan Fouts, Chargers	1981	609	360	59.1	4,802
Dan Marino, Dolphins	1986	623	378	60.7	4,746
Dan Fouts, Chargers	1980	589	348	59.1	4,715
Warren Moon, Oilers	1991	655	404	61.7	4,690
Warren Moon, Oilers	1990	584	362	62.0	4,689
Rich Gannon, Raiders	2002	618	418	67.6	4,684
Neil Lomax, Cardinals	1984	560	345	61.6	4,614
Drew Bledsoe, Patriots	1994	691	400	57.9	4,555

Passer Rating

Player	YEAR	RATING
Steve Young, 49ers	1994	112.8
Joe Montana, 49ers	1989	112.4
Milt Plum, Browns	1960	110.4
Sammy Baugh, Redskins	1945	109.9
Kurt Warner, Rams	1999	109.2

Passing—Touchdowns

Player	YEAR	NO.
Dan Marino, Dolphins	1984	48
Dan Marino, Dolphins	1986	44
Kurt Warner, Rams	1999	41
Brett Favre, Packers	1995	38

Four tied with 36.

Receiving—Receptions

Player	YEAR	NO.	YDS
Marvin Harrison, Colts	2002	143	1,722
Herman Moore, Lions	1995	123	1,686
Cris Carter, Vikings	1994	122	1,256
Jerry Rice, 49ers	1995	122	1,848
Cris Carter, Vikings	1995	122	1,371
Isaac Bruce, Rams	1995	119	1,781
Jimmy Smith, Jaguars	1999	116	1,636
Marvin Harrison, Colts	1999	115	1,663
Rod Smith, Broncos	2001	113	1,343

Four tied with 112.

Receiving—Yards Gained

Player	YEAR	YDS
Jerry Rice, 49ers	1995	1,848
Isaac Bruce, Rams	1995	1,781
Charley Hennigan, Oilers	1961	1,746
Marvin Harrison, Colts	2002	1,722
Herman Moore, Lions	1995	1,686
Marvin Harrison, Colts	1999	1,663

Receiving—Touchdowns

Player	YEAR	NO.
Jerry Rice, 49ers	1987	22
Mark Clayton, Dolphins	1984	18
Sterling Sharpe, Packers	1994	18

Six tied with 17.

Interceptions

Player	YEAR	NO.
Dick "Night Train" Lane, Rams	1952	14
Dan Sandifer, Redskins	1948	13
Spec Sanders, N.Y. Yankees	1950	13
Lester Hayes, Raiders	1980	13

Nine tied with 12.

Sacks

Player	YEAR	NO.
Michael Strahan, N.Y.Giants	2001	22.5
Mark Gastineau, Jets	1984	22
Reggie White, Eagles	1987	21
Chris Doleman, Vikings	1989	21
Lawrence Taylor, N.Y. Giants	1986	20.5

Pro Bowl Results

Date	Result	Date	Result	Date	Result
2-2-03	AFC 45, NFC 20	2-5-95	AFC 41, NFC 13	2-1-87	AFC 10, NFC 6
2-9-02	AFC 38, NFC 30	2-6-94	NFC 17, AFC 3	2-2-86	NFC 28, AFC 24
2-4-01	AFC 38, NFC 17	2-7-93	AFC 23, NFC 20	1-27-85	AFC 22, NFC 14
2-6-00	NFC 51, AFC 31	2-2-92	NFC 21, AFC 15	1-29-84	NFC 45, AFC 3
2-7-99	AFC 23, NFC 10	2-3-91	AFC 23, NFC 21	2-6-83	NFC 20, AFC 19
2-1-98	AFC 29, NFC 24	2-4-90	NFC 27, AFC 21	1-31-82	AFC 16, NFC 13
2-2-97	AFC 26, NFC 23	1-29-89	NFC 34, AFC 3	2-1-81	NFC 21, AFC 7
2-4-96	NFC 20, AFC 13	2-7-88	AFC 15, NFC 6	1-27-80	NFC 37, AFC 27

Pro Bowl Results (cont.)

Date	Result	Date	Result	Date	Result
1-29-79	NFC 13, AFC 7	1-22-67	NFL East 20, West 10	1-12-58	West 26, East 7
1-23-78	NFC 14, AFC 13	1-21-67	AFL East 30, West 23	1-13-57	West 19, East 10
1-17-77	AFC 24, NFC 14	1-15-66	NFL East 36, West 7	1-15-56	East 31, West 30
1-26-76	NFC 23, AFC 20	1-15-66	AFL All-Stars 30, Buffalo 19	1-16-55	West 26, East 19
1-20-75	NFC 17, AFC 10	1-16-65	AFL West 38, East 14	1-17-54	East 20, West 9
1-20-74	AFC 15, NFC 13	1-10-65	NFL West 34, East 14	1-10-53	N. Conf. 27, A. Conf. 7
1-21-73	AFC 33, NFC 28	1-19-64	AFL West 27, East 24	1-12-52	N. Conf. 30, A. Conf. 13
1-23-72	AFC 26, NFC 13	1-12-64	NFL West 31, East 17	1-14-51	A. Conf. 28, N. Conf. 27
1-24-71	NFC 27, AFC 6	1-13-63	NFL East 30, West 20	12-27-42	NFL All-Stars 17, Washington 14
1-18-70	NFL West 16, East 13	1-13-63	AFL West 21, East 14	1-4-42	Chi. Bears 35, NFL All-Stars 24
1-17-70	AFL West 26, East 3	1-14-62	NFL West 31, East 27	12-29-40	Chi. Bears 28, NFL All-Stars 14
1-19-69	NFL West 10, East 7	1-7-62	AFL West 47, East 27	1-14-40	Green Bay 16, NFL All-Stars 7
1-19-69	AFL West 38, East 25	1-15-61	West 35, East 31	1-15-39	N.Y. Giants 13, Pro All-Stars 10
1-21-68	NFL West 38, East 20	1-17-60	West 38, East 21		
1-21-68	AFL East 25, West 24	1-11-59	East 28, West 21		

2003 NFL Draft—First Round

April 26-27, 2003, New York, NY

Pick	Team	Player	Pos.	Ht.	Wt.	School
1	Cincinnati	Carson Palmer	QB	6-5	232	USC
2	Detroit	Charles Rogers	WR	6-2	202	Michigan State
3	Houston	Andre Johnson	WR	6-2	230	Miami (Florida)
4	N.Y. Jets (from Chicago)	Dewayne Robertson	DT	6-1	317	Kentucky
5	Dallas	Terence Newman	CB	5-10	189	Kansas State
6	New Orleans (from Arizona)	Johnathan Sullivan	DT	6-3	313	Georgia
7	Jacksonville	Byron Leftwich	QB	6-5	241	Marshall
8	Carolina	Jordan Gross	OT	6-5	300	Utah
9	Minnesota (Passed at 7, pick exercised here)	Kevin Williams	DE	6-5	304	Oklahoma State
10	Baltimore	Terrell Suggs	DE	6-3	262	Arizona State
11	Seattle	Marcus Trufant	CB	5-11	199	Washington State
12	St. Louis	Jimmy Kennedy	DT	6-4	322	Penn State
13	New England (from Washington through N.Y. Jets and Chicago)	Ty Warren	DT	6-5	307	Texas A&M
14	Chicago (from Buffalo through New England)	Michael Haynes	DE	6-4	281	Penn State
15	Philadelphia (from San Diego)	Jerome McDougle	DE	6-2	264	Miami (Florida)
16	Pittsburgh (from Kansas City)	Troy Polamalu	SS	5-10	206	USC
17	Arizona (from New Orleans)	Bryant Johnson	WR	6-2	214	Penn State
18	Arizona (from Miami through New Orleans)	Calvin Pace	DE	6-4	269	Wake Forest
19	Baltimore (from New England)	Kyle Boller	QB	6-3	234	California
20	Denver	George Foster	OT	6-5	338	Georgia
21	Cleveland	Jeff Faine	C	6-3	303	Notre Dame
22	Chicago (from N.Y. Jets)	Rex Grossman	QB	6-1	217	Florida
23	Buffalo (from Atlanta)	Willis McGahee	RB	6-0	223	Miami (Florida)
24	Indianapolis	Dallas Clark	TE	6-3	257	Iowa
25	N.Y. Giants	William Joseph	DT	6-5	308	Miami (Florida)
26	San Francisco	Kwame Harris	OT	6-7	310	Stanford
27	Kansas City (from Pittsburgh)	Larry Johnson	RB	6-1	228	Penn State
28	Tennessee	Andre Woolfolk	CB	6-1	197	Oklahoma
29	Green Bay	Nick Barnett	OLB	6-2	236	Oregon State
30	San Diego (from Philadelphia)	Sammy Davis	CB	6-0	186	Texas A&M
31	Oakland	Nnamdi Asomugha	CB	6-2	213	California
32	Oakland (from Tampa Bay)	Tyler Brayton	DE	6-6	277	Colorado

KEY QB=quarterback; WR=wide receiver; DT=defensive tackle; CB=cornerback; OT=offensive tackle; DE=defensive end; SS=strong safety; C=center; RB=running back; TE=tight end; OLB=outside linebacker

FOOTBALL

The Notre Dame Fighting Irish, the University of Southern California Trojans, and the Ohio State Buckeyes have won a total of 12 national championships in the past 50 years but only one since 1978. The year 2002 was a return to glory for all three programs.

For a time, the Fighting Irish and their suffocating defense were the story of the year. Notre Dame opened the season with eight straight wins for the first time in 10 years. But they stumbled down the stretch and lost three of their last five games.

While the Irish lost their footing, the Trojans hit their stride, winning their final eight games. Powered by the cannon arm of Heisman Trophy-winning quarterback Carson Palmer, USC was ranked Number 4 in the final AP poll, the school's first Top 5 final ranking since 1979.

All season long, Ohio State claimed it got no respect. That changed after the Buckeyes ended the Miami Hurricanes' 34-game winning streak in the national championship game. Ohio State won, 31–24, in double overtime, the first time a national championship game went into overtime. Maurice Clarett, Ohio State's star freshman running back, ran for two touchdowns, including the game-winner.

As a true freshman, in 2002, Maurice Clarett ran for 1,237 yards and 16 touchdowns.

BOB ROSATO/SPORTS ILLUSTRATED

Final 2002 College Football Polls

Associated Press

Team	Record	Points
1. Ohio St.	14−0	1,775
2. Miami (Florida)	12−1	1,693
3. Georgia	13−1	1,598
4. USC	11−2	1,590
5. Oklahoma	12−2	1,476
6. Texas	11−2	1,363
7. Kansas St.	11−2	1,356
8. Iowa	11−2	1,334
9. Michigan	10−3	1,182
10. Washington St.	10−3	1,085
11. Alabama	10−3	988
12. North Carolina St.	11−3	943
13. Maryland	11−3	844
14. Auburn	9−4	821
15. Boise St.	12−1	692
16. Penn St.	9−4	675
17. Notre Dame	10−3	657
18. Virginia Tech	10−4	544
19. Pittsburgh	9−4	520
20. Colorado	9−5	307
21. Florida St.	9−5	291
22. Virginia	9−5	250
23. TCU	10−2	231
24. Marshall	11−2	201
25. West Virginia	9−4	195

ESPN/USA Today Coaches

Team	Record	Points
1. Ohio St.	14−0	1,525
2. Miami (Florida)	12−1	1,451
3. Georgia	13−1	1,378
4. USC	11−2	1,362
5. Oklahoma	12−2	1,244
6. Kansas St.	11−2	1,230
7. Texas	11−2	1,140
8. Iowa	11−2	1,105
9. Michigan	10−3	1,011
10. Washington St.	10−3	932
11. North Carolina St.	11−3	876
12. Boise St.	12−1	808
13. Maryland	11−3	803
14. Virginia Tech	10−4	644
15. Penn St.	9−4	619
16. Auburn	9−4	579
17. Notre Dame	10−3	525
18. Pittsburgh	9−4	486
19. Marshall	11−2	333
20. West Virginia	9−4	297
21. Colorado	9−5	291
22. TCU	10−2	274
23. Florida St.	9−5	219
24. Florida	8−5	145
25. Virginia	9−5	141

2002–03 College Bowl and Playoff Results

Bowl Games

Bowl	Date	Site	Result
Fiesta	Jan. 3	Tempe, Arizona	Ohio St. 31, Miami (Florida) 24 (2 OT)
Orange	Jan. 2	Miami, Florida	USC 38, Iowa 17
Sugar	Jan. 1	New Orleans, Louisiana	Georgia 26, Florida St. 13
Rose	Jan. 1	Pasadena, California	Oklahoma, 34, Washington St. 14
Capital One	Jan. 1	Orlando, Florida	Auburn 13, Penn St. 9
Gator	Jan. 1	Jacksonville, Florida	North Carolina St. 28, Notre Dame 6
Cotton	Jan. 1	Dallas, Texas	Texas 35, LSU 20
Outback	Jan. 1	Tampa, Florida	Michigan 38, Florida 30
San Francisco	Dec. 31	San Francisco, California	Virginia Tech 20, Air Force 13
Peach	Dec. 31	Atlanta, Georgia	Maryland 30, Tennessee 3
Silicon Valley Classic	Dec. 31	San Jose, California	Fresno St. 30, Georgia Tech 21
Liberty	Dec. 31	Memphis, Tennessee	TCU 17, Colorado St. 3
Sun	Dec. 31	El Paso, Texas	Purdue 34, Washington 24
Humanitarian	Dec. 31	Boise, Idaho	Boise St. 34, Iowa St. 16
Seattle	Dec. 30	Seattle, Washington	Wake Forest 38, Oregon 17
Music City	Dec. 30	Nashville, Tennessee	Minnesota 29, Arkansas 14
Alamo	Dec. 28	San Antonio, Texas	Wisconsin 31, Colorado 28 (OT)
Continental Tire	Dec. 28	Charlotte, North Carolina	Virginia 48, West Virginia 22
Holiday	Dec. 27	San Diego, California	Kansas St. 34, Arizona St. 27
Independence	Dec. 27	Shreveport, Louisiana	Mississippi 27, Nebraska 23
Houston	Dec. 27	Houston, Texas	Oklahoma St. 33, Southern Miss 23
Insight	Dec. 26	Tempe, Arizona	Pittsburgh 38, Oregon St. 13
Motor City	Dec. 26	Detroit, Michigan	Boston College 51, Toledo 25
Hawaii	Dec. 25	Honolulu, Hawaii	Tulane 36, Hawaii 28
Las Vegas	Dec. 25	Las Vegas, Nevada	UCLA 27, New Mexico 13
Tangerine	Dec. 23	Orlando, Florida	Texas Tech 55, Clemson 15
GMAC	Dec. 18	Mobile, Alabama	Marshall 38, Louisville 15
New Orleans	Dec. 17	New Orleans, Louisiana	North Texas 24, Cincinnati 19

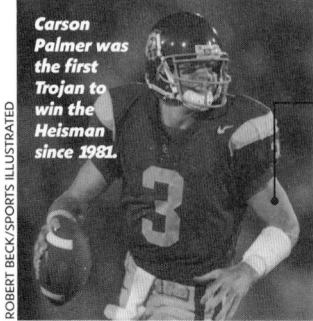

Carson Palmer was the first Trojan to win the Heisman since 1981.

ROBERT BECK/SPORTS ILLUSTRATED

2002 Heisman Voting

Player, School	Position	1st	2nd	3rd	Total
Carson Palmer, USC	QB	242	224	154	1,328
Brad Banks, Iowa	QB	199	173	152	1,095
Larry Johnson, Penn St.	RB	108	130	142	726
Willis McGahee, Miami (Florida)	RB	101	118	121	660
Ken Dorsey, Miami (Florida)	QB	122	89	99	643
Byron Leftwitch, Marshall	QB	22	26	34	125
Jason Gesser, Washington St.	QB	5	22	15	74
Chris Brown, Colorado	RB	5	11	11	48
Kliff Kingsbury, Texas Tech	QB	6	2	11	33
Quentin Griffin, Oklahoma	RB	1	8	9	28

2002 AP All-America Team

Offense

QB Carson Palmer, USC, Sr.
RB Larry Johnson, Penn St., Sr.
  Willis McGahee, Miami (Florida), So.
WR Charles Rogers, Michigan St., Jr.
  Reggie Williams, Washington, So.
TE Dallas Clark, Iowa, Sr.
C Brett Romberg, Miami, Sr.
OL Shawn Andrews, Arkansas, So.
  Derrick Dockery, Texas, Sr.
  Jordan Gross, Utah, Sr.
  Eric Steinbach, Iowa, Sr.
K Mike Nugent, Ohio St., So.
All-Purpose Derek Abney, Kentucky, Jr.

Defense

DL Tommie Harris, Oklahoma, So.
  Rien Long, Washington St., Jr.
  David Pollack, Georgia, So.
  Terrell Suggs, Arizona St., Jr.
LB E.J. Henderson, Maryland, Sr.
  Teddy Lehman, Oklahoma, Jr.
  Matt Wilhelm, Ohio St., Sr.
DB Mike Doss, Ohio St., Sr.
  Terence Newman, Kansas St., Sr.
  Troy Polamalu, USC, Sr.
  Shane Walton, Notre Dame, Sr.
P Mark Mariscal, Colorado, Sr.

▷**Random Fact:** University of Illinois back Howard Griffith ran for a Division I record eight touchdowns (three on consecutive carries) on September 22, 1990, against Southern Illinois University.

KEY QB=quarterback; RB=running back; WR=wide receiver; TE=tight end; C=center; OL=offensive lineman; K=kicker; DL=defensive lineman; LB=linebacker; DB=defensive back; P=punter; Sr.=senior; Jr.=junior; So.=sophomore

2002 NCAA Division I-A Conference Standings

Atlantic Coast Conference

Team	Conference				Overall			
	W	L	PF	PA	W	L	PF	PA
Florida State	7	1	275	142	9	4	415	275
Maryland	6	2	247	161	10	3	421	225
Virginia	6	2	220	185	8	5	354	326
North Carolina State	5	3	192	127	10	3	432	232
Clemson	4	4	197	223	7	5	315	294
Georgia Tech	4	4	148	150	7	5	259	237
Wake Forest	3	5	196	198	6	6	318	310
North Carolina	1	7	113	285	3	9	223	421
Duke	0	8	137	254	2	10	227	353

Big East Conference

Team	Conference				Overall			
	W	L	PF	PA	W	L	PF	PA
Miami (Florida)	7	0	297	140	12	0	503	217
West Virginia	6	1	212	116	9	3	374	254
Pittsburgh	5	2	185	138	8	4	293	219
Virginia Tech	3	4	209	202	9	4	409	250
Boston College	3	4	180	157	8	4	341	228
Syracuse	2	5	169	245	4	8	347	406
Temple	2	5	124	208	4	8	242	351
Rutgers	0	7	79	249	1	11	167	397

KEY W=win; L=loss; PF=points for; PA=points against

Big Ten Conference

Team	Conference				Overall			
	W	L	PF	PA	W	L	PF	PA
Ohio State	8	0	185	88	13	0	379	159
Iowa	8	0	302	130	11	1	467	218
Michigan	6	2	224	162	9	3	323	235
Penn State	5	3	286	152	9	3	437	214
Purdue	4	4	235	182	6	6	352	264
Illinois	4	4	212	206	5	7	346	307
Minnesota	3	5	198	256	7	5	347	305
Wisconsin	2	6	202	218	7	6	341	294
Michigan State	2	6	194	314	4	8	316	398
Indiana	1	7	164	332	3	9	258	445
Northwestern	1	7	170	332	3	9	272	493

Big 12 Conference

NORTH

Team	Conference				Overall			
	W	L	PF	PA	W	L	PF	PA
Colorado	7	1	281	175	9	4	370	294
Kansas State	6	2	342	91	10	2	548	127
Iowa State	4	4	201	238	7	6	388	362
Nebraska	3	5	192	215	7	6	360	308
Missouri	2	6	214	268	5	7	360	352
Kansas	0	8	125	380	2	10	248	507

SOUTH

Team	Conference				Overall			
	W	L	PF	PA	W	L	PF	PA
Oklahoma	6	2	305	154	11	2	507	202
Texas	6	2	235	160	10	2	404	192
Texas Tech	5	3	298	286	8	5	482	424
Oklahoma State	5	3	256	230	7	5	413	333
Texas A&M	3	5	266	245	6	6	345	280
Baylor	1	7	93	366	3	9	202	496

Conference USA

Team	Conference				Overall			
	W	L	PF	PA	W	L	PF	PA
Texas Christian University (TCU)	6	2	263	179	9	2	344	219
Cincinnati	6	2	259	174	7	6	390	305
Louisville	5	3	243	200	7	5	359	281
Southern Mississippi	5	3	161	142	7	5	259	205
Tulane	4	4	185	147	7	5	325	254
Alabama-Birmingham	4	4	218	233	5	7	268	370
East Carolina	4	4	250	266	4	8	335	399
Houston	3	5	235	293	5	7	320	393
Memphis	2	6	190	223	3	9	303	327
Army	1	7	163	310	1	11	226	491

Mid-American Conference

EAST

Team	Conference				Overall			
	W	L	PF	PA	W	L	PF	PA
Marshall	8	1	324	229	10	2	419	300
University of Central Florida (UCF)	6	2	271	187	7	5	391	315
Miami (Ohio)	5	3	295	216	7	5	384	325
Ohio	4	4	260	245	4	8	299	374
Akron	3	5	212	209	4	8	325	379
Kent State	1	7	93	269	3	9	202	424
Buffalo	0	8	134	303	1	11	214	416

WEST

Team	Conference				Overall			
	W	L	PF	PA	W	L	PF	PA
Northern Illinois	7	1	280	167	8	4	375	298
Toledo	7	2	348	222	9	4	470	327
Bowling Green	6	2	352	224	9	3	490	304
Ball State	4	4	218	220	6	6	278	333
Western Michigan	3	5	219	220	4	8	303	330
Central Michigan	2	6	172	272	4	8	267	384
Eastern Michigan	1	7	193	388	3	9	286	566

2002 NCAA Division I-A Conference Standings (cont.)

Mountain West Conference

Team	Conference				Overall			
	W	L	PF	PA	W	L	PF	PA
Colorado State	6	1	244	149	10	3	415	315
New Mexico	5	2	196	155	7	6	328	331
Air Force	4	3	241	201	8	4	427	283
San Diego State	4	3	168	190	4	9	309	411
Utah	3	4	162	177	5	6	249	226
University of Nevada-Las Vegas (UNLV)	3	4	195	217	5	7	292	366
Brigham Young University (BYU)	2	5	113	187	5	7	272	333
Wyoming	1	6	207	250	2	10	288	432

Pacific Ten Conference

Team	Conference				Overall			
	W	L	PF	PA	W	L	PF	PA
University of Southern California (USC)	7	1	299	163	10	2	427	223
Washington State	7	1	285	188	10	2	417	262
Arizona State	5	3	257	244	8	5	425	373
Oregon State	4	4	211	180	8	4	401	229
California	4	4	256	238	7	5	427	318
University of California-Los Angeles (UCLA)	4	4	232	232	7	5	360	313
Washington	4	4	232	233	7	5	374	308
Oregon	3	5	237	266	7	5	400	324
Arizona	1	7	143	250	4	8	227	310
Stanford	1	7	128	286	2	9	225	377

Southeastern Conference

EAST

Team	Conference				Overall			
	W	L	PF	PA	W	L	PF	PA
Georgia	8	1	256	147	12	1	424	199
Florida	6	2	191	160	8	4	306	241
Tennessee	5	3	182	147	8	4	293	197
Kentucky	3	5	215	228	7	5	385	301
South Carolina	3	5	108	156	5	7	225	262
Vanderbilt	0	8	121	260	2	10	221	368

WEST

Team	Conference				Overall			
	W	L	PF	PA	W	L	PF	PA
Alabama	6	2	227	99	10	3	367	200
Auburn	5	3	213	150	8	4	375	222
Louisiana State University (LSU)	5	3	179	160	8	4	303	203
Arkansas	5	4	226	214	9	4	356	248
Mississippi	3	5	175	230	6	6	324	308
Mississippi State	0	8	123	265	3	9	227	339

Sun Belt Conference

Team	Conference				Overall			
	W	L	PF	PA	W	L	PF	PA
North Texas	6	0	159	59	7	5	225	173
New Mexico State	5	1	177	160	7	5	327	328
Arkansas State	3	3	125	109	6	7	259	361
Middle Tennessee State	2	4	158	151	3	8	252	304
Lousiana-Lafayette	2	4	117	178	3	9	203	352
Louisiana-Monroe	2	4	140	176	3	9	236	451
Idaho	1	5	123	166	2	10	285	428

2002 NCAA Division I-A Conference Standings (cont.)

Western Athletic Conference

Team	Conference				Overall			
	W	L	PF	PA	W	L	PF	PA
Boise State	8	0	409	111	11	1	559	224
Hawaii	7	1	304	202	10	3	474	353
Fresno State	6	2	236	204	8	5	348	358
San Jose State	4	4	262	271	6	7	376	467
Nevada	4	4	248	259	5	7	331	371
Rice	3	5	216	235	4	7	253	296
Louisiana Tech	3	5	248	277	4	8	320	426
Southern Methodist University (SMU)	3	5	164	247	3	9	207	378
Texas-El Paso	1	7	147	305	2	10	220	511
Tulsa	1	7	156	279	1	11	233	417

Independents

Team	Overall			
	W	L	PF	PA
Notre Dame	10	2	284	189
South Florida	9	2	339	204
Connecticut	6	6	373	270
Utah State	4	7	305	432
Troy State	4	8	218	252
Navy	2	10	290	436

NCAA Division I-AA Conference Standings

Atlantic 10 Conference

Team	Conference				Overall			
	W	L	PF	PA	W	L	PF	PA
Maine	7	2	195	150	10	2	322	172
Northeastern	7	2	283	165	10	2	379	179
Villanova	6	3	277	169	9	3	351	191
Massachusetts	6	3	209	178	8	4	327	250
William & Mary	5	4	247	228	6	5	326	284
Delaware	4	5	218	174	6	6	291	227
Hofstra	4	5	211	218	6	6	270	255
Richmond	4	5	185	151	4	7	199	202
James Madison	4	6	152	228	5	7	196	272
New Hampshire	2	7	163	285	3	8	199	345
Rhode Island	1	8	104	298	3	9	187	389

Big Sky Conference

Team	Conference				Overall			
	W	L	PF	PA	W	L	PF	PA
Montana	5	2	173	125	10	2	376	222
Idaho State	5	2	184	112	8	3	331	188
Montana State	5	2	169	125	7	5	284	261
Eastern Washington	3	4	209	198	6	5	365	276
Northern Arizona	3	4	154	197	6	5	252	284
Portland State	3	4	166	161	6	5	236	245
Sacramento State	3	4	211	228	5	7	325	380
Weber State	1	6	116	236	3	8	266	309

Big South Conference

Team	Conference				Overall			
	W	L	PF	PA	W	L	PF	PA
Gardner Webb	3	0	126	63	9	1	278	204
Elon	2	1	104	86	4	7	249	352
Liberty	1	2	87	104	2	9	230	364
Charleston South	0	3	45	109	4	8	189	327

NCAA Division I-AA Conference Standings (cont.)

Gateway Conference

Team	Conference				Overall			
	W	L	PF	PA	W	L	PF	PA
Western Illinois	6	1	222	127	10	1	394	201
Western Kentucky	6	1	156	63	8	3	277	156
Youngstown State	4	3	114	113	7	4	215	201
Illinois State	4	3	150	121	6	5	249	250
Indiana State	3	4	121	180	5	7	226	318
Northern Iowa	2	5	123	191	5	6	227	286
Southern Illinois	2	5	177	228	4	8	414	360
Southwest Missouri State	1	6	149	189	4	7	255	294

Ivy League

Team	Conference				Overall			
	W	L	PF	PA	W	L	PF	PA
Pennsylvania	7	0	284	73	9	1	363	132
Harvard	6	1	190	154	7	3	267	230
Princeton	4	3	154	176	6	4	226	236
Yale	4	3	173	141	6	4	257	188
Cornell	3	4	119	205	4	6	169	292
Dartmouth	2	5	151	200	3	7	247	295
Brown	2	5	135	160	2	8	222	278
Columbia	0	7	121	218	1	9	161	295

Metro Atlantic Athletic Conference

Team	Conference				Overall			
	W	L	PF	PA	W	L	PF	PA
Duquesne	8	0	304	27	11	1	397	115
Marist	5	3	196	163	7	4	282	230
St. Peter's	5	3	207	118	6	5	234	207
Fairfield	5	3	181	170	5	6	210	266
Iona	4	4	130	160	5	6	156	243
Siena	3	5	109	148	3	7	112	194
St. John's	2	6	167	258	2	8	184	308
Canisius	2	6	86	201	2	9	113	329
La Salle	2	6	162	297	2	9	200	388

Mid-Eastern Athletic Conference

Team	Conference				Overall			
	W	L	PF	PA	W	L	PF	PA
Bethune Cookman	7	1	263	133	11	1	407	166
Florida A&M	5	3	196	202	7	5	321	319
Hampton	5	3	276	167	7	5	405	250
Morgan State	5	3	235	207	7	5	364	345
South Carolina State	4	4	187	166	7	5	321	212
Howard	4	4	148	198	6	5	243	286
Norfolk State	2	6	111	240	5	6	209	286
Delaware State	2	6	134	233	4	8	218	313
North Carolina A&T	2	6	155	159	4	8	281	271

Northeast Conference

Team	Conference				Overall			
	W	L	PF	PA	W	L	PF	PA
Albany (New York)	6	1	214	102	8	4	357	245
Stony Brook	5	2	142	102	8	2	232	118
Sacred Heart	5	2	152	85	7	3	241	129
Wagner	4	3	98	89	7	4	232	134
Central Connecticut	3	4	87	112	5	6	139	251
Robert Morris	2	5	56	142	3	7	128	227
Monmouth (New Jersey)	2	5	66	92	2	8	115	177
St. Francis (Pennsylvania)	1	6	59	150	2	8	101	229

Ohio Valley Conference

Team	Conference				Overall			
	W	L	PF	PA	W	L	PF	PA
Eastern Illinois	5	1	248	207	8	3	415	366
Murray State	5	1	206	141	7	4	362	292
Eastern Kentucky	4	2	198	90	8	4	383	220
Southeast Missouri State	4	2	228	193	8	4	416	349
Tennessee Tech	2	4	160	142	5	7	328	333
Tennessee State	1	5	160	227	2	10	308	403
Tennessee-Martin	0	6	99	299	2	10	186	459

Patriot League

Team	Conference				Overall			
	W	L	PF	PA	W	L	PF	PA
Fordham	6	1	250	141	9	2	379	177
Colgate	6	1	181	137	9	3	301	216
Lafayette	5	2	183	111	7	5	303	270
Lehigh	4	3	180	100	8	4	319	216
Towson	3	4	129	141	6	5	285	245
Georgetown	2	5	118	277	5	6	190	345
Holy Cross	2	5	161	201	4	8	293	344
Bucknell	0	7	86	180	2	9	163	254

Pioneer Conference

NORTH

Team	Conference				Overall			
	W	L	PF	PA	W	L	PF	PA
Dayton	4	0	183	27	11	1	423	118
San Diego	3	1	162	126	5	5	297	309
Butler	2	2	126	142	4	6	294	374
Drake	1	3	149	169	5	6	355	429
Valparaiso	0	4	87	215	1	10	268	498

SOUTH

Team	Conference				Overall			
	W	L	PF	PA	W	L	PF	PA
Morehead State	3	0	132	74	9	3	347	218
Davidson	2	1	84	77	7	3	320	227
Austin Peay	1	2	73	110	7	5	287	333
Jacksonville (Florida)	0	3	40	96	3	7	185	314

Southern Conference

Team	Conference				Overall			
	W	L	PF	PA	W	L	PF	PA
Georgia Southern	7	1	284	127	9	2	400	152
Wofford	6	2	201	145	9	3	298	197
Appalachian State	6	2	219	159	8	3	301	259
Furman	6	2	235	147	8	3	327	210
Virginia Military Institute	3	5	177	299	6	6	314	415
Western Carolina	3	5	209	232	5	6	279	294
East Tennessee State	2	6	106	214	4	8	167	286
Chattanooga	2	6	175	241	2	10	232	377
Citadel	1	7	188	230	3	9	305	338

Southland Conference

Team	Conference				Overall			
	W	L	PF	PA	W	L	PF	PA
McNeese State	6	0	224	74	10	1	380	177
Northwestern State	4	2	154	132	9	3	345	238
Nicholls State	3	3	121	114	7	4	283	195
Stephen F. Austin	3	3	138	157	6	5	322	245
Jacksonville State	2	4	121	137	5	6	229	298
Sam Houston State	2	4	89	168	4	7	197	313
Southwest Texas	1	5	117	182	4	7	211	290

NCAA Division I-AA Conference Standings (cont.)

Southwestern Athletic Conference

EAST Team	W	L	PF	PA	W	L	PF	PA
			Conference				Overall	
Alabama A&M	6	1	172	110	8	3	242	186
Jackson State	5	2	214	142	7	4	330	267
Alcorn State	3	4	196	199	6	5	280	283
Mississippi Valley State	3	4	124	137	5	6	241	260
Alabama State	2	5	181	202	6	6	337	277

WEST Team	W	L	PF	PA	W	L	PF	PA
			Conference				Overall	
Grambling	6	0	258	143	10	1	451	288
Southern	4	2	131	141	5	6	231	272
Texas Southern	3	4	219	188	4	7	314	277
Arkansas-Pine Bluff	2	5	167	209	3	8	284	368
Prairie View	0	7	81	272	1	10	123	413

Independents

Team	W	L	PF	PA
		Overall		
St. Mary's (California)	6	6	318	267
Florida International	5	6	241	228
Samford	4	7	285	385
California Polytech	3	8	247	302
Florida Atlantic	2	9	176	339
Savannah State	1	9	106	341
Southern Utah	1	10	202	427
Morris Brown	1	11	225	431

2002 NCAA Individual Leaders: Division I-A

Scoring

	TD	PTS
Kliff Kingsbury, Texas Tech	47	282
Josh Harris, Bowling Green	40	240
Carson Palmer, USC	37	222
Josh Fields, Oklahoma St.	34	204
Kyle Boller, California	33	198
Ryan Schneider, UCF	33	198
Byron Leftwich, Marshall	33	198
Chance Harridge, Air Force	32	192
Brock Forsey, Boise St.	32	192
Brad Banks, Iowa	31	186
Cody Pickett, Washington	31	186

Field Goals

	FGM	FGA	PCT
Billy Bennett, Georgia	26	33	78.8
Mike Nugent, Ohio St.	25	28	89.3
Nick Novak, Maryland	24	28	85.7
Jeff Babcock, Colorado St.	24	32	75.0
Four tied with 23.			

Trivia Challenge

Who is the only Division I player to pass for more than 700 yards in one game?

David Klingler of the University of Houston Cougars. On December 2, 1990, Klingler threw for 716 yards against the Arizona State Sun Devils.

KEY TD=touchdowns; PTS=points; FGM=field goals made; FGA=field goals attempted; PCT=percentage

BOB ROSATO/SPORTS ILLUSTRATED

Today's Stars

Eli Manning, quarterback, b. January 3, 1981, New Orleans, Louisiana. Manning earned the starting spot at Ole Miss as a sophomore, in 2001, and set or matched 17 school records, including passing yards (2,948), completions (259), and touchdown passes (31). In 2002, he reset five of those records and broke seven more, including two his father had held. Manning's father, Archie, was a two-time All-America at Ole Miss. His older brother, Peyton Manning, is a three-time Pro Bowl quarterback with the Indianapolis Colts.

Eli Manning was the first Ole Miss QB to pass for at least 2,000 yards in back-to-back seasons.

Mike Williams, wide receiver, b. January 4, 1984, Tampa, Florida. In 2002, the 6'5" University of Southern California receiver had one of the best freshman seasons in Division I-A history. Williams caught 81 passes for 1,265 yards, both of which are Division I-A freshman records. He also tied the freshman record for touchdown receptions (14).

Kevin Jones, running back, b. August 21, 1982, Chester, Pennsylvania. At 6 feet, 211 pounds, Jones is big enough to run over opponents, but it's his quickness that makes defenses look silly. In 2002, he had back-to-back 100-yard games for Virginia Tech and gained 871 yards for the season. Jones was named Big East rookie of the year in 2001, after setting the Tech record for rushing yards by a freshman (957). As a high school senior, he won the first High School Heisman for the northeast region.

BOB ROSATO/SPORTS ILLUSTRATED

2002 NCAA Individual Leaders: Division I-A (cont.)

Rushing

	G	Carries	YDS	AVG	TD
Larry Johnson, Penn St.	13	271	2,087	7.7	20
Michael Turner, Northern Illinois	12	338	1,915	5.7	19
Quentin Griffin, Oklahoma	14	287	1,884	6.6	15
Chris Brown, Colorado	12	304	1,840	6.1	19
Willis McGahee, Miami (Florida)	13	282	1,753	6.2	28
Avon Cobourne, West Virginia	13	335	1,710	5.1	17
Steven Jackson, Oregon St.	13	319	1,690	5.3	15
Marcus Merriweather, Ball St.	12	332	1,618	4.9	12
Brock Forsey, Boise St.	13	295	1,611	5.5	26
Cecil Sapp, Colorado St.	14	347	1,601	4.6	17

Passing Efficiency

	ATTS	COMP PCT	YDS	INT	TD	Rating
Brad Banks, Iowa	294	57.8	2,573	5	26	157.1
Byron Leftwich, Marshall	491	67.4	4,268	10	30	156.5
Brian Jones, Toledo	423	70.2	3,446	9	23	152.3
Ryan Schneider, UCF	429	61.5	3,758	16	31	151.5
Carson Palmer, USC	489	63.2	3,942	10	33	149.1
Matt Schaub, Virginia	418	68.9	2,976	7	28	147.5
Jason Gesser, Washington St.	402	58.7	3,408	13	28	146.4
Ken Dorsey, Miami (Florida)	393	56.5	3,369	12	28	145.9
Kliff Kingsbury, Texas Tech	712	67.3	5,017	13	45	143.7
Bryan Randall, Virginia Tech	248	63.7	2,134	11	12	143.1

Ken Dorsey was 38–2 as a starter for the Hurricanes.

KEY G=games; YDS=yards; AVG=average; TD=touchdowns; ATTS=attempts; COMP PCT=completion percentage; INT=interceptions

2002 NCAA Individual Leaders: Division I-A (cont.)

Receiving

	G	REC	YDS	YDS/G	TD
J.R. Tolver, San Diego St.	13	128	1,785	137.3	13
Rashaun Woods, Oklahoma St.	13	107	1,695	130.4	17
Nate Burleson, Nevada	12	138	1,627	135.6	12
Kassim Osgood, San Diego St.	13	108	1,552	119.4	8
Reggie Williams, Washington	13	94	1,454	111.8	11
Bobby Wade, Arizona	12	93	1,389	115.8	8
Shaun McDonald, Arizona St.	14	86	1,387	99.1	13
Kevin Walter, Eastern Michigan	12	92	1,359	113.3	9
Charles Rogers, Michigan St.	12	68	1,351	112.6	13
John Standeford, Purdue	13	75	1,307	100.5	13

Interceptions

	INT	YDS	TD
Jim Leonhard, Wisconsin	10	114	0
Lynaris Elpheage, Tulane	8	133	1
Gerald Jones, San Jose St.	8	116	1
Gabe Franklin, Boise St.	8	70	0
Randee Drew, Northern Illinois	7	103	0
Jason David, Washington St.	7	101	0
Shane Walton, Notre Dame	7	84	2
Corey Webster, LSU	7	75	1
Justin Miller, Clemson	7	68	0
Jason Goss, TCU	7	27	0

▷Random Fact: In 1999, the University of Hawaii had the best one-year turnaround in NCAA history, posting a 9–4 record after going 0–12 in 1998.

2002 NCAA Individual Leaders: Division I-AA

Scoring

	TD	PTS
Bruce Eugene, Grambling	52	312
Brett Gordon, Villanova	37	222
Chaz Williams, Georgia Southern	36	216
Robert Kent, Jackson State	35	210
Tony Romo, Eastern Illinois	35	210
Ira Vandever, Drake	35	210
Niel Loebig, Duquesne	31	186
David Caudill, Morehead St.	31	186
Josh Blankenship, Eastern Washington	30	180
Jack Tomco, S.E. Missouri St.	29	174

Trivia Challenge

Can you name the only two schools that have won more than 800 football games?

The University of Michigan Wolverines (823 games) and the Yale University Bulldogs (815 games).

Field Goals

	FGM	FGA	PCT
Mackenzie Hoambrecker, Northern Iowa	25	28	89.3
Justin Langan, Western Illinois	20	27	74.1
Chris Snyder, Montana	19	32	59.4
Peter Martinez, Western Kentucky	18	25	72.0
Matt Fordyce, Fordham	18	26	69.2

Rushing

	G	Carries	YDS	AVG	TD
Jay Bailey, Austin Peay	12	317	1,680	140.0	18
J.R. Taylor, Eastern Illinois	12	254	1,522	126.8	18
Gary Jones, Albany (New York)	12	231	1,509	125.8	22
Kirwin Watson, Fordham	13	287	1,463	112.5	18
Jon Frazier, Western Kentucky	15	292	1,435	95.7	11
Chaz Williams, Georgia Southern	14	290	1,422	101.6	27
Jermaine Austin, Georgia Southern	14	244	1,416	101.1	8
Marcus Williams, Maine	14	263	1,406	100.4	7
Joe McCourt, Lafayette	12	314	1,393	116.1	13
Jermaine Pugh, Lehigh	12	261	1,335	111.3	11

KEY G=games; REC=receptions; YDS=yards; YDS/G=yards per game; TD=touchdowns; INT=interceptions; PTS=points; FGM=field goals made; FGA=field goals attempted; PCT=percentage; AVG=average

Passing Efficiency

	ATTS	COMP PCT	YDS	INT	TD	Rating
Eric Rasmussen, San Diego	279	60.9	2,473	1	24	163.1
Billy Napier, Furman	275	68.7	2,475	7	16	158.4
Ira Vandever, Drake	361	56.8	3,239	11	32	155.3
Russ Michna, Western Illinois	331	57.1	3,037	5	24	155.1
Jack Tomco, S.E. Missouri St.	372	65.1	3,132	16	29	152.9
Robert Kent, Jackson St.	395	58.7	3,386	12	31	150.6
Tony Romo, Eastern Illinois	407	63.4	3,165	18	34	147.4
Josh Blankenship, Eastern Washington	418	59.8	3,243	7	30	145.3
Ryan Fitzpatrick, Harvard	150	62.7	1,155	0	8	144.9
Kyle Slager, Brown	340	67.6	2,609	10	19	144.7

Receiving

	G	REC	YDS	YDS/G	TD
Tramon Douglas, Grambling	12	92	1,704	142.0	18
Willie Ponder, S.E. Missouri St.	12	86	1,450	120.8	15
Carl Morris, Harvard	10	90	1,288	128.8	8
Cortez Hankton, Texas Southern	11	64	1,270	115.5	13
Jeremy Conley, Duquesne	12	71	1,196	99.7	14
Luke Graham, Colgate	12	65	1,182	98.5	7
Aaron Overton, Drake	11	71	1,180	107.3	12
Chas Gessner, Brown	10	114	1,166	116.6	11
Aryvia Holmes, Samford	10	84	1,158	115.8	9
Rich Musinski, William & Mary	11	58	1,140	103.6	9

Interceptions

	INT	YDS	TD
Rashean Mathis, Bethune Cookman	14	455	3
Mark Kasmer, Dayton	11	157	2
Antwan Hill, Alabama St.	10	199	1
Rod Gulley, McNeese St.	9	160	2
Levy Brown, Florida A&M	8	38	0
Octavius Bond, Grambling	7	66	0
Leigh Bodden, Duquesne	7	71	0
Chad King, Stony Brook	7	109	1
Tyrone Parsons, Alcorn St.	7	75	0
Corey Oaks, Robert Morris	7	130	2

Did You Know?

The Lehigh Mountain Hawks and the Lafayette Leopards have the nation's longest Division I rivalry, playing each other 138 times. The series began in 1884. Lafayette leads it, 72-61-5.

KEY ATTS=attempts; COMP PCT=completion percentage; YDS=yards; INT=interceptions; TD=touchdowns; G=games; REC=receptions; YDS/G=yards per game; INT=interceptions

National Championships

Year	Champion	Record	Head Coach	Year	Champion	Record	Head Coach
2002	Ohio St.	14-0	Jim Tressel	1980	Georgia	12-0-0	Vince Dooley
2001	Miami (Florida)	12-0	Larry Croker	1979	Alabama	12-0-0	Bear Bryant
2000	Oklahoma	13-0	Bob Stoops	1978	Alabama	11-1-0	Bear Bryant
1999	Florida St.	12-0	Bobby Bowden		USC (UPI)	12-1-0	John Robinson
1998	Tennessee	13-0	Phillip Fulmer	1977	Notre Dame	11-1-0	Dan Devine
1997	Michigan	12-0	Lloyd Carr	1976	Pittsburgh	12-0-0	Johnny Majors
	Nebraska (ESPN)	13-0	Tom Osborne	1975	Oklahoma	11-1-0	Barry Switzer
1996	Florida	12-1	Steve Spurrier	1974	Oklahoma (AP)	11-0-0	Barry Switzer
1995	Nebraska	12-0-0	Tom Osborne		USC (UPI)	10-1-1	John McKay
1994	Nebraska	13-0-0	Tom Osborne	1973	Notre Dame	11-0-0	Ara Parseghian
1993	Florida St.	12-1-0	Bobby Bowden		Alabama (UPI)	11-1-0	Bear Bryant
1992	Alabama	13-0-0	Gene Stallings	1972	USC	12-0-0	John McKay
1991	Miami (Florida)	12-0-0	Dennis Erickson	1971	Nebraska	13-0-0	Bob Devaney
	Washington (CNN)	12-0-0	Don James	1970	Nebraska	11-0-1	Bob Devaney
1990	Colorado	11-1-1	Bill McCartney		Texas (UPI)	10-1-0	Darrell Royal
	Georgia Tech (UPI)	11-0-1	Bobby Ross	1969	Texas	11-0-0	Darrell Royal
1989	Miami (Florida)	1-1-0	Dennis Erickson	1968	Ohio St.	10-0-0	Woody Hayes
1988	Notre Dame	12-0-0	Lou Holtz	1967	USC	10-1-0	John McKay
1987	Miami (Florida)	12-0-0	Jimmy Johnson	1966	Notre Dame	9-0-1	Ara Parseghian
1986	Penn St.	12-0-0	Joe Paterno	1965	Alabama	9-1-1	Bear Bryant
1985	Oklahoma	11-1-0	Barry Switzer		Michigan St. (UPI)	10-1-0	Duffy Daugherty
1984	Brigham Young	13-0-0	LaVell Edwards	1964	Alabama	10-1-0	Bear Bryant
1983	Miami (Florida)	11-1-0	Howard Schnellenberger	1963	Texas	11-0-0	Darrell Royal
1982	Penn St.	11-1-0	Joe Paterno	1962	USC	11-0-0	John McKay
1981	Clemson	12-0-0	Danny Ford	1961	Alabama	11-0-0	Bear Bryant

Note: National Champion selectors: Helms Athletic Foundation (H) 1883-1935, The Dickinson System (D) 1924-40; The Associated Press (AP) 1936-present, United Press International (UPI) 1958-90, *USA Today*/CNN (CNN) 1991-96, and *USA Today*/ESPN (ESPN) 1997-present.

National Championships (cont.)

Year	Champion	Record	Head Coach	Year	Champion	Record	Head Coach
1960	Minnesota	8-2-0	Murray Warmath	1925	Alabama (H)	10-0-0	Wallace Wade
1959	Syracuse	11-0-0	Ben Schwartzwalder		Dartmouth (D)	8-0-0	Jesse Hawley
1958	Louisiana St.	11-0-0	Paul Dietzel	1924	Notre Dame	10-0-0	Knute Rockne
1957	Auburn	10-0-0	Shug Jordan	1923	Illinois	8-0-0	Bob Zuppke
	Ohio St. (UPI)	9-1-0	Woody Hayes	1922	Cornell	8-0-0	Gil Dobie
1956	Oklahoma	10-0-0	Bud Wilkinson	1921	Cornell	8-0-0	Gil Dobie
1955	Oklahoma	11-0-0	Bud Wilkinson	1920	California	9-0-0	Andy Smith
1954	Ohio St.	10-0-0	Woody Hayes	1919	Harvard	9-0-1	Bob Fisher
	UCLA (UPI)	9-0-0	Red Sanders	1918	Pittsburgh	4-1-0	Pop Warner
1953	Maryland	10-1-0	Jim Tatum	1917	Georgia Tech	9-0-0	John Heisman
1952	Michigan St.	9-0-0	Biggie Munn	1916	Pittsburgh	8-0-0	Pop Warner
1951	Tennessee	10-0-0	Robert Neyland	1915	Cornell	9-0-0	Al Sharpe
1950	Oklahoma	10-1-0	Bud Wilkinson	1914	Army	9-0-0	Charley Daly
1949	Notre Dame	10-0-0	Frank Leahy	1913	Harvard	9-0-0	Percy Haughton
1948	Michigan	9-0-0	Bennie Oosterbaan	1912	Harvard	9-0-0	Percy Haughton
1947	Notre Dame	9-0-0	Frank Leahy	1911	Princeton	8-0-2	Bill Roper
	Michigan	10-0-0	Fritz Crisler	1910	Harvard	8-0-1	Percy Haughton
1946	Notre Dame	8-0-1	Frank Leahy	1909	Yale	12-1-0	Howard Jones
1945	Army	9-0-0	Red Blaik	1908	Pennsylvania	11-0-1	Sol Metzger
1944	Army	9-0-0	Red Blaik	1907	Yale	9-0-1	Bill Knox
1943	Notre Dame	9-1-0	Frank Leahy	1906	Princeton	9-0-1	Bill Roper
1942	Ohio St.	9-1-0	Paul Brown	1905	Chicago	10-0-0	Amos Alonzo Stagg
1941	Minnesota	8-0-0	Bernie Bierman	1904	Pennsylvania	12-0-0	Carl Williams
1940	Minnesota	8-0-0	Bernie Bierman	1903	Princeton	11-0-0	Art Hillebrand
1939	Texas A&M (AP)	11-0-0	Homer Norton	1902	Michigan	11-0-0	Fielding Yost
	USC (D)	8-0-2	Howard Jones	1901	Michigan	11-0-0	Fielding Yost
1938	TCU (AP)	11-0-0	Dutch Meyer	1900	Yale	12-0-0	Malcolm McBride
	Notre Dame (D)	8-1-0	Elmer Layden	1899	Harvard	10-0-1	Benjamin H. Dibblee
1937	Pittsburgh	9-0-1	Jock Sutherland	1898	Harvard	11-0-0	W. Cameron Forbes
1936	Minnesota	7-1-0	Bernie Bierman	1897	Pennsylvania	15-0-0	George W. Woodruff
1935	Minnesota (H)	8-0-0	Bernie Bierman	1896	Princeton	10-0-1	Garrett Cochran
	SMU (D)	12-1-0	Matty Bell	1895	Pennsylvania	14-0-0	George W. Woodruff
1934	Minnesota	8-0-0	Bernie Bierman	1894	Yale	16-0-0	William C. Rhodes
1933	Michigan	8-0-0	Harry Kipke	1893	Princeton	11-0-0	Tom Trenchard
1932	USC (H)	10-0-0	Howard Jones	1892	Yale	13-0-0	Walter Camp
	Michigan (D)	8-0-0	Harry Kipke	1891	Yale	13-0-0	Walter Camp
1931	USC	10-1-0	Howard Jones	1890	Harvard	11-0-0	G. Stewart/G. Adams
1930	Notre Dame	10-0-0	Knute Rockne	1889	Princeton	10-0-0	Edgar Poe
1929	Notre Dame	9-0-0	Knute Rockne	1888	Yale	13-0-0	Walter Camp
1928	Georgia Tech (H)	10-0-0	Bill Alexander	1887	Yale	9-0-0	Harry W. Beecher
	USC (D)	9-0-1	Howard Jones	1886	Yale	9-0-1	Robert N. Corwin
1927	Illinois	7-0-1	Bob Zuppke	1885	Princeton	9-0-0	Charles DeCamp
1926	Alabama (H)	9-0-1	Wallace Wade	1884	Yale	8-0-1	Eugene L. Richards
	Stanford (D)(H)	10-0-1	Pop Warner	1883	Yale	8-0-0	Ray Tompkins

Major Bowl Game Results

Rose Bowl

Date	Result	Date	Result
2003	Oklahoma 34, Washington St. 14	1991	Washington 46, Iowa 34
2002	Miami 37, Nebraska 14	1990	USC 17, Michigan 10
2001	Washington 34, Purdue 24	1989	Michigan 22, USC 14
2000	Wisconsin 17, Stanford 9	1988	Michigan St. 20, USC 17
1999	Wisconsin 38, UCLA 31	1987	Arizona St. 22, Michigan 15
1998	Michigan 21, Washington St. 16	1986	UCLA 45, Iowa 28
1997	Ohio St. 20, Arizona St. 17	1985	USC 20, Ohio St. 17
1996	USC 41, Northwestern 32	1984	UCLA 45, Illinois 9
1995	Penn St. 38, Oregon 20	1983	UCLA 24, Michigan 14
1994	Wisconsin 21, UCLA 16	1982	Washington 28, Iowa 0
1993	Michigan 38, Washington 31	1981	Michigan 23, Washington 6
1992	Washington 34, Michigan 14	1980	USC 17, Ohio St. 16

Rose Bowl (cont.)

Date	Result	Date	Result
1979	USC 17, Michigan 10	1946	Alabama 34, USC 14
1978	Washington 27, Michigan 20	1945	USC 25, Tennessee 0
1977	USC 14, Michigan 6	1944	USC 29, Washington 0
1976	UCLA 23, Ohio St. 10	1943	Georgia 9, UCLA 0
1975	USC 18, Ohio St. 17	1942	Oregon St. 20, Duke 16
1974	Ohio St. 42, USC 21	1941	Stanford 21, Nebraska 13
1973	USC 42, Ohio St. 17	1940	USC 14, Tennessee 0
1972	Stanford 13, Michigan 12	1939	USC 7, Duke 3
1971	Stanford 27, Ohio St. 17	1938	California 13, Alabama 0
1970	USC 10, Michigan 3	1937	Pittsburgh 21, Washington 0
1969	Ohio St. 27, USC 16	1936	Stanford 7, SMU 0
1968	USC 14, Indiana 3	1935	Alabama 29, Stanford 13
1967	Purdue 14, USC 13	1934	Columbia 7, Stanford 0
1966	UCLA 14, Michigan St. 12	1933	USC 35, Pittsburgh 0
1965	Michigan 34, Oregon St. 7	1932	USC 21, Tulane 12
1964	Illinois 17, Washington 7	1931	Alabama 24, Washington St. 0
1963	USC 42, Wisconsin 37	1930	USC 47, Pittsburgh 14
1962	Minnesota 21, UCLA 3	1929	Georgia Tech 8, California 7
1961	Washington 17, Minnesota 7	1928	Stanford 7, Pittsburgh 6
1960	Washington 44, Wisconsin 8	1927	Stanford 7, Alabama 7
1959	Iowa 38, California 12	1926	Alabama 20, Washington 19
1958	Ohio St. 10, Oregon 7	1925	Notre Dame 27, Stanford 10
1957	Iowa 35, Oregon St. 19	1924	Washington 14, Navy 14
1956	Michigan St. 17, UCLA 14	1923	USC 14, Penn St. 3
1955	Ohio St. 20, USC 7	1922	California 0, Washington & Jefferson 0
1954	Michigan St. 28, UCLA 20	1921	California 28, Ohio St. 0
1953	USC 7, Wisconsin 0	1920	Harvard 7, Oregon 6
1952	Illinois 40, Stanford 7	1919	Great Lakes 17, Mare Island 0
1951	Michigan 14, California 6	1918	Mare Island 19, Camp Lewis 7
1950	Ohio St. 17, California 14	1917	Oregon 14, Pennsylvania 0
1949	Northwestern 20, California 14	1916	Washington St. 14, Brown 0
1948	Michigan 49, USC 0	1902	Michigan 49, Stanford 0
1947	Illinois 45, UCLA 14		

Note: From 1903–15, no Rose Bowl football game was held. In 1903, polo replaced football. From 1904 through 1915, chariot races were held. Football returned in 1916.

Orange Bowl

Date	Result	Date	Result
January 2, 2003	USC 38, Iowa 17	January 1, 1974	Penn St. 16, LSU 9
January 2, 2002	Florida 56, Maryland 23	January 1, 1973	Nebraska 40, Notre Dame 6
January 3, 2001	Oklahoma 13, Florida St. 2	January 1, 1972	Nebraska 38, Alabama 6
January 1, 2000	Michigan 35, Alabama 34 (OT)	January 1, 1971	Nebraska 17, LSU 12
January 2, 1999	Florida 31, Syracuse 10	January 1, 1970	Penn St. 10, Missouri 3
January 2, 1998	Nebraska 42, Tennessee 17	January 1, 1969	Penn St. 15, Kansas 14
December 31, 1996	Nebraska 41, Virginia Tech 21	January 1, 1968	Oklahoma 26, Tennessee 24
January 1, 1996	Florida St. 31, Notre Dame 26	January 2, 1967	Florida 27, Georgia Tech 12
January 1, 1995	Nebraska 24, Miami (Florida) 17	January 1, 1966	Alabama 39, Nebraska 28
January 1, 1994	Florida St. 18, Nebraska 16	January 1, 1965	Texas 21, Alabama 17
January 1, 1993	Florida St. 27, Nebraska 14	January 1, 1964	Nebraska 13, Auburn 7
January 1, 1992	Miami (Florida) 22, Nebraska 0	January 1, 1963	Alabama 17, Oklahoma 0
January 1, 1991	Colorado 10, Notre Dame 9	January 1, 1962	LSU 25, Colorado 7
January 1, 1990	Notre Dame 21, Colorado 6	January 2, 1961	Missouri 21, Navy 14
January 2, 1989	Miami (Florida) 23, Nebraska 3	January 1, 1960	Georgia 14, Missouri 0
January 1, 1988	Miami (Florida) 20, Oklahoma 14	January 1, 1959	Oklahoma 21, Syracuse 6
January 1, 1987	Oklahoma 42, Arkansas 8	January 1, 1958	Oklahoma 48, Duke 21
January 1, 1986	Oklahoma 25, Penn St. 10	January 1, 1957	Colorado 27, Clemson 21
January 1, 1985	Washington 28, Oklahoma 17	January 2, 1956	Oklahoma 20, Maryland 6
January 2, 1984	Miami (Florida) 31, Nebraska 30	January 1, 1955	Duke 34, Nebraska 7
January 1, 1983	Nebraska 21, LSU 20	January 1, 1954	Oklahoma 7, Maryland 0
January 1, 1982	Clemson 22, Nebraska 15	January 1, 1953	Alabama 61, Syracuse 6
January 1, 1981	Oklahoma 18, Florida St. 17	January 1, 1952	Georgia Tech 17, Baylor 14
January 1, 1980	Oklahoma 24, Florida St. 7	January 1, 1951	Clemson 15, Miami (Florida) 14
January 1, 1979	Oklahoma 31, Nebraska 24	January 2, 1950	Santa Clara 21, Kentucky 13
January 2, 1978	Arkansas 31, Oklahoma 0	January 1, 1949	Texas 41, Georgia 28
January 1, 1977	Ohio St. 27, Colorado 10	January 1, 1948	Georgia Tech 20, Kansas 14
January 1, 1976	Oklahoma 14, Michigan 6	January 1, 1947	Rice 8, Tennessee 0
January 1, 1975	Notre Dame 13, Alabama 11	January 1, 1946	Miami (Florida) 13, Holy Cross 6

Major Bowl Game Results (cont.)

Orange Bowl (cont.)

Date	Result
January 1, 1945	Tulsa 26, Georgia Tech 12
January 1, 1944	LSU 19, Texas A&M 14
January 1, 1943	Alabama 37, Boston College 21
January 1, 1942	Georgia 40, TCU 26
January 1, 1941	Mississippi St. 14, Georgetown 7
January 1, 1940	Georgia Tech 21, Missouri 7

Date	Result
January 2, 1939	Tennessee 17, Oklahoma 0
January 1, 1938	Auburn 6, Michigan St. 0
January 1, 1937	Duquesne 13, Mississippi St. 12
January 1, 1936	Catholic 20, Mississippi 19
January 1, 1935	Bucknell 26, Miami (Florida) 0

Sugar Bowl

Date	Result
January 1, 2003	Georgia 26, Florida St. 13
January 1, 2002	LSU 47, Illinois 34
January 2, 2001	Miami (Florida) 37, Florida 20
January 4, 2000	Florida St. 46, Virginia Tech 29
January 1, 1999	Ohio St. 24, Texas A&M 14
January 1, 1998	Florida St. 31, Ohio St. 14
January 2, 1997	Florida 52, Florida St. 20
December 31, 1995	Virginia Tech 28, Texas 10
January 2, 1995	Florida St. 23, Florida 17
January 1, 1994	Florida 41, West Virginia 7
January 1, 1993	Alabama 34, Miami (Florida) 13
January 1, 1992	Notre Dame 39, Florida 28
January 1, 1991	Tennessee 23, Virginia 22
January 1, 1990	Miami (Florida) 33, Alabama 25
January 2, 1989	Florida St. 13, Auburn 7
January 1, 1988	Auburn 16, Syracuse 16
January 1, 1987	Nebraska 30, LSU 15
January 1, 1986	Tennessee 35, Miami (Florida) 7
January 1, 1985	Nebraska 28, LSU 10
January 2, 1984	Auburn 9, Michigan 7
January 1, 1983	Penn St. 27, Georgia 23
January 1, 1982	Pittsburgh 24, Georgia 20
January 1, 1981	Georgia 17, Notre Dame 10
January 1, 1980	Alabama 24, Arkansas 9
January 1, 1979	Alabama 14, Penn St. 7
January 2, 1978	Alabama 35, Ohio St. 6
January 1, 1977	Pittsburgh 27, Georgia 3
December 31, 1975	Alabama 13, Penn St. 6
December 31, 1974	Nebraska 13, Florida 10
December 31, 1973	Notre Dame 24, Alabama 23
December 31, 1972	Oklahoma 14, Penn St. 0
January 1, 1972	Oklahoma 40, Auburn 22
January 1, 1971	Tennessee 34, Air Force 13
January 1, 1970	Mississippi 27, Arkansas 22
January 1, 1969	Arkansas 16, Georgia 2

Date	Result
January 1, 1968	LSU 20, Wyoming 13
January 2, 1967	Alabama 34, Nebraska 7
January 1, 1966	Missouri 20, Florida 18
January 1, 1965	LSU 13, Syracuse 10
January 1, 1964	Alabama 12, Mississippi 7
January 1, 1963	Mississippi 17, Arkansas 3
January 1, 1962	Alabama 10, Arkansas 3
January 2, 1961	Mississippi 14, Rice 6
January 1, 1960	Mississippi 21, LSU 0
January 1, 1959	LSU 7, Clemson 0
January 1, 1958	Mississippi 39, Texas 7
January 1, 1957	Baylor 13, Tennessee 7
January 2, 1956	Georgia Tech 7, Pittsburgh 0
January 1, 1955	Navy 21, Mississippi 0
January 1, 1954	Georgia Tech 42, West Virginia 19
January 1, 1953	Georgia Tech 24, Mississippi 7
January 1, 1952	Maryland 28, Tennessee 13
January 1, 1951	Kentucky 13, Oklahoma 7
January 2, 1950	Oklahoma 35, LSU 0
January 1, 1949	Oklahoma 14, North Carolina 6
January 1, 1948	Texas 27, Alabama 7
January 1, 1947	Georgia 20, North Carolina 10
January 1, 1946	Oklahoma St. 33, Saint Mary's (Colorado) 13
January 1, 1945	Duke 29, Alabama 26
January 1, 1944	Georgia Tech 20, Tulsa 18
January 1, 1943	Tennessee 14, Tulsa 7
January 1, 1942	Fordham 2, Missouri 0
January 1, 1941	Boston College 19, Tennessee 13
January 1, 1940	Texas A&M 14, Tulane 13
January 2, 1939	TCU 15, Carnegie Mellon 7
January 1, 1938	Santa Clara 6, LSU 0
January 1, 1937	Santa Clara 21, LSU 14
January 1, 1936	TCU 3, LSU 2
January 1, 1935	Tulane 20, Temple 14

Cotton Bowl

Date	Result
January 1, 2003	Texas 35, LSU 20
January 1, 2002	Oklahoma 10, Arkansas 3
January 1, 2001	Kansas St. 35, Tennessee 21
January 1, 2000	Arkansas 27, Texas 6
January 1, 1999	Texas 38, Mississippi St. 11
January 1, 1998	UCLA 29, Texas A&M 23
January 1, 1997	BYU 19, Kansas St. 15
January 1, 1996	Colorado 38, Oregon 6
January 2, 1995	USC 55, Texas Tech 14
January 1, 1994	Notre Dame 24, Texas A&M 21

Date	Result
January 1, 1993	Notre Dame 28, Texas A&M 3
January 1, 1992	Florida St. 10, Texas A&M 2
January 1, 1991	Miami (Florida) 46, Texas 3
January 1, 1990	Tennessee 31, Arkansas 27
January 2, 1989	UCLA 17, Arkansas 3
January 1, 1988	Texas A&M 35, Notre Dame 10
January 1, 1987	Ohio St. 28, Texas A&M 12
January 1, 1986	Texas A&M 36, Auburn 16
January 1, 1985	Boston College 45, Houston 28
January 2, 1984	Georgia 10, Texas 9

Legends

Barry Sanders, running back, b. July 16, 1968, Wichita, Kansas. In 1988, as an Oklahoma State junior, Sanders averaged 238.9 yards per game and set 25 NCAA records. He led the nation in rushing yards (2,628) and scored 39 touchdowns. Both records still stand. He also won the Heisman Trophy in 1988 and was the Detroit Lions' top pick and the third pick overall in the 1989 NFL draft.

Barry Sanders holds eleven Division I-A single-season rushing records.

DAMIAN STROHMEYER/SPORTS ILLUSTRATED

Archie Griffin, running back, b. August 21, 1954, Columbus, Ohio. Griffin is the only player to win the Heisman Trophy twice (1974, 1975) and is the only Ohio State Buckeye to lead the team in rushing for four straight seasons. Griffin is eighth on the all-time NCAA list for career rushing yards (5,177) and holds the NCAA record for consecutive 100-yard rushing games (31).

Tony Dorsett, running back, b. April 7, 1954, Rochester, Pennsylvania. Dorsett was an All-America in each of his four seasons at Pittsburgh. He set the NCAA Division I record for rushing yards (1,586) as a freshman. He became the first college running back to rush for 1,000 yards in four straight seasons. Dorsett was also the first back to rush for more than 6,000 career yards (6,082). As a senior, in 1976, he led the Panthers to an undefeated season and their first national championship in nearly 40 years. He also won the Heisman Trophy that year.

Major Bowl Game Results (cont.)

Cotton Bowl (cont.)

Date	Result	Date	Result
January 1, 1983	SMU 7, Pittsburgh 3	January 1, 1963	LSU 13, Texas 0
January 1, 1982	Texas 14, Alabama 12	January 1, 1962	Texas 12, Mississippi 7
January 1, 1981	Alabama 30, Baylor 2	January 2, 1961	Duke 7, Arkansas 6
January 1, 1980	Houston 17, Nebraska 14	January 1, 1960	Syracuse 23, Texas 14
January 1, 1979	Notre Dame 35, Houston 34	January 1, 1959	TCU 0, Air Force 0
January 2, 1978	Notre Dame 38, Texas 10	January 1, 1958	Navy 20, Rice 7
January 1, 1977	Houston 30, Maryland 21	January 1, 1957	TCU 28, Syracuse 27
January 1, 1976	Arkansas 31, Georgia 10	January 2, 1956	Mississippi 14, TCU 13
January 1, 1975	Penn St. 41, Baylor 20	January 1, 1955	Georgia Tech 14, Arkansas 6
January 1, 1974	Nebraska 19, Texas 3	January 1, 1954	Rice 28, Alabama 6
January 1, 1973	Texas 17, Alabama 13	January 1, 1953	Texas 16, Tennessee 0
January 1, 1972	Penn St. 30, Texas 6	January 1, 1952	Kentucky 20, TCU 7
January 1, 1971	Notre Dame 24, Texas 11	January 1, 1951	Tennessee 20, Texas 14
January 1, 1970	Texas 21, Notre Dame 17	January 2, 1950	Rice 27, North Carolina 13
January 1, 1969	Texas 36, Tennessee 13	January 1, 1949	SMU 21, Oregon 13
January 1, 1968	Texas A&M 20, Alabama 16	January 1, 1948	SMU 13, Penn St. 13
December 31, 1966	Georgia 24, SMU 9	January 1, 1947	Arkansas 0, LSU 0
January 1, 1966	LSU 14, Arkansas 7	January 1, 1946	Texas 40, Missouri 27
January 1, 1965	Arkansas 10, Nebraska 7	January 1, 1945	Oklahoma St. 34, TCU 0
January 1, 1964	Texas 28, Navy 6	January 1, 1944	Texas 7, Randolph Field 7

Major Bowl Game Results (cont.)

Cotton Bowl (cont.)

Date	Result	Date	Result
January 1, 1943	Texas 14, Georgia Tech 7	January 2, 1939	St. Mary's (Calif.) 20, Texas Tech 13
January 1, 1942	Alabama 29, Texas A&M 21	January 1, 1938	Rice 28, Colorado 14
January 1, 1941	Texas A&M 13, Fordham 12	January 1, 1937	TCU 16, Marquette 6
January 1, 1940	Clemson 6, Boston College 3		

Fiesta Bowl

Date	Result	Date	Result
January 3, 2003	Ohio St. 31, Miami 24	January 2, 1987	Penn St. 14, Miami (Florida) 10
January 1, 2002	Oregon 38, Colorado 16	January 1, 1986	Michigan 27, Nebraska 23
January 1, 2001	Oregon St. 41, Notre Dame 9	January 1, 1985	UCLA 39, Miami (Florida) 37
January 2, 2000	Nebraska 31, Tennessee 21	January 2, 1984	Ohio St. 28, Pittsburgh 23
January 4, 1999	Tennessee 23, Florida St. 16	January 1, 1983	Arizona St. 32, Oklahoma 21
December 31, 1997	Kansas St. 35, Syracuse 18	January 1, 1982	Penn St. 26, USC 10
January 1, 1997	Penn St. 38, Texas 15	December 26, 1980	Penn St. 31, Ohio St. 19
January 2, 1996	Nebraska 62, Florida 24	December 25, 1979	Pittsburgh 16, Arizona 10
January 2, 1995	Colorado 41, Notre Dame 24	December 25, 1978	Arkansas 10, UCLA 10
January 1, 1994	Arizona 29, Miami (Florida) 0	December 25, 1977	Penn St. 42, Arizona St. 30
January 1, 1993	Syracuse 26, Colorado 22	December 25, 1976	Oklahoma 41, Wyoming 7
January 1, 1992	Penn St. 42, Tennessee 17	December 26, 1975	Arizona St. 17, Nebraska 14
January 1, 1991	Louisville 34, Alabama 7	December 28, 1974	Oklahoma 16, BYU 6
January 1, 1990	Florida St. 41, Nebraska 17	December 21, 1973	Arizona St. 28, Pittsburgh 7
January 2, 1989	Notre Dame 34, West Virginia 21	December 23, 1972	Arizona St. 49, Missouri 35
January 1, 1988	Florida St. 31, Nebraska 28	December 27, 1971	Arizona St. 45, Florida St. 38

NCAA Division I-AA Championships

Year	Winner	Runner-up	Score	Year	Winner	Runner-up	Score
2002	Western Kentucky	McNeese St.	34–14	1989	Georgia Southern	Stephen F. Austin	37–34
2001	Montana	Furman	13–6				
2000	Georgia Southern	Montana	27–25	1988	Furman	Georgia Southern	17–12
1999	Georgia Southern	Youngstown St.	59–24	1987	Northeast Louisiana	Marshall	43–42
1998	Massachusetts	Georgia Southern	55–43	1986	Georgia Southern	Arkansas St.	48–21
1997	Youngstown St.	McNeese St.	10–9	1985	Georgia Southern	Furman	44–42
1996	Marshall	Montana	49–29	1984	Montana St.	Louisiana Tech	19–6
1995	Montana	Marshall	22–20	1983	Southern Illinois	Western Carolina	43–7
1994	Youngstown St.	Boise St.	28–14	1982	Eastern Kentucky	Delaware	17–14
1993	Youngstown St.	Marshall	17–5	1981	Idaho St.	Eastern Kentucky	34–23
1992	Marshall	Youngstown St.	31–28	1980	Boise St.	Eastern Kentucky	31–29
1991	Youngstown St.	Marshall	25–17	1979	Eastern Kentucky	Lehigh	30–7
1990	Georgia Southern	Nevada-Reno	36–13	1978	Florida A&M	Massachusetts	35–28

Heisman Memorial Trophy

Awarded to the best college player by the Downtown Athletic Club (DAC) of New York City. The trophy is named after John W. Heisman, who coached Georgia Tech to the national championship in 1917 and later served as DAC athletic director.

Year	Winner, College	Runner-up, College
2002	Carson Palmer, USC	Brad Banks, Iowa
2001	Eric Crouch, Nebraska	Rex Grossman, Florida
2000	Chris Weinke, Florida St.	Josh Heupel, Oklahoma
1999	Ron Dayne, Wisconsin	Joe Hamilton, Georgia Tech
1998	Ricky Williams, Texas	Michael Bishop, Kansas St.

Heisman Memorial Trophy (cont.)

Year	Winner, College	Runner-up, College
1997	† Charles Woodson, Michigan	Peyton Manning, Tennessee
1996	† Danny Wuerffel, Florida	Troy Davis, Iowa St.
1995	Eddie George, Ohio St.	Tommie Frazier, Nebraska
1994	Rashaan Salaam, Colorado	Ki-Jana Carter, Penn St.
1993	† Charlie Ward, Florida St.	Heath Shuler, Tennessee
1992	Gino Torretta, Miami (Florida)	Marshall Faulk, San Diego St.
1991	* Desmond Howard, Michigan	Casey Weldon, Florida St.
1990	* Ty Detmer, BYU	Raghib Ismail, Notre Dame
1989	* Andre Ware, Houston	Anthony Thompson, Indiana
1988	* Barry Sanders, Oklahoma St.	Rodney Peete, USC
1987	Tim Brown, Notre Dame	Don McPherson, Syracuse
1986	Vinny Testaverde, Miami (Florida)	Paul Palmer, Temple
1985	Bo Jackson, Auburn	Chuck Long, Iowa
1984	Doug Flutie, Boston College	Keith Byars, Ohio St.
1983	Mike Rozier, Nebraska	Steve Young, BYU
1982	* Herschel Walker, Georgia	John Elway, Stanford
1981	Marcus Allen, USC	Herschel Walker, Georgia
1980	George Rogers, South Carolina	Hugh Green, Pittsburgh
1979	Charles White, USC	Billy Sims, Oklahoma
1978	* Billy Sims, Oklahoma	Chuck Fusina, Penn St.
1977	Earl Campbell, Texas	Terry Miller, Oklahoma St.
1976	† Tony Dorsett, Pittsburgh	Ricky Bell, USC
1975	Archie Griffin, Ohio St.	Chuck Muncie, California
1974	* Archie Griffin, Ohio St.	Anthony Davis, USC
1973	John Cappelletti, Penn St.	John Hicks, Ohio St.
1972	Johnny Rodgers, Nebraska	Greg Pruitt, Oklahoma
1971	Pat Sullivan, Auburn	Ed Marinaro, Cornell
1970	Jim Plunkett, Stanford	Joe Theismann, Notre Dame
1969	Steve Owens, Oklahoma	Mike Phipps, Purdue
1968	O.J. Simpson, USC	Leroy Keyes, Purdue
1967	Gary Beban, UCLA	O.J. Simpson, USC
1966	Steve Spurrier, Florida	Bob Griese, Purdue
1965	Mike Garrett, USC	Howard Twilley, Tulsa
1964	John Huarte, Notre Dame	Jerry Rhome, Tulsa
1963	* Roger Staubach, Navy	Billy Lothridge, Georgia Tech
1962	Terry Baker, Oregon St.	Jerry Stovall, LSU
1961	Ernie Davis, Syracuse	Bob Ferguson, Ohio St.
1960	Joe Bellino, Navy	Tom Brown, Minnesota
1959	Billy Cannon, LSU	Rich Lucas, Penn St.
1958	Pete Dawkins, Army	Randy Duncan, Iowa
1957	John David Crow, Texas A&M	Alex Karras, Iowa
1956	Paul Hornung, Notre Dame	Johnny Majors, Tennessee
1955	Howard Cassady, Ohio St.	Jim Swink, TCU
1954	Alan Ameche, Wisconsin	Kurt Burris, Oklahoma
1953	John Lattner, Notre Dame	Paul Giel, Minnesota
1952	Billy Vessels, Oklahoma	Jack Scarbath, Maryland
1951	Dick Kazmaier, Princeton	Hank Lauricella, Tennessee
1950	* Vic Janowicz, Ohio St.	Kyle Rote, SMU
1949	† Leon Hart, Notre Dame	Charlie Justice, North Carolina
1948	* Doak Walker, SMU	Charlie Justice, North Carolina
1947	† John Lujack, Notre Dame	Bob Chappius, Michigan
1946	Glenn Davis, Army	Charley Trippi, Georgia
1945	* † Doc Blanchard, Army	Glenn Davis, Army
1944	Les Horvath, Ohio St.	Glenn Davis, Army
1943	Angelo Bertelli, Notre Dame	Bob Odell, Pennsylvania
1942	Frank Sinkwich, Georgia	Paul Governali, Columbia
1941	† Bruce Smith, Minnesota	Angelo Bertelli, Notre Dame
1940	Tom Harmon, Michigan	John Kimbrough, Texas A&M
1939	Nile Kinnick, Iowa	Tom Harmon, Michigan
1938	† Davey O'Brien, TCU	Marshall Goldberg, Pittsburgh
1937	Clint Frank, Yale	Byron White, Colorado
1936	Larry Kelley, Yale	Sam Francis, Nebraska
1935	Jay Berwanger, Chicago	Monk Meyer, Army

*Juniors (all others were seniors)
†Winners who played for national championship teams the same year
Note: Former Heisman winners and members of the national media cast votes with ballots allowing for three names (3 points for first, 2 points for second, and 1 point for third).

Maxwell Award

Given to the nation's outstanding college football player by the Maxwell Football Club of Philadelphia.

Year	Player, College	Year	Player, College
2002	Larry Johnson, Penn St.	1969	Mike Reid, Penn St.
2001	Ken Dorsey, Miami (Florida)	1968	O.J. Simpson, USC
2000	Drew Brees, Purdue	1967	Gary Beban, UCLA
1999	Ron Dayne, Wisconsin	1966	Jim Lynch, Notre Dame
1998	Ricky Williams, Texas	1965	Tommy Nobis, Texas
1997	Peyton Manning, Tennessee	1964	Glenn Ressler, Penn St.
1996	Danny Wuerffel, Florida	1963	Roger Staubach, Navy
1995	Eddie George, Ohio St.	1962	Terry Baker, Oregon St.
1994	Kerry Collins, Penn St.	1961	Bob Ferguson, Ohio St.
1993	Charlie Ward, Florida St.	1960	Joe Bellino, Navy
1992	Gino Torretta, Miami (Florida)	1959	Rich Lucas, Penn St.
1991	Desmond Howard, Michigan	1958	Pete Dawkins, Army
1990	Ty Detmer, BYU	1957	Bob Reifsnyder, Navy
1989	Anthony Thompson, Indiana	1956	Tommy McDonald, Oklahoma
1988	Barry Sanders, Oklahoma St.	1955	Howard Cassady, Ohio St.
1987	Don McPherson, Syracuse	1954	Ron Beagle, Navy
1986	Vinny Testaverde, Miami (Florida)	1953	John Lattner, Notre Dame
1985	Chuck Long, Iowa	1952	John Lattner, Notre Dame
1984	Doug Flutie, Boston College	1951	Dick Kazmaier, Princeton
1983	Mike Rozier, Nebraska	1950	Reds Bagnell, Pennsylvania
1982	Herschel Walker, Georgia	1949	Leon Hart, Notre Dame
1981	Marcus Allen, USC	1948	Chuck Bednarik, Pennsylvania
1980	Hugh Green, Pittsburgh	1947	Doak Walker, SMU
1979	Charles White, USC	1946	Charley Trippi, Georgia
1978	Chuck Fusina, Penn St.	1945	Doc Blanchard, Army
1977	Ross Browner, Notre Dame	1944	Glenn Davis, Army
1976	Tony Dorsett, Pittsburgh	1943	Bob Odell, Pennsylvania
1975	Archie Griffin, Ohio St.	1942	Paul Governali, Columbia
1974	Steve Joachim, Temple	1941	Bill Dudley, Virginia
1973	John Cappelletti, Penn St.	1940	Tom Harmon, Michigan
1972	Brad Van Pelt, Michigan St.	1939	Nile Kinnick, Iowa
1971	Ed Marinaro, Cornell	1938	Davey O'Brien, TCU
1970	Jim Plunkett, Stanford	1937	Clint Frank, Yale

Davey O'Brien National Quarterback Award

Given to the top quarterback in the nation by the Davey O'Brien Educational and Charitable Trust of Fort Worth. Named for TCU Hall of Fame quarterback Davey O'Brien (1936-38).

Year	Player, College	Year	Player, College
2002	Brad Banks, Iowa	1991	Ty Detmer, BYU
2001	Eric Crouch, Nebraska	1990	Ty Detmer, BYU
2000	Chris Weinke, Florida St.	1989	Andre Ware, Houston
1999	Joe Hamilton, Georgia Tech	1988	Troy Aikman, UCLA
1998	Michael Bishop, Kansas St.	1987	Don McPherson, Syracuse
1997	Peyton Manning, Tennessee	1986	Vinny Testaverde, Miami (Florida)
1996	Danny Wuerffel, Florida	1985	Chuck Long, Iowa
1995	Danny Wuerffel, Florida	1984	Doug Flutie, Boston College
1994	Kerry Collins, Penn St.	1983	Steve Young, BYU
1993	Charlie Ward, Florida St.	1982	Todd Blackledge, Penn St.
1992	Gino Torretta, Miami (Florida)	1981	Jim McMahon, BYU

Did You Know?

Notre Dame has had the most Heisman Trophy winners (7). The last Irish player to win it was wide receiver Tim Brown, in 1987.

Vince Lombardi/Rotary Award

The award, given to the outstanding college lineman of the year, is sponsored by the Rotary Club of Houston.

Year	Player, College	Year	Player, College
2002	Terrell Suggs, Arizona St.	1986	Cornelius Bennett, Alabama
2001	Julius Peppers, North Carolina	1985	Tony Casillas, Oklahoma
2000	Jamal Reynolds, Florida St.	1984	Tony Degrate, Texas
1999	Corey Moore, Virginia Tech	1983	Dean Steinkuhler, Nebraska
1998	Dat Nguyen, Texas A&M	1982	Dave Rimington, Nebraska
1997	Grant Wistrom, Nebraska	1981	Kenneth Sims, Texas
1996	Orlando Pace, Ohio St.	1980	Hugh Green, Pittsburgh
1995	Orlando Pace, Ohio St.	1979	Brad Budde, USC
1994	Warren Sapp, Miami (Florida)	1978	Bruce Clark, Penn St.
1993	Aaron Taylor, Notre Dame	1977	Ross Browner, Notre Dame
1992	Marvin Jones, Florida St.	1976	Wilson Whitley, Houston
1991	Steve Emtman, Washington	1975	Lee Roy Selmon, Oklahoma
1990	Chris Zorich, Notre Dame	1974	Randy White, Maryland
1989	Percy Snow, Michigan St.	1973	John Hicks, Ohio St.
1988	Tracy Rocker, Auburn	1972	Rich Glover, Nebraska
1987	Chris Spielman, Ohio St.	1971	Walt Patulski, Notre Dame
		1970	Jim Stillwagon, Ohio St.

2002-03 TIMELINE

August 22, 2002: College football begins its earliest season as Colorado State beats Virginia, 35 – 29. CSU running back Cecil Sapp rushes for 178 yards and a pair of touchdowns.

September 7, 2002: The University of Texas-El Paso gives up an NCAA Division I-A season-high 77 points in a loss to the Kentucky Wildcats. UTEP gives up 68 points to the Oklahoma Sooners the next week.

October 5, 2002: The Tennessee Volunteers outlast the Arkansas Razorbacks, 41 – 38, in six overtimes. In 2001, the Razorbacks and Mississippi set a Division I record for the longest game (seven overtimes). The Razorbacks won that game.

October 26, 2002: Notre Dame improves its record to 8 – 0 with a 34 – 24 win over Florida State. It is the best start for the Irish in 10 seasons.

November 9, 2002: LSU receiver Devery Henderson hauls in a deflected 75-yard Hail Mary touchdown pass as time expires. The catch gives LSU 33 – 30 win over the University of Kentucky.

November 20, 2002: Virginia Tech running back Lee Suggs runs for a touchdown in a 21 – 18 loss to West Virginia. The TD breaks the Division I record for games in a row with a touchdown (23). Suggs goes on to score in every game in which he plays: 27 straight games with a touchdown.

December 14, 2002: University of Southern California (USC) quarterback Carson Palmer wins the Heisman Trophy. He is the fifth winner from USC. The award is the first Heisman for USC since Marcus Allen won it in 1981.

December 25, 2002: Katie Hnida becomes the first woman to play in a Division I-A football game. The junior kicker attempts an extra point for the University of New Mexico in the Las Vegas Bowl. The kick is blocked, and the Lobos lose the game to the University of California at Los Angeles (UCLA) Bruins, 27 – 13.

January 3, 2003: In the national championship game, the Ohio State Buckeyes beat the Miami Hurricanes, 31 – 24, in two overtimes.

BASEBALL

World Series MVP Troy Glaus and the Anaheim Angels defeated the San Francisco Giants in seven games in 2002.

V.J. LOVERO/SPORTS ILLUSTRATED

The 2002 major league baseball season was full of suspense and surprises. The season looked as if it might be cut short when the players said they would strike if they and the owners couldn't agree on a new contract. Both sides reached an agreement on August 30, and no games were missed. Commissioner Bud Selig wanted to "contract," or shrink, the major leagues by eliminating two financially struggling teams in small markets: the Minnesota Twins and the Montreal Expos. In the end, both teams were saved.

The season's biggest surprise was how well the Anaheim Angels played. They seemed to come from nowhere to win the World Series for the first time in the team's 42-year history.

Great pitching made a welcome return after almost a decade of awesome hitting. A group of talented young hurlers, including American League Cy Young Award-winner Barry Zito (23–5) of the Oakland A's, held hitters to the lowest total batting average (.261) since 1992. Zito was one of seven A.L. pitchers to win at least 19 games.

But sluggers' bats were not kept totally silent. Barry Bonds of the San Francisco Giants had another monster season, winning his first major league batting title (.370), hitting his 600th career home run, playing in his first World Series, and winning a N.L. and major league record fifth MVP award. Rising offensive stars included A.L. MVP shortstop Miguel Tejada of the A's (.308, 34 homers, 131 RBIs) and second baseman Alfonso Soriano (39 homers, 41 steals) of the New York Yankees.

2002 Major League Baseball Final Standings

National League

EASTERN DIVISION

Team	Won	Lost	Pct	GB	Home	Away
Braves	101	59	.631	—	52–28	49–31
Expos	83	79	.512	19	49–32	34–47
Phillies	80	81	.497	21½	40–40	40–41
Marlins	79	83	.488	23	46–35	33–48
Mets	75	86	.466	26½	38–43	37–43

CENTRAL DIVISION

Team	Won	Lost	Pct	GB	Home	Away
Cardinals	97	65	.599	—	52–29	45–36
Astros	84	78	.519	13	47–34	37–44
Reds	78	84	.481	19	38–43	40–41
Pirates	72	89	.447	24½	38–42	34–47
Cubs	67	95	.414	30	36–45	31–50
Brewers	56	106	.346	41	31–50	25–56

WESTERN DIVISION

Team	Won	Lost	Pct	GB	Home	Away
Diamondbacks	98	64	.605	—	55–26	43–38
†Giants	95	66	.590	2½	50–31	45–35
Dodgers	92	70	.568	6	46–35	46–35
Rockies	73	89	.451	25	47–34	26–55
Padres	66	96	.407	32	41–40	25–56

†Wild-card team

American League

EASTERN DIVISION

Team	Won	Lost	Pct	GB	Home	Away
Yankees	103	58	.640	—	52–28	51–30
Red Sox	93	69	.574	10½	42–39	51–30
Blue Jays	78	84	.481	25½	42–39	36–45
Orioles	67	95	.414	36½	34–47	33–48
Devil Rays	55	106	.342	48	30–51	25–55

CENTRAL DIVISION

Team	Won	Lost	Pct	GB	Home	Away
Twins	94	67	.584	—	54–27	40–40
White Sox	81	81	.500	13.5	47–34	34–47
Indians	74	88	.457	20.5	39–42	35–46
Royals	62	100	.383	32.5	37–44	25–56
Tigers	55	106	.342	39	33–47	22–59

WESTERN DIVISION

Team	Won	Lost	Pct	GB	Home	Away
Athletics	103	59	.636	—	54–27	49–32
†Angels	99	63	.611	4	54–27	45–36
Mariners	93	69	.574	10	48–33	45–36
Rangers	72	90	.444	31	42–39	30–51

†Wild-card team

MLB TEAMS

NATIONAL LEAGUE
Arizona Diamondbacks
Atlanta Braves
Chicago Cubs
Cincinnati Reds
Colorado Rockies
Florida Marlins
Houston Astros
Los Angeles Dodgers
Milwaukee Brewers
Montreal Expos
New York Mets
Philadelphia Phillies
Pittsburgh Pirates
San Diego Padres
San Francisco Giants
St. Louis Cardinals

AMERICAN LEAGUE
Anaheim Angels
Baltimore Orioles
Boston Red Sox
Chicago White Sox
Cleveland Indians
Detroit Tigers
Kansas City Royals
Minnesota Twins
New York Yankees
Oakland Athletics
Seattle Mariners
Tampa Bay Devil Rays
Texas Rangers
Toronto Blue Jays

In 2002, Barry Bonds of the Giants was named National League MVP a record fifth time.

BRAD MANGIN

MLB 2002 Playoffs

National League Division Series

Oct 1	Cardinals 12 at Diamondbacks 2	Oct 5	Diamondbacks 3 at Cardinals 6
Oct 3	Cardinals 2 at Diamondbacks 1		

(St. Louis Cardinals won series 3–0)

Oct 2	Giants 8 at Braves 5	Oct 6	Braves 3 at Giants 8
Oct 3	Giants 3 at Braves 7	Oct 7	Giants 3 at Braves 1
Oct 5	Braves 10 at Giants 2		

(San Francisco Giants won series 3–2)

National League Championship Series

Oct 9	Giants 9 at Cardinals 6	Oct 13	Cardinals 3 at Giants 4
Oct 10	Giants 4 at Cardinals 1	Oct 14	Cardinals 1 at Giants 2
Oct 12	Cardinals 5 at Giants 4		

(San Francisco Giants won series 4–1)

GAME 1

Giants	1	4	1	0	1	2	0	0	0	**9**	**11**	**0**
Cardinals	0	1	0	0	2	2	0	1	0	**6**	**11**	**0**

W— Rueter. **L—** Morris. **SV—** Nen.
LOB— SF: 6, StL: 8. **2B—** StL: Marrero, Edmonds. **3B—** SF: Bonds. **HR—** SF: Lofton, Bell, Santiago; StL: Pujols, Cairo, Drew. **S—** SF: Aurilia; StL: Morris. **SB—** SF: Lofton. **CS—** StL: Robinson. **HBP—** StL: Renteria. **GIDP—** SF: Santiago; StL: Renteria. **T—** 3:31. **A—** 52,175.

Recap: Barry Bonds' two-run triple highlighted a four-run second inning as San Francisco jumped on St. Louis's ace, Matt Morris, early. The Giants hammered Morris for seven runs and 10 hits in 4 ⅓ innings. Bonds contributed to a big night by the middle of the San Francisco order, going 1-for-2 with three walks, two runs scored, and two RBIs. Jeff Kent, Bonds, and Benito Santiago combined for six hits, six RBIs, and four runs scored.

GAME 2

Giants	1	0	0	0	2	0	0	0	1	**4**	**7**	**0**
Cardinals	0	0	0	0	0	0	0	1	0	**1**	**6**	**0**

W— Schmidt. **L—** Williams. **SV—** Nen.
LOB— SF: 7, StL: 5. **2B—** StL: Edmonds. **3B—** SF: Snow. **HR—** SF: Aurilia 2; StL: Perez. **S—** SF: Schmidt, Martinez; StL: Williams. **T—** 3:17. **A—** 52,195.

Recap: Jason Schmidt carried a shutout into the eighth inning and Rich Aurilia homered twice as San Francisco swept the first two games in St. Louis. Schmidt allowed only four hits and a walk while whiffing eight Cardinals in eight-plus innings. Aurilia's two-run shot in the fifth gave him 11 RBIs for the postseason, tying the record for most runs driven in by a shortstop in the playoffs.

GAME 3

Cardinals	0	0	2	1	1	1	0	0	0	**5**	**6**	**1**
Giants	0	1	0	0	3	0	0	0	0	**4**	**10**	**0**

W— Finley. **L—** Witasick. **SV—** Isringhausen.
E— StL: Renteria. **LOB—** StL: 5, SF: 11. **2B—** StL: Pujols, Vina, SF: Aurilia. **HR—** StL: Matheny, Edmonds, Marrero; SF: Bonds. **S—** SF: Aurilia, Dunston, Ortiz. **SF—** StL: Renteria; SF: Aurilia. **GIDP—** SF: Snow. **T—** 3:32. **A—** 42,177.

Recap: After a solo homer by Eli Marrero snapped a sixth-inning tie, St. Louis got a fine effort from its bullpen to get back into the series. Dave Veres, Steve Kline, Rick White, and Jason Isringhausen shut down the Giants in the final four innings to preserve the 5–4 win. Barry Bonds was a factor again, hitting a three-run homer in the fifth inning that erased a 4–1 deficit. He also walked three times but popped up with the bases loaded and two outs in the second.

GAME 4

Cardinals	2	0	0	0	0	0	0	0	1	**3**	**12**	**0**
Giants	0	0	0	0	0	2	0	2	x	**4**	**4**	**1**

W— Worrell. **L—** White. **SV—** Nen.
E— SF: Aurilia. **LOB—** StL: 11, SF: 5. **2B—** StL: Vina, Matheny; SF: Snow. **HR—** SF: Santiago. **S—** StL: Renteria, Benes; SF: Hernandez. **GIDP—** StL: Drew, Vina. **SB—** StL: Martinez. **T—** 3:26. **A—** 42,676.

Recap: After an intentional walk to Barry Bonds with two outs in the eighth inning, Benito Santiago, who would be named MVP of the series, rose to the challenge and hit a two-run homer that lifted San Francisco to a 4–3 win. Robb Nen escaped danger in the top of the ninth to nail down his third save of the LCS. After Jim Edmonds singled in a run, Nen struck out Albert Pujols and J.D. Drew with the tying run on third to end the threat.

GAME 5

Cardinals	0	0	0	0	0	0	1	0	0	**1**	**9**	**0**
Giants	0	0	0	0	0	0	1	1	x	**2**	**7**	**0**

W— Worrell. **L—** Morris.
LOB— StL: 10, SF: 9. **2B—** StL: Matheny; SF: Bell. **S—** StL: Morris; SF: Aurilia. **SF—** StL: Vina; SF: Bonds. **GIDP—** SF: Kent. **HBP—** SF: Lofton, Aurilia, Kent. **T—** 3:01. **A—** 42,673.

Recap: Kenny Lofton hit an RBI single with two outs in the ninth inning, sending San Francisco to the World Series for the first time since 1989. Barry Bonds, who has underperformed in recent postseasons, did his part by hitting a game-tying sacrifice fly in the eighth off Matt Morris. Morris got the first two outs in the ninth, but after two singles, he was lifted in favor of Steve Kline. Lofton connected on Kline's first offering.

KEY   W=winning pitcher; L=losing pitcher; SV=save; LOB=left on base; S=single; 2B=doubles; 3B=triples; HR=home runs; SAC=sacrifice; SB=stolen bases; CS=caught stealing; HBP=hit by pitch; GIDP=grounded into double plays; E=errors; WP=wild pitch; PB=passed ball; T=time; A=attendance

MLB 2002 Playoffs

American League Division Series

Oct 1	Twins 7 at Athletics 5	Oct 5	Athletics 2 at Twins 11
Oct 2	Twins 1 at Athletics 9	Oct 6	Twins 5 at Athletics 4
Oct 4	Athletics 6 at Twins 3		

(Minnesota Twins won series 3–2)

Oct 1	Angels 5 at Yankees 8	Oct 4	Yankees 6 at Angels 9
Oct 2	Angels 8 at Yankees 6	Oct 5	Yankees 5 at Angels 9

(Anaheim Angels won series 3–1)

American League Championship Series

Oct 8	Angels 1 at Twins 2	Oct 12	Twins 1 at Angels 7
Oct 9	Angels 6 at Twins 3	Oct 13	Twins 5 at Angels 13
Oct 11	Twins 1 at Angels 2		

(Anaheim Angels won series 4–1)

GAME 1

										R	H	E
Angels	0	0	1	0	0	0	0	0	0	1	4	0
Twins	0	1	0	0	1	0	0	0	x	2	5	1

W— Mays. **L—** Appier. **SV—** Guardado.
E— Minn: Guzman. **LOB—** Ana: 4, Minn: 7. **2B—** Minn:
Hunter, Koskie. **Sac—** Minn: Hunter. **SF—** Minn:
Pierzynski. **HBP—** Minn: Guzman. **GIDP—** Ana: Salmon.
T— 2:58. **A—** 55,562.

Recap: Joe Mays limited Anaheim to four singles in
eight innings, and more than 55,000 fans cheered the
Twins to a 2–1 Game 1 victory. Minnesota improved to
13–2 alltime in the Metrodome during the postseason.
The Twins took the lead in the second when Torii
Hunter doubled, advanced on a wild pitch and came
home on A.J. Pierzynski's sacrifice fly. After Anaheim
tied the score on an unearned run in the third, Corey
Koskie scored Luis Rivas with a double in the fifth to put
Minnesota back on top for good.

GAME 2

										R	H	E
Angels	1	3	0	0	0	2	0	0	0	6	10	0
Twins	0	0	0	0	0	3	0	0	0	3	11	1

W— Ortiz. **L—** Reed. **SV—** Percival.
E— Minn: Pierzynski. **LOB—** Ana: 6, Minn: 7. **2B—** Ana:
Fullmer, Spiezio; Minn: Guzman, Hunter. **3B—** Ana:
Glaus. **HR—** Ana: Erstad, Fullmer. **GIDP—** Minn: Hunter,
Rivas. **CS—** Ana: Spiezio. **WP—** Minn: Santana. **T—** 3:13.
A— 55,990.

Recap: Anaheim jumped out to a six-run lead and
escaped the Metrodome with a 1–1 split after the first
two games of ALCS. The Angels scored three runs in the
second when Minnesota bungled a rundown play and
catcher A.J. Pierzynski couldn't hold onto the ball on a
play at the plate. Minnesota crept back into the game
with three runs in the sixth, only to see Anaheim closer
Troy Percival extinguish the threat in the ninth.

GAME 3

										R	H	E
Twins	0	0	0	0	0	0	1	0	0	1	6	0
Angels	0	1	0	0	0	0	0	1	x	2	7	2

W— Rodriguez. **L—** Romero. **SV—** Percival.
E— Ana: Eckstein, Gil. **LOB—** Minn: 7, Ana: 9. **2B—** Minn:
Jones; Ana: Anderson. **HR—** Ana: Anderson, Glaus. **S—**
Ana: Gil. **SB—** Minn: Mohr. **WP—** Minn: Santana. **T—**
3:13. **A—** 44,234.

Recap: Troy Glaus hit a solo homer in the bottom of the
eighth inning to give Anaheim a 2–1 victory. Jarrod
Washburn and Eric Milton locked in a pitchers' duel as
the Angels took a 1–0 lead to the seventh. Anaheim's
Washburn left after that inning, having allowed one run
and six hits while striking out seven and walking none.
Milton was almost as good, yielding a run and five hits
with two walks and four strikeouts in six innings. With the
help of two superb catches in the outfield, Troy Percival
fired a perfect ninth for his second straight save and fourth
of the playoffs.

GAME 4

										R	H	E
Twins	0	0	0	0	0	0	0	0	1	1	6	2
Angels	0	0	0	0	0	0	2	5	x	7	10	0

W— Lackey. **L—** Radke.
E— Minn: Pierzynski, Santana. **LOB—** Minn: 4, Ana: 5.
2B— Minn: Mientkiewicz, Koskie; Ana: Spiezio, Fullmer.
3B— Ana: Molina. **S—** Ana: Kennedy. **HBP—** Ana:
Molina. **SB—** Ana: Erstad. **CS—** Minn: Pierzynski. **T—** 2:49.
A— 44,830.

Recap: Troy Glaus delivered a key late-inning hit for the
second straight night, singling in the go-ahead run in
the seventh inning, as Anaheim pulled away for a 7–1
victory. The Angels broke open the game with five runs
in the eighth, but the cushion proved unnecessary as
rookie John Lackey went seven innings, limiting the
Twins to three hits and striking out seven without
issuing a single walk.

GAME 5

										R	H	E
Twins	1	1	0	0	0	0	3	0	0	5	9	0
Angels	0	0	1	0	2	0	10	0	x	13	18	0

W— Rodriguez. **L—** Santana.
LOB— Minn: 3, Ana: 5. **2B—** Minn: Ortiz, Mohr. **HR—**
Kennedy 3, Spiezio. **S—** Minn: Guzman. **GIDP—** Minn:
Rivas, Hunter; Ana: Fullmer. **HBP—** Ana: Eckstein. **CS—**
Ana: Anderson. **WP—** Minn: Romero; Ana: Appier,
Donnelly, Rodriguez. **T—** 3:30. **A—** 44,835.

Recap: Adam Kennedy tied a playoff record with three
home runs, including a go-ahead three-run shot in a
10-run seventh inning, as Anaheim advanced to their first
World Series. After Minnesota rallied for three runs in the
top of the seventh to take a 5–3 lead, the Angels blitzed
the Twins' bullpen in the bottom of the inning. Kennedy,
who was only 1 for 10 in the first four games, went 4 for
4 with five RBIs and was named MVP of the series.

MLB 2002 Playoffs Composite Box Scores

National League Championship Series

SAN FRANCISCO GIANTS

BATTING	AB	R	H	HR	RBI	BA
Dunston	2	0	1	0	0	.500
Bell	17	4	7	1	1	.412
Aurilia	15	4	5	2	5	.333
Santiago	20	2	6	2	6	.300
Bonds	11	5	3	1	6	.273
Kent	19	3	5	0	0	.263
Snow	20	1	5	0	2	.250
Lofton	21	4	5	1	2	.238
Sanders	16	0	1	0	0	.063
Feliz	1	0	0	0	0	.000
Goodwin	3	0	0	0	0	.000
Martinez	1	0	0	0	1	.000
Shinjo	1	0	0	0	0	.000
Pitchers	11	0	1	0	0	.091
Totals	158	23	39	7	23	.247

PITCHING	G	IP	H	BB	SO	ERA
Eyre	4	1 2/3	2	0	0	0.00
Fultz	1	1/3	0	0	0	0.00
Schmidt (1-0)	1	7 2/3	4	1	8	1.17
Rodriguez	4	4 2/3	3	2	2	1.93
Worrell (2-0)	4	4 1/3	2	0	3	2.08
Nen (3 SV)	3	3 1/3	3	1	4	2.70
Hernandez	1	6 1/3	9	1	0	2.84
Rueter (1-0)	2	11	15	2	3	4.09
Ortiz	1	4 2/3	5	3	3	7.71
Witasick (0-1)	1	1	1	0	0	9.00
Totals	5	45	44	10	23	3.20

ST. LOUIS CARDINALS

BATTING	AB	R	H	HR	RBI	BA
Edmonds	20	2	8	1	4	.400
Cairo	13	2	5	1	2	.385
Drew	13	1	5	1	1	.385
Matheny	19	2	6	1	1	.316
Pujols	19	2	5	1	2	.263
Vina	23	2	6	0	2	.261
Perez	4	1	1	1	1	.250
Marrero	16	1	3	1	1	.188
Renteria	19	0	3	0	1	.158
Martinez	14	1	2	0	1	.143
DiFelice	1	0	0	0	0	.000
Robinson	2	1	0	0	0	.000
Pitchers	8	1	0	0	0	.125
Totals	171	16	44	7	16	.257

PITCHING	G	IP	H	BB	SO	ERA
Fassero	1	2/3	0	0	1	0.00
Kline	4	2 1/3	2	0	1	0.00
Veres	2	3 2/3	2	1	5	0.00
Benes	1	5 1/3	2	4	5	3.38
Isringhausen (1 SV)	2	2	1	3	3	4.50
White (0-1)	3	4	2	2	5	4.50
Williams (0-1)	1	6	6	1	7	4.50
Morris (0-2)	2	13	16	6	6	6.23
Finley (1-0)	1	5	7	3	1	7.20
Crudale	1	1 2/3	1	1	2	10.80
Totals	5	43 2/3	39	21	36	4.74

American League Championship Series

ANAHEIM ANGELS

BATTING	AB	R	H	HR	RBI	BA
Figgins	1	2	1	0	0	1.000
Erstad	22	4	8	1	2	.364
Kennedy	14	5	5	3	5	.357
Spiezio	17	5	6	1	5	.353
Fullmer	12	2	4	1	4	.333
Glaus	19	4	6	1	2	.316
Eckstein	21	1	6	0	2	.286
Anderson	20	3	5	1	3	.250
Wooten	8	1	2	0	1	.250
B. Molina	14	0	3	0	2	.214
Salmon	14	0	3	0	0	.214
Ochoa	4	2	0	0	0	.000
Gil	2	0	0	0	0	.000
Palmeiro	2	0	0	0	0	.000
J. Molina	1	0	0	0	0	.000
Totals	171	29	49	8	26	.287

PITCHING	G	IP	H	BB	SO	ERA
Lackey (1-0)	1	7	3	0	7	0.00
Rodriguez (2-0)	4	4 1/3	2	2	7	0.00
Percival (2 SV)	3	3 1/3	0	0	3	0.00
Schoeneweis	1	2/3	0	0	0	0.00
Washburn	1	7	6	0	7	1.29
Weber	3	2 2/3	3	0	3	3.38
Appier (0-1)	2	10 1/3	10	4	3	3.48
Ortiz (1-0)	1	5 1/3	10	1	3	5.06
Donnelly	3	3 1/3	3	0	5	8.10
Totals	5	44	37	7	38	2.45

MINNESOTA TWINS

BATTING	AB	R	H	HR	RBI	BA
Mohr	12	3	5	0	0	.417
LeCroy	3	0	1	0	0	.333
Ortiz	16	0	5	0	2	.313
Koskie	18	3	5	0	2	.278
Mientkiewicz	18	1	5	0	2	.278
Pierzynski	16	1	4	0	2	.250
Rivas	12	1	3	0	0	.250
Cuddyer	5	0	1	0	0	.200
Guzman	18	1	3	0	0	.167
Hunter	18	2	3	0	0	.167
Jones	20	0	2	0	2	.100
Kielty	3	0	0	0	1	.000
Prince	1	0	0	0	0	.000
Totals	160	12	37	0	11	.231

PITCHING	G	IP	H	BB	SO	ERA
Guardado (1 SV)	1	1	0	1	2	0.00
Lohse	1	1	0	0	1	0.00
Milton	1	6	5	2	4	1.50
Mays (1-0)	2	13 1/3	12	0	3	2.03
Radke (0-1)	1	6 2/3	5	1	4	2.70
Wells	2	1	2	0	2	9.00
Reed (0-1)	1	5 1/3	8	0	0	10.13
Santana (0-1)	4	3 1/3	4	0	4	10.80
Hawkins	4	1 1/3	4	1	1	20.25
Romero (0-1)	4	2	4	2	3	22.50
Jackson	3	1	5	2	2	27.00
Totals	5	42	49	9	26	5.57

KEY AB=at-bats; R=runs; H=hits; HR=home runs; RBI=runs batted in; BA=batting average; G=Games; IP=innings pitched; H=hits; BB=bases on balls; SO=strikeouts; ERA=earned run average

2002 World Series

Oct 19	Giants 4 at Angels 3	Oct 24	Angels 4 at Giants 16
Oct 20	Giants 10 at Angels 11	Oct 26	Giants 5 at Angels 6
Oct 22	Angels 10 at Giants 4	Oct 27	Giants 1 at Angels 4
Oct 23	Angels 3 at Giants 4		

(Anaheim Angels won series 4–3)

GAME 1

Giants	0	2	0	0	0	2	0	0	0	**4**	**6**	**0**
Angels	0	1	0	0	0	2	0	0	0	**3**	**9**	**0**

W— Schmidt. **L—** Washburn. **SV—** Nen.
LOB— SF: 5, Ana: 8. **2B—** Ana: Kennedy, Spiezio. **HR—** SF: Bonds, Sanders, Snow; Ana: Glaus 2. **Sac—** SF: Lofton. **SB—** Ana: Fullmer. **T—** 3:44. **A—** 44,603.

Recap: The game's first three hits were home runs, including a 418-foot drive by Barry Bonds in his first World Series at-bat, and the San Francisco bullpen shut down all of the Angels except Troy Glaus en route to a 4–3 victory in Game 1. Bolstered by 3 ⅓ innings of hitless relief and a sparkling defensive play from first baseman J.T. Snow, the Giants handed the Angels their first home loss of the postseason.

GAME 2

Giants	0	4	1	0	4	0	0	0	1	**10**	**12**	**1**
Angels	5	2	0	0	1	1	0	2	x	**11**	**16**	**1**

W— Rodriguez. **L—** Rodriguez. **SV—** Percival.
E— SF: Lofton; Ana: Anderson. **LOB—** SF: 4, Ana: 5. **2B—** SF: Aurilia; Ana: Erstad 2, Glaus. **HR—** SF: Sanders, Bell, Kent, Bonds; Ana: Salmon 2. **SF—** Ana: Spiezio. **GIDP—** Ana: Molina. **SB—** SF: Sanders; Ana: Spiezio, Fullmer. **PB—** SF: Santiago. **T—** 3:57. **A—** 44,584.

Recap: Anaheim squandered a 5–0 lead and needed two Tim Salmon home runs to pull out an 11–10 victory and even the Series at one win apiece. Anaheim's 20-year-old Francisco Rodriguez became the youngest pitcher to earn a World Series victory, throwing three perfect innings of relief. Salmon went 4 for 4 with a walk, driving in four runs and scoring three.

GAME 3

Angels	0	0	4	4	0	1	0	1	0	**10**	**16**	**0**
Giants	1	0	0	0	3	0	0	0	0	**4**	**6**	**2**

W— Ortiz. **L—** Hernandez.
E— SF: Bell, Santiago. **LOB—** Ana: 15, SF: 7. **2B—** Ana: Kennedy, Erstad, Salmon. **3B—** Ana: Spiezio. **HR—** SF: Aurilia, Bonds. **S—** SF: Hernandez. **GIDP—** SF: Bell; Ana: Spiezio. **SB—** SF: Lofton; Ana: Salmon, Erstad. **HBP—** Ana: Kennedy. **T—** 3:37. **A—** 42,707.

Recap: The Angels became the first team in Series history to bat around in consecutive innings, unleashing a torrent of hits, walks, and steals to take an 8–1 lead by the fourth inning. Barry Bonds set a postseason record with his seventh home run.

GAME 4

Angels	0	1	2	0	0	0	0	0	0	**3**	**10**	**1**
Giants	0	0	0	0	3	0	0	1	x	**4**	**12**	**1**

W— Worrell. **L—** Rodriguez. **SV—** Nen.
E— Ana: Salmon; SF: Bell. **LOB—** Ana: 5, SF: 8. **2B—** SF: Aurilia. **HR—** Ana: Glaus. **SF—** Ana: Eckstein; SF: Kent. **GIDP—** Ana: Glaus, Molina, Fullmer; SF: Santiago 2. **SB—**

SF: Goodwin. **CS—** SF: Bell. **PB—** Ana: Molina. **T—** 3:02. **A—** 42,703.

Recap: David Bell lined a tiebreaking single off rookie sensation Francisco Rodriguez in the eighth inning, and the Giants came back from a 3–0 deficit to even the Series. Kenny Lofton had three hits, including a bunt single that extended a fifth-inning rally.

GAME 5

Angels	0	0	0	0	3	1	0	0	0	**4**	**10**	**2**
Giants	3	3	0	0	0	2	4	4	x	**16**	**16**	**0**

W— Zerbe. **L—** Washburn.
E— Ana: Erstad, Glaus. **LOB—** Ana: 9, SF: 8. **2B—** Ana: Palmeiro, Glaus, Gil; SF: Bonds 2, Kent. **3B—** SF: Lofton. **HR—** SF: Kent 2, Aurilia. **S—** SF: Schmidt, Shinjo. **SF—** Ana: Erstad; SF: Santiago, Sanders. **SB—** Ana: Eckstein. **T—** 3:53. **A—** 42,713.

Recap: San Francisco jumped all over Angels' ace Jarrod Washburn, and Jeff Kent sealed the victory with a pair of two-run homers. The Giants tied a Series record with their 12th home run, and the total of 17 by both teams equaled another record.

GAME 6

Giants	0	0	0	0	3	1	1	0	0	**5**	**8**	**1**
Angels	0	0	0	0	0	0	3	3	x	**6**	**10**	**1**

W— Donnelly. **L—** Worrell. **SV—** Percival.
E— SF: Bonds; Ana: B Molina. **LOB—** SF: 6, Ana: 6. **2B—** SF: Lofton; Ana: Glaus. **HR—** SF: Dunston, Bonds; Ana: Spiezio, Erstad. **S—** Ana: J Molina. **GIDP—** SF: Santiago; Ana: Anderson. **SB—** SF: Lofton 2. **WP—** Ana: Rodriguez. **T—** 3:48. **A—** 44,506.

Recap: World Series MVP Troy Glaus lined a two-run double after a key misplay by Barry Bonds in the eighth, capping a wild rally that forced a Game 7. After spotting the Giants a 5–0 lead, the Angels got a homer from Scott Spiezio in the seventh to make it 5–3. A solo shot by Darin Erstad started the rally in the eighth.

GAME 7

Giants	0	1	0	0	0	0	0	0	0	**1**	**6**	**0**
Angels	0	1	3	0	0	0	0	0	x	**4**	**5**	**0**

W— Lackey. **L—** Hernandez. **SV—** Percival.
LOB— SF: 9, Ana: 6. **2B—** SF: Snow; Ana: Molina 2, Anderson. **S—** Ana: Erstad. **SF—** SF: Sanders. **HBP—** Ana: Salmon. **T—** 3:16. **A—** 44,598.

Recap: Pitching on three days' rest, John Lackey became only the second rookie ever to win Game 7 of the World Series, and the Angels became the eighth straight home team to win that decisive game. Garret Anderson delivered the big hit, sending a line drive into the rightfield corner that scored three runs. Anaheim and San Francisco combined for a record 85 runs and a record 21 homers in the Series.

Today's Stars

ALEX RODRIGUEZ, short-stop, b. July 27, 1975, New York, New York. Widely considered baseball's best all-around player. In 2002, "A-Rod" smashed 57 homers to become the first shortstop in major league history to have back-to-back 50-plus-homer seasons. He also played in his fifth consecutive All-Star Game and won the Gold Glove award for the first time. Rodriguez signed a record-breaking $252-million, 10-year-free-agent contract with the Texas Rangers before the 2001 season. He played the first six full seasons of his career (1995-00) with the Seattle Mariners, becoming the first shortstop to hit 40 or more homers and steal 40 or more bases in a season (1998).

BARRY BONDS, outfielder, b. July 24, 1964, Riverside, California. Bonds was named the Player of the Decade for the 1990's by *The Sporting News*. Heading into the 2003 season, he had won the Gold Glove eight times, the N.L. MVP award a National League and major league record five times, and was named an All-Star 11 times. In 2002, the San Francisco Giant led the majors in batting (.370), and set the big-league records for walks (198) and on-base percentage (.582). He also hit his 600th career homer and won the N.L. MVP award. Bonds set the major league's single-season homer record (73) in 2001.

In 2002, Alex Rodriguez led the majors in homers (57), RBIs (142), and total bases (389), the first player to lead in all three categories since 1984.

RANDY JOHNSON, pitcher, b. September 10, 1963, Walnut Creek, California. His 100-m.p.h. fastball and intimidating glare make the 6' 10" flamethrower baseball's most feared pitcher. In 2002, Johnson won the Cy Young Award for an N.L. record-tying fourth straight season (it was his fifth overall). He also helped the Arizona Diamondbacks win the N.L. West title for the third time in four seasons. He was named co-MVP of the 2001 World Series after tying the record for most wins in one Series (3). Johnson began his career in 1988, with the Montreal Expos, but blossomed into a star with the Seattle Mariners, winning 20 games in 1997.

JOHN BIEVER/SPORTS ILLUSTRATED

2002 World Series Composite Box Score

ANAHEIM ANGELS

BATTING	AB	R	H	HR	RBI	BA
Gil	5	1	4	0	0	.800
Wooten	2	0	1	0	0	.500
Glaus	26	7	10	3	8	.385
Salmon	26	7	9	2	5	.346
Eckstein	29	6	9	0	3	.310
Erstad	30	6	9	1	3	.300
B. Molina	21	2	6	0	2	.286
Anderson	32	3	9	0	6	.281
Kennedy	25	1	7	0	2	.280
Fullmer	15	3	4	0	1	.267
Spiezio	23	3	6	1	8	.261
Palmiero	4	1	1	0	0	.250
Ochoa	1	0	0	0	0	.000
J. Molina	0	0	0	0	0	—
Figgins	0	1	0	0	0	—
Pitchers	6	0	1	0	0	.167
Totals	**245**	**41**	**76**	**7**	**38**	**.310**

SAN FRANCISCO GIANTS

BATTING	AB	R	H	HR	RBI	BA
Bonds	17	8	8	4	6	.471
Snow	27	6	11	1	4	.407
Bell	23	4	7	1	4	.304
Lofton	31	7	9	0	2	.290
Kent	29	6	8	3	7	.276
Aurilia	32	5	8	2	5	.250
Sanders	21	3	5	2	6	.238
Santiago	26	2	6	0	5	.231
Dunston	9	1	2	1	3	.222
Shinjo	6	1	1	0	0	.167
Feliz	5	0	0	0	0	.000
Goodwin	4	0	0	0	0	.000
Martinez	2	0	0	0	0	.000
Pitchers	3	1	1	0	0	.333
Totals	**235**	**44**	**66**	**14**	**42**	**.281**

ANAHEIM ANGELS

PITCHING	G	IP	H	BB	SO	ERA
Donnelly (1–0)	5	7⅔	1	4	6	0.00
Schoeneweis	2	2	1	1	2	0.00
Rodriguez (1–1)	4	8⅔	6	1	13	2.08
Percival (3 SV)	3	3	2	1	3	3.00
Lackey (1–0)	3	12⅓	15	5	7	4.38
Shields	1	1⅔	5	0	1	5.40
Ortiz (1–0)	1	5	5	4	3	7.20
Washburn (0–2)	2	9⅔	12	7	6	9.31
Appier	2	6⅓	9	5	4	11.37
Weber	4	4⅔	10	2	5	13.50
Totals	**7**	**61**	**66**	**30**	**50**	**5.75**

SAN FRANCISCO GIANTS

PITCHING	G	IP	H	BB	SO	ERA
Eyre	3	3	5	1	2	0.00
Nen (2 SV)	3	3	2	1	3	0.00
Rueter	2	10	10	1	5	2.70
Zerbe (1–0)	3	6	6	0	0	3.00
Worrell (1–1)	6	5⅔	4	1	4	3.18
Fultz	2	2⅓	4	1	0	3.86
Rodriguez (0–1)	6	5⅔	4	1	3	4.76
Schmidt (1–0)	2	10⅓	16	4	14	5.23
Ortiz	2	8	13	2	2	10.12
Hernandez (0–2)	2	5⅔	9	9	4	14.29
Witasick	2	⅓	3	2	1	54.00
Totals	**7**	**60**	**76**	**23**	**38**	**5.55**

Trivia Challenge

The Anaheim Angels ended a 41-year world championship drought in 2002 by winning the World Series for the first time. Name the eight teams that have still not won the Series.

San Diego Padres, Texas Rangers, Houston Astros, Montreal Expos, Milwaukee Brewers, Seattle Mariners, Colorado Rockies, Tampa Bay Devil Rays

2002 MLB Individual leaders

National League Batting

BATTING AVERAGE

Barry Bonds, SF	.370
Larry Walker, Col	.338
Vladimir Guerrero, Mtl	.336
Todd Helton, Col	.329
Chipper Jones, Atl	.327
Jose Vidro, Mtl	.315
Albert Pujols, StL	.314
Jeff Kent, SF	.313
Jim Edmonds, StL	.311
Edgardo Alfonzo, NY	.308

HITS

Vladimir Guerrero, Mtl	206
Jeff Kent, SF	195
Jose Vidro, Mtl	190
Luis Castillo, Fla	185
Albert Pujols, StL	185
Todd Walker, Cin	183
Todd Helton, Col	182
Chipper Jones, Atl	179
Bobby Abreu, Phil	176
Rafael Furcal, Atl	175

DOUBLES

Bobby Abreu, Phil	50
Mike Lowell, Fla	44
Orlando Cabrera, Mtl	43
Jose Vidro, Mtl	43
Todd Walker, Cin	42
Jeff Kent, SF	42

TRIPLES

Jimmy Rollins, Phil	10
Kenny Lofton, SF	9
Quinton McCracken, Ariz	8
Rafael Furcal, Atl	8
Brad Wilkerson, Mtl	8
Scott Rolen, StL	8

HOME RUNS

Sammy Sosa, Chi	49
Barry Bonds, SF	46
Lance Berkman, Hou	42
Shawn Green, LA	42
Vladimir Guerrero, Mtl	39
Brian Giles, Pitt	38
Pat Burrell, Phil	37
Jeff Kent, SF	37
Andruw Jones, Atl	35
Albert Pujols, StL	34

RUNS SCORED

Sammy Sosa, Chi	122
Albert Pujols, StL	118
Barry Bonds, SF	117
Shawn Green, LA	110
Todd Helton, Col	107
Lance Berkman, Hou	106
Vladimir Guerrero, Mtl	106
Junior Spivey, Ariz	103
Jose Vidro, Mtl	103
Bobby Abreu, Phil	102
Jeff Kent, SF	102

TOTAL BASES

Vladimir Guerrero, Mtl	364
Jeff Kent, SF	352
Lance Berkman, Hou	334
Albert Pujols, StL	331
Sammy Sosa, Chi	330

STOLEN BASES

Luis Castillo, Fla	48
Juan Pierre, Col	47
Dave Roberts, LA	45
Vladimir Guerrero, Mtl	40
Alex Sanchez, Mil	37

RUNS BATTED IN

Lance Berkman, Hou	128
Albert Pujols, StL	127
Pat Burrell, Phil	116
Shawn Green, LA	114
Vladimir Guerrero, Mtl	111
Barry Bonds, SF	110
Scott Rolen, StL	110
Todd Helton, Col	109
Sammy Sosa, Chi	108
Jeff Kent, SF	108

SLUGGING PERCENTAGE

Barry Bonds, SF	.799
Brian Giles, Pitt	.622
Larry Walker, Col	.602
Sammy Sosa, Chi	.594
Vladimir Guerrero, Mtl	.593

ON-BASE PERCENTAGE

Barry Bonds, SF	.582
Brian Giles, Pitt	.450
Chipper Jones, Atl	.435
Todd Helton, Col	.429
Larry Walker, Col	.421

BASES ON BALLS

Barry Bonds, SF	198
Brian Giles, Pitt	135
Adam Dunn, Cin	128
Chipper Jones, Atl	107
Lance Berkman, Hou	107

Randy Johnson

National League Pitching

EARNED RUN AVERAGE

Randy Johnson, Ariz	2.32
Greg Maddux, Atl	2.62
Tom Glavine, Atl	2.96
Odalis Perez, LA	3.00
Roy Oswalt, Hou	3.01
Elmer Dessens, Cin	3.03
Toma Ohka, Mtl	3.18
Randy Wolf, Phil	3.20
Kirk Rueter, SF	3.23
Curt Schilling, Ariz	3.23

SAVES

John Smoltz, Atl	55
Eric Gagne, LA	52
Mike Williams, Pitt	46
Jose Mesa, Phil	45
Robb Nen, SF	43
Jose Jimenez, Col	41
Trevor Hoffman, SD	38
Byung-Hyun Kim, Ariz	36
Billy Wagner, Hou	35
Armando Benitez, NY	33

WINS

Randy Johnson, Ariz	24
Curt Schilling, Ariz	23
Roy Oswalt, Hou	19
Tom Glavine, Atl	18
Kevin Millwood, Atl	18
Matt Morris, StL	17
Jason Jennings, Col	16
Greg Maddux, Atl	16
Hideo Nomo, LA	16
Three tied with 15.	

GAMES PITCHED

Paul Quantrill, LA	86
Octavio Dotel, Hou	83
Tim Worrell, SF	80
Todd Jones, Col	79
Three tied with 78.	

INNINGS PITCHED

Randy Johnson, Ariz	260
Curt Schilling, Ariz	$259\frac{1}{3}$
Roy Oswalt, Hou	233
Javier Vazquez, Mtl	$230\frac{1}{3}$
Tom Glavine, Atl	$224\frac{2}{3}$

STRIKEOUTS

Randy Johnson, Ariz	334
Curt Schilling, Ariz	316
Kerry Wood, Chi	217
Matt Clement, Chi	215
Roy Oswalt, Hou	208
A.J. Burnett, Fla	203
Jason Schmidt, SF	196
Hideo Nomo, LA	193
Javier Vazquez, Mtl	179
Kevin Millwood, Atl	178

COMPLETE GAMES

Randy Johnson, Ariz	8
A.J Burnett, Fla	7
Livan Hernandez, SF	5
Curt Schilling, Ariz	5
Five tied with 4.	

SHUTOUTS

A.J Burnett, Fla	5
Randy Johnson, Ariz	4
Livan Hernandez, SF	3
Six tied with 2.	

JOHN W. MCDONOUGH/SPORTS ILLUSTRATED

2002 MLB Individual leaders

American League Batting

BATTING AVERAGE

Manny Ramirez, Bos	.349
Mike Sweeney, KC	.340
Bernie Williams, NY	.333
Ichiro Suzuki, Sea	.321
Magglio Ordonez, Chi	.320
Jason Giambi, NY	.314
Adam Kennedy, Ana	.312
Nomar Garciaparra, Bos	.310
Miguel Tejada, Oak	.308
Garret Anderson, Ana	.306

HITS

Alfonso Soriano, NY	209
Ichiro Suzuki, Sea	208
Bernie Williams, NY	204
Miguel Tejada, Oak	204
Nomar Garciaparra, Bos	197
Garret Anderson, Ana	195
Derek Jeter, NY	191
Magglio Ordonez, Chi	189
Alex Rodriguez, Tex	187
Shea Hillenbrand, Bos	186

DOUBLES

Garret Anderson, Ana	56
Nomar Garciaparra, Bos	56
Alfonso Soriano, NY	51
Magglio Ordonez, Chi	47
Carlos Beltran, KC	44

TRIPLES

Johnny Damon, Bos	11
Randy Winn, TB	9
Mike Young, Tex	8
Ichiro Suzuki, Sea	8
Carlos Beltran, KC	7

HOME RUNS

Alex Rodriguez, Tex	57
Jim Thome, Clev	52
Rafael Palmeiro, Tex	43
Jason Giambi, NY	41
Alfonso Soriano, NY	39
Magglio Ordonez, Chi	38
Miguel Tejada, Oak	34
Eric Chavez, Oak	34
Manny Ramirez, Bos	33
Carlos Delgado, Tor	33

RUNS SCORED

Alfonso Soriano, NY	128
Alex Rodriguez, Tex	125
Derek Jeter, NY	124
Jason Giambi, NY	120
Johnny Damon, Bos	118
Magglio Ordonez, Chi	116
Ray Durham, Oak	114
Carlos Beltran, KC	114
Ichiro Suzuki, Sea	111
Miguel Tejada, Oak	108

TOTAL BASES

Alex Rodriguez, Tex	389
Alfonso Soriano, NY	381
Magglio Ordonez, Chi	352
Garret Anderson, Ana	344
Miguel Tejada, Oak	336

STOLEN BASES

Alfonso Soriano, NY	41
Carlos Beltran, KC	35
Derek Jeter, NY	32
Johnny Damon, Bos	31
Mike Cameron, Sea	31
Ichiro Suzuki, Sea	31

RUNS BATTED IN

Alex Rodriguez, Tex	142
Magglio Ordonez, Chi	135
Miguel Tejada, Oak	131
Garret Anderson, Ana	123
Jason Giambi, NY	122
Nomar Garciaparra, Bos	120
Jim Thome, Clev	118
Troy Glaus, Ana	111
Eric Chavez, Oak	109
Carlos Delgado, Tor	108

SLUGGING PERCENTAGE

Jim Thome, Clev	.677
Manny Ramirez, Bos	.647
Alex Rodriguez, Tex	.623
Jason Giambi, NY	.598
Magglio Ordonez, Chi	.597

ON-BASE PERCENTAGE

Manny Ramirez, Bos	.450
Jim Thome, Clev	.445
Jason Giambi, NY	.435
Mike Sweeney, KC	.417
Bernie Williams, NY	.415

BASES ON BALLS

Jim Thome, Clev	122
Jason Giambi, NY	109
Rafael Palmeiro, Tex	104
Carlos Delgado, Tor	102
John Olerud, Sea	98

American League Pitching

Pedro Martinez, Bos	20
David Wells, NY	19
Roy Halladay, Tor	19
Mark Mulder, Oak	19
Mark Buehrle, Chi	19
Mike Mussina, NY	18
Jarrod Washburn, Ana	18
Paul Byrd, KC	17

EARNED RUN AVERAGE

Pedro Martinez, Bos	2.26
Derek Lowe, Bos	2.58
Barry Zito, Oak	2.75
Tim Wakefield, Bos	2.81
Roy Halladay, Tor	2.93
Tim Hudson, Oak	2.98
Jarrod Washburn, Ana	3.15
Joel Pineiro, Sea	3.24
Jamie Moyer, Sea	3.32
Mark Mulder, Oak	3.47

SAVES

Eddie Guardado, Minn	45
Billy Koch, Oak	44
Troy Percival, Ana	40
Ugueth Urbina, Bos	40
Kelvim Escobar, Tor	38
Kazuhiro Sasaki, Sea	37
Juan Acevedo, Det	28
Mariana Rivera, NY	28
Roberto Hernandez, KC	26
Jorge Julio, Balt	25

WINS

Barry Zito, Oak	23
Derek Lowe, Bos	21

GAMES PITCHED

Billy Koch, Oak	84
JC Romero, Minn	81
Mike Stanton, NY	79
Steve Karsay, NY	78
Kelvim Escobar, Tor	76

INNINGS PITCHED

Roy Halladay, Tor	239⅓
Mark Buehrle, Chi	239
Tim Hudson, Oak	238⅓
Jamie Moyer, Sea	230⅔
Barry Zito, Oak	229⅓

STRIKEOUTS

Pedro Martinez, Bos	239
Roger Clemens, NY	192
Mike Mussina, NY	182
Barry Zito, Oak	182

Alfonso Soriano

Freddy Garcia, Sea	181
Roy Halladay, Tor	168
Ramon Ortiz, Ana	162
Mark Mulder, Oak	159
Tim Hudson, Oak	152
C.C. Sabathia, Clev	149

COMPLETE GAMES

Paul Byrd, KC	7
Mark Buehrle, Chi	5
Joe Kennedy, TB	5
Five tied with 4.	

SHUTOUTS

Jeff Weaver, NY	3
Seven tied with 2.	

HEINZ KLUETMEIER/SPORTS ILLUSTRATED

BASEBALL

2002 Regular Season Team Stats
National League

TEAM BATTING	G	AB	R	H	2B	3B	HR	RBI	TB	BB	SO	SB	OBP	SLG	BA
Colorado	162	5,512	778	1,508	283	41	152	726	2,329	497	1,043	103	.337	.423	.274
St. Louis	162	5,505	787	1,475	285	26	175	758	2,337	542	927	86	.338	.425	.268
Arizona	162	5,508	819	1,471	283	41	165	783	2,331	643	1,016	92	.346	.423	.267
San Francisco	162	5,497	783	1,465	300	35	198	751	2,429	616	961	74	.344	.442	.267
Los Angeles	162	5,619	722	1,477	291	30	155	700	2,293	430	961	96	.319	.408	.263
Houston	162	5,503	749	1,441	291	32	167	719	2,297	589	1,120	71	.338	.417	.262
Florida	162	5,496	699	1,433	280	32	146	653	2,215	595	1,130	177	.337	.403	.261
Montreal	162	5,553	744	1,447	304	36	162	699	2,309	583	1,118	119	.334	.416	.261
Atlanta	161	5,495	708	1,428	280	25	164	669	2,250	558	1,028	76	.331	.409	.260
Philadelphia	161	5,523	710	1,428	325	41	165	676	2,330	640	1,095	104	.339	.422	.259
New York	161	5,496	690	1,409	238	22	160	650	2,171	486	1,044	87	.322	.395	.256
Cincinnati	162	5,470	709	1,386	297	21	169	678	2,232	583	1,188	116	.330	.408	.253
Milwaukee	162	5,415	627	1,369	269	29	139	597	2,113	500	1,125	94	.320	.390	.253
San Diego	162	5,515	662	1,393	243	29	136	627	2,102	547	1,062	71	.321	.381	.253
Chicago	162	5,496	706	1,351	259	29	200	676	2,268	585	1,269	63	.321	.413	.246
Pittsburgh	161	5,330	641	1,300	263	20	142	610	2,029	537	1,109	86	.319	.381	.244

TEAM PITCHING	W	L	ERA	CG	Sho	SV	Inn	H	R	ER	BB	SO
Atlanta	101	59	3.13	3	15	57	1,467⅓	1,302	565	511	554	1,058
San Francisco	95	66	3.54	10	13	43	1,437⅓	1,349	616	566	523	992
Los Angeles	92	70	3.69	4	15	56	1,457⅔	1,311	643	598	555	1,132
St. Louis	97	65	3.70	4	9	42	1,446⅓	1,355	648	595	547	1,009
New York	75	86	3.89	9	10	36	1,442⅔	1,408	703	624	543	1,107
Arizona	98	64	3.92	14	10	40	1,446⅔	1,361	674	630	421	1,303
Montreal	83	79	3.97	9	3	39	1,453	1,475	718	641	508	1,088
Houston	84	78	4.00	2	11	43	1,445	1,423	695	643	546	1,219
Philadelphia	80	81	4.17	5	9	47	1,449⅔	1,381	724	671	570	1,075
Pittsburgh	72	89	4.23	2	7	47	1,412⅔	1,447	730	664	572	920
Cincinnati	78	84	4.27	2	8	42	1,453⅔	1,502	774	690	550	980
Chicago	67	95	4.29	11	9	23	1,441⅓	1,373	759	687	606	1,333
Florida	79	83	4.36	11	12	36	1,456⅓	1,449	763	706	631	1,104
San Diego	66	96	4.62	5	10	40	1,436⅓	1,522	815	738	582	1,108
Milwaukee	56	106	4.72	7	4	32	1,432⅓	1,468	821	751	666	1,026
Colorado	73	89	5.20	1	8	43	1,426⅔	1,554	898	825	582	920

American League

TEAM BATTING	G	AB	R	H	2B	3B	HR	RBI	TB	BB	SO	SB	OBP	SLG	BA
Anaheim	162	5,678	851	1,603	333	32	152	811	2,456	462	805	117	.341	.433	.282
Boston	162	5,640	859	1,560	348	33	177	810	2,505	545	944	80	.345	.444	.277
New York	161	5,601	897	1,540	314	12	223	857	2,547	640	1171	100	.354	.455	.275
Seattle	162	5,569	814	1,531	285	31	152	771	2,334	629	1,003	137	.350	.419	.275
Minnesota	161	5,582	768	1,518	348	36	167	731	2,439	472	1,089	79	.332	.437	.272
Chicago	162	5,847	927	1,578	309	31	226	867	2,627	604	1,011	95	.341	.449	.270
Texas	162	5,618	843	1,510	304	27	230	806	2,558	554	1,055	62	.338	.455	.269
Oakland	162	5,558	800	1,450	279	28	205	772	2,400	609	1,008	46	.339	.432	.261
Toronto	162	5,581	813	1,457	305	38	187	771	2,399	522	1,142	71	.327	.430	.261
Kansas City	162	5,535	737	1,415	285	42	140	695	2,204	524	921	140	.323	.398	.256
Tampa Bay	161	5,605	673	1,419	297	35	133	641	2,185	456	1,115	102	.314	.390	.253
Cleveland	162	5,423	739	1,349	255	26	192	706	2,232	542	1,000	52	.321	.412	.249
Detroit	161	5,406	575	1,340	265	37	124	546	2,051	363	1,035	65	.300	.379	.248
Baltimore	162	5,491	667	1,353	311	27	165	636	2,213	452	993	110	.309	.405	.246

TEAM PITCHING	W	L	ERA	CG	Sho	SV	Inn	H	R	ER	BB	SO
Oakland	103	59	3.68	9	19	48	1,452	1,391	654	593	474	1,021
Anaheim	99	63	3.69	7	14	54	1,452⅔	1,345	644	595	509	999
Boston	93	69	3.75	5	17	51	1,446	1,339	665	603	430	1,157
New York	103	58	3.87	9	11	53	1,452	1,441	697	625	403	1,135
Seattle	93	69	4.07	8	12	43	1,445⅓	1,422	699	654	441	1,063
Minnesota	94	67	4.12	8	9	47	1,444⅔	1,454	712	662	439	1,026
Baltimore	67	95	4.46	8	3	31	1,450⅔	1,491	773	719	549	967
Chicago	81	81	4.55	7	7	35	1,423	1,422	798	720	528	945
Toronto	78	84	4.80	6	6	41	1,438⅓	1,504	828	767	590	991
Cleveland	74	88	4.91	9	4	34	1,424⅔	1,508	837	777	603	1,058
Detroit	55	106	4.92	11	7	33	1,414	1,593	864	773	463	794
Texas	72	90	5.15	4	4	33	1,439⅔	1,528	882	824	669	1,030
Kansas City	62	100	5.21	11	6	30	1,441	1,587	891	834	572	909
Tampa Bay	55	106	5.29	12	3	25	1,440⅓	1,567	918	846	620	925

KEY TB=total bases; OBP=on-base percentage; SLG=slugging percentage; BA=batting average; W=win; L=loss; CG=complete games; Sho=shutouts; Inn=innings; ER=earned runs; GS=games started

NATIONAL LEAGUE TEAM-BY-TEAM STATS

ARIZONA DIAMONDBACKS

BATTING	G	AB	R	H	2B	3B	HR	RBI	TB	BB	SO	SB	OBP	SLG	BA
Greg Colbrunn	72	171	30	57	16	2	10	27	107	13	19	0	.378	.626	.333
Danny Bautista	40	154	22	50	5	2	6	23	77	11	21	4	.367	.500	.325
Quinton McCracken	123	348	60	108	27	8	3	40	160	32	67	5	.368	.460	.310
Junior Spivey	143	538	103	162	34	6	16	78	256	65	100	11	.389	.476	.301
Luis Gonzalez	148	524	90	151	19	3	28	103	260	97	76	9	.400	.496	.288
Steve Finley	150	505	82	145	24	4	25	89	252	65	73	16	.370	.499	.287
Craig Counsell	112	436	63	123	22	1	2	51	153	45	52	7	.348	.351	.282
Tony Womack	153	590	90	160	23	5	5	57	208	46	80	29	.325	.353	.271
Erubial Durazo	76	222	46	58	12	2	16	48	122	49	60	0	.395	.550	.261
Matt Williams	60	215	29	56	7	2	12	40	103	21	41	3	.324	.479	.260
Mark Grace	124	298	43	75	19	0	7	48	115	46	30	2	.351	.386	.252
Damian Miller	101	297	40	74	22	0	11	42	129	38	88	0	.340	.434	.249
Dave Dellucci	97	229	34	56	11	2	7	29	92	28	55	2	.326	.402	.245
Rod Barajas	70	154	12	36	10	0	3	23	55	10	25	1	.288	.357	.234

PITCHING	W–L	ERA	G	GS	CG	SV	Inn	H	R	ER	BB	SO
Byung-Hyun Kim	8–3	2.04	72	0	0	36	84	64	20	19	26	92
Randy Johnson	24–5	2.32	35	35	8	0	260	197	78	67	71	334
Curt Schilling	23–7	3.23	36	35	5	0	$259^1/_3$	218	95	93	33	316
Mike Koplove	6–1	3.36	55	0	0	0	$61^2/_3$	47	24	23	23	46
Mike Fetters	3–3	4.09	65	0	0	0	55	53	31	25	37	53
Miguel Batista	8–9	4.29	36	29	1	0	$184^2/_3$	172	99	88	70	112
Mike Myers	4–3	4.38	69	0	0	4	37	39	18	18	17	31
Rick Helling	10–12	4.51	30	30	0	0	$175^2/_3$	180	94	88	48	120
Brian Anderson	6–11	4.79	35	24	0	0	156	174	86	83	32	81
Mike Morgan	1–1	5.29	29	0	0	0	34	41	22	20	9	13

ATLANTA BRAVES

BATTING	G	AB	R	H	2B	3B	HR	RBI	TB	BB	SO	SB	OBP	SLG	BA
Chipper Jones	158	548	90	179	35	1	26	100	294	107	89	8	.435	.536	.327
Matt Franco	81	205	25	65	15	4	6	30	106	27	31	1	.395	.517	.317
Gary Sheffield	135	492	82	151	26	0	25	84	252	72	53	12	.404	.512	.307
Mark DeRosa	72	212	24	63	9	2	5	23	91	12	24	2	.339	.429	.297
Julio Franco	125	338	51	96	13	1	6	30	129	39	75	5	.357	.382	.284
Rafael Furcal	154	636	95	175	31	8	8	47	246	43	114	27	.323	.387	.275
Darren Bragg	109	212	34	57	15	2	3	15	85	24	52	5	.347	.401	.269
Andruw Jones	154	560	91	148	34	0	35	94	287	83	135	8	.366	.513	.264
Wes Helms	85	210	20	51	16	0	6	22	85	11	57	1	.283	.405	.243
Javy Lopez	109	347	31	81	15	0	11	52	129	26	63	0	.299	.372	.233
Vinny Castilla	143	543	56	126	23	2	12	61	189	22	69	4	.268	.348	.232
Keith Lockhart	128	296	34	64	13	3	5	32	98	27	50	0	.282	.331	.216

PITCHING	W–L	ERA	G	GS	CG	SV	Inn	H	R	ER	BB	SO
Chris Hammond	7–2	0.95	63	0	0	0	76	53	15	8	31	63
Darren Holmes	2–2	1.81	55	0	0	1	$54^2/_3$	41	12	11	12	47
Mike Remlinger	7–3	1.99	73	0	0	0	68	48	17	15	28	69
Greg Maddux	16–6	2.62	34	34	0	0	$199^1/_3$	194	67	58	45	118
Tom Glavine	18–11	2.96	36	36	2	0	$224^2/_3$	210	85	74	78	127
Kerry Ligtenberg	3–4	2.97	52	0	0	0	$66^2/_3$	52	23	22	33	51
Kevin Millwood	18–8	3.24	35	34	1	0	217	186	83	78	65	178
John Smoltz	3–2	3.25	75	0	0	55	$80^1/_3$	59	30	29	24	85
Damian Moss	12–6	3.42	33	29	0	0	179	140	80	68	89	111
Albie Lopez	1–4	4.37	30	4	0	0	$55^2/_3$	66	29	27	18	39
Jason Marquis	8–9	5.04	22	22	0	0	$114^1/_3$	127	66	64	49	84

BASEBALL

CHICAGO CUBS

BATTING	G	AB	R	H	2B	3B	HR	RBI	TB	BB	SO	SB	OBP	SLG	BA
Sammy Sosa	150	556	122	160	19	2	49	108	330	103	144	2	.399	.594	.288
Moises Alou	132	484	50	133	23	1	15	61	203	47	61	8	.337	.419	.275
Fred McGriff	146	523	67	143	27	2	30	103	264	63	99	1	.353	.505	.273
Mark Bellhorn	146	445	86	115	24	4	27	56	228	76	144	7	.374	.512	.258
Bobby Hill	59	190	26	48	7	2	4	20	71	17	42	6	.327	.374	.253
Corey Patterson	153	592	71	150	30	5	14	54	232	19	142	18	.284	.392	.253
Alex Gonzalez	142	513	58	127	27	5	18	61	218	46	136	5	.312	.425	.248
Chris Stynes	98	195	25	47	9	1	5	26	73	21	29	1	.314	.374	.241
Joe Girardi	90	234	19	53	10	1	1	13	68	16	35	1	.275	.291	.226
Roosevelt Brown	111	204	14	43	12	0	3	23	64	23	50	2	.299	.314	.211
Todd Hundley	92	266	32	56	8	0	16	35	112	32	80	0	.301	.421	.211
Chad Hermansen	100	237	25	49	14	1	8	18	89	22	82	7	.276	.376	.207

PITCHING	W–L	ERA	G	GS	CG	SV	Inn	H	R	ER	BB	SO
Joe Borowski	4–4	2.73	73	0	0	2	95²/₃	84	31	29	29	97
Mark Prior	6–6	3.32	19	19	1	0	116²/₃	98	45	43	38	147
Matt Clement	12–11	3.60	32	32	3	0	205	162	84	82	85	215
Kerry Wood	12–11	3.66	33	33	4	0	213²/₃	169	92	87	97	217
Carlos Zambrano	4–8	3.66	32	16	0	0	108¹/₃	94	53	44	63	93
Jon Lieber	6–8	3.70	21	21	3	0	141	153	64	58	12	87
Juan Cruz	3–11	3.98	45	9	0	1	97¹/₃	84	56	43	59	81
Antonio Alfonseca	2–5	4.00	66	0	0	19	74¹/₃	73	34	33	36	61
Jason Bere	1–10	5.67	16	16	0	0	85²/₃	98	63	54	28	65

CINCINNATI REDS

BATTING	G	AB	R	H	2B	3B	HR	RBI	TB	BB	SO	SB	OBP	SLG	BA
Austin Kearns	107	372	66	117	24	3	13	56	186	54	81	6	.407	.500	.315
Todd Walker	155	612	79	183	42	3	11	64	264	50	81	8	.353	.431	.299
Ken Griffey	70	197	17	52	8	0	8	23	84	28	39	1	.358	.426	.264
Sean Casey	120	425	56	111	25	0	6	42	154	43	47	2	.334	.362	.261
Corky Miller	39	114	9	29	10	0	3	15	48	9	20	0	.328	.421	.254
Reggie Taylor	135	287	41	73	15	4	9	38	123	14	79	11	.291	.429	.254
Adam Dunn	158	535	84	133	28	2	26	71	243	128	170	19	.400	.454	.249
Jason LaRue	113	353	42	88	17	1	12	52	143	27	117	1	.324	.405	.249
Barry Larkin	145	507	72	124	37	2	7	47	186	44	57	13	.305	.367	.245
Russell Branyan	84	217	34	53	9	1	16	39	112	34	86	3	.349	.516	.244
Aaron Boone	162	606	83	146	38	2	26	87	266	56	111	32	.314	.439	.241
Jose Guillen	85	240	25	57	7	0	8	31	88	14	43	4	.287	.367	.238

PITCHING	W–L	ERA	G	GS	CG	SV	Inn	H	R	ER	BB	SO
Scott Williamson	3–4	2.92	63	0	0	8	74	46	27	24	36	84
Gabe White	6–1	2.98	62	0	0	0	54¹/₃	49	19	18	10	41
Elmer Dessens	7–8	3.03	30	30	0	0	178	173	70	60	49	93
Danny Graves	7–3	3.19	68	4	0	32	98²/₃	99	37	35	25	58
Chris Reitsma	6–12	3.64	32	21	1	0	138¹/₃	144	73	56	45	84
Jimmy Haynes	15–10	4.12	34	34	0	0	196²/₃	210	97	90	81	126
Shawn Estes	5–12	5.10	29	29	1	0	160²/₃	171	94	91	83	109
Jose Rijo	5–4	5.14	31	9	0	0	77	89	48	44	20	38
Joey Hamilton	4–10	5.27	39	17	0	1	124²/₃	136	78	73	50	85
Ryan Dempster	10–13	5.38	33	33	4	0	209	228	127	125	93	153
Bruce Chen	2–5	5.56	55	6	0	0	77²/₃	85	53	48	43	80
Scott Sullivan	6–5	6.06	71	0	0	1	78²/₃	93	60	53	31	78

COLORADO ROCKIES

BATTING	G	AB	R	H	2B	3B	HR	RBI	TB	BB	SO	SB	OBP	SLG	BA
Larry Walker	136	477	95	161	40	4	26	104	287	65	73	6	.421	.602	.338
Todd Helton	156	553	107	182	39	4	30	109	319	99	91	5	.429	.577	.329
Gabe Kapler	40	119	12	37	4	3	2	17	53	8	23	6	.359	.445	.311
Jay Payton	134	445	69	135	22	7	16	59	217	29	54	7	.351	.488	.303
Juan Pierre	152	592	90	170	20	5	1	35	203	31	52	47	.332	.343	.287
Todd Zeile	144	506	61	138	23	0	18	87	215	66	92	1	.353	.425	.273
Sandy Alomar	38	116	8	31	4	0	0	12	35	4	19	0	.292	.302	.267
Gary Bennett	90	291	26	77	10	2	4	26	103	15	45	1	.314	.354	.265
Brent Butler	113	344	55	89	18	4	9	42	142	10	40	2	.287	.413	.259
Junior Ortiz	65	192	22	48	7	1	1	12	60	16	30	2	.315	.313	.250
Juan Uribe	155	566	69	136	25	7	6	49	193	34	120	9	.286	.341	.240
Terry Shumpert	106	234	30	55	12	1	6	21	87	21	41	4	.304	.372	.235
Greg Norton	113	168	19	37	8	1	7	37	68	24	52	2	.314	.405	.220
Benny Agbayani	48	117	10	24	5	0	4	19	41	10	35	1	.266	.350	.205

PITCHING	W-L	ERA	G	GS	CG	SV	Inn	H	R	ER	BB	SO
Jose Jimenez	2-10	3.56	74	0	0	41	73$\frac{1}{3}$	76	34	29	11	47
Denny Stark	11-4	4.00	32	20	0	0	128$\frac{1}{3}$	108	69	57	64	64
Justin Speier	5-1	4.33	63	0	0	1	62$\frac{1}{3}$	51	31	30	19	47
Jason Jennings	16-8	4.52	32	32	0	0	185$\frac{1}{3}$	201	102	93	70	127
Todd Jones	1-4	4.70	79	0	0	1	82$\frac{1}{3}$	84	43	43	28	73
Denny Neagle	8-11	5.26	35	28	1	0	164$\frac{1}{3}$	170	101	96	63	111
Shawn Chacon	5-11	5.73	21	21	0	0	119$\frac{1}{3}$	122	84	76	60	67
Sean Lowe	5-3	5.79	51	1	0	0	79$\frac{1}{3}$	101	58	51	41	64
Kent Mercker	3-1	6.14	58	0	0	0	44	55	33	30	22	37
Mike Hampton	7-15	6.15	30	30	0	0	178$\frac{2}{3}$	228	135	122	91	74

FLORIDA MARLINS

BATTING	G	AB	R	H	2B	3B	HR	RBI	TB	BB	SO	SB	OBP	SLG	BA
Kevin Millar	126	438	58	134	41	0	16	57	223	40	74	0	.366	.509	.306
Luis Castillo	146	606	86	185	18	5	2	39	219	55	76	48	.364	.361	.305
Mike Redmond	89	256	19	78	15	0	2	28	99	21	34	0	.372	.387	.305
Mike Lowell	160	597	88	165	44	0	24	92	281	65	92	4	.346	.471	.276
Juan Encarnacion	152	584	77	158	22	5	24	85	262	46	113	21	.324	.449	.271
Derrek Lee	162	581	95	157	35	7	27	86	287	98	164	19	.378	.494	.270
Eric Owens	131	385	44	104	15	5	4	37	141	31	33	26	.324	.366	.270
Andy Fox	133	435	55	109	14	5	4	41	145	49	94	31	.338	.333	.251
Preston Wilson	141	510	80	124	22	2	23	65	219	58	140	20	.329	.429	.243
Ramon Castro	54	101	11	24	4	0	6	18	46	14	24	0	.322	.455	.238
Alex Gonzalez	42	151	15	34	7	1	2	18	49	12	32	3	.296	.325	.225
Charles Johnson	83	244	18	53	19	0	6	36	90	31	61	0	.301	.369	.217

PITCHING	W-L	ERA	G	GS	CG	SV	Inn	H	R	ER	BB	SO
Vladimir Nunez	4-5	2.74	52	3	0	0	92	79	33	28	30	64
Braden Looper	2-5	3.14	78	0	0	13	86	73	31	30	28	55
A.J. Burnett	12-9	3.30	31	29	7	0	204$\frac{1}{3}$	153	84	75	90	203
Vladimir Nunez	6-5	3.41	77	0	0	20	97$\frac{2}{3}$	80	38	37	37	73
Josh Beckett	6-7	4.10	23	21	0	0	107$\frac{1}{3}$	93	56	49	44	113
Michael Tejera	8-8	4.45	47	18	0	1	139$\frac{2}{3}$	144	71	69	60	95
Kevin Olsen	0-5	4.53	17	8	0	0	55$\frac{2}{3}$	57	31	28	31	38
Brad Penny	8-7	4.66	24	24	1	0	129$\frac{1}{3}$	148	76	67	50	93
Carl Pavano	6-10	5.16	37	22	0	0	136	174	88	78	45	92
Graeme Lloyd	4-5	5.21	66	0	0	5	57	67	34	33	19	37
Julian Tavarez	10-12	5.39	29	27	0	0	153$\frac{2}{3}$	188	100	92	15	74

 **BASEBALL**

HOUSTON ASTROS

BATTING	G	AB	R	H	2B	3B	HR	RBI	TB	BB	SO	SB	OBP	SLG	BA
Mark Loretta	107	283	33	86	18	0	4	27	116	32	37	1	.381	.410	.304
Jose Vizcaino	125	406	53	123	19	2	5	37	161	24	40	3	.342	.397	.303
Lance Berkman	158	578	106	169	35	2	42	128	334	107	118	8	.405	.578	.292
Jeff Bagwell	158	571	94	166	33	2	31	98	296	101	130	7	.401	.518	.291
Orlando Merced	123	251	35	72	13	3	6	30	109	26	50	4	.350	.434	.287
Geoff Blum	130	368	45	104	20	4	10	52	162	49	70	2	.367	.440	.283
Daryl Ward	136	453	41	125	31	0	12	72	192	33	82	1	.324	.424	.276
Brian L. Hunter	98	201	32	54	16	3	3	20	85	16	39	5	.329	.423	.269
Julio Lugo	88	322	45	84	15	1	8	3	125	28	74	9	.322	.388	.261
Brad Ausmus	130	447	57	115	19	3	6	50	158	38	71	2	.322	.353	.257
Craig Biggio	145	577	96	146	36	3	15	58	233	50	111	16	.330	.404	.253
Richard Hidalgo	114	388	54	91	17	4	15	48	161	43	85	6	.319	.415	.235
Gregg Zaun	76	185	18	41	7	1	3	24	59	12	36	1	.275	.319	.222

PITCHING	W–L	ERA	G	GS	CG	SV	Inn	H	R	ER	BB	SO
Octavio Dotel	6–4	1.85	83	0	0	6	97 1/3	58	21	20	27	118
Billy Wagner	4–2	2.52	70	0	0	35	75	51	21	21	22	88
Roy Oswalt	19–9	3.01	35	34	0	0	233	215	86	78	62	208
Wade Miller	15–4	3.28	26	26	1	0	164 2/3	151	63	60	62	144
Peter Munro	5–5	3.57	19	4	0	0	80 2/3	89	37	32	23	45
Ricky Stone	3–3	3.61	78	0	0	1	77 1/3	78	36	31	34	63
Carlos Hernandez	7–5	4.38	23	21	0	0	111	112	56	54	61	93
Nelson Cruz	2–6	4.48	43	5	0	0	78 1/3	90	44	39	29	61
Shane Reynolds	3–6	4.86	13	13	0	0	74	80	43	40	26	47
Dave Mlicki	4–10	5.34	22	16	0	0	86	101	57	51	34	57
Tim Redding	3–6	5.40	18	14	0	0	73 1/3	78	49	44	35	63
Kirk Saarloos	6–7	6.01	17	17	1	0	85 1/3	100	59	57	27	54

LOS ANGELES DODGERS

BATTING	G	AB	R	H	2B	3B	HR	RBI	TB	BB	SO	SB	OBP	SLG	BA
Tyler Houston	76	255	25	77	15	2	7	33	117	14	41	1	.347	.459	.302
Dave Hansen	96	120	15	35	6	0	2	17	47	14	22	1	.363	.392	.292
Alex Cora	115	258	37	75	14	4	5	28	112	26	3	7	.371	.434	.291
Shawn Green	158	582	110	166	31	4	42	114	325	93	112	8	.385	.558	.285
Brian Jordan	128	471	65	134	27	3	18	80	221	34	86	2	.338	.469	.285
Paul Lo Duca	149	580	74	163	38	1	10	64	233	34	31	3	.330	.402	.281
Marquis Grissom	111	343	57	95	21	4	17	60	175	22	68	5	.321	.510	.277
Dave Roberts	127	422	63	117	14	7	3	34	154	48	51	45	.353	.365	.277
Mark Grudzielanek	150	536	56	145	23	0	9	50	195	22	89	4	.301	.364	.271
Eric Karros	142	524	52	142	26	1	13	73	209	37	74	4	.323	.399	.271
Adrian Beltre	159	587	70	151	26	5	21	75	250	37	96	7	.303	.426	.257
Cesar Izturis	135	439	43	102	24	2	1	31	133	14	39	7	.253	.303	.232

PITCHING	W–L	ERA	G	GS	CG	SV	Inn	H	R	ER	BB	SO
Eric Gagne	4–1	1.97	77	0	0	52	82 1/3	55	18	18	16	114
Paul Quantrill	5–4	2.70	86	0	0	1	76 2/3	80	27	23	25	53
Odalis Perez	15–10	3.00	32	32	4	0	222 1/3	182	76	74	38	155
Giovanni Carrara	6–3	3.28	63	1	0	1	90 2/3	83	34	33	32	56
Hideo Nomo	16–6	3.39	34	34	0	0	220 1/3	189	92	83	101	193
Omar Daal	11–9	3.90	39	23	0	0	161 1/3	142	73	70	54	105
Andy Ashby	9–13	3.91	30	30	0	0	181 2/3	179	85	79	65	107
Guillermo Mota	1–3	4.15	43	0	0	0	60 2/3	45	30	28	27	49
Kazuhisa Ishii	14–10	4.27	28	28	0	0	154	137	82	73	106	143
Kevin Brown	3–4	4.81	17	10	0	0	63 2/3	68	36	34	23	58

MILWAUKEE BREWERS

BATTING	G	AB	R	H	2B	3B	HR	RBI	TB	BB	SO	SB	OBP	SLG	BA
Lenny Harris	122	197	23	60	8	2	3	17	81	14	17	4	.355	.411	.305
Alex Sanchez	112	394	55	114	10	7	1	33	141	31	62	37	.343	.358	.289
Jose Hernandez	152	525	72	151	24	2	24	73	251	52	188	3	.356	.478	.288
Eric Young	138	496	57	139	29	3	3	28	183	39	38	31	.338	.369	.280
Richie Sexson	157	570	86	159	37	2	29	102	287	70	136	0	.363	.504	.279
Robert Machado	73	211	19	55	14	1	3	22	80	17	41	0	.316	.379	.261
Jeff Hammonds	128	448	47	115	26	5	9	41	178	52	86	4	.332	.397	.257
Alex Ochoa	85	215	32	55	9	0	6	21	82	32	30	8	.357	.381	.256
Ryan Thompson	62	137	16	34	9	2	8	24	71	7	38	1	.295	.518	.248
Matt Stairs	107	270	41	66	15	0	16	41	129	36	50	2	.349	.478	.244
Geoff Jenkins	67	243	35	59	17	1	10	29	108	22	60	1	.320	.444	.243
Paul Bako	87	234	24	55	8	1	4	20	77	20	46	0	.295	.329	.235
Ron Belliard	104	289	30	61	13	0	3	26	83	18	46	2	.257	.287	.211

PITCHING	W–L	ERA	G	GS	CG	SV	Inn	H	R	ER	BB	SO
Luis Vizcaino	5–3	2.99	76	0	0	5	81 1/3	55	27	27	30	79
Ray King	3–2	3.05	76	0	0	0	65	61	24	22	24	50
Valerio De Los Santos	2–3	3.12	51	0	0	0	57 2/3	42	21	20	2	38
Mike DeJean	1–5	3.12	68	0	0	27	75	66	28	26	39	65
Ben Sheets	11–16	4.15	34	34	1	0	216 2/3	237	105	100	70	170
Glendon Rusch	10–16	4.70	34	34	4	0	210 2/3	227	118	110	76	140
Nick Neugebauer	1–7	4.72	12	12	0	0	55 1/3	56	33	29	44	47
Nelson Figueroa	1–7	5.03	30	11	0	0	93	96	59	52	37	51
Ruben Quevedo	6–11	5.76	26	25	1	0	139	159	100	89	68	93
Jose Cabrera	6–10	6.79	50	11	0	0	103 1/3	131	84	78	36	61

MONTREAL EXPOS

BATTING	G	AB	R	H	2B	3B	HR	RBI	TB	BB	SO	SB	OBP	SLG	BA
Vladimir Guerrero	161	614	106	206	37	2	39	111	364	84	70	40	.417	.593	.336
Jose Vidro	152	604	103	190	43	3	19	96	296	60	70	2	.378	.490	.315
Endy Chavez	36	125	20	37	8	5	1	9	58	5	16	3	.321	.464	.296
Troy O'Leary	97	273	27	78	12	2	3	37	103	34	47	1	.371	.377	.286
Cliff Floyd	99	349	56	96	22	0	21	61	181	61	78	11	.394	.519	.275
Brian Schneider	73	207	21	57	19	2	5	29	95	21	41	1	.339	.459	.275
Wil Cordero	66	143	21	39	9	0	6	29	66	17	26	2	.349	.462	.273
Brad Wilkerson	153	507	92	135	27	8	20	59	238	81	161	7	.370	.469	.266
Michael Barrett	117	376	44	99	20	1	12	49	157	40	65	6	.332	.418	.263
Orlando Cabrera	153	563	64	148	43	1	7	56	214	48	53	25	.321	.380	.263
Andres Galarraga	104	292	30	76	12	0	9	40	115	30	81	2	.344	.394	.260
Chris Truby	35	105	12	27	5	2	2	7	42	5	27	1	.297	.400	.257
Jose Macias	90	231	33	59	17	1	7	33	99	13	44	5	.294	.429	.255
Fernando Tatis	114	381	43	87	18	1	15	55	152	35	90	2	.303	.399	.228
Lee Stevens	63	205	28	39	6	1	10	31	77	39	57	1	.318	.376	.190
Peter Bergeron	31	123	24	23	3	2	0	7	30	22	44	10	.310	.244	.187

PITCHING	W–L	ERA	G	GS	CG	SV	Inn	H	R	ER	BB	SO
Joey Eischen	6–1	1.34	59	0	0	2	53 2/3	43	11	8	18	51
Scott Stewart	4–2	3.09	67	0	0	17	64	49	29	22	22	67
Toma Ohka	13–8	3.18	32	31	2	0	192 2/3	194	83	68	45	118
Bartolo Colon	10–4	3.31	17	17	4	0	117	11	48	43	39	74
Javier Vazquez	10–13	3.91	34	34	2	0	230 1/3	243	111	100	49	179
Matt Herges	2–5	4.04	62	0	0	6	64 2/3	80	33	29	26	50
T.J. Tucker	6–3	4.11	57	0	0	4	61 1/3	69	32	28	31	42
Masato Yoshii	4–9	4.11	31	20	1	0	131 1/3	143	66	60	32	74
Jim Brower	3–2	4.37	52	0	0	0	80 1/3	77	40	39	32	57
Tony Armas	12–12	4.44	29	9	0	0	164 1/3	149	8	81	78	131
Britt Reames	1–4	5.03	42	6	0	0	68	70	4	38	38	76

NEW YORK METS

BATTING	G	AB	R	H	2B	3B	HR	RBI	TB	BB	SO	SB	OBP	SLG	BA
Edgardo Alfonzo	135	490	78	151	26	0	16	56	225	62	55	6	.391	.459	.308
Ty Wigginton	46	116	18	35	8	0	6	18	61	8	19	2	.354	.526	.302
Timo Perez	136	444	52	131	27	6	8	47	194	23	36	10	.331	.437	.295
Mike Piazza	135	478	69	134	23	2	33	98	260	57	82	0	.359	.544	.280
Roberto Alomar	149	590	73	157	24	4	11	53	222	57	83	16	.331	.376	.266
Roger Cedeno	149	511	65	133	19	2	7	41	177	42	92	25	.318	.346	.260
Raul Gonzalez	40	104	13	27	3	0	3	12	39	6	22	4	.297	.375	.260
Mo Vaughn	139	487	67	126	18	0	26	72	222	59	145	0	.349	.456	.259
Rey Ordonez	144	460	53	117	25	2	1	42	149	24	46	2	.292	.324	.254
Vance Wilson	74	163	19	40	7	0	5	26	62	5	32	0	.301	.380	.245
John Valentin	114	208	18	50	15	0	3	30	74	22	37	0	.339	.356	.240
Jeromy Burnitz	154	479	65	103	15	0	19	54	175	58	135	10	.311	.365	.215
Joe McEwing	105	196	22	39	8	1	3	26	58	9	50	4	.242	.296	.199

PITCHING	W–L	ERA	G	GS	CG	SV	Inn	H	R	ER	BB	SO
Steve Reed	2–5	2.01	64	0	0	1	67	56	15	15	14	50
Armando Benitez	1–0	2.27	62	0	0	33	67⅓	46	20	17	25	79
David Weathers	6–3	2.91	71	0	0	0	77⅓	69	30	25	36	61
Steve Trachsel	11–11	3.37	30	30	1	0	173⅔	170	80	65	69	105
Al Leiter	13–13	3.48	33	33	2	0	204⅓	194	99	79	69	172
Scott Strickland	6–9	3.54	69	0	0	2	68⅔	61	29	27	33	69
Mike Bacsik	3–2	4.37	11	9	1	0	55⅔	63	29	27	19	30
John Thomson	9–14	4.71	30	30	0	0	181⅓	201	116	95	44	107
Jason Middlebrook	2–3	4.73	15	5	0	0	51⅓	44	27	27	22	42
Pedro Astacio	12–11	4.79	31	31	3	0	191⅔	192	106	102	63	152
Jeff D'Amico	6–10	4.94	29	22	1	0	145⅔	152	84	80	37	101

PHILADELPHIA PHILLIES

BATTING	G	AB	R	H	2B	3B	HR	RBI	TB	BB	SO	SB	OBP	SLG	BA
Todd Pratt	39	106	14	33	11	0	3	16	53	24	28	2	.449	.500	.311
Bobby Abreu	157	572	102	176	50	6	20	85	298	104	117	31	.413	.521	.308
Placido Polanco	147	548	75	158	32	2	9	49	221	26	41	5	.330	.403	.288
Pat Burrell	157	586	96	165	39	2	37	116	319	89	153	1	.376	.544	.282
Mike Lieberthal	130	476	46	133	29	2	15	52	211	38	58	0	.349	.443	.279
Jason Michaels	81	105	16	28	10	3	2	11	50	13	33	1	.347	.476	.267
Travis Lee	153	536	55	142	26	2	13	70	211	54	104	5	.331	.394	.265
Marlon Anderson	145	539	64	139	30	6	8	48	205	42	71	5	.315	.380	.258
Tomas Perez	92	212	22	53	13	1	5	20	83	21	40	1	.319	.392	.250
Jimmy Rollins	154	637	82	156	33	10	11	60	242	54	103	31	.306	.380	.245
Jeremy Giambi	82	156	32	38	10	0	12	28	84	52	54	0	.435	.538	.244
Ricky Ledee	96	203	33	46	13	1	8	23	85	35	50	1	.342	.419	.227

PITCHING	W–L	ERA	G	GS	CG	SV	Inn	H	R	ER	BB	SO
Jose Mesa	4–6	2.97	74	0	0	45	75.2	65	26	25	39	64
Mike Timlin	4–6	2.98	72	1	0	0	96⅔	75	35	32	14	50
Randy Wolf	11–9	3.20	31	31	3	0	210⅔	172	77	75	63	172
Carlos Silva	5–0	3.21	68	0	0	1	84	88	34	30	22	41
Vicente Padilla	14–11	3.28	32	32	1	0	206	198	83	75	53	128
Joe Roa	4–4	4.04	14	11	0	0	71⅓	78	33	32	13	35
Brett Myers	4–5	4.25	12	12	1	0	72	73	38	34	29	34
Terry Adams	7–9	4.35	46	19	0	0	136⅔	132	76	66	58	96
Dave Coggin	2–5	4.68	38	7	0	0	77	65	42	40	51	64
Rheal Cormier	5–6	5.25	54	0	0	0	60	61	38	35	32	49
Brandon Duckworth	8–9	5.41	30	29	0	0	163	167	103	98	69	167
Robert Person	4–5	5.44	16	16	0	0	87⅔	79	58	53	51	61

PITTSBURGH PIRATES

BATTING	G	AB	R	H	2B	3B	HR	RBI	TB	BB	SO	SB	OBP	SLG	BA
Brian Giles	153	497	95	148	37	5	38	103	309	135	74	15	.450	.622	.298
Jason Kendall	145	545	59	154	25	3	3	44	194	49	29	15	.350	.356	.283
Pokey Reese	119	421	46	111	25	0	4	50	148	41	81	12	.330	.352	.264
Armando Rios	76	208	20	55	11	0	1	24	69	16	39	1	.319	.332	.264
Craig Wilson	131	368	48	97	16	1	16	57	163	32	116	2	.355	.443	.264
Jack Wilson	147	527	77	133	22	4	4	47	175	37	74	5	.306	.332	.252
Kevin Young	146	468	60	115	26	1	6	51	191	50	101	4	.322	.408	.246
Aramis Ramirez	142	522	51	122	26	0	18	71	202	29	95	2	.279	.387	.234
Abraham Nunez	112	253	28	59	14	1	2	15	81	27	44	3	.311	.320	.233
Adam Hyzdu	59	155	24	36	6	0	11	34	75	21	44	0	.324	.484	.232
Adrian Brown	91	208	20	45	10	2	1	21	62	19	34	10	.284	.298	.216
Keith Osik	55	100	6	16	3	0	2	11	25	6	25	0	.211	.250	.160
Mike Benjamin	108	120	7	18	2	1	0	3	22	7	31	0	.202	.183	.150

PITCHING	W–L	ERA	G	GS	CG	SV	Inn	H	R	ER	BB	SO
Scott Sauerbeck	5–4	2.30	78	0	0	0	62 2/3	50	18	16	27	70
Mike Williams	2–6	2.93	59	0	0	46	61 1/3	54	24	20	21	43
Mike Lincoln	2–4	3.11	55	0	0	0	72 1/3	80	28	25	27	50
Brian Boehringer	4–4	3.39	70	0	0	1	79 2/3	65	30	30	33	65
Kip Wells	12–14	3.58	33	33	1	0	198 1/3	197	92	79	71	134
Brian Meadows	1–6	3.88	11	11	0	0	62 2/3	62	29	27	14	31
Josh Fogg	12–12	4.35	33	33	0	0	194 1/3	199	102	94	69	113
Joe Beimel	2–5	4.64	53	8	0	0	85 1/3	88	49	44	45	53
Kris Benson	9–6	4.70	25	25	0	0	130 1/3	152	76	68	50	79
Jimmy Anderson	8–13	5.44	28	25	1	0	140 2/3	167	91	85	63	47
Ron Villone	4–6	5.81	45	7	0	0	93	95	63	60	34	55

ST. LOUIS CARDINALS

BATTING	G	AB	R	H	2B	3B	HR	RBI	TB	BB	SO	SB	OBP	SLG	BA
Albert Pujols	157	590	118	185	40	2	34	127	331	72	69	2	.394	.561	.314
Jim Edmonds	144	476	96	148	31	2	28	83	267	86	134	4	.420	.561	.311
Edgar Renteria	152	544	77	166	36	2	11	83	239	49	57	22	.364	.439	.305
Fernando Vina	150	622	75	168	29	5	1	54	210	44	36	17	.333	.338	.270
Scott Rolen	155	580	89	154	29	8	31	110	292	72	102	8	.357	.503	.266
Eli Marrero	131	397	63	104	19	1	18	66	179	40	72	14	.327	.451	.262
Tino Martinez	150	511	63	134	25	1	21	75	224	58	71	3	.337	.438	.262
Kerry Robinson	124	181	27	47	7	4	1	15	65	11	29	7	.301	.359	.260
J.D. Drew	135	424	61	107	19	1	18	56	182	57	104	8	.34	.429	.252
Miguel Cairo	108	184	28	46	9	2	2	23	65	13	36	1	.307	.353	.250
Mike Matheny	110	315	31	77	12	1	3	35	100	32	49	1	.313	.317	.244
Mike DiFelice	70	174	17	40	11	0	4	19	63	17	42	0	.297	.362	.230
Eduardo Perez	96	154	22	31	9	0	10	26	70	17	36	0	.290	.455	.201

PITCHING	W–L	ERA	G	GS	CG	SV	Inn	H	R	ER	BB	SO
Jason Isringhausen	3–2	2.48	60	0	0	32	65 1/3	46	22	18	18	68
Woody Williams	9–4	2.53	17	17	1	0	103 1/3	84	30	29	25	76
Andy Benes	5–4	2.78	18	17	1	0	97	80	39	30	51	64
Steve Kline	2–1	3.39	66	0	0	6	58 1/3	54	23	22	21	41
Matt Morris	17–9	3.42	32	32	1	0	210 1/3	210	86	80	64	171
Dave Veres	5–8	3.48	71	0	0	4	82 2/3	67	34	32	39	68
Darryl Kile	5–4	3.72	14	14	0	0	84 2/3	82	36	35	28	50
Chuck Finley	7–4	3.80	14	14	1	0	85 1/3	69	41	36	30	83
Jason Simontacchi	11–5	4.02	24	24	0	0	143 1/3	134	68	64	54	72
Luther Hackman	5–4	4.11	43	6	0	0	81	90	42	37	39	46
Rick White	5–7	4.31	61	0	0	0	62 2/3	62	33	30	21	41
Jamey Wright	7–13	5.29	23	22	1	0	129 1/3	130	80	76	75	77
Jeff Fassero	8–6	5.35	73	0	0	0	69	81	43	41	27	56

BASEBALL

SAN DIEGO PADRES

BATTING	G	AB	R	H	2B	3B	HR	RBI	TB	BB	SO	SB	OBP	SLG	BA
Ryan Klesko	146	540	90	162	39	1	29	95	290	76	86	6	.388	.537	.300
Mark Kotsay	153	578	82	169	27	7	17	61	261	59	89	11	.359	.452	.292
Phil Nevin	107	407	53	116	16	0	12	57	168	38	87	4	.344	.413	.285
Gene Kingsale	89	216	27	60	10	3	2	28	82	20	47	9	.346	.380	.278
Ramon Vazquez	128	423	50	116	21	5	2	32	153	45	79	7	.344	.362	.274
Sean Burroughs	63	192	18	52	5	1	1	11	62	12	30	2	.317	.323	.271
Deivi Cruz	151	514	49	135	28	2	7	47	188	22	58	2	.294	.366	.263
Ron Gant	102	309	58	81	14	1	18	59	151	36	59	4	.338	.489	.262
Bubba Trammell	133	403	54	98	16	1	17	56	167	53	71	1	.333	.414	.243
D'Angelo Jimenez	87	321	39	77	11	4	3	33	105	34	63	4	.311	.327	.240
Julius Matos	76	185	19	44	3	0	2	19	53	9	33	1	.279	.286	.238
Ray Lankford	81	205	20	46	7	1	6	26	73	30	61	2	.326	.356	.224
Wiki Gonzalez	56	164	16	36	8	1	1	20	49	27	24	0	.330	.299	.220
Tom Lampkin	104	281	32	61	10	1	10	37	103	38	59	4	.313	.367	.217
Trenidad Hubbard	89	129	16	27	5	0	1	7	35	14	28	9	.285	.271	.209

PITCHING	W-L	ERA	G	GS	CG	SV	Inn	H	R	ER	BB	SO
Trevor Hoffman	2-5	2.73	61	0	0	38	59 ⅓	52	20	18	18	69
Oliver Perez	4-5	3.50	16	15	0	0	90	71	37	35	48	94
Brian Lawrence	12-12	3.69	35	31	2	0	210	230	97	86	52	149
Brett Tomko	10-10	4.49	32	32	3	0	204 ⅓	212	107	102	60	126
Jake Peavy	6-7	4.52	17	17	0	0	97 ⅔	106	54	49	33	90
Jeremy Fikac	4-7	5.48	65	0	0	0	69	74	50	42	34	66
Bobby J. Jones	7-8	5.50	19	18	0	0	108	134	68	66	21	60
Brian Tollberg	1-5	6.13	12	11	0	0	61 ⅔	88	47	42	19	33
Dennis Tankersley	1-4	8.06	17	9	0	0	51 ⅓	59	46	46	40	39

SAN FRANCISCO GIANTS

BATTING	G	AB	R	H	2B	3B	HR	RBI	TB	BB	SO	SB	OBP	SLG	BA
Barry Bonds	143	403	117	149	31	2	46	110	322	198	47	9	.582	.799	.370
Jeff Kent	152	623	102	195	42	2	37	108	352	52	101	5	.368	.565	.313
Benito Santiago	126	478	56	133	24	5	16	74	215	27	73	4	.315	.450	.278
Ramon E. Martinez	72	181	26	49	10	2	4	25	75	14	26	2	.335	.414	.271
Kenny Lofton	46	180	30	48	10	3	3	9	73	23	22	7	.353	.406	.267
Bill Mueller	111	366	51	96	19	4	7	38	144	52	42	0	.350	.393	.262
David Bell	154	552	82	144	29	2	20	73	237	54	80	1	.333	.429	.261
Tom Goodwin	78	154	23	40	5	2	1	17	52	14	25	16	.321	.338	.260
Rich Aurilia	133	538	76	138	35	2	15	61	222	37	90	1	.305	.413	.257
Pedro Feliz	67	146	14	37	4	1	2	13	49	6	27	0	.281	.336	.253
Reggie Sanders	140	505	75	126	23	6	23	85	230	47	121	18	.324	.455	.250
J.T. Snow	143	422	47	104	26	2	6	53	152	59	90	0	.344	.360	.246
Tsuyoshi Shinjo	118	362	42	86	15	3	9	37	134	24	46	5	.294	.370	.238
Damon Minor	83	173	21	41	6	0	10	24	77	24	34	0	.333	.445	.237
Shawon Dunston	72	147	7	34	5	0	1	9	42	3	33	1	.250	.286	.231

PITCHING	W-L	ERA	G	GS	CG	SV	Inn	H	R	ER	BB	SO
Robb Nen	6-2	2.20	68	0	0	43	73 ⅔	64	19	18	20	81
Tim Worrell	8-2	2.25	80	0	0	0	72	55	21	18	30	55
Jay Witasick	1-0	2.37	44	0	0	0	68 ⅓	58	19	18	21	54
Chad Zerbe	2-0	3.04	50	0	0	0	56 ⅓	52	22	19	21	26
Kirk Rueter	14-8	3.23	33	33	0	0	203 ⅓	204	83	73	54	76
Jason Schmidt	13-8	3.45	29	29	2	0	185 ⅓	148	78	71	73	196
Russ Ortiz	14-10	3.61	33	33	2	0	214 ⅓	191	89	86	94	137
Felix Rodriguez	8-6	4.17	71	0	0	0	69	53	33	32	29	58
Livan Hernandez	12-16	4.38	33	33	5	0	216	233	113	105	71	134
Ryan Jensen	13-8	4.51	32	30	1	0	171 ⅔	183	93	86	66	105

AMERICAN LEAGUE TEAM-BY-TEAM STATS

ANAHEIM ANGELS

BATTING	G	AB	R	H	2B	3B	HR	RBI	TB	BB	SO	SB	OBP	SLG	BA
Adam Kennedy	144	474	65	148	32	6	7	52	213	19	80	17	.345	.449	.312
Garret Anderson	158	638	93	195	56	3	29	123	344	30	80	6	.332	.539	.306
Orlando Palmeiro	110	263	35	79	12	1	0	31	93	30	22	7	.368	.354	.300
David Eckstein	152	608	107	178	22	6	8	63	236	45	44	21	.363	.388	.293
Shawn Wooten	49	113	13	33	8	0	3	19	50	7	24	2	.336	.442	.292
Brad Fullmer	129	429	75	124	35	6	19	59	228	31	44	10	.356	.531	.289
Tim Salmon	38	483	84	138	37	1	22	88	243	71	102	6	.380	.503	.286
Benji Gil	61	130	11	37	8	1	3	20	56	5	33	2	.307	.431	.285
Scott Spiezio	153	491	80	140	34	2	12	82	214	67	52	6	.371	.436	.285
Darin Erstad	150	625	99	177	28	4	10	73	243	27	67	23	.313	.389	.283
Troy Glaus	156	569	99	142	24	1	30	111	258	88	144	10	.352	.453	.250
Ben Molina	122	428	34	105	18	0	5	47	138	15	34	0	.274	.322	.245

PITCHING	W-L	ERA	G	GS	CG	SV	Inn	H	R	ER	BB	SO
Troy Percival	4-1	1.92	58	0	0	40	56 1/3	38	12	12	25	68
Brendan Donnelly	1-1	2.17	46	0	0	1	49 2/3	32	13	12	19	54
Scot Shields	5-3	2.20	29	1	0	0	49	31	13	12	21	30
Ben Weber	7-2	2.54	63	0	0	7	78	70	25	22	22	43
Jarrod Washburn	18-6	3.15	32	32	1	0	206	183	75	72	59	139
Lou Pote	0-2	3.22	31	0	0	0	50 1/3	33	20	18	26	32
John Lackey	9-4	3.66	18	18	1	0	108 1/3	113	52	44	33	69
Ramon Ortiz	15-9	3.77	32	32	4	0	217 1/3	188	97	91	68	162
Kevin Appier	14-12	3.92	32	32	0	0	188 1/3	191	89	82	64	132
Al Levine	4-4	4.24	52	0	0	5	63 2/3	61	35	30	34	40
Scott Schoeneweis	9-8	4.88	54	15	0	1	118	119	68	64	49	65
Aaron Sele	8-9	4.89	26	26	1	0	160	190	92	87	49	82

BALTIMORE ORIOLES

BATTING	G	AB	R	H	2B	3B	HR	RBI	TB	BB	SO	SB	OBP	SLG	BA
Gary Matthews Jr.	109	344	54	95	25	3	7	38	147	43	69	15	.355	.427	.276
Jeff Conine	116	451	44	123	26	4	15	63	202	25	66	8	.307	.448	.273
Jerry Hairston	122	426	55	114	25	3	5	32	160	34	55	21	.329	.376	.268
Chris Singleton	136	466	67	122	30	6	9	50	191	21	83	20	.296	.410	.262
Marty Cordova	131	458	55	116	25	2	18	64	199	47	111	1	.325	.434	.253
Jay Gibbons	136	490	71	121	29	1	28	69	236	45	66	1	.311	.482	.247
Tony Batista	161	615	90	150	36	1	31	87	281	50	107	5	.309	.457	.244
Melvin Mora	149	557	86	130	30	4	19	64	225	70	108	16	.338	.404	.233
Mike Bordick	117	367	37	85	19	3	8	36	134	35	63	7	.302	.365	.232
Geronimo Gil	125	422	33	98	19	0	12	45	153	21	88	2	.270	.363	.232
Chris Richard	50	155	15	36	11	0	4	21	59	12	30	0	.292	.381	.232
Brook Fordyce	56	130	7	30	8	0	1	8	41	9	19	1	.301	.315	.231
Brian Roberts	37	128	18	29	6	0	1	11	38	15	21	9	.308	.297	.227

PITCHING	W-L	ERA	G	GS	CG	SV	Inn	H	R	ER	BB	SO
Buddy Groom	3-2	1.60	70	0	0	2	62	44	11	11	12	48
Jorge Julio	5-6	1.99	67	0	0	25	68	55	22	15	27	55
Willis Roberts	5-4	3.36	66	0	0	1	75	79	34	28	32	51
Rodrigo Lopez	15-9	3.57	33	28	1	0	196 2/3	172	83	78	62	136
Rick Bauer	6-7	3.98	56	1	0	1	83 2/3	84	41	37	36	45
Sidney Ponson	7-9	4.09	28	28	3	0	176	172	84	80	63	120
Jason Johnson	5-14	4.59	22	22	1	0	131 1/3	141	68	67	41	97
B.J. Ryan	2-1	4.68	67	0	0	1	57 2/3	51	31	30	33	56
Travis Driskill	8-8	4.95	29	19	0	0	132 2/3	150	78	73	48	78
Scott Erickson	5-12	5.55	29	28	3	0	160 2/3	192	109	99	68	74
Calvin Maduro	2-5	5.56	12	10	0	0	56 2/3	64	37	35	22	29
John Stephens	2-5	6.09	12	11	0	0	65	68	44	44	22	56

BASEBALL

BOSTON RED SOX

BATTING	G	AB	R	H	2B	3B	HR	RBI	TB	BB	SO	SB	OBP	SLG	BA
Manny Ramirez	120	436	84	152	31	0	33	107	282	73	85	0	.450	.647	.349
Cliff Floyd	47	171	30	54	21	0	7	18	96	15	28	4	.374	.561	.316
Nomar Garciaparra	156	635	101	197	56	5	24	120	335	41	63	5	.352	.528	.310
Shea Hillenbrand	156	634	94	186	43	4	18	83	291	25	95	4	.330	.459	.293
Carlos Baerga	73	182	17	52	11	0	2	19	69	7	20	6	.316	.379	.286
Johnny Damon	154	623	118	178	34	11	14	63	276	65	70	31	.356	.443	.286
Rey Sanchez	107	357	46	102	12	3	1	38	123	17	31	2	.318	.345	.286
Brian Daubach	137	444	62	118	24	2	20	78	206	51	126	2	.348	.464	.266
Jason Varitek	132	467	58	124	27	1	10	61	183	41	95	4	.332	.392	.266
Trot Nixon	152	532	81	136	36	3	24	94	250	65	109	4	.338	.470	.256
Lou Merloni	84	194	28	48	12	2	4	18	76	20	35	1	.332	.392	.247
Doug Mirabelli	57	151	17	34	7	0	7	25	62	17	33	0	.312	.411	.225
Ricky Henderson	72	179	40	40	6	1	5	16	63	38	47	8	.369	.352	.223
Tony Clark	90	275	25	57	12	1	3	29	80	21	57	0	.265	.291	.207

PITCHING	W–L	ERA	G	GS	CG	SV	Inn	H	R	ER	BB	SO
Pedro Martinez	20–4	2.26	30	30	2	0	199⅓	144	62	50	40	239
Derek Lowe	21–8	2.58	32	32	1	0	219⅔	166	65	63	48	127
Tim Wakefield	11–5	2.81	45	15	0	3	163⅓	121	57	51	51	134
Ugueth Urbina	1–6	3.00	61	0	0	40	60	44	21	20	20	71
Casey Fossum	5–4	3.46	43	12	0	1	106⅔	113	56	41	30	101
Bob Howry	3–5	4.19	67	0	0	0	68⅔	67	37	32	21	45
John Burkett	13–8	4.53	29	29	1	0	173	199	93	87	50	124
Darren Oliver	4–5	4.66	14	9	1	0	58	70	30	30	27	32
Rolando Arrojo	4–3	4.98	29	8	0	1	81⅓	83	47	45	27	51
Frank Castillo	6–15	5.07	36	23	0	1	163⅓	174	101	92	58	112

CHICAGO WHITE SOX

BATTING	G	AB	R	H	2B	3B	HR	RBI	TB	BB	SO	SB	OBP	SLG	BA
Magglio Ordonez	153	590	116	189	47	1	38	135	352	53	77	7	.381	.597	.320
Paul Konerko	151	570	81	173	30	0	27	104	284	44	72	0	.359	.498	.304
Sandy Alomar	51	167	21	48	10	1	7	25	81	5	14	0	.309	.485	.287
D'Angelo Jimenez	27	108	22	31	4	3	1	11	44	16	10	2	.384	.407	.287
Joe Crede	53	200	28	57	10	0	12	35	103	8	40	0	.311	.515	.285
Carlos Lee	140	492	82	130	26	2	26	80	238	75	73	1	.359	.484	.264
Tony Graffanino	70	229	35	60	12	4	6	31	98	22	38	2	.329	.428	.262
Kenny Lofton	93	352	68	91	20	6	8	42	147	49	51	22	.348	.418	.259
Aaron Rowand	126	302	41	78	16	2	7	29	119	12	54	0	.298	.394	.258
Frank Thomas	148	523	77	132	29	1	28	92	247	88	115	3	.361	.472	.252
Royce Clayton	112	342	51	86	14	2	7	35	125	20	67	5	.295	.365	.251
Jose Valentin	135	474	70	118	26	4	25	75	227	43	99	3	.311	.479	.249
Willie Harris	49	163	14	38	4	0	2	12	48	9	21	8	.270	.294	.233
Jeff Liefer	76	204	28	47	8	0	7	26	76	19	60	0	.295	.373	.230
Mark Johnson	86	263	31	55	8	1	4	18	77	30	52	0	.297	.293	.209

PITCHING	W–L	ERA	G	GS	CG	SV	Inn	H	R	ER	BB	SO
Damaso Marte	1–1	2.83	68	0	0	10	60⅓	44	19	19	18	72
Keith Foulke	2–4	2.90	65	0	0	11	77⅔	65	26	25	13	58
Mark Buehrle	19–12	3.58	34	34	5	0	239	236	102	95	61	134
Antonio Osuna	8–2	3.86	59	0	0	11	67⅔	64	32	29	28	66
Rocky Biddle	3–4	4.06	44	7	0	1	77⅔	7	42	35	39	64
Matt Ginter	1–0	4.47	33	0	0	1	54⅓	59	34	27	21	37
Jon Garland	12–12	4.58	33	33	1	0	192⅔	188	109	98	83	112
Danny Wright	14–12	5.18	33	33	1	0	196⅓	200	124	113	71	136
Gary Glover	7–8	5.20	41	22	0	1	138⅓	136	86	80	52	70
Todd Ritchie	5–15	6.06	26	23	0	0	133⅔	176	104	90	52	77

CLEVELAND INDIANS

BATTING	G	AB	R	H	2B	3B	HR	RBI	TB	BB	SO	SB	OBP	SLG	BA
Jim Thome	147	480	101	146	19	2	52	118	325	122	139	1	.445	.677	.304
Ellis Burks	138	518	92	156	28	0	32	91	280	44	108	2	.362	.541	.301
Karim Garcia	53	202	30	60	8	0	16	52	116	6	41	0	.314	.574	.297
Ricky Gutierrez	94	353	38	97	13	0	4	38	122	20	48	0	.325	.346	.275
Omar Vizquel	151	582	85	160	31	5	14	72	243	56	64	18	.341	.418	.275
John McDonald	93	264	35	66	11	3	1	12	86	10	50	3	.288	.326	.250
Milton Bradley	98	325	48	81	18	3	9	38	132	32	58	6	.317	.406	.249
Matt Lawton	114	416	71	98	19	2	15	57	166	59	34	8	.342	.399	.236
Lee Stevens	53	153	22	34	7	1	5	26	58	15	32	0	.285	.379	.222
Travis Fryman	118	397	42	86	14	3	11	55	139	40	82	0	.292	.350	.217
Chris Magruder	87	258	34	56	15	1	6	29	91	15	55	2	.261	.353	.217
Bill Selby	65	159	15	34	7	2	6	21	63	15	27	0	.278	.396	.214
Einar Diaz	102	320	34	66	19	0	2	16	91	17	27	0	.258	.284	.206
Russell Branyan	50	161	16	33	4	0	8	17	61	17	65	1	.278	.379	.205

PITCHING	W–L	ERA	G	GS	CG	SV	Inn	H	R	ER	BB	SO
Bartolo Colon	10–4	2.55	16	16	4	0	116 1/3	104	37	33	31	75
C.C. Sabathia	13–11	4.37	33	33	2	0	210	198	109	102	88	149
Danys Baez	10–11	4.41	39	26	1	6	165 1/3	160	84	81	82	130
Chuck Finley	4–11	4.44	18	18	1	0	105 1/3	114	56	52	48	91
Bob Wickman	1–3	4.46	36	0	0	20	34 1/3	42	22	17	10	36
Terry Mulholland	3–2	4.60	16	3	0	0	47	56	27	24	14	21
Mark Wohlers	3–4	4.79	64	0	0	7	71 1/3	71	41	38	26	46
Dave Burba	5–5	5.20	35	21	1	0	145 1/3	155	91	84	57	95
David Riske	2–2	5.26	51	0	0	1	51 1/3	49	32	30	35	65
Ryan Drese	10–9	6.55	26	26	1	0	137 1/3	176	104	100	62	102

DETROIT TIGERS

BATTING	G	AB	R	H	2B	3B	HR	RBI	TB	BB	SO	SB	OBP	SLG	BA
Randall Simon	130	482	51	145	17	1	19	82	221	13	30	0	.320	.459	.301
Dmitri Young	54	201	25	57	14	0	7	27	92	12	39	2	.329	.458	.284
Bobby Higginson	119	444	50	125	24	3	10	63	185	41	45	12	.345	.417	.282
Wendall Magee	97	347	34	94	19	1	6	35	133	10	64	2	.289	.383	.271
Robert Fick	148	556	66	150	36	2	17	63	241	46	90	0	.331	.433	.270
Damian Jackson	81	245	31	63	20	1	1	25	88	21	36	12	.320	.359	.257
Ramon Santiago	65	222	33	54	5	5	4	20	81	13	48	8	.306	.365	.243
Carlos Pena	115	397	43	96	17	4	19	52	178	41	111	2	.316	.448	.242
George Lombard	72	241	34	58	11	3	5	13	90	20	78	13	.300	.373	.241
Shane Halter	122	410	46	98	22	6	10	39	162	39	92	0	.309	.395	.239
Mike Rivera	39	132	11	30	8	1	1	11	43	4	35	0	.254	.326	.227
Damian Easley	85	304	29	68	14	1	8	30	108	27	43	1	.307	.355	.224
Brandon Inge	95	321	27	65	15	3	7	24	107	24	101	1	.266	.333	.202
Chris Truby	89	277	23	55	13	2	2	15	78	5	71	1	.215	.282	.199
Craig Paquette	72	252	20	49	14	1	4	20	77	10	53	1	.223	.306	.194

PITCHING	W–L	ERA	G	GS	CG	SV	Inn	H	R	ER	BB	SO
Juan Acevedo	1–5	2.65	65	0	0	28	74 2/3	68	33	22	23	43
Julio Santana	3–5	2.84	38	0	0	0	57	49	19	18	28	38
Mark Redman	8–15	4.21	30	30	3	0	203	211	107	95	51	109
Mike Maroth	6–10	4.48	21	21	0	0	128 2/3	136	68	64	36	58
Brian Powell	1–5	4.84	13	9	0	0	57 2/3	64	34	31	21	30
Nate Cornejo	1–5	5.04	9	9	1	0	50	63	33	28	18	23
Steve Sparks	8–16	5.52	32	30	3	0	189	238	134	116	67	98
Jeff Farnsworth	2–3	5.79	44	0	0	0	70	100	47	45	29	28
Adam Bernero	4–7	6.20	28	11	0	0	101 2/3	128	74	70	31	69
Jose Lima	4–6	7.77	20	12	0	0	68 1/3	86	60	59	21	33

BASEBALL

KANSAS CITY ROYALS

BATTING

BATTING	G	AB	R	H	2B	3B	HR	RBI	TB	BB	SO	SB	OBP	SLG	BA
Mike Sweeney	126	471	81	160	31	1	24	86	265	61	46	9	.417	.563	.340
Raul Ibanez	137	497	70	146	37	6	24	103	267	40	76	5	.346	.537	.294
Joe Randa	151	549	63	155	36	5	11	80	234	46	69	2	.341	.426	.282
Carlos Beltran	162	637	114	174	44	7	29	105	319	71	135	35	.346	.501	.273
A.J. Hinch	72	197	25	49	7	1	7	27	79	18	35	3	.321	.401	.249
Michael Tucker	144	475	65	118	27	6	12	56	193	56	105	23	.330	.406	.248
Carlos Febles	119	351	44	86	16	4	4	26	122	41	63	16	.336	.348	.245
Brent Mayne	101	326	35	77	8	2	4	30	101	34	54	4	.309	.310	.236
Neifi Perez	145	554	65	131	20	4	3	37	168	20	53	8	.260	.303	.236
Aaron Guiel	70	240	30	56	13	0	4	38	81	19	61	1	.296	.338	.233
Luis Alicea	94	237	28	54	8	2	1	23	69	32	34	2	.322	.291	.228
Chuck Knoblauch	80	300	41	63	9	0	6	22	90	28	32	19	.284	.300	.210
Brandon Berger	51	134	16	27	5	1	6	17	52	8	32	1	.255	.388	.201

PITCHING

PITCHING	W-L	ERA	G	GS	CG	SV	Inn	H	R	ER	BB	SO
Paul Byrd	17-11	3.90	33	33	7	0	228 ⅓	224	111	99	38	129
Jason Grimsley	4-7	3.91	70	0	0	1	71 ⅓	64	32	31	37	59
Cory Bailey	3-4	4.11	37	0	0	1	46	53	24	21	31	24
Roberto Hernandez	1-3	4.33	53	0	0	26	52	62	29	25	12	39
Runelvys Hernandez	4-4	4.36	12	12	0	0	74 ⅓	79	36	36	22	45
Jeremy Affeldt	3-4	4.64	34	7	0	0	77 ⅔	85	41	40	37	67
Miguel Asencio	4-7	5.11	31	21	0	0	123 ⅓	136	73	70	64	58
Dan Reichert	3-5	5.32	30	6	0	0	66	77	48	39	25	36
Jeff Suppan	9-16	5.32	33	33	3	0	208	229	134	123	68	109
Darrell May	4-10	5.35	30	21	1	0	131 ⅓	144	83	78	50	95
Shawn Sedlacek	3-5	6.72	16	14	0	0	84 ⅓	99	64	63	36	52
Blake Stein	0-4	7.91	27	2	0	1	46 ⅔	59	41	41	27	42

MINNESOTA TWINS

BATTING

BATTING	G	AB	R	H	2B	3B	HR	RBI	TB	BB	SO	SB	OBP	SLG	BA
Jacque Jones	149	577	96	173	37	2	27	85	295	37	129	6	.341	.511	.300
A.J. Pierzynski	130	440	54	132	31	6	6	49	193	13	61	1	.334	.439	.300
Bobby Kielty	112	289	49	84	14	3	12	46	140	52	66	4	.405	.484	.291
Torii Hunter	148	561	89	162	37	4	29	94	294	35	118	23	.334	.524	.289
Cristian Guzman	148	623	80	170	31	6	9	59	240	17	79	12	.292	.385	.273
David Ortiz	125	412	52	112	32	1	20	75	206	43	87	1	.339	.500	.272
Dustan Mohr	120	383	55	103	23	2	12	45	166	31	86	6	.325	.433	.269
Corey Koskie	140	490	71	131	37	3	15	69	219	72	127	10	.368	.447	.267
Doug Mientkiewicz	143	467	60	122	29	1	10	64	183	74	69	1	.365	.392	.261
Matt LeCroy	63	181	19	47	11	1	7	27	81	13	38	0	.306	.448	.260
Luis Rivas	93	316	46	81	23	4	4	35	124	19	51	9	.305	.392	.256
Brian Buchanan	44	135	19	34	5	1	5	15	56	6	33	2	.294	.415	.252
Denny Hocking	102	260	28	65	13	0	2	25	84	24	44	0	.310	.323	.250

PITCHING

PITCHING	W-L	ERA	G	GS	CG	SV	Inn	H	R	ER	BB	SO
J.C. Romero	9-2	1.89	81	0	0	1	81	62	17	17	36	76
LaTroy Hawkins	6-0	2.13	65	0	0	0	80 ⅓	63	23	19	15	63
Eddie Guardado	1-3	2.93	68	0	0	45	67 ⅔	53	22	22	18	70
Johan Santana	8-6	2.99	27	14	0	1	108 ⅓	84	41	36	49	137
Tony Fiore	10-3	3.16	48	2	0	0	91	74	32	32	43	55
Mike Jackson	2-3	3.27	58	0	0	0	55	59	20	20	13	29
Rick Reed	15-7	3.78	33	32	2	0	188	192	89	79	26	121
Kyle Lohse	13-8	4.23	32	31	1	0	180 ⅔	181	92	85	70	124
Matt Kinney	2-7	4.64	14	12	0	0	66	78	39	34	33	45
Brad Radke	9-5	4.72	21	21	2	0	118 ⅓	124	64	62	20	62
Eric Milton	13-9	4.84	29	29	2	0	171	173	96	92	30	121
Joe Mays	4-8	5.38	17	17	1	0	95 ⅓	113	60	57	25	38

NEW YORK YANKEES

BATTING	G	AB	R	H	2B	3B	HR	RBI	TB	BB	SO	SB	OBP	SLG	BA
Bernie Williams	154	612	102	204	37	2	19	102	302	83	97	8	.415	.493	.333
Jason Giambi	155	560	120	176	34	1	41	122	335	109	112	2	.435	.598	.314
Alfonso Soriano	156	696	128	209	51	2	39	102	381	23	157	41	.332	.547	.300
Derek Jeter	157	644	124	191	26	0	18	75	271	73	114	32	.373	.421	.297
Jorge Posada	143	511	79	137	40	1	20	99	239	81	143	1	.370	.468	.268
Juan Rivera	28	83	9	22	5	0	1	6	30	6	10	1	.311	.361	.265
Ron Coomer	55	148	14	39	7	0	3	17	55	6	23	0	.290	.372	.264
John Vander Wal	84	219	30	57	17	1	6	20	94	23	58	1	.327	.429	.260
Shane Spencer	94	288	32	71	15	2	6	34	108	31	62	0	.324	.375	.247
Robin Ventura	141	465	68	115	17	0	27	93	213	90	101	3	.368	.458	.247
Nick Johnson	129	378	56	92	15	0	15	58	152	48	98	1	.347	.402	.243
Rondell White	126	455	59	109	21	0	14	62	172	25	86	1	.288	.378	.240
Raul Mondesi	146	569	90	132	34	1	26	88	246	59	103	15	.308	.432	.232
Enrique Wilson	60	105	17	19	2	2	2	11	31	8	22	1	.239	.295	.181

PITCHING	W–L	ERA	G	GS	CG	SV	Inn	H	R	ER	BB	SO
Mariano Rivera	1–4	2.74	45	0	0	28	46	35	16	14	11	41
Mike Stanton	7–1	3.00	79	0	0	6	78	73	29	26	28	44
Steve Karsay	6–4	3.26	78	0	0	12	88 1/3	87	33	32	30	65
Andy Pettitte	13–5	3.27	22	22	3	0	134 2/3	144	58	49	32	97
Ramiro Mendoza	8–4	3.44	62	0	0	4	91 2/3	102	43	35	16	61
Jeff Weaver	11–11	3.52	32	25	3	2	199 2/3	193	88	78	48	132
Orlando Hernandez	8–5	3.64	24	22	0	1	146	131	63	59	36	113
David Wells	19–7	3.75	31	31	2	0	206 1/3	210	100	86	45	137
Mike Mussina	18–10	4.05	33	33	2	0	215 2/3	208	103	97	48	182
Roger Clemens	13–6	4.35	29	29	0	0	180	172	94	87	63	192

OAKLAND ATHLETICS

BATTING	G	AB	R	H	2B	3B	HR	RBI	TB	BB	SO	SB	OBP	SLG	BA
Miguel Tejada	162	662	108	204	30	0	34	131	336	38	84	7	.354	.508	.308
Ray Durham	150	564	114	163	34	6	15	70	254	73	93	26	.374	.450	.289
Scott Hatteberg	136	492	58	138	22	4	15	61	213	68	56	0	.374	.433	.280
Olmedo Saenz	68	156	15	43	10	1	6	18	73	13	31	1	.354	.468	.276
Eric Chavez	153	585	87	161	31	3	34	109	300	65	119	8	.348	.513	.275
John Mabry	89	193	27	53	13	1	11	40	101	14	37	1	.322	.523	.275
Jeremy Giambi	42	157	26	43	7	0	8	17	74	27	40	0	.390	.471	.274
Mark Ellis	98	345	58	94	16	4	6	35	136	44	54	4	.359	.394	.272
David Justice	118	398	54	106	18	3	11	49	163	70	66	4	.376	.410	.266
Jermaine Dye	131	488	74	123	27	1	24	86	224	52	108	2	.333	.459	.252
Terrence Long	162	587	71	141	32	4	16	67	229	48	96	3	.298	.390	.240
Adam Piatt	55	137	18	32	8	0	5	18	55	12	33	2	.303	.401	.234
Ramon Hernandez	136	403	51	94	20	0	7	42	135	43	64	0	.313	.335	.233
Randy Velarde	56	133	22	30	8	0	2	8	44	15	32	3	.325	.331	.226
Greg Myers	65	144	15	32	5	0	6	21	55	26	36	0	.341	.382	.222

PITCHING	W–L	ERA	G	GS	CG	SV	Inn	H	R	ER	BB	SO
Barry Zito	23–5	2.75	35	35	1	0	229 1/3	182	79	70	78	182
Tim Hudson	15–9	2.98	34	34	4	0	238 1/3	237	87	79	62	152
Chad Bradford	4–2	3.11	75	0	0	2	75 1/3	73	29	26	14	56
Billy Koch	11–4	3.27	84	0	0	44	93 2/3	73	38	34	46	93
Mark Mulder	19–7	3.47	30	30	2	0	207 1/3	182	88	80	55	159
Ted Lilly	5–7	3.69	22	16	2	0	100	80	43	41	31	77
Cory Lidle	8–10	3.89	31	30	2	0	192	191	90	83	39	111
Ricardo Rincon	1–4	4.18	71	0	0	1	56	47	28	26	11	49
Jim Mecir	6–4	4.26	61	0	0	1	67 2/3	68	36	32	29	53
Aaron Harang	5–4	4.83	16	15	0	0	78 1/3	78	44	42	45	64

BASEBALL

SEATTLE MARINERS

BATTING	G	AB	R	H	2B	3B	HR	RBI	TB	BB	SO	SB	OBP	SLG	BA
Ichiro Suzuki	157	647	111	208	27	8	8	51	275	68	62	31	.388	.425	.321
John Olerud	154	553	85	166	39	0	22	102	271	98	66	0	.403	.490	.300
Dan Wilson	115	359	35	106	16	1	6	44	142	18	81	1	.326	.396	.295
Bret Boone	155	608	88	169	34	3	24	107	281	53	102	12	.339	.462	.278
Edgar Martinez	97	328	42	91	23	0	15	59	159	67	69	1	.403	.485	.277
Mark McLemore	104	337	54	91	17	2	7	41	133	61	63	18	.380	.395	.270
Ruben Sierra	122	419	47	113	23	0	13	60	175	31	66	4	.319	.418	.270
Desi Relaford	112	329	55	88	13	2	6	43	123	33	51	10	.339	.374	.267
Carlos Guillen	134	475	73	124	24	6	9	56	187	46	91	4	.326	.394	.261
Ben Davis	80	228	24	59	10	1	7	43	92	18	58	1	.313	.404	.259
Jeff Cirillo	146	485	51	121	20	0	6	54	159	31	67	8	.301	.328	.249
Mike Cameron	158	545	84	130	26	5	25	80	241	79	176	31	.340	.442	.239
Jose Offerman	101	284	48	66	12	1	5	31	95	37	38	9	.320	.335	.232

PITCHING	W–L	ERA	G	GS	CG	SV	Inn	H	R	ER	BB	SO
Arthur Rhodes	10–4	2.33	66	0	0	2	69 2/3	45	18	18	13	81
Kazuhiro Sasaki	4–5	2.52	61	0	0	37	60 2/3	44	24	17	20	73
Shigetoshi Hasegawa	8–3	3.20	53	0	0	1	70 1/3	60	26	25	30	39
Joel Pineiro	14–7	3.24	37	28	2	0	194 1/3	189	75	70	54	136
Jamie Moyer	13–8	3.32	34	34	4	0	230 2/3	198	89	85	50	147
John Halama	6–5	3.56	31	10	0	0	101	112	45	40	33	70
Jeff Nelson	3–2	3.94	41	0	0	2	45 2/3	36	20	20	27	55
Ryan Franklin	7–5	4.02	41	12	0	0	118 2/3	117	62	53	22	65
Ismael Valdes	8–12	4.18	31	31	1	0	196	194	94	91	47	102
Freddy Garcia	16–10	4.39	34	34	1	0	223 2/3	227	110	109	63	181
James Baldwin	7–10	5.28	30	23	0	0	150	179	95	88	49	88
Doug Creek	3–2	5.82	52	0	0	0	55 2/3	57	37	36	35	56

TAMPA BAY DEVIL RAYS

BATTING	G	AB	R	H	2B	3B	HR	RBI	TB	BB	SO	SB	OBP	SLG	BA
Aubrey Huff	113	454	67	142	25	0	23	59	236	37	55	4	.364	.520	.313
Randy Winn	152	607	87	181	39	9	14	75	280	55	109	27	.360	.461	.298
Chris Gomez	130	461	51	122	31	3	10	46	189	21	58	1	.305	.410	.265
John Flaherty	76	281	27	73	20	0	4	33	105	15	50	2	.296	.374	.260
Carl Crawford	63	259	23	67	11	6	2	30	96	9	41	9	.290	.371	.259
Toby Hall	85	330	37	85	19	1	6	42	124	17	27	0	.293	.376	.258
Jason Conti	78	222	26	57	15	2	3	21	85	18	55	4	.315	.383	.257
Steve Cox	148	560	65	142	30	1	16	72	222	60	116	5	.330	.396	.254
Ben Grieve	136	482	62	121	30	0	19	64	208	69	121	8	.353	.432	.251
Andy Sheets	41	149	18	37	4	0	4	22	53	12	41	2	.301	.356	.248
Brent Abernathy	117	463	46	112	18	4	2	40	144	25	46	10	.288	.311	.242
Jared Sandberg	102	358	55	82	21	1	18	54	159	39	139	3	.305	.444	.229
Felix Escalona	59	157	17	34	8	2	0	9	46	3	44	7	.262	.293	.217
Jason Tyner	44	168	17	36	2	1	0	9	40	7	19	7	.249	.238	.214
Greg Vaughn	69	251	28	41	10	2	8	29	79	41	82	3	.286	.315	.163

PITCHING	W–L	ERA	G	GS	CG	SV	Inn	H	R	ER	BB	SO
Esteban Yan	7–8	4.30	55	0	0	19	69	70	35	33	29	53
Joe Kennedy	8–11	4.53	30	30	5	0	196 2/3	204	114	99	55	109
Paul Wilson	6–12	4.83	30	30	1	0	193 2/3	219	113	104	67	111
Tanyon Sturtze	4–18	5.18	33	33	4	0	224	271	141	129	89	137
Wilson Alvarez	2–3	5.28	23	10	0	1	75	80	47	44	36	56
Travis Harper	5–9	5.46	37	7	0	1	85 2/3	101	54	52	27	60
Jorge Sosa	2–7	5.53	31	14	0	0	99 1/3	88	63	61	54	48
Victor Zambrano	8–8	5.53	42	11	0	1	114	120	77	70	68	73
Ryan Rupe	5–10	5.60	15	15	2	0	90	83	60	56	25	67
Steve Kent	0–2	5.65	34	0	0	1	57 1/3	67	41	36	38	41

TEXAS RANGERS

BATTING	G	AB	R	H	2B	3B	HR	RBI	TB	BB	SO	SB	OBP	SLG	BA
Ivan Rodriguez	108	408	67	128	32	2	19	60	221	25	71	5	.353	.542	.314
Alex Rodriguez	162	624	125	187	27	2	57	142	389	87	122	9	.392	.623	.300
Rusty Greer	51	199	24	59	9	2	1	17	75	19	17	1	.356	.377	.296
Mike Lamb	115	314	54	89	13	0	9	33	129	33	48	0	.354	.411	.283
Juan Gonzalez	70	277	38	78	21	1	8	35	125	17	56	2	.324	.451	.282
Herbert Perry	132	450	64	124	24	1	22	77	216	34	66	4	.333	.480	.276
Rafael Palmeiro	155	546	99	149	34	0	43	105	312	104	94	2	.391	.571	.273
Frank Catalanotto	68	212	42	57	16	6	3	23	94	25	27	9	.364	.443	.269
Carl Everett	105	374	47	100	16	0	16	62	164	33	77	2	.333	.439	.267
Mike Young	156	573	77	150	26	8	9	62	219	41	112	6	.308	.382	.262
Gabe Kapler	72	196	25	51	12	1	0	17	65	8	30	5	.285	.332	.260
Kevin Mench	110	366	52	95	20	2	15	60	164	31	83	1	.327	.448	.260
Bill Haselman	69	179	16	44	7	0	3	18	60	11	25	0	.297	.335	.246
Hank Blalock	49	147	16	31	8	0	3	17	48	20	43	0	.306	.327	.211
Ruben Rivera	69	158	17	33	4	0	4	14	49	17	45	4	.302	.310	.209

PITCHING	W-L	ERA	G	GS	CG	SV	Inn	H	R	ER	BB	SO
Francisco Cordero	2-0	1.79	39	0	0	10	45 1/3	33	12	9	13	41
Jay Powell	3-2	3.44	51	0	0	0	49 2/3	50	28	19	24	35
Kenny Rogers	13-8	3.84	33	33	2	0	210 2/3	212	101	90	70	107
Doug Davis	3-5	4.98	10	10	1	0	59 2/3	67	36	33	22	28
Joaquin Benoit	4-5	5.31	17	13	0	1	84 2/3	91	51	50	58	59
Todd Van Poppel	3-2	5.45	50	0	0	1	72 1/3	80	44	44	29	85
Hideki Irabu	3-8	5.74	38	2	0	16	47	51	30	30	16	30
Chan Ho Park	9-8	5.75	25	25	0	0	145 2/3	154	95	9	78	121
Rob Bell	4-3	6.22	17	15	0	0	94	113	69	65	35	70
Aaron Myette	2-5	10.06	15	12	0	0	48 1/3	64	57	54	41	48

TORONTO BLUE JAYS

BATTING	G	AB	R	H	2B	3B	HR	RBI	TB	BB	SO	SB	OBP	SLG	BA
Josh Phelps	74	265	41	82	20	1	15	58	149	19	82	0	.362	.562	.309
Shannon Stewart	141	577	103	175	38	6	10	45	255	54	60	14	.371	.442	.303
Eric Hinske	151	566	99	158	38	2	24	84	272	77	138	13	.365	.481	.279
Carlos Delgado	143	505	103	140	34	2	33	108	277	102	126	1	.406	.549	.277
Orlando Hudson	54	192	20	53	10	5	4	23	85	11	27	0	.319	.443	.276
Chris Woodward	90	312	48	86	13	4	13	45	146	26	72	3	.330	.468	.276
Vernon Wells	159	608	87	167	34	4	23	100	278	27	85	9	.305	.457	.275
Dave Berg	109	374	42	101	26	2	4	39	143	26	57	0	.322	.382	.270
Tom Wilson	96	265	33	68	10	0	8	37	102	28	79	0	.334	.385	.257
Jose Cruz	124	466	64	114	26	5	18	70	204	51	106	7	.317	.438	.245
Kevin Huckaby	88	273	29	67	6	1	3	22	84	9	44	0	.270	.308	.245
Felipe Lopez	85	282	35	64	15	3	8	34	109	23	90	5	.287	.387	.227
Darrin Fletcher	45	127	8	28	6	0	3	22	43	4	13	0	.239	.339	.220
Joe Lawrence	55	150	16	27	4	0	2	15	37	16	38	2	.262	.247	.180

PITCHING	W-L	ERA	G	GS	CG	SV	Inn	H	R	ER	BB	SO
Roy Halladay	19-7	2.93	34	34	2	0	239 1/3	223	93	78	62	168
Felix Heredia	1-2	3.61	53	0	0	0	52 1/3	51	29	21	26	31
Cliff Politte	1-3	3.61	55	0	0	1	57 1/3	38	23	23	19	57
Kelvim Escobar	5-7	4.27	76	0	0	38	78	75	39	37	44	85
Pete Walker	10-5	4.33	37	20	0	1	139 1/3	143	72	67	51	80
Corey Thurman	2-3	4.37	43	1	0	0	68	65	34	33	45	56
Scott Eyre	2-4	4.97	49	3	0	0	63	69	37	35	29	51
Chris Carpenter	4-5	5.28	13	13	1	0	73 1/3	89	45	43	27	45
Justin Miller	9-5	5.54	25	18	0	0	102 1/3	103	70	63	66	68
Esteban Loaiza	9-10	5.71	25	25	3	0	151 1/3	192	102	96	38	87
Scott Cassidy	1-4	5.73	58	0	0	0	66	52	42	42	32	48
Steve Parris	5-5	5.97	14	14	0	0	75 1/3	96	50	50	35	48
Brandon Lyon	1-4	6.53	15	10	0	0	62	78	47	45	19	30
Luke Prokopec	2-9	6.78	22	12	0	0	71 2/3	90	57	54	25	41

BASEBALL

World Series All-time Results

2002	Anaheim (A) 4, San Francisco (N) 3	1952	New York (A) 4, Brooklyn (N) 3
2001	Arizona (N) 4, New York (A) 3	1951	New York (A) 4, New York (N) 2
2000	New York (A) 4, New York (N) 1	1950	New York (A) 4, Philadelphia (N) 0
1999	New York (A) 4, Atlanta (N) 0	1949	New York (A) 4, Brooklyn (N) 1
1998	New York (A) 4, San Diego (N) 0	1948	Cleveland (A) 4, Boston (N) 2
1997	Florida (N) 4, Cleveland (A) 3	1947	New York (A) 4, Brooklyn (N) 3
1996	New York (A) 4, Atlanta (N) 2	1946	St. Louis (N) 4, Boston (A) 3
1995	Atlanta (N) 4, Cleveland (A) 2	1945	Detroit (A) 4, Chicago (N) 3
1994	Series canceled due to players' strike.	1944	St. Louis (N) 4, St. Louis (A) 2
1993	Toronto (A) 4, Philadelphia (N) 2	1943	New York (A) 4, St. Louis (N) 1
1992	Toronto (A) 4, Atlanta (N) 2	1942	St. Louis (N) 4, New York (A) 1
1991	Minnesota (A) 4, Atlanta (N) 3	1941	New York (A) 4, Brooklyn (N) 1
1990	Cincinnati (N) 4, Oakland (A) 0	1940	Cincinnati (N) 4, Detroit (A) 3
1989	Oakland (A) 4, San Francisco (N) 0	1939	New York (A) 4, Cincinnati (N) 0
1988	Los Angeles (N) 4, Oakland (A) 1	1938	New York (A) 4, Chicago (N) 0
1987	Minnesota (A) 4, St. Louis (N) 3	1937	New York (A) 4, New York (N) 1
1986	New York (N) 4, Boston (A) 3	1936	New York (A) 4, New York (N) 2
1985	Kansas City (A) 4, St. Louis (N) 3	1935	Detroit (A) 4, Chicago (N) 2
1984	Detroit (A) 4, San Diego (N) 1	1934	St. Louis (N) 4, Detroit (A) 3
1983	Baltimore (A) 4, Philadelphia (N) 1	1933	New York (N) 4, Washington (A) 1
1982	St. Louis (N) 4, Milwaukee (A) 3	1932	New York (A) 4, Chicago (N) 0
1981	Los Angeles (N) 4, New York (A) 2	1931	St. Louis (N) 4, Philadelphia (A) 3
1980	Philadelphia (N) 4, Kansas City (A) 2	1930	Philadelphia (A) 4, St. Louis (N) 2
1979	Pittsburgh (N) 4, Baltimore (A) 3	1929	Philadelphia (A) 4, Chicago (N) 1
1978	New York (A) 4, Los Angeles (N) 2	1928	New York (A) 4, St. Louis (N) 0
1977	New York (A) 4, Los Angeles (N) 2	1927	New York (A) 4, Pittsburgh (N) 0
1976	Cincinnati (N) 4, New York (A) 0	1926	St. Louis (N) 4, New York (A) 3
1975	Cincinnati (N) 4, Boston (A) 3	1925	Pittsburgh (N) 4, Washington (A) 3
1974	Oakland (A) 4, Los Angeles (N) 1	1924	Washington (A) 4, New York (N) 3
1973	Oakland (A) 4, New York (N) 3	1923	New York (A) 4, New York (N) 2
1972	Oakland (A) 4, Cincinnati (N) 3	1922	New York (N) 4, New York (A) 0; 1 tie
1971	Pittsburgh (N) 4, Baltimore (A) 3	1921	New York (N) 5, New York (A) 3
1970	Baltimore (A) 4, Cincinnati (N) 1	1920	Cleveland (A) 5, Brooklyn (N) 2
1969	New York (N) 4, Baltimore (A) 1	1919	Cincinnati (N) 5, Chicago (A) 3
1968	Detroit (A) 4, St. Louis (N) 3	1918	Boston (A) 4, Chicago (N) 2
1967	St. Louis (N) 4, Boston (A) 3	1917	Chicago (A) 4, New York (N) 2
1966	Baltimore (A) 4, Los Angeles (N) 0	1916	Boston (A) 4, Brooklyn (N) 1
1965	Los Angeles (N) 4, Minnesota (A) 3	1915	Boston (A) 4, Philadelphia (N) 1
1964	St. Louis (N) 4, New York (A) 3	1914	Boston (N) 4, Philadelphia (A) 0
1963	Los Angeles (N) 4, New York (A) 0	1913	Philadelphia (A) 4, New York (N) 1
1962	New York (A) 4, San Francisco (N) 3	1912	Boston (A) 4, New York (N) 3; 1 tie
1961	New York (A) 4, Cincinnati (N) 1	1911	Philadelphia (A) 4, New York (N) 2
1960	Pittsburgh (N) 4, New York (A) 3	1910	Philadelphia (A) 4, Chicago (N) 1
1959	Los Angeles (N) 4, Chicago (A) 2	1909	Pittsburgh (N) 4, Detroit (A) 3
1958	New York (A) 4, Milwaukee (N) 3	1908	Chicago (N) 4, Detroit (A) 1
1957	Milwaukee (N) 4, New York (A) 3	1907	Chicago (N) 4, Detroit (A) 0; 1 tie
1956	New York (A) 4, Brooklyn (N) 3	1906	Chicago (A) 4, Chicago (N) 2
1955	Brooklyn (N) 4, New York (A) 3	1905	New York (N) 4, Philadelphia (A) 1
1954	New York (N) 4, Cleveland (A) 0	1904	No series
1953	New York (A) 4, Brooklyn (N) 2	1903	Boston (A) 5, Pittsburgh (N) 3

Note: A=American League; N=National League

The World Series
Most Valuable Players

2002	Troy Glaus, Ana		1979	Willie Stargell, Pitt
2001	Randy Johnson, Ariz		1978	Bucky Dent, NY (A)
	Curt Schilling, Ariz		1977	Reggie Jackson, NY (A)
2000	Derek Jeter, NY (A)		1976	Johnny Bench, Cin
1999	Mariano Rivera, NY (A)		1975	Pete Rose, Cin
1998	Scott Brosius, NY (A)		1974	Rollie Fingers, Oak
1997	Livan Hernandez, Fla		1973	Reggie Jackson, Oak
1996	John Wetteland, NY (A)		1972	Gene Tenace, Oak
1995	Tom Glavine, Atl		1971	Roberto Clemente, Pitt
1994	Series canceled due to labor dispute.		1970	Brooks Robinson, Balt
1993	Paul Molitor, Tor		1969	Donn Clendenon, NY (N)
1992	Pat Borders, Tor		1968	Mickey Lolich, Det
1991	Jack Morris, Minn		1967	Bob Gibson, StL
1990	Jose Rijo, Cin		1966	Frank Robinson, Balt
1989	Dave Stewart, Oak		1965	Sandy Koufax, LA
1988	Orel Hershiser, LA		1964	Bob Gibson, StL
1987	Frank Viola, Minn		1963	Sandy Koufax, LA
1986	Ray Knight, NY (N)		1962	Ralph Terry, NY (A)
1985	Bret Saberhagen, KC		1961	Whitey Ford, NY (A)
1984	Alan Trammell, Det		1960	Bobby Richardson, NY (A)
1983	Rick Dempsey, Balt		1959	Larry Sherry, LA
1982	Darrell Porter, StL		1958	Bob Turley, NY (A)
1981	Ron Cey, LA; Steve Yeager, LA;		1957	Lew Burdette, Mil
	Pedro Guerrero, LA		1956	Don Larsen, NY (A)
1980	Mike Schmidt, Phil		1955	Johnny Podres, Bklyn

League Championship Series

	National League			American League
2002	San Francisco (WC) 4, St. Louis (C) 1		2002	Anaheim (WC) 4, Minnesota (C) 1
2001	Arizona (W) 4, Atlanta (E) 1		2001	New York (E) 4, Seattle (W) 1
2000	New York (WC) 4, St. Louis (C) 1		2000	New York (E) 4, Seattle (WC) 2
1999	Atlanta (E) 4, New York (wc) 2		1999	New York (E) 4, Boston (WC) 1
1998	San Diego (W) 4, Atlanta (E) 2		1998	New York (E) 4, Cleveland (C) 2
1997	Florida (WC) 4, Atlanta (E) 2		1997	Cleveland (C) 4, Baltimore (E) 2
1996	Atlanta (E) 4, St. Louis (C) 3		1996	New York (E) 4, Baltimore (WC) 1
1995	Atlanta (E) 4, Cincinnati (C) 0		1995	Cleveland (C) 4, Seattle (W) 2
1994	Playoffs canceled due to labor dispute.		1994	Playoffs canceled due to labor dispute.
1993	Philadelphia (E) 4, Atlanta (W) 2		1993	Toronto (E) 4, Chicago (W) 2
1992	Atlanta (W) 4, Pittsburgh (E) 3		1992	Toronto (E) 4, Oakland (W) 2
1991	Atlanta (W) 4, Pittsburgh (E) 3		1991	Minnesota (W) 4, Toronto (E) 1
1990	Cincinnati (W) 4, Pittsburgh (E) 2		1990	Oakland (W) 4, Boston (E) 0
1989	San Francisco (W) 4, Chicago (E) 1		1989	Oakland (W) 4, Toronto (E) 1
1988	Los Angeles (W) 4, New York (E) 3		1988	Oakland (W) 4, Boston (E) 0
1987	St. Louis (E) 4, San Francisco (W) 3		1987	Minnesota (W) 4, Detroit (E) 1
1986	New York (E) 4, Houston (W) 2		1986	Boston (E) 4, California (W) 3
1985	St. Louis (E) 4, Los Angeles (W) 2		1985	Kansas City (W) 4, Toronto (E) 3
1984	San Diego (W) 4, Chicago (E) 2		1984	Detroit (E) 3, Kansas City (W) 0
1983	Philadelphia (E) 3, Los Angeles (W) 1		1983	Baltimore (E) 3, Chicago (W) 1
1982	St. Louis (E) 3, Atlanta (W) 0		1982	Milwaukee (E) 3, California (W) 2
1981	Los Angeles (W) 3, Montreal (E) 2		1981	New York (E) 3, Oakland (W) 0
1980	Philadelphia (E) 3, Houston (W) 2		1980	Kansas City (W) 3, New York (E) 0
1979	Pittsburgh (E) 3, Cincinnati (W) 0		1979	Baltimore (E) 3, California (W) 1
1978	Los Angeles (W) 3, Philadelphia (E) 1		1978	New York (E) 3, Kansas City (W) 1
1977	Los Angeles (W) 3, Philadelphia (E) 1		1977	New York (E) 3, Kansas City (W) 2
1976	Cincinnati (W) 3, Philadelphia (E) 0		1976	New York (E) 3, Kansas City (W) 2
1975	Cincinnati (W) 3, Pittsburgh (E) 0		1975	Boston (E) 3, Oakland (W) 0
1974	Los Angeles (W) 3, Pittsburgh (E) 1		1974	Oakland (W) 3, Baltimore (E) 1
1973	New York (E) 3, Cincinnati (W) 2		1973	Oakland (W) 3, Baltimore (E) 2
1972	Cincinnati (W) 3, Pittsburgh (E) 2		1972	Oakland (W) 3, Detroit (E) 2
1971	Pittsburgh (E) 3, San Francisco (W) 1		1971	Baltimore (E) 3, Oakland (W) 0
1970	Cincinnati (W) 3, Pittsburgh (E) 0		1970	Baltimore (E) 3, Minnesota (W) 0
1969	New York (E) 3, Atlanta (W) 0		1969	Baltimore (E) 3, Minnesota (W) 0

Note: WC=wild-card team; W=Western Division; E=Eastern Division; C=Central Division

NLCS Most Valuable Player

2002	Benito Santiago, SF	1993	Curt Schilling, Phil	1984	Steve Garvey, SD
2001	Craig Counsell, Ariz	1992	John Smoltz, Atl	1983	Gary Matthews, Phil
2000	Mike Hampton, NY	1991	Steve Avery, Atl	1982	Darrell Porter, StL
1999	Eddie Perez, Atl	1990	R. Myers/R. Dibble, Cin	1981	Burt Hooton, LA
1998	Sterling Hitchcock, SD	1989	Will Clark, SF	1980	Manny Trillo, Phil
1997	Livan Hernandez, Fla	1988	Orel Hershiser, LA	1979	Willie Stargell, Pitt
1996	Javier Lopez, Atl	1987	Jeffrey Leonard, SF	1978	Steve Garvey, LA
1995	Mike Devereaux, Atl	1986	Mike Scott, Hou	1977	Dusty Baker, LA
1994	Playoffs canceled	1985	Ozzie Smith, StL		

ALCS Most Valuable Player

2002	Adam Kennedy, Ana	1994	Playoffs canceled	1986	Marty Barrett, Bos
2001	Andy Pettitte, NY	1993	Dave Stewart, Tor	1985	George Brett, KC
2000	David Justice, NY	1992	Roberto Alomar, Tor	1984	Kirk Gibson, Det
1999	Orlando Hernandez, NY	1991	Kirby Puckett, Minn	1983	Mike Boddicker, Balt
1998	David Wells, NY	1990	Dave Stewart, Oak	1982	Fred Lynn, Calif
1997	Marquis Grissom, Clev	1989	Rickey Henderson, Oak	1981	Graig Nettles, NY
1996	Bernie Williams, NY	1988	Dennis Eckersley, Oak	1980	Frank White, KC
1995	Orel Hershiser, Clev	1987	Gary Gaetti, Minn		

All-Star Game

Date	Winner	Score	Site	Date	Winner	Score	Site
7-15-03	American	7–6	U.S. Cellular Field, Chi	7-7-64	National	7–4	Shea Stadium, NY
7-9-02	Tie (11 inn)	7–7	Miller Park, Milwaukee	7-9-63	National	5–3	Municipal Stadium, Clev
7-10-01	American	4–1	Safeco Field, Sea	7-30-62	American	9–4	Wrigley Field, Chi
7-11-00	American	6–3	Turner Field, Atl	7-10-62	National	3–1	D.C. Stadium, Wash
7-13-99	American	4–1	Fenway Park, Bos	7-31-61	Tie*	1–1	Fenway Park, Bos
7-7-98	American	13–8	Coors Field, Col	7-11-61	National	5–4	Candlestick Park, SF
7-8-97	American	3–1	Jacobs Field, Clev	7-13-60	National	6–0	Yankee Stadium, NY
7-9-96	National	6–0	Veterans Stadium, Phil	7-11-60	National	5–3	Municipal Stadium, KC
7-11-95	National	3–2	The Ballpark in Arlington, Tex	8-3-59	American	5–3	Memorial Coliseum, LA
				7-7-59	National	5–4	Forbes Field, Pitt
7-12-94	National	8–7	Three Rivers Stadium, Pitt	7-8-58	American	4–3	Memorial Stadium, Balt
7-13-93	American	9–3	Camden Yards, Balt	7-9-57	American	6–5	Busch Stadium, StL
7-14-92	American	13–6	Jack Murphy Stadium, SD	7-10-56	National	7–3	Griffith Stadium, Wash
7-9-91	American	4–2	SkyDome, Tor	7-12-55	National	6–5	County Stadium, Mil
7-10-90	American	2–0	Wrigley Field, Chi	7-13-54	American	11–9	Municipal Stadium, Clev
7-11-89	American	5–3	Anaheim Stadium, Cal	7-14-53	National	5–1	Crosley Field, Cin
7-12-88	American	2–1	Riverfront Stadium, Cin	7-8-52	National	3–2	Shibe Park, Phil
7-14-87	National	2–0	Oakland Coliseum, Oak	7-10-51	National	8–3	Briggs Stadium, Det
7-15-86	American	3–2	Astrodome, Hou	7-11-50	National	4–3	Comiskey Park, Chi
7-16-85	National	6–1	Metrodome, Minn	7-12-49	American	11–7	Ebbets Field, Bklyn
7-10-84	National	3–1	Candlestick Park, SF	7-13-48	American	5–2	Sportsman's Park, StL
7-6-83	American	13–3	Comiskey Park, Chi	7-8-47	American	2–1	Wrigley Field, Chi
7-13-82	National	4–1	Olympic Stadium, Mtl	7-9-46	American	12–0	Fenway Park, Bos
8-9-81	National	5–4	Municipal Stadium, Clev	1945	No game due to wartime travel restrictions.		
7-8-80	National	4–2	Dodger Stadium, LA	7-11-44	National	7–1	Forbes Field, Pitt
7-17-79	National	7–6	Kingdome, Sea	7-13-43	American	5–3	Shibe Park, Phil
7-11-78	National	7–3	Jack Murphy Stadium, SD	7-6-42	American	3–1	Polo Grounds, NY
7-19-77	National	7–5	Yankee Stadium, NY	7-8-41	American	7–5	Briggs Stadium, Det
7-13-76	National	7–1	Veterans Stadium, Phil	7-10-40	National	4–0	Sportsman's Park, StL
7-15-75	National	6–3	County Stadium, Mil	7-11-39	American	3–1	Yankee Stadium, NY
7-23-74	National	7–2	Three Rivers Stadium, Pitt	7-6-38	National	4–1	Crosley Field, Cin
7-24-73	National	7–1	Royals Stadium, KC	7-7-37	American	8–3	Griffith Stadium, Wash
7-25-72	National	4–3	Atlanta Stadium, Atl	7-7-36	National	4–3	Braves Field, Bos
7-13-71	American	6–4	Tiger Stadium, Det	7-8-35	American	4–1	Municipal Stadium, Clev
7-14-70	National	5–4	Riverfront Stadium, Cin	7-10-34	American	9–7	Polo Grounds, NY
7-23-69	National	9–3	R.F.K. Memorial Stadium, Wash	7-6-33	American	4–2	Comiskey Park, Chi
7-9-68	National	1–0	Astrodome, Hou				
7-11-67	National	2–1	Anaheim Stadium, Cal				
7-12-66	National	2–1	Busch Stadium, StL				
7-13-65	National	6–5	Metropolitan Stadium, Minn				

Did You Know?

Between 1959 and 1962, two All-Star Games were played each year. The reason? Money. Revenue made from the games was divided among the players' pension fund, youth baseball, and older players who had played before the pension plan was started.

*Game called because of rain after nine innings.

All-Star Game
Most Valuable Players

Year	Name and Team	League	Year	Name and Team	League	Year	Name and Team	League
2003	Garret Anderson, Ana	AL	1988	Terry Steinbach, Oak	AL	1974	Steve Garvey, LA	NL
2002	Not selected		1987	Tim Raines, Mtl	NL	1973	Bobby Bonds, SF	NL
2001	Cal Ripken Jr., Balt	AL	1986	Roger Clemens, Bos	AL	1972	Joe Morgan, Cin	NL
2000	Derek Jeter, NY	AL	1985	LaMarr Hoyt, SD	NL	1971	Frank Robinson, Balt	AL
1999	Pedro Martinez, Bos	AL	1984	Gary Carter, Mtl	NL	1970	Carl Yastrzemski, Bos	AL
1998	Roberto Alomar, Balt	AL	1983	Fred Lynn, Calif	AL	1969	Willie McCovey, SF	NL
1997	Sandy Alomar, Clev	AL	1982	Dave Concepcion, Cin	NL	1968	Willie Mays, SF	NL
1996	Mike Piazza, LA	NL	1981	Gary Carter, Mtl	NL	1967	Tony Perez, Cin	NL
1995	Jeff Conine, Fla	NL	1980	Ken Griffey, Cin	NL	1966	Brooks Robinson, Balt	AL
1994	Fred McGriff, Atl	NL	1979	Dave Parker, Pitt	NL	1965	Juan Marichal, SF	NL
1993	Kirby Puckett, Minn	AL	1978	Steve Garvey, LA	NL	1964	Johnny Callison, Phil	NL
1992	Ken Griffey Jr., Sea	AL	1977	Don Sutton, LA	NL	1963	Willie Mays, SF	NL
1991	Cal Ripken Jr., Balt	AL	1976	George Foster, Cin	NL	1962	Maury Wills, LA	NL
1990	Julio Franco, Tex	AL	1975	Bill Madlock, Chi	NL		Leon Wagner, LA	AL
1989	Bo Jackson, KC	AL		Jon Matlack, NY	NL			

Trivia Challenge

The 2002 All-Star Game was declared a tie after 11 innings because both sides ran out of pitchers. There has been only one other tie in All-Star Game history. Name it.

In 1961, the game was called because of rain after nine innings. The American League and National League were tied, 1–1.

Regular Season
Most Valuable Players

NATIONAL LEAGUE

Year	Name and Team	Position	Year	Name and Team	Position
2002	Barry Bonds, SF	Outfield	1965	Willie Mays, SF	Outfield
2001	Barry Bonds, SF	Outfield	1964	Ken Boyer, StL	Third Base
2000	Jeff Kent, SF	Second Base	1963	Sandy Koufax, LA	Pitcher
1999	Chipper Jones, Atl	Third Base	1962	Maury Wills, LA	Shortstop
1998	Sammy Sosa, Chi	Outfield	1961	Frank Robinson, Cin	Outfield
1997	Larry Walker, Col	Outfield	1960	Dick Groat, Pitt	Shortstop
1996	Ken Caminiti, SD	Third base	1959	Ernie Banks, Chi	Shortstop
1995	Barry Larkin, Cin	Shortstop	1958	Ernie Banks, Chi	Shortstop
1994	Jeff Bagwell, Hou	First base	1957	Hank Aaron, Mil	Outfield
1993	Barry Bonds, SF	Outfield	1956	Don Newcombe, Bklyn	Pitcher
1992	Barry Bonds, Pitt	Outfield	1955	Roy Campanella, Bklyn	Catcher
1991	Terry Pendleton, Atl	Third base	1954	Willie Mays, NY	Outfield
1990	Barry Bonds, Pitt	Outfield	1953	Roy Campanella, Bklyn	Catcher
1989	Kevin Mitchell, SF	Outfield	1952	Hank Sauer, Chi	Outfield
1988	Kirk Gibson, LA	Outfield	1951	Roy Campanella, Bklyn	Catcher
1987	Andre Dawson, Chi	Outfield	1950	Jim Konstanty, Phil	Pitcher
1986	Mike Schmidt, Phil	Third base	1949	Jackie Robinson, Bklyn	Second base
1985	Willie McGee, StL	Outfield	1948	Stan Musial, StL	Outfield
1984	Ryne Sandberg, Chi	Second base	1947	Bob Elliott, Bos	Third base
1983	Dale Murphy, Atl	Outfield	1946	Stan Musial, StL	First base, Outfield
1982	Dale Murphy, Atl	Outfield	1945	Phil Cavarretta, Chi	First base
1981	Mike Schmidt, Phil	Third base	1944	Marty Marion, StL	Shortstop
1980	Mike Schmidt, Phil	Third base	1943	Stan Musial, StL	Outfield
1979	Keith Hernandez, StL	First base	1942	Mort Cooper, StL	Pitcher
	Willie Stargell, Pitt	First base	1941	Dolph Camilli, Bklyn	First base
1978	Dave Parker, Pitt	Outfield	1940	Frank McCormick, Cin	First base
1977	George Foster, Cin	Outfield	1939	Bucky Walters, Cin	Pitcher
1976	Joe Morgan, Cin	Second base	1938	Ernie Lombardi, Cin	Catcher
1975	Joe Morgan, Cin	Second base	1937	Joe Medwick, StL	Outfield
1974	Steve Garvey, LA	First base	1936	Carl Hubbell, NY	Pitcher
1973	Pete Rose, Cin	Outfield	1935	Gabby Hartnett, Chi	Catcher
1972	Johnny Bench, Cin	Catcher	1934	Dizzy Dean, StL	Pitcher
1971	Joe Torre, StL	Third base	1933	Carl Hubbell, NY	Pitcher
1970	Johnny Bench, Cin	Catcher	1932	Chuck Klein, Phil	Outfield
1969	Willie McCovey, SF	First base	1931	Frankie Frisch, StL	Second base
1968	Bob Gibson, StL	Pitcher	1930	No selection	
1967	Orlando Cepeda, StL	First base	1929	Rogers Hornsby, Chi	Second base
1966	Roberto Clemente, Pitt	Outfield	1928	Jim Bottomley, StL	First base

Regular Season
Most Valuable Players (cont.)

Miguel Tejada of the A's was 2002 A.L. MVP.

Year	Name and Team	Position
1927	Paul Waner, Pitt	Outfield
1926	Bob O'Farrell, StL	Catcher
1925	Rogers Hornsby, StL	Second base, Manager
1924	Dazzy Vance, Bklyn	Pitcher
1915-23	No selections	
1914	Johnny Evers, Bos	Second base
1913	Jake Daubert, Bklyn	First base
1912	Larry Doyle, NY	Second base
1911	Wildfire Schulte, Chi	Outfield

AMERICAN LEAGUE

Year	Name and Team	Position
2002	Miguel Tejada, Oak	Shortstop
2001	Ichiro Suzuki, Sea	Outfield
2000	Jason Giambi, Oak	First Base
1999	Ivan Rodriguez, Tex	Catcher
1998	Juan Gonzalez, Tex	Outfield
1997	Ken Griffey Jr., Sea	Outfield
1996	Juan Gonzalez, Tex	Outfield
1995	Mo Vaughn, Bos	First base
1994	Frank Thomas, Chi	First base
1993	Frank Thomas, Chi	First base
1992	Dennis Eckersley, Oak	Pitcher
1991	Cal Ripken, Jr., Balt	Shortstop
1990	Rickey Henderson, Oak	Outfield
1989	Robin Yount, Mil	Outfield
1988	Jose Canseco, Oak	Outfield
1987	George Bell, Tor	Outfield
1986	Roger Clemens, Bos	Pitcher
1985	Don Mattingly, NY	First base
1984	Willie Hernandez, Det	Pitcher
1983	Cal Ripken, Jr., Balt	Shortstop
1982	Robin Yount, Mil	Shortstop
1981	Rollie Fingers, Mil	Pitcher
1980	George Brett, KC	Third base
1979	Don Baylor, Calif	Outfield, DH
1978	Jim Rice, Bos	Outfield, DH
1977	Rod Carew, Minn	First base

Year	Name and Team	Position
1976	Thurman Munson, NY	Catcher
1975	Fred Lynn, Bos	Outfield
1974	Jeff Burroughs, Tex	Outfield
1973	Reggie Jackson, Oak	Outfield
1972	Dick Allen, Chi	First base
1971	Vida Blue, Oak	Pitcher
1970	Boog Powell, Balt	First base
1969	Harmon Killebrew, Minn	Third base, First base
1968	Denny McLain, Det	Pitcher
1967	Carl Yastrzemski, Bos	Outfield
1966	Frank Robinson, Balt	Outfield
1965	Zoilo Versalles, Minn	Shortstop
1964	Brooks Robinson, Balt	Third base
1963	Elston Howard, NY	Catcher
1962	Mickey Mantle, NY	Outfield
1961	Roger Maris, NY	Outfield
1960	Roger Maris, NY	Outfield
1959	Nellie Fox, Chi	Second base
1958	Jackie Jensen, Bos	Outfield
1957	Mickey Mantle, NY	Outfield
1956	Mickey Mantle, NY	Outfield
1955	Yogi Berra, NY	Catcher
1954	Yogi Berra, NY	Catcher
1953	Al Rosen, Clev	Third base
1952	Bobby Shantz, Phil	Pitcher
1951	Yogi Berra, NY	Catcher
1950	Phil Rizzuto, NY	Shortstop
1949	Ted Williams, Bos	Outfield
1948	Lou Boudreau, Clev	Shortstop
1947	Joe DiMaggio, NY	Outfield
1946	Ted Williams, Bos	Outfield
1945	Hal Newhouser, Det	Pitcher
1944	Hal Newhouser, Det	Pitcher
1943	Spud Chandler, NY	Pitcher
1942	Joe Gordon, NY	Second base
1941	Joe DiMaggio, NY	Outfield
1940	Hank Greenberg, Det	Outfield
1939	Joe DiMaggio, NY	Outfield
1938	Jimmie Foxx, Bos	First base
1937	Charlie Gehringer, Det	Second base
1936	Lou Gehrig, NY	First base
1935	Hank Greenberg, Det	First base
1934	Mickey Cochrane, Det	Catcher
1933	Jimmie Foxx, Phil	First base
1932	Jimmie Foxx, Phil	First base
1931	Lefty Grove, Phil	Pitcher
1930	No selection	
1929	No selection	
1928	Mickey Cochrane, Phil	Catcher
1927	Lou Gehrig, NY	First base
1926	George Burns, Clev	First base
1925	Roger Peckinpaugh, Wash	Shortstop
1924	Walter Johnson, Wash	Pitcher
1923	Babe Ruth, NY	Outfield
1922	George Sisler, StL	First base
1915-21	No selections	
1914	Eddie Collins, Phil	Second base
1913	Walter Johnson, Wash	Pitcher
1912	Tris Speaker, Bos	Outfield
1911	Ty Cobb, Det	Outfield

The Regular Season
Rookies of the Year

NATIONAL LEAGUE		AMERICAN LEAGUE	
2002	Jason Jennings, Col (P)	2002	Eric Hinske, Tor (3B)
2001	Albert Pujols, StL (OF)	2001	Ichiro Suzuki, Sea (OF)
2000	Rafael Furcal, Atl (SS)	2000	Kazuhiro Sasaki, Sea (P)
1999	Scott Williamson, Cin (P)	1999	Carlos Beltran, KC (OF)
1998	Kerry Wood, Chi (P)	1998	Ben Grieve, Oak (OF)
1997	Scott Rolen, Phil (3B)	1997	Nomar Garciaparra, Bos (SS)
1996	Todd Hollandsworth, LA (OF)	1996	Derek Jeter, NY (SS)
1995	Hideo Nomo, LA (P)	1995	Marty Cordova, Minn (OF)
1994	Raul Mondesi, LA (OF)	1994	Bob Hamelin, KC (DH)
1993	Mike Piazza, LA (C)	1993	Tim Salmon, Calif (OF)
1992	Eric Karros, LA (1B)	1992	Pat Listach, Mil (SS)
1991	Jeff Bagwell, Hou (3B)	1991	Chuck Knoblauch, Minn (2B)
1990	Dave Justice, Atl (OF)	1990	Sandy Alomar Jr, Clev (C)
1989	Jerome Walton, Chi (OF)	1989	Gregg Olson, Balt (P)
1988	Chris Sabo, Cin (3B)	1988	Walt Weiss, Oak (SS)
1987	Benito Santiago, SD (C)	1987	Mark McGwire, Oak (1B)
1986	Todd Worrell, StL (P)	1986	Jose Canseco, Oak (OF)
1985	Vince Coleman, StL (OF)	1985	Ozzie Guillen, Chi (SS)
1984	Dwight Gooden, NY (P)	1984	Alvin Davis, Sea (1B)
1983	Darryl Strawberry, NY (OF)	1983	Ron Kittle, Chi (OF)
1982	Steve Sax, LA (2B)	1982	Cal Ripken, Jr., Balt (SS)
1981	Fernando Valenzuela, LA (P)	1981	Dave Righetti, NY (P)
1980	Steve Howe, LA (P)	1980	Joe Charboneau, Clev (OF)
1979	Rick Sutcliffe, LA (P)	1979	Alfredo Griffin, Tor (SS)
1978	Bob Horner, Atl (3B)		John Castino, Minn (3B)
1977	Andre Dawson, Mtl (OF)	1978	Lou Whitaker, Det (2B)
1976	Pat Zachry, Cin (P)	1977	Eddie Murray, Balt (DH)
	Butch Metzger, SD (P)	1976	Mark Fidrych, Det (P)
1975	John Montefusco, SF (P)	1975	Fred Lynn, Bos (OF)
1974	Bake McBride, StL (OF)	1974	Mike Hargrove, Tex (1B)
1973	Gary Matthews, SF (OF)	1973	Al Bumbry, Balt (OF)
1972	Jon Matlack, NY (P)	1972	Carlton Fisk, Bos (C)
1971	Earl Williams, Atl (C)	1971	Chris Chambliss, Clev (1B)
1970	Carl Morton, Mtl (P)	1970	Thurman Munson, NY (C)
1969	Ted Sizemore, LA (2B)	1969	Lou Piniella, KC (OF)
1968	Johnny Bench, Cin (C)	1968	Stan Bahnsen, NY (P)
1967	Tom Seaver, NY (P)	1967	Rod Carew, Minn (2B)
1966	Tommy Helms, Cin (2B)	1966	Tommie Agee, Chi (OF)
1965	Jim Lefebvre, LA (2B)	1965	Curt Blefary, Balt (OF)
1964	Dick Allen, Phil (3B)	1964	Tony Oliva, Minn (OF)
1963	Pete Rose, Cin (2B)	1963	Gary Peters, Chi (P)
1962	Ken Hubbs, Chi (2B)	1962	Tom Tresh, NY (SS)
1961	Billy Williams, Chi (OF)	1961	Don Schwall, Bos (P)
1960	Frank Howard, LA (OF)	1960	Ron Hansen, Balt (SS)
1959	Willie McCovey, SF (1B)	1959	Bob Allison, Wash (OF)
1958	Orlando Cepeda, SF (1B)	1958	Albie Pearson, Wash (OF)
1957	Jack Sanford, Phil (P)	1957	Tony Kubek, NY (OF, SS)
1956	Frank Robinson, Cin (OF)	1956	Luis Aparicio, Chi (SS)
1955	Bill Virdon, StL (OF)	1955	Herb Score, Clev (P)
1954	Wally Moon, StL (OF)	1954	Bob Grim, NY (P)
1953	Junior Gilliam, Bklyn (2B)	1953	Harvey Kuenn, Det (SS)
1952	Joe Black, Bklyn (P)	1952	Harry Byrd, Phil (P)
1951	Willie Mays, NY (OF)	1951	Gil McDougald, NY (3B)
1950	Sam Jethroe, Bos (OF)	1950	Walt Dropo, Bos (1B)
1949	Don Newcombe, Bklyn (P)	1949	Roy Sievers, StL (OF)
* 1948	Alvin Dark, Bos (SS)		
* 1947	Jackie Robinson, Bklyn (1B)		

*Just one selection for both leagues

BASEBALL

The Regular Season
Cy Young Award Winners

National League

Year	Pitcher	W–L	Sv	ERA
2002	Randy Johnson, Ariz	24–5	0	2.32
2001	Randy Johnson, Ariz	21–6	0	2.49
2000	Randy Johnson, Ariz	19–7	0	2.64
1999	Randy Johnson, Ariz	17–9	0	2.48
1998	Tom Glavine, Atl	20–6	0	2.47
1997	Pedro Martinez, Mtl	17–8	0	1.90
1996	John Smoltz, Atl	24–8	0	2.94
1995	Greg Maddux, Atl	19–2	0	1.63
1994	Greg Maddux, Atl	16–6	0	1.56
1993	Greg Maddux, Atl	20–10	0	2.36
1992	Greg Maddux, Chi	20–11	0	2.18
1991	Tom Glavine, Atl	20–11	0	2.55
1990	Doug Drabek, Pitt	22–6	0	2.76
1989	Mark Davis, SD	4–3	44	1.85
1988	Orel Hershiser, LA	23–8	1	2.26
1987	Steve Bedrosian, Phil	5–3	40	2.83
1986	Mike Scott, Hou	18–10	0	2.22
1985	Dwight Gooden, NY	24–4	0	1.53
1984	†Rick Sutcliffe, Chi	16–1	0	2.69
1983	John Denny, Phil	19–6	0	2.37
1982	Steve Carlton, Phil	23–11	0	3.10
1981	Fernando Valenzuela, LA	13–7	0	2.48
1980	Steve Carlton, Phil	24–9	0	2.34
1979	Bruce Sutter, Chi	6–6	37	2.23
1978	Gaylord Perry, SD	21–6	0	2.72
1977	Steve Carlton, Phil	23–10	0	2.64
1976	Randy Jones, SD	22–14	0	2.74
1975	Tom Seaver, NY	22–9	0	2.38
1974	Mike Marshall, LA	15–12	21	2.42
1973	Tom Seaver, NY	19–10	0	2.08
1972	Steve Carlton, Phil	27–10	0	1.97
1971	Ferguson Jenkins, Chi	24–13	0	2.77
1970	Bob Gibson, StL	23–7	0	3.12
1969	Tom Seaver, NY	25–7	0	2.21
1968	*Bob Gibson, StL	22–9	0	1.12
1967	Mike McCormick, SF	22–10	0	2.85

American League

Year	Pitcher	W–L	Sv	ERA
2002	Barry Zito, Oak	23–5	0	2.75
2001	Roger Clemens, NY	20–3	0	3.51
2000	Pedro Martinez, Bos	18–6	0	1.74
1999	Pedro Martinez, Bos	23–4	0	1.55
1998	Roger Clemens, Tor	20–6	0	2.65
1997	Roger Clemens, Tor	21–7	0	2.05
1996	Pat Hentgen, Tor	20–10	0	3.22
1995	Randy Johnson, Sea	18–2	0	2.48
1994	David Cone, KC	16–4	0	2.94
1993	Jack McDowell, Chi	22–10	0	3.37
1992	*Dennis Eckersley, Oak	7–1	51	1.91
1991	Roger Clemens, Bos	18–10	0	2.62
1990	Bob Welch, Oak	27–6	0	2.95
1989	Bret Saberhagen, KC	23–6	0	2.16
1988	Frank Viola, Minn	24–7	0	2.64
1987	Roger Clemens, Bos	20–9	0	2.97
1986	*Roger Clemens, Bos	24–4	0	2.48
1985	Bret Saberhagen, KC	20–6	0	2.87
1984	*Willie Hernandez, Det	9–3	32	1.92
1983	LaMarr Hoyt, Chi	24–10	0	3.66
1982	Pete Vuckovich, Mil	18–6	0	3.34
1981	*Rollie Fingers, Mil	6–3	28	1.04
1980	Steve Stone, Balt	25–7	0	3.23
1979	Mike Flanagan, Balt	23–9	0	3.08
1978	Ron Guidry, NY	25–3	0	1.74
1977	Sparky Lyle, NY	13–5	26	2.17
1976	Jim Palmer, Balt	22–13	0	2.51
1975	Jim Palmer, Balt	23–11	1	2.09
1974	Catfish Hunter, Oak	25–12	0	2.49
1973	Jim Palmer, Balt	22–9	1	2.40
1972	Gaylord Perry, Clev	24–16	1	1.92
1971	*Vida Blue, Oak	24–8	0	1.82
1970	Jim Perry, Minn	24–12	0	3.03
1969	Denny McLain, Det	24–9	0	2.80
	(tie) Mike Cuellar, Balt	23–11	0	2.38
1968	*Denny McLain, Det	31–6	0	1.96
1967	Jim Lonborg, Bos	22–9	0	3.16

Year	Pitcher**	W–L	Sv	ERA
1966	Sandy Koufax, LA (NL)	27–9	0	1.73
1965	Sandy Koufax, LA (NL)	26–8	2	2.04
1964	Dean Chance, LA (AL)	20–9	4	1.65
1963	*Sandy Koufax, LA (NL)	25–5	0	1.88
1962	Don Drysdale, LA (NL)	25–9	1	2.83
1961	Whitey Ford, NY (AL)	25–4	0	3.21
1960	Vernon Law, Pitt (NL)	20–9	0	3.08
1959	Early Wynn, Chi (AL)	22–10	0	3.17
1958	Bob Turley, NY (AL)	21–7	1	2.97
1957	Warren Spahn, Mil (NL)	21–11	3	2.69
1956	*Don Newcombe, Bklyn (NL)	27–7	0	3.06

* Won the MVP and Cy Young awards in the same season.
** One award presented for both leagues.
† NL games only. Sutcliffe pitched 15 games with Cleveland before being traded to the Cubs.

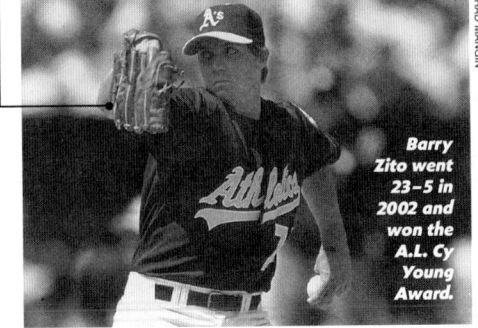

Barry Zito went 23–5 in 2002 and won the A.L. Cy Young Award.

BRAD MANGIN

The Regular Season
Career Individual Batting

Hank Aaron is the career leader in home runs (755).

HARRY HARRIS/AP

Lou Brock	10,332
Cap Anson	10,278
Luis Aparicio	10,230
Tris Speaker	10,208
Al Kaline	10,116

HOME RUNS

Hank Aaron	755
Babe Ruth	714
Willie Mays	660
*Barry Bonds	613
Frank Robinson	586
Mark McGwire	583
Harmon Killebrew	573
Reggie Jackson	563
Mike Schmidt	548
Mickey Mantle	536
Jimmie Foxx	534
Ted Williams	521
Willie McCovey	521
Eddie Mathews	512
Ernie Banks	512
Mel Ott	511
Eddie Murray	504
*Sammy Sosa	499
Lou Gehrig	493
*Rafael Palmeiro	490

HITS

Pete Rose	4,256
Ty Cobb	4,189
Hank Aaron	3,771
Stan Musial	3,630
Tris Speaker	3,515
Carl Yastrzemski	3,419
Cap Anson	3,418
Honus Wagner	3,415
Paul Molitor	3,319
Eddie Collins	3,313
Willie Mays	3,283
Eddie Murray	3,255
Nap Lajoie	3,251
Cal Ripken, Jr.	3,184
George Brett	3,154
Paul Waner	3,152
Robin Yount	3,142
Tony Gwynn	3,141
Dave Winfield	3,110
Rod Carew	3,053

BATTING AVERAGE (5,000 AB)

Ty Cobb	.367
Rogers Hornsby	.358
Ed Delahanty	.346
Tris Speaker	.345
Ted Williams	.344
Billy Hamilton	.344
Dan Brouthers	.342
Jesse Burkett	.342
Babe Ruth	.342
Harry Heilmann	.342
Willie Keeler	.341
Bill Terry	.341
George Sisler	.340

Lou Gehrig	.340
Jesse Burkett	.338
Tony Gwynn	.338
Nap Lajoie	.338
Al Simmons	.334
Paul Waner	. .333
Eddie Collins	.333

RUNS

*Rickey Henderson	2,288
Ty Cobb	2,245
Babe Ruth	2,174
Hank Aaron	2,174
Pete Rose	2,165
Willie Mays	2,062
Cap Anson	1,996
Stan Musial	1,949
Lou Gehrig	1,888
Tris Speaker	1,881
Mel Ott	1,859
*Barry Bonds	1,830
Frank Robinson	1,829
Eddie Collins	1,820
Carl Yastrzemski	1,816
Ted Williams	1,798
Paul Molitor	1,782
Charlie Gehringer	1,774
Jimmie Foxx	1,751
Honus Wagner	1,740

DOUBLES

Tris Speaker	793
Pete Rose	746
Stan Musial	725
Ty Cobb	724
George Brett	665
Nap Lajoie	657
Carl Yastrzemski	646
Honus Wagner	640
Hank Aaron	624
Paul Molitor	605
Paul Waner	604
Cal Ripken, Jr.	603
Robin Yount	583
Cap Anson	581
Wade Boggs	578
Charlie Gehringer	574
Eddie Murray	560
Tony Gwynn	543
Harry Heilmann	542
Rogers Hornsby	541

GAMES

Pete Rose	3,562
Carl Yastrzemski	3,308
Hank Aaron	3,298
*Rickey Henderson	3,051
Ty Cobb	3,034
Stan Musial	3,026
Eddie Murray	3,026
Cal Ripken, Jr.	3,001
Willie Mays	2,992
Dave Winfield	2,973
Rusty Staub	2,951
Brooks Robinson	2,896
Robin Yount	2,856
Al Kaline	2,834
Harold Baines	2,830
Eddie Collins	2,826
Reggie Jackson	2,820
Frank Robinson	2,808
Honus Wagner	2,792
Tris Speaker	2,789

AT-BATS

Pete Rose	14,053
Hank Aaron	12,364
Carl Yastrzemski	11,988
Cal Ripken, Jr.	11,551
Ty Cobb	11,429
Eddie Murray	11,336
Robin Yount	11,008
Dave Winfield	11,003
Stan Musial	10,972
*Rickey Henderson	10,889
Willie Mays	10,881
Paul Molitor	10,835
Brooks Robinson	10,654
Honus Wagner	10,427
George Brett	10,349

*Active in 2002.

Note: Stats were compiled after the 2002 season.

Visit **www.sikids.com** for the latest sports stats and info. Site code: slamdunk AOL keyword: sikids

Regular Season
Career Individual Batting (cont.)

TRIPLES	
Sam Crawford	312
Ty Cobb	297
Honus Wagner	252
Jake Beckley	244
Roger Connor	233
Tris Speaker	223
Fred Clarke	223
Dan Brouthers	206
Joe Kelley	194
Paul Waner	190
Bid McPhee	189
Eddie Collins	187
Ed Delahanty	185
Sam Rice	184
Jesse Burkett	182
Edd Roush	182
Ed Konetchy	182
Buck Ewing	178
Rabbit Maranville	177
Stan Musial	177

BASES ON BALLS	
*Rickey Henderson	2,179
Babe Ruth	2,062
Ted Williams	2,019
*Barry Bonds	1,922
Joe Morgan	1,865
Carl Yastrzemski	1,845
Mickey Mantle	1,735
Mel Ott	1,708
Eddie Yost	1,614
Darrell Evans	1,605
Stan Musial	1,599
Pete Rose	1,566
Harmon Killebrew	1,559
Lou Gehrig	1,508
Mike Schmidt	1,507
Eddie Collins	1,503
Willie Mays	1,463
Jimmie Foxx	1,452
Eddie Mathews	1,444
Frank Robinson	1,420

RUNS BATTED IN	
Hank Aaron	2,297
Babe Ruth	2,213
Cap Anson	2,076
Lou Gehrig	1,995
Stan Musial	1,951
Ty Cobb	1,937
Jimmie Foxx	1,922
Eddie Murray	1,917
Willie Mays	1,903
Mel Ott	1,860
Carl Yastrzemski	1,844
Ted Williams	1,839
Dave Winfield	1,833
Al Simmons	1,827
Frank Robinson	1,812

Honus Wagner	1,732
Reggie Jackson	1,702
Cal Ripken, Jr.	1,695
Tony Perez	1,652
*Barry Bonds	1,652

SLUGGING AVERAGE (5,000 AB)	
Babe Ruth	.690
Ted Williams	.634
Lou Gehrig	.632
Jimmie Foxx	.609
Hank Greenberg	.605
*Barry Bonds	.595
Mark McGwire	.588
Joe DiMaggio	.579
Rogers Hornsby	.577
*Mike Piazza	.575
*Larry Walker	.574
*Frank Thomas	.568
Albert Belle	.564
*Juan Gonzalez	.563
*Ken Griffey, Jr.	.562
Johnny Mize	.562
Stan Musial	.559
Willie Mays	.557
Mickey Mantle	.557
Hank Aaron	.555

STOLEN BASES	
*Rickey Henderson	1,403
Lou Brock	938
Billy Hamilton	912
Ty Cobb	892
*Tim Raines	808
Vince Coleman	752
Eddie Collins	744
Arlie Latham	739
Max Carey	738
Honus Wagner	722
Joe Morgan	689
Willie Wilson	668
Tom Brown	657
Bert Campaneris	649
Otis Nixon	620
George Davis	616
Dummy Hoy	594
Maury Wills	586
George Van Haltren	583
Ozzie Smith	580

ON-BASE PERCENTAGE (5,000 AB)	
Ted Williams	.482
Babe Ruth	.474
Billy Hamilton	.455
Lou Gehrig	.447
Rogers Hornsby	.434
Ty Cobb	.433
*Frank Thomas	.432
Jimmie Foxx	.428

Tris Speaker	.428
*Barry Bonds	.428
*Edgar Martinez	.424
Eddie Collins	.424
Dan Brouthers	.423
Mickey Mantle	.421
Mickey Cochrane	.419
Stan Musial	.417
Cupid Childs	.416
Jesse Burkett	.415
Wade Boggs	.415
*Jeff Bagwell	.414

TOTAL BASES	
Hank Aaron	6,856
Stan Musial	6,134
Willie Mays	6,066
Ty Cobb	5,854
Babe Ruth	5,793
Pete Rose	5,752
Carl Yastrzemski	5,539
Eddie Murray	5,397
Frank Robinson	5,373
Dave Winfield	5,221
Cal Ripken, Jr.	5,168
Tris Speaker	5,101
Lou Gehrig	5,060
George Brett	5,044
Mel Ott	5,041
*Barry Bonds	4,961
Jimmie Foxx	4,956
Ted Williams	4,884
Honus Wagner	4,862
Paul Molitor	4,854

STRIKEOUTS	
Reggie Jackson	2,597
Jose Canseco	1,942
*Andres Galarraga	1,939
Willie Stargell	1,936
Mike Schmidt	1,883
Tony Perez	1,867
*Sammy Sosa	1,832
Dave Kingman	1,816
*Fred McGriff	1,797
Bobby Bonds	1,757
Dale Murphy	1,748
Lou Brock	1,730
Mickey Mantle	1,710
Harmon Killebrew	1,699
Chili Davis	1,698
Dwight Evans	1,697
Dave Winfield	1,686
*Rickey Henderson	1,678
Gary Gaetti	1,602
Mark McGwire	1,596

*Active in 2002.

Regular Season
Career Individual Pitching

GAMES	
*Jesse Orosco	1,187
Dennis Eckersley	1,071
Hoyt Wilhelm	1,070
Kent Tekulve	1,050
*Dan Plesac	1,046
Lee Smith	1,022
Goose Gossage	1,002
*John Franco	998
Lindy McDaniel	987
*Mike Jackson	960
Rollie Fingers	944
Gene Garber	931
Cy Young	906
Sparky Lyle	899
Jim Kaat	898
Paul Assenmacher	884
Jeff Reardon	880
Don McMahon	874
Phil Niekro	864
Charlie Hough	858

INNINGS PITCHED	
Cy Young	7,356⅔
Pud Galvin	5,941⅓
Walter Johnson	5,914⅔
Phil Niekro	5,404⅓
Nolan Ryan	5,386
Gaylord Perry	5,350⅓
Don Sutton	5,282⅓
Warren Spahn	5,243⅔
Steve Carlton	5,217⅓
Grover Alexander	5,190
Kid Nichols	5,056⅓
Tim Keefe	5,047⅓
Bert Blyleven	4,970
Bobby Mathews	4,956
Mickey Welch	4,802
Tom Seaver	4,782⅔
Christy Mathewson	4,780⅔
Tommy John	4,710⅓
Robin Roberts	4,688⅔
Early Wynn	4,564

WINS	
Cy Young	511
Walter Johnson	417
Grover Alexander	373
Christy Mathewson	373
Pud Galvin	365
Warren Spahn	363
Kid Nichols	361
Tim Keefe	342
Steve Carlton	329
John Clarkson	328
Eddie Plank	326
Nolan Ryan	324
Don Sutton	324
Phil Niekro	318
Gaylord Perry	314
Tom Seaver	311
Charley Radbourn	309
Mickey Welch	307
Lefty Grove	300
Early Wynn	300

LOSSES	
Cy Young	316
Pud Galvin	308
Nolan Ryan	292
Walter Johnson	279
Phil Niekro	274
Gaylord Perry	265
Don Sutton	256
Jack Powell	254
Eppa Rixey	251
Bert Blyleven	250
Bobby Mathews	248
Robin Roberts	245
Warren Spahn	245
Steve Carlton	244
Early Wynn	244
Jim Kaat	237
Frank Tanana	236
Gus Weyhing	232
Tommy John	231
Bob Friend	230
Ted Lyons	230

WINNING PERCENTAGE**	
Al Spalding	.796
Spud Chandler	.717
*Pedro Martinez	.707
Whitey Ford	.690
Dave Foutz	.690
Bob Caruthers	.688
Don Gullett	.686
Lefty Grove	.680
*Randy Johnson	.679
Joe Wood	.671
Vic Raschi	.667
Larry Corcoran	.665
Christy Mathewson	.665
Sam Leever	.660
*Roger Clemens	.660
Sal Maglie	.658
Dick McBride	.656
Sandy Koufax	.655
Johnny Allen	.654
Ron Guidry	.651

SAVES	
Lee Smith	478
*John Franco	422
Dennis Eckersley	390
Jeff Reardon	367
*Trevor Hoffman	352
Randy Myers	347
Rollie Fingers	341
John Wetteland	330
*Roberto Hernandez	320
Rick Aguilera	318
*Robb Nen	314
Tom Henke	311
Goose Gossage	310
Jeff Montgomery	304
Doug Jones	303
Bruce Sutter	300
Rod Beck	266
Todd Worrell	256
Dave Righetti	252
*Troy Percival	250

EARNED RUN AVERAGE (2,000 IP)	
Ed Walsh	1.82
Addie Joss	1.89
Al Spalding	2.04
Three Finger Brown	2.06
John Ward	2.10
Christy Mathewson	2.13
Tommy Bond	2.14
Rube Waddell	2.16
Walter Johnson	2.17
Ed Reulbach	2.28
Will White	2.28
Eddie Plank	2.35
Larry Corcoran	2.36
Eddie Cicotte	2.38
Candy Cummings	2.39
Doc White	2.39
Nap Rucker	2.42
George Bradley	2.43
Jim McCormick	2.43
Chief Bender	2.46

SHUTOUTS	
Walter Johnson	110
Grover Alexander	90
Christy Mathewson	79
Cy Young	76
Eddie Plank	69
Warren Spahn	63
Nolan Ryan	61
Tom Seaver	61
Bert Blyleven	60
Don Sutton	58
Pud Galvin	57
Ed Walsh	57
Bob Gibson	56
Three Finger Brown	55
Steve Carlton	55
Jim Palmer	53
Gaylord Perry	53
Juan Marichal	52
Rube Waddell	50
Vic Willis	50

COMPLETE GAMES	
Cy Young	749
Pud Galvin	639
Tim Keefe	554
Walter Johnson	531
Kid Nichols	531
Mickey Welch	525
Bobby Mathews	525
Charley Radbourn	489
John Clarkson	485
Tony Mullane	468
Jim McCormick	466
Gus Weyhing	448
Grover Alexander	437
Christy Mathewson	434
Jack Powell	422
Eddie Plank	410
Will White	394
Amos Rusie	392
Vic Willis	388
Tommy Bond	386

*Active in 2002. **Minimum 100 victories.

Regular Season
Career Individual Pitching (cont.)

STRIKEOUTS	
Nolan Ryan	5,714
Steve Carlton	4,136
*Roger Clemens	3,909
*Randy Johnson	3,746
Bert Blyleven	3,701
Tom Seaver	3,640
Don Sutton	3,574
Gaylord Perry	3,534
Walter Johnson	3,509
Phil Niekro	3,342
Ferguson Jenkins	3,192
Bob Gibson	3,117
Jim Bunning	2,855
Mickey Lolich	2,832
Cy Young	2,803

Frank Tanana	2,773
David Cone	2,655
*Greg Maddux	2,641
*Chuck Finley	2,610
Warren Spahn	2,583

BASES ON BALLS	
Nolan Ryan	2,795
Steve Carlton	1,833
Phil Niekro	1,809
Early Wynn	1,775
Bob Feller	1,764
Bobo Newsom	1,732
Amos Rusie	1,704
Charlie Hough	1,665
Gus Weyhing	1,566
Red Ruffing	1,541

Bump Hadley	1,442
Warren Spahn	1,434
Earl Whitehill	1,431
Tony Mullane	1,408
Sad Sam Jones	1,396
Jack Morris	1,390
Tom Seaver	1,390
Gaylord Perry	1,379
Bobby Witt	1,375
Mike Torrez	1,371

□▷**Random Fact:**
On April 30, 2002, Al Leiter of the New York Mets beat the Arizona Diamondbacks, 10–1. The win made him the only pitcher to beat all 30 major league teams at least once during his career.

Individual Batting, Single Season

HITS	
George Sisler, 1920	257
Lefty O'Doul, 1929	254
Bill Terry, 1930	254
Al Simmons, 1925	253
Rogers Hornsby, 1922	250
Chuck Klein, 1930	250
Ty Cobb, 1911	248
George Sisler, 1922	246
Ichiro Suzuki, 2001	242
Heinie Manush, 1928	241
Babe Herman, 1930	241

BATTING AVERAGE	
Hugh Duffy, 1894	.440
Tip O'Neill, 1887	.435
Ross Barnes, 1876	.429
Nap Lajoie, 1901	.426
Willie Keeler, 1897	.424
Rogers Hornsby, 1924	.424
George Sisler, 1922	.420
Ty Cobb, 1911	.420
Fred Dunlap, 1884	.412
Ed Delahanty, 1899	.410

DOUBLES	
Earl Webb, 1931	67
George Burns, 1926	64
Joe Medwick, 1936	64
Hank Greenberg, 1934	63
Paul Waner, 1932	62
Charlie Gehringer, 1936	60
Tris Speaker, 1923	59
Chuck Klein, 1930	59
Todd Helton, 2000	59
Billy Herman, 1936	57
Billy Herman, 1935	57
Carlos Delgado, 2000	57

TRIPLES	
Chief Wilson, 1912	36
Dave Orr, 1886	31
Heinie Reitz, 1894	31
Perry Werden, 1893	29
Harry Davis, 1897	28
George Davis, 1893	27
Sam Thompson, 1894	27
Jimmy Williams, 1899	27
John Reilly, 1890	26
George Treadway, 1894	26
Joe Jackson, 1912	26
Sam Crawford, 1914	26
Kiki Cuyler, 1925	26

HOME RUNS	
Barry Bonds, 2001	73
Mark McGwire, 1998	70
Sammy Sosa, 1998	66
Mark McGwire, 1999	65
Sammy Sosa, 2001	64
Sammy Sosa, 1999	63
Roger Maris, 1961	61
Babe Ruth, 1927	60
Babe Ruth, 1921	59
Jimmie Foxx, 1932	58
Hank Greenberg, 1938	58
Mark McGwire, 1997	58

TOTAL BASES	
Babe Ruth, 1921	457
Rogers Hornsby, 1922	450
Lou Gehrig, 1927	447
Chuck Klein, 1930	445
Jimmie Foxx, 1932	438
Stan Musial, 1948	429
Sammy Sosa, 2001	425
Hack Wilson, 1930	423
Chuck Klein, 1932	420
Luis Gonzalez, 2001	419
Lou Gehrig, 1930	419

RUNS BATTED IN	
Hack Wilson, 1930	190
Lou Gehrig, 1931	184
Hank Greenberg, 1937	183
Lou Gehrig, 1927	175
Jimmie Foxx, 1938	175
Lou Gehrig, 1930	174
Babe Ruth, 1921	171
Chuck Klein, 1930	170
Hank Greenberg, 1935	170
Jimmie Foxx, 1932	169

STRIKEOUTS	
Bobby Bonds, 1970	189
Jose Hernandez, 2002	188
Bobby Bonds, 1969	187
Preston Wilson, 2000	187
Rob Deer, 1987	186
Jose Hernandez, 2001	185
Jim Thome, 2001	185
Pete Incaviglia, 1986	185
Cecil Fielder, 1990	182
Mo Vaughn, 2000	181

RUNS	
Billy Hamilton, 1894	192
Tom Brown, 1891	177
Babe Ruth, 1921	177
Tip O'Neill, 1887	167
Lou Gehrig, 1936	167
Billy Hamilton, 1895	166
Willie Keeler, 1894	165
Joe Kelley, 1894	165
Arlie Latham, 1887	163
Babe Ruth, 1928	163
Lou Gehrig, 1931	163

Regular Season
Individual Batting, Single Season (cont.)

STOLEN BASES		BASES ON BALLS		SLUGGING AVERAGE	
Hugh Nicol, 1887	138	Barry Bonds, 2002	198	Barry Bonds, 2001	.863
Rickey Henderson, 1982	130	Barry Bonds, 2001	177	Babe Ruth, 1920	.847
Arlie Latham, 1887	129	Babe Ruth, 1923	170	Babe Ruth, 1921	.846
Lou Brock, 1974	118	Ted Williams, 1947	162	Barry Bonds, 2002	.799
Charlie Comiskey, 1887	117	Ted Williams, 1949	162	Babe Ruth, 1927	.772
John Ward, 1887	111	Mark McGwire, 1998	162	Lou Gehrig, 1927	.765
Billy Hamilton, 1889	111	Ted Williams, 1946	156	Babe Ruth, 1923	.764
Billy Hamilton, 1891	111	Eddie Yost, 1956	151	Rogers Hornsby, 1925	.756
Vince Coleman, 1985	110	Eddie Joost, 1949	149	Mark McGwire, 1998	.752
Arlie Latham, 1888	109	Jeff Bagwell, 1999	149	Jeff Bagwell, 1994	.750
Vince Coleman, 1987	109				

Individual Pitching, Single Season

GAMES		LOSSES		SHUTOUTS	
Mike Marshall, 1974	106	John Coleman, 1883	48	George Bradley, 1876	16
Kent Tekulve, 1979	94	Will White, 1880	42	Grover Alexander, 1916	16
Mike Marshall, 1973	92	Larry McKeon, 1884	41	Jack Coombs, 1910	13
Kent Tekulve, 1978	91	George Bradley, 1879	40	Bob Gibson, 1968	13
Wayne Granger, 1969	90	Jim McCormick, 1879	40	Jim Galvin, 1884	12
Mike Marshall, 1979	90	Henry Porter, 1888	37	Ed Morris, 1886	12
Kent Tekulve, 1987	90	Kid Carsey, 1891	37	Grover Alexander, 1915	12
Steve Kline, 2001	89	George Cobb, 1892	37	Tommy Bond, 1879	11
Mark Eichhorn, 1987	89	Stump Weidman, 1886	36	Charley Radbourn, 1884	11
Wilbur Wood, 1968	88	Bill Hutchison, 1892	36	Dave Foutz, 1886	11
Mike Myers, 1997	88			Christy Mathewson, 1908	11

GAMES STARTED		WINNING PERCENTAGE			
				Ed Walsh, 1908	11
Will White, 1879	75	Roy Face, 1959	.947	Walter Johnson, 1913	11
Jim Galvin, 1883	75	Johnny Allen, 1937	.938	Sandy Koufax, 1963	11
Jim McCormick, 1880	74	Greg Maddux, 1995	.905	Dean Chance, 1964	11
Charley Radbourn, 1884	73	Randy Johnson, 1995	.900		
Guy Hecker, 1884	73	Ron Guidry, 1978	.893	COMPLETE GAMES	
Jim Galvin, 1884	72	Freddie Fitzsimmons, 1940	.889		
John Clarkson, 1889	72	Lefty Grove, 1931	.886	Will White, 1879	75
Bill Hutchison, 1892	71	Bob Stanley, 1978	.882	Charley Radbourn, 1884	73
John Clarkson, 1885	70	Preacher Roe, 1951	.880	Jim McCormick, 1880	72
Matt Kilroy, 1887	69	Fred Goldsmith, 1880	.875	Jim Galvin, 1883	72
		Tom Seaver, 1981	.875	Guy Hecker, 1884	72

INNINGS PITCHED		SAVES		Jim Galvin, 1884	71
				Tim Keefe, 1883	68
Will White, 1878	680	Bobby Thigpen, 1990	57	John Clarkson, 1885	68
Charley Radbourn, 1884	678⅔	John Smoltz, 2002	55	John Clarkson, 1889	68
Guy Hecker, 1884	670⅔	Randy Myers, 1993	53	Bill Hutchison, 1892	67
Jim McCormick, 1880	657⅔	Trevor Hoffman, 1998	53		
Jim Galvin, 1883	656⅓	Eric Gagne, 2002	52	STRIKEOUTS	
Jim Galvin, 1884	636⅓	Dennis Eckersley, 1992	51		
Charley Radbourn, 1883	632⅓	Rod Beck, 1998	51	Matt Kilroy, 1886	513
Bill Hutchison, 1892	627	Mariano Rivera, 2001	50	Toad Ramsey, 1886	499
John Clarkson, 1885	623	Dennis Eckersley, 1990	48	Hugh Daily, 1884	483
Jim Devlin, 1876	622	Rod Beck, 1993	48	Dupee Shaw, 1884	451
		Jeff Shaw, 1998	48	Charley Radbourn, 1884	441
				Charlie Buffinton, 1884	417
WINS		EARNED RUN AVERAGE		Guy Hecker, 1884	385
				Nolan Ryan, 1973	383
Charley Radbourn, 1884	59	Tim Keefe, 1880	0.86	Sandy Koufax, 1965	382
John Clarkson, 1885	53	Dutch Leonard, 1914	0.96	Bill Sweeney, 1884	374
Guy Hecker, 1884	52	Three Finger Brown, 1906	1.04		
John Clarkson, 1889	49	Bob Gibson, 1968	1.12	BASES ON BALLS	
Charley Radbourn, 1883	48	Christy Mathewson, 1909	1.14		
Charlie Buffinton, 1884	48	Walter Johnson, 1913	1.14	Amos Rusie, 1890	289
Al Spalding, 1876	47	Jack Pfiester, 1907	1.15	Mark Baldwin, 1889	274
John Ward, 1879	47	Addie Joss, 1908	1.16	Amos Rusie, 1892	267
Jim Galvin, 1883	46	Carl Lundgren, 1907	1.17	Amos Rusie, 1891	262
Jim Galvin, 1884	46	Denny Driscoll, 1882	1.21	Mark Baldwin, 1890	249
Matt Kilroy, 1887	46			Jack Stivetts, 1891	232
				Mark Baldwin, 1891	227
				Phil Knell, 1891	226
				Bob Barr, 1890	219
				Amos Rusie 1893	218

BASEBALL

Regular Season
Individual Batting, Single Game

MOST RUNS	
7 Guy Hecker, Lou	Aug 15, 1886

MOST HITS	
7 Wilbert Robinson, Balt	June 10, 1892
Rennie Stennett, Pitt	Sept 16, 1975

MOST HOME RUNS	
4 Bobby Lowe, Bos (N)	May 30, 1894
Ed Delahanty, Phil	July 13, 1896
Lou Gehrig, NY (A)	June 3, 1932
Gil Hodges, Bklyn	Aug 31, 1950
Joe Adcock, Mil (N)	July 31, 1954
Rocky Colavito, Clev	June 10, 1959
Willie Mays, SF	April 30, 1961
Bob Horner, Atl	July 6, 1986
Mark Whiten, StL	Sept 7, 1993
Mike Cameron, Sea	May 2, 2002
Shawn Green, LA	May 23, 2002

MOST GRAND SLAMS	
2 Tony Lazzeri, NY (A)	May 24, 1936
Jim Tabor, Bos (A)	July 4, 1939
Rudy York, Bos (A)	July 27, 1946
Jim Gentile, Balt	May 9, 1961
Tony Cloninger, Atl	July 3, 1966
Jim Northrup, Det	June 24, 1968
Frank Robinson, Balt	June 26, 1970
Robin Ventura, Chi (A)	Sept 4, 1995
Chris Hoiles, Balt	Aug 14, 1998
Fernando Tatis, StL	Apr 23, 1999
Nomar Garciaparra, Bos	May 10, 1999

MOST RBIs	
12 Jim Bottomley, StL	Sept 16, 1924
Mark Whiten, StL	Sept 7, 1993

Individual Pitching, Single Game

MOST INNINGS PITCHED	
26 Leon Cadore, Bklyn	May 1, 1920, tie 1–1
Joe Oeschger, Bos (N)	May 1, 1920, tie 1–1

MOST RUNS ALLOWED	
24 Al Travers, Det	May 18, 1912

MOST HITS ALLOWED	
36 Jack Wadsworth, Lou	Aug 17, 1894

MOST STRIKEOUTS	
20 Roger Clemens, Bos	April 29, 1986
20 Roger Clemens, Bos	Sept 18, 1996
20 Kerry Wood, Chi (N)	May 6, 1998
20 Randy Johnson, Ariz	May 8, 2001

MOST WALKS ALLOWED	
16 Bill George, NY (N)	May 30, 1887
George Van Haltren, Chi (N)	June 27, 1887
Henry Gruber, Clev	Apr 19, 1890
Bruno Haas, Phil (A)	June 2, 1915

MOST WILD PITCHES	
6 J.R. Richard, Hou	April 10, 1979
Phil Niekro, Atl	Aug 14, 1979
Bill Gullickson, Mtl	April 10, 1982

Notable Achievements
No-Hit Games, Nine Innings or More

National League

Date		Pitcher and Game	Date		Pitcher and Game
1876	July 15	George Bradley, StL vs Hart 2–0	1892	Aug 6	Jack Stivetts, Bos vs Bklyn 11–0
1880	June 12	John Richmond, Wor vs Clev 1–0		Aug 22	Alex Sanders, Lou vs Balt 6–2
		(perfect game)		Oct 15	Bumpus Jones, Cin vs Pitt 7–1
	June 17	Monte Ward, Prov vs Buff 5–0			(first major league game)
		(perfect game)	1893	Aug 16	Bill Hawke, Balt vs Wash 5–0
	Aug 19	Larry Corcoran, Chi vs Bos 6–0	1897	Sept 18	Cy Young, Clev vs Cin 6–0
	Aug 20	Pud Galvin, Buff vs Wor 1–0	1898	Apr 22	Ted Breitenstein, Cin vs Pitt 11–0
1882	Sept 20	Larry Corcoran, Chi vs Wor 5–0		Apr 22	Jim Hughes, Balt vs Bos 8–0
	Sept 22	Tim Lovett, Bklyn vs NY 4–0		July 8	Frank Donahue, Phil vs Bos 5–0
1883	July 25	Hoss Radbourn, Prov vs Clev 8–0		Aug 21	Walter Thornton, Chi vs Bklyn 2–0
	Sept 13	Hugh Daily, Clev vs Phil 1–0	1899	May 25	Deacon Phillippe, Lou vs NY 7–0
1884	June 27	Larry Corcoran, Chi vs Prov 6–0		Aug 7	Vic Willis, Bos vs Wash 7–1
	Aug 4	Pud Galvin, Buff vs Det 18–0	1900	July 12	Noodles Hahn, Cin vs Phil 4–0
1885	July 27	John Clarkson, Chi vs Prov 4–0	1901	July 15	Christy Mathewson, NY vs StL 5–0
	Aug 29	Charles Ferguson, Phil vs Prov 1–0	1903	Sept 18	Chick Fraser, Phil vs Chi 10–0
1891	July 31	Amos Rusie, NY vs Bklyn 6–0	1904	June 11	Bob Wicker, Chi at NY 1–0
	June 22	Tom Lovett, Bklyn vs NY 4–0			(hit in 10th; won in 12th)

Notable Achievements
No-Hit Games, Nine Innings or More (cont.)

National League

Date		Pitcher and Game	Date		Pitcher and Game
1905	June 13	Christy Mathewson, NY vs Chi 1–0	1969	Apr 17	Bill Stoneman, Mtl vs Phil 7–0
1906	May 1	John Lush, Phil vs Bklyn 6–0		Apr 30	Jim Maloney, Cin vs Hou 10–0
	July 20	Mal Eason, Bklyn vs StL 2–0		May 1	Don Wilson, Hou vs Cin 4–0
	Aug 1	Harry McIntire, Bklyn vs Pitt 0–1		Aug 19	Ken Holtzman, Chi vs Atl 3–0
		(hit in 11th; lost in 13th)		Sept 20	Bob Moose, Pitt vs NY 4–0
1907	May 8	Frank Pfeffer, Bos vs Cin 6–0	1970	June 12	Dock Ellis, Pitt vs SD 2–0
	Sept 20	Nick Maddox, Pitt vs Bklyn 2–1		July 20	Bill Singer, LA vs Phil 5–0
1908	July 4	George Wiltse, NY vs Phil 1–0	1971	June 3	Ken Holtzman, Chi vs Cin 1–0
		(10 innings)		June 23	Rick Wise, Phil vs Cin 4–0
	Sept 5	Nap Rucker, Bklyn vs Bos 6–0		Aug 14	Bob Gibson, StL vs Pitt 11–0
1909	Apr 15	Leon Ames, NY vs Bklyn 0–3	1972	Apr 16	Burt Hooton, Chi vs Phil 4–0
		(hit in 10th; lost in 13th)		Sept 2	Milt Pappas, Chi vs SD 8–0
1912	Sept 6	Jeff Tesreau, NY vs Phil 3–0		Oct 2	Bill Stoneman, Mtl vs NY 7–0
1914	Sept 9	George Davis, Bos vs Phil 7–0	1973	Aug 5	Phil Niekro, Atl vs SD 9–0
1915	Apr 15	Rube Marquard, NY vs Bklyn 2–0	1975	Aug 24	Ed Halicki, SF vs NY 6–0
	Aug 31	Jimmy Lavender, Chi vs NY 2–0	1976	July 9	Larry Dierker, Hou vs Mtl 6–0
1916	June 16	Tom Hughes, Bos vs Pitt 2–0		Aug 9	John Candelaria, Pitt vs LA 2–0
1917	May 2	Jim Vaughn, Chi vs Cin 0–1		Sept 29	John Montefusco, SF vs Atl 9–0
		(hit in 10th; lost in 10th)	1978	Apr 16	Bob Forsch, StL vs Phil 5–0
	May 2	Fred Toney, Cin vs Chi 1–0		June 16	Tom Seaver, Cin vs StL 4–0
		(10 innings)	1979	Apr 7	Ken Forsch, Hou vs Atl 6–0
1919	May 11	Hod Eller, Cin vs StL 6–0	1980	June 27	Jerry Reuss, LA vs SF 8–0
1922	May 7	Jesse Barnes, NY vs Phil 6–0	1981	May 10	Charlie Lea, Mtl vs SF 4–0
1924	July 17	Jesse Haines, StL vs Bos 5–0		Sept 26	Nolan Ryan, Hou vs LA 5–0
1925	Sept 13	Dazzy Vance, Bklyn vs Phil 10–1	1983	Sept 26	Bob Forsch, StL vs Mtl 3–0
1929	May 8	Carl Hubbell, NY vs Pitt 11–0	1986	Sept 25	Mike Scott, Hou vs SF 2–0
1934	Sept 21	Paul Dean, StL vs Bklyn 3–0	1988	Sept 16	Tom Browning, Cin vs LA 1–0
1938	June 11	Johnny Vander Meer, Cin vs Bos3–0			(perfect game)
	June 15	Johnny Vander Meer, Cin vs Bklyn 6-0	1990	June 29	Fernando Valenzuela, LA vs StL 6–0
1940	Apr 30	Tex Carleton, Bklyn vs Cin, 3–0		Aug 15	Terry Mulholland, Phil vs SF 6–0
1941	Aug 30	Lon Warneke, StL vs Cin 2–0	1991	May 23	Tommy Greene, Phil vs Mtl 2–0
1944	Apr 27	Jim Tobin, Bos vs Bklyn 2–0		July 26	Mark Gardner, Mtl vs LA 0–1
	May 15	Clyde Shoun, Cin vs Bos 1–0			(hit in 10th, lost in 10th)
1946	Apr 23	Ed Head, Bklyn vs Bos 5–0		July 28	Dennis Martinez, Mtl vs LA 2–0
1947	June 18	Ewell Blackwell, Cin vs Bos 6–0			(perfect game)
1948	Sept 9	Rex Barney, Bklyn vs NY 2–0		Sept 11	Kent Mercker (6), Mark Wohlers (2),
1950	Aug 11	Vern Bickford, Bos vs Bklyn 7–0			and Alejandro Pena (1), Atl vs SD 1–0
1951	May 6	Cliff Chambers, Pitt vs Bos 3–0	1992	Aug 17	Kevin Gross, LA vs SF 2–0
1952	June 19	Carl Erskine, Bklyn vs Chi 5–0	1993	Sept 8	Darryl Kile, Hou vs NY 7–1
1954	June 12	Jim Wilson, Mil vs Phil 2–0	1994	Apr 8	Kent Mercker, Atl vs LA 6–0
1955	May 12	Sam Jones, Chi vs Pitt 4–0	1995	June 3	Pedro Martinez, Mtl vs SD 1–0
1956	May 12	Carl Erskine, Bklyn vs NY 3–0			(perfect through nine, hit in 10th)
	Sept 25	Sal Maglie, Bklyn vs Phil 5–0		July 14	Ramon Martinez, LA vs Fla 7–0
1959	May 26	Harvey Haddix, Pitt vs Mil 0–1	1996	May 11	Al Leiter, Fla vs Col 11–0
		(hit in 13th; lost in 13th)		Sept 17	Hideo Nomo, LA vs Col 9–0
1960	May 15	Don Cardwell, Chi vs StL 4–0	1997	June 10	Kevin Brown, Fla vs SF 9–0
	Aug 18	Lew Burdette, Mil vs Phil 1–0		July 12	Francisco Cordova (9) and
	Sept 16	Warren Spahn, Mil vs Phil 4–0			Ricardo Rincon (1), Pitt vs Col 3–0
1961	Apr 28	Warren Spahn, Mil vs SF 1–0	1999	June 25	Jose Jimenez, StL vs Ariz 1–0
1962	June 30	Sandy Koufax, LA vs NY 5–0	2001	May 12	A.J. Burnett, Fla vs SD 3–0
1963	May 11	Sandy Koufax, LA vs SF 8–0		Sept 3	Bud Smith, StL vs SD 4–0
	May 17	Don Nottebart, Hou vs Phil 4–1			
	June 15	Juan Marichal, SF vs Hou 1–0			
1964	Apr 23	Ken Johnson, Hou vs Cin 0–1			
	June 4	Sandy Koufax, LA vs Phil 3–0			
	June 21	Jim Bunning, Phil vs NY 6–0			
		(perfect game)			
1965	June 14	Jim Maloney, Cin vs NY 0–1			
		(hit in 11th; lost in 11th)			
	Aug 19	Jim Maloney, Cin vs Chi 1–0 (10 innings)			
	Sept 9	Sandy Koufax, LA vs Chi 1–0 (perfect game)			
1967	June 18	Don Wilson, Hou vs Atl 2–0			
1968	July 29	George Culver, Cin vs Phil 6–1			
	Sept 17	Gaylord Perry, SF vs StL 1–0			
	Sept 18	Ray Washburn, StL vs SF 2–0			

Notable Achievements
No-Hit Games, Nine Innings or More (cont.)

American League

Date		Pitcher and Game
1901	May 9	Earl Moore, Clev vs Chi 2–4 (hit in 10th; lost in 10th)
1902	Sept 20	Jimmy Callahan, Chi vs Det 3–0
1904	May 5	Cy Young, Bos vs Phil 3–0 (perfect game)
	Aug 17	Jesse Tannehill, Bos vs Chi 6–0
1905	July 22	Weldon Henley, Phil vs StL 6–0
	Sept 6	Frank Smith, Chi vs Det 15–0
	Sept 27	Bill Dinneen, Bos vs Chi 2–0
1908	June 30	Cy Young, Bos vs NY 8–0
	Sept 18	Bob Rhoades, Clev vs Bos 2–1
	Sept 20	Frank Smith, Chi vs Phil 1–0
1908	Oct 2	Addie Joss, Clev vs Chi 1–0 (perfect game)
1910	Apr 20	Addie Joss, Clev vs Chi 1–0
	May 12	Chief Bender, Phil vs Clev 4–0
	Aug 30	Tom Hughes, NY vs Clev 0–5 (hit in 10th; lost in 11th)
1911	July 29	Joe Wood, Bos vs StL 5–0
	Aug 27	Ed Walsh, Chi vs Bos 5–0
1912	July 4	George Mullin, Det vs StL 7–0
	Aug 30	Earl Hamilton, StL vs Det 5–1
1914	May 14	Jim Scott, Chi vs Wash 0–1 (hit in 10th; lost in 10th)
	May 31	Joe Benz, Chi vs Clev 6–1
1916	June 21	George Foster, Bos vs NY 2–0
	Aug 26	Joe Bush, Phil vs Clev 5–0
	Aug 30	Dutch Leonard, Bos vs StL 4–0
1917	Apr 14	Ed Cicotte, Chi vs StL 11–0
	Apr 24	George Mogridge, NY vs Bos 2–1
	May 5	Ernie Koob, StL vs Chi 1–0
	May 6	Bob Groom, StL vs Chi 3–0
	June 23	Ernie Shore, Bos vs Wash 4–0 (perfect game)
1918	June 3	Dutch Leonard, Bos vs Det 5–0
1919	Sept 10	Ray Caldwell, Clev vs NY 3–0
1920	July 1	Walter Johnson, Wash vs Bos 1–0
1922	Apr 30	Charlie Robertson, Chi vs Det 2–0 (perfect game)
1923	Sept 4	Sam Jones, NY vs Phil 2–0
	Sept 7	Howard Ehmke, Bos vs Phil 4–0
1926	Aug 21	Ted Lyons, Chi vs Bos 6–0
1931	Apr 29	Wes Ferrell, Clev vs StL 9–0
	Aug 8	Bob Burke, Wash vs Bos 5–0
1934	Sept 18	Bobo Newsom, StL vs Bos 1–2 (hit in 10th; lost in 10th)
1935	Aug 31	Vern Kennedy, Chi vs Clev 5–0
1937	June 1	Bill Dietrich, Chi vs StL 8–0
1938	Aug 27	Mtle Pearson, NY vs Clev 13–0
1940	Apr 16	Bob Feller, Clev vs Chi 1–0 (opening day)
1945	Sept 9	Dick Fowler, Phil vs StL 1–0
1946	Apr 30	Bob Feller, Clev vs NY 1–0
1947	July 10	Don Black, Clev vs Phil 3–0
	Sep 3	Bill McCahan, Phil vs Wash 3–0
1948	June 30	Bob Lemon, Clev vs Det 2–0
1951	July 1	Bob Feller, Clev vs Det 2–1
	July 12	Allie Reynolds, NY vs Clev 1–0
	Sept 28	Allie Reynolds, NY vs Bos 8–0
1952	May 15	Virgil Trucks, Det vs Wash 1–0
	Aug 25	Virgil Trucks, Det vs NY 1–0

Date		Pitcher and Game
1953	May 6	Bobo Holloman, StL vs Phil 6–0 (first major league start)
1956	July 14	Mel Parnell, Bos vs Chi 4–0
	Oct 8	Don Larsen, NY (A) vs Bklyn (N) 2–0 (World Series) (perfect game)
1957	Aug 20	Bob Keegan, Chi vs Wash 6–0
1958	July 20	Jim Bunning, Det vs Bos 3–0
	Sept 20	Hoyt Wilhelm, Balt vs NY 1–0
1962	May 5	Bo Belinsky, LA vs Balt 2–0
	June 26	Earl Wilson, Bos vs LA 2–0
	Aug 1	Bill Monbouquette, Bos vs Chi 1–0
	Aug 26	Jack Kralick, Minn vs KC 1–0
1965	Sept 16	Dave Morehead, Bos vs Clev 2–0
1966	June 10	Sonny Siebert, Clev vs Wash 2–0
1967	Apr 30	Steve Barber (8⅔) and Stu Miller (⅓), Balt vs Det 1–2
	Aug 25	Dean Chance, Minn vs Clev 2–1
	Sept 10	Joel Horlen, Chi vs Det 6–0
1968	Apr 27	Tom Phoebus, Balt vs Bos 6–0
	May 8	Catfish Hunter, Oak vs Minn 4–0 (perfect game)
1969	Aug 13	Jim Palmer, Balt vs Oak 8–0
1970	July 3	Clyde Wright, Cal vs Oak 4–0
	Sept 21	Vida Blue, Oak vs Minn 6–0
1973	Apr 27	Steve Busby, KC vs Det 3–0
	May 15	Nolan Ryan, Cal vs KC 3–0
	July 15	Nolan Ryan, Cal vs Det 6–0
	July 30	Jim Bibby, Tex vs Oak 6–0
1974	June 19	Steve Busby, KC vs Mil 2–0
	July 19	Dick Bosman, Clev vs Oak 4–0
	Sept 28	Nolan Ryan, Cal vs Minn 4–0
1975	June 1	Nolan Ryan, Cal vs Balt 1–0
	Sept 28	Vida Blue (5), Glenn Abbott and Paul Lindblad (1), Rollie Fingers (2), Oak vs Cal 5–0
1976	July 28	John Odom (5) and Francisco Barrios (4), Chi vs Oak 2–1
1977	May 14	Jim Colborn, KC vs Tex 6–0
	May 30	Dennis Eckersley, Clev vs Cal 1–0
	Sept 22	Bert Blyleven, Tex vs Cal 6–0
1981	May 15	Len Barker, Clev vs Tor 3–0 (perfect game)
1983	July 4	Dave Righetti, NY vs Bos 4–0
	Sept 29	Mike Warren, Oak vs Chi 3–0
1984	Apr 7	Jack Morris, Det vs Chi 4–0
	Sept 30	Mike Witt, Cal vs Tex 1–0 (perfect game)
1986	Sept 19	Joe Cowley, Chi vs Cal 7–1
1987	Apr 15	Juan Nieves, Mil vs Balt 7–0
1990	Apr 11	Mark Langston (7), Mike Witt (2), Cal vs Sea 1–0
	June 2	Randy Johnson, Sea vs Det 2–0
	June 11	Nolan Ryan, Tex vs Oak 5–0
	June 29	Dave Stewart, Oak vs Tor 5–0
1990	July 1	Andy Hawkins, NY vs Chi 0–4 (pitched eight of nine-inning game)
	Sept 2	Dave Stieb, Tor vs Clev 3–0
1991	May 1	Nolan Ryan, Tex vs Tor 3–0
	July 13	Bob Milacki (6), Mike Flanagan (1), Mark Williamson (1), and Gregg Olson (1), Balt vs Oak 2–0

Notable Achievements
No-Hit Games, Nine Innings or More (cont.)

American League

Date		Pitcher and Game	Date		Pitcher and Game
	Aug 11	Wilson Alvarez, Chi vs Balt 7–0	1996	May 14	Dwight Gooden, NY vs Sea 2–0
	Aug 26	Bret Saberhagen, KC vs Chi 7–0	1998	May 17	David Wells, NY vs Minn 4–0
1993	Apr 22	Chris Bosio, Sea vs Bos 7–0			(perfect game)
	Sept 4	Jim Abbott, NY vs Clev 4–0	1999	July 18	David Cone, NY vs Mtl 6–0
1994	Apr 27	Scott Erickson, Minn vs Mil 6–0			(perfect game)
	July 28	Kenny Rogers, Texas vs Cal 4–0		Sept 11	Eric Milton, Minn vs Ana 7–0
		(perfect game)	2001	Apr 4	Hideo Nomo, Bos vs Balt 3–0
			2002	Apr 27	Derek Lowe, Bos vs TB 10–0

Longest Hitting Streaks

National League

Player and Team	Year	G
Willie Keeler, Balt	1897	44
Pete Rose, Cin	1978	44
Bill Dahlen, Chi	1894	42
Tommy Holmes, Bos	1945	37
Billy Hamilton, Phil	1894	36
Luis Castillo, Fla	2002	35
Fred Clarke, Lou	1895	35
Benito Santiago, SD	1987	34
George Davis, NY	1893	33
Rogers Hornsby, StL	1922	32

American League

Player and Team	Year	G
Joe DiMaggio, NY	1941	56
George Sisler, StL	1922	41
Ty Cobb, Det	1911	40
Paul Molitor, Mil	1987	39
Ty Cobb, Det	1917	35
Ty Cobb, Det	1912	34
George Sisler, StL	1925	34
John Stone, Det	1930	34
George McQuinn, StL	1938	34
Dom DiMaggio, Bos	1949	34

Triple Crown Winners*

National League

Player and Team	Year	HR	RBI	BA
Paul Hines, Prov	1878	4	50	.358
Hugh Duffy, Bos	1894	18	145	.438
Heinie Zimmerman, Chi**	1912	14	103	.372
Rogers Hornsby, StL	1922	42	152	.401
Rogers Hornsby, StL	1925	39	143	.403
Chuck Klein, Phil	1933	28	120	.368
Joe Medwick, StL	1937	31	154	.374

American League

Player and Team	Year	HR	RBI	BA
Nap Lajoie, Phil	1901	14	125	.422
Ty Cobb, Det	1909	9	115	.377
Jimmie Foxx, Phil	1933	48	163	.356
Lou Gehrig, NY	1934	49	165	.363
Ted Williams, Bos	1942	36	137	.356
Ted Williams, Bos	1947	32	114	.343
Mickey Mantle, NY	1956	52	130	.353
Frank Robinson, Balt	1966	49	122	.316
Carl Yastrzemski, Bos	1967	44	121	.326

*Player who leads in three categories: home runs, RBIs, and batting average.
**Zimmerman ranked first in RBIs as calculated by Ernie Lanigan, but only third as calculated by Information Concepts Inc.

Triple Crown Pitchers***

National League

Player and Team	Year	W	L	SO	ERA	Player and Team	Year	W	L	SO	ERA
Tommy Bond, Bos	1877	40	17	170	2.11	Hippo Vaughn, Chi	1918	22	10	148	1.74
Hoss Radbourn, Prov	1884	60	12	441	1.38	Grover Alexander, Chi	1920	27	14	173	1.91
Tim Keefe, NY	1888	35	12	333	1.74	Dazzy Vance, Bklyn	1924	28	6	262	2.16
John Clarkson, Bos	1889	49	19	284	2.73	Bucky Walters, Cin	1939	27	11	137	2.29
Amos Rusie, NY	1894	36	13	195	2.78	Sandy Koufax, LA	1963	25	5	306	1.88
Christy Mathewson, NY	1905	31	8	206	1.27	Sandy Koufax, LA	1965	26	8	382	2.04
Christy Mathewson, NY	1908	37	11	259	1.43	Sandy Koufax, LA	1966	27	9	317	1.73
Grover Alexander, Phil	1915	31	10	241	1.22	Steve Carlton, Phil	1972	27	10	310	1.97
Grover Alexander, Phil	1916	33	12	167	1.55	Dwight Gooden, NY	1985	24	4	268	1.53
Grover Alexander, Phil	1917	30	13	201	1.86	Randy Johnson, Ariz	2002	24	5	334	2.32

American League

Player and Team	Year	W	L	SO	ERA	Player and Team	Year	W	L	SO	ERA
Cy Young, Bos	1901	33	10	158	1.62	Lefty Gomez, NY	1934	26	5	158	2.33
Rube Waddell, Phil	1905	26	11	287	1.48	Lefty Gomez, NY	1937	21	11	194	2.33
Walter Johnson, Wash	1913	36	7	303	1.09	Hal Newhouser, Det	1945	25	9	212	1.81
Walter Johnson, Wash	1918	23	13	162	1.27	Roger Clemens, Tor	1997	21	7	292	2.05
Walter Johnson, Wash	1924	23	7	158	2.72	Roger Clemens, Tor	1998	20	6	271	2.64
Lefty Grove, Phil	1930	28	5	209	2.54	Pedro Martinez, Bos	1999	23	4	313	2.07
Lefty Grove, Phil	1931	31	4	175	2.06						

***Pitcher who leads in three categories: ERA, wins, and strikeouts.

BASEBALL

▷**Random Fact:**
In 1997, Jackie Robinson became the first and only player whose jersey number (42) was retired by every major league team.

Notable Achievements
Consecutive Games Played, 500 or More Games

Cal Ripken, Jr.	2,632	Frank McCormick	652
Lou Gehrig	2,130	Sandy Alomar, Sr.	648
Everett Scott	1,307	Eddie Brown	618
Steve Garvey	1,207	Roy McMillan	585
Billy Williams	1,117	George Pinckney	577
Joe Sewell	1,103	Steve Brodie	574
Stan Musial	895	Aaron Ward	565
Eddie Yost	829	Candy LaChance	540
Gus Suhr	822	Buck Freeman	535
Nellie Fox	798	Fred Luderus	533
Pete Rose	745	Clyde Milan	511
Dale Murphy	740	Charlie Gehringer	511
Richie Ashburn	730	Vada Pinson	508
Ernie Banks	717	Tony Cuccinello	504
Pete Rose	678	Charlie Gehringer	504
Earl Averill	673	Omar Moreno	503

Unassisted Triple Play

Player and Team	Date	Pos	Opp	Opp Batter
Neal Ball, Clev	7-19-09	SS	Bos	Amby McConnell
Bill Wambsganss, Clev	10-10-20	2B	Bklyn	Clarence Mitchell
George Burns, Bos	9-14-23	1B	Clev	Frank Brower
Ernie Padgett, Bos	10-6-23	SS	Phil	Walter Holke
Glenn Wright, Pitt	5-7-25	SS	StL	Jim Bottomley
Jimmy Cooney, Chi	5-30-27	SS	Pitt	Paul Waner
Johnny Neun, Det	5-31-27	1B	Clev	Homer Summa
Ron Hansen, Wash	7-30-68	SS	Clev	Joe Azcue
Mickey Morandini, Phil	9-20-92	2B	Pitt	Jeff King
John Valentin, Bos	7-15-94	SS	Minn	Marc Newfield
Randy Velarde, Oak	5-29-00	2B	NYY	Shane Spencer

National League
Pennant Winners (past 50 years)

Year	Team	Manager	W	L	Pct	GA
2002	††San Francisco (WC)	Dusty Baker	95	66	.590	-2½
2001	††Arizona (W)	Bob Brenly	92	70	.568	2
2000	††New York Mets (WC)	Bobby Valentine	94	68	.580	-6½
1999	††Atlanta Braves (E)	Bobby Cox	103	59	.636	6½
1998	††San Diego (W)	Bruce Bochy	98	64	.605	9½
1997	††Florida (WC)	Jim Leyland	92	70	.568	-9
1996	††Atlanta (E)	Bobby Cox	96	66	.593	8
1995	††Atlanta (E)	Bobby Cox	90	54	.625	21
1994	Season ended Aug. 11 due to labor dispute.					
1993	††Philadelphia (E)	Jim Fregosi	97	65	.599	3
1992	††Atlanta (W)	Bobby Cox	98	64	.605	8
1991	††Atlanta (W)	Bobby Cox	94	68	.580	1
1990	††Cincinnati (W)	Lou Piniella	91	71	.562	5
1989	††San Francisco (W)	Roger Craig	92	70	.568	3
1988	††Los Angeles (W)	Tommy Lasorda	94	67	.584	7
1987	††St. Louis (E)	Whitey Herzog	95	67	.586	3
1986	††New York (E)	Dave Johnson	108	54	.667	21½
1985	††St. Louis (E)	Whitey Herzog	101	61	.623	3
1984	††San Diego (W)	Dick Williams	92	70	.568	12
1983	††Philadelphia (E)	Pat Corrales/Paul Owens	90	72	.556	6
1982	††St. Louis (E)	Whitey Herzog	92	70	.568	3
1981	††Los Angeles (W)	Tommy Lasorda	63	47	.573	* *
1980	††Philadelphia (E)	Dallas Green	91	71	.562	1
1979	††Pittsburgh (E)	Chuck Tanner	98	64	.605	2
1978	††Los Angeles (W)	Tommy Lasorda	95	67	.586	2½
1977	††Los Angeles (W)	Tommy Lasorda	98	64	.605	10
1976	††Cincinnati (W)	Sparky Anderson	102	60	.630	10
1975	††Cincinnati (W)	Sparky Anderson	108	54	.667	20

††Won championship series.

Legends

BABE RUTH, pitcher/outfielder, b. February 6, 1895, Baltimore, Maryland; d. August 16, 1948, New York, New York. Ruth's awesome power and larger-than-life personality made him baseball's most famous player. He was a star pitcher for the Boston Red Sox before being sold to the New York Yankees prior to the start of the 1920 season. He switched to the outfield and became the greatest slugger of his time. He set the major league's single-season homer record four times in nine seasons. In 1927, he hit 60, a record that stood for 34 years. He retired in 1935 as the major league leader in homers (714). He also compiled a .344 lifetime batting average. Ruth played on 10 A.L. pennant winners and seven World Series championship teams. In 1936, he was one of the first five players elected to the Baseball Hall of Fame.

Babe Ruth set the single-season homer record four times in nine seasons.

JACKIE ROBINSON, infielder, b. January 13, 1919, Cairo, Georgia; d. October 24, 1972, Stamford, Connecticut. On April 15, 1947, Robinson broke the major league "color barrier" with the Brooklyn Dodgers by becoming the first African American to play in the majors in the modern era. That season, the speedy, daring Robinson overcame racist taunts to win the first Rookie of the Year award. His league-leading .342 average earned him the N.L. MVP award in 1949. During his 10-season career, he played on six pennant winners and won the World Series in 1955 with the Dodgers. He was elected to the Hall of Fame in 1962, his first year of eligibility.

CY YOUNG, pitcher, b. March 29, 1867, Gilmore, Ohio; d. November 4, 1955, Newcomerstown, Ohio. There are plenty of reasons why the award given to the best pitcher in each league each season bears his name. Young set untouchable major league records during his 22 seasons: most wins (511), most innings pitched (7,356 2/3), and most complete games (749). He pitched three no-hitters, including a perfect game in 1904. In 1903, Young and the Boston Pilgrims won the first World Series. (The Pilgrims became the Red Sox in 1907.) He was elected to the Hall of Fame in 1936.

National League
Pennant Winners (cont.)

Year	Team	Manager	W	L	Pct	GA
1974	††Los Angeles (W)	Walt Alston	102	60	.630	4
1973	††New York (E)	Yogi Berra	82	79	.509	1½
1972	††Cincinnati (W)	Sparky Anderson	95	59	.617	10½
1971	††Pittsburgh (E)	Danny Murtaugh	97	65	.599	7
1970	††Cincinnati (W)	Sparky Anderson	102	60	.630	14½
1969	††New York (E)	Gil Hodges	100	62	.617	8
1968	St. Louis	Red Schoendienst	97	65	.599	9
1967	St. Louis	Red Schoendienst	101	60	.627	10½
1966	Los Angeles	Walt Alston	95	67	.586	1½
1965	Los Angeles	Walt Alston	97	65	.599	2
1964	St. Louis	Johnny Keane	93	69	.574	1
1963	Los Angeles	Walt Alston	99	63	.611	6
1962	#San Francisco	Al Dark	103	62	.624	1
1961	Cincinnati	Fred Hutchinson	93	61	.604	4
1960	Pittsburgh	Danny Murtaugh	95	59	.617	7
1959	‡Los Angeles	Walt Alston	88	68	.564	2
1958	Milwaukee	Fred Haney	92	62	.597	8
1957	Milwaukee	Fred Haney	95	59	.617	8
1956	Brooklyn	Walt Alston	93	61	.604	1
1955	Brooklyn	Walt Alston	98	55	.641	13½
1954	New York	Leo Durocher	97	57	.630	5
1953	Brooklyn	Chuck Dressen	105	49	.682	13
1952	Brooklyn	Chuck Dressen	96	57	.627	4½

††Won championship series. #Defeated Los Angeles, two games to one, in playoff for pennant. ‡Defeated Milwaukee, two games to none, in playoff for pennant.

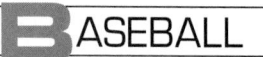

BASEBALL

American League
Pennant Winners (past 50 years)

Year	Team	Manager	W	L	Pct	GA
2002	‡Anaheim (WC)	Mike Scioscia	99	63	.611	-4
2001	‡New York (E)	Joe Torre	95	65	.594	13 ½
2000	‡New York (E)	Joe Torre	87	74	.540	2 ½
1999	‡New York (E)	Joe Torre	98	64	.605	4
1998	‡New York (E)	Joe Torre	114	48	.704	22
1997	‡Cleveland (C)	Mike Hargrove	86	75	.534	6
1996	‡New York (E)	Joe Torre	92	70	.568	4
1995	‡Cleveland (C)	Mike Hargrove	100	44	.694	30
1994	Season ended Aug. 11 due to labor dispute.					
1993	‡Toronto	Cito Gaston	95	67	.586	7
1992	‡Toronto	Cito Gaston	96	66	.593	4
1991	‡Minnesota (W)	Tom Kelly	95	67	.586	8
1990	‡Oakland (W)	Tony La Russa	103	59	.636	9
1989	‡Oakland (W)	Tony La Russa	99	63	.611	7
1988	‡Oakland (W)	Tony La Russa	104	58	.642	13
1987	‡Minnesota (W)	Tom Kelly	85	77	.525	2
1986	‡Boston (E)	John McNamara	95	66	.590	5 ½
1985	‡Kansas City (W)	Dick Howser	91	71	.562	1
1984	‡Detroit (E)	Sparky Anderson	104	58	.642	15
1983	‡Baltimore (E)	Joe Altobelli	98	64	.605	6
1982	‡Milwaukee (E)	Buck Rodgers, Harvey Kuenn	95	67	.586	1
1981	‡New York (E)	Gene Michael, Bob Lemon	59	48	.551	#
1980	‡Kansas City (W)	Jim Frey	97	65	.599	14
1979	‡Baltimore (E)	Earl Weaver	102	57	.642	8
1978	†‡New York (E)	Billy Martin, Bob Lemon	100	63	.613	1
1977	‡New York (E)	Billy Martin	100	62	.617	2 ½
1976	‡New York (E)	Billy Martin	97	62	.610	10 ½
1975	‡Boston (E)	Darrell Johnson	95	65	.594	4 ½
1974	‡Oakland (W)	Al Dark	90	72	.556	5
1973	‡Oakland (W)	Dick Williams	94	68	.580	6
1972	‡Oakland (W)	Dick Williams	93	62	.600	5 ½
1971	‡Baltimore (E)	Earl Weaver	101	57	.639	12
1970	‡Baltimore (E)	Earl Weaver	108	54	.667	15
1969	‡Baltimore (E)	Earl Weaver	109	53	.673	19
1968	Detroit	Mayo Smith	103	59	.636	12
1967	Boston	Dick Williams	92	70	.568	1
1966	Baltimore	Hank Bauer	97	63	.606	9
1965	Minnesota	Sam Mele	102	60	.630	7
1964	New York	Yogi Berra	99	63	.611	1
1963	New York	Ralph Houk	104	57	.646	10 ½
1962	New York	Ralph Houk	96	66	.593	5
1961	New York	Ralph Houk	109	53	.673	8
1960	New York	Casey Stengel	97	57	.630	8
1959	Chicago	Al Lopez	94	60	.610	5
1958	New York	Casey Stengel	92	62	.597	10
1957	New York	Casey Stengel	98	56	.636	8
1956	New York	Casey Stengel	97	57	.630	9
1955	New York	Casey Stengel	96	58	.623	3
1954	Cleveland	Al Lopez	111	43	.721	8
1953	New York	Casey Stengel	99	52	.656	8 ½
1952	New York	Casey Stengel	95	59	.617	2

‡Won championship series. †Defeated Boston in a one-game playoff. #First half 34-22; second half 25-26, in season split by strike; defeated Milwaukee in playoff for Eastern Division title.

The following is a list of big-time players who switched teams for the 2003 season.

JIM THOME, first baseman, Philadelphia Phillies After 12 seasons with the Cleveland Indians, in December 2002, Thome signed a six-year contract with Philly worth $85 million. Thome's power (52 home runs in 2002) will be a welcome addition to the Phillies' lineup. His ability to draw fans will help lead the Phils into their new stadium for the 2004 season.

TOM GLAVINE, pitcher, New York Mets Glavine spent his whole career (16 seasons until 2003) helping to turn the Atlanta Braves from a laughingstock to a perennial champion. In December 2002, he headed north to New York. Glavine, a two-time Cy Young Award winner who posted five 20-win seasons with the Braves, signed a three-year $35 million contract with the Mets, giving the team the top-notch starter they hoped would help them make a run for their first National League East title since 1988.

JEFF KENT, second baseman, Houston Astros Kent won the 2000 National League MVP with the San Francisco Giants. Over the next two seasons, however, his relationship with Giants management — and teammate Barry Bonds — disintegrated. In December 2002, he signed with Houston for $18.2 million over two years. Kent, who hit .313 with 37 homers and 108 RBIs in 2002, joined a stacked Astro lineup that includes first baseman Jeff Bagwell, centerfielder Craig Biggio, and leftfielder Lance Berkman.

MIKE HAMPTON, pitcher, Atlanta Braves The Colorado Rockies gave up on the disappointing Hampton, whom they had signed in 2001 for a then-record $121 million for a pitcher, and traded him to the Braves (by way of the Florida Marlins), in November 2002. Though he went just 7 – 15 with a 6.15 ERA in 2002, Hampton had been a proven winner with the Astros (2.90 ERA in 1999) and Mets (3.14 ERA in 2000). Plus, he can hit. His .344 average was tops for all major league pitchers in 2002.

IVAN "PUDGE" RODRIGUEZ, catcher, Florida Marlins Easily the best defensive catcher in baseball, Rodriguez was a prime example of the lack of interest in the free-agent market in 2002. Despite batting .314, he got one known offer, from the Baltimore Orioles. He nearly signed to play in Japan before agreeing to a one-year, $10 million contract with the Marlins in January 2003. Rodriguez's ability to work with young pitchers will be crucial with Florida's inexperienced staff.

Other noteworthy transactions: Third baseman **David Bell** (San Francisco Giants) and pitcher **Kevin Millwood** (Atlanta Braves) both moved to Philadelphia, giving the Phillies a legitimate shot at their first division title in 10 years. The Oakland A's and Chicago White Sox traded closers, with **Billy Koch** going to Chicago and **Keith Foulke** moving to Oakland. Centerfielder **Kenny Lofton** is the new leadoff hitter for the Pittsburgh Pirates. First baseman **Fred McGriff** will try to reach the 500 home-run mark with the Los Angeles Dodgers. The Mets added All-Star outfielder **Cliff Floyd,** and the Rockies picked up catcher **Charles Johnson** from the Marlins.

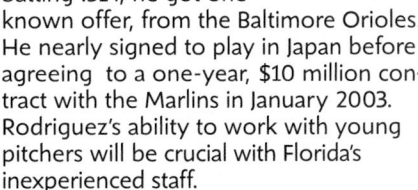

AL TIELEMANS/SPORTS ILLUSTRATED

FRANK FRANKLIN II/AP

HEINZ KLUETMEIER/SPORTS ILLUSTRATED

2003 Rookies to Watch

FRANCISCO RODRIGUEZ, pitcher, Anaheim Angels K-Rod pitched just 5⅔ regular-season innings in 2002, but he was vital in Anaheim's drive to its first-ever World Series championship, winning a record-tying five post-season games. His high-90s fastball and fierce slider have already earned him a reputation as a dangerous pitcher.

HIDEKI MATSUI, leftfielder, New York Yankees Despite their recent success, the Yankees have had a revolving door of leftfielders (Shane Spencer, Tim Raines, Chuck Knoblauch, Rondell White, and Ricky Ledee, to name just a few). The signing of Matsui, known as "Godzilla" from his 10 hugely productive seasons with the Yomiuri Giants, in Japan, should change that. He hit a career-high .334, with a league-leading and career-best 50 home runs in 2002. In his Yankee Stadium debut on April 8, 2003, Matsui hit a grand slam to defeat the Minnesota Twins, 7–3.

HEE SEOP CHOI, first baseman, Chicago Cubs The Chicago Cubs called up Choi from the minors in September 2002 to patrol first base before taking over the job permanently in 2003. At the time of his Cub debut, he was the first Korean-born position player to appear in a major league game. In four minor league seasons, Choi had 82 homers and 307 RBIs.

MARK TEIXEIRA, third baseman, Texas Rangers Teixeira was a hitting star in college at Georgia Tech, but the Rangers are bringing him along slowly. Last year, Ranger third baseman Hank Blalock was billed as the league's top rookie and wound up being sent back to the minors. Teixeira batted .318 with 19 homers and 69 RBIs in 86 games in the minor leagues in 2002.

V.J. LOVERO/SPORTS ILLUSTRATED

BERNIE NUNEZ/AP

MATT YORK/AP

2002-03 TIMELINE

January 8, 2002: Team owners and players begin new contract talks. Major issues on the table: how to help small-market teams compete with big-market teams and the owners' plan to eliminate two teams, most likely the Minnesota Twins and Montreal Expos.

March 31, 2002: The season opens with the Cleveland Indians whitewashing the Anaheim Angels, 6–0, in Anaheim, California.

April 27, 2002: Derek Lowe of the Boston Red Sox pitches a no-hitter against the Tampa Bay Devil Rays. The 10–0 win makes Lowe the first pitcher since 1965 to toss a no-hitter in Boston's Fenway Park.

May 2, 2002: Centerfielder Mike Cameron of the Seattle Mariners ties the single-game record by belting four homers as Seattle trounces the Chicago White Sox, 15–4. Twenty-one days later, rightfielder Shawn Green of the Los Angeles Dodgers hits four homers against the Milwaukee Brewers. It is the first time in major league history that there have been two four-homer games in one season.

June 21, 2002: Luis Castillo of the Florida Marlins hits safely in his 35th straight game, setting a major league record for most consecutive games with a hit by a second baseman. The streak is snapped by the Detroit Tigers on June 22.

July 5, 2002: Hall of Fame slugger Ted Williams of the Boston Red Sox dies at age 83. "The Splendid Splinter" hit .406 in 1941. Since then, no major leaguer has hit .400 or higher in a season.

July 9, 2002: The All-Star Game at Miller Park, in Milwaukee, Wisconsin, is declared a 7–7 tie when both teams run out of pitchers after 11 innings of play. No game MVP is chosen.

July 28, 2002: Shortstop Ozzie Smith is the only player inducted into the Hall of Fame. The 15-time All-Star and 13-time Gold Glove winner was called The Wizard because of his magical defensive play. He played 19 major league seasons with the San Diego Padres and St. Louis Cardinals.

August 9, 2002: Barry Bonds of the San Francisco Giants becomes only the fourth player in major league history to hit at least 600 homers, when he knocks one out at Pac Bell Park, in San Francisco, California. Only Hank Aaron (755), Babe Ruth (714), and Bonds' godfather, Willie Mays (660), hit at least 600 round-trippers.

August 30, 2002: Players and owners prevent a strike by reaching a four-year collective-bargaining agreement.

October 14, 2002: The San Francisco Giants win the N.L. pennant by downing the St. Louis Cardinals, 2–1, in Game 5 of the N.L. Championship Series.

October 27, 2002: The Angels win the World Series after rallying from a three-games-to-two deficit to beat the Giants, 4–1, in Game 7. Angel third base-man Troy Glaus is named Series MVP.

November 11, 2002: Barry Bonds is named the N.L. MVP for the fifth time, a National League and major league record.

March 31, 2003: The major league season opens on a bad note for the New York Yankees. They beat the Toronto Blue Jays, 8–4, but Derek Jeter dislocates his shoulder and is out until May 13.

April 2, 2003: Alex Rodriguez of the Texas Rangers becomes the youngest player to reach 300 home runs. Rodriguez, 27 years 249 days old, hit a three-run homer off Ramon Ortiz of the Anaheim Angels.

May 11, 2003: Rafael Palmeiro of the Texas Rangers becomes the 19th player to hit 500 career home runs. Palmeiro hits his 500th in a 17–10 win over the Cleveland Indians. He and Sammy Sosa are the only players born outside the U.S. in the 500-homer club.

June 13, 2003: Roger Clemens of the New York Yankees becomes the 21st major league pitcher to reach 300 career wins. His 300th victory comes against the St. Louis Cardinals. On this night of milestones, the Rocket also throws his 4,000th strikeout.

July 15, 2003: The American League de-feats the National League, 7-6, in the All-Star Game at U.S Cellular Field, in Chicago, Illinois. For the first time, the winning league is awarded home-field advantage in the World Series.

BASKETBALL

The 2002-03 NBA season began with three burning questions: 1. Would the Los Angeles Lakers win their fourth straight title? 2. Could Michael Jordan lead the Washington Wizards to the playoffs in his final season? 3. Would the Number 1 pick, 7' 5" center Yao Ming of China and the Houston Rockets, be a legit NBA player?

The third question was answered first. Yao broke out with 30 points and 16 rebounds against the Dallas Mavericks on November 21, 2002, putting to rest any talk that he didn't have the skills to play in the NBA. Even though Yao averaged a modest 13.5 points and 8.2 rebounds for the season, he showed that he definitely has the talent to become a dominant player in the near future.

Forty-year-old Michael Jordan still showed flashes of brilliance (averaging 20 points per game), but the Wizards fizzled to a 37–45 record and failed to make the playoffs. Jordan's competitive personality reportedly rubbed teammates and management the wrong way. After the season, he retired (again) and was let go from his job as Wizards' team president.

In 2002-03, Tim Duncan led the Spurs to their second NBA title and was named league and NBA Finals MVPs.

DAVID E. KLUTHO/SPORTS ILLUSTRATED

NBA TEAMS

EASTERN CONFERENCE
Atlanta Hawks
Boston Celtics
Chicago Bulls
Cleveland Cavaliers
Detroit Pistons
Indiana Pacers
Miami Heat
Milwaukee Bucks
New Jersey Nets
New Orleans Hornets
New York Knicks
Orlando Magic
Philadelphia 76ers
Toronto Raptors
Washington Wizards

WESTERN CONFERENCE
Dallas Mavericks
Denver Nuggets
Golden State Warriors
Houston Rockets
Los Angeles Clippers
Los Angeles Lakers
Memphis Grizzlies
Minnesota Timberwolves
Phoenix Suns
Portland Trail Blazers
Sacramento Kings
San Antonio Spurs
Seattle SuperSonics
Utah Jazz

There was also plenty of friction during the Lakers' season. Up-and-down play, plus injuries to center Shaquille O'Neal (foot) and guard Kobe Bryant (shoulder), led the team to a 50–32 record (fifth-best in the West). The Lakers' three-season dynasty ended when they lost to the San Antonio Spurs, led by MVP Tim Duncan, in the second round of the playoffs.

Duncan showed that he is the league's most unstoppable player. He carried the Spurs to their second title in five seasons, leading the team in scoring (24.7 points per game), rebounding (15.4), assists (5.3), and blocks (3.29) during the post-season. The Spurs' opponent in the Finals was the New Jersey Nets, making their second-straight appearance in the championship series. The Nets put up a decent fight as star point guard Jason Kidd led his team with 19.7 points and 7.8 assists per game. But in the end, they were outplayed by the Spurs and bowed out of the Finals four games to two.

The burning questions have been answered for 2002-03. Next season will start with a Yao Ming-sized one: How will high-school phenom LeBron James fare in his first NBA season?

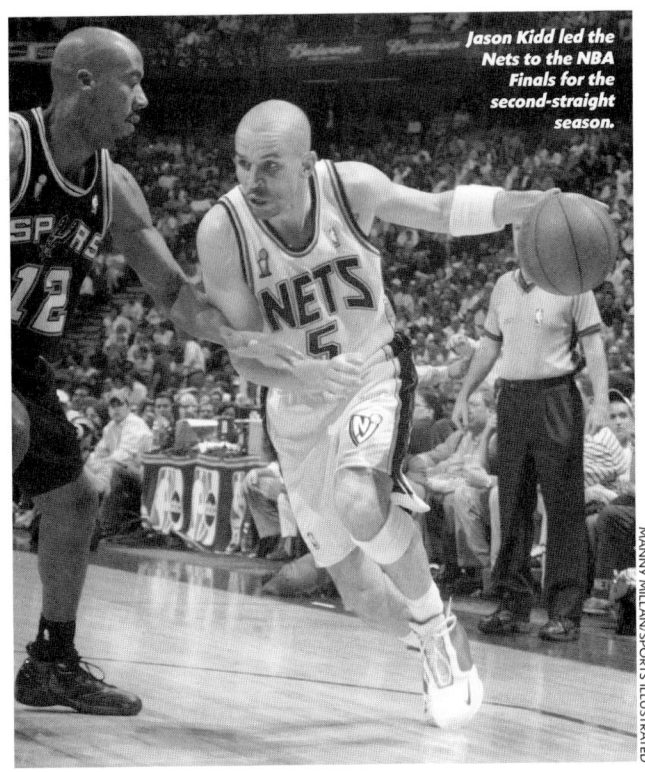

Jason Kidd led the Nets to the NBA Finals for the second-straight season.

MANNY MILLAN/SPORTS ILLUSTRATED

2002-03 NBA Final Standings

Eastern Conference

ATLANTIC	W	L	PCT	GB
a-Nets (2)	49	33	.598	0.0
x-76ers (4)	48	34	.585	1.0
x-Celtics (6)	44	38	.537	5.0
x-Magic (8)	42	40	.512	7.0
Wizards	37	45	.451	12.0
Knicks	37	45	.451	12.0
Heat	25	57	.305	24.0

CENTRAL	W	L	PCT	GB
e,c-Pistons (1)	50	32	.610	0.0
x-Pacers (3)	48	34	.585	2.0
x-Hornets (5)	47	35	.573	3.0
x-Bucks (7)	42	40	.512	8.0
Hawks	35	47	.427	15.0
Bulls	30	52	.366	20.0
Raptors	24	58	.293	26.0
Cavaliers	17	65	.207	33.0

Western Conference

MIDWEST	W	L	PCT	GB
w,m-Spurs (1)	60	22	.732	0.0
x-Mavericks (3)	60	22	.732	0.0
x-Timberwolves (4)	51	31	.622	9.0
x-Jazz (7)	47	35	.573	13.0
Rockets	43	39	.524	17.0
Grizzlies	28	54	.341	32.0
Nuggets	17	65	.207	43.0

PACIFIC	W	L	PCT	GB
p-Kings (2)	59	23	.720	0.0
x-Lakers (5)	50	32	.610	9.0
x-Trail Blazers (6)	50	32	.610	9.0
x-Suns (8)	44	38	.537	15.0
SuperSonics	40	42	.488	19.0
Warriors	38	44	.463	21.0
Clippers	27	55	.329	32.0

Note: Numbers in parentheses are seedings for the playoffs.

KEY x=clinched playoff berth; e=clinched Eastern Conference; a=clinched Atlantic Division; c=clinched Central Division; w=clinched Western Conference; m=clinched Midwest Division; p=clinched Pacific Division; W=win; L=loss; PCT=winning percentage; GB=games back

2003 NBA Playoffs

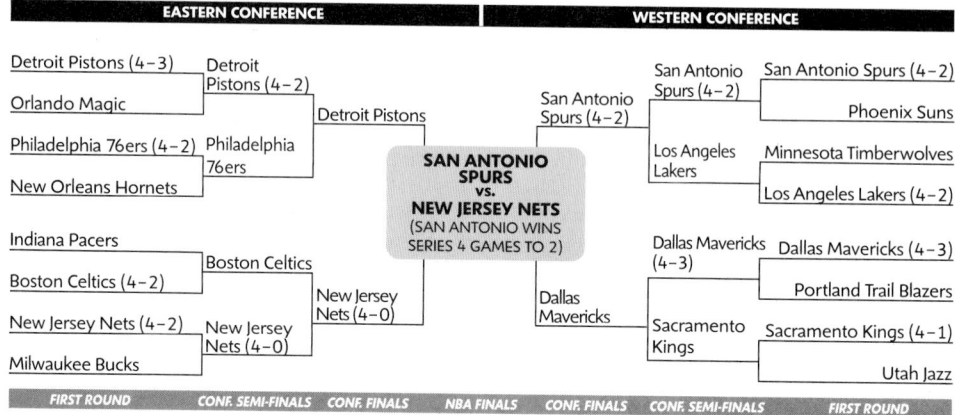

EASTERN CONFERENCE			WESTERN CONFERENCE

Detroit Pistons (4–3)
Orlando Magic
— Detroit Pistons (4–2)
— Detroit Pistons

Philadelphia 76ers (4–2)
New Orleans Hornets
— Philadelphia 76ers

SAN ANTONIO SPURS vs. NEW JERSEY NETS
(SAN ANTONIO WINS SERIES 4 GAMES TO 2)

Indiana Pacers
Boston Celtics (4–2)
— Boston Celtics

New Jersey Nets (4–2)
Milwaukee Bucks
— New Jersey Nets (4–0)
— New Jersey Nets (4–0)

San Antonio Spurs (4–2)
San Antonio Spurs (4–2)
— San Antonio Spurs (4–2)
— Phoenix Suns

Los Angeles Lakers
— Minnesota Timberwolves
— Los Angeles Lakers (4–2)

Dallas Mavericks (4–3)
Dallas Mavericks (4–3)
— Dallas Mavericks
— Portland Trail Blazers

Sacramento Kings
— Sacramento Kings (4–1)
— Utah Jazz

FIRST ROUND	CONF. SEMI-FINALS	CONF. FINALS	NBA FINALS	CONF. FINALS	CONF. SEMI-FINALS	FIRST ROUND

NBA Playoff Results

First Round

EASTERN CONFERENCE

Detroit Pistons vs. Orlando Magic
GAME 1 April 20, 2003: Orlando 99, Detroit 94
GAME 2 April 23, 2003: Detroit 89, Orlando 77
GAME 3 April 25, 2003: Orlando 89, Detroit 80
GAME 4 April 27, 2003: Orlando 100, Detroit 92
GAME 5 April 30, 2003: Detroit 98, Orlando 67
GAME 6 May 2, 2003: Detroit 103, Orlando 88
GAME 7 May 4, 2003: Detroit 103, Orlando 93
Detroit Pistons win series 4–3

New Jersey Nets vs. Milwaukee Bucks
GAME 1 April 19, 2003: New Jersey 109, Milwaukee 96
GAME 2 April 22, 2003: Milwaukee 88, New Jersey 85
GAME 3 April 24, 2003: New Jersey 103, Milwaukee 101
GAME 4 April 26, 2003: Milwaukee 119, New Jersey 114 (OT)
GAME 5 April 29, 2003: New Jersey 89, Milwaukee 82
GAME 6 May 1, 2003: New Jersey 113, Milwaukee 101
New Jersey Nets win series 4–2

Indiana Pacers vs. Boston Celtics
GAME 1 April 19, 2003: Boston 103, Indiana 100
GAME 2 April 21, 2003: Indiana 89, Boston 77
GAME 3 April 24, 2003: Boston 101, Indiana 83
GAME 4 April 27, 2003: Boston 102, Indiana 92
GAME 5 April 29, 2003: Indiana 93, Boston 88 (OT)
GAME 6 May 1, 2003: Boston 110, Indiana 90
Boston Celtics win series 4–2

Philadelphia 76ers vs. New Orleans Hornets
GAME 1 April 20, 2003: Philadelphia 98, New Orleans 90
GAME 2 April 23, 2003: Philadelphia 90, New Orleans 85
GAME 3 April 26, 2003: New Orleans 99, Philadelphia 85
GAME 4 April 28, 2003: Philadelphia 96, New Orleans 87
GAME 5 April 30, 2003: New Orleans 93, Philadelphia 91
GAME 6 May 2, 2003: Philadelphia 107, New Orleans 103
Philadelphia 76ers win series 4–2

WESTERN CONFERENCE

San Antonio Spurs vs. Phoenix Suns
GAME 1 April 19, 2003: Phoenix 96, San Antonio 95 (OT)
GAME 2 April 21, 2003: San Antonio 84, Phoenix 76
GAME 3 April 25, 2003: San Antonio 99, Phoenix 86
GAME 4 April 27, 2003: Phoenix 86, San Antonio 84
GAME 5 April 29, 2003: San Antonio 94, Phoenix 82
GAME 6 May 1, 2003: San Antonio 87, Phoenix 85
San Antonio Spurs win series 4–2

Sacramento Kings vs. Utah Jazz
GAME 1 April 19, 2003: Sacramento 96, Utah 90
GAME 2 April 21, 2003: Sacramento 108, Utah 95
GAME 3 April 26, 2003: Utah 107, Sacramento 104
GAME 4 April 28, 2003: Sacramento 99, Utah 82
GAME 5 April 30, 2003: Sacramento 111, Utah 91
Sacramento Kings win series 4–1

Dallas Mavericks vs. Portland Trail Blazers
GAME 1 April 19, 2003: Dallas 96, Portland 86
GAME 2 April 23, 2003: Dallas 103, Portland 99
GAME 3 April 25, 2003: Dallas 115, Portland 103
GAME 4 April 27, 2003: Portland 98, Dallas 79
GAME 5 April 30, 2003: Portland 103, Dallas 99
GAME 6 May 2, 2003: Portland 125, Dallas 103
GAME 7 May 4, 2003: Dallas 107, Portland 95
Dallas Mavericks win series 4–3

Minnesota Timberwolves vs. Los Angeles Lakers
GAME 1 April 20, 2003: Los Angeles 117, Minnesota 98
GAME 2 April 22, 2003: Minnesota 119, Los Angeles 91
GAME 3 April 24, 2003: Minnesota 114, Los Angeles 110 (OT)
GAME 4 April 27, 2003: Los Angeles 102, Minnesota 97
GAME 5 April 29, 2003: Los Angeles 120, Minnesota 90
GAME 6 May 1, 2003: Los Angeles 101, Minnesota 85
Los Angeles Lakers win series 4–2

Conference Semi-finals

EASTERN CONFERENCE
Detroit Pistons vs. Philadelphia 76ers
GAME 1 May 6, 2003: Detroit 98, Philadelphia 87
GAME 2 May 8, 2003: Detroit 104, Philadelphia 97 (OT)
GAME 3 May 10, 2003: Philadelphia 93, Detroit 83

NBA Playoff Results (cont.)

GAME 4 May 11, 2003: Philadelphia 95, Detroit 82
GAME 5 May 14, 2003: Detroit 78, Philadelphia 77
GAME 6 May 16, 2003: Detroit 93, Philadelphia 89
Detroit Pistons win series 4–2

New Jersey Nets vs. Boston Celtics
GAME 1 May 5, 2003: New Jersey 97, Boston 93
GAME 2 May 7, 2003: New Jersey 104, Boston 95
GAME 3 May 9, 2003: New Jersey 94, Boston 76
GAME 4 May 12, 2003: New Jersey 110, Boston 101 (2OT)
New Jersey Nets win series 4–0

WESTERN CONFERENCE
San Antonio Spurs vs. Los Angeles Lakers
GAME 1 May 5, 2003: San Antonio 87, Los Angeles 82
GAME 2 May 7, 2003: San Antonio 114, Los Angeles 95
GAME 3 May 9, 2003: Los Angeles 110, San Antonio 95
GAME 4 May 11, 2003: Los Angeles 99, San Antonio 95
GAME 5 May 13, 2003: San Antonio 96, Los Angeles 94
GAME 6 May 15, 2003: San Antonio 110, Los Angeles 82
San Antonio Spurs win series 4–2

Sacramento Kings vs. Dallas Mavericks
GAME 1 May 6, 2003: Sacramento 124, Dallas 113
GAME 2 May 8, 2003: Dallas 132, Sacramento 110
GAME 3 May 10, 2003: Dallas 141, Sacramento 137 (2OT)
GAME 4 May 11, 2003: Sacramento 99, Dallas 83
GAME 5 May 13, 2003: Dallas 112, Sacramento 93
GAME 6 May 15, 2003: Sacramento 115, Dallas 109
GAME 7 May 17, 2003: Dallas 112, Sacramento 99
Dallas Mavericks win series 4–3

Conference Finals

EASTERN CONFERENCE
Detroit Pistons vs. New Jersey Nets
GAME 1 May 18, 2003: New Jersey 76, Detroit 74
GAME 2 May 20, 2003: New Jersey 88, Detroit 86
GAME 3 May 22, 2003: New Jersey 97, Detroit 85
GAME 4 May 24, 2003: New Jersey 102, Detroit 82
New Jersey Nets win series 4–0

WESTERN CONFERENCE
San Antonio Spurs vs. Dallas Mavericks
GAME 1 May 19, 2003: Dallas 113, San Antonio 110
GAME 2 May 21, 2003: San Antonio 119, Dallas 106
GAME 3 May 23, 2003: San Antonio 96, Dallas 83
GAME 4 May 25, 2003: San Antonio 102, Dallas 95
GAME 5 May 27, 2003: Dallas 103, San Antonio 91
GAME 6 May 29, 2003: San Antonio 90, Dallas 78
San Antonio Spurs win series 4–2

Finals

San Antonio Spurs vs. New Jersey Nets
GAME 1 June 4, 2003: San Antonio 101, New Jersey 89
GAME 2 June 6, 2003: New Jersey 87, San Antonio 85
GAME 3 June 8, 2003: San Antonio 84, New Jersey 79
GAME 4 June 11, 2003: New Jersey 77, San Antonio 76
GAME 5 June 13, 2003: San Antonio 93, New Jersey 83
GAME 6 June 15, 2003: San Antonio 88, New Jersey 77
San Antonio Spurs win series 4–2

NBA FINALS COMPOSITE BOX SCORE

NEW JERSEY NETS

Player	GP	Field Goals		3-PT FG		Free Throws		Rebounds		A	STL	TO	BLK	AVG
		FGM	PCT	FGM	PCT	FTM	PCT	OFF	TOTAL					
Kidd	6	44	36.4	10	27.0	20	83.3	14	37	47	7	18	1	19.7
Martin	6	36	34.3	0	00.0	16	66.7	15	60	13	10	22	14	14.7
Jefferson	6	30	41.7	0	00.0	19	79.2	8	39	11	8	14	2	13.2
Kittles	6	23	37.7	7	30.4	12	80.0	6	25	8	11	3	3	10.8
Harris	6	11	30.6	2	33.3	15	78.9	7	16	7	2	6	0	6.5
Williams	5	11	42.3	0	00.0	6	75.0	10	21	4	1	1	7	5.6
Rogers	6	10	32.3	3	37.5	5	83.3	4	10	3	0	5	0	4.7
Collins	6	7	33.3	0	00.0	8	80.0	15	28	6	4	5	3	3.7
Mutombo	6	5	50.0	0	00.0	4	100.0	7	17	0	3	5	8	2.3
Johnson	5	5	55.6	1	50.0	0	00.0	0	1	1	1	3	0	2.2
Scalabrine	1	0	00.0	0	00.0	0	00.0	0	1	0	0	0	0	0.0
Slay	1	0	00.0	0	00.0	0	00.0	0	0	0	0	0	0	0.0
Totals	**6**	**182**	**37.0**	**23**	**27.7**	**105**	**78.4**	**86**	**255**	**100**	**47**	**85**	**38**	**82.0**

SAN ANTONIO SPURS

Player	GP	Field Goals		3-PT FG		Free Throws		Rebounds		A	STL	TO	BLK	AVG
		FGM	PCT	FGM	PCT	FTM	PCT	OFF	TOTAL					
Duncan	6	54	49.5	0	00.0	37	68.5	23	102	32	6	23	32	24.2
Parker	6	32	38.6	6	42.9	14	60.9	2	19	25	2	11	1	14.0
Robinson	6	22	61.1	0	00.0	21	70.0	15	44	4	7	3	11	10.8
Jackson	6	23	37.7	10	35.7	6	50.0	4	25	16	7	26	2	10.3
Ginobili	6	16	34.8	3	21.4	17	81.0	9	27	12	13	10	3	8.7
Rose	6	19	44.2	0	00.0	8	100.0	10	23	4	3	11	3	7.7
Claxton	6	14	56.0	0	00.0	9	75.0	1	6	9	4	4	4	6.2
Bowen	6	7	23.3	4	28.6	2	100.0	2	19	5	4	4	2	3.3
Kerr	4	3	75.0	1	100.0	1	50.0	1	1	2	1	0	0	2.0
Willis	5	3	33.3	0	00.0	2	100.0	7	9	0	0	3	1	1.6
Ferry	3	0	00.0	0	00.0	0	00.0	0	0	0	0	0	0	0.0
Smith	1	0	00.0	0	00.0	0	00.0	0	0	0	0	0	0	0.0
Totals	**6**	**193**	**43.2**	**24**	**32.0**	**117**	**70.5**	**74**	**275**	**109**	**47**	**99**	**59**	**87.8**

KEY GP=games played; FGM=field goals made; PCT=percentage; FTM=free throws made; OFF=offensive; A=assists; STL=steals; TO=turnovers; BLK=blocks; AVG=average

NBA Finals Box Scores

Game 1

SAN ANTONIO SPURS 101

	MIN	FG M-A	FT M-A	REB O-T	A	PF	STL	TO	PTS
Jackson	42	5-15	2-5	1-3	5	3	2	3	12
Parker	40	6-14	3-4	0-3	5	0	1	2	16
Duncan	44	11-17	10-14	3-20	6	1	3	1	32
Bowen	26	2-3	0-0	0-2	1	4	0	1	6
Robinson	27	6-8	2-3	2-6	1	2	0	0	14
Ginobili	28	3-8	0-0	1-7	3	3	0	3	7
Rose	24	5-11	2-2	3-6	2	5	1	2	12
Claxton	8	1-3	0-0	0-0	1	2	0	0	2
Ferry	1	0-0	0-0	0-0	0	0	0	0	0
Kerr									DNP
Smith									DNP
Willis									DNP
Totals	240	39-79	19-28	10-47	24	20	7	12	101

Percentages: Field goals— 49.4%, Free throws— 67.9%, 3-point field goals— 4-10, 40.0% (Jackson 0-4, Parker 1-2, Bowen 2-2, Ginobili 1-2). Team rebounds: 8. Blocked shots: 12 (Duncan 7, Robinson 4, Claxton 1).

NEW JERSEY NETS 89

	MIN	FG M-A	FT M-A	REB O-T	A	PF	STL	TO	PTS
Kidd	44	4-17	1-2	0-8	10	1	2	3	10
Kittles	30	2-7	3-4	2-3	2	1	0	1	8
Jefferson	36	5-10	5-6	0-4	1	3	2	3	15
Martin	33	10-24	1-2	4-12	2	6	1	1	21
Collins	31	1-4	3-4	4-9	3	4	0	0	5
Harris	24	4-10	6-7	0-1	0	1	0	0	15
Rogers	21	5-10	0-0	1-2	1	3	0	0	11
Williams	11	2-5	0-0	2-4	0	4	0	0	4
Mutombo	6	0-1	0-0	0-2	0	2	0	0	0
Johnson	4	0-1	0-0	0-0	0	1	0	0	0
Slay									DNP
Scalabrine									DNP
Totals	240	33-89	19-25	13-45	19	26	5	8	89

Percentages: Field goals— 37.1%, Free throws— 76.0%, 3-point field goals— 4-13, 30.8% (Kidd 1-5, Kittles 1-3, Martin 0-1, Harris 1-2, Rogers 1-2). Team rebounds: 11. Blocked shots: 5 (Kidd 1, Martin 2, Williams 1, Mutombo 1).

Game 2

NEW JERSEY NETS 87

	MIN	FG M-A	FT M-A	REB O-T	A	PF	STL	TO	PTS
Kidd	42	11-24	6-8	4-7	3	1	0	4	30
Kittles	21	3-7	1-2	1-4	1	1	3	1	8
Jefferson	39	3-10	2-2	1-3	3	3	2	3	8
Martin	33	6-16	2-2	3-5	4	5	2	1	14
Collins	34	3-6	0-0	1-4	1	2	1	1	6
Harris	27	5-8	0-0	2-7	1	1	1	1	10
Mutombo	20	2-3	0-0	1-4	0	3	0	0	4
Rogers	18	2-8	2-2	2-5	2	4	0	1	7
Johnson	6	0-1	0-0	0-0	1	1	0	1	0
Slay									DNP
Williams									DNP
Scalabrine									DNP
Totals	240	35-83	13-16	15-39	16	21	9	13	87

Percentages: Field goals— 42.2%, Free throws— 81.3%, 3-point field goals— 4-11, 36.4% (Kidd 2-4, Kittles 1-2, Collins 0-1, Harris 0-1, Rogers 1-3). Team rebounds: 5. Blocked shots: 5 (Martin 2, Mutombo 3).

SAN ANTONIO SPURS 85

	MIN	FG M-A	FT M-A	REB O-T	A	PF	STL	TO	PTS
Parker	41	9-17	3-4	1-5	5	3	0	1	21
Jackson	40	6-10	0-0	0-2	3	2	2	7	16
Duncan	43	8-19	3-10	2-12	3	3	0	4	19
Bowen	26	1-2	0-0	0-5	0	1	0	2	3
Robinson	33	3-6	4-6	4-8	1	0	2	1	10
Ginobili	29	1-6	2-2	4-6	3	4	1	3	4
Rose	19	3-4	1-1	2-3	1	1	1	2	7
Claxton	7	2-2	1-2	0-0	0	0	0	1	5
Kerr	1	0-1	0-0	0-0	1	2	0	0	0
Willis	1	0-1	0-0	1-2	0	0	0	0	0
Ferry									DNP
Smith									DNP
Totals	240	33-68	14-25	14-43	17	16	6	21	85

Percentages: Field goals— 48.5%, Free throws— 56.0%, 3-point field goals— 5-13, 38.5% (Parker 0-2, Jackson 4-7, Duncan 0-1, Bowen 1-1, Ginobili 0-2). Team rebounds: 10. Blocked shots: 7 (Parker 1, Jackson 1, Duncan 3, Robinson 2).

Game 3

SAN ANTONIO SPURS 84

	MIN	FG M-A	FT M-A	REB O-T	A	PF	STL	TO	PTS
Parker	43	9-21	4-8	1-3	6	0	0	1	26
Jackson	36	2-7	2-4	0-6	2	3	1	4	7
Duncan	45	6-13	9-12	3-16	7	3	1	5	21
Bowen	32	0-5	0-0	1-4	0	3	1	1	0
Robinson	26	1-5	6-8	1-3	0	2	1	0	8
Ginobili	28	3-6	2-3	2-2	4	2	4	1	8
Rose	22	4-7	0-0	0-2	0	2	1	3	8
Claxton	5	2-2	0-0	0-1	0	1	1	1	4
Willis	3	1-1	0-0	1-1	0	1	0	1	2
Kerr									DNP
Ferry									DNP
Smith									DNP
Totals	240	28-67	23-35	9-38	19	17	10	17	84

Percentages: Field goals— 41.8%, Free throws— 65.7%, 3-point field goals— 5-10, 50.0% (Parker 4-6, Jackson 1-2, Bowen 0-2). Team rebounds: 15. Blocked shots: 8 (Duncan 3, Bowen 2, Ginobili 2, Rose 1).

NEW JERSEY NETS 79

	MIN	FG M-A	FT M-A	REB O-T	A	PF	STL	TO	PTS
Kidd	42	6-19	0-0	2-3	11	3	2	4	12
Kittles	34	8-16	2-3	1-4	1	2	3	0	21
Martin	42	8-18	7-8	2-11	0	5	4	5	23
Jefferson	36	3-11	0-0	2-9	0	2	2	1	6
Collins	25	0-3	0-0	4-5	1	6	0	3	0
Harris	22	1-6	4-4	1-1	3	2	1	2	7
Mutombo	18	1-1	0-0	1-3	0	3	1	1	2
Rogers	11	0-3	2-2	0-2	0	2	0	2	2
Johnson	6	2-2	0-0	0-1	0	0	0	0	4
Williams	4	1-2	0-0	1-2	1	1	0	0	2
Slay									DNP
Scalabrine									DNP
Totals	240	30-81	15-17	14-41	17	26	13	18	79

Percentages: Field goals— 37.0%, Free throws— 88.2%, 3-point field goals— 4-13, 30.8% (Kidd 0-5, Kittles 3-5, Martin 0-1, Harris 1-2). Team rebounds: 10. Blocked shots: 5 (Kittles 2, Martin 2, Collins 1).

KEY MIN=minutes played; FG M-A=field goals made-attempted; FT M-A=free throws made-attempted; REB O-T=rebounds offensive-total; A=assists; PF=personal fouls; STL=steals; TO=turnovers; PTS=points; DNP=did not play

Game 4

NEW JERSEY NETS 77

	MIN	FG M-A	FT M-A	REB O-T	A	PF	STL	TO	PTS
Kidd	47	5-18	6-6	3-8	9	3	0	5	16
Kittles	35	2-10	0-0	1-6	1	0	1	0	4
Martin	40	7-16	6-12	5-13	3	5	1	5	20
Jefferson	40	8-15	2-4	1-10	1	1	0	3	18
Collins	10	0-0	0-0	2-2	1	4	1	0	0
Mutombo	21	1-3	2-2	2-3	0	3	2	1	4
Williams	17	2-6	4-5	2-7	1	3	0	0	8
Harris	15	0-4	0-0	3-4	3	1	0	1	0
Rogers	11	2-5	0-0	0-0	0	2	0	1	4
Johnson	4	1-1	0-0	0-0	0	0	0	0	3
Slay									DNP
Scalabrine									DNP
Totals	240	28-78	20-29	19-53	19	22	5	16	77

Percentages: Field goals— 35.9%, Free throws— 69.0%, 3-point field goals— 1-9, 11.1% (Kidd 0-4, Kittles 0-4, Johnson 1-1). Team rebounds: 9. Blocked shots: 13 (Martin 3, Jefferson 2, Collins 1, Mutombo 3, Williams 4).

SAN ANTONIO SPURS 76

	MIN	FG M-A	FT M-A	REB O-T	A	PF	STL	TO	PTS
Parker	31	1-12	1-2	0-4	3	3	0	2	3
Jackson	28	1-9	2-3	2-4	3	3	1	2	5
Bowen	40	2-9	0-0	1-7	1	2	2	0	5
Duncan	39	10-23	3-3	8-17	2	4	1	3	23
Robinson	24	4-5	6-7	3-7	1	6	1	0	14
Ginobili	28	3-10	2-3	1-2	1	1	4	1	10
Claxton	17	3-6	4-4	1-3	2	1	1	0	10
Willis	16	2-7	2-2	5-5	0	3	0	2	6
Rose	15	0-9	0-0	1-4	0	3	0	1	0
Kerr	1	0-0	0-0	0-0	1	1	0	0	0
Ferry	1	0-0	0-0	0-0	0	0	0	0	0
Smith									DNP
Totals	240	26-90	20-24	22-53	14	27	10	11	76

Percentages: Field goals— 28.9%, Free throws— 83.3%, 3-point field goals— 4-18, 22.2% (Parker 0-2, Jackson 1-4, Bowen 1-5, Ginobili 2-6, Rose 0-1). Team rebounds: 12. Blocked shots: 10 (Jackson 1, Duncan 7, Robinson 1, Willis 1).

Game 5

SAN ANTONIO SPURS 93

	MIN	FG M-A	FT M-A	REB O-T	A	PF	STL	TO	PTS
Parker	33	5-13	3-5	0-2	4	3	1	2	14
Jackson	32	2-7	0-0	1-7	3	2	0	4	5
Duncan	46	10-18	9-10	3-17	4	3	1	6	29
Bowen	29	1-4	2-2	0-1	1	4	0	0	4
Robinson	20	2-4	2-2	1-3	0	6	3	1	6
Rose	29	6-9	2-2	2-3	1	2	0	1	14
Ginobili	26	4-8	4-4	0-3	0	5	2	1	12
Claxton	15	1-4	1-2	0-1	2	4	2	0	3
Kerr	9	2-2	1-2	1-1	0	0	1	0	6
Willis	1	0-0	0-0	0-1	0	0	0	0	0
Ferry									DNP
Smith									DNP
Totals	240	33-69	24-29	8-39	15	29	10	15	93

Percentages: Field goals— 47.8%, Free throws— 82.8%, 3-point field goals— 3-9, 33.3% (Parker 1-2, Jackson 1-4, Bowen 0-2, Kerr 1-1). Team rebounds: 8. Blocked shots: 9 (Duncan 4, Robinson 2, Ginobili 1, Claxton 2).

NEW JERSEY NETS 83

	MIN	FG M-A	FT M-A	REB O-T	A	PF	STL	TO	PTS
Kidd	48	10-23	5-6	3-7	7	2	2	2	29
Kittles	34	3-9	2-2	1-4	1	3	1	1	8
Martin	38	2-8	0-0	1-9	3	5	1	8	4
Jefferson	37	5-11	9-11	2-6	4	4	2	1	19
Collins	26	1-3	5-6	4-5	0	5	1	0	7
Williams	23	4-9	2-3	4-7	0	4	0	0	10
Harris	22	1-7	3-4	0-1	0	0	0	1	5
Mutombo	7	0-1	0-0	1-2	0	2	0	2	0
Rogers	5	0-3	1-2	1-1	0	0	0	1	1
Slay									DNP
Johnson									DNP
Scalabrine									DNP
Totals	240	26-74	27-34	17-42	15	25	7	16	83

Percentages: Field goals— 35.1%, Free throws— 79.4%, 3-point field goals— 4-16, 25.0% (Kidd 4-10, Kittles 0-3, Martin 0-1, Rogers 0-2). Team rebounds: 7. Blocked shots: 5 (Kittles 1, Martin 3, Williams 1).

Game 6

SAN ANTONIO SPURS 88

	MIN	FG M-A	FT M-A	REB O-T	A	PF	STL	TO	PTS
Jackson	35	7-13	0-0	0-3	0	3	1	6	17
Parker	24	2-6	0-0	0-2	2	0	0	3	4
Duncan	46	9-19	3-5	4-20	10	2	0	4	21
Bowen	18	1-7	0-0	0-0	2	0	1	0	2
Robinson	31	6-8	1-4	4-17	1	2	0	1	13
Ginobili	33	2-8	7-9	1-7	3	3	2	1	11
Claxton	23	5-8	3-4	0-1	4	2	0	2	13
Rose	18	1-3	3-3	2-5	0	1	0	2	5
Kerr	9	1-1	0-0	0-0	0	1	0	0	2
Ferry	1	0-0	0-0	0-0	0	0	0	0	0
Smith	1	0-1	0-0	0-0	0	0	0	0	0
Willis	1	0-0	0-0	0-0	0	0	0	0	0
Totals	240	34-74	17-25	11-55	20	14	4	19	88

Percentages: Field goals— 45.9%, Free throws— 68.0%, 3-point field goals— 3-15, 20.0% (Jackson 3-7, Duncan 0-1, Bowen 0-2, Ginobili 0-4, Smith 0-1). Team rebounds: 6. Blocked shots: 13 (Duncan 8, Robinson 2, Claxton 1, Rose 2).

NEW JERSEY NETS 77

	MIN	FG M-A	FT M-A	REB O-T	A	PF	STL	TO	PTS
Kidd	42	8-20	2-2	2-4	7	4	1	0	21
Kittles	34	5-12	4-4	0-4	2	3	0	0	16
Jefferson	41	6-15	1-1	2-7	2	5	0	3	13
Martin	39	3-23	0-0	0-10	1	3	1	2	6
Collins	25	2-5	0-0	0-3	0	4	1	1	4
Williams	16	2-4	0-0	1-1	2	4	1	0	4
Harris	15	0-1	2-4	1-2	0	1	0	1	2
Mutombo	10	1-1	2-2	2-3	0	1	0	1	4
Rogers	8	1-2	0-0	0-0	0	1	0	0	3
Johnson	8	2-4	0-0	0-0	0	0	1	2	4
Slay	1	0-0	0-0	0-0	0	0	0	0	0
Scalabrine	1	0-0	0-0	0-1	0	0	0	0	0
Totals	240	30-87	11-13	8-35	14	25	8	11	77

Percentages: Field goals— 34.5%, Free throws— 84.6%, 3-point field goals— 6-21, 28.6% (Kidd 3-9, Kittles 2-6, Jefferson 0-1, Martin 0-2, Harris 0-1, Rogers 1-1, Johnson 0-1). Team rebounds: 11. Blocked shots: 5 (Martin 2, Collins 1, Williams 1, Mutombo 1).

Legends

Larry Bird, forward, b. December 7, 1956, West Baden, Indiana. Bird was one of the best pure shooters in NBA history. He led the Boston Celtics to three championships (1980-81, 1983-84, 1985-86) and won three straight MVP awards (1984, 1985, 1986) in his 13-year career. Bird retired shortly after winning the gold medal as a member of the 1992 Olympic "Dream Team." A career 24.3 points-per-game scorer, Bird was elected to the Basketball Hall of Fame in 1998.

Larry Bird was a nine-time All-Star and a two-time Finals MVP (1984, 1986).

MANNY MILLAN/SPORTS ILLUSTRATED

Kareem Abdul-Jabbar, center, b. April 16, 1947, New York, New York. Abdul-Jabbar's graceful sky-hook made him a power in the paint for the Milwaukee Bucks and, later, the Los Angeles Lakers. The 7' 3" center won a record six MVP awards, along with six championships. Abdul-Jabbar retired in 1989, after 20 seasons. He is the NBA's all-time leading scorer (38,387 points) and was inducted into the Basketball Hall of Fame in 1995. Abdul-Jabbar also played on three straight NCAA championship teams with UCLA, where he was known as Lew Alcindor.

Oscar Robertson, guard, b. November 24, 1938, Charlotte, Tennessee. Robertson was one of the most versatile players in NBA history. In 1961-62, "The Big O" averaged a triple-double for the *entire* season (30.8 points per game, 12.5 rebounds per game, and 11.4 assists per game). Over the first five seasons of his career, he averaged 30.3 points, 10.4 rebounds, and 10.6 assists. Robertson led the Milwaukee Bucks to the NBA championship in 1971. He also led the league in assists eight times and was MVP of the NBA All-Star Game three times. Robertson retired in 1974 and was inducted into the Basketball Hall of Fame in 1979.

MANNY MILLAN/SPORTS ILLUSTRATED

Tracy McGrady, Orlando Magic

2002-03 NBA Individual Leaders

Scoring

Scoring	GP	PTS	AVG
Tracy McGrady, Orlando Magic	75	2,407	32.1
Kobe Bryant, Los Angeles Lakers	82	2,461	30.0
Allen Iverson, Phildelphia 76ers	82	2,262	27.6
Shaquille O'Neal, Los Angeles Lakers	67	1,841	27.5
Paul Pierce, Boston Celtics	79	2,048	25.9

Rebounds	GP	REB	AVG
Ben Wallace, Detroit Pistons	73	1,126	15.4
Kevin Garnett, Minnesota Timberwolves	82	1,102	13.4
Tim Duncan, San Antonio Spurs	81	1,043	12.9
Jermaine O'Neal, Indiana Pacers	77	796	10.3
Brian Grant, Miami Heat	82	837	10.2
Troy Murphy, Golden State Warriors	79	806	10.2

Assists	GP	A	AVG
Jason Kidd, New Jersey Nets	80	711	8.9
Jason Williams, Memphis Grizzlies	76	631	8.3
Gary Payton, Milwaukee Bucks	80	663	8.3
Stephon Marbury, Phoenix Suns	81	654	8.1
John Stockton, Utah Jazz	82	629	7.7

Field-goal Percentage	FGA	FGM	PCT
Eddy Curry, Chicago Bulls	573	335	58.5
Shaquille O'Neal, Los Angeles Lakers	1,211	695	57.4
Carlos Boozer, Cleveland Cavaliers	618	331	53.6
P.J. Brown, New Orleans Hornets	601	319	53.1
Radoslav Nesterovic, Minnesota Timberwolves	762	400	52.5

Free-throw Percentage	FTA	FTM	PCT
Allan Houston, New York Knicks	395	363	91.9
Ray Allen, Seattle SuperSonics	345	316	91.6
Steve Nash, Dallas Mavericks	339	308	90.9
Troy Hudson, Minnesota Timberwolves	231	208	90.0
Reggie Miller, Indiana Pacers	230	207	90.0

KEY GP=games played; PTS=points; AVG=average; REB=rebounds; A=assists; FGA=field-goal attempts; FGM=field goals made; FTA=free-throw attempts; FTM=free throws made; PCT=percentage

2002-03 NBA Individual Leaders (cont.)

3-point Field-goal Percentage	FGA	FGM	PCT
Bruce Bowen, San Antonio Spurs	229	101	44.1
Michael Redd, Milwaukee Bucks	416	182	43.8
Wesley Person, Memphis Grizzlies	231	100	43.3
David Wesley, New Orleans Hornets	316	134	42.4
Wally Szczerbiak, Minnesota Timberwolves	145	61	42.1

Blocks	GP	BLK	AVG
Theo Ratliff, Atlanta Hawks	81	262	3.23
Ben Wallace, Detroit Pistons	73	230	3.15
Tim Duncan, San Antonio Spurs	81	237	2.93
Elton Brand, Los Angeles Clippers	62	158	2.55
Adonal Foyle, Golden State Warriors	82	205	2.50

Steals	GP	STL	AVG
Allen Iverson, Philadelphia 76ers	82	225	2.74
Ron Artest, Indiana Pacers	69	159	2.30
Shawn Marion, Phoenix Suns	81	185	2.28
Doug Christie, Sacramento Kings	80	180	2.25
Jason Kidd, New Jersey Nets	80	179	2.24

Allen Iverson, Philadelphia 76ers

KEY GP=games played; STL=steals; BLK=blocks; AVG=average

NBAE/GETTY IMAGES

2002-03 TIMELINE

September 4, 2002: The U.S. Men's National Team loses to Argentina, 87–80, in the world championships. It is the first loss for the U.S. when using NBA players. The U.S. loses two more games in the tournament and finishes in sixth place, its worst showing since the event began in 1950. Yugoslavia wins the gold medal and Dirk Nowitzki of Germany (and the Dallas Mavericks) is named MVP of the tournament.

October 30, 2002: Number 1 draft pick Yao Ming makes his NBA debut for the Houston Rockets against the Indiana Pacers. Yao goes scoreless in 11 minutes. He averages 13.5 points and 8.2 rebounds for the season.

November 28, 2002: After winning their first 14 games, the Dallas Mavericks lose to the Indiana Pacers, 110–98. The Mavs fall one victory short of the NBA record for most wins to start a season.

February 9, 2003: The Western Conference wins the All-Star Game, 155–145, in double overtime. Forward Kevin Garnett of the Minnesota Timberwolves scores 37 points and is named MVP. The night before, Jason Richardson of the Golden State Warriors wins the Slam Dunk Contest and Peja Stojakovic of the Sacramento Kings wins the Three-Point Shootout.

March 5, 2003: Kobe Bryant scores 20 points in a 97–95 win over the Indiana Pacers, becoming the youngest player (24 years, 193 days) in history to score at least 10,000 career points.

April 16, 2003: Michael Jordan plays his final game, a 107–87 loss to the Philadelphia 76ers. Jordan scores 15 points and retires (again) with the highest career scoring average in NBA history (30.1).

April 30, 2003: John Stockton announces his retirement after the Jazz are knocked out of the first round of the playoffs by the Sacramento Kings. Stockton finishes his 19-year career as the NBA's career leader in assists (15,806) and steals (3,265).

May 15, 2003: The San Antonio Spurs beat the Los Angeles Lakers, 110–82, to win its Western Conference semi-final series, four games to two. The win ends the Lakers' run of 13 straight playoff series wins.

June 15, 2003: The San Antonio Spurs defeat the New Jersey Nets in the Finals, four games to two. Forward Tim Duncan is named Finals MVP. Center David Robinson retires after 14 seasons with a ring, the second championship of his career.

June 26, 2003: The Cleveland Cavaliers select 6'7" guard/forward LeBron James with the Number 1 pick of the draft. In 2002-03, James averaged 30.4 points and 9.8 rebounds for St. Vincent–St. Mary High School, in Akron, Ohio.

BASKETBALL *PRO*

TEAM-BY-TEAM STATS

ATLANTA HAWKS

Player	GP	MIN	Field Goals FGM	PCT	3-PT FG FGA-FGM	Free Throws FTM	PCT	Rebounds OFF	TOTAL	A	STL	TO	BLK	AVG
Shareef Abdur-Rahim	81	3,087	566	47.8	60-21	455	84.1	175	677	242	87	212	38	19.9
Glenn Robinson	69	2,591	539	43.2	263-90	268	87.6	86	457	205	91	248	26	20.8
Jason Terry	81	3,081	488	42.8	431-160	259	88.7	37	279	600	126	249	14	17.2
Dion Glover	76	1,890	277	42.7	158-56	127	78.4	62	282	141	71	108	15	9.7
Theo Ratliff	81	2,518	276	46.4	0-0	154	72.0	154	607	73	56	137	262	8.7
Ira Newble	73	1,931	231	49.5	84-32	70	77.8	86	271	99	50	69	26	7.7
Alan Henderson	82	1,494	153	46.8	2-0	88	63.8	156	398	41	33	61	32	4.8
Dan Dickau	50	515	70	41.2	61-22	21	80.8	9	43	85	14	53	2	3.7
Darvin Ham	75	926	71	44.7	3-0	38	48.1	73	153	38	16	65	19	2.4
Nazr Mohammed	35	445	67	42.1	0-0	26	63.4	47	129	6	16	25	21	4.6
Emanual Davis	24	340	32	36.4	29-7	17	77.3	5	43	36	12	25	2	3.7
Jermaine Jackson	29	273	19	45.2	1-0	17	60.7	9	32	35	10	15	3	1.9
Corey Benjamin	9	152	13	30.2	13-2	12	75.0	10	31	10	1	6	2	4.4
Chris Crawford	5	38	8	61.5	3-1	7	87.5	3	7	1	2	2	3	4.8
Matt Maloney	14	103	8	32.0	15-5	3	60.0	1	7	17	4	5	0	1.7
Mikki Moore	5	31	5	41.7	0-0	8	80.0	5	7	3	0	2	2	3.6
Amal McCaskill	11	70	4	23.5	0-0	3	75.0	7	22	5	3	2	1	1.0
Antonio Harvey	4	32	2	40.0	0-0	0	00.0	1	6	0	1	3	4	1.0
Brandon Williams	6	19	1	14.3	1-0	0	00.0	2	2	0	2	3	0	.3
Paul Shirley	2	5	0	00.0	0-0	0	00.0	0	1	0	0	0	0	.0
Team Totals	82	19,905	2,859	44.4	1,141-402	1,594	79.3	937	3,495	1,679	611	1,367	473	94.1
Opponents	82	-	3,015	43.6	1,243-446	1,530	76.0	1,073	3,493	1,771	738	1,068	409	97.6

BOSTON CELTICS

Player	GP	MIN	Field Goals FGM	PCT	3-PT FG FGA-FGM	Free Throws FTM	PCT	Rebounds OFF	TOTAL	A	STL	TO	BLK	AVG
Paul Pierce	79	3,096	663	41.6	391-118	604	80.2	106	578	349	139	288	62	25.9
Antoine Walker	78	3,235	603	38.8	582-188	176	61.5	99	563	373	116	260	31	20.1
Eric Williams	82	2,350	254	44.2	110-37	201	75.0	143	382	140	86	97	19	9.1
Tony Delk	67	1,873	233	41.6	304-120	68	78.2	41	232	146	72	69	10	9.8
J.R. Bremer	64	1,503	171	36.9	286-101	85	76.6	18	145	164	38	59	3	8.3
Walter McCarty	82	1,949	173	41.4	248-91	61	62.2	64	288	106	78	67	28	6.1
Tony Battie	67	1,683	199	53.9	5-1	88	74.6	148	433	49	33	48	81	7.3
Vin Baker	52	942	99	47.8	4-0	72	67.3	90	198	29	22	61	30	5.2
Kedrick Brown	51	666	61	35.7	39-3	20	62.5	45	140	20	34	23	13	2.8
Mark Blount	27	518	45	56.3	0-0	30	75.0	49	125	21	20	33	17	4.4
Grant Long	41	488	27	38.6	3-0	18	78.3	24	83	25	9	19	1	1.8
Bimbo Coles	14	175	22	44.9	7-0	8	100.0	1	11	16	6	10	0	3.7
Bruno Sundov	26	138	14	25.0	16-4	0	00.0	8	28	7	6	9	3	1.2
Ruben Wolkowyski	7	24	2	50.0	1-0	1	25.0	1	5	1	0	1	0	.7
Mark Bryant	2	9	0	00.0	0-0	0	00.0	0	2	1	0	0	0	.0
Team Totals	82	19,830	2,700	41.5	2,155-719	1,480	74.2	849	3,320	1,575	720	1,147	303	92.7
Opponents	82	-	2,804	43.5	1,400-463	1,560	74.9	937	3,687	1,824	617	1,315	367	93.1

KEY GP=games played; MIN=minutes played; FGM=field goals made; PCT=percentage; FGA=field goals attempted; FTM=free throws made; OFF=offensive; A=assists; STL=steals; TO=turnovers; BLK=blocks; AVG=average

CHICAGO BULLS

Player	GP	MIN	Field Goals FGM	PCT	3-PT FG FGA-FGM	Free Throws FTM	PCT	Rebounds OFF	TOTAL	A	STL	TO	BLK	AVG
Jalen Rose	82	3,351	642	40.6	359-133	399	85.4	68	351	395	72	285	23	22.1
Donyell Marshall	78	2,378	421	45.9	87-33	167	75.6	234	699	137	95	135	85	13.4
Jamal Crawford	80	1,992	334	41.3	242-86	104	80.6	21	185	334	77	134	25	10.7
Eddy Curry	81	1,571	335	58.5	0-0	179	62.4	116	353	37	18	137	62	10.5
Jay Williams	75	1,961	273	39.9	202-65	103	64.0	27	195	350	86	171	17	9.5
Tyson Chandler	75	1,827	257	53.1	0-0	177	60.8	169	514	76	37	135	106	9.2
Marcus Fizer	38	809	178	46.5	6-1	88	65.7	80	216	48	14	57	17	11.7
Eddie Robinson	64	1,355	155	49.2	14-3	51	81.0	76	200	66	62	52	13	5.7
Trenton Hassell	82	1,999	144	36.7	40-13	41	74.5	37	255	151	45	83	61	4.2
Lonny Baxter	55	682	96	46.6	2-0	70	68.0	65	165	16	9	46	22	4.8
Corie Blount	50	836	65	48.5	0-0	20	57.1	68	205	50	33	43	19	3.0
Fred Hoiberg	63	784	49	38.9	21-5	41	82.0	11	137	70	40	25	5	2.3
Rick Brunson	17	196	23	46.0	6-4	10	83.3	4	19	36	10	17	3	3.5
Roger Mason, Jr.	17	113	11	35.5	18-6	2	100.0	2	12	12	4	5	0	1.8
Dalibor Bagaric	10	76	8	30.8	0-0	3	75.0	7	20	4	3	5	3	1.9
Team Totals	82	19,930	2,991	44.5	349	1,455	72.2	985	3,526	1,782	605	1,388	461	95.0
Opponents	82	-	2,991	43.9	431	1,794	74.9	1,117	3,689	1,949	768	1,208	413	100.1

CLEVELAND CAVALIERS

Player	GP	MIN	Field Goals FGM	PCT	3-PT FG FGA-FGM	Free Throws FTM	PCT	Rebounds OFF	TOTAL	A	STL	TO	BLK	AVG
Ricky Davis	79	3,131	602	41.0	204-74	348	74.8	97	390	436	125	277	36	20.6
Zydrunas Ilgauskas	81	2,432	495	44.1	5-0	400	78.1	240	611	127	56	210	152	17.2
Carlos Boozer	81	2,049	331	53.6	1-0	148	77.1	202	609	106	59	103	50	10.0
Jumaine Jones	80	2,204	308	43.4	314-111	57	68.7	106	405	112	67	107	22	9.8
Dajuan Wagner	47	1,385	223	36.9	174-55	128	80.0	20	82	130	38	85	7	13.4
Darius Miles	67	2,008	263	41.0	14-0	92	59.4	113	363	176	67	178	69	9.2
Smush Parker	66	1,103	136	40.2	118-38	98	83.1	29	119	162	48	133	12	6.2
Milt Palacio	80	1,976	162	41.8	37-8	65	74.7	48	235	259	68	131	16	5.0
Chris Mihm	52	809	116	40.4	3-0	76	72.4	93	231	28	18	48	38	5.9
DeSagana Diop	80	943	54	35.1	0-0	11	36.7	63	215	43	33	56	81	1.5
Tierre Brown	15	168	27	45.8	1-0	11	78.6	8	30	39	13	22	0	4.3
Michael Stewart	47	251	14	37.8	0-0	8	66.7	19	55	6	2	10	15	.8
Team Totals	82	19,830	2,850	42.2	896-293	1,502	74.7	1,118	3,660	1,712	636	1,501	521	91.4
Opponents	82	-	3,072	45.3	1,197-428	1,712	77.2	932	3,423	1,972	802	1,162	494	101.0

Did You Know?

Kobe Bryant scored 40 or more points in nine straight games, from February 6 to February 23, 2003. It was the third-longest streak of 40 or more points in NBA history. Wilt Chamberlain set the record (14 straight games), in 1961-62.

DALLAS MAVERICKS

Player	GP	MIN	Field Goals		3-PT FG	Free Throws		Rebounds		A	STL	TO	BLK	AVG
			FGM	PCT	FGA-FGM	FTM	PCT	OFF	TOTAL					
Dirk Nowitzki	80	3,117	690	46.3	390-148	483	88.1	81	791	239	111	152	82	25.1
Steve Nash	82	2,711	518	46.5	269-111	308	90.9	63	234	598	85	192	6	17.7
Michael Finley	69	2,642	507	42.5	322-119	198	86.1	107	402	205	76	114	21	19.3
Nick Van Exel	73	2,026	342	41.2	312-118	110	76.4	35	208	312	42	123	4	12.5
Raef LaFrentz	69	1,611	266	51.8	116-47	60	68.2	125	330	54	35	46	91	9.3
Shawn Bradley	81	1,731	201	53.6	1-0	141	80.6	151	476	54	65	67	170	6.7
Walt Williams	66	1,161	134	39.3	171-64	31	62.0	53	207	59	42	35	26	5.5
Adrian Griffin	74	1,373	146	43.3	24-6	27	84.4	88	264	105	77	47	6	4.4
Eduardo Najera	48	1,103	129	55.8	1-0	62	68.1	90	223	47	40	23	22	6.7
Raja Bell	75	1,173	93	44.1	51-21	23	67.6	47	145	57	52	43	8	3.1
Avery Johnson	48	430	63	42.0	2-0	30	76.9	10	31	64	15	29	1	3.3
Tariq Abdul-Wahad	14	204	27	46.6	1-0	3	50.0	14	40	21	6	7	3	4.1
Popeye Jones	26	222	24	38.7	0-0	5	45.5	29	59	8	5	15	1	2.0
Evan Eschmeyer	17	135	7	36.8	0-0	3	75.0	10	29	6	10	6	7	1.0
Antoine Rigaudeau	11	91	8	22.9	5-1	0	00.0	4	8	6	3	6	0	1.5
Mark Strickland	4	13	2	40.0	0-0	0	00.0	5	7	0	0	1	0	1.0
Team Totals	82	19,780	3,161	45.3	1,668-636	1,486	82.9	912	3,456	1,837	665	949	449	103.0
Opponents	82	-	2,926	43.8	1401-477	1,477	72.7	1,045	3,727	1,781	547	1,316	322	95.2

DENVER NUGGETS

Player	GP	MIN	Field Goals		3-PT FG	Free Throws		Rebounds		A	STL	TO	BLK	AVG
			FGM	PCT	FGA-FGM	FTM	PCT	OFF	TOTAL					
Juwan Howard	77	2,730	567	45.0	4-2	282	80.3	181	585	234	77	189	27	18.4
Nene Hilario	80	2,258	321	51.9	3-0	197	57.8	208	491	149	127	181	65	10.5
Rodney White	72	1,563	260	40.8	134-32	98	78.4	43	213	121	45	156	32	9.0
Donnell Harvey	77	1,613	246	44.6	7-1	118	67.0	125	409	100	48	123	27	7.9
Junior Harrington	82	2,003	169	36.2	28-7	73	65.2	44	250	277	80	157	15	5.1
Vincent Yarbrough	59	1,381	168	39.3	78-21	49	79.0	36	162	130	57	81	33	6.9
Nikoloz Tskitishvili	81	1,320	115	29.3	152-37	48	73.8	64	181	91	31	84	29	3.9
Chris Andersen	59	907	114	40.0	1-0	77	55.0	109	274	32	30	60	60	5.2
Shammond Williams	27	712	94	39.0	102-37	30	66.7	12	61	138	16	53	3	9.4
Ryan Bowen	62	996	97	49.2	7-2	27	65.9	78	157	54	65	43	29	3.6
Marcus Camby	29	616	93	41.0	5-2	33	66.0	75	208	47	20	27	40	7.6
Predrag Savovic	27	256	29	31.2	26-4	21	72.4	9	25	22	14	21	1	3.1
Jeff Trepagnier	8	97	17	42.5	8-4	7	100.0	8	16	6	8	8	0	5.6
John Crotty	12	180	14	34.1	13-4	9	60.0	1	15	29	3	9	0	3.4
Adam Harrington	6	74	7	35.0	11-4	1	50.0	1	6	10	1	0	0	3.2
Devin Brown	3	71	7	28.0	1-0	4	66.7	4	11	5	4	4	1	6.0
Team Totals	82	19,730	2,689	41.1	824-229	1,294	69.9	1,112	3,475	1,737	712	1,514	422	84.2
Opponents	82	-	2,696	44.3	1,134-420	1,768	75.7	861	3,304	1,764	742	1,405	538	92.4

DETROIT PISTONS

Player	GP	MIN	FGM	PCT	FGA-FGM	FTM	PCT	OFF	TOTAL	A	STL	TO	BLK	AVG
			Field Goals		3-PT FG	Free Throws		Rebounds						
Richard Hamilton	82	2,640	570	44.3	119-32	440	83.3	88	318	208	64	200	13	19.7
Chauncey Billups	74	2,327	366	42.1	380-149	318	87.8	38	273	287	63	134	15	16.2
Clifford Robinson	81	2,825	372	39.8	259-87	161	67.6	81	318	268	87	158	88	12.2
Corliss Williamson	82	2,061	374	45.3	11-2	237	79.0	147	358	104	44	126	27	12.0
Jon Barry	80	1,473	191	45.0	214-87	86	86.0	33	180	206	63	81	14	6.9
Ben Wallace	73	2,873	210	48.1	6-1	85	45.0	293	1,126	120	104	88	230	6.9
Mehmet Okur	72	1,366	180	42.6	112-38	96	73.3	117	335	71	25	66	39	6.9
Chucky Atkins	65	1,398	168	36.1	242-86	40	81.6	21	96	175	27	77	4	7.1
Michael Curry	78	1,555	92	40.2	54-16	36	80.0	16	127	104	44	43	4	3.0
Zeljko Rebraca	30	488	80	55.2	0-0	38	79.2	27	92	9	6	29	17	6.6
Tayshaun Prince	42	435	53	44.9	47-20	11	64.7	5	45	24	10	21	14	3.3
Hubert Davis	43	328	31	39.2	36-12	5	83.3	6	36	29	5	11	0	1.8
Danny Manning	13	89	13	40.6	8-3	5	83.3	7	18	7	9	7	3	2.6
Don Reid	1	10	0	00.0	0-0	1	50.0	0	0	0	0	0	0	1.0
Pepe Sanchez	9	37	0	00.0	0-0	0	00.0	4	6	8	5	2	0	.0
Team Totals	82	19,905	2,700	43.0	1,488-533	1,559	77.1	883	3,328	1,620	556	1,104	468	91.4
Opponents	82	-	2,744	43.8	839-289	1,413	74.6	859	3,387	1,501	568	1,149	355	87.7

GOLDEN STATE WARRIORS

Player	GP	MIN	FGM	PCT	FGA-FGM	FTM	PCT	OFF	TOTAL	A	STL	TO	BLK	AVG
			Field Goals		3-PT FG	Free Throws		Rebounds						
Antawn Jamison	82	3,226	691	47.0	209-65	375	78.9	195	578	156	76	177	45	22.2
Gilbert Arenas	82	2,866	509	43.1	313-109	370	79.1	97	386	514	124	290	17	18.3
Jason Richardson	82	2,698	476	41.0	334-123	207	76.4	111	378	247	90	179	23	15.6
Troy Murphy	79	2,510	338	45.1	14-3	244	84.1	228	806	106	65	111	30	11.7
Erick Dampier	82	1,978	259	49.6	2-0	155	69.8	248	543	58	27	112	154	8.2
Earl Boykins	68	1,321	199	42.9	77-29	173	86.5	35	88	221	38	73	4	8.8
Mike Dunleavy, Jr.	82	1,305	168	40.3	150-52	78	78.0	66	214	106	53	86	19	5.7
Adonal Foyle	82	1,787	185	53.6	1-0	70	67.3	176	490	37	40	73	205	5.4
Bob Sura	55	1,130	135	41.2	85-28	103	69.6	58	167	177	45	82	2	7.3
Chris Mills	21	262	39	36.8	25-7	16	88.9	19	50	22	7	10	3	4.8
Jiri Welsch	37	234	19	25.3	4-1	22	75.9	12	28	27	8	19	2	1.6
Danny Fortson	17	223	20	37.0	1-0	19	65.5	28	73	12	9	15	0	3.5
Oscar Torres	17	109	16	44.4	13-7	14	70.0	3	12	3	4	8	2	3.1
Dean Oliver	15	93	7	24.1	6-1	7	87.5	8	16	23	7	10	0	1.5
A.J. Guyton	2	9	0	00.0	1-0	0	00.0	0	0	2	1	1	0	.0
Guy Rucker	3	4	0	00.0	0-0	0	00.0	0	1	1	0	0	0	.0
Team Totals	82	19,755	3,061	44.1	1,235-425	1,853	77.8	1,284	3,830	1,712	594	1,295	506	102.4
Opponents	82	-	3,240	45.2	1,177-438	1,575	75.6	1,204	3,592	1,934	710	1,121	491	103.6

HOUSTON ROCKETS

Player	GP	MIN	Field Goals FGM	PCT	3-PT FG FGA-FGM	Free Throws FTM	PCT	Rebounds OFF	TOTAL	A	STL	TO	BLK	AVG
Steve Francis	81	3,318	571	43.5	240-85	476	80.0	159	499	502	141	299	41	21.0
Cuttino Mobley	73	3,044	463	43.4	318-112	242	85.8	70	303	208	95	166	36	17.5
Yao Ming	82	2,382	401	49.8	2-1	301	81.1	196	675	137	31	173	147	13.5
Eddie Griffin	77	1,890	271	40.0	192-64	58	61.7	138	461	86	52	76	111	8.6
Maurice Taylor	67	1,377	231	43.2	2-0	100	72.5	95	238	66	22	100	22	8.4
Glen Rice	62	1,532	196	42.9	254-101	63	75.9	28	154	65	23	55	5	9.0
James Posey	58	1,646	188	43.9	141-46	119	82.6	52	281	106	77	78	9	9.3
Moochie Norris	82	1,375	134	40.6	45-11	78	68.4	37	159	196	55	86	4	4.4
Kelvin Cato	73	1,247	133	52.0	4-0	66	53.2	132	428	20	38	56	85	4.5
Terence Morris	49	632	82	46.6	32-7	11	78.6	40	128	25	8	29	17	3.7
Juaquin Hawkins	58	685	57	38.5	24-10	10	50.0	16	78	47	29	29	6	2.3
Jason Collier	13	104	17	47.2	0-0	2	100.0	12	29	1	2	2	1	2.8
Bostjan Nachbar	14	77	11	35.5	10-2	5	50.0	3	11	3	2	6	2	2.1
Tito Maddox	9	35	3	25.0	3-0	5	62.5	1	7	5	3	3	1	1.2
Team Totals	82	19,930	2,840	44.0	1,267-439	1,569	76.8	1,024	3,588	1,506	594	1,276	493	93.8
Opponents	82	-	2,891	43.3	1,113-386	1,399	77.5	979	3,332	1,683	663	1,082	381	92.3

INDIANA PACERS

Player	GP	MIN	Field Goals FGM	PCT	3-PT FG FGA-FGM	Free Throws FTM	PCT	Rebounds OFF	TOTAL	A	STL	TO	BLK	AVG
Jermaine O'Neal	77	2,864	610	48.4	21-7	373	73.1	202	796	155	66	180	178	20.8
Ron Artest	69	2,317	362	42.8	211-71	273	73.6	101	362	198	159	145	50	15.5
Al Harrington	82	2,467	389	43.4	46-13	211	77.0	159	511	125	71	163	33	12.2
Brad Miller	73	2,270	329	49.3	16-5	292	81.8	185	603	193	65	118	43	13.1
Reggie Miller	70	2,117	281	44.1	318-113	207	90.0	21	172	170	62	66	4	12.6
Jamaal Tinsley	73	2,237	220	39.6	166-46	80	71.4	58	260	548	125	192	18	7.8
Ron Mercer	72	1,671	244	40.9	16-3	65	80.2	32	154	112	49	54	14	7.7
Erick Strickland	71	1,275	163	42.9	160-62	70	80.5	23	145	209	38	98	7	6.5
Jonathan Bender	46	819	112	44.1	53-19	60	71.4	42	133	42	8	42	56	6.6
Austin Croshere	49	633	86	41.1	69-27	53	81.5	40	155	56	6	28	13	5.1
Jeff Foster	77	802	64	36.0	2-0	34	54.0	118	279	51	28	34	21	2.1
Tim Hardaway	10	127	18	36.7	31-11	2	50.0	1	15	24	9	11	0	4.9
Primoz Brezec	22	111	15	39.5	1-0	12	60.0	13	23	4	2	7	4	1.9
Fred Jones	19	115	9	37.5	7-2	3	75.0	4	9	5	6	6	1	1.2
Jamison Brewer	10	80	9	52.9	2-0	4	44.4	5	9	18	2	6	1	2.2
Team Totals	82	19,905	2,911	44.1	1,119-379	1,739	76.6	1,004	3,626	1,910	696	1,210	443	96.8
Opponents	82	-	2,860	42.8	1,197-407	1,527	76.7	1,006	3,464	1,696	620	1,258	513	93.3

LOS ANGELES CLIPPERS

Player	GP	MIN	Field Goals FGM	PCT	3-PT FG FGA-FGM	Free Throws FTM	PCT	Rebounds OFF	TOTAL	A	STL	TO	BLK	AVG
Elton Brand	62	2,454	451	50.2	1-0	244	68.5	283	703	157	71	161	158	18.5
Andre Miller	80	2,913	377	40.6	108-23	311	79.5	84	316	537	99	206	11	13.6
Corey Maggette	64	2,006	343	44.4	177-62	325	80.2	77	322	123	55	147	16	16.8
Lamar Odom	49	1,679	268	43.9	129-42	136	77.7	59	326	178	42	140	41	14.6
Eric Piatkowski	62	1,360	210	47.1	201-80	101	82.8	44	156	70	33	56	9	9.7
Quentin Richardson	59	1,368	203	37.2	198-61	85	68.5	98	281	52	35	64	10	9.4
Marko Jaric	66	1,379	179	40.1	166-53	79	75.2	35	160	193	97	103	11	7.4
Michael Olowokandi	36	1,369	186	42.7	0-0	69	65.7	57	328	47	18	98	79	12.3
Keyon Dooling	55	969	128	38.9	139-50	44	77.2	9	72	89	24	60	6	6.4
Sean Rooks	70	1,344	125	42.1	1-0	47	81.0	53	216	69	34	66	44	4.2
Melvin Ely	52	802	92	49.5	0-0	52	70.3	64	174	15	10	50	32	4.5
Cherokee Parks	30	648	82	50.3	2-1	23	60.5	46	132	21	16	18	20	6.3
Wang Zhizhi	41	412	62	38.3	47-16	42	72.4	26	77	10	8	31	10	4.4
Chris Wilcox	46	479	73	52.1	0-0	25	50.0	32	104	21	7	26	12	3.7
Tremaine Fowlkes	37	573	56	43.8	9-2	50	84.7	41	103	23	25	20	2	4.4
Team Totals	82	19,755	2,835	43.7	1,178-390	1,633	75.0	1,008	3,470	1,605	574	1,291	461	93.8
Opponents	82	-	3,035	44.7	1,244-454	1,507	77.4	1,046	3,506	1,840	652	1,152	418	97.9

LOS ANGELES LAKERS

Player	GP	MIN	Field Goals FGM	PCT	3-PT FG FGA-FGM	Free Throws FTM	PCT	Rebounds OFF	TOTAL	A	STL	TO	BLK	AVG
Kobe Bryant	82	3,401	868	45.1	324-124	601	84.3	106	564	481	181	288	67	30.0
Shaquille O'Neal	67	2,535	695	57.4	0-0	451	62.2	259	742	206	38	196	159	27.5
Derek Fisher	82	2,829	339	43.7	212-85	100	80.0	40	239	298	93	94	15	10.5
Rick Fox	76	2,181	262	42.2	280-105	52	75.4	64	323	253	69	121	14	9.0
Robert Horry	80	2,343	184	38.7	177-51	103	76.9	181	514	233	96	112	61	6.5
Devean George	71	1,613	180	39.0	132-49	83	79.0	91	286	92	56	65	38	6.9
Samaki Walker	67	1,243	115	42.0	1-0	66	65.3	115	368	64	20	56	55	4.4
Stanislav Medvedenko	58	620	112	43.4	2-0	31	72.1	66	141	18	11	37	8	4.4
Brian Shaw	72	900	101	38.7	109-38	10	66.7	20	119	103	32	54	13	3.5
Kareem Rush	76	872	96	39.3	68-19	16	69.6	26	94	68	10	63	11	3.0
Mark Madsen	54	781	69	42.3	0-0	36	59.0	86	159	38	15	27	19	3.2
Jannero Pargo	34	342	37	39.8	24-7	4	100.0	9	37	39	13	23	2	2.5
Tracy Murray	31	193	23	32.4	38-8	7	77.8	5	23	12	5	14	3	2.0
Soumaila Samake	13	77	10	41.7	0-0	2	100.0	10	23	4	0	2	5	1.7
Team Totals	82	19,930	3,091	45.1	1,367-486	1,562	73.4	1,078	3,632	1,909	639	1,192	470	100.4
Opponents	82	-	2,976	44.3	1,223-465	1,622	76.0	957	3,452	1,753	644	1,190	311	98.0

▷**Random Fact**: Tim Duncan became the second player in history to be named to both an All-NBA Team and an All-Defensive Team in each of his first six seasons (1997-98 to 2002-03). David Robinson was the first. He did it in each of his first seven seasons.

BASKETBALL PRO

MEMPHIS GRIZZLIES

Player	GP	MIN	Field Goals		3-PT FG	Free Throws		Rebounds		A	STL	TO	BLK	AVG
			FGM	PCT	FGA-FGM	FTM	PCT	OFF	TOTAL					
Pau Gasol	82	2,948	569	51.0	10-1	416	73.6	192	720	229	34	213	148	19.0
Jason Williams	76	2,407	333	38.8	404-143	110	84.0	25	212	631	91	168	10	12.1
Lorenzen Wright	70	1,982	325	45.4	5-0	147	65.9	170	528	80	51	110	54	11.4
Shane Battier	78	2,383	275	48.3	216-86	120	82.8	128	345	105	102	68	88	9.7
Wesley Person	66	1,941	274	45.6	231-100	79	81.4	24	192	112	42	56	19	11.0
Stromile Swift	67	1,478	235	48.1	2-0	177	72.2	114	384	45	55	99	104	9.7
Mike Batiste	75	1,248	197	42.2	81-18	69	78.4	82	257	52	42	69	16	6.4
Earl Watson	79	1,366	170	43.5	91-31	62	72.1	46	164	225	89	88	14	5.5
Brevin Knight	55	928	97	42.5	8-2	20	54.1	15	81	233	69	94	2	3.9
Mike Miller	16	360	77	51.0	44-22	29	80.6	6	55	31	6	26	5	12.8
Michael Dickerson	6	87	10	41.7	11-4	5	100.0	1	6	8	5	6	1	4.8
Ryan Humphrey	13	122	12	34.3	0-0	5	45.5	4	30	4	5	2	2	2.2
Robert Archibald	12	72	6	30.0	0-0	7	38.9	6	17	3	0	7	3	1.6
Cezary Trybanski	15	86	5	25.0	0-0	4	40.0	6	14	1	0	8	6	.9
Chris Owens	1	6	2	66.7	0-0	0	00.0	1	1	0	0	1	0	4.0
Team Totals	82	19,930	3,049	45.2	1,279-467	1,430	73.9	943	3,409	1,892	651	1,262	500	97.5
Opponents	82	-	3,224	46.0	1,188-431	1,381	75.9	1,126	3,681	1,991	714	1,213	430	100.7

MIAMI HEAT

Player	GP	MIN	Field Goals		3-PT FG	Free Throws		Rebounds		A	STL	TO	BLK	AVG
			FGM	PCT	FGA-FGM	FTM	PCT	OFF	TOTAL					
Caron Butler	78	2,858	429	41.6	107-34	309	82.4	135	397	213	137	192	31	15.4
Eddie Jones	47	1,789	291	42.3	241-98	189	82.2	35	226	173	64	85	31	18.5
Brian Grant	82	2,641	344	50.9	0-0	158	77.1	241	837	104	63	129	47	10.3
Malik Allen	80	2,318	335	42.4	4-0	97	80.2	134	425	54	37	128	78	9.6
Mike James	78	1,722	218	37.3	228-67	104	73.2	26	149	246	64	108	5	7.8
Travis Best	72	1,807	231	39.6	109-36	105	85.4	26	147	255	44	106	7	8.4
Rasual Butler	72	1,514	207	36.2	171-50	76	73.1	29	186	93	21	77	43	7.5
Vladimir Stepania	79	1,594	185	43.3	0-0	71	53.0	211	554	24	45	69	40	5.6
Eddie House	55	1,025	172	38.7	120-36	31	86.1	17	101	87	44	46	1	7.5
LaPhonso Ellis	55	784	100	38.2	107-27	50	75.8	44	157	15	15	31	15	5.0
Anthony Carter	49	912	83	35.6	8-0	33	66.0	12	83	203	45	81	5	4.1
Sean Lampley	35	487	56	43.4	4-0	57	69.5	26	83	31	7	25	3	4.8
Sean Marks	23	223	22	37.3	1-0	10	66.7	8	35	3	5	14	6	2.3
Ken Johnson	16	156	15	40.5	0-0	2	33.3	4	32	0	1	6	12	2.0
Team Totals	82	19,830	2,688	41.2	1,100-348	1,292	76.5	948	3,412	1,501	592	1,167	324	85.6
Opponents	82	-	2,713	43.7	1,149-406	1,598	75.1	872	3,459	1,482	626	1,173	436	90.6

MILWAUKEE BUCKS

Player	GP	MIN	Field Goals		3-PT FG	Free Throws		Rebounds		A	STL	TO	BLK	AVG
			FGM	PCT	FGA-FGM	FTM	PCT	OFF	TOTAL					
Sam Cassell	78	2,700	546	47.0	163-59	385	86.1	57	342	450	88	177	14	19.7
Michael Redd	82	2,316	455	46.9	416-182	149	80.5	98	371	117	100	74	13	15.1
Tim Thomas	80	2,358	412	44.3	265-97	145	78.0	97	389	102	70	133	49	13.3
Toni Kukoc	63	1,704	249	43.2	263-95	137	70.6	67	266	230	81	122	29	11.6
Gary Payton	28	1,085	221	46.6	68-20	88	74.6	23	86	206	40	56	8	19.6
Anthony Mason	65	2,119	191	48.6	1-0	84	71.8	90	416	209	32	79	12	7.2
Desmond Mason	28	952	166	47.4	17-5	78	76.5	66	188	68	20	41	11	14.8
Jason Caffey	51	894	113	45.6	0-0	69	65.1	68	176	38	19	56	15	5.8
Dan Gadzuric	49	760	70	48.3	1-0	29	51.8	66	197	9	22	27	52	3.4
Marcus Haislip	39	441	66	43.1	12-3	26	68.4	21	53	9	7	21	18	4.1
Ervin Johnson	69	1,170	61	45.2	0-0	30	68.2	117	294	24	34	34	63	2.2
Joel Przybilla	32	546	18	39.1	0-0	12	50.0	48	145	12	10	19	45	1.5
Jamal Sampson	5	8	0	00.0	0-0	0	00.0	1	2	1	1	0	0	.0
Team Totals	82	19,905	3,045	45.7	1,526-585	1,483	77.6	876	3,243	1,823	622	1,044	344	99.5
Opponents	82	-	3,043	45.8	1,278-479	1,574	74.5	1,021	3,562	1,892	543	1,182	333	99.3

MINNESOTA TIMBERWOLVES

Player	GP	MIN	Field Goals		3-PT FG	Free Throws		Rebounds		A	STL	TO	BLK	AVG
			FGM	PCT	FGA-FGM	FTM	PCT	OFF	TOTAL					
Kevin Garnett	82	3,321	743	50.2	71-20	377	75.1	244	1,102	495	113	229	129	23.0
Troy Hudson	79	2,600	409	42.8	266-97	208	90.0	42	183	452	60	182	7	14.2
Wally Szczerbiak	52	1,836	351	48.1	145-61	150	86.7	53	241	136	44	87	22	17.6
Radoslav Nesterovic	77	2,337	400	52.5	2-0	61	64.2	146	504	114	39	99	116	11.2
Kendall Gill	82	2,068	286	42.2	59-19	123	76.4	51	248	156	78	108	15	8.7
Anthony Peeler	82	2,245	252	41.4	212-87	39	78.0	40	241	244	72	82	13	7.7
Gary Trent	80	1,222	208	53.5	2-0	60	59.4	106	291	77	32	59	23	6.0
Marc Jackson	77	1,041	153	43.8	1-1	114	76.5	86	225	37	24	59	30	5.5
Joe Smith	54	1,117	151	46.0	2-0	102	77.9	111	270	38	14	43	55	7.5
Rod Strickland	47	956	120	43.2	11-1	79	73.8	20	95	215	46	76	6	6.8
Reggie Slater	26	141	27	54.0	0-0	27	60.0	18	31	4	6	9	1	3.1
Loren Woods	38	353	29	38.2	3-1	21	77.8	27	95	19	10	23	13	2.1
Igor Rakocevic	42	244	22	37.9	12-5	29	80.6	4	17	33	4	23	0	1.9
Mike Wilks	31	324	21	31.3	18-4	16	88.9	11	30	50	11	12	3	2.0
Team Totals	82	19,805	3,172	46.6	804-296	1,406	77.0	959	3,573	2,070	553	1,124	433	98.1
Opponents	82	-	3,005	43.7	1,362-472	1,394	75.2	974	3,418	1,871	571	1,116	405	96.0

Did You Know?

On May 8, 2003, the Dallas Mavericks set the playoff record for most points in a half. They dropped 83 points in the first half against the Sacramento Kings.

NEW JERSEY NETS

Player	GP	MIN	Field Goals FGM	PCT	3-PT FG FGA-FGM	Free Throws FTM	PCT	Rebounds OFF	TOTAL	A	STL	TO	BLK	AVG
Jason Kidd	80	2,989	515	41.4	370-126	339	84.1	110	504	711	179	296	25	18.7
Kenyon Martin	77	2,628	509	47.0	43-9	256	65.3	164	640	185	98	192	70	16.7
Richard Jefferson	80	2,879	456	50.1	24-6	324	74.3	150	514	201	80	156	44	15.5
Kerry Kittles	65	1,951	332	46.7	219-78	106	78.5	52	252	170	101	55	30	13.0
Lucious Harris	77	1,973	298	41.3	136-47	152	80.4	63	232	155	53	71	8	10.3
Aaron Williams	81	1,597	199	45.3	1-0	102	78.5	137	331	88	27	85	57	6.2
Rodney Rogers	68	1,303	183	40.2	132-44	68	75.6	61	263	107	50	91	31	7.0
Jason Collins	81	1,900	140	41.4	4-0	180	76.3	136	368	87	47	85	44	5.7
Anthony Johnson	66	842	103	44.6	35-13	51	68.9	13	78	86	37	41	5	4.1
Brian Scalabrine	59	724	68	40.2	39-14	30	83.3	40	141	46	16	46	18	3.1
Dikembe Mutombo	24	514	49	37.4	0-0	40	72.7	54	153	19	4	34	37	5.8
Tamar Slay	36	274	39	37.9	25-7	7	70.0	8	31	14	14	20	3	2.6
Brandon Armstrong	17	69	9	33.3	6-1	5	83.3	0	4	2	3	5	1	1.4
Chris Childs	12	106	6	30.0	6-1	2	66.7	3	5	16	8	6	1	1.3
Donny Marshall	3	6	0	00.0	1-0	0	00.0	0	3	0	0	1	0	.0
Team Totals	82	19,755	2,906	44.1	1,041-346	1,662	75.7	991	3,519	1,887	717	1,212	374	95.4
Opponents	82	-	2,757	42.7	1,185-425	1,453	74.9	932	3,393	1,607	693	1,358	423	90.1

NEW ORLEANS HORNETS

Player	GP	MIN	Field Goals FGM	PCT	3-PT FG FGA-FGM	Free Throws FTM	PCT	Rebounds OFF	TOTAL	A	STL	TO	BLK	AVG
Jamal Mashburn	82	3,321	670	42.2	306-119	313	84.8	66	498	462	83	230	17	21.6
David Wesley	73	2,710	449	43.3	316-134	185	78.1	38	175	251	109	132	9	16.7
Baron Davis	50	1,889	332	41.6	283-99	93	71.0	56	186	320	91	140	22	17.1
Jamaal Magloire	82	2,443	305	48.0	3-0	231	71.7	260	724	88	49	158	111	10.3
P.J. Brown	78	2,609	319	53.1	3-0	194	83.6	243	701	147	67	98	80	10.7
Courtney Alexander	66	1,360	193	38.2	57-19	118	80.8	39	118	79	31	68	6	7.9
George Lynch	81	1,497	147	40.9	79-28	41	55.4	139	353	104	66	52	19	4.5
Robert Traylor	69	851	105	44.3	3-1	57	64.8	108	262	50	45	53	37	3.9
Stacey Augmon	70	862	79	41.1	7-0	54	75.0	26	119	69	27	40	9	3.0
Jerome Moiso	51	644	89	52.0	0-0	27	65.9	59	178	22	19	46	44	4.0
Robert Pack	28	440	52	40.3	5-0	41	74.5	11	51	81	25	40	0	5.2
Kenny Anderson	23	446	61	40.7	2-1	16	72.7	14	45	77	18	42	4	6.0
Bryce Drew	13	79	8	29.6	7-3	0	00.0	4	13	11	2	3	0	1.5
Kirk Haston	12	57	2	11.8	3-0	2	50.0	0	7	3	0	7	5	.5
Randy Livingston	2	12	2	50.0	0-0	2	100.0	0	0	1	0	0	0	3.0
Team Totals	82	19,905	2,914	43.5	1,075-404	1,467	76.8	1,097	3,572	1,807	656	1,212	394	93.9
Opponents	82	-	2,857	43.8	1,001-338	1,474	76.6	909	3,277	1,630	647	1,196	427	91.8

NEW YORK KNICKS

Player	GP	MIN	Field Goals		3-PT FG	Free Throws		Rebounds						
			FGM	PCT	FGA-FGM	FTM	PCT	OFF	TOTAL	A	STL	TO	BLK	AVG
Allan Houston	82	3,108	652	44.5	450-178	363	91.9	26	231	220	54	178	7	22.5
Latrell Sprewell	74	2,859	454	40.3	360-134	173	79.4	45	285	332	102	172	22	16.4
Kurt Thomas	81	2,577	497	48.3	3-2	138	75.0	160	637	162	81	138	97	14.0
Howard Eisley	82	2,243	262	41.7	337-131	89	84.8	24	186	444	71	149	9	9.1
Shandon Anderson	82	1,731	248	46.2	140-52	139	73.2	64	254	87	73	114	20	8.4
Othella Harrington	74	1,850	225	50.8	0-0	123	82.0	165	476	62	12	90	23	7.7
Clarence Weatherspoon	79	2,024	186	44.9	0-0	149	76.8	214	599	68	69	63	36	6.6
Charlie Ward	66	1,465	165	39.9	267-101	41	77.4	25	177	306	78	95	11	7.2
Michael Doleac	75	1,041	146	42.6	0-0	36	78.3	65	219	42	16	49	16	4.4
Lee Nailon	38	405	84	44.2	1-0	42	82.4	32	70	26	6	32	3	5.5
Travis Knight	32	287	25	38.5	1-0	10	76.9	18	62	14	8	10	9	1.9
Lavor Postell	12	98	14	36.8	7-2	13	86.7	1	4	3	2	7	0	3.6
Frank Williams	21	167	9	27.3	16-6	4	66.7	3	18	34	7	17	2	1.3
Team Totals	82	19,855	2,967	44.1	1,582-606	1,320	81.5	842	3,218	1,800	579	1,149	255	95.9
Opponents	82	-	2,961	45.7	1,053-358	1,691	77.1	935	3,548	1,732	627	1,179	308	97.2

ORLANDO MAGIC

Player	GP	MIN	Field Goals		3-PT FG	Free Throws		Rebounds						
			FGM	PCT	FGA-FGM	FTM	PCT	OFF	TOTAL	A	STL	TO	BLK	AVG
Tracy McGrady	75	2,954	829	45.7	448-173	576	79.3	121	488	411	124	195	59	32.1
Pat Garrity	81	2,584	312	41.9	407-161	83	83.0	72	306	121	62	77	20	10.7
Darrell Armstrong	82	2,350	263	40.9	232-78	165	87.8	91	295	323	135	160	13	9.4
Shawn Kemp	79	1,633	211	41.8	1-0	115	74.2	147	451	55	66	102	33	6.8
Jacque Vaughn	80	1,686	184	44.8	34-8	97	77.6	26	118	232	64	97	2	5.9
Grant Hill	29	843	151	49.2	4-1	118	81.9	40	206	122	28	84	13	14.5
Gordan Giricek	27	961	143	44.0	119-39	62	81.6	18	130	67	30	51	2	14.3
Andrew DeClercq	77	1,327	149	53.4	0-0	67	64.4	142	339	52	39	84	36	4.7
Pat Burke	62	783	113	38.2	7-1	40	69.0	57	146	23	19	47	25	4.3
Drew Gooden	19	544	100	49.8	2-0	59	73.8	58	160	20	15	45	13	13.6
Jeryl Sasser	75	1,025	64	30.9	44-13	53	67.9	64	184	65	45	39	12	2.6
Steven Hunter	33	447	56	54.4	0-0	18	40.9	38	93	6	9	15	36	3.9
Chris Whitney	22	290	30	34.1	36-7	11	91.7	2	21	21	12	16	1	3.5
Olumide Oyedeji	27	145	10	43.5	0-0	7	63.6	10	50	5	5	5	3	1.0
Horace Grant	5	85	13	52.0	0-0	0	00.0	2	8	7	3	1	0	5.2
Team Totals	82	19,805	2,947	43.6	1,590-568	1,616	77.7	958	3,350	1,676	696	1,177	300	98.5
Opponents	82	-	3,007	45.5	1,211-405	1,648	76.7	970	3,566	1,837	643	1,341	411	98.4

PHILADELPHIA 76ers

Player	GP	MIN	Field Goals FGM	PCT	3-PT FG FGA-FGM	Free Throws FTM	PCT	Rebounds OFF	TOTAL	A	STL	TO	BLK	AVG
Allen Iverson	82	3,485	804	41.4	303-84	570	77.4	68	344	454	225	286	13	27.6
Keith Van Horn	74	2,337	459	48.2	176-65	193	80.4	159	524	93	63	150	30	15.9
Eric Snow	82	3,108	361	45.2	32-7	325	85.8	71	301	544	133	194	11	12.9
Aaron McKie	80	2,374	286	42.9	112-37	112	83.6	61	350	278	131	109	9	9.0
Derrick Coleman	64	1,742	223	44.8	67-22	134	78.4	151	450	87	53	96	69	9.4
Kenny Thomas	46	1,392	178	48.2	0-0	114	75.0	140	392	73	46	76	22	10.2
Brian Skinner	77	1,381	182	55.0	0-0	97	60.2	136	366	19	47	62	53	6.0
Greg Buckner	75	1,514	185	46.5	55-15	65	80.2	72	216	96	72	62	16	6.0
Todd MacCulloch	42	812	123	51.7	0-0	53	67.1	66	196	20	19	35	32	7.1
John Salmons	64	504	48	41.4	31-10	26	74.3	16	59	47	17	29	6	2.1
Tyrone Hill	24	496	44	40.4	0-0	21	60.0	56	124	9	15	16	7	4.5
Monty Williams	21	276	34	42.5	2-0	24	75.0	12	45	26	12	17	5	4.4
Efthimios Rentzias	35	144	20	33.9	8-4	8	88.9	10	26	7	6	4	2	1.5
Kenny Satterfield	17	82	4	22.2	0-0	1	50.0	4	8	15	2	7	0	.5
Team Totals	82	19,855	2,975	44.8	787-245	1,746	77.5	1,042	3,457	1,771	844	1,212	284	96.8
Opponents	82	-	2,876	45.2	1,278-453	1,547	76.0	908	3,308	1,809	639	1,405	521	94.5

PHOENIX SUNS

Player	GP	MIN	Field Goals FGM	PCT	3-PT FG FGA-FGM	Free Throws FTM	PCT	Rebounds OFF	TOTAL	A	STL	TO	BLK	AVG
Stephon Marbury	81	3,240	671	43.9	296-89	375	80.3	53	263	654	108	263	20	22.3
Shawn Marion	81	3,373	662	45.2	364-141	251	85.1	199	773	198	185	157	95	21.2
Amare Stoudemire	82	2,570	392	47.2	10-2	320	66.1	250	721	78	62	189	87	13.5
Joe Johnson	82	2,255	316	39.7	205-75	96	79.4	57	264	210	62	108	19	9.8
Anfernee Hardaway	58	1,777	256	44.7	73-26	77	79.4	66	258	235	66	145	26	10.6
Bo Outlaw	80	1,800	153	55.0	2-0	72	62.1	134	368	112	50	76	71	4.7
Casey Jacobsen	72	1,147	122	37.3	165-52	72	68.6	29	83	73	35	55	6	5.1
Scott Williams	69	872	120	41.1	2-0	33	78.6	72	193	22	27	32	21	4.0
Jake Voskuhl	65	947	92	56.4	0-0	64	66.7	97	225	36	18	48	29	3.8
Dan Langhi	60	541	81	40.1	31-9	12	60.0	19	87	21	15	16	6	3.1
Jake Tsakalidis	33	543	61	45.2	0-0	39	75.0	45	122	13	6	26	17	4.9
Tom Gugliotta	27	447	60	45.5	1-0	9	67.2	25	100	31	14	31	5	4.8
Randy Brown	32	262	16	37.2	0-0	9	100.0	3	26	35	17	17	2	1.3
Alton Ford	11	31	3	33.3	0-0	1	33.3	0	6	1	0	2	0	.6
Team Totals	82	19,805	3,005	44.3	1,149-394	1,430	74.2	1,049	3,489	1,719	665	1,208	404	95.5
Opponents	82	-	2,913	43.8	1,361-436	1,479	76.6	1,031	3,518	1,824	639	1,309	453	94.4

▷**Random Fact:** Karl Malone holds the record for most consecutive seasons (11) in which a player scores 2,000 or more points each season.

PORTLAND TRAIL BLAZERS

Player	GP	MIN	Field Goals FGM	PCT	3-PT FG FGA-FGM	Free Throws FTM	PCT	Rebounds OFF	TOTAL	A	STL	TO	BLK	AVG
Rasheed Wallace	74	2,684	515	47.1	307-110	200	73.5	113	548	153	70	140	77	18.1
Bonzi Wells	75	2,396	437	44.1	130-38	226	72.2	98	394	246	123	215	18	15.2
Derek Anderson	76	2,556	355	42.7	331-116	231	85.9	53	264	325	90	128	16	13.9
Scottie Pippen	64	1,911	265	44.4	133-38	121	81.8	57	278	285	105	164	25	10.8
Zach Randolph	77	1,301	264	51.3	5-0	122	75.8	139	343	41	42	62	14	8.4
Ruben Patterson	78	1,655	254	49.2	20-3	138	62.7	120	264	101	73	117	29	8.3
Dale Davis	78	2,282	237	54.1	0-0	105	63.3	233	564	94	51	71	70	7.4
Arvydas Sabonis	78	1,209	172	47.6	6-3	129	78.7	88	335	142	61	75	49	6.1
Jeff McInnis	75	1,311	188	44.4	35-6	50	74.6	22	97	170	21	75	2	5.8
Damon Stoudamire	59	1,315	156	37.6	114-44	53	79.1	40	155	204	39	82	6	6.9
Antonio Daniels	67	872	84	45.2	59-18	65	85.5	11	72	85	33	32	9	3.7
Qyntel Woods	53	334	59	50.0	9-3	7	35.0	15	53	12	15	23	1	2.4
Charles Smith	3	13	1	25.0	1-0	3	75.0	0	0	1	1	1	0	1.7
Chris Dudley	3	11	0	00.0	0-0	0	00.0	2	2	0	0	0	0	.0
Ruben Boumtje-Boumtje	2	5	0	00.0	0-0	0	00.0	1	1	1	1	0	0	.0
Team Totals	82	19,855	2,987	46.0	1,150-379	1,450	74.5	992	3,370	1,860	725	1,248	316	95.2
Opponents	82	-	2,942	45.0	1,285-438	1,267	76.4	912	3,204	1,863	683	1,270	391	92.5

SACRAMENTO KINGS

Player	GP	MIN	Field Goals FGM	PCT	3-PT FG FGA-FGM	Free Throws FTM	PCT	Rebounds OFF	TOTAL	A	STL	TO	BLK	AVG
Chris Webber	67	2,622	661	46.1	21-5	215	60.7	160	704	364	106	215	88	23.0
Predrag Stojakovic	72	2,450	497	48.1	406-155	231	87.5	61	397	141	72	101	5	19.2
Bobby Jackson	59	1,676	340	46.4	235-89	126	84.6	57	219	182	71	106	3	15.2
Mike Bibby	55	1,835	329	47.0	137-56	161	86.1	34	147	285	72	127	8	15.9
Vlade Divac	80	2,384	305	46.6	25-6	179	71.3	157	574	274	83	152	105	9.9
Doug Christie	80	2,710	267	47.9	185-73	141	81.0	61	342	376	180	144	37	9.4
Keon Clark	80	1,780	226	50.1	4-0	84	65.6	138	451	80	38	94	150	6.7
Jim Jackson	63	1,309	204	44.2	71-32	47	85.5	84	262	118	31	80	4	7.7
Hidayet Turkoglu	67	1,175	165	42.2	78-29	88	80.0	35	188	87	25	50	12	6.7
Damon Jones	49	709	80	38.1	121-44	20	74.1	11	70	80	18	23	4	4.6
Gerald Wallace	47	571	90	49.2	4-1	39	52.7	38	128	23	24	44	15	4.7
Scot Pollard	23	325	40	46.0	0-0	23	60.5	46	106	6	13	15	15	4.5
Lawrence Funderburke	27	229	32	44.4	0-0	10	58.8	17	55	8	1	6	11	2.7
Mateen Cleaves	12	55	6	26.1	1-1	3	75.0	1	8	10	2	14	0	1.3
Team Totals	82	19,830	3,242	46.4	1,288-491	1,367	74.6	900	3,651	2,034	736	1,192	457	101.7
Opponents	82	-	2,991	42.0	1,166-373	1,454	74.1	1,145	3,759	1,759	684	1,262	356	95.2

SAN ANTONIO SPURS

Player	GP	MIN	Field Goals		3-PT FG	Free Throws		Rebounds		A	STL	TO	BLK	AVG
			FGM	PCT	FGA-FGM	FTM	PCT	OFF	TOTAL					
Tim Duncan	81	3,181	714	51.3	22-6	450	71.0	259	1,043	316	55	248	237	23.3
Tony Parker	82	2,774	484	46.4	243-82	219	75.5	33	216	432	71	198	4	15.5
Stephen Jackson	80	2,254	356	43.5	297-95	139	76.0	66	286	183	125	176	30	11.8
Malik Rose	79	1,933	289	45.9	5-2	242	79.1	148	506	124	57	170	40	10.4
Bruce Bowen	82	2,566	223	46.6	220-101	36	40.4	59	239	113	66	72	42	7.1
David Robinson	64	1,676	197	46.9	0-0	152	71.0	163	508	61	52	83	111	8.5
Emanuel Ginobili	69	1,431	174	43.8	148-51	126	73.7	47	161	138	96	100	17	7.6
Steve Smith	53	1,032	113	38.8	118-39	95	83.3	21	99	70	28	43	9	6.8
Steve Kerr	75	952	110	43.0	124-49	30	88.2	12	60	70	27	35	3	4.0
Kevin Willis	71	840	123	47.9	2-0	51	61.4	83	226	24	20	60	20	4.2
Speedy Claxton	30	471	67	46.2	11-0	39	68.4	22	56	75	22	35	7	5.8
Danny Ferry	64	601	44	35.5	60-21	10	76.9	20	75	21	7	27	9	1.9
Mengke Bateer	12	46	4	23.5	3-1	0	00.0	2	10	4	0	6	0	.8
Team Totals	82	19,830	2,908	46.2	1,270-449	1,591	72.5	939	3,495	1,636	629	1,295	529	95.8
Opponents	82	-	2,862	42.7	1,043-354	1,334	76.8	1,029	3,351	1,559	665	1,231	422	90.4

SEATTLE SUPERSONICS

Player	GP	MIN	Field Goals		3-PT FG	Free Throws		Rebounds		A	STL	TO	BLK	AVG
			FGM	PCT	FGA-FGM	FTM	PCT	OFF	TOTAL					
Rashard Lewis	77	3,044	519	45.2	217-75	283	82.0	152	503	133	99	143	35	18.1
Brent Barry	75	2,480	264	45.8	293-118	128	79.5	48	301	384	113	142	15	10.3
Predrag Drobnjak	82	1,984	325	41.2	85-30	91	79.1	111	320	86	48	65	38	9.4
Vladimir Radmanovic	72	1,910	274	41.0	293-104	72	70.6	76	323	97	64	100	22	10.1
Ray Allen	29	1,197	247	44.1	222-78	138	92.0	49	163	170	46	81	3	24.5
Jerome James	51	766	111	47.8	0-0	54	58.7	78	216	27	12	75	82	5.4
Kevin Ollie	29	770	82	44.1	1-1	66	75.9	13	83	110	32	36	1	8.0
Reggie Evans	67	1,365	66	47.1	0-0	80	51.9	167	445	34	38	52	11	3.2
Calvin Booth	47	575	52	43.7	2-0	34	72.3	32	109	12	11	22	33	2.9
Vitaly Potapenko	26	403	41	44.1	0-0	22	75.9	25	89	4	9	25	8	4.0
Ansu Sesay	45	448	41	38.3	0-0	12	57.1	34	73	23	14	25	5	2.1
Elden Campbell	15	184	16	33.3	0-0	16	76.2	13	39	9	9	8	8	3.2
Joseph Forte	17	86	10	28.6	3-0	4	66.7	4	11	11	4	10	0	1.4
Ronald Murray	2	20	2	40.0	1-0	0	00.0	0	3	2	0	4	0	2.0
Team Totals	82	19,855	2,887	43.7	1,291-456	1,326	74.4	963	3,348	1,775	679	1,085	295	92.1
Opponents	82	-	2,871	44.7	1,371-472	1,351	74.2	936	3,400	1,703	500	1,209	409	92.3

Trivia Challenge

Which four teams from the American Basketball Association (ABA) joined the NBA in 1976-77 and remain today?

The Denver Nuggets, the San Antonio Spurs, the New Jersey Nets, and the Indiana Pacers.

TORONTO RAPTORS

Player	GP	MIN	Field Goals		3-PT FG	Free Throws		Rebounds		A	STL	TO	BLK	AVG
			FGM	PCT	FGA-FGM	FTM	PCT	OFF	TOTAL					
Morris Peterson	82	2,949	421	39.2	344-116	195	78.9	97	363	188	88	128	32	14.1
Alvin Williams	78	2,638	396	43.8	146-48	187	78.2	55	245	416	111	128	21	13.2
Voshon Lenard	63	1,929	325	40.2	252-92	156	80.4	48	212	144	59	103	21	14.3
Vince Carter	43	1,471	355	46.7	131-45	129	80.6	59	188	143	48	74	41	20.6
Antonio Davis	53	1,894	261	40.7	0-0	216	77.1	130	437	131	23	118	62	13.9
Jerome Williams	71	2,346	267	49.9	6-1	156	55.5	231	650	95	116	98	26	9.7
Jelani McCoy	67	1,367	194	49.1	0-0	69	54.8	95	355	43	28	96	60	6.8
Rafer Alston	47	980	139	41.5	130-51	37	68.5	21	107	192	38	86	15	7.8
Michael Bradley	67	1,314	151	48.1	6-1	35	52.2	162	409	67	16	76	32	5.0
Lindsey Hunter	29	673	106	35.1	107-34	34	72.3	15	59	71	35	57	5	9.7
Chris Jefferies	51	666	75	38.7	54-18	29	67.4	16	59	22	19	45	16	3.9
Greg Foster	29	539	47	38.5	4-1	26	81.3	30	102	13	1	30	9	4.2
Mamadou N'diaye	22	364	43	44.8	0-0	34	72.3	29	82	7	8	21	32	5.5
Maceo Baston	16	106	15	60.0	0-0	10	83.3	4	23	0	4	6	11	2.5
Damone Brown	5	115	11	31.4	2-0	6	75.0	3	15	3	1	6	0	5.6
Nate Huffman	7	76	9	36.0	0-0	5	62.5	9	23	5	1	3	3	3.3
Art Long	7	80	9	36.0	2-1	1	20.0	8	20	4	3	11	3	2.9
Zendon Hamilton	3	12	2	40.0	0-0	2	100.0	1	4	0	1	1	0	2.0
Team Totals	82	19,805	2,847	42.7	1,193-409	1,350	71.8	1,023	3,378	1,583	609	1,181	392	90.9
Opponents	82	-	3,037	46.1	986-370	1,490	75.9	976	3,577	1,729	604	1,125	406	96.8

UTAH JAZZ

Player	GP	MIN	Field Goals		3-PT FG	Free Throws		Rebounds		A	STL	TO	BLK	AVG
			FGM	PCT	FGA-FGM	FTM	PCT	OFF	TOTAL					
Karl Malone	81	2,936	595	46.2	14-3	474	76.3	113	628	379	136	210	31	20.6
Matt Harpring	78	2,557	521	51.1	160-66	262	79.2	190	514	133	73	160	17	17.6
Andrei Kirilenko	80	2,213	315	49.1	114-37	296	80.0	147	420	138	118	136	175	12.0
John Stockton	82	2,275	309	48.3	80-29	237	82.6	51	201	629	137	182	16	10.8
Calbert Cheaney	81	2,351	325	49.9	25-10	40	58.0	73	284	163	65	108	13	8.6
Scott Padgett	82	1,321	170	40.2	133-45	81	75.7	83	272	86	41	70	24	5.7
Greg Ostertag	81	1,926	169	51.8	0-0	100	51.0	180	503	55	20	104	147	5.4
Mark Jackson	82	1,467	147	39.8	95-27	61	76.3	34	176	375	48	152	3	4.7
DeShawn Stevenson	61	760	114	40.1	12-4	47	69.1	22	85	40	22	49	8	4.6
Tony Massenburg	58	792	104	44.8	0-0	65	77.4	59	156	17	17	50	19	4.7
Carlos Arroyo	44	287	50	45.9	7-3	18	81.8	11	26	53	12	30	1	2.8
Jarron Collins	22	421	38	44.2	1-0	44	71.0	32	60	14	5	19	6	5.5
John Amaechi	50	474	37	31.4	0-0	25	48.1	26	77	21	14	34	7	2.0
Team Totals	82	19,780	2,894	46.8	641-224	1,750	74.5	1,021	3,402	2,103	708	1,374	467	94.7
Opponents	82	-	2,751	43.4	1,252-437	1,627	75.9	1,011	3,131	1,601	723	1,305	427	92.3

WASHINGTON WIZARDS

Player	GP	MIN	Field Goals FGM	PCT	3-PT FG FGA-FGM	Free Throws FTM	PCT	Rebounds OFF	TOTAL	A	STL	TO	BLK	AVG
Michael Jordan	82	3,031	679	44.5	55-16	266	82.1	71	497	311	123	173	39	20.0
Jerry Stackhouse	70	2,747	491	40.9	245-71	455	87.8	61	258	316	65	193	28	21.5
Larry Hughes	67	2,137	346	46.7	79-29	136	73.1	67	308	205	86	136	24	12.8
Tyronn Lue	75	1,986	248	43.3	176-60	91	87.5	22	149	263	47	77	1	8.6
Christian Laettner	76	2,215	255	49.4	16-2	120	83.3	114	502	235	82	87	40	8.3
Kwame Brown	80	1,773	224	44.6	3-0	145	66.8	128	426	58	50	110	80	7.4
Brendan Haywood	81	1,930	173	51.0	0-0	155	63.3	192	404	29	32	65	119	6.2
Bryon Russell	70	1,388	108	35.3	140-46	53	76.8	43	208	72	70	55	7	4.5
Juan Dixon	42	647	104	38.4	84-25	37	80.4	13	72	40	26	42	3	6.4
Etan Thomas	38	513	61	49.2	0-0	60	63.8	70	165	3	8	33	23	4.8
Bobby Simmons	36	378	44	39.3	5-0	32	91.4	33	77	20	10	8	3	3.3
Jared Jeffries	20	292	30	47.6	6-3	16	55.2	26	58	16	8	21	5	4.0
Charles Oakley	42	514	23	41.8	0-0	28	82.4	37	107	40	13	21	6	1.8
Jahidi White	16	230	25	47.2	0-0	17	68.0	37	73	2	1	9	12	4.2
Anthony Goldwire	5	34	4	57.1	1-1	4	80.0	0	3	1	0	4	0	2.6
Brian Cardinal	5	15	1	25.0	1-0	2	100.0	3	5	1	0	1	0	.8
Team Totals	82	19,830	2,816	44.0	811-253	1,617	77.9	917	3,312	1,612	621	1,095	390	91.5
Opponents	82	-	2,877	44.2	1,242-449	1,382	77.1	949	3,396	1,776	612	1,171	358	92.5

Today's Stars

In 2002-03, Kevin Garnett was second in the NBA in rebounds (13.4 per game) and tied for eighth in points (23 per game).

JOHN W. McDONOUGH/SPORTS ILLUSTRATED

Kevin Garnett, forward, b. May 19, 1976, Mauldin, South Carolina. K.G. was already one of the premier players in the league before he exploded for the best season of his career in 2002-03. The 6' 11" phenom averaged 23 points and 13.4 rebounds per game and was named MVP of the 2003 All-Star Game. He made the All-NBA First Team for the second time in his career and was named to the All-Defensive First Team for the fourth-straight season. Garnett jumped straight from high school to the NBA in 1995.

Allen Iverson, guard, b. June 7, 1975, Hampton, Virginia. A.I. crosses up opponents with his quick first step and nasty crossover. The Philadelphia 76ers' four-time All-Star was third in the NBA in scoring in 2002-03 (27.6 points per game) and first in steals (2.74). Iverson was the All-Star and regular-season MVPs in 2000-01, leading the league in scoring (31.1) and steals (2.51). He also led the 76ers to the NBA Finals that season.

Dirk Nowitzki, forward, b. June 19, 1978, Wurzburg, Germany. Nowitzki is the best-shooting 7-footer ever in the NBA. He has averaged 146 treys in the past three seasons for the Dallas Mavericks. No other 7-footer in NBA history has ever had more than 49 three-pointers in a season. Nowitzki's numbers have improved steadily since his rookie season in 1998-99. He averaged 25.1 points and 9.9 rebounds per game in 2002-03 and led Dallas to the Western Conference Finals.

NBA Champions

Season	Champion	Series	Runner-up	Winning Coach	Finals MVP
2002-03	San Antonio	4-2	New Jersey	Gregg Popovich	Tim Duncan, SA
2001-02	LA Lakers	4-0	New Jersey	Phil Jackson	Shaquille O'Neal, LA
2000-01	LA Lakers	4-1	Philadelphia	Phil Jackson	Shaquille O'Neal, LA
1999-00	LA Lakers	4-2	Indiana	Phil Jackson	Shaquille O'Neal, LA
1998-99	San Antonio	4-1	New York	Gregg Popovich	Tim Duncan, SA
1997-98	Chicago	4-2	Utah	Phil Jackson	Michael Jordan, Chi
1996-97	Chicago	4-2	Utah	Phil Jackson	Michael Jordan, Chi
1995-96	Chicago	4-2	Seattle	Phil Jackson	Michael Jordan, Chi
1994-95	Houston	4-0	Orlando	Rudy Tomjanovich	Hakeem Olajuwon, Hou
1993-94	Houston	4-3	New York	Rudy Tomjanovich	Hakeem Olajuwon, Hou
1992-93	Chicago	4-2	Phoenix	Phil Jackson	Michael Jordan, Chi
1991-92	Chicago	4-2	Portland	Phil Jackson	Michael Jordan, Chi
1990-91	Chicago	4-1	LA Lakers	Phil Jackson	Michael Jordan, Chi
1989-90	Detroit	4-1	Portland	Chuck Daly	Isiah Thomas, Det
1988-89	Detroit	4-0	LA Lakers	Chuck Daly	Joe Dumars, Det
1987-88	LA Lakers	4-3	Detroit	Pat Riley	James Worthy, LA
1986-87	LA Lakers	4-2	Boston	Pat Riley	Magic Johnson, LA
1985-86	Boston	4-2	Houston	K.C. Jones	Larry Bird, Bos
1984-85	LA Lakers	4-2	Boston	Pat Riley	Kareem Abdul-Jabbar, LA
1983-84	Boston	4-3	LA Lakers	K.C. Jones	Larry Bird, Bos
1982-83	Philadelphia	4-0	LA Lakers	Billy Cunningham	Moses Malone, Phil
1981-82	LA Lakers	4-2	Philadelphia	Pat Riley	Magic Johnson, LA
1980-81	Boston	4-2	Houston	Bill Fitch	Cedric Maxwell, Bos
1979-80	LA Lakers	4-2	Philadelphia	Paul Westhead	Magic Johnson, LA
1978-79	Seattle	4-1	Washington	Lenny Wilkens	Dennis Johnson, Sea
1977-78	Washington	4-3	Seattle	Dick Motta	Wes Unseld, Wash
1976-77	Portland	4-2	Philadelphia	Jack Ramsay	Bill Walton, Port
1975-76	Boston	4-2	Phoenix	Tom Heinsohn	Jo Jo White, Bos
1974-75	Golden State	4-0	Washington	Al Attles	Rick Barry, GS
1973-74	Boston	4-3	Milwaukee	Tom Heinsohn	John Havlicek, Bos
1972-73	New York	4-1	LA Lakers	Red Holzman	Willis Reed, NY
1971-72	LA Lakers	4-1	New York	Bill Sharman	Wilt Chamberlain, LA
1970-71	Milwaukee	4-0	Baltimore	Larry Costello	Kareem Abdul-Jabbar, Mil
1969-70	New York	4-3	LA Lakers	Red Holzman	Willis Reed, NY
1968-69	Boston	4-3	LA Lakers	Bill Russell	Jerry West, LA
1967-68	Boston	4-2	LA Lakers	Bill Russell	—
1966-67	Philadelphia	4-2	San Francisco	Alex Hannum	—
1965-66	Boston	4-3	LA Lakers	Red Auerbach	—
1964-65	Boston	4-1	LA Lakers	Red Auerbach	—
1963-64	Boston	4-1	San Francisco	Red Auerbach	—
1962-63	Boston	4-2	LA Lakers	Red Auerbach	—
1961-62	Boston	4-3	LA Lakers	Red Auerbach	—
1960-61	Boston	4-1	St. Louis	Red Auerbach	—
1959-60	Boston	4-3	St. Louis	Red Auerbach	—
1958-59	Boston	4-0	Minneapolis	Red Auerbach	—
1957-58	St. Louis	4-2	Boston	Alex Hannum	—
1956-57	Boston	4-3	St. Louis	Red Auerbach	—
1955-56	Philadelphia	4-1	Ft. Wayne	George Senesky	—
1954-55	Syracuse	4-3	Ft. Wayne	Al Cervi	—
1953-54	Minneapolis	4-3	Syracuse	John Kundla	—
1952-53	Minneapolis	4-1	New York	John Kundla	—
1951-52	Minneapolis	4-3	New York	John Kundla	—
1950-51	Rochester	4-3	New York	Les Harrison	—
1949-50	Minneapolis	4-2	Syracuse	John Kundla	—
1948-49	Minneapolis	4-2	Washington	John Kundla	—
1947-48	Baltimore	4-2	Philadelphia	Buddy Jeannette	—
1946-47	Philadelphia	4-1	Chicago	Ed Gottlieb	—

JOHN W. McDONOUGH/SPORTS ILLUSTRATED

WALTER IOOSS JR./SPORTS ILLUSTRATED

All-time Individual Leaders

Michael Jordan

Wilt Chamberlain

Scoring

Most Points, Career

	PTS	AVG
Kareem Abdul-Jabbar	38,387	24.6
Karl Malone	36,374	25.4
Michael Jordan	32,292	30.1
Wilt Chamberlain	31,419	30.1
Moses Malone	27,409	20.6
Elvin Hayes	27,313	21.0
Hakeem Olajuwon	26,946	21.8
Oscar Robertson	26,710	25.7
Dominique Wilkins	26,668	24.8
John Havlicek	26,395	20.8

Highest Scoring Average, Career

Michael Jordan	30.1	1,072 games
Wilt Chamberlain	30.1	1,045 games
Shaquille O'Neal	27.6	742 games
Elgin Baylor	27.4	846 games
Jerry West	27.0	932 games
Allen Iverson	27.0	487 games
Bob Pettit	26.4	792 games
George Gervin	26.2	791 games
Oscar Robertson	25.7	1,040 games
Karl Malone	25.4	1,434 games

Note: Minimum 400 games.

Most Points, Game

		Opponent	Date
100	Wilt Chamberlain, Phil	NY	3/2/62
78	Wilt Chamberlain, Phil	LA	12/8/61
73	Wilt Chamberlain, Phil	Chi	1/13/62
73	Wilt Chamberlain, SF	NY	11/16/62
73	David Thompson, Den	Det	4/9/78
72	Wilt Chamberlain, SF	LA	11/3/62
71	Elgin Baylor, LA	NY	11/15/60
71	David Robinson, SA	LAC	4/24/94
70	Wilt Chamberlain, SF	Syr	3/10/63
69	Michael Jordan, Chi	Clev	3/28/90

Highest Field-goal Percentage, Career

.599 —Artis Gilmore

Highest Free-throw Percentage, Career

.904 —Mark Price

Note: Minimum 1,200 free throws made.

3-point Field Goals

Most 3-point Field Goals, Career: 2,330 —Reggie Miller, Indiana

Highest 3-point Field-goal Percentage, Career: .454 —Steve Kerr, San Antonio

Most 3-point Field Goals, Game: 12 —Kobe Bryant, LA Lakers vs. Seattle, 1/7/03

Note: First year of shot: 1979-80.

Steals

Most Steals, Career: 3,265 —John Stockton, Utah
Most Steals, Game: 11 —Kendall Gill, New Jersey vs. Miami, 4/3/99; Larry Kenon, San Antonio vs. Kansas City, 12/26/76

Rebounds

Most Rebounds, Career

	NO	YRS	AVG
Wilt Chamberlain	23,924	14	22.9
Bill Russell	21,620	13	22.5
Kareem Abdul-Jabbar	17,440	20	11.2
Elvin Hayes	16,279	16	12.5
Moses Malone	16,212	19	12.2
Robert Parish	14,715	21	9.1
Karl Malone	14,601	18	10.2
Nate Thurmond	14,464	14	15.0
Walt Bellamy	14,241	14	13.7
Wes Unseld	13,769	13	14.0

Most Rebounds, Game

NO	PLAYER, TEAM	OPPONENT	DATE
55	Wilt Chamberlain, Phil	Bos	11/24/60
51	Bill Russell, Bos	Syr	2/5/60
49	Bill Russell, Bos	Phil	11/16/57
49	Bill Russell, Bos	Det	3/11/65
45	Wilt Chamberlain, Phil	Syr	2/6/60
45	Wilt Chamberlain, Phil	LA	1/21/61

Assists

Most Assists, Career

John Stockton	15,806
Mark Jackson	10,215
Magic Johnson	10,141
Oscar Robertson	9,887
Isiah Thomas	9,061

Most Assists, Game

30 —Scott Skiles, Orlando vs. Denver, 12/30/90

Blocks

Most Blocks, Career

Hakeem Olajuwon	3,830
Kareem Abdul-Jabbar	3,189
Mark Eaton	3,064
David Robinson	2,954
Patrick Ewing	2,894

Most Blocks, Game

17 —Elmore Smith, LA Lakers vs. Portland, 10/28/73

KEY PTS=points; AVG=average; NO=number; YRS=years

Most Valuable Player: Maurice Podoloff Trophy

Season	Player, Team
2002–03	Tim Duncan, San Antonio
2001–02	Tim Duncan, San Antonio
2000–01	Allen Iverson, Philadelphia
1999–00	Shaquille O'Neal, LA Lakers
1998–99	Karl Malone, Utah
1997–98	Michael Jordan, Chicago
1996–97	Karl Malone, Utah
1995–96	Michael Jordan, Chicago
1994–95	David Robinson, San Antonio
1993–94	Hakeem Olajuwon, Houston
1992–93	Charles Barkley, Phoenix
1991–92	Michael Jordan, Chicago
1990–91	Michael Jordan, Chicago
1989–90	Magic Johnson, LA Lakers
1988–89	Magic Johnson, LA Lakers
1987–88	Michael Jordan, Chicago
1986–87	Magic Johnson, LA Lakers
1985–86	Larry Bird, Boston
1984–85	Larry Bird, Boston
1983–84	Larry Bird, Boston
1982–83	Moses Malone, Philadelphia
1981–82	Moses Malone, Houston
1980–81	Julius Erving, Philadelphia
1979–80	Kareem Abdul-Jabbar, LA Lakers
1978–79	Moses Malone, Houston
1977–78	Bill Walton, Portland
1976–77	Kareem Abdul-Jabbar, LA Lakers
1975–76	Kareem Abdul-Jabbar, LA Lakers
1974–75	Bob McAdoo, Buffalo
1973–74	Kareem Abdul-Jabbar, Milwaukee
1972–73	Dave Cowens, Boston
1971–72	Kareem Abdul-Jabbar, Milwaukee
1970–71	Kareem Abdul-Jabbar, Milwaukee
1969–70	Willis Reed, New York
1968–69	Wes Unseld, Baltimore
1967–68	Wilt Chamberlain, Philadelphia
1966–67	Wilt Chamberlain, Philadelphia
1965–66	Wilt Chamberlain, Philadelphia
1964–65	Bill Russell, Boston
1963–64	Oscar Robertson, Cincinnati
1962–63	Bill Russell, Boston
1961–62	Bill Russell, Boston
1960–61	Bill Russell, Boston
1959–60	Wilt Chamberlain, Philadelphia
1958–59	Bob Pettit, St. Louis
1957–58	Bill Russell, Boston
1956–57	Bob Cousy, Boston
1955–56	Bob Pettit, St. Louis

Rookie of the Year: Eddie Gottlieb Trophy

Amare Stoudemire, Phoenix Suns

Season	Player, Team
2002–03	Amare Stoudemire, Phoenix
2001–02	Pau Gasol, Memphis
2000–01	Mike Miller, Orlando
1999–00	Steve Francis, Houston; Elton Brand, Chicago
1998–99	Vince Carter, Toronto
1997–98	Tim Duncan, San Antonio
1996–97	Allen Iverson, Philadelphia
1995–96	Damon Stoudamire, Toronto
1994–95	Jason Kidd, Dallas; Grant Hill, Detroit
1993–94	Chris Webber, Golden State
1992–93	Shaquille O'Neal, Orlando
1991–92	Larry Johnson, Charlotte
1990–91	Derrick Coleman, New Jersey
1989–90	David Robinson, San Antonio
1988–89	Mitch Richmond, Golden State
1987–88	Mark Jackson, New York
1986–87	Chuck Person, Indiana
1985–86	Patrick Ewing, New York
1984–85	Michael Jordan, Chicago
1983–84	Ralph Sampson, Houston
1982–83	Terry Cummings, San Diego
1981–82	Buck Williams, New Jersey
1980–81	Darrell Griffith, Utah
1979–80	Larry Bird, Boston
1978–79	Phil Ford, Kansas City
1977–78	Walter Davis, Phoenix
1976–77	Adrian Dantley, Buffalo
1975–76	Alvan Adams, Phoenix
1974–75	Keith Wilkes, Golden State
1973–74	Ernie DiGregorio, Buffalo
1972–73	Bob McAdoo, Buffalo
1971–72	Sidney Wicks, Portland
1970–71	Dave Cowens, Boston; Geoff Petrie, Portland
1969–70	Kareem Abdul-Jabbar, Milwaukee
1968–69	Wes Unseld, Baltimore
1967–68	Earl Monroe, Baltimore
1966–67	Dave Bing, Detroit
1965–66	Rick Barry, San Francisco
1964–65	Willis Reed, New York
1963–64	Jerry Lucas, Cincinnati
1962–63	Terry Dischinger, Chicago
1961–62	Walt Bellamy, Chicago
1960–61	Oscar Robertson, Cincinnati
1959–60	Wilt Chamberlain, Philadelphia
1958–59	Elgin Baylor, Minnesota
1957–58	Woody Sauldsberry, Philadelphia
1956–57	Tom Heinsohn, Boston
1955–56	Maurice Stokes, Rochester
1954–55	Bob Pettit, Milwaukee
1953–54	Ray Felix, Baltimore
1952–53	Don Meineke, Ft. Wayne

Note: There were co-winners in 1999–00, 1994–95, and 1970–71.

Defensive Player of the Year

Season	Player, Team
2002–03	Ben Wallace, Detroit
2001–02	Ben Wallace, Detroit
2000–01	Dikembe Mutombo, Philadelphia/Atlanta
1999–00	Alonzo Mourning, Miami
1998–99	Alonzo Mourning, Miami
1997–98	Dikembe Mutombo, Atlanta
1996–97	Dikembe Mutombo, Atlanta
1995–96	Gary Payton, Seattle
1994–95	Dikembe Mutombo, Denver
1993–94	Hakeem Olajuwon, Houston
1992–93	Hakeem Olajuwon, Houston
1991–92	David Robinson, San Antonio
1990–91	Dennis Rodman, Detroit
1989–90	Dennis Rodman, Detroit
1988–89	Mark Eaton, Utah
1987–88	Michael Jordan, Chicago
1986–87	Michael Cooper, LA Lakers
1985–86	Alvin Robertson, San Antonio
1984–85	Mark Eaton, Utah
1983–84	Sidney Moncrief, Milwaukee
1982–83	Sidney Moncrief, Milwaukee

Bobby Jackson, Sacramento Kings

Sixth Man Award

JOHN W. McDONOUGH/SPORTS ILLUSTRATED

Trivia Challenge

Who is the youngest player ever to play in an NBA game?

Jermaine O'Neal of the Indiana Pacers, O'Neal, then with the Portland Trail Blazers, played in his first game on December 5, 1996, against the Denver Nuggets. He was 18 years, 1 month, and 22 days old.

Season	Player, Team	Season	Player, Team	Season	Player, Team
2002–03	Bobby Jackson, Sacramento	1996–97	John Starks, New York	1986–87	Ricky Pierce, Milwaukee
2001–02	Corliss Williamson, Detroit	1995–96	Toni Kukoc, Chicago	1985–86	Bill Walton, Boston
2000–01	Aaron McKie, Philadelphia	1994–95	Anthony Mason, New York	1984–85	Kevin McHale, Boston
		1993–94	Dell Curry, Charlotte	1983–84	Kevin McHale, Boston
1999–00	Rodney Rogers, Phoenix	1992–93	Cliff Robinson, Portland	1982–83	Bobby Jones, Philadelphia
1998–99	Darrell Armstrong, Orlando	1991–92	Detlef Schrempf, Indiana		
		1990–91	Detlef Schrempf, Indiana		
1997–98	Danny Manning, Phoenix	1989–90	Ricky Pierce, Milwaukee		
		1988–89	Eddie Johnson, Phoenix		
		1987–88	Roy Tarpley, Dallas		

Most Improved Player

Season	Player, Team	Season	Player, Team	Season	Player, Team
2002–03	Gilbert Arenas, Golden State	1995–96	Gheorghe Muresan, Washington	1990–91	Scott Skiles, Orlando
2001–02	Jermaine O'Neal, Indiana			1989–90	Rony Seikaly, Miami
2000–01	Tracy McGrady, Orlando	1994–95	Dana Barros, Philadelphia	1988–89	Kevin Johnson, Phoenix
1999–00	Jalen Rose, Indiana			1987–88	Kevin Duckworth, Portland
1998–99	Darrell Armstrong, Orlando	1993–94	Don MacLean, Washington		
		1992–93	Chris Jackson, Denver	1986–87	Dale Ellis, Seattle
1997–98	Alan Henderson, Atlanta	1991–92	Pervis Ellison, Washington	1985–86	Alvin Robertson, San Antonio
1996–97	Isaac Austin, Miami				

All-Star Game Results

Year	Result	Site	Winning Coach	Most Valuable Player
2003	West 155, East 145 (OT)	Atlanta, GA	Rick Adelman	Kevin Garnett, Minnesota
2002	West 135, East 120	Philadelphia, PA	Don Nelson	Kobe Bryant, LA Lakers
2001	East 111, West 110	Washington, DC	Larry Brown	Allen Iverson, Philadelphia
2000	West 137, East 126	Oakland, CA	Phil Jackson	Shaquille O'Neal, LA Lakers/Tim Duncan, San Antonio
1999	Cancelled due to lockout			
1998	East 135, West 114	New York, NY	Larry Bird	Michael Jordan, Chicago
1997	East 132, West 120	Cleveland, OH	Doug Collins	Glen Rice, Charlotte
1996	East 129, West 118	San Antonio, TX	Phil Jackson	Michael Jordan, Chicago
1995	West 139, East 112	Phoenix, AZ	Paul Westphal	Mitch Richmond, Sacramento
1994	East 127, West 118	Minneapolis, MN	Lenny Wilkens	Scottie Pippen, Chicago
1993	West 135, East 132	Salt Lake City, UT	Paul Westphal	Karl Malone/John Stockton, Utah
1992	West 153, East 113	Orlando, FL	Don Nelson	Magic Johnson, LA Lakers
1991	East 116, West 114	Charlotte, NC	Chris Ford	Charles Barkley, Philadelphia
1990	East 130, West 113	Miami, FL	Chuck Daly	Magic Johnson, LA Lakers
1989	West 143, East 134	Houston, TX	Pat Riley	Karl Malone, Utah
1988	East 138, West 133	Chicago, IL	Mike Fratello	Michael Jordan, Chicago
1987	West 154, East 149 (OT)	Seattle, WA	Pat Riley	Tom Chambers, Seattle
1986	East 139, West 132	Dallas, TX	K.C. Jones	Isiah Thomas, Detroit
1985	West 140, East 129	Indianapolis, IN	Pat Riley	Ralph Sampson, Houston
1984	East 154, West 145 (OT)	Denver, CO	K.C. Jones	Isiah Thomas, Detroit
1983	East 132, West 123	Los Angeles, CA	Billy Cunningham	Julius Erving, Philadelphia
1982	East 120, West 118	East Rutherford, NJ	Bill Fitch	Larry Bird, Boston
1981	East 123, West 120	Cleveland, OH	Billy Cunningham	Nate Archibald, Boston
1980	East 144, West 135 (OT)	Washington, DC	Billy Cunningham	George Gervin, San Antonio
1979	West 134, East 129	Detroit, MI	Lenny Wilkens	David Thompson, Denver

All-Star Game Results (cont.)

Year	Result	Site	Winning Coach	Most Valuable Player
1978	East 133, West 125	Atlanta, GA	Billy Cunningham	Randy Smith, Buffalo
1977	West 125, East 124	Milwaukee, WI	Larry Brown	Julius Erving, Philadelphia
1976	East 123, West 109	Philadelphia, PA	Tom Heinsohn	Dave Bing, Washington
1975	East 108, West 102	Phoenix, AZ	K.C. Jones	Walt Frazier, New York
1974	West 134, East 123	Seattle, WA	Larry Costello	Bob Lanier, Detroit
1973	East 104, West 84	Chicago, IL	Tom Heinsohn	Dave Cowens, Boston
1972	West 112, East 110	Los Angeles, CA	Bill Sharman	Jerry West, LA Lakers
1971	West 108, East 107	San Diego, CA	Larry Costello	Lenny Wilkens, Seattle
1970	East 142, West 135	Philadelphia, PA	Red Holzman	Willis Reed, New York
1969	East 123, West 112	Baltimore, MD	Gene Shue	Oscar Robertson, Cincinnati
1968	East 144, West 124	New York, NY	Alex Hannum	Hal Greer, Philadelphia
1967	West 135, East 120	San Francisco, CA	Fred Schaus	Rick Barry, San Francisco
1966	East 137, West 94	Cincinnati, OH	Red Auerbach	Adrian Smith, Cincinnati
1965	East 124, West 123	St. Louis, MO	Red Auerbach	Jerry Lucas, Cincinnati
1964	East 111, West 107	Boston, MA	Red Auerbach	Oscar Robertson, Cincinnati
1963	East 115, West 108	Los Angeles, CA	Red Auerbach	Bill Russell, Boston
1962	West 150, East 130	St. Louis, MO	Fred Schaus	Bob Pettit, St. Louis
1961	West 153, East 131	Syracuse, NY	Paul Seymour	Oscar Robertson, Cincinnati
1960	East 125, West 115	Philadelphia, PA	Red Auerbach	Wilt Chamberlain, Philadelphia
1959	West 124, East 108	Detroit, MI	Ed Macauley	Bob Pettit, St. Louis/Elgin Baylor, Minnesota
1958	East 130, West 118	St. Louis, MO	Red Auerbach	Bob Pettit, St. Louis
1957	East 109, West 97	Boston, MA	Red Auerbach	Bob Cousy, Boston
1956	West 108, East 94	Rochester, NY	Charley Eckman	Bob Pettit, St. Louis
1955	East 100, West 91	New York, NY	Al Cervi	Bill Sharman, Boston
1954	East 98, West 93 (OT)	New York, NY	Joe Lapchick	Bob Cousy, Boston
1953	West 79, East 75	Ft. Wayne, IN	John Kundla	George Mikan, Minnesota
1952	East 108, West 91	Boston, MA	Al Cervi	Paul Arizin, Philadelphia
1951	East 111, West 94	Boston, MA	Joe Lapchick	Ed Macauley, Boston

2003 NBA Draft—First Round

June 26, 2003, New York, NY

1. LeBron James, Cleveland
2. Darko Milicic, Detroit (from Memphis)
3. Carmelo Anthony, Denver
4. Chris Bosh, Toronto
5. Dwyane Wade, Miami
6. Chris Kaman, LA Clippers
7. Kirk Hinrich, Chicago
8. T.J. Ford, Milwaukee (from Atlanta)
9. Mike Sweetney, New York
10. Jarvis Hayes, Washington
11. Mickael Pietrus, Golden State
12. Nick Collison, Seattle
13. Marcus Banks, Memphis (from Houston; traded to Boston)
14. Luke Ridnour, Seattle (from Milwaukee)
15. Reece Gaines, Orlando
16. Troy Bell, Boston (traded to Memphis)
17. Zarko Cabarkapa, Phoenix
18. David West, New Orleans
19. Aleksandar Pavlovic, Utah
20. Dahntay Jones, Boston (from Philadelphia; traded to Memphis)
21. Boris Diaw-Riffiod, Atlanta (from Indiana)
22. Zoran Planinic, New Jersey
23. Travis Outlaw, Portland
24. Brian Cook, LA Lakers
25. Carlos Delfino, Detroit
26. Ndudi Ebi, Minnesota
27. Kendrick Perkins, Memphis (from Sacramento; traded to Boston)
28. Leandrinho Barbosa, San Antonio (traded to Phoenix)
29. Josh Howard, Dallas

World Championship of Basketball

Year	Winner	Runner-up	Score	Site
2002	Yugoslavia	Argentina	84–77 (OT)	Indianapolis, Indiana
1998	Yugoslavia	Russia	64–62	Athens, Greece
1994 *	United States	Russia	137–91	Toronto, Ontario, Canada
1990	Yugoslavia	Soviet Union	92–75	Buenos Aires, Argentina
1986	United States	Soviet Union	87–85	Madrid, Spain
1982	Soviet Union	United States	95–94	Cali, Colombia
1978	Yugoslavia	Soviet Union	82–81 (OT)	Manila, Philippines
1974	Soviet Union	Yugoslavia	†	San Juan, Puerto Rico
1970	Yugoslavia	Brazil	†	Ljubljana, Yugoslavia
1967	Soviet Union	Yugoslavia	†	Montevideo, Uruguay
1963	Brazil	Yugoslavia	†	Rio de Janeiro, Brazil
1959	Brazil	United States	†	Santiago, Chile
1954	United States	Brazil	†	Rio de Janeiro, Brazil
1950	Argentina	United States	†	Rio de Janeiro, Brazil

* U.S. professionals began competing in 1994. In 1998, a labor dispute resulted in a boycott of the World Championship by NBA stars; the U.S. roster was filled by members of the Continental Basketball Association and European professional leagues and college players.
† Result determined by overall record in final round of competition.

BASKETBALL   *WOMEN'S*

The 2002 WNBA regular season began and ended with the defending champion Los Angeles Sparks dueling the New York Liberty. Between those bookends was a season filled with exciting debuts, historic firsts, and the making of a dynasty.

After being drafted in 2001, Tamika Catchings of the Indiana Fever sat out that season with a knee injury. Her jaw-dropping comeback performance in 2002 earned her Rookie of the Year honors.

Veteran center Lisa Leslie of the Los Angeles Sparks became the first WNBA player to dunk in a game, on July 30, against the Miami Sol. One month later, Leslie helped dunk the Liberty in the WNBA Finals for the Sparks' second-straight championship. And if winning her second Finals MVP award wasn't enough, Leslie also earned MVP honors at the FIBA Women's World Championship in September. She averaged team-highs in points (17.2 per game) and rebounds (8.1) for the U.S., which won its record seventh gold medal.

Some troubling news was announced in the WNBA's off-season. Four teams — the Miami Sol, the Orlando Miracle, the Portland Fire, and the Utah Starzz — ceased operations. The good news was that the Starzz moved to San Antonio and are now the Silver Stars. The Miracle relocated north to become the Connecticut Sun.

Two-time Finals MVP Lisa Leslie led the Sparks to their second-straight WNBA championship.

LUCY NICHOLSON/AP

WNBA TEAMS

EASTERN CONFERENCE
Charlotte Sting
Cleveland Rockers
Detroit Shock
Indiana Fever
Miami Sol*
New York Liberty
Orlando Miracle**
Washington Mystics

WESTERN CONFERENCE
Houston Comets
Los Angeles Sparks
Minnesota Lynx
Phoenix Mercury
Portland Fire***
Sacramento Monarchs
Seattle Storm
Utah Starzz****

*Team ceased operations in November 2002.
**Team relocated to Connecticut for the 2003 season.
***Team ceased operations in December 2002.
****Team relocated to San Antonio for the 2003 season.

Trivia Challenge

Name the two WNBA Rookies of the Year who attended the University of Tennessee.

Chamique Holdsclaw (1999) and Tamika Catchings (2002)

Ticha Penicheiro of the Sacramento Monarchs led the WNBA in assists in 2002 (8 per game).

RICK PEDRONCELLI/AP

2002 WNBA Final Standings

Eastern Conference

TEAM	W	L	PCT	GB
Liberty	18	14	.563	0.0
Sting	18	14	.563	0.0
Mystics	17	15	.531	1.0
Fever	16	16	.500	2.0
Miracle	16	16	.500	2.0
Sol	15	17	.469	3.0
Rockers	10	22	.313	8.0
Shock	9	23	.281	9.0

Western Conference

TEAM	W	L	PCT	GB
Sparks	25	7	.781	0.0
Comets	24	8	.750	1.0
Starzz	20	12	.625	5.0
Storm	17	15	.531	8.0
Fire	16	16	.500	9.0
Monarchs	14	18	.438	11.0
Mercury	11	21	.344	14.0
Lynx	10	22	.313	15.0

2002 WNBA Playoffs

EASTERN CONFERENCE			WESTERN CONFERENCE	
New York Liberty (1)	New York Liberty		Los Angeles Sparks	Los Angeles Sparks (1)
Indiana Fever (4)		**LOS ANGELES SPARKS**		Seattle Storm (4)
Charlotte Sting (2)	Washington Mystics	New York Liberty	Utah Starzz	Houston Comets (2)
Washington Mystics (3)				Utah Starzz (3)
CONF. SEMI-FINALS	CONF. FINALS	FINALS	CONF. FINALS	CONF. SEMI-FINALS

2002 WNBA Playoff Results

EASTERN CONFERENCE SEMI-FINALS

| August 15: | Sting: 62 | at Mystics: 74 |
| August 17: | Mystics: 62 | at Sting: 59 |

Washington Mystics won series 2–0

August 16:	Liberty: 55	at Fever: 73
August 18:	Fever: 65	at Liberty: 84
August 20:	Fever: 60	at Liberty: 75

New York Liberty won series 2–1

WESTERN CONFERENCE SEMI-FINALS

| August 15: | Sparks: 78 | at Storm: 61 |
| August 17: | Storm: 59 | at Sparks: 69 |

Los Angeles Sparks won series 2–0

August 16:	Comets: 59	at Starzz: 66
August 18:	Starzz: 77	at Comets: 83 (2OT)
August 20:	Starzz: 75	at Comets: 72

Utah Starzz won series 2–1

EASTERN CONFERENCE FINALS

August 22:	Liberty: 74	at Mystics: 79
August 24:	Mystics: 79	at Liberty: 96
August 25:	Mystics: 57	at Liberty: 64

New York Liberty won series 2–1

WESTERN CONFERENCE FINALS

| August 22: | Sparks: 75 | at Starzz: 67 |
| August 24: | Starzz: 77 | at Sparks: 103 |

Los Angeles Sparks won series 2–0

WNBA FINALS

| August 29: | Sparks: 71 | at Liberty: 63 |
| August 31: | Liberty: 66 | at Sparks: 69 |

Los Angeles Sparks won series 2–0

Did You Know?

Los Angeles, California, is the only city to boast both a WNBA (Sparks) and an NBA (Lakers) championship in the same year (2001, 2002).

WNBA FINALS COMPOSITE BOX SCORE

NEW YORK LIBERTY

PLAYER	GP	MPG	FG%	3P%	FT%	REBOUNDS OFF	REBOUNDS DEF	TOTAL	APG	SPG	BPG	TO	PF	PPG
Becky Hammon	2	24.5	.556	.417	1.000	.50	2.00	2.50	2.0	.50	.00	1.00	2.50	13.5
Vickie Johnson	2	32.5	.474	.429	.600	1.00	3.00	4.00	2.5	.50	.00	1.50	2.50	12.0
Tari Phillips	2	32.5	.318	.000	.714	2.50	3.50	6.00	1.5	1.00	1.50	3.00	3.50	12.0
Tamika Whitmore	2	36.5	.318	.000	.727	.00	5.00	5.00	1.0	.00	.00	2.50	3.00	11.0
Crystal Robinson	2	31.0	.278	.300	.000	2.00	.50	2.50	1.0	.50	1.00	1.50	2.00	6.5
Teresa Weatherspoon	2	31.0	.300	.000	.750	1.00	4.00	5.00	4.0	1.50	.00	.50	3.00	6.0
Sue Wicks	2	12.0	.429	1.000	.000	1.50	1.00	2.50	.5	.50	.00	.50	2.00	3.5
Korie Hlede	DNP - Coach's Decision													
Camille Cooper	DNP - Coach's Decision													
Linda Frohlich	DNP - Coach's Decision													
Bernadette Ngoyisa	DNP - Coach's Decision													
TEAM AVERAGES	2	200.0	.379	.343	.725	8.5	19.0	27.5	12.5	4.5	2.5	11.0	18.5	64.5

LOS ANGELES SPARKS

PLAYER	GP	MPG	FG%	3P%	FT%	REBOUNDS OFF	REBOUNDS DEF	TOTAL	APG	SPG	BPG	TO	PF	PPG
Lisa Leslie	2	40.0	.500	.500	.700	1.00	7.00	8.00	1.5	.50	2.00	1.50	4.00	16.0
Mwadi Mabika	2	38.0	.333	.400	.769	2.00	4.50	6.50	3.5	1.00	.00	2.00	2.50	16.0
DeLisha Milton	2	36.5	.526	.333	.800	1.00	4.50	5.50	1.0	1.50	2.50	1.00	4.50	12.5
Nikki Teasley	2	38.0	.333	.125	.750	.50	2.00	2.50	11.0	1.50	.00	5.50	3.00	9.5
Latasha Byears	2	32.5	.500	.000	.400	5.00	6.00	11.00	.5	1.50	.50	1.00	4.00	8.0
Tamecka Dixon	1	14.0	1.000	.000	.000	.00	2.00	2.00	1.0	2.00	.00	4.00	6.00	6.0
Sophia Witherspoon	2	7.0	.500	.667	1.000	.00	.50	.50	.0	.00	.00	.00	.50	4.0
Nicky McCrimmon	1	2.0	.500	.000	.000	.00	.00	.00	.0	.00	.00	.00	1.00	2.0
Ericka DeSouza	DNP - Coach's Decision													
Marlies Askamp	DNP - Coach's Decision													
Vedrana Grgin-Fonseca	DNP - Coach's Decision													
TEAM AVERAGES	2	200.0	.450	.346	.721	9.5	25.5	35.0	18.0	7.0	5.0	13.5	22.0	70.0

KEY GP=games played; MPG=minutes per game; FG%=field-goal percentage; 3P%=three-point percentage; FT%=free-throw percentage; OFF=offensive; DEF=defensive; APG=assists per game; SPG=steals per game; BPG=blocks per game; TO=turnovers; PF=personal fouls; PPG=points per game

WNBA FINALS GAME 1 Liberty 63, Sparks 71 Time of Game: 2:02 Attendance: 17,666

8/29/2002 Madison Square Garden, New York, NY Officials: Bob Trammell, Patty Broderick, Matthew Boland

SPARKS

PLAYER	POS	MIN	FGM-A	3GM-A	FTM-A	REBOUNDS OFF	DEF	TOT	A	STL	BLK	TO	PF	PTS
Nikki Teasley	G	38	2-7	0-3	4-6	1	1	2	11	2	0	7	3	8
Latasha Byears	G	34	2-8	0-0	2-3	5	6	11	0	3	0	1	3	6
Mwadi Mabika	F	40	6-18	3-7	5-7	4	4	8	5	1	0	0	3	20
DeLisha Milton	F	40	7-11	0-1	3-3	2	4	6	0	2	3	0	4	17
Lisa Leslie	C	40	6-12	1-1	2-2	1	8	9	2	1	3	2	4	15
Sophia Witherspoon		6	1-3	1-2	0-0	0	1	1	0	0	0	0	1	3
Nicky McCrimmon		2	1-2	0-0	0-0	0	0	0	0	0	0	0	1	2
Tamecka Dixon		DNP - COACH'S DECISION												
Ericka DeSouza		DNP - COACH'S DECISION												
Marlies Askamp		DNP - COACH'S DECISION												
Vedrana Grgin-Fonseca		DNP - COACH'S DECISION												
TOTAL		200	25-61 (41.0%)	5-14 (35.7%)	16-21 (76.2%)	13	24	37	18	9	6	10	19	71

LIBERTY

PLAYER	POS	MIN	FGM-A	3GM-A	FTM-A	REBOUNDS OFF	DEF	TOT	A	STL	BLK	TO	PF	PTS
Vickie Johnson	G	30	3-7	1-3	0-0	1	3	4	3	1	0	2	2	7
Teresa Weatherspoon	G	29	0-4	0-0	3-4	0	7	7	3	1	0	1	3	3
Tamika Whitmore	F	38	2-9	0-0	1-2	0	6	6	2	0	0	2	2	5
Crystal Robinson	F	36	5-12	3-7	0-0	2	0	2	1	0	2	3	3	13
Tari Phillips	C	35	4-13	0-2	4-6	1	3	4	3	0	2	3	3	12
Becky Hammon		23	7-9	4-6	0-0	0	1	1	2	0	0	1	3	18
Sue Wicks		9	2-3	1-1	0-0	1	0	1	1	0	0	1	1	5
Korie Hlede		DNP - COACH'S DECISION												
Camille Cooper		DNP - COACH'S DECISION												
Linda Frohlich		DNP - COACH'S DECISION												
Bernadette Ngoyisa		DNP - COACH'S DECISION												
TOTAL		200	23-57 (40.4%)	9-19 (47.4%)	8-12 (66.7%)	5	20	25	15	2	4	13	17	63

FINAL	1	2	T
Sparks	35	36	71
Liberty	35	28	63

WNBA FINALS GAME 2 Sparks 69, Liberty 66 Time of Game: 2:07 Attendance: 13,493

8/31/2002 STAPLES Center, Los Angeles, CA Officials: June Courteau, Lisa Mattingly, Roy Gulbeyan

LIBERTY

PLAYER	POS	MIN	FGM-A	3GM-A	FTM-A	REBOUNDS OFF	DEF	TOT	A	STL	BLK	TO	PF	PTS
Vickie Johnson	G	35	6-12	2-4	3-5	1	3	4	2	0	0	1	3	17
Teresa Weatherspoon	G	33	3-6	0-2	3-4	2	1	3	5	2	0	3	3	9
Tamika Whitmore	F	35	5-13	0-1	7-9	0	4	4	0	0	0	3	4	17
Crystal Robinson	F	26	0-6	0-3	0-0	2	1	3	1	1	0	0	1	0
Tari Phillips	C	30	3-9	0-0	6-8	4	4	8	0	2	1	3	4	12
Becky Hammon		26	3-9	1-6	2-2	1	3	4	2	1	0	1	2	9
Sue Wicks		15	1-4	0-0	0-0	2	2	4	0	1	0	0	3	2
Korie Hlede		DNP - COACH'S DECISION												
Camille Cooper		DNP - COACH'S DECISION												
Linda Frohlich		DNP - COACH'S DECISION												
Bernadette Ngoyisa		DNP - COACH'S DECISION												
TOTAL		200	21-59 (35.6%)	3-16 (18.8%)	21-28 (75.0%)	12	18	30	10	7	1	8	20	66

SPARKS

PLAYER	POS	MIN	FGM-A	3GM-A	FTM-A	REBOUNDS OFF	DEF	TOT	A	STL	BLK	TO	PF	PTS
Nikki Teasley	G	38	4-11	1-5	2-2	0	3	3	11	1	0	4	3	11
Mwadi Mabika	G	36	3-9	1-3	5-6	0	5	5	2	1	0	4	2	12
DeLisha Milton	F	33	3-8	1-2	1-2	0	5	5	2	1	2	2	5	8
Latasha Byears	F	31	5-6	0-0	0-2	5	6	11	1	0	1	1	5	10
Lisa Leslie	C	40	6-12	0-1	5-8	1	6	7	1	0	1	1	4	17
Tamecka Dixon		14	3-3	0-0	0-0	0	2	2	1	2	0	4	6	6
Sophia Witherspoon		8	1-1	1-1	2-2	0	0	0	0	0	0	0	0	5
Ericka DeSouza		DNP - COACH'S DECISION												
Marlies Askamp		DNP - COACH'S DECISION												
Nicky McCrimmon		DNP - COACH'S DECISION												
Vedrana Grgin-Fonseca		DNP - COACH'S DECISION												
TOTAL		200	25-50 (50.0%)	4-12 (33.3%)	15-22 (68.2%)	6	27	33	18	5	4	16	25	69

FINAL	1	2	T
Liberty	24	42	66
Sparks	31	38	69

TECHNICAL FOUL—INDIVIDUAL

NYL	1st Qtr 12:58	Richie Adubato
	2nd Qtr 1:55	Tari Phillips
	2nd Qtr 1:55	Lisa Leslie
LAS		

KEY POS=position; MIN=minutes; FGM-A=field goals made-attempts; 3GM-A=three-point field goals made-attempts; FTM-A=free throws made-attempts; TOT=total; A=assists; STL=steals; BLK=blocks; PTS=points

Award Winners

YEAR	MVP	ROOKIE	DEFENSIVE	IMPROVED	SPORTSMANSHIP	COACH
2002	Sheryl Swoopes	Tamika Catchings	Sheryl Swoopes	Coco Miller	Jennifer Gillom	Marianne Stanley
2001	Lisa Leslie	Jackie Stiles	Debbie Black	Janeth Arcain	Sue Wicks	Dan Hughes
2000	Sheryl Swoopes	Betty Lennox	Sheryl Swoopes	Tari Phillips	Susie McConnell Serio	Michael Cooper
1999	Yolanda Griffith	Chamique Holdsclaw	Yolanda Griffith	N/A	Dawn Staley	Van Chancellor
1998	Cynthia Cooper	Tracy Reid	Teresa Weatherspoon	N/A	Susie McConnell Serio	Van Chancellor
1997	Cynthia Cooper	N/A	Teresa Weatherspoon	N/A	Haixia Zheng	Van Chancellor

NEWCOMER*

1998   Susie McConnell Serio
1999   Yolanda Griffith
*No longer awarded

> ☐▷**Random Fact:** The Houston Comets are the only team in professional basketball history to win its league's first four championships (1997 through 2000).

Legends

Cheryl Miller, forward, b. January 3, 1964, Riverside, California. Miller was the first player, male or female, to have her number retired by the University of Southern California (USC, number 31). In 1984, she led USC to its second-straight NCAA Division I women's basketball title and guided the U.S. women to their first-ever Olympic gold medal. Miller was inducted into the Naismith Memorial Basketball Hall of Fame in 1995.

Nancy Lieberman, guard, b. July 1, 1958, Brooklyn, New York. At age 18, Lieberman became the youngest basketball player to win an Olympic medal when the U.S. women's team earned silver in 1976. The three-time All-America led Old Dominion University to back-to-back AIAW national championships (1979 and 1980). In 1986, she became the first woman to play in a men's pro league when she suited up for the Springfield Fame of the USBL. She was inducted into the Naismith Memorial Basketball Hall of Fame in 1996.

Cynthia Cooper, guard, b. April 14, 1963, Chicago, Illinois. Cooper won two national titles with USC (1983 and 1984) and was a member of the U.S. teams that won the Olympic gold medal in 1988 and the bronze medal in 1992. She spent 11 seasons in European pro leagues before joining the WNBA in 1997. The 5' 10" scorer led the Houston Comets to four consecutive WNBA championships (1997-00) in the league's first four seasons and won the Finals MVP each time. She also earned two regular-season MVP awards and three scoring titles.

Cheryl Miller led USC to two straight NCAA titles in 1983 and 1984.

PETER READ MILLER

TEAM-BY-TEAM STATS

CHARLOTTE STING

PLAYER	GP	MIN	FIELD GOALS FGM	PCT	3-PT FG FGA	FGM	FREE THROWS FTM	PCT	REBOUNDS OFF	TOTAL	A	STL	TO	BLK	AVG
Andrea Stinson	32	950	159	45.6	70	29	64	68.8	37	177	91	37	52	9	12.8
Tammy Sutton-Brown	32	885	129	53.1	0	0	124	71.3	76	191	15	29	49	36	11.9
Allison Feaster	32	956	115	39.4	189	79	70	82.4	37	118	61	39	40	12	11.8
Dawn Staley	32	1,061	84	36.4	83	33	77	76.2	8	56	164	48	80	0	8.7
Charlotte Smith	32	890	91	41.0	91	34	40	74.1	39	121	53	21	60	17	8.0
Kelly Miller	32	554	79	44.6	51	24	29	76.3	31	68	49	22	27	1	6.6
Shalonda Enis	4	59	5	27.8	3	0	9	100.0	6	9	3	1	1	2	4.8
Tonya Edwards	29	303	36	36.4	25	7	33	71.7	11	41	24	16	17	2	3.9
Erin Buescher	29	392	33	40.2	11	4	25	69.4	32	91	18	13	27	15	3.3
Summer Erb	31	342	35	56.5	0	0	18	72.0	20	71	10	13	35	11	2.8
Keisha Anderson	7	31	3	25.0	4	1	0	0.0	2	6	5	0	3	0	1.0
Elena Shakirova	1	5	0	0.0	0	0	1	50.0	1	1	0	1	0	0	1.0
Sheila Lambert	3	16	1	33.3	0	0	0	0.0	2	3	3	1	2	0	.7
Shantia Owens	2	6	0	0.0	0	0	0	0.0	0	2	0	0	0	0	.0
STING	32	6,450	770	43.0	527	211	490	73.9	302	955	496	241	408	105	70.0
OPPONENTS	32	-	778	43.1	372	133	444	74.2	295	915	489	208	424	103	66.7

CLEVELAND ROCKERS

PLAYER	GP	MIN	FIELD GOALS FGM	PCT	3-PT FG FGA	FGM	FREE THROWS FTM	PCT	REBOUNDS OFF	TOTAL	A	STL	TO	BLK	AVG
Penny Taylor	30	908	133	41.6	111	38	87	85.3	51	158	68	37	58	11	13.0
Chastity Melvin	32	1,055	153	46.4	6	3	90	68.7	84	194	57	28	74	18	12.5
Merlakia Jones	32	1,094	157	39.9	54	15	62	78.5	33	176	72	44	55	4	12.2
Ann Wauters	28	802	120	55.3	1	0	74	85.1	45	140	39	16	59	21	11.2
Jennifer Rizzotti	26	695	54	40.0	99	38	32	80.0	5	70	85	23	45	3	6.8
Rushia Brown	28	468	42	40.0	1	0	28	73.7	29	75	27	21	39	8	4.0
Deanna Jackson	18	143	19	41.3	3	0	17	70.8	10	27	6	2	9	1	3.1
Mery Andrade	32	665	34	30.6	26	5	18	78.3	17	56	67	29	41	6	2.8
Brandi McCain	31	392	25	29.1	58	21	12	75.0	4	26	41	11	34	3	2.7
Lucienne Berthieu	5	16	3	42.9	1	0	2	50.0	3	4	0	0	0	0	1.6
Tracy Henderson	23	173	16	39.0	0	0	3	100.0	12	34	3	3	18	7	1.5
Tricia Bader Binford	18	132	4	15.4	14	1	5	83.3	1	7	15	6	7	1	.8
Paige Sauer	1	7	0	0.0	0	0	0	0.0	1	2	0	1	1	0	.0
ROCKERS	32	6,550	760	41.8	374	121	430	77.8	295	969	480	221	451	83	64.7
OPPONENTS	32	-	797	43.5	441	149	397	76.2	278	918	530	242	428	109	66.9

KEY FGM=field goals made; PCT=percentage; FGA=field goal attempts; FTM=free throws made; A=assists; STL=steals; BLK=blocks; AVG=average

DETROIT SHOCK

PLAYER	GP	MIN	FIELD GOALS		3-PT FG		FREE THROWS		REBOUNDS		A	STL	TO	BLK	AVG
			FGM	PCT	FGA	FGM	FTM	PCT	OFF	TOTAL					
Swin Cash	32	1,079	144	40.8	63	13	173	76.2	77	222	86	37	100	31	14.8
Wendy Palmer	16	464	65	42.5	60	19	35	66.0	27	96	20	13	34	2	11.5
Elaine Powell	15	397	54	44.6	22	6	34	85.0	26	63	60	23	41	8	9.9
Deanna Nolan	32	804	103	41.5	114	42	29	80.6	17	87	62	27	61	12	8.7
Astou Ndiaye	32	776	126	46.7	2	0	23	59.0	44	162	39	17	58	12	8.6
Dominique Canty	28	625	52	33.8	5	1	55	72.4	24	69	83	21	56	4	5.7
Ayana Walker	32	548	63	37.7	9	2	34	69.4	56	118	17	12	29	34	5.1
Barbara Farris	32	564	49	41.9	1	0	45	73.8	29	94	16	12	38	9	4.5
Edwina Brown	28	549	43	32.8	12	6	23	71.9	29	82	58	25	60	7	4.1
Kelly Santos	12	169	16	38.1	0	0	12	60.0	12	32	7	3	14	9	3.7
Lenae Williams	27	177	30	29.7	54	13	0	00.0	7	19	4	4	14	0	2.7
Stacy Clinesmith	12	105	8	38.1	15	6	5	83.3	1	5	17	1	6	1	2.3
Jill Chapman	19	119	10	37.0	1	0	2	66.7	11	26	0	3	8	2	1.2
Begona Garcia	8	64	2	18.2	6	2	2	50.0	0	4	9	3	11	0	1.0
Oksana Zakaluzhnaya	3	10	1	33.3	0	0	0	00.0	0	0	0	0	0	1	.7
SHOCK	32	6,450	766	39.9	364	110	472	72.5	360	1,079	478	201	541	132	66.1
OPPONENTS	32	-	828	41.7	447	146	464	76.7	314	983	465	277	443	139	70.8

HOUSTON COMETS

PLAYER	GP	MIN	FIELD GOALS		3-PT FG		FREE THROWS		REBOUNDS		A	STL	TO	BLK	AVG
			FGM	PCT	FGA	FGM	FTM	PCT	OFF	TOTAL					
Sheryl Swoopes	32	1,154	221	43.4	80	23	127	82.5	30	158	107	88	87	23	18.5
Tina Thompson	29	1,052	176	43.1	108	40	93	82.3	67	217	62	25	92	20	16.7
Janeth Arcain	32	1,116	128	42.4	37	10	98	88.3	42	126	86	51	71	6	11.4
Tiffani Johnson	32	815	77	43.3	2	0	47	81.0	73	173	39	17	38	24	6.3
Michelle Snow	32	480	45	46.9	2	1	34	59.6	31	119	13	12	22	26	3.9
Grace Daley	23	185	16	43.2	8	2	29	61.7	13	23	16	3	17	1	2.7
Kelley Gibson	29	276	21	38.2	36	14	4	66.7	3	20	14	8	21	7	2.1
Rita Williams	9	85	5	45.5	6	2	7	70.0	0	6	7	11	10	0	2.1
Coquese Washington	21	349	17	34.0	21	8	2	100.0	7	41	31	13	20	0	2.1
Tynesha Lewis	17	145	13	43.3	8	3	5	62.5	6	18	9	3	9	3	2.0
Sonja Henning	23	521	18	34.6	12	3	5	45.5	10	58	51	23	36	6	1.9
Rebecca Lobo	21	132	15	46.9	7	3	1	25.0	9	23	12	1	11	5	1.6
Tammy Jackson	5	69	3	37.5	0	0	0	00.0	7	13	1	3	6	3	1.2
Amanda Lassiter	6	46	0	00.0	5	0	1	50.0	1	6	2	2	2	2	.2
COMETS	32	6,425	755	42.5	332	109	453	77.4	299	1,001	450	260	455	126	64.8
OPPONENTS	32	-	705	37.5	489	151	331	73.2	309	973	446	262	464	71	59.1

INDIANA FEVER

PLAYER	GP	MIN	FIELD GOALS FGM	PCT	3-PT FG FGA	FGM	FREE THROWS FTM	PCT	REBOUNDS OFF	TOTAL	A	STL	TO	BLK	AVG
Tamika Catchings	32	1,167	184	41.9	193	76	150	81.5	92	276	118	94	82	43	18.6
Nikki McCray	32	1,058	132	41.5	66	21	84	81.6	29	97	70	28	82	3	11.5
Olympia Scott-Richardson	31	975	113	48.7	4	0	66	80.5	80	211	52	38	69	13	9.4
Coquese Washington	11	325	26	37.1	31	14	14	70.0	7	33	48	23	24	2	7.3
Rita Williams	20	484	39	28.9	67	17	25	73.5	10	37	43	21	29	2	6.0
Nadine Malcolm	29	599	58	36.7	41	12	28	75.7	22	61	21	13	34	3	5.4
Alicia Thompson	18	314	39	35.8	29	7	12	70.6	12	42	14	7	18	2	5.4
Bridget Pettis	32	375	38	35.5	43	9	28	71.8	17	39	17	8	24	0	3.5
Kelly Schumacher	31	352	45	50.6	1	0	18	69.2	18	59	13	7	21	23	3.5
Niele Ivey	31	439	25	35.2	50	19	17	81.0	6	28	39	16	22	3	2.8
Jackie Moore	18	128	16	42.1	1	0	10	71.4	9	29	3	5	14	1	2.3
Monica Maxwell	18	170	14	29.8	17	5	2	100.0	12	31	7	7	6	4	1.9
Zuzi Klimesova	11	39	2	16.7	0	0	1	100.0	1	5	2	1	2	1	.5
FEVER	32	6,425	731	40.1	543	180	455	78.4	315	948	447	268	438	100	65.5
OPPONENTS	32	-	804	44.2	464	162	359	71.4	288	932	507	226	470	145	66.5

LOS ANGELES SPARKS

PLAYER	GP	MIN	FIELD GOALS FGM	PCT	3-PT FG FGA	FGM	FREE THROWS FTM	PCT	REBOUNDS OFF	TOTAL	A	STL	TO	BLK	AVG
Lisa Leslie	31	1,060	189	46.6	37	12	133	72.7	78	322	83	46	108	90	16.9
Mwadi Mabika	32	1,050	188	42.3	175	64	99	83.9	32	167	92	38	62	9	16.8
DeLisha Milton	32	966	132	48.7	50	21	77	74.0	65	211	45	50	94	35	11.3
Tamecka Dixon	30	958	125	39.1	57	20	49	83.1	18	92	119	28	82	5	10.6
Latasha Byears	26	486	76	61.8	0	0	30	56.6	65	141	13	19	20	4	7.0
Nikki Teasley	32	882	67	40.4	100	40	30	75.0	17	84	140	25	68	9	6.4
Sophia Witherspoon	31	358	49	41.5	67	28	35	76.1	9	29	29	13	22	2	5.2
Marlies Askamp	20	215	26	47.3	1	0	9	64.3	24	49	4	11	11	4	3.1
Vedrana Grgin-Fonseca	12	79	12	38.7	12	5	2	66.7	3	8	1	1	8	0	2.6
Vicki Hall	3	19	2	50.0	1	0	3	75.0	1	2	1	1	1	0	2.3
Nicky McCrimmon	32	356	20	40.8	15	4	7	63.6	9	23	53	22	24	3	1.6
Erika Desouza	11	41	5	35.7	0	0	2	20.0	8	14	2	3	6	0	1.1
Katryna Gaither	1	5	0	00.0	0	0	0	00.0	0	1	1	0	1	0	.0
SPARKS	32	6,475	891	44.5	515	194	476	73.8	329	1,143	583	257	517	161	76.6
OPPONENTS	32	-	796	39.0	521	163	480	74.0	314	959	508	275	453	111	69.8

MIAMI SOL

PLAYER	GP	MIN	FIELD GOALS		3-PT FG		FREE THROWS		REBOUNDS		A	STL	TO	BLK	AVG
			FGM	PCT	FGA	FGM	FTM	PCT	OFF	TOTAL					
Sheri Sam	32	1,073	191	43.4	76	26	55	61.8	58	155	83	69	71	6	14.5
Betty Lennox	26	581	110	35.8	131	46	44	75.9	18	73	47	25	62	5	11.9
Sandy Brondello	30	763	97	36.5	44	14	55	82.1	7	41	46	26	40	4	8.8
Pollyanna Johns	31	801	78	52.3	0	0	61	62.9	58	140	32	27	53	15	7.0
Ruth Riley	26	519	60	46.5	0	0	28	60.9	24	90	25	11	49	41	5.7
Tamara Moore	5	83	8	32.0	9	2	10	100.0	3	7	10	7	11	0	5.6
Kristen Rasmussen	31	674	64	55.2	7	3	39	84.8	41	117	41	18	37	16	5.5
Debbie Black	32	899	64	40.0	3	0	25	75.8	41	123	137	59	32	5	4.8
Vanessa Nygaard	29	443	43	42.6	64	24	10	76.9	27	67	9	11	13	1	4.1
Iziane Castro Marques	19	182	24	33.3	17	1	17	68.0	7	17	7	7	18	0	3.5
Lindsey Yamasaki	15	147	19	44.2	17	9	5	50.0	3	15	9	4	10	1	3.5
Claudia Neves	20	194	11	35.5	21	4	11	68.8	0	7	25	8	13	0	1.9
Marlies Askamp	6	72	4	42.0	0	0	3	27.3	6	11	3	1	1	1	1.8
Trisha Stafford-Odom	6	38	1	16.7	0	0	6	75.0	3	6	2	1	6	0	1.3
Carolyn Moos	2	6	0	00.0	0	0	0	00.0	0	0	0	0	0	1	.0
SOL	32	6,475	774	41.7	389	129	369	69.8	296	869	476	274	435	96	63.9
OPPONENTS	32	-	745	43.3	382	129	469	76.4	278	971	446	222	515	104	65.3

MINNESOTA LYNX

PLAYER	GP	MIN	FIELD GOALS		3-PT FG		FREE THROWS		REBOUNDS		A	STL	TO	BLK	AVG
			FGM	PCT	FGA	FGM	FTM	PCT	OFF	TOTAL					
Katie Smith	31	1,138	162	40.4	188	62	126	82.4	24	92	79	32	70	7	16.5
Svetlana Abrosimova	27	805	119	37.7	60	20	56	48.3	45	146	60	42	92	10	11.6
Tamika Williams	31	1,023	124	56.1	11	3	63	58.3	96	229	51	44	74	13	10.1
Tamara Moore	26	653	63	36.6	68	26	44	83.0	20	76	78	23	74	9	7.5
Betty Lennox	5	138	10	20.8	23	5	6	60.0	2	16	16	5	20	0	6.2
Michele Van Gorp	22	352	41	45.6	7	2	16	72.7	29	64	14	6	20	11	4.5
Georgia Schweitzer	30	509	42	48.3	33	14	26	86.7	7	51	37	15	27	5	4.1
Lynn Pride	31	589	57	38.5	10	1	8	47.1	25	103	43	25	47	25	4.0
Kristi Harrower	27	481	37	38.9	54	18	4	40.0	9	46	54	12	28	0	3.6
Shaunzinski Gortman	29	369	35	36.1	43	14	7	77.8	16	61	21	13	25	6	3.1
Janell Burse	31	344	31	37.3	1	0	21	58.3	29	60	7	7	18	13	2.7
Val Whiting-Raymond	6	52	4	30.8	0	0	5	41.7	3	9	5	2	4	2	2.2
Shanele Stires	9	22	2	50.0	2	1	1	50.0	4	6	1	0	2	1	.7
LYNX	32	6,475	727	41.0	500	166	383	66.3	309	959	466	226	529	102	62.6
OPPONENTS	32	-	747	41.3	389	141	469	76.5	302	914	495	273	465	117	65.8

NEW YORK LIBERTY

PLAYER	GP	MIN	FIELD GOALS FGM	PCT	3-PT FG FGA	FGM	FREE THROWS FTM	PCT	REBOUNDS OFF	TOTAL	A	STL	TO	BLK	AVG
Tari Phillips	32	1,009	183	49.1	2	0	85	67.5	69	223	41	58	93	14	14.1
Tamika Whitmore	32	977	148	47.7	1	0	110	73.3	43	141	23	27	49	43	12.7
Crystal Robinson	32	1,068	126	41.7	181	67	59	81.9	22	92	81	48	52	12	11.8
Vickie Johnson	31	1,028	139	45.6	76	32	49	80.3	42	109	86	27	45	4	11.6
Becky Hammon	32	659	87	44.2	114	44	38	67.9	18	68	54	25	55	0	8.0
Teresa Weatherspoon	32	954	39	34.2	20	2	28	51.9	23	86	181	42	78	3	3.4
Sue Wicks	30	428	24	34.3	1	0	18	66.7	30	101	14	22	30	15	2.2
Korie Hlede	16	129	11	42.3	1	0	4	44.4	4	16	12	6	21	2	1.6
Camille Cooper	23	119	11	39.3	0	0	5	62.5	5	16	3	4	10	5	1.2
Bernadette Ngoyisa	7	12	3	60.0	0	0	0	00.0	1	5	0	0	0	2	.9
Linda Frohlich	16	67	1	10.0	4	0	4	100.0	3	13	1	2	4	0	.4
LIBERTY	32	6,450	772	44.4	400	145	400	70.5	260	870	496	261	458	100	65.3
OPPONENTS	32	-	691	39.9	434	149	484	75.0	312	961	410	228	478	88	63.0

ORLANDO MIRACLE

PLAYER	GP	MIN	FIELD GOALS FGM	PCT	3-PT FG FGA	FGM	FREE THROWS FTM	PCT	REBOUNDS OFF	TOTAL	A	STL	TO	BLK	AVG
Shannon Johnson	31	1,110	157	40.4	77	21	164	76.6	49	129	163	51	98	7	16.1
Nykesha Sales	32	1,042	155	41.2	115	37	84	79.2	36	120	60	60	71	7	13.5
Wendy Palmer	16	501	65	43.9	60	23	27	69.2	20	93	21	22	23	6	11.3
Katie Douglas	32	830	92	44.9	79	29	58	86.6	41	135	53	49	42	13	8.5
Taj McWilliams-Franklin	13	383	41	50.0	3	1	27	87.1	21	63	13	19	22	14	8.5
Jessie Hicks	31	471	73	47.7	0	0	44	69.8	60	102	23	19	51	25	6.1
Elaine Powell	15	308	35	35.4	11	2	16	61.5	7	32	30	20	30	4	5.9
Adrienne Johnson	32	602	68	37.6	61	18	12	70.6	14	46	22	15	26	2	5.2
Clarisse Machanguana	29	428	61	53.5	0	0	16	64.0	26	64	17	12	33	4	4.8
Cintia Dos Santos	26	260	26	49.1	1	0	36	78.3	15	35	10	4	20	13	3.4
Carla McGhee	2	4	2	50.0	0	0	1	100.0	1	1	0	0	0	0	2.5
Brooke Wyckoff	32	514	31	32.6	50	14	5	71.4	28	90	32	19	30	18	2.5
Tiffany McCain	16	51	2	20.0	4	0	3	75.0	1	3	2	3	3	0	.4
Davalyn Cunningham	6	21	0	00.0	0	0	0	00.0	1	2	0	2	1	0	.0
MIRACLE	32	6,525	808	42.2	461	145	493	76.3	320	915	446	295	456	113	70.4
OPPONENTS	32	-	804	43.2	422	156	491	73.5	362	1,046	519	251	541	108	70.5

PHOENIX MERCURY

PLAYER	GP	MIN	FIELD GOALS FGM	PCT	3-PT FG FGA	FGM	FREE THROWS FTM	PCT	REBOUNDS OFF	TOTAL	A	STL	TO	BLK	AVG
Jennifer Gillom	31	874	166	41.5	93	36	105	80.2	36	116	37	29	61	21	15.3
Gordana Grubin	32	859	114	38.4	92	29	60	75.9	16	64	104	36	58	3	9.9
Lisa Harrison	32	899	120	49.6	6	2	20	87.0	43	126	40	31	45	3	8.2
Brandy Reed	5	85	15	36.6	5	0	8	72.7	1	4	4	2	8	3	7.6
Adrain Williams	32	878	79	46.7	0	0	42	70.0	64	220	35	48	63	29	6.3
Adriana Moises Pinto	32	619	63	38.4	66	19	48	80.0	15	60	79	30	72	3	6.0
Susanna Bonfiglio	22	306	43	48.3	6	0	19	76.0	16	37	23	12	18	0	4.8
Tracy Reid	24	421	48	41.0	1	0	17	60.7	33	77	14	22	36	2	4.7
Kayte Christensen	30	413	48	50.5	1	0	24	68.6	39	80	15	24	32	13	4.0
Jaynetta Saunders	27	302	39	37.9	4	0	21	65.6	10	38	23	9	20	4	3.7
Slobodanka Tuvic	26	320	30	39.0	6	1	25	78.1	11	63	11	9	31	9	3.3
Kristen Veal	23	361	24	30.4	47	13	10	76.9	6	27	41	14	42	2	3.1
Shea Mahoney	3	13	2	66.7	1	0	1	100.0	2	2	1	0	1	0	1.7
Quacy Barnes	2	13	0	00.0	0	0	3	75.0	0	1	0	1	0	2	1.5
Oksana Zakaluzhnaya	5	37	2	33.3	0	0	2	50.0	0	3	0	0	4	0	1.2
MERCURY	32	6,400	793	42.0	328	100	405	75.3	292	918	427	267	501	94	65.3
OPPONENTS	32	-	850	45.5	388	155	436	71.7	309	1,001	532	268	491	127	71.6

PORTLAND FIRE

PLAYER	GP	MIN	FIELD GOALS FGM	PCT	3-PT FG FGA	FGM	FREE THROWS FTM	PCT	REBOUNDS OFF	TOTAL	A	STL	TO	BLK	AVG
DeMya Walker	31	848	139	48.4	12	2	59	62.1	55	154	51	26	90	33	10.9
Tamicha Jackson	32	692	122	41.9	76	24	46	69.7	20	59	95	55	64	1	9.8
Alisa Burras	32	633	117	62.9	0	0	44	84.6	52	147	7	10	49	7	8.7
Sylvia Crawley	32	819	114	40.1	17	7	44	69.8	46	134	47	18	62	37	8.7
Ukari Figgs	31	866	83	35.6	120	39	59	90.8	13	80	104	25	44	2	8.5
Jackie Stiles	21	382	43	31.9	44	15	24	80.0	7	18	20	4	21	0	6.0
LaQuanda Barksdale	17	285	36	35.6	22	5	23	88.5	18	40	12	8	23	7	5.9
Kristin Folkl	32	602	62	49.2	3	0	31	88.6	41	148	32	18	32	17	4.8
Stacey Thomas	32	621	51	34.5	39	10	31	50.8	34	94	67	42	36	12	4.5
Carolyn Young	19	186	26	35.1	22	10	21	87.5	5	14	12	4	18	0	4.4
Tully Bevilaqua	27	421	25	41.0	36	15	19	65.5	7	33	44	22	27	3	3.1
Amber Hall	20	104	11	45.8	0	0	8	50.0	8	26	1	7	12	1	1.5
Jenny Mowe	5	16	0	00.0	0	0	1	50.0	1	1	0	0	1	0	.2
FIRE	32	6,475	829	42.5	391	127	410	72.7	307	948	492	239	493	120	68.6
OPPONENTS	32	-	819	43.4	348	126	463	71.6	334	1,012	486	272	508	139	69.6

SACRAMENTO MONARCHS

PLAYER	GP	MIN	FIELD GOALS FGM	PCT	3-PT FG FGA	FGM	FREE THROWS FTM	PCT	REBOUNDS OFF	TOTAL	A	STL	TO	BLK	AVG
Yolanda Griffith	17	577	93	52.0	0	0	102	80.3	66	148	19	16	45	13	16.9
Tangela Smith	32	1,063	184	42.3	42	15	86	85.1	56	188	40	27	59	46	14.7
Ruthie Bolton	32	737	125	39.6	132	43	56	72.7	31	94	37	45	35	2	10.9
Kedra Holland-Corn	32	902	102	34.1	157	38	54	75.0	28	90	63	41	81	5	9.3
Ticha Penicheiro	24	853	60	37.7	32	8	75	72.8	7	102	192	64	69	1	8.5
Lady Grooms	32	850	78	43.1	1	0	71	85.5	38	99	39	21	46	8	7.1
La'Keshia Frett	32	648	84	44.9	15	5	14	82.4	30	95	23	5	27	19	5.8
Edna Campbell	1	12	2	40.0	2	0	0	00.0	0	1	0	1	0	0	4.0
Cass Bauer-Bilodeau	25	233	17	29.8	0	0	9	60.0	14	41	1	2	25	5	1.7
Kara Wolters	14	78	9	32.1	0	0	6	60.0	8	23	3	0	6	3	1.7
Hamchetou Maiga	23	197	13	24.5	0	0	14	46.7	18	37	9	15	23	3	1.7
Andrea Nagy	24	409	12	27.3	14	3	7	43.8	3	29	73	10	31	4	1.4
Stacey Ford	5	12	1	50.0	0	0	0	00.0	2	2	1	0	1	0	.4
Monique Ambers	2	4	0	00.0	0	0	0	00.0	0	0	0	0	0	0	.0
MONARCHS	32	6,575	780	40.1	395	112	494	75.7	301	949	500	247	456	109	67.7
OPPONENTS	32	-	815	41.9	453	149	515	75.6	352	1,075	493	233	496	128	71.7

SEATTLE STORM

PLAYER	GP	MIN	FIELD GOALS FGM	PCT	3-PT FG FGA	FGM	FREE THROWS FTM	PCT	REBOUNDS OFF	TOTAL	A	STL	TO	BLK	AVG
Lauren Jackson	28	882	186	40.3	120	42	68	75.6	66	190	41	30	47	81	17.2
Sue Bird	32	1,121	151	40.3	142	57	102	91.1	17	83	191	55	109	3	14.4
Kamila Vodichkova	32	817	114	46.5	38	13	54	80.6	61	176	47	36	55	18	9.2
Simone Edwards	32	694	84	53.2	1	1	54	74.0	46	141	19	21	44	12	7.0
Semeka Randall	21	458	47	35.3	19	4	36	70.6	38	68	29	20	36	1	6.4
Kate Starbird	9	186	20	45.5	11	5	8	88.9	3	19	12	6	11	4	5.9
Amanda Lassiter	24	554	47	36.2	66	20	12	70.6	23	63	55	27	49	19	5.3
Jamie Redd	10	112	17	50.0	18	9	9	75.0	8	13	7	2	7	0	5.2
Felicia Ragland	31	432	48	38.4	55	22	23	82.1	27	48	23	27	29	1	4.5
Adia Barnes	26	493	37	33.3	4	1	15	51.7	45	102	28	32	25	9	3.5
Michelle Marciniak	23	280	24	35.3	8	2	22	75.9	8	28	38	11	25	2	3.1
Sonja Henning	8	207	8	36.4	4	0	2	50.0	8	26	15	9	7	1	2.3
Takeisha Lewis	14	57	4	40.0	1	0	10	55.6	7	24	3	2	7	0	1.3
Kate Paye	19	114	7	36.8	16	6	1	50.0	2	7	5	3	8	0	1.1
Danielle McCulley	4	43	0	00.0	3	0	2	100.0	3	7	1	1	2	0	.5
STORM	32	6,450	794	40.8	506	182	418	77.0	362	995	514	282	477	151	68.4
OPPONENTS	32	-	783	43.1	342	102	435	74.1	307	969	488	254	531	125	65.7

UTAH STARZZ

PLAYER	GP	MIN	FIELD GOALS FGM	PCT	3-PT FG FGA	FGM	FREE THROWS FTM	PCT	REBOUNDS OFF	TOTAL	A	STL	TO	BLK	AVG
Adrienne Goodson	32	1,101	189	45.1	28	8	117	74.5	91	181	67	45	102	6	15.7
Marie Ferdinand	32	1,065	176	47.4	34	5	132	77.2	19	107	91	51	89	7	15.3
Margo Dydek	30	876	139	43.6	8	2	114	84.4	52	262	71	25	96	107	13.1
Natalie Williams	31	1,008	124	43.5	12	5	98	74.2	105	255	38	38	72	16	11.3
Jennifer Azzi	32	1,151	91	46.0	92	41	83	79.8	15	69	158	27	67	14	9.6
Semeka Randall	8	135	18	45.0	2	0	22	75.9	4	21	8	4	10	1	7.3
LaTonya Johnson	28	269	25	32.9	32	10	15	75.0	8	19	10	7	15	2	2.7
LaNeishea Caufield	8	65	6	40.0	9	5	2	100.0	3	5	1	7	8	0	2.4
Amy Herrig	28	269	23	43.4	0	0	22	73.3	15	57	4	9	21	14	2.4
Andrea Gardner	30	198	18	36.7	0	0	21	55.3	29	61	5	3	13	3	1.9
Kate Starbird	15	88	10	40.0	8	2	4	57.1	0	7	7	9	2	4	1.7
Danielle Crockrom	18	84	10	35.7	1	0	9	75.0	6	13	2	0	3	2	1.6
Elisa Aguilar	28	141	14	42.4	21	11	4	57.1	0	11	16	3	11	2	1.5
STARZZ	32	6,450	843	44.1	247	89	643	76.2	347	1,068	478	228	522	178	75.6
OPPONENTS	32	-	851	41.2	377	126	516	75.0	361	1,006	489	260	444	149	73.3

WASHINGTON MYSTICS

PLAYER	GP	MIN	FIELD GOALS FGM	PCT	3-PT FG FGA	FGM	FREE THROWS FTM	PCT	REBOUNDS OFF	TOTAL	A	STL	TO	BLK	AVG
Chamique Holdsclaw	20	634	149	45.2	28	11	88	83.0	54	232	45	20	45	6	19.9
Stacey Dales-Schuman	31	805	93	40.4	109	43	74	74.0	26	81	84	16	68	4	9.8
Coco Miller	32	904	114	43.3	64	24	46	82.1	44	116	82	33	59	2	9.3
Vicky Bullett	32	958	109	46.2	48	19	34	82.9	46	186	53	54	56	37	8.5
Asjha Jones	32	612	93	39.9	10	2	20	60.6	39	89	28	13	39	17	6.5
Murriel Page	32	750	88	45.1	4	2	30	56.6	55	155	37	14	45	15	6.5
Helen Luz	32	474	65	43.9	106	42	15	78.9	9	32	48	18	43	5	5.8
Annie Burgess	26	632	39	38.6	33	12	35	77.8	16	62	93	34	41	4	4.8
Tonya Washington	25	291	28	32.6	18	6	11	84.6	27	38	15	3	16	2	2.9
Kiesha Brown	18	108	12	34.3	11	1	3	100.0	4	12	6	5	5	0	1.6
Audrey Sauret	15	165	10	41.7	5	1	3	60.0	3	11	18	8	15	2	1.6
Maren Walseth	18	104	6	24.0	7	1	0	00.0	7	21	7	2	9	0	.7
Katryna Gaither	1	1	0	00.0	0	0	0	00.0	0	0	0	0	0	0	.0
Tausha Mills	4	17	0	00.0	0	0	0	00.0	0	3	0	1	2	0	.0
MYSTICS	32	6,450	806	42.2	443	164	359	75.1	330	1,038	516	221	455	94	66.7
OPPONENTS	32	-	786	41.3	446	147	397	73.8	309	989	442	237	441	101	66.1

Today's Stars

Sue Bird, guard, b. October 16, 1980, Syosset, New York. In 2002, Bird led the Connecticut Huskies to a perfect 35–0 record and her second — the team's third — NCAA Division I women's basketball championship. Three weeks later, the Seattle Storm selected her with the Number 1 pick in the WNBA draft. Bird led all rookies in assists per game (6) and free-throw percentage (.911).

Tamika Catchings, forward, b. July 21, 1979, Stratford, New Jersey. Catchings earned 2002 WNBA Rookie of the Year honors as a member of the Indiana Fever. She ranked first in the league in steals per game (2.94), second in points (18.6) and minutes (36.5), fourth in rebounds (8.6), sixth in blocks (1.34), and tenth in assists (3.7). The four-time Kodak All-American helped Tennessee win the NCAA Division I women's title in 1998.

Sheryl Swoopes, forward, b. March 25, 1971, Brownfield, Texas. One of the most decorated players in the history of women's basketball. Between 1993 through 2002, Swoopes won an NCAA Division I women's championship with Texas Tech, two Olympic gold medals with the U.S. women's national team, four straight WNBA championships with the Houston Comets, two league MVP awards, and two WNBA Defensive Player of t he Year honors.

Sue Bird was the Number 1 pick in the 2002 WNBA draft.

JEFF ZELEVANSKY/AP

□▷**Random Fact:** The league's most talented rookie class (2002) featured the University of Connecticut's Fab Four: Sue Bird (Number 1 draft pick), Swin Cash (2), Asjha Jones (4), and Tamika Williams (6). They became the first college teammates to be chosen among the first six picks in draft history.

WNBA Champions

YEAR	CHAMPION	RUNNER-UP	MVP
2002	Los Angeles Sparks	New York Liberty	Lisa Leslie
2001	Los Angeles Sparks	Charlotte Sting	Lisa Leslie
2000	Houston Comets	New York Liberty	Cynthia Cooper
1999	Houston Comets	New York Liberty	Cynthia Cooper
1998	Houston Comets	Phoenix Mercury	Cynthia Cooper
1997	Houston Comets	New York Liberty	Cynthia Cooper

STEVE YEATER/AP

Visit **www.sikids.com** for the latest sports stats and info.
Site code: slamdunk
AOL keyword: sikids

2002 WNBA Individual Leaders

POINTS

	GP	PTS	AVG
Chamique Holdsclaw, Washington Mystics	20	397	19.9
Tamika Catchings, Indiana Fever	32	594	18.6
Sheryl Swoopes, Houston Comets	32	592	18.5
Lauren Jackson, Seattle Storm	28	482	17.2
Lisa Leslie, Los Angeles Sparks	31	523	16.9

REBOUNDS

	GP	REB	AVG
Chamique Holdsclaw, Washington Mystics	20	232	11.6
Lisa Leslie, Los Angeles Sparks	31	322	10.4
Margo Dydek, Utah Starzz	30	262	8.7
Tamika Catchings, Indiana Fever	32	276	8.6
Natalie Williams, Utah Starzz	31	255	8.2

ASSISTS

	GP	A	AVG
Ticha Penicheiro, Sacramento Monarchs	24	192	8.0
Sue Bird, Seattle Storm	32	191	6.0
Teresa Weatherspoon, New York Liberty	32	181	5.7
Shannon Johnson, Orlando Miracle	31	163	5.3
Dawn Staley, Charlotte Sting	32	164	5.1

FIELD-GOAL PERCENTAGE

	FGA	FGM	PCT
Alisa Burras, Portland Fire	186	117	62.9
Tamika Williams, Minnesota Lynx	221	124	56.1
Ann Wauters, Cleveland Rockers	217	120	55.3
Tammy Sutton-Brown, Charlotte Sting	243	129	53.1
Yolanda Griffith, Sacramento Monarchs	179	93	52.0

FREE-THROW PERCENTAGE

	FTA	FTM	PCT
Sue Bird, Seattle Storm	112	102	91.1
Ukari Figgs, Portland Fire	65	59	90.8
Janeth Arcain, Houston Comets	111	98	88.3
Katie Douglas, Orlando Miracle	67	58	86.6
Tamara Moore, Minnesota Lynx	63	54	85.7

3-POINT FIELD-GOAL PERCENTAGE

	FGA	FGM	PCT
Kelly Miller, Charlotte Sting	51	24	47.1
Jennifer Azzi, Utah Starzz	92	41	44.6
Coquese Washington, Indiana Fever	52	22	42.3
Vickie Johnson, New York Liberty	76	32	42.1
DeLisha Milton, Los Angeles Sparks	50	21	42.0

STEALS

	GP	STL	AVG
Tamika Catchings, Indiana Fever	32	94	2.94
Sheryl Swoopes, Houston Comets	32	88	2.75
Ticha Penicheiro, Sacramento Monarchs	24	64	2.67
Sheri Sam, Miami Sol	32	69	2.16
Nykesha Sales, Orlando Miracle	32	60	1.88

BLOCKS

	GP	BLK	AVG
Margo Dydek, Utah Starzz	30	107	3.57
Lisa Leslie, Los Angeles Sparks	31	90	2.90
Lauren Jackson, Seattle Storm	28	81	2.89
Ruth Riley, Miami Sol	26	41	1.58
Tangela Smith, Sacramento Monarchs	32	46	1.44

WNBA All-Star Game Results

YEAR	RESULT	SITE	WINNING COACH	MVP
2003	West 84, East 75	New York, NY	Michael Cooper	Nikki Teasley, Los Angeles Sparks
2002	West 81, East 76	Washington, D.C.	Michael Cooper	Lisa Leslie, Los Angeles Sparks
2001	West 80, East 72	Orlando, FL	Van Chancellor	Lisa Leslie, Los Angeles Sparks
2000	West 73, East 61	Phoenix, AZ	Van Chancellor	Tina Thompson, Houston Comets
1999	West 79, East 61	New York, NY	Van Chancellor	Lisa Leslie, Los Angeles Sparks

2002-03 TIMELINE

May 25, 2002: The Los Angeles Sparks host the New York Liberty in a WNBA season opener for the second time. The first time was the league's inaugural game, on June 21, 1997 (Liberty 67, Sparks, 57). The Sparks win this one, 72–64.

June 5, 2002: Liberty point guard Teresa Weatherspoon becomes the first WNBA player to reach 1,000 career assists.

July 15, 2002: Sparks center Lisa Leslie is named All-Star Game MVP for a record third time. She has 18 points, 14 rebounds, and 4 blocks. The Western Conference beats the Eastern Conference, 81–76, to remain perfect in All-Star competition (4–0).

July 30, 2002: Lisa Leslie becomes the first player to dunk in a WNBA game. Her dunk comes on a breakaway basket against the Miami Sol.

August 13, 2002: Rookie forward Tamika Catchings of the Indiana Fever is the first WNBA player to finish a season among the Top 5 leaders in points, rebounds, steals, and minutes per game.

August 31, 2002: The Sparks complete a two-game sweep of the Liberty to clinch their second-straight WNBA championship. Lisa Leslie is named Finals MVP for the second season in a row.

September 25, 2002: The USA Basketball Women's World Championship Team, which is made up of 12 WNBA players, defeats Russia, 79–74, to win its record seventh gold medal. Lisa Leslie is named tournament MVP.

April 25, 2003: The Cleveland Rockers choose forward LaToya Thomas of Mississippi State with the first pick in the WNBA draft.

April 29, 2003: Four-time WNBA Finals MVP Cynthia Cooper, who retired in 2000, announces her return to the Houston Comets.

May 22, 2003: The seventh WNBA season begins with four teams in action. The Houston Comets beat the Seattle Storm, 75-64, and the Sacramento Monarchs defeat the Pheonix Mercury, 65-56.

Did You Know?

The first woman to dunk in a college game was West Virginia's Georgeann Wells, who did it on December 21, 1984. Charlotte Smith dunked while at the University of North Carolina in 1994. Michelle Snow of the Houston Comets dunked three times during her college career at the University of Tennessee.

World Championship All-time Results

YEAR	WINNER	RUNNER-UP	SCORE	SITE
2002	United States	Russia	79–74	China
1998	United States	Russia	71–65	Germany
1994	Brazil	China	96–87	Australia
1990	United States	Yugoslavia	88–78	Malaysia
1986	United States	Soviet Union	108–88	Soviet Union
1983	Soviet Union	United States	84–82	Brazil
1979	United States	South Korea	77–61	South Korea
1975	Soviet Union	Japan	106–75	Colombia
1971	Soviet Union	Czechoslovakia	88–69	Brazil
1967	Soviet Union	South Korea	83–50	Czechoslovakia
1964	Soviet Union	Czechoslovakia	70–35	Peru
1959 *	Soviet Union	Bulgaria	51–38	Soviet Union
1957	United States	Soviet Union	51–48	Brazil
1953	United States	Chile	49–36	Chile

*The United States did not compete at the 1959 World Championships because they were held in Moscow, Soviet Union.

2002 World Championship Final Standings

1.	USA	(9–0)
2.	Russia	(7–2)
3.	Australia	(7–2)
4.	South Korea	(4–5)
5.	Spain	(6–3)
6.	China	(5–4)
7.	Brazil	(6–3)
8.	France	(4–5)
9.	Cuba	(3–5)
10.	Argentina	(2–6)
11.	Lithuania	(3–5)
12.	Yugoslavia	(2–6)
13.	Japan	(2–3)
14.	Chinese Taipei	(1–4)
15.	Senegal	(1–4)
16.	Tunisia	(0–5)

World Championship Individual Leaders

Lauren Jackson of Australia led all scorers (23.1 points per game) at the 2002 World Championships.

VINCENT YU/AP

POINTS

PLAYER	TEAM	GP	PTS	AVG
Lauren Jackson	Australia	9	208	23.1
Elena Baranova	Russia	9	163	18.1
Matsuko Nagata	Japan	5	87	17.4
Lisa Leslie	United States	9	155	17.2
Awa Gueye	Senegal	5	86	17.2

REBOUNDS

PLAYER	TEAM	GP	REB	AVG
Elena Baranova	Russia	9	99	11.0
Cheng Hui-Yun	Chinese Taipei	5	46	9.2
Alessandra Oliveira	Brazil	9	73	8.1
Lisa Leslie	United States	9	73	8.1
Chen Nan	China	9	71	7.9

ASSISTS

PLAYER	TEAM	GP	A	AVG
Chien Wei-Chuan	Chinese Taipei	4	22	5.5
Kahori Kawakami	Japan	5	24	4.8
Biljana Stankovic	Yugoslavia	8	27	3.4
Kaouthar Abid	Tunisia	5	16	3.2
Kristi Harrower	Australia	9	28	3.1

FIELD-GOAL PERCENTAGE

PLAYER	TEAM	GP	FGA	FGM	PCT
Alessandra Oliveira	Brazil	9	79	56	70.9
Ingrid Pons Molina	Spain	9	54	36	66.7
Daliborka Vilipic	Yugoslavia	8	55	36	65.5
Kelly Santos	Brazil	9	43	27	62.8
Chen Nan	China	9	101	58	57.4

FREE-THROW PERCENTAGE

PLAYER	TEAM	GP	FTA	FTM	PCT
Sun-Min Jung	South Korea	9	48	46	95.8
Chen Xiaoli	China	9	22	21	95.5
Janeth Arcain	Brazil	9	23	21	91.3
Garcia Pinero	Spain	9	21	19	90.5
R. Sanchez Lujan	Spain	9	21	19	90.5

3-POINT FIELD-GOAL PERCENTAGE

PLAYER	TEAM	GP	FGA	FGM	PCT
Gordana Bogojevic	Yugoslavia	8	18	13	72.2
Chien Wei-Chuan	Chinese Taipei	4	12	7	58.3
Ljubica Draljaca	Yugoslavia	7	18	10	55.6
Lauren Jackson	Australia	9	20	11	55.0
Edwige Lawson	France	9	20	11	55.0

STEALS

PLAYER	TEAM	GP	STL	AVG
Awa Gueye	Senegal	5	17	3.40
Cheng Hui-Yun	Chinese Taipei	5	17	3.40
Yuliseni Baro	Cuba	8	25	3.13
Kaouthar Abid	Tunisia	5	14	2.80
Catherine Melain	France	9	25	2.78

BLOCKS

PLAYER	TEAM	GP	BLK	AVG
Irina Issipova	Russia	9	14	1.56
I. Baranauskaite	Lithuania	8	8	1.00
Cheng Hui-Yun	Chinese Taipei	5	5	1.00
Lisa Leslie	United States	9	8	.89
Nicole Antibe	France	9	7	.78

2003 WNBA Draft

April 25, 2003, Secaucus, NJ

FIRST ROUND PICK TEAM	NAME/POSITION	SCHOOL/ FORMER TEAM
1. Cleveland	LaToya Thomas, F	Mississippi State
2. Sacramento	Chantelle Anderson, C	Vanderbilt
3. Detroit	Cheryl Ford, C	Louisiana Tech
4. Phoenix	Plenette Pierson, F	Texas Tech
5. Detroit	Kara Lawson, G	Tennessee
6. Indiana	Gwen Jackson, F	Tennessee
7. Washington	Aiysha Smith, C	Louisiana State
8. Seattle	Sun-Min Jung, C	Korea
9. Charlotte	Jocelyn Penn, F	South Carolina
10. New York	Molly Creamer, G	Bucknell
11. San Antonio	Coretta Brown, G	North Carolina
12. Houston	Allison Curtin, G	Tulsa

KEY G=guard; F=forward; C=center

BASKETBALL

The 2002-03 season was *supposed* to be the Year of the Senior. And for a while, it was. Arizona, led by senior forward Luke Walton and senior guard Jason Gardner, was the Number 1 team for 13 weeks of the 19-week college season. Kentucky and its senior guard, Keith Bogans, reeled off 26 straight wins from December 30 to March 27.

But things changed once the NCAA tournament got rolling. Top-seeded Arizona was upset by Number 2 Kansas in the Elite Eight. The same day, Number 1 Kentucky fell to Number 3 Marquette. When the hype and hoopla of March Madness finally quieted down, the scene was very "Melo" — as in Syracuse freshman sensation Carmelo Anthony. Anthony carried Syracuse to its first national title. He racked up 20 points, 10 rebounds, and 7 assists in 'Cuse's 81–78 win over Kansas in the championship game. The Orangemen were lent a helping hand by another freshman, point guard Gerry McNamara, who drained six first-half 3-pointers.

Anthony had one of the most eye-popping seasons by a freshman in recent years, averaging 22.2 points and 10 rebounds per game. He was named National Freshman of the Year. Sophomore point guard T.J. Ford of Texas won the Wooden and Naismith National Player of the Year awards.

Freshman Carmelo Anthony led Syracuse to its first national championship, in 2002-03.

BOB ROSATO/SPORTS ILLUSTRATED

▷**Random Fact:** Marquette guard Dwyane Wade became the third player in history to have a triple-double in the NCAA tournament. Michigan State guard Magic Johnson and Utah guard Andre Miller were the other two.

NCAA Men's Division I Championship Box Score

SYRACUSE ORANGEMEN 81

Player	POS	MIN	FG M-A	3-PT M-A	FT M-A	PF	PTS
Carmelo Anthony	F	37	7-16	3-5	3-4	2	20
Gerry McNamara	G	34	6-13	6-10	0-0	2	18
Hakim Warrick	F	31	2-4	0-0	2-4	3	6
Billy Edelin	G	27	4-10	0-0	4-6	1	12
Craig Forth	C	24	3-4	0-1	0-1	5	6
Josh Pace	G	21	4-9	0-0	0-0	2	8
Kueth Duany	G	13	4-6	2-3	1-2	3	11
Jeremy McNeil	F	13	0-1	0-0	0-0	4	0
Xzavier Gaines	G	0	0-0	0-0	0-0	0	0
Tyrone Albright	G	0	0-0	0-0	0-0	0	0
Josh Brooks	F	0	0-0	0-0	0-0	0	0
Matt Gorman	F	0	0-0	0-0	0-0	0	0
Gary Hall	F	0	0-0	0-0	0-0	0	0
Ronneil Herron	G	0	0-0	0-0	0-0	0	0
Andrew Kouwe	G	0	0-0	0-0	0-0	0	0
Totals			30-63 (47.6%)	11-19 (57.9%)	10-17 (58.8%)		

KANSAS JAYHAWKS 78

Player	POS	MIN	FG M-A	3-PT M-A	FT M-A	PF	PTS
Nick Collison	F	39	8-14	0-0	3-10	5	19
Kirk Hinrich	G	38	6-20	3-12	1-1	1	16
Jeff Graves	F	37	7-13	0-0	2-7	2	16
Aaron Miles	G	34	1-5	0-2	0-0	1	2
Keith Langford	G	23	7-9	0-1	5-10	5	19
Michael Lee	G	23	2-8	1-5	0-0	1	5
Bryant Nash	F	5	0-2	0-0	1-2	1	1
Brett Olson	F	0	0-0	0-0	0-0	0	0
Jeff Hawkins	G	0	0-0	0-0	0-0	0	0
Christian Moody	F	0	0-0	0-0	0-0	0	0
Moulaye Niang	F	0	0-0	0-0	0-0	0	0
Wayne Simien	F	0	0-0	0-0	0-0	0	0
Stephen Vinson	G	0	0-0	0-0	0-0	0	0
Totals			31-71 (43.7%)	4-20 (20.0%)	12-30 (40.0%)		

KEY POS=position; MIN=minutes played; FG M-A=field goals made-attempted; 3-PT M-A=3-point field goals made-attempted; FT M-A=free throws made-attempted; PF=personal fouls; PTS=points; F=forward; G=guard; C=center

Nick Collison of Kansas averaged 18.5 points and 10 rebounds per game in 2002-03.

SUE OGROCKI/AP

Did You Know?

Carmelo Anthony became the third freshman to win the Final Four's Most Outstanding Player award. The other two players to win were Louisville's Pervis Ellison (1986) and Utah's Arnie Ferrin (1944).

USA TODAY/ESPN Top 25 Final Poll

Rank	School	Final Record	Points
1	Syracuse	30–5	775
2	Kansas	30–8	742
3	Texas	26–7	694
4	Kentucky	32–4	666
5	Arizona	28–4	654
6	Marquette	27–6	626
7	Oklahoma	27–7	595
8	Pittsburgh	28–5	559
9	Duke	26–7	493
10	Maryland	21–10	384
11	Connecticut	23–10	371
12	Wake Forest	25–6	361
13	Illinois	25–7	345
13	Wisconsin	24–8	345
15	Notre Dame	24–10	333
16	Florida	25–8	309
17	Xavier	26–6	253
18	Michigan State	22–13	252
19	Louisville	25–7	244
20	Stanford	24–9	164
21	Butler	27–6	133
22	Missouri	22–11	122
23	Creighton	29–5	121
24	Oklahoma State	22–10	94
25	Dayton	24–6	81

NCAA Men's Division I Individual Leaders

Scoring

	Class	GP	FG	3FG	FT	PTS	AVG
Ruben Douglas, New Mexico	Sr.	28	218	94	253	783	28.0
Henry Domercant, Eastern Illinois	Sr.	29	252	84	222	810	27.9
Mike Helms, Oakland	Jr.	28	241	74	196	752	26.9
Michael Watson, Missouri–Kansas City	Jr.	29	247	118	128	740	25.5
Troy Bell, Boston College	Sr.	31	224	106	227	781	25.2
Keydren Clark, St. Peter's	Fr.	29	231	109	151	722	24.9
Luis Flores, Manhattan	Jr.	30	231	109	151	722	24.6
Chris Williams, Ball State	Sr.	30	226	64	220	736	24.5
Mike Sweetney, Georgetown	Jr.	34	264	0	248	776	22.8
Kevin Martin, Western Carolina	So.	24	161	50	174	546	22.8

KEY GP=games played; FG=field goals; 3FG=3-point field goals; FT=free throws; PTS=points; AVG=average; Sr.=senior; Jr.=junior; So.=sophomore; Fr.=freshman

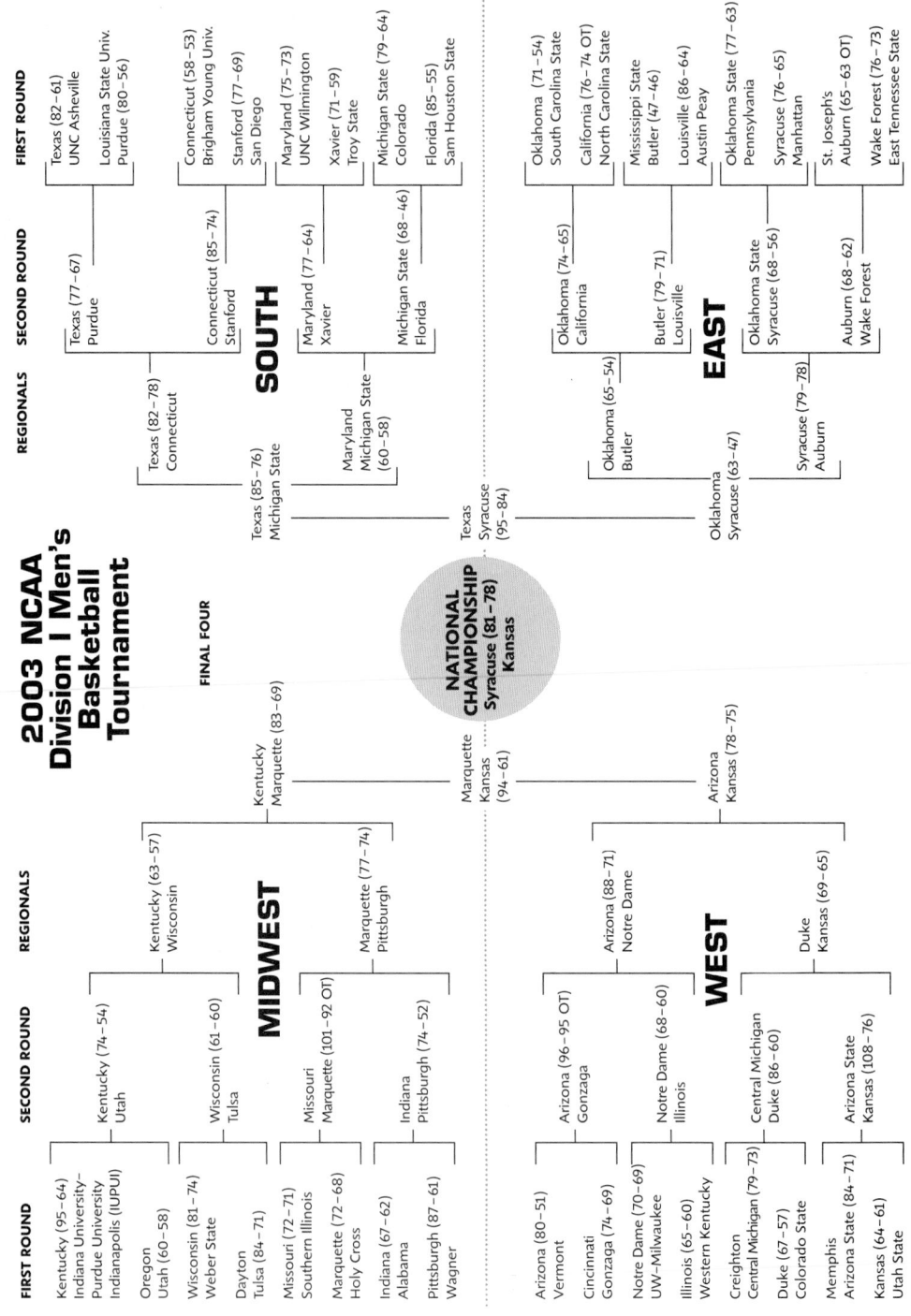

2003 NCAA Division I Men's Basketball Tournament

Vick-torious

In just his second NFL season, Michael Vick of the Atlanta Falcons set the NFL single-game rushing record for a quarterback when he ran for 173 yards against the Minnesota Vikings on December 1, 2002. He led the Falcons to their first playoff appearance since 1999 and was named to the Pro Bowl.

BOB ROSATO/SPORTS ILLUSTRATED

G-o-o-o-o-oals!

Ronaldo earned the Golden Boot award as the leading scorer at the 2002 World Cup tournament (8 goals). Two of those goals came in the championship match against Germany, which Brazil won, 2-0. The victory gave Brazil its fifth World Cup title, the most of any country.

ANTONIO SCORZA/AFP

BOB ROSATO/SPORTS ILLUSTRATED

M av-e-lous

Forward Dirk Nowitzki and the Dallas Mavericks began the 2002-03 season on fire — an NBA-best 14–0. Nowitzki, who made his second straight All-Star appearance, in 2003, was named the top international player in a 2002-03 survey of NBA general managers.

PAUL BUCKLEY

Mx King

Ricky Carmichael won his third straight 250cc motocross championship, in 2002, becoming the first rider to win both motos (or heats) of all 12 races on the AMA National Series schedule. (The term "cc," or "cubic centimeters," refers to the size of a bike's engine.) Carmichael also won his second straight 250cc supercross championship. He is now an eight-time AMA national champion.

Williams Wins All

Serena Williams dominated women's tennis in 2002. She had a 56–5 record and finished the year ranked Number 1 in the world. Williams completed the "Serena Slam" in January 2003. She won four straight Grand Slam titles — the French Open, Wimbledon, the U.S. Open, and the Australian Open — defeating her sister Venus (ranked Number 2) in each final.

HEINZ KLUETMEIER/SPORTS ILLUSTRATED

Stunt Man

At the 2002 Summer X Games, Mat Hoffman soared to a silver medal in the vert event by pulling the first hands-free 900. "The Condor," a two-time X Games gold medalist and the inventor of more than 50 tricks, landed the first hands-on 900 thirteen years earlier.

 **www.hoffmanbikes.com**

HOFFMAN BIKES

Super Woman

On July 30, 2002, center Lisa Leslie of the Los Angeles Sparks became the first player to dunk in a WNBA game. Leslie also led the Sparks to their second-straight WNBA title in 2002. She was named the Finals and All-Star Game MVPs.

LISA BLUMENFELD/GETTY IMAGES

MICHEL EULER/AP

Record Run

Sprinter Tim Montgomery of the United States earned the title World's Fastest Human on September 14, 2002. He clocked 9.78 seconds in the 100-meter dash at the IAAF Grand Prix Final, in Paris, France. Montgomery's blistering time broke the previous record of 9.79 seconds, which had been set by U.S. sprinter Maurice Greene in 1999.

SIMON BRUTY/SPORTS ILLUSTRATED

Miracle on Ice

U.S. figure skater Sarah Hughes propelled herself from fourth place to the gold medal at the 2002 Winter Olympics with a near-flawless performance in the women's long program. Hughes edged out Russia's Irina Slutskaya (silver) and the U.S.'s Michelle Kwan (bronze).

KOJI SASAHARA/AP

Making a Splash

At the 2002 U.S. summer nationals, Natalie Coughlin won five events and became the first woman to swim the 100-meter backstroke in under one minute. Coughlin won four gold medals at the Pan Pacific Championships, where she became the first U.S. woman to break 54 seconds in the 100-meter freestyle.

AL TIELEMANS/SPORTS ILLUSTRATED

Freshman Phenom

In 2002, Maurice Clarett became the first true freshman (a player who is playing college ball in his first year out of high school) to start at tailback for the Ohio State Buckeyes. The 19-year-old helped lead the Buckeyes to their first football national championship since 1968. Along the way, Clarett set OSU freshman records in rushing yards (1,237), points (108), touchdowns (18), and 100-yard rushing games (6).

Soccer Sensation

Landon Donovan is the future of U.S. soccer. He jump-started the U.S. team at the 2002 World Cup. The 20-year-old forward's clinching goal in the 2–0 win against Mexico led the U.S. to the quarterfinals for the first time since 1930. Donovan scored two goals in the tournament, tying the team lead.

SIMON BRUTY/SPORTS ILLUSTRATED

JOSE FERNANDEZ/AP; RUSS HAMILTON/AP (INSET)

Dominant Driver

NASCAR driver Tony Stewart won the 2002 Winston Cup championship by finishing tied for third on the circuit in victories (3) and first in Top 5 finishes (15). The Winston Cup title was Stewart's ninth career championship.

KRISTA NILES/AP

Tiger Who?

Annika Sorenstam of Sweden won 11 LPGA titles in 2002. She is the first woman golfer to have eight or more victories in back-to-back seasons since 1978 and 1979, when Nancy Lopez did it.

Ride On

Kelly Clark of the U.S. soared to the top of snowboarding. In January 2003, she won a silver medal in the superpipe event at the Winter X Games. At the 2002 Winter X Games, Clark won gold in the superpipe. At the 2002 Winter Olympics, she won the gold medal in the halfpipe. It was the first medal of the Games for the U.S.

DOUGLAS C. PIZAC/AP

Devilish Duhon

Duke point guard Chris Duhon's slick passing and tight D in 2002-03 helped the Blue Devils roll to the top of the nation. The team reached the Number 1 ranking for the sixth consecutive season. Only the UCLA Bruins have reached Number 1 in more consecutive seasons (1963-64 through 1974-75).

JOHN BIEVER/SPORTS ILLUSTRATED

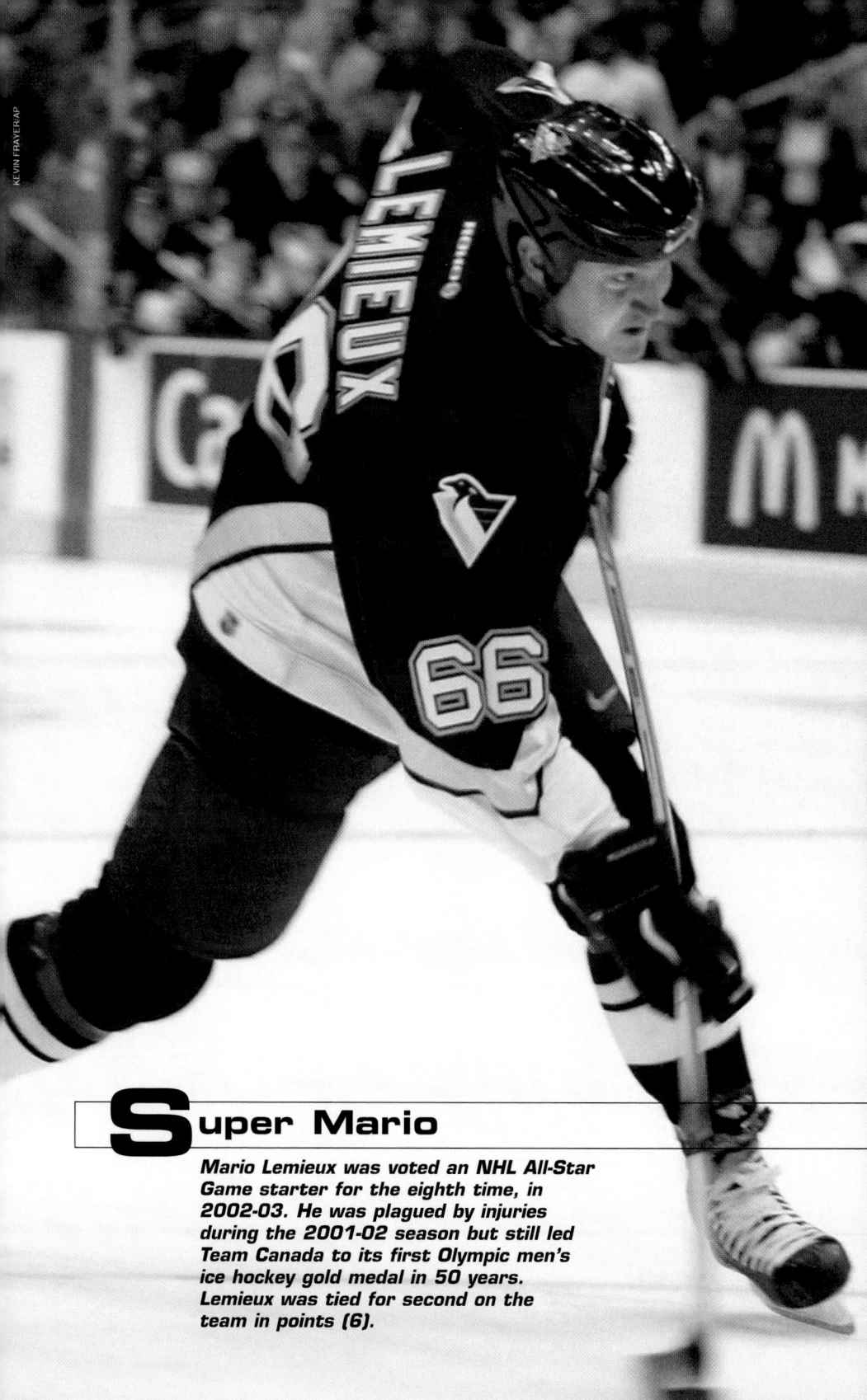

KEVIN FRAYER/AP

Super Mario

Mario Lemieux was voted an NHL All-Star Game starter for the eighth time, in 2002-03. He was plagued by injuries during the 2001-02 season but still led Team Canada to its first Olympic men's ice hockey gold medal in 50 years. Lemieux was tied for second on the team in points (6).

Bonds Blasts Off

Barry Bonds became a member of an elite club in 2002. The San Francisco Giant leftfielder hit his 600th home run on August 9. Hank Aaron (755 career homers), Babe Ruth (714), and Willie Mays (660) are the only other major league players to reach 600 homers.

PETER READ MILLER/SPORTS ILLUSTRATED

Field-Goal Percentage

	Class	GP	FGM	FGA	PCT
Adam Mark, Belmont	Jr.	28	199	297	67.0
Rickey White, Maine	Sr.	24	131	198	66.2
Matt Nelson, Colorado State	So.	31	205	319	64.3
Armond Williams, Illinois–Chicago	Jr.	30	168	263	63.9
Michael Harris, Rice	So.	28	172	276	62.3
Chris Kaman, Central Michigan	Jr.	31	244	392	62.2
David Gruber, Northern Iowa	Jr.	28	141	231	61.0
Ike Diogu, Arizona State	Fr.	32	209	344	60.8
Omar Barlett, Jacksonville State	Sr.	30	178	293	60.8
Jason Keep, San Diego	Sr.	30	195	323	60.4

Note: Minimum five field goals made per game.

Free-Throw Percentage

	Class	GP	FTM	FTA	PCT
Steve Drabyn, Belmont	Jr.	29	78	82	95.1
Matt Logie, Lehigh	Sr.	28	91	96	94.8
Hollis Price, Oklahoma	Sr.	34	130	140	92.9
Brian Dux, Canisius	Sr.	28	115	125	92.0
J.J. Redick, Duke	Fr.	33	102	111	91.9
Tim Parker, Chattanooga	Sr.	30	78	85	91.8
Dwayne Byfield, Monmouth	So.	28	72	79	91.1
Gerry McNamara, Syracuse	Fr.	35	90	99	90.9
Kyle Korver, Creighton	Sr.	34	109	120	90.8
Jeb Ivey, Portland State	Sr.	27	69	76	90.8

Note: Minimum 2.5 free throws made per game.

Rebounds

	Class	GP	REB	AVG
Brandon Hunter, Ohio	Sr.	30	378	12.6
Amien Hicks, Morris Brown	Sr.	24	298	12.4
Adam Sonn, Belmont	Sr.	29	352	12.1
Chris Kaman, Central Michigan	Jr.	31	373	12.0
David West, Xavier	Sr.	32	379	11.8
Louis Truscott, Houston	Sr.	28	315	11.3
Emeka Okafor, Connecticut	So.	33	370	11.2
Kenny Adeleke, Hofstra	So.	29	320	11.0
James Singleton, Murray State	Sr.	29	320	11.0
James Thomas, Texas	Jr.	33	363	11.0

T.J. Ford, Texas

Assists

	Class	GP	A	APG
Martell Bailey, Illinois–Chicago	Jr.	30	244	8.1
Marques Green, St. Bonaventure	Jr.	27	216	8.0
T.J. Ford, Texas	So.	33	254	7.7
Elliott Prasse-Freeman, Harvard	Sr.	27	207	7.7
Antawn Dobie, Long Island	Sr.	26	193	7.4

3-Point Field-Goal Percentage

	Class	GP	3FGM	3FGA	PCT
Jeff Schiffner, Pennsylvania	Jr.	28	74	150	49.3
Kyle Korver, Creighton	Sr.	34	129	269	48.0
Terrence Woods, Florida A&M	Jr.	28	139	304	45.7
Chez Marks, Morehead State	Sr.	29	82	180	45.6
Tyson Dorsey, Samford	Jr.	27	75	165	45.5

Note: Minimum 2.5 three-point field goals made per game.

KEY GP=games played; FGM=field goals made; FGA=field goals attempted; PCT=percentage; FTM=free throws made; FTA=free throws attempted; REB=rebounds; AVG=average; A=assists; APG=assists per game; 3FGM=3-point field goals made; 3FGA=3-point field goals attempted

JOHN BIEVER/SPORTS ILLUSTRATED

NCAA Men's Division I Individual Leaders (cont.)

Steals

	Class	GP	STL	SPG
Alexis McMillan, Stetson	Sr.	22	87	4.0
Zakee Wadood, East Tenn. St.	Jr.	29	93	3.2
Jay Heard, Jacksonville St.	Sr.	30	95	3.2
Eric Bush, UAB	Sr.	34	106	3.1
Marcus Hatten, St. John's (N.Y.)	Sr.	34	100	2.9
Rawle Marshall, Oakland	So.	28	80	2.9

Blocks

	Class	GP	BLK	BPG
Emeka Okafor, Connecticut	So.	33	156	4.7
Nick Billings, Binghamton	So.	27	117	4.3
Justin Rowe, Maine	Sr.	25	105	4.2
Deng Gai, Fairfield	So.	25	96	3.8
Robert Battle, Drexel	Sr.	31	116	3.7

KEY GP=games played; STL=steals; SPG=steals per game; BLK=blocks; BPG=blocks per game

▷**Random Fact:** The National Invitation Tournament (NIT) is the oldest tournament in college basketball. It was first played in 1938. The NCAA tournament began in 1939.

2002-03 TIMELINE

November 12, 2002: Arizona begins the season ranked Number 1 in the Associated Press and ESPN/*USA Today* polls. Syracuse is unranked.

November 14, 2002: Memphis defeats Syracuse, 70–63, in the first Division I game of the season. Freshman Carmelo Anthony scores 27 points in his college debut.

February 5, 2003: Texas Tech coach Bobby Knight gets his 800th career win. He becomes the fourth Division I men's coach to win at least 800 games.

February 13, 2003: Tennessee State athletic director Teresa Phillips becomes the first woman to coach a Division I men's team. Phillips replaces interim coach Hosea Lewis for one game, after Lewis is suspended for participating in a bench-clearing brawl.

February 22, 2003: Guard Michael Watson of Missouri–Kansas City scores 54 points, the most of any Division I player in 2002-03.

March 21, 2003: In the most exciting finish of the NCAA tournament, defending champion Maryland staves off an upset by UNC Wilmington. With the Terps down by one with less than five seconds left, senior guard Drew Nicholas dribbles the length of the floor and hits an off-balance, game-winning 3-pointer as time expires. Maryland wins, 75–73.

March 23, 2003: Butler (Number 12 seed) is the only double-digit seed to make it to the Sweet Sixteen of the NCAA tournament.

April 3, 2003: St. John's wins the National Invitation Tournament (NIT) championship, defeating Georgetown in the title game, 70–67. Red Storm guard Marcus Hatten is named MVP.

April 7, 2003: Syracuse wins its first national championship, defeating Kansas, 81–78.

NCAA Men's Division I Championship Results

Year	Winner	Score	Runner-up	Third Place	Fourth Place	Winning Coach
2003	Syracuse	81–78	Kansas	Texas	Marquette	Jim Boeheim
2002	Maryland	64–52	Indiana	* Kansas	* Oklahoma	Gary Williams
2001	Duke	82–72	Arizona	* Maryland	* Michigan St.	Mike Krzyzewski
2000	Michigan St.	89–76	Florida	* Wisconsin	* North Carolina	Tom Izzo
1999	Connecticut	77–74	Duke	* Michigan St.	* Ohio St.	Jim Calhoun
1998	Kentucky	78–69	Utah	* Stanford	* North Carolina	Tubby Smith
1997	Arizona	84–79 (OT)	Kentucky	* Minnesota	* North Carolina	Lute Olson
1996	Kentucky	76–67	Syracuse	Vacated‡	Mississippi St.	Rick Pitino
1995	UCLA	89–78	Arkansas	* North Carolina	* Oklahoma St.	Jim Harrick
1994	Arkansas	76–72	Duke	* Arizona	* Florida	Nolan Richardson
1993	North Carolina	77–71	Michigan	* Kansas	* Kentucky	Dean Smith
1992	Duke	71–51	Michigan	* Cincinnati	* Indiana	Mike Krzyzewski
1991	Duke	72–65	Kansas	* UNLV	* North Carolina	Mike Krzyzewski
1990	UNLV	103–73	Duke	* Arkansas	* Georgia Tech	Jerry Tarkanian
1989	Michigan	80–79 (OT)	Seton Hall	* Duke	* Illinois	Steve Fisher
1988	Kansas	83–79	Oklahoma	* Arizona	* Duke	Larry Brown
1987	Indiana	74–73	Syracuse	* UNLV	* Providence	Bobby Knight
1986	Louisville	72–69	Duke	* Kansas	* Louisiana St.	Denny Crum
1985	Villanova	66–64	Georgetown	St. John's (N.Y.)	Vacated‡	Rollie Massimino
1984	Georgetown	84–75	Houston	* Kentucky	* Virginia	John Thompson
1983	North Carolina St.	54–52	Houston	* Georgia	* Louisville	Jim Valvano
1982	North Carolina	63–62	Georgetown	* Houston	* Louisville	Dean Smith
1981	Indiana	63–50	North Carolina	Virginia	Louisiana St.	Bobby Knight
1980	Louisville	59–54	Vacated‡	Purdue	Iowa	Denny Crum
1979	Michigan St.	75–64	Indiana St.	DePaul	Penn	Jud Heathcote
1978	Kentucky	94–88	Duke	Arkansas	Notre Dame	Joe Hall
1977	Marquette	67–59	North Carolina	UNLV	NC-Charlotte	Al McGuire
1976	Indiana	86–68	Michigan	UCLA	Rutgers	Bobby Knight
1975	UCLA	92–85	Kentucky	Louisville	Syracuse	John Wooden
1974	North Carolina St.	76–64	Marquette	UCLA	Kansas	Norm Sloan
1973	UCLA	87–66	Memphis St.	Indiana	Providence	John Wooden
1972	UCLA	81–76	Florida St.	North Carolina	Louisville	John Wooden
1971	UCLA	68–62	Vacated‡	Vacated‡	Kansas	John Wooden
1970	UCLA	80–69	Jacksonville	New Mexico St.	St. Bonaventure	John Wooden
1969	UCLA	92–72	Purdue	Drake	North Carolina	John Wooden
1968	UCLA	78–55	North Carolina	Ohio St.	Houston	John Wooden
1967	UCLA	79–64	Dayton	Houston	North Carolina	John Wooden
1966	UTEP	72–65	Kentucky	Duke	Utah	Don Haskins
1965	UCLA	91–80	Michigan	Princeton	Wichita St.	John Wooden
1964	UCLA	98–83	Duke	Michigan	Kansas St.	John Wooden
1963	Loyola (Illinois)	60–58 (OT)	Cincinnati	Duke	Oregon St.	George Ireland
1962	Cincinnati	71–59	Ohio St.	Wake Forest	UCLA	Edwin Jucker
1961	Cincinnati	70–65 (OT)	Ohio St.	Vacated‡	Utah	Edwin Jucker
1960	Ohio St.	75–55	California	Cincinnati	NYU	Fred Taylor
1959	California	71–70	West Virginia	Cincinnati	Louisville	Pete Newell
1958	Kentucky	84–72	Seattle	Temple	Kansas St.	Adolph Rupp
1957	North Carolina	54–53 (3OT)	Kansas	San Francisco	Michigan St.	Frank McGuire
1956	San Francisco	83–71	Iowa	Temple	SMU	Phil Woolpert
1955	San Francisco	77–63	La Salle	Colorado	Iowa	Phil Woolpert
1954	La Salle	92–76	Bradley	Penn St.	USC	Kenneth Loeffler
1953	Indiana	69–68	Kansas	Washington	Louisiana St.	Branch McCracken
1952	Kansas	80–63	St. John's (N.Y.)	Illinois	Santa Clara	Forrest Allen
1951	Kentucky	68–58	Kansas St.	Illinois	Oklahoma St.	Adolph Rupp
1950	CCNY	71–68	Bradley	North Carolina St.	Baylor	Nat Holman
1949	Kentucky	46–36	Oklahoma St.	Illinois	Oregon St.	Adolph Rupp
1948	Kentucky	58–42	Baylor	Holy Cross	Kansas St.	Adolph Rupp
1947	Holy Cross	58–47	Oklahoma	Texas	CCNY	Alvin Julian
1946	Oklahoma St.	43–40	North Carolina	Ohio St.	California	Hank Iba
1945	Oklahoma St.	49–45	NYU	* Arkansas	* Ohio St.	Hank Iba
1944	Utah	42–40 (OT)	Dartmouth	* Iowa St.	* Ohio St.	Vadal Peterson
1943	Wyoming	46–34	Georgetown	* Texas	* DePaul	Everett Shelton
1942	Stanford	53–38	Dartmouth	* Colorado	* Kentucky	Everett Dean
1941	Wisconsin	39–34	Washington St.	* Pittsburgh	* Arkansas	Harold Foster
1940	Indiana	60–42	Kansas	* Duquesne	* USC	Branch McCracken
1939	Oregon	46–33	Ohio St.	* Oklahoma	* Villanova	Howard Hobson

* Tied for third place. ‡Student-athletes representing St. Joseph's (PA) in 1961, Villanova in 1971, Western Kentucky in 1971, UCLA in 1980, Memphis State in 1985, and Massachusetts in 1996 were declared ineligible subsequent to the tournament. Under NCAA rules, the teams' and ineligible student-athletes' records were deleted, and the teams' places in the standings were vacated.

Today's Stars

Emeka Okafor, center, b. September 28, 1982, Houston, Texas. Okafor's strength and smarts make him college basketball's most intimidating force in the paint. He led the nation in blocks (4.7 per game) in 2002-03, as a sophomore. The 6' 9" UConn Huskie also topped the Big East in rebounding (11.2).

J.J. Redick, guard, b. June 24, 1984, Cookeville, Tennessee. It would be fitting if one of the J's in Redick's name stood for "jumper," because his is a treat to watch. As a freshman at Duke in 2002-03, Redick averaged 15 points per game and led the Atlantic Coast Conference (ACC) in 3-pointers (95) and free-throw percentage (91.9 percent).

Luke Jackson, guard, b. November 6, 1981, Eugene, Oregon. In 2002-03, Jackson helped the Oregon Ducks win their first-ever Pacific 10 tournament championship. The 6' 7" junior averaged 16 points and a team-leading 6.9 rebounds per game for the season. Jackson will be the go-to guy for the Ducks in 2003-04, now that star point guard Luke Ridnour has taken his act to the NBA.

In 2002-03, Emeka Okafor of UConn set a school record for most blocks in a season (155).

BOB CHILD/AP

NCAA Final Four Most Outstanding Players

Year	Winner, School	Year	Winner, School	Year	Winner, School
2003	Carmelo Anthony, Syracuse	1980	Darrell Griffith, Louisville	1957	* Wilt Chamberlain, Kansas
2002	Juan Dixon, Maryland	1979	Earvin Johnson, Michigan St.	1956	* Hal Lear, Temple
2001	Shane Battier, Duke	1978	Jack Givens, Kentucky	1955	Bill Russell, San Francisco
2000	Mateen Cleaves, Michigan St.	1977	Butch Lee, Marquette	1954	Tom Gola, La Salle
1999	Richard Hamilton, Connecticut	1976	Kent Benson, Indiana	1953	* B.H. Horn, Kansas
1998	Jeff Sheppard, Kentucky	1975	Richard Washington, UCLA	1952	Clyde Lovellette, Kansas
1997	Miles Simon, Arizona	1974	David Thompson, North Carolina St.	1951	Bill Spivey, Kentucky
1996	Tony Delk, Kentucky	1973	Bill Walton, UCLA	1950	Irwin Dambrot, CCNY
1995	Ed O'Bannon, UCLA	1972	Bill Walton, UCLA	1949	Alex Groza, Kentucky
1994	Corliss Williamson, Arkansas	1971	* † Howard Porter, Villanova	1948	Alex Groza, Kentucky
1993	Donald Williams, North Carolina	1970	Sidney Wicks, UCLA	1947	George Kaftan, Holy Cross
1992	Bobby Hurley, Duke	1969	* * Lew Alcindor, UCLA	1946	Bob Kurland, Oklahoma St.
1991	Christian Laettner, Duke	1968	Lew Alcindor, UCLA	1945	Bob Kurland, Oklahoma St.
1990	Anderson Hunt, UNLV	1967	Lew Alcindor, UCLA	1944	Arnie Ferrin, Utah
1989	Glen Rice, Michigan	1966	* Jerry Chambers, Utah	1943	Ken Sailors, Wyoming
1988	Danny Manning, Kansas	1965	* Bill Bradley, Princeton	1942	Howard Dallmar, Stanford
1987	Keith Smart, Indiana	1964	Walt Hazzard, UCLA	1941	John Kotz, Wisconsin
1986	Pervis Ellison, Louisville	1963	Art Heyman, Duke	1940	Marv Huffman, Indiana
1985	Ed Pinckney, Villanova	1962	Paul Hogue, Cincinnati	1939	* Jimmy Hull, Ohio St.
1984	Patrick Ewing, Georgetown	1961	* Jerry Lucas, Ohio St.		
1983	* Akeem Olajuwon, Houston	1960	Jerry Lucas, Ohio St.		* Not a member of the championship-winning team.
1982	James Worthy, North Carolina	1959	* Jerry West, West Virginia		† Record later vacated.
1981	Isiah Thomas, Indiana	1958	* Elgin Baylor, Seattle		* * Now known as Kareem Abdul-Jabbar.

National Invitation Tournament (NIT) Championship Results

Year	Winner	Score	Runner-up	Year	Winner	Score	Runner-up
2003	St. John's (N.Y.)	70–67	Georgetown	1970	Marquette	65–53	St. John's (N.Y.)
2002	Memphis	72–62	South Carolina	1969	Temple	89–76	Boston College
2001	Tulsa	79–60	Alabama	1968	Dayton	61–48	Kansas
2000	Wake Forest	71–61	Notre Dame	1967	Southern Illinois	71–56	Marquette
1999	California	61–60	Clemson	1966	BYU	97–84	NYU
1998	Minnesota	79–72	Penn St.	1965	St. John's (N.Y.)	55–51	Villanova
1997	Michigan	82–73	Florida St.	1964	Bradley	86–54	New Mexico
1996	Nebraska	60–56	St. Joseph's	1963	Providence	81–66	Canisius
1995	Virginia Tech	65–64 (OT)	Marquette	1962	Dayton	73–67	St. John's (N.Y.)
1994	Villanova	80–73	Vanderbilt	1961	Providence	62–59	St. Louis
1993	Minnesota	62–61	Georgetown	1960	Bradley	88–72	Providence
1992	Virginia	81–76	Notre Dame	1959	St. John's (N.Y.)	76–71(OT)	Bradley
1991	Stanford	78–72	Oklahoma	1958	Xavier	78–74 (OT)	Dayton
1990	Vanderbilt	74–72	St. Louis	1957	Bradley	84–83	Memphis St.
1989	St. John's (N.Y.)	73–65	St. Louis	1956	Louisville	93–80	Dayton
1988	Connecticut	72–67	Ohio St.	1955	Duquesne	70–58	Dayton
1987	Southern Miss.	84–80	La Salle	1954	Holy Cross	71–62	Duquesne
1986	Ohio St.	73–63	Wyoming	1953	Seton Hall	58–46	St. John's (N.Y.)
1985	UCLA	65–62	Indiana	1952	La Salle	75–64	Dayton
1984	Michigan	83–63	Notre Dame	1951	BYU	62–43	Dayton
1983	Fresno State	69–60	DePaul	1950	CCNY	69–61	Bradley
1982	Bradley	67–58	Purdue	1949	San Francisco	48–47	Loyola (Illinois)
1981	Tulsa	86–84 (OT)	Syracuse	1948	St. Louis	65–52	NYU
1980	Virginia	58–55	Minnesota	1947	Utah	49–45	Kentucky
1979	Indiana	53–52	Purdue	1946	Kentucky	46–45	Rhode Island
1978	Texas	101–93	North Carolina St.	1945	DePaul	71–54	Bowling Green
1977	St. Bonaventure	94–91	Houston	1944	St. John's (N.Y.)	47–39	DePaul
1976	Kentucky	71–67	North Carolina-Charlotte	1943	St. John's (N.Y.)	48–27	Toledo
1975	Princeton	80–69	Providence	1942	West Virginia	47–45	Western Kentucky
1974	Purdue	87–81	Utah	1941	Long Island Univ.	56–42	Ohio University
1973	Virginia Tech	92–91 (OT)	Notre Dame	1940	Colorado	51–40	Duquesne
1972	Maryland	100–69	Niagara	1939	Long Island Univ.	44–32	Loyola (Illinois)
1971	North Carolina	84–66	Georgia Tech	1938	Temple	60–36	Colorado

Trivia Challenge

What was the last school to reach three straight Final Fours (1998-99, 1999-00, 2000-01)?

Michigan State

Pete Maravich, LSU

NCAA Men's Division I Single-Season Leaders

Points

Player	Year	GP	FG	3FG	FT	PTS
Pete Maravich, LSU	1970	31	522	—	337	1,381
Elvin Hayes, Houston	1968	33	519	—	176	1,214
Frank Selvy, Furman	1954	29	427	—	355	1,209
Pete Maravich, LSU	1969	26	433	—	282	1,148
Pete Maravich, LSU	1968	26	432	—	274	1,138
Bo Kimble, Loyola Marymount	1990	32	404	92	231	1,131
Hersey Hawkins, Bradley	1988	31	377	87	284	1,125
Austin Carr, Notre Dame	1970	29	444	—	218	1,106
Austin Carr, Notre Dame	1971	29	430	—	241	1,101
Otis Birdsong, Houston	1977	36	452	—	186	1,090

Scoring Average

Player	Year	GP	FG	FT	PTS	AVG
Pete Maravich, LSU	1970	31	522	337	1,381	44.5
Pete Maravich, LSU	1969	26	433	282	1,148	44.2
Pete Maravich, LSU	1968	26	432	274	1,138	43.8
Frank Selvy, Furman	1954	29	427	355	1,209	41.7
Johnny Neumann, Mississippi	1971	23	366	191	923	40.1

KEY GP=games played; FG=field goals; 3FG=3-point field goals; FT=free throws; PTS=points; AVG=average

RICH CLARKSON/SPORTS ILLUSTRATED

NCAA Men's Division I Single-Season Leaders (cont.)

Scoring Average (cont.)

Player	Year	GP	FG	FT	PTS	AVG
Freeman Williams, Portland St.	1977	26	417	176	1,010	38.8
Billy McGill, Utah	1962	26	394	221	1,009	38.8
Calvin Murphy, Niagara	1968	24	337	242	916	38.2
Austin Carr, Notre Dame	1970	29	444	218	1,106	38.1
Austin Carr, Notre Dame	1971	29	430	241	1,101	38.0

Rebound Average (before 1973)

Player	Year	GP	REB	AVG
Charlie Slack, Marshall	1955	21	538	25.6
Leroy Wright, Pacific	1959	26	652	25.1
Art Quimby, Connecticut	1955	25	611	24.4
Charlie Slack, Marshall	1956	22	520	23.6
Ed Conlin, Fordham	1953	26	612	23.5

Rebound Average (since 1973*)

Player	Year	GP	REB	AVG
Kermit Washington, American	1973	25	511	20.4
Marvin Barnes, Providence	1973	30	571	19.0
Marvin Barnes, Providence	1974	32	597	18.7
Pete Padgett, Nevada–Reno	1973	26	462	17.8
Jim Bradley, Northern Illinois	1973	24	426	17.8

*Freshmen became eligible for varsity play before the 1972-73 season.

Assists

Player	Year	GP	A
Mark Wade, UNLV	1987	38	406
Avery Johnson, Southern University	1988	30	399
Anthony Manuel, Bradley	1988	31	373
Avery Johnson, Southern University	1987	31	333
Mark Jackson, St. John's (N.Y.)	1986	32	328

Field-Goal Percentage

Player	Year	FGM	FGA	PCT
Steve Johnson, Oregon St.	1981	235	315	74.6
Dwayne Davis, Florida	1989	179	248	72.2
Keith Walker, Utica	1985	154	216	71.3
Steve Johnson, Oregon St.	1980	211	297	71.0
Adam Mark, Belmont	2002	150	212	70.8

Free-Throw Percentage

Player	Year	FTM	FTA	PCT
Craig Collins, Penn St.	1985	94	98	95.9
Steve Drabyn, Belmont	2003	78	82	95.1
Rod Foster, UCLA	1982	95	100	95.0
Clay McKnight, Pacific	2000	74	78	94.9
Matt Logie, Lehigh	2003	91	96	94.8

3-Point Field-Goal Percentage

Player	Year	3FGM	3FGA	PCT
Glenn Tropf, Holy Cross	1988	52	82	63.4
Sean Wightman, Western Michigan	1992	48	76	63.2

KEY GP=games played; FG=field goals; FT=free throws; PTS=points; AVG=average; REB=rebounds; A=assists; FGM=field goals made; FGA=field goals attempted; PCT=percentage; FTM=free throws made; FTA=free throws attempted; 3FGM=3-point field goals made; 3FGA=3-point field goals attempted

Trivia Challenge

In 2002, which player became the all-time leader in minutes played in the NCAA tournament?

Junior guard Steve Blake of Maryland

3-Point Field-Goal Percentage (cont.)

Player	Year	3FGM	3FGA	PCT
Keith Jennings, East Tennessee St.	1991	84	142	59.2
Dave Calloway, Monmouth	1989	48	82	58.5
Steve Kerr, Arizona	1988	114	199	57.3

Steals

Player	Year	GP	STL
Desmond Cambridge, Alabama A&M	2002	29	160
Mookie Blaylock, Oklahoma	1988	39	150
Aldwin Ware, Florida A&M	1988	29	142
Darron Brittman, Chicago St.	1986	28	139
John Linehan, Providence	2002	31	139

Blocks

Player	Year	GP	BLK
David Robinson, Navy	1986	35	207
Adonal Foyle, Colgate	1997	28	180
Keith Closs, Central Connecticut St.	1996	28	178
Shawn Bradley, BYU	1991	34	177
Wojciech Myrda, LA-Monroe	2002	32	172

KEY 3FGM=3-point field goals made; 3FGA=3-point field goals attempted; PCT=percentage; GP=games played; STL=steals; BLK=blocks

Legends

Bill Walton led UCLA to two national championships (1972, 1973).

Bill Walton, center, b. November 5, 1952, La Mesa, California. Walton is arguably the greatest college hoopster in history. During his three-year varsity career, he led UCLA to an 86–4 record and two national titles. In the 1973 national championship game, Walton shot 21 of 22 from the field for 44 points. He averaged 20.3 points and 15.7 rebounds per game for his college career, and was named Naismith Player of the Year three times.

Christian Laettner, forward, b. August 17, 1969, Angola, New York. Laettner was the main man behind the dominant Duke teams of the early 1990's. In 1992, he became the first player to start in four straight Final Fours. Laettner led Duke to championships in 1991 and 1992, and is the NCAA tournament's all-time leading scorer (407 points).

Patrick Ewing, center, b. August 5, 1962, Kingston, Jamaica. At 7' and 255 pounds, Ewing was a looming presence for the tenacious Georgetown defense of the early 1980's. He carried the Hoyas to three Final Fours and the 1984 NCAA championship. He averaged 15.3 points and 9.2 rebounds per game in four seasons, and was named the 1985 Naismith Player of the Year. After his senior season, Ewing was so sought after that the NBA created the draft lottery. That way, teams wouldn't intentionally lose games in order to qualify for the Number 1 pick.

SHEEDY & LONG/SPORTS ILLUSTRATED

BASKETBALL WOMEN'S COLLEGE

The 2002-03 women's college hoops season can be summed up in one word: *Huskies.* Led by All-America junior guard Diana Taurasi, the University of Connecticut had a Division I-leading 37–1 record and won its second consecutive national championship by defeating Tennessee, 73–68, in the title game. UConn didn't get all the ink during the season, though. Junior guard/forward Alana Beard of Duke led the Blue Devils to their first Number 1 ranking and second-straight NCAA Final Four. She ended the season with 22 points and 6.9 rebounds per game. Jody Conradt of Texas and Pat Summitt of Tennessee became the first female college hoops coaches to win their 800th game. Villanova made some noise during the Big East tournament by snapping UConn's 70-game victory streak with a 52–48 upset win. No matter. The Huskies rebounded to win the six games that mattered most: the six they played in the NCAA tournament.

Diana Taurasi scored a game-high 28 points as UConn defeated Tennessee 73–68 for the 2002-03 national championship.

BOB CHILD/AP

Trivia Challenge

When was the first women's NCAA tournament held, and which school won the championship game?

In 1982, Louisiana Tech won the first women's NCAA tournament.

NCAA Women's Division I Championship Box Score

CONNECTICUT HUSKIES 73

Player	MIN	FGM-A	FTM-A	OFF	REB	A	PF	PTS
Diana Taurasi	37	8-15	8-8	1	4	1	2	28
Barbara Turner	21	5-7	0-0	1	1	1	3	10
Jessica Moore	35	2-5	0-0	1	4	3	2	4
Maria Conlon	39	3-7	2-4	0	4	6	2	11
Ann Strother	32	6-11	2-2	0	3	3	2	17
Ashley Battle	12	0-3	0-0	0	1	0	0	0
Willnett Crockett	24	1-1	1-2	2	6	0	5	3
Totals	**200**	**25-49**	**13-16**	**5**	**22**	**15**	**16**	**73**
		(51.0%)	(81.3%)					

TENNESSEE VOLUNTEERS 68

Player	MIN	FGM-A	FTM-A	OFF	REB	A	PF	PTS
Gwen Jackson	36	6-14	3-6	6	9	4	3	15
Shyra Ely	25	3-6	0-0	0	2	0	1	6
Tasha Butts	16	2-4	0-0	1	1	2	3	4
Kara Lawson	40	5-13	5-5	1	5	5	1	18
Loree Moore	24	2-4	0-0	1	2	1	1	5
Shanna Zolman	11	0-0	0-0	1	2	0	2	0
Brittany Jackson	21	4-10	2-2	1	5	0	3	13
Ashley Robinson	17	1-2	1-6	4	8	1	2	3
Courtney McDaniel	6	1-3	0-0	1	2	0	2	2
Tye'sha Fluker	4	1-1	0-0	1	1	0	0	2
Totals	**200**	**25-57**	**11-19**	**17**	**37**	**13**	**18**	**68**
		(43.9%)	(57.9%)					

KEY MIN=minutes played; FGM-A=field goals made-attempted; FTM-A=free throws made-attempted; OFF=offensive rebounds; REB=rebounds; A=assists; PF=personal fouls; PTS=points

Kara Lawson and the Tennessee Lady Vols finished the 2002-03 season with a 31–4 record.

DAMIAN STROHMEYER/SPORTS ILLUSTRATED

USA TODAY/ESPN Top 25 Final Poll

Rank	Team	Record
1.	Connecticut	34–1
2.	Tennessee	31–4
3.	Texas	28–5
4.	Duke	34–1
5.	LSU	30–3
6.	Texas Tech	29–5
7.	Purdue	29–5
8.	Villanova	28–5
9.	Louisiana Tech	31–3
10.	Kansas State	29–5
11.	Georgia	21–10
12.	Penn State	26–9
13.	Minnesota	25–6
14.	Stanford	27–5
15.	North Carolina	28–6
16.	Mississippi State	24–8
17.	Boston College	22–9
18.	South Carolina	23–8
19.	Colorado	24–8
20.	Vanderbilt	22–10
21.	Notre Dame	21–11
22.	UC–Santa Barbara	27–5
23.	New Mexico	24–9
24.	Wisconsin–Green Bay	28–4
25.	Arkansas	22–11

▷**Random Fact:** During the 2002-03 season, Duke became the second school whose men's and women's teams were ranked Number 1 at the same time. Both of Connecticut's teams held the top ranking during the 1994-95 season. UConn also accomplished the feat in 1998-99.

Did You Know?

The first school to win the national championship two seasons in a row was the University of Southern California (1982-83 and 1983-84).

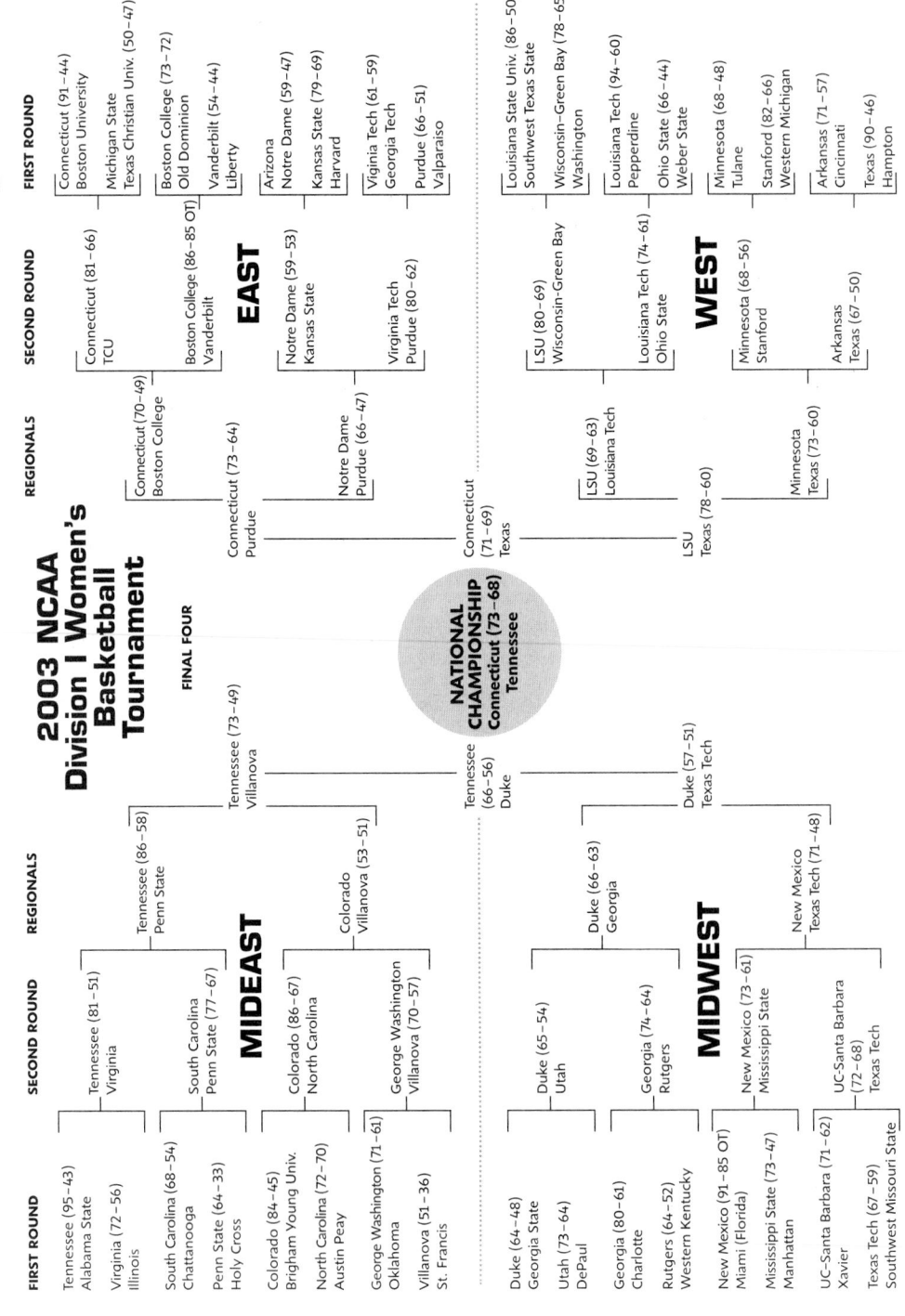

2003 NCAA Division I Women's Basketball Tournament

EAST

FIRST ROUND
- Connecticut (91–44)
- Boston University
- Michigan State
- Texas Christian Univ. (50–47)
- Boston College (73–72)
- Old Dominion
- Vanderbilt (54–44)
- Liberty
- Arizona
- Notre Dame (59–47)
- Kansas State (79–69)
- Harvard
- Virginia Tech (61–59)
- Georgia Tech
- Purdue (66–51)
- Valparaiso

SECOND ROUND
- Connecticut (81–66)
- TCU
- Boston College (86–85 OT)
- Vanderbilt
- Notre Dame (59–53)
- Kansas State
- Virginia Tech
- Purdue (80–62)

REGIONALS
- Connecticut (70–49)
- Boston College
- Notre Dame
- Purdue (66–47)

Connecticut (73–64)
Purdue

WEST

FIRST ROUND
- Louisiana State Univ. (86–50)
- Southwest Texas State
- Wisconsin–Green Bay (78–65)
- Washington
- Louisiana Tech (94–60)
- Pepperdine
- Ohio State (66–44)
- Weber State
- Minnesota (68–48)
- Tulane
- Stanford (82–66)
- Western Michigan
- Arkansas (71–57)
- Cincinnati
- Texas (90–46)
- Hampton

SECOND ROUND
- LSU (80–69)
- Wisconsin–Green Bay
- Louisiana Tech (74–61)
- Ohio State
- Minnesota (68–56)
- Stanford
- Arkansas
- Texas (67–50)

REGIONALS
- LSU (69–63)
- Louisiana Tech
- Minnesota
- Texas (73–60)

LSU
Texas (78–60)

Connecticut (71–69)
Texas

FINAL FOUR

Tennessee (73–49)
Villanova

Connecticut (73–68)

NATIONAL CHAMPIONSHIP
Connecticut (73–68)
Tennessee

Tennessee (66–56)
Duke

MIDEAST

REGIONALS
- Tennessee (86–58)
- Penn State
- Colorado
- Villanova (53–51)

SECOND ROUND
- Tennessee (81–51)
- Virginia
- South Carolina
- Penn State (77–67)
- Colorado (86–67)
- North Carolina
- George Washington
- Villanova (70–57)

FIRST ROUND
- Tennessee (95–43)
- Alabama State
- Virginia (72–56)
- Illinois
- South Carolina (68–54)
- Chattanooga
- Penn State (64–33)
- Holy Cross
- Colorado (84–45)
- Brigham Young Univ.
- North Carolina (72–70)
- Austin Peay
- George Washington (71–61)
- Oklahoma
- Villanova (51–36)
- St. Francis

MIDWEST

REGIONALS
- Duke (66–63)
- Georgia
- New Mexico
- Texas Tech (71–48)

Duke (57–51)
Texas Tech

SECOND ROUND
- Duke (65–54)
- Utah
- Georgia (74–64)
- Rutgers
- New Mexico (73–61)
- Mississippi State
- UC-Santa Barbara (72–68)
- Texas Tech

FIRST ROUND
- Duke (64–48)
- Georgia State
- Utah (73–64)
- DePaul
- Georgia (80–61)
- Charlotte
- Rutgers (64–52)
- Western Kentucky
- New Mexico (91–85 OT)
- Miami (Florida)
- Mississippi State (73–47)
- Manhattan
- UC-Santa Barbara (71–62)
- Xavier
- Texas Tech (67–59)
- Southwest Missouri State

Scoring

	Class	GP	FG	3FG	FT	PTS	AVG
Chandi Jones, Houston	Jr.	28	275	52	168	770	27.5
Molly Creamer, Bucknell	Sr.	28	239	62	219	759	27.1
LaToya Thomas, Mississippi St.	Sr.	31	297	18	182	794	25.6
Tiffany Webb, Wright St.	So.	28	246	50	132	674	24.1
Kelly Mazzante, Penn St.	Jr.	35	292	98	155	837	23.9
Jocelyn Penn, South Carolina	Sr.	30	282	14	138	716	23.9
Allison Curtin, Tulsa	Sr.	30	231	56	174	692	23.1
Alana Beard, Duke	Jr.	37	294	24	201	813	22.0
Shanika Freeman, Jacksonville St.	So.	29	212	21	184	629	21.7
Hana Peljito, Harvard	Jr.	24	178	24	130	510	21.3

KEY GP=games played; FG=field goals; 3FG=3-point field goals; FT=free throws; PTS=points; AVG=average

Alana Beard,
Duke University

Legends

In 1994-95, Rebecca Lobo led UConn to its first national championship.

Rebecca Lobo, forward, b. September 6, 1973, Southwick, Massachusetts. Lobo helped establish the Connecticut Huskies as a serious women's college hoops program. As a senior All-America in 1994-95, she averaged 17.1 points and 9.8 rebounds to lead them to a 35–0 record and their first national championship. Lobo left UConn as the school's all-time leader in rebounds (1,268) and blocks (396), second in points (2,133), and third in games played (126). She now plays in the WNBA for the Connecticut Sun.

Chamique Holdsclaw, forward, b. August 9, 1977, Flushing, New York. Holdsclaw was one of the most hyped high school players in women's hoops history. She arrived in Knoxville, Tennessee, with a reputation for greatness. She lived up to the billing by becoming a two-time National Player of the Year, three-time A.P. first-team All-America selection, and two-time Southeastern Conference Player of the Year. She led Tennessee to the national championship three seasons in a row (1996, 1997, 1998). Tennessee was 131–17 during Holdsclaw's remarkable four-season run. She now plays in the WNBA for the Washington Mystics and was the league's Rookie of the Year in 1999.

Anne Donovan, center, b. November 1, 1961, Ridgewood, New Jersey. Donovan was one of the early stars of women's college hoops and is one of only four basketball players — male or female — to be named to three Olympic teams (1980, 1984, 1988). The three-time All-America led Old Dominion University to the NCAA Final Four in 1982-83 and was named National Player of the Year that season. Donovan led ODU to the 1980 AIAW national title and is still the school's all-time leader in scoring (2,179 points), rebounding (1,976), and blocks (801). She was inducted into the Basketball Hall of Fame in 1995. Donovan also found success coaching college, pro, and U.S. national teams. She now coaches the WNBA's Seattle Storm.

NCAA Women's Division I Individual Leaders (cont.)

Field-Goal Percentage

	Class	GP	FGM	FGA	PCT
Courtney Coleman, Ohio St.	Sr.	32	184	278	66.2
Janel McCarville, Minnesota	So.	30	155	236	65.7
Chantelle Anderson, Vanderbilt	Sr.	32	217	341	63.6
Gerlonda Hardin, Austin Peay	Jr.	31	198	312	63.5
Jocelyn Penn, South Carolina	Sr.	30	282	449	62.8
Beth Swink, St. Francis (Pennsylvania)	So.	31	199	318	62.6
Michelle Smith, UAB	Sr.	26	151	242	62.4
Shawntinice Polk, Arizona	Fr.	31	218	358	60.9
Liene Jansone, Siena	Jr.	33	234	388	60.3
Khara Smith, DePaul	Fr.	32	181	301	60.1

Note: Minimum 5.0 field goals made per game.

Free-Throw Percentage

	Class	GP	FTM	FTA	PCT
Jill Marano, La Salle	So.	29	88	93	94.6
Kandi Brown, Morehead St.	Jr.	28	104	111	93.7
Kim McDonough, St. Peter's	Sr.	28	81	88	92.0
Erin Thorn, BYU	Sr.	31	87	95	91.6
Carey Sauer, San Francisco	Jr.	29	112	123	91.1
Molly McDowell, Southern Illinois	Sr.	27	113	125	90.4
Casey Rost, Western Mich.	So.	32	121	134	90.3
Jen Perugini, Youngstown St.	So.	28	81	91	89.0
Katie Houlehan, Missouri–KC	So.	28	72	81	88.9
Jennifer Youngblood, Northern Illinois	Jr.	28	70	79	88.6

Note: Minimum 2.5 free throws made per game.

Rebounds

	Class	GP	REB	AVG
Jennifer Butler, Massachusetts	Sr.	28	412	14.7
Angela Buckner, Wichita St.	Jr.	28	366	13.1
Cheryl Ford, Louisiana Tech	Sr.	34	438	12.9
Ashlee Kelly, Quinnipiac	Jr.	28	338	12.1
Tori Talbert, Southwest Texas St.	So.	32	385	12.0
Alex Cook, Northern Iowa	So.	30	360	12.0
Rosalee Mason, Manhattan	Jr.	30	342	11.4
Amie Williams, Jackson St.	Jr.	29	318	11.0
Jamie Gray, Evansville	Jr.	27	296	11.0

Assists

	Class	GP	A	APG
La'Terrica Dobin, Northwestern St.	Jr.	28	298	10.6
Latesha Lee, Jackson St.	Jr.	29	214	7.4
Laura Ingham, Nevada	Sr.	29	212	7.3
Ashley McElhiney, Vanderbilt	Sr.	30	219	7.3
Ivelina Vrancheva, Florida International	Jr.	30	217	7.2
Yolanda Paige, West Virginia	So.	28	199	7.1
Jess Cichowicz, James Madison	Sr.	28	194	6.9
Sara Nord, Louisville	Jr.	29	199	6.9
Cricket Williams, San Jose St.	Jr.	28	192	6.9
Cristina Ciocan, South Carolina	Jr.	31	207	6.7

KEY GP=games played; FGM=field goals made; FGA=field goals attempted; PCT=percentage; FTM=free throws made; FTA=free throws attempted; REB=rebounds; AVG=average; A=assists; APG=assists per game

▷**Random Fact**: In 2002-03, forward LaToya Thomas of Mississippi State became the sixth player to be named a four-time Kodak All-America. The last quadruple winner was Tennessee forward Tamika Catchings, who earned number four in 2000-01.

3-Point Field-Goal Percentage

	Class	GP	3FGM	3FGA	PCT
Sinnamonn Garrett, New Mexico St.	Jr.	28	68	137	49.6
Jess Hansen, UC–Santa Barbara	Sr.	32	67	142	47.2
Kate Bulger, West Virginia	Jr.	28	77	164	47.0
Lindsay Bowen, Michigan St.	Fr.	29	77	166	46.4
Laura Spanheimer, Creighton	So.	33	77	168	45.8
Sara Potts, Kentucky	So.	27	74	163	45.4
Caity Matter, Ohio St.	So.	32	106	235	45.1
Kara Lawson, Tennessee	Sr.	38	77	171	45.0
Angela Davidson, Northwestern St.	Sr.	27	54	123	43.9
Katie Davis, Villanova	Sr.	34	104	237	43.9

Note: Minimum 2.0 three-point field goals made per game.

Steals

	Class	GP	STL	SPG
Teresa McNair, Eastern Kentucky	Sr.	29	131	4.5
Toccara Williams, Texas A&M	Jr.	27	117	4.3
Maria Jilian, Western Michigan	So.	32	124	3.9
Melanie Boeglin, Indiana St.	Fr.	31	117	3.8
Jocelyn Penn, South Carolina	Sr.	30	112	3.7
Chanel Spriggs, American	Jr.	29	107	3.7
Meghan Saake, Miami (Florida)	Sr.	31	114	3.7
Shrieka Evans, Grambling	Sr.	30	110	3.7
Nicole Rhem, South Carolina St.	Jr.	24	87	3.6
Mandy Clark, Delaware St.	So.	26	94	3.6

Blocks

	Class	GP	BLK	BPG
Amie Williams, Jackson St.	Jr.	29	152	5.2
Sandora Irvin, TCU	So.	33	128	3.9
Christen Roper, Hawaii	Sr.	30	110	3.7
Amy Collins, Stephen F. Austin	Sr.	28	91	3.3
Alyssa Shriver, Tulsa	Sr.	30	96	3.2
Sonja Brown, Southern Mississippi	Sr.	28	89	3.2
Ugo Oha, George Washington	Jr.	32	93	2.9
Hollie Tyler, Montana	So.	30	86	2.9
Teana McKiver, Tulane	Sr.	29	80	2.8
Brooke McAfee, IUPUI	Fr.	28	75	2.7

KEY 3FGM=3-point field goals made; 3FGA=3-point field goals attempted; PCT=percentage; STL=steals; SPG=steals per game; BLK=blocks; BPG=blocks per game

NCAA Women's Division I Championship Results

Year	Winner	Score	Runner-up	Winning Coach
2003	Connecticut	73–68	Tennessee	Geno Auriemma
2002	Connecticut	82–70	Oklahoma	Geno Auriemma
2001	Notre Dame	68–66	Purdue	Muffet McGraw
2000	Connecticut	71–52	Tennessee	Geno Auriemma
1999	Purdue	62–45	Duke	Carolyn Peck
1998	Tennessee	93–75	Louisiana Tech	Pat Summitt
1997	Tennessee	68–59	Old Dominion	Pat Summitt
1996	Tennessee	83–65	Georgia	Pat Summitt
1995	Connecticut	70–64	Tennessee	Geno Auriemma
1994	North Carolina	60–59	Louisiana Tech	Sylvia Hatchell
1993	Texas Tech	84–82	Ohio State	Marsha Sharp
1992	Stanford	78–62	Western Kentucky	Tara VanDerveer
1991	Tennessee	70–67(OT)	Virginia	Pat Summitt
1990	Stanford	88–81	Auburn	Tara VanDerveer
1989	Tennessee	76–60	Auburn	Pat Summitt
1988	Louisiana Tech	56–54	Auburn	Leon Barmore
1987	Tennessee	67–44	Louisiana Tech	Pat Summitt
1986	Texas	97–81	USC	Jody Conradt
1985	Old Dominion	70–65	Georgia	Marianne Stanley
1984	USC	72–61	Tennessee	Linda Sharp
1983	USC	69–67	Louisiana Tech	Linda Sharp
1982	Louisiana Tech	76–62	Cheyney	Sonja Hogg

2002-03 TIMELINE

November 10, 2002: In his first game as Louisiana Tech's coach, Kurt Budke guides the Number 16 Lady Techsters to an 85–76 upset of Number 7 Texas Tech. Budke had replaced Hall of Fame coach Leon Barmore, who retired after the 2001-02 season with 576 wins in 20 seasons.

December 31, 2002: Texas Christian roars over Texas Southern in a 76–16 blowout. Texas Southern's 16 points (on 10.3 percent shooting) are the fewest scored in a Division I game. The team commits 29 turnovers.

January 4, 2003: In the best regular-season game of the year, Connecticut rallies to beat archrival Tennessee, 63–62, in overtime. UConn's Diana Taurasi scores 25 points, including a 60-foot 3-pointer at the end of the first half. She also banks in a trey to force overtime.

January 14, 2003: The Lady Vols cruise past DePaul, 76–57, making Tennessee's Pat Summitt the first female head coach — and fourth Division I coach, male or female — to win at least 800 college games. Summitt did it in 29 seasons, and six of her victories have been in the national championship game.

January 22, 2003: Texas coach Jody Conradt joins Summitt as the only other female coach with at least 800 wins when her Longhorns beat Texas Tech, 69–58. Conradt's 800th victory comes in her 34th season as a head coach.

February 1, 2003: In an eagerly anticipated battle, Number 2 UConn withstands a late rally to beat Number 1 Duke, 77–65. The game is shown on national TV, and Duke's Cameron Indoor Stadium is sold out for a women's game for the first time.

March 11, 2003: In the Big East tournament final, the Villanova Wildcats pull the biggest upset of the season by ending Connecticut's NCAA-record 70-game winning streak. The 52–48 win gives the Lady Wildcats their third Big East championship and first since 1987.

April 5, 2003: Le'Coe Willingham's running jumper with 3.2 seconds to play completes Auburn's 13-point comeback and gives the Tigers a 64–63 win over Baylor in the National Invitation Tournament (NIT) championship game.

April 6, 2003: Connecticut and Tennessee are ready to square off for the NCAA championship after the Huskies knock off Texas and the Lady Vols drop Duke in their Final Four games.

April 8, 2003: For the first time, the women's national championship game is the last game of the college basketball season, played one day after the men's championship game. Connecticut's 73–68 triumph over Tennessee gives the Huskies their fourth championship in nine seasons and their second in a row. Diana Taurasi is named Most Outstanding Player of the Final Four.

Did You Know?

Patricia Hoskins of Mississippi Valley State holds the NCAA record for career scoring average (28.4 points per game).

Trivia Challenge

Connecticut's 70-game winning streak ended in 2003. Before UConn's loss to Villanova, when was the last time the Huskies lost a game?

Notre Dame beat UConn, 90–75, on March 30, 2001, at the Final Four.

NCAA Women's Divison I All-time Individual Leaders

Points

Player	YRS	GP	PTS
Jackie Stiles, SW Missouri St.	1997–01	129	3,393
Patricia Hoskins, Miss. Valley St.	1985–89	110	3,122
Lorri Bauman, Drake	1981–84	120	3,115
Chamique Holdsclaw, Tennessee	1995–99	148	3,025
Cheryl Miller, USC	1983–86	128	3,018
Cindy Blodgett, Maine	1994–98	118	3,005
Valorie Whiteside, Appalachian St.	1984–88	116	2,944
Joyce Walker, Louisiana St.	1981–84	117	2,906
Sandra Hodge, New Orleans	1981–84	107	2,860
Andrea Congreaves, Mercer	1989–93	108	2,796

Jackie Stiles,
Southwest
Missouri State

DAVID E. KLUTHO/SPORTS ILLUSTRATED

Scoring Average

Player	YRS	GP	FG	3FG	FT	PTS	AVG
Patricia Hoskins, Miss. Valley St.	1985–89	110	1,196	24	706	3,122	28.4
Sandra Hodge, New Orleans	1981–84	107	1,194	—	472	2,860	26.7
Jackie Stiles, SW Missouri St.	1997–01	129	1,160	221	852	3,393	26.3
Lorri Bauman, Drake	1981–84	120	1,104	—	907	3,115	26.0
Andrea Congreaves, Mercer	1989–93	108	1,107	153	429	2,796	25.9
Cindy Blodgett, Maine	1994–98	118	1,055	219	676	3,005	25.5
Valorie Whiteside, Appalachian St.	1984–88	116	1,153	0	638	2,944	25.4
Joyce Walker, LSU	1981–84	117	1,259	—	388	2,906	24.8
Tarcha Hollis, Grambling	1988–91	85	904	3	247	2,058	24.2
Korie Hlede, Duquesne	1994–98	109	1,045	162	379	2,631	24.1

Today's Stars

Kelly Mazzante led the nation in scoring (24.9 points per game) as a sophomore in 2001-02.

Kelly Mazzante, guard, b. February 2, 1982, Williamsport, Pennsylvania. Mazzante is the only player in Penn State history to ring up 2,000 points and 200 steals in her career, and was 16 points shy of setting the school's career scoring record heading into the 2003-04 season. She has led the Big Ten in scoring in each of her three seasons and led the nation in 2001-02 (24.9 points per game). Mazzante led the Nittany Lions to the Sweet 16 in 2001-02 and 2002-03. It was the first time the school made back-to-back Sweet 16 appearances since 1985 and 1986.

Diana Taurasi, guard, b. June 11, 1982, Chino, California. By the time Taurasi had finished her sophomore season (2001-02), she was an All-America on an undefeated national championship team (39–0) and being called one of the best players in UConn history. She was named Naismith Player of the Year as a junior, in 2002-03, after leading the Huskies to a 37–1 record and their second-straight national championship. Taurasi scored 28 points in the championship game and was named the Final Four's Most Outstanding Player.

Alana Beard, guard/forward, b. May 14, 1982, Shreveport, Louisiana. As a junior in 2002-03, Beard guided the Blue Devils to their first Number 1 national ranking by leading the team in scoring (22 points per game), steals (2.8), and blocks (1.3). She also became the first female Duke player to be named a first-team A.P. All-America. Beard led Duke to the Final Four in 2001-02 and 2002-03.

PAT LITTLE/AP

HOCKEY

Youth ruled during the 2002-03 NHL season. Four players under age 25 finished among the top 15 in goal-scoring. Among them were right wing Marian Hossa (45 goals) of the Ottawa Senators, right wing Dany Heatley (41) and left wing Ilya Kovalchuk (38) of the Atlanta Thrashers, and center Joe Thornton (36) of the Boston Bruins.

At the same time, the league continued to struggle with the problem of a scoring drought during the regular season. The average goals per game were just 5.31, up only slightly from 5.24 in 2001-02.

In the Stanley Cup playoffs, the Cinderella story was the Mighty Ducks of Anaheim. After missing the post-season for three straight seasons, the Ducks qualified as the seventh seed in the Western Conference. Behind the brilliant play of goalie Jean-Sebastien Giguere, Anaheim whipped

In 2002-03, Martin Brodeur won the Vezina Trophy as the NHL's top goalie. He led the New Jersey Devils to their third Stanley Cup championship.

DAVID E. KLUTHO/SPORTS ILLUSTRATED

NHL TEAMS

EASTERN CONFERENCE
Atlanta Thrashers
Boston Bruins
Buffalo Sabres
Carolina Hurricanes
Florida Panthers
Montreal Canadiens
New Jersey Devils
New York Islanders
New York Rangers
Ottawa Senators
Philadelphia Flyers
Pittsburgh Penguins
Tampa Bay Lightning
Toronto Maple Leafs
Washington Capitals

WESTERN CONFERENCE
Anaheim Mighty Ducks
Calgary Flames
Chicago Blackhawks
Colorado Avalanche
Columbus Blue Jackets
Dallas Stars
Detroit Red Wings
Edmonton Oilers
Los Angeles Kings
Minnesota Wild
Nashville Predators
Phoenix Coyotes
San Jose Sharks
St. Louis Blues
Vancouver Canucks

the Detroit Red Wings, the Dallas Stars, and the Minnesota Wild, giving up just 21 goals in the first three rounds. But the clock struck midnight for "Giggy" and the Ducks when they met the New Jersey Devils in the finals. New Jersey beat Anaheim in seven games to win their third Stanley Cup in the past nine seasons.

Goalies dominated the finals. Martin Brodeur of the Devils tied a finals record with three shutouts. He also set a record for most shutouts (7) in the playoffs. Giguere was tops among all postseason goalies with a 1.62 goals-against average and won the Conn Smythe Trophy as playoff MVP. He was the first player from a losing team to win the award since 1987.

Finally, Patrick Roy, age 37, announced he was hanging up his skates after 19 standout seasons. The Colorado Avalanche legend owns numerous NHL records, including most career wins (551) and playoff shutouts (23). He won the Stanley Cup four times (1985-86, 1992-93, 1995-96, 2000-01), and the Conn Smythe Trophy three times (1986, 1993, 2001). Roy also won the Vezina Trophy three times as the NHL's best goalie.

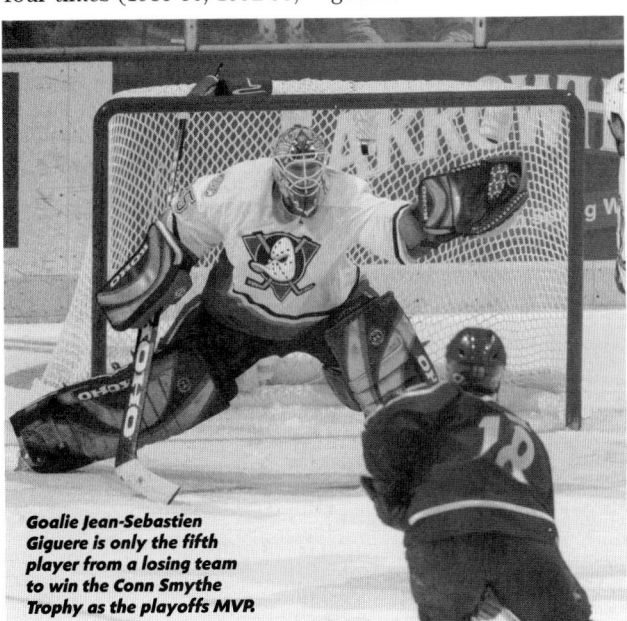

DAVID E. KLUTHO/SPORTS ILLUSTRATED

Goalie Jean-Sebastien Giguere is only the fifth player from a losing team to win the Conn Smythe Trophy as the playoffs MVP.

NHL 2002-03 Final Standings

DIVISION STANDINGS

Northeast Division

	GP	W	L	T	OTL	GF	GA	PTS
z-Senators	82	52	21	8	1	263	182	113
x-Maple Leafs	82	44	28	7	3	236	208	98
x-Bruins	82	36	31	11	4	245	237	87
Canadiens	82	30	35	8	9	206	234	77
Sabres	82	27	37	10	8	190	219	72

Southeast Division

	GP	W	L	T	OTL	GF	GA	PTS
y-Lightning	82	36	25	16	5	219	210	93
x-Capitals	82	39	29	8	6	224	220	92
Thrashers	82	31	39	7	5	226	284	74
Panthers	82	24	36	13	9	176	237	70
Hurricanes	82	22	43	11	6	171	240	61

Atlantic Division

	GP	W	L	T	OTL	GF	GA	PTS
y-Devils	82	46	20	10	6	216	166	108
x-Flyers	82	45	20	13	4	211	166	107
x-Islanders	82	35	34	11	2	224	231	83
Rangers	82	32	36	10	4	210	231	78
Penguins	82	27	44	6	5	189	255	65

Central Division

	GP	W	L	T	OTL	GF	GA	PTS
y-Red Wings	82	48	20	10	4	269	203	110
x-Blues	82	41	24	11	6	253	222	99
Blackhawks	82	30	33	13	6	207	226	79
Predators	82	27	35	13	7	183	206	74
Blue Jackets	82	29	42	8	3	213	263	69

Northwest Division

	GP	W	L	T	OTL	GF	GA	PTS
y-Avalanche	82	42	19	13	8	251	194	105
x-Canucks	82	45	23	13	1	264	208	104
x-Wild	82	42	29	10	1	198	178	95
x-Oilers	82	36	26	11	9	231	230	92
Flames	82	29	36	13	4	186	228	75

Pacific Division

	GP	W	L	T	OTL	GF	GA	PTS
z-Stars	82	46	17	15	4	245	169	111
x-Mighty Ducks	82	40	27	9	6	203	193	95
Kings	82	33	37	6	6	203	221	78
Coyotes	82	31	35	11	5	204	230	78
Sharks	82	28	37	9	8	214	239	73

KEY GP=games played; W=win; L=loss; T=tie; OTL=overtime loss; GF=goals for; GA=goals against; PTS=points; x-clinched playoff spot; y-clinched division; z-clinched conference

2003 Stanley Cup Playoffs

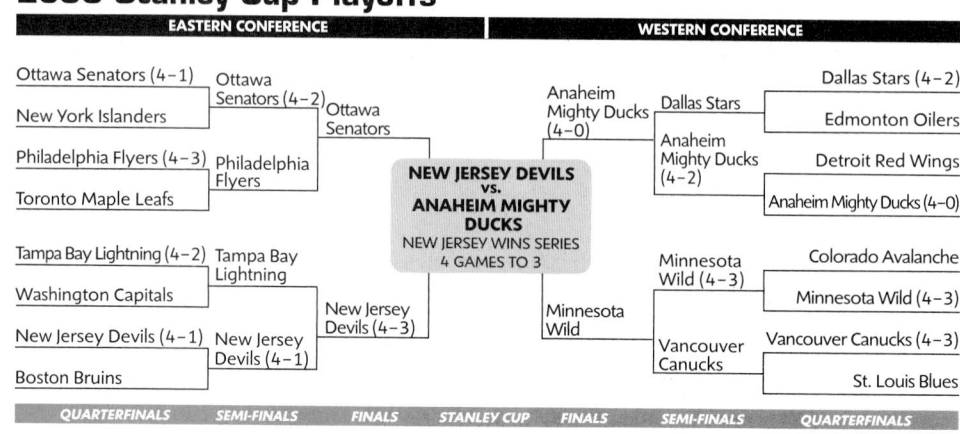

EASTERN CONFERENCE

Ottawa Senators (4–1)

New York Islanders

Ottawa Senators (4–2)

Ottawa Senators

Philadelphia Flyers (4–3)

Toronto Maple Leafs

Philadelphia Flyers

Tampa Bay Lightning (4–2)

Washington Capitals

Tampa Bay Lightning

New Jersey Devils (4–1)

Boston Bruins

New Jersey Devils (4–1)

New Jersey Devils (4–3)

NEW JERSEY DEVILS vs. ANAHEIM MIGHTY DUCKS
NEW JERSEY WINS SERIES 4 GAMES TO 3

WESTERN CONFERENCE

Dallas Stars (4–2)

Edmonton Oilers

Anaheim Mighty Ducks (4–0)

Dallas Stars

Detroit Red Wings

Anaheim Mighty Ducks (4–2)

Anaheim Mighty Ducks (4–0)

Colorado Avalanche

Minnesota Wild (4–3)

Minnesota Wild (4–3)

Vancouver Canucks (4–3)

St. Louis Blues

Minnesota Wild

Vancouver Canucks

QUARTERFINALS   SEMI-FINALS   FINALS   STANLEY CUP   FINALS   SEMI-FINALS   QUARTERFINALS

Stanley Cup Playoff Results

Conference Quarterfinals

EASTERN CONFERENCE

Ottawa Senators vs. New York Islanders
GAME 1: April 9, 2003: New York 3, Ottawa 0
GAME 2: April 12, 2003: Ottawa 3, New York 0
GAME 3: April 14, 2003: Ottawa 3, New York 2 (2OT)
GAME 4: April 16, 2003: Ottawa 3, New York 1
GAME 5: April 17, 2003: Ottawa 4, New York 1
Ottawa Senators win series 4–1

New Jersey Devils vs. Boston Bruins
GAME 1: April 9, 2003: New Jersey 2, Boston 1
GAME 2: April 11, 2003: New Jersey 4, Boston 2
GAME 3: April 13, 2003: New Jersey 3, Boston 0
GAME 4: April 15, 2003: Boston 5, New Jersey 1
GAME 5: April 17, 2003: New Jersey 3, Boston 0
New Jersey Devils win series 4–1

Tampa Bay Lightning vs. Washington Capitals
GAME 1: April 10, 2003: Washington 3, Tampa Bay 0
GAME 2: April 12, 2003: Washington 6, Tampa Bay 3
GAME 3: April 15, 2003: Tampa Bay 4, Washington 3 (OT)
GAME 4: April 16, 2003: Tampa Bay 3, Washington 1
GAME 5: April 18, 2003: Tampa Bay 2, Washington 1
GAME 6: April 20, 2003: Tampa Bay 2, Washington 1 (3OT)
Tampa Bay Lightning wins series 4–2

Philadelphia Flyers vs. Toronto Maple Leafs
GAME 1: April 9, 2003: Toronto 5, Philadelphia 3
GAME 2: April 11, 2003: Philadelphia 4, Toronto 1
GAME 3: April 14, 2003: Toronto 4, Philadelphia 3 (2OT)
GAME 4: April 16, 2003: Philadelphia 3, Toronto 2 (3OT)
GAME 5: April 19, 2003: Philadelphia 4, Toronto 1
GAME 6: April 21, 2003: Toronto 2, Philadelphia 1 (2OT)
GAME 7: April 22, 2003: Philadelphia 6, Toronto 1
Philadelphia Flyers win series 4–3

WESTERN CONFERENCE

Dallas Stars vs. Edmonton Oilers
GAME 1: April 9, 2003: Edmonton 2, Dallas 1
GAME 2: April 11, 2003: Dallas 6, Edmonton 1
GAME 3: April 13, 2003: Edmonton 3, Dallas 2
GAME 4: April 15, 2003: Dallas 3, Edmonton 1
GAME 5: April 17, 2003: Dallas 5, Edmonton 2
GAME 6: April 19, 2003: Dallas 3, Edmonton 2
Dallas Stars win series 4–2

Detroit Red Wings vs. Anaheim Mighty Ducks
GAME 1: April 10, 2003: Anaheim 2, Detroit 1 (3OT)
GAME 2: April 12, 2003: Anaheim 3, Detroit 2
GAME 3: April 14, 2003: Anaheim 2, Detroit 1
GAME 4: April 16, 2003: Anaheim 3, Detroit 2 (OT)
Anaheim Mighty Ducks win series 4–0

Colorado Avalanche vs. Minnesota Wild
GAME 1: April 10, 2003: Minnesota 4, Colorado 2
GAME 2: April 12, 2003: Colorado 3, Minnesota 2
GAME 3: April 14, 2003: Colorado 3, Minnesota 0
GAME 4: April 16, 2003: Colorado 3, Minnesota 1
GAME 5: April 19, 2003: Minnesota 3, Colorado 2
GAME 6: April 21, 2003: Minnesota 3, Colorado 2 (OT)
GAME 7: April 22, 2003: Minnesota 3, Colorado 2 (OT)
Minnesota Wild wins series 4–3

Vancouver Canucks vs. St. Louis Blues
GAME 1: April 10, 2003: St. Louis 6, Vancouver 0
GAME 2: April 12, 2003: Vancouver 2, St. Louis 1
GAME 3: April 14, 2003: St. Louis 3, Vancouver 1
GAME 4: April 16, 2003: St. Louis 4, Vancouver 1
GAME 5: April 18, 2003: Vancouver 5, St. Louis 3
GAME 6: April 20, 2003: Vancouver 4, St. Louis 3
GAME 7: April 22, 2003: Vancouver 4, St. Louis 1
Vancouver Canucks win series 4–3

Stanley Cup Playoff Results (cont.)

Conference Semi-finals

EASTERN CONFERENCE

Ottawa Senators vs. Philadelphia Flyers
GAME 1: April 25, 2003: Ottawa 4, Philadelphia 2
GAME 2: April 27, 2003: Philadelphia 2, Ottawa 0
GAME 3: April 29, 2003: Ottawa 3, Philadelphia 2 (OT)
GAME 4: May 1, 2003: Philadelphia 1, Ottawa 0
GAME 5: May 3, 2003: Ottawa 5, Philadelphia 2
GAME 6: May 5, 2003: Ottawa 5, Philadelphia 1

Ottawa Senators win series 4-2

New Jersey Devils vs. Tampa Bay Lightning
GAME 1: April 24, 2003: New Jersey 3, Tampa Bay 0
GAME 2: April 26, 2003: New Jersey 3, Tampa Bay 2 (OT)
GAME 3: April 28, 2003: Tampa Bay 4, New Jersey 3
GAME 4: April 30, 2003: New Jersey 3, Tampa Bay 1
GAME 5: May 2, 2003: New Jersey 2, Tampa Bay 1 (3OT)

New Jersey Devils win series 4-1

WESTERN CONFERENCE

Dallas Stars vs. Anaheim Mighty Ducks
GAME 1: April 24, 2003: Anaheim 4, Dallas 3 (5OT)
GAME 2: April 26, 2003: Anaheim 3, Dallas 2 (OT)
GAME 3: April 28, 2003: Dallas 2, Anaheim 1
GAME 4: April 30, 2003: Anaheim 1, Dallas 0
GAME 5: May 3, 2003: Dallas 4, Anaheim 1
GAME 6: May 5, 2003: Anaheim 4, Dallas 3

Anaheim Mighty Ducks win series 4-2

Vancouver Canucks vs. Minnesota Wild
GAME 1: April 25, 2003: Vancouver 4, Minnesota 3 (OT)
GAME 2: April 27, 2003: Minnesota 3, Vancouver 2
GAME 3: April 29, 2003: Vancouver 3, Minnesota 2
GAME 4: May 2, 2003: Vancouver 3, Minnesota 2 (OT)
GAME 5: May 5, 2003: Minnesota 7, Vancouver 2
GAME 6: May 7, 2003: Minnesota 5, Vancouver 1
GAME 7: May 8, 2003: Minnesota 4, Vancouver 2

Minnesota Wild wins series 4-3

Eastern Finals

Ottawa Senators vs. New Jersey Devils
GAME 1: May 10, 2003: Ottawa 3, New Jersey 2 (OT)
GAME 2: May 13, 2003: New Jersey 4, Ottawa 1
GAME 3: May 15, 2003: New Jersey 1, Ottawa 0
GAME 4: May 17, 2003: New Jersey 5, Ottawa 2
GAME 5: May 19, 2003: Ottawa 3, New Jersey 1
GAME 6: May 21, 2003: Ottawa 2, New Jersey 1 (OT)
GAME 7: May 23, 2003: New Jersey 3, Ottawa 2

New Jersey Devils win series 4-3

Western Finals

Minnesota Wild vs. Anaheim Mighty Ducks
GAME 1: May 10, 2003: Anaheim 1, Minnesota 0 (2OT)
GAME 2: May 12, 2003: Anaheim 2, Minnesota 0
GAME 3: May 14, 2003: Anaheim 4, Minnesota 0
GAME 4: May 16, 2003: Anaheim 2, Minnesota 1

Anaheim Mighty Ducks win series 4-0

Stanley Cup Finals

New Jersey Devils vs. Anaheim Mighty Ducks
GAME 1: May 27, 2003: New Jersey 3, Anaheim 0
GAME 2: May 29, 2003: New Jersey 3, Anaheim 0
GAME 3: May 31, 2003: Anaheim 3, New Jersey 2 (OT)
GAME 4: June 2, 2003: Anaheim 1, New Jersey 0 (OT)
GAME 5: June 5, 2003: New Jersey 6, Anaheim 3
GAME 6: June 7, 2003: Anaheim 5, New Jersey 2
GAME 7: June 9, 2003: New Jersey 3, Anaheim 0

New Jersey Devils win series 4-3

Stanley Cup Championship Box Scores

GAME 1
May 27, 2003
NEW JERSEY 3, ANAHEIM 0

	1ST	2ND	3RD	TOTAL
ANAHEIM	0	0	0	0
NEW JERSEY	0	1	2	3

FIRST PERIOD SCORING
None

SECOND PERIOD SCORING
Jeff Friesen, New Jersey (1:45) Assists: Sergei Brylin, Brian Gionta

THIRD PERIOD SCORING
Grant Marshall, New Jersey (5:34) Assists: Patrik Elias, Scott Gomez
Jeff Friesen, New Jersey (19:38) Assists: Colin White, Martin Brodeur

GAME 2
May 29, 2003
NEW JERSEY 3, ANAHEIM 0

	1ST	2ND	3RD	TOTAL
ANAHEIM	0	0	0	0
NEW JERSEY	0	2	1	3

FIRST PERIOD SCORING
None

SECOND PERIOD SCORING
Patrick Elias, New Jersey (4:42) Assists: Oleg Tverdovsky, Scott Gomez
Scott Gomez, New Jersey (12:11) Assists: Oleg Tverdovsky, Patrik Elias

THIRD PERIOD SCORING
Jeff Friesen, New Jersey (4:22) Assists: Brian Gionta, Scott Niedermayer

GAME 3
May 31, 2003
ANAHEIM 3, NEW JERSEY 2 (OT)

	1ST	2ND	3RD	OT	TOTAL
NEW JERSEY	0	1	1	0	2
ANAHEIM	0	2	0	1	3

FIRST PERIOD SCORING
None

SECOND PERIOD SCORING
Marc Chouinard, Anaheim (3:39) Assist: Sandis Ozolinsh
Patrik Elias, New Jersey (14:02) Assists: Jamie Langenbrunner, Brian Rafalski
Sandis Ozolinsh, Anaheim (14:47) Assist: Jean-Sebastien Giguere

THIRD PERIOD SCORING
Scott Gomez, New Jersey (9:11) Assists: Grant Marshall, Patrik Elias

OVERTIME SCORING
Ruslan Salei, Anaheim (6:59) Assist: Adam Oates

Stanley Cup Championship Box Scores (cont.)

GAME 4
June 2, 2003
ANAHEIM 1, NEW JERSEY 0 (OT)

	1ST	2ND	3RD	OT	TOTAL
NEW JERSEY	0	0	0	0	0
ANAHEIM	0	0	0	1	1

FIRST PERIOD SCORING
None

SECOND PERIOD SCORING
None

THIRD PERIOD SCORING
None

OVERTIME SCORING
Steve Thomas, Anaheim (:39) Assists: Samuel Pahlsson, Sandis Ozolinsh

GAME 5
June 5, 2003
NEW JERSEY 6, ANAHEIM 3

	1ST	2ND	3RD	TOTAL
ANAHEIM	2	1	0	3
NEW JERSEY	2	2	2	6

FIRST PERIOD SCORING
Petr Sykora, Anaheim (:42) Assist: Adam Oates
Pascal Rheaume, New Jersey (3:35) Assists: Turner Stevenson, Sergei Brylin
Patrik Elias, New Jersey (7:45) Assists: Brian Rafalski, Scott Gomez
Steve Rucchin, Anaheim (12:50) Assists: Petr Sykora, Paul Kariya

SECOND PERIOD SCORING
Brian Gionta, New Jersey (3:12) Assists: Jay Pandolfo, Scott Niedermayer
Samuel Pahlsson, Anaheim (6:35) Assists: Rob Niedermayer, Keith Carney
Jay Pandolfo, New Jersey (9:02) Assists: Brian Gionta, Scott Stevens

THIRD PERIOD SCORING
Jamie Langenbrunner, New Jersey (5:39) Assists: Mike Rupp, Scott Niedermayer
Jamie Langenbrunner, New Jersey (12:52) Assist: Brian Gionta

GAME 6
June 7, 2003
ANAHEIM 5, NEW JERSEY 2

	1ST	2ND	3RD	TOTAL
NEW JERSEY	0	1	1	2
ANAHEIM	3	1	1	5

FIRST PERIOD SCORING
Steve Rucchin, Anaheim (4:26) Assists: Paul Kariya, Petr Sykora
Steve Rucchin, Anaheim (13:42) Assists: Mike Leclerc, Rob Niedermayer
Steve Thomas, Anaheim (15:59) Assists: Paul Kariya, Keith Carney

SECOND PERIOD SCORING
Jay Pandolfo, New Jersey (2:18) Assists: John Madden, Brian Gionta
Paul Kariya, Anaheim (17:15) Assists: Petr Sykora, Adam Oates

THIRD PERIOD SCORING
Petr Sykora, Anaheim (3:57) Assists: Stanislav Chistov, Niclas Havelid
Grant Marshall, New Jersey (10:46) Assists: Brian Rafalski, Patrik Elias

GAME 7
June 9, 2003
NEW JERSEY 3, ANAHEIM 0

	1ST	2ND	3RD	TOTAL
ANAHEIM	0	0	0	0
NEW JERSEY	0	2	1	3

FIRST PERIOD SCORING
None

SECOND PERIOD SCORING
Mike Rupp, New Jersey (2:22) Assists: Scott Niedermayer, Colin White
Jeff Friesen, New Jersey (12:18) Assists: Mike Rupp, Scott Niedermayer

THIRD PERIOD SCORING
Jeff Friesen, New Jersey (16:16) Assists: Mike Rupp, Scott Stevens

2002-03 NHL Individual Leaders

Scoring

POINTS

POINTS	GP	PTS
Peter Forsberg, Avalanche	75	106
Markus Naslund, Canucks	82	104
Joe Thornton, Bruins	77	101
Milan Hejduk, Avalanche	82	98
Todd Bertuzzi, Canucks	82	97
Pavol Demitra, Blues	78	93
Glen Murray, Bruins	82	92
Mario Lemieux, Penguins	67	91
Dany Heatley, Thrashers	77	89
Mike Modano, Stars	79	85
Zigmund Palffy, Kings	76	85
Sergei Fedorov, Red Wings	80	83
Paul Kariya, Mighty Ducks	82	81

POINTS (cont.)	GP	PTS
Marian Hossa, Senators	80	80
Alexander Mogilny, Maple Leafs	73	79
Vaclav Prospal, Lightning	80	79
Daniel Alfredsson, Senators	78	78
Vincent LeCavalier, Lightning	80	78
Jaromir Jagr, Capitals	75	77
Alexei Kovalev, Rangers	78	77

GOALS	GP	G
Milan Hejduk, Avalanche	82	50
Markus Naslund, Canucks	82	48
Todd Bertuzzi, Canucks	82	46
Marian Hossa, Senators	80	45
Glen Murray, Bruins	82	44

KEY GP=games played; PTS=points; G=goals

GOALS (cont.)

	GP	G
Dany Heatley, Thrashers	77	41
Ilya Kovalchuk, Thrashers	81	38
Brett Hull, Red Wings	82	37
Mats Sundin, Maple Leafs	75	37
Zigmund Palffy, Kings	76	37
Alexei Kovalev, Rangers	78	37

GENE J. PUSKAR/AP

Mario Lemieux, Pittsburgh Penguins

ASSISTS

	GP	A
Peter Forsberg, Avalanche	75	77
Joe Thornton, Bruins	77	65
Mario Lemieux, Penguins	67	63
Mike Modano, Stars	79	57
Pavol Demitra, Blues	78	57
Vaclav Prospal, Lightning	80	57
Brad Richards, Lightning	80	57
Markus Naslund, Canucks	82	56
Paul Kariya, Mighty Ducks	82	56
Al MacInnis, Blues	80	52
Doug Weight, Blues	70	52
Ray Whitney, Blue Jackets	81	52

PLUS/MINUS

	GP	+/-
Peter Forsberg, Avalanche	75	52
Milan Hejduk, Avalanche	82	52
Nicklas Lidstrom, Red Wings	82	40
Jere Lehtinen, Stars	80	39
Derian Hatcher, Stars	82	37
Mike Modano, Stars	79	34
Alex Tanguay, Avalanche	82	34
Eric Desjardins, Flyers	79	30
Adam Foote, Avalanche	78	30
Zdeno Chara, Senators	74	29

Note: +/-=plus-minus rating (a player is awarded a plus (+1) each time he is on the ice when his team scores an even-strength or shorthanded goal. He receives a minus (-1) each time he is on the ice when the opposing team scores an even-strength or shorthanded goal. Power-play goals are not included in the rating.)

Did You Know?

No player in NHL history has served longer as his team's captain than center Steve Yzerman of the Detroit Red Wings. "Stevie Y" first began wearing the C on his jersey in 1986-87 and has been the Wings' main man ever since.

Goaltending

GOALS-AGAINST AVERAGE

	GP	GAA
Marty Turco, Stars	55	1.72
Roman Cechmanek, Flyers	58	1.83
Dwayne Roloson, Wild	50	2.00
Martin Brodeur, Devils	73	2.02
Patrick Lalime, Senators	67	2.16
Patrick Roy, Avalanche	63	2.18
Tomas Vokoun, Predators	69	2.20
Robert Esche, Flyers	30	2.20
Emmanuel Fernandez, Wild	35	2.24
Ed Belfour, Maple Leafs	62	2.26
Jean-Sebastien Giguere, Mighty Ducks	65	2.30
Garth Snow, Islanders	43	2.31
Jocelyn Thibault, Blackhawks	62	2.37
Olaf Kolzig, Capitals	66	2.40
Dan Cloutier, Canucks	57	2.42
Ron Tugnutt, Stars	31	2.47
Nikolai Khabibulin, Lightning	65	2.47
Brent Johnson, Blues	38	2.47
Curtis Joseph, Red Wings	61	2.49
Mike Dunham, Rangers	58	2.50

SHUTOUTS

	GP	W	L	T	SO
Martin Brodeur, Devils	73	41	23	9	9
Patrick Lalime, Senators	67	39	20	7	8
Jean-Sebastien Giguere, Mighty Ducks	65	34	22	6	8
Jocelyn Thibault, Blackhawks	62	26	28	7	8
Marty Turco, Stars	55	31	10	10	7
Ed Belfour, Maple Leafs	62	37	20	5	7
Roman Cechmanek, Flyers	58	33	15	10	6
Roberto Luongo, Panthers	65	20	34	7	6

Five tied with five.

SAVE PERCENTAGE

	GP	GA	SA	SAVE PCT	W	L	T
Marty Turco, Stars	55	92	1,359	.932	31	10	10
Dwayne Roloson, Wild	50	98	1,334	.927	23	16	8
Roman Cechmanek, Flyers	58	102	1,368	.925	33	15	10
Emmanuel Fernandez, Wild	35	74	972	.924	19	13	2
Ed Belfour, Maple Leafs	62	141	1,816	.922	37	20	5
Patrick Roy, Avalanche	63	137	1,723	.920	35	15	13
Jean-Sebastien Giguere, Mighty Ducks	65	145	1,820	.920	34	22	6
Olaf Kolzig, Capitals	66	156	1,925	.919	33	25	6
Tomas Vokoun, Predators	69	146	1,771	.918	25	31	11
Garth Snow, Islanders	43	92	1,120	.918	16	17	5
Roberto Luongo, Panthers	65	164	2,011	.916	20	34	7
Mike Dunham, Rangers	58	137	1,626	.916	21	26	7
Jocelyn Thibault, Blackhawks	62	144	1,690	.915	26	28	7
Martin Brodeur, Devils	73	147	1,706	.914	41	23	9

WINS

	GP	W	L	T
Martin Brodeur, Devils	73	41	23	9
Patrick Lalime, Senators	67	39	20	7
Ed Belfour, Maple Leafs	62	37	20	5
Patrick Roy, Avalanche	63	35	15	13
Jean-Sebastien Giguere, Mighty Ducks	65	34	22	6
Curtis Joseph, Red Wings	61	34	19	6
Roman Cechmanek, Flyers	58	33	15	10
Olaf Kolzig, Capitals	66	33	25	6
Dan Cloutier, Canucks	57	33	16	7
Marty Turco, Stars	55	31	10	10

KEY G=goals; A=assists; GAA=goals-against average; W=win; L=loss; T=tie; SO=shutout; GA=goals allowed; SA=shots allowed; SAVE PCT=save percentage

2002-03 NHL TEAM-BY-TEAM STATS

ANAHEIM MIGHTY DUCKS

	GP	G	A	PTS	+/-	PIM
Paul Kariya	82	25	56	81	-3	48
Petr Sykora	82	34	25	59	-7	24
Steve Rucchin	82	20	38	58	-14	12
Adam Oates	67	9	36	45	-1	16
Sandis Ozolinsh	82	12	32	44	-6	56
Niclas Havelid	82	11	22	33	5	30
Steve Thomas	81	14	16	30	10	53
Stanislav Chistov	79	12	18	30	4	54
Mike LeClerc	57	9	19	28	-8	34
Jason Krog	67	10	15	25	1	12
Keith Carney	81	4	18	22	8	65
Rob Niedermayer	66	10	12	22	-10	57
Andy McDonald	46	10	11	21	-1	14
Patric Kjellberg	76	8	11	19	-9	16
Samuel Pahlsson	34	4	11	15	10	18
Ruslan Salei	61	4	8	12	2	78
Fredrik Olausson	44	2	6	8	0	22
Vitaly Vishnevski	80	2	6	8	-8	76
Marc Chouinard	70	3	4	7	-9	40
Dan Bylsma	39	1	4	5	-1	12

	GP	G	A	PTS	+/-	PIM
Alexei Smirnov	44	3	2	5	-1	18
Lance Ward	65	3	2	5	-6	121
Kevin Sawyer	31	2	1	3	-2	115
Kurt Sauer	80	1	2	3	-23	74
Mike Brown	16	1	1	2	0	44
Rob Valicevic	10	1	0	1	1	2
Chris O'Sullivan	2	0	1	1	0	0
Cam Severson	2	0	0	0	0	8
Jonathan Hedstrom	4	0	0	0	-1	0

GOALIES	GP	W	L	T	GAA
Martin Gerber	22	6	11	3	1.95
Jean-Sebastien Giguere	65	34	22	6	2.30

ATLANTA THRASHERS

	GP	G	A	PTS	+/-	PIM
Dany Heatley	77	41	48	89	-8	58
Vyacheslav Kozlov	79	21	49	70	-10	66
Ilya Kovalchuk	81	38	29	67	-24	57
Marc Savard	67	17	33	50	-14	85
Patrik Stefan	71	13	21	34	-10	12
Yannick Tremblay	75	8	22	30	-27	32
Tony Hrkac	80	9	17	26	-16	14
Shawn McEachern	46	10	16	26	-27	28
Frantisek Kaberle	79	7	19	26	-19	32
Andy Sutton	53	3	18	21	-8	114
Lubos Bartecko	37	7	9	16	3	8
Daniel Tjarnqvist	75	3	12	15	-20	26
Dan Snyder	36	10	4	14	-4	34
Brad Tapper	35	10	4	14	2	23
Chris Tamer	72	1	9	10	-10	118
Per Svartvadet	62	1	7	8	-11	8
Jeff Cowan	66	3	5	8	-15	115
Mark Hartigan	23	5	2	7	-8	6
Jeff Odgers	74	2	4	6	-13	171
Chris Herperger	27	4	1	5	-11	7

	GP	G	A	PTS	+/-	PIM
Kamil Piros	3	3	2	5	4	2
Mike Weaver	40	0	5	5	-5	20
Kirill Safronov	32	2	2	4	-10	14
Yuri Butsayev	16	2	0	2	-5	8
Joe DiPenta	3	1	1	2	3	0
Garnet Exelby	15	0	2	2	0	41
Francis Lessard	18	0	2	2	1	61
Benjamin Simon	10	0	1	1	0	9
Uwe Krupp	4	0	0	0	-2	10
Kurtis Foster	2	0	0	0	-2	0

GOALIES	GP	W	L	T	GAA
Pasi Nurminen	52	21	19	5	2.88
Milan Hnilicka	21	4	13	1	3.56
Byron Dafoe	17	5	11	1	4.36
Frederic Cassivi	2	1	1	0	5.37

Note: Players are listed under the teams with which they finished the 2002-03 season.

KEY GP=games played; G=goals; A=assists; PTS=points; +/-=plus-minus rating; PIM=penalty minutes; W=win; L=loss; T=tie; GAA=goals-against average

BOSTON BRUINS

	GP	G	A	PTS	+/-	PIM
Joe Thornton	77	36	65	101	12	109
Glen Murray	82	44	48	92	9	64
Mike Knuble	75	30	29	59	18	45
Brian Rolston	81	27	32	59	1	32
Jozef Stumpel	78	14	37	51	E	12
Bryan Berard	80	10	28	38	-4	64
P.J. Axelsson	66	17	19	36	8	24
Nicholas Boynton	78	7	17	24	8	99
Jonathan Girard	73	6	16	22	4	21
Dan McGillis	71	3	17	20	3	60
Michal Grosek	63	2	18	20	2	71
Marty McInnis	77	9	10	19	-11	38
Martin Lapointe	59	8	10	18	-19	87
Hal Gill	76	4	13	17	21	56
Ivan Huml	41	6	11	17	3	30
Sean O'Donnell	70	1	15	16	8	76
Rob Zamuner	55	10	6	16	2	18
Sergei Samsonov	8	5	6	11	8	2
P.J. Stock	71	1	9	10	-5	160
Don Sweeney	67	3	5	8	-1	24

	GP	G	A	PTS	+/-	PIM
Ian Moran	78	0	8	8	-18	48
Sean Brown	69	1	5	6	-6	117
Lee Goren	14	2	1	3	-2	7
Andy Hilbert	14	0	3	3	-1	7
Rich Brennan	7	0	1	1	3	6
Martin Samuelsson	8	0	1	1	-1	2
Kris Vernarsky	14	1	0	1	-2	2
Zdenek Kutlak	4	1	0	1	E	0
Brantt Myhres	1	0	0	0	E	31
Matt Herr	3	0	0	0	E	0

GOALIES	GP	W	L	T	GAA
Andrew Raycroft	5	2	3	0	2.40
Steve Shields	36	12	13	9	2.76
Jeff Hackett	36	15	17	2	2.86
Tim Thomas	4	3	1	0	3.01

BUFFALO SABRES

	GP	G	A	PTS	+/-	PIM
Miroslav Satan	79	26	49	75	-3	20
Daniel Briere	82	24	34	58	-20	62
J.P. Dumont	76	14	21	35	-14	44
Ales Kotalik	68	21	14	35	-2	30
Curtis Brown	74	15	16	31	4	40
Taylor Pyatt	78	14	14	28	-8	38
Jochen Hecht	49	10	16	26	4	30
Tim Connolly	80	12	13	25	-28	32
Alexei Zhitnik	70	3	18	21	-5	85
Dmitri Kalinin	65	8	13	21	-7	57
Brian Campbell	65	2	17	19	-8	20
Adam Mair	79	6	11	17	-4	146
James Patrick	69	4	12	16	-3	26
Henrik Tallinder	46	3	10	13	-3	28
Maxim Afinogenov	35	5	6	11	-12	21
Rhett Warrener	50	0	9	9	1	63
Eric Boulton	58	1	5	6	1	178
Jason Botterill	17	1	4	5	1	14
Jay McKee	59	0	5	5	-16	49
Chris Taylor	11	1	2	3	-1	2

	GP	G	A	PTS	+/-	PIM
Rory Fitzpatrick	36	1	3	4	-7	16
Denis Hamel	25	2	0	2	-4	17
Norm Milley	8	0	2	2	-2	6
Milan Bartovic	3	1	0	1	E	0
Doug Houda	1	0	0	0	-2	2
Jaroslav Kristek	6	0	0	0	-2	4
Doug Janik	6	0	0	0	1	2
Paul Gaustad	1	0	0	0	E	0
Sean McMorrow	1	0	0	0	E	0
Radoslav Hecl	14	0	0	0	E	2

GOALIES	GP	W	L	T	GAA
Mika Noronen	16	4	9	3	2.42
Martin Biron	54	17	28	6	2.56
Ryan Miller	15	6	8	1	2.63

HOCKEY

CALGARY FLAMES

	GP	G	A	PTS	+/-	PIM
Jarome Iginla	75	35	32	67	-10	49
Craig Conroy	79	22	37	59	-4	36
Chris Drury	80	23	30	53	-9	33
Martin Gelinas	81	21	31	52	-3	51
Toni Lydman	81	6	20	26	-7	28
Stephane Yelle	82	10	15	25	-10	50
Oleg Saprykin	52	8	15	23	5	46
Chris Clark	81	10	12	22	-11	126
Dave Lowry	34	5	14	19	4	22
Bob Boughner	69	3	14	17	5	126
Jordan Leopold	58	4	10	14	-15	12
Shean Donovan	65	5	7	12	-8	37
Robyn Regehr	76	0	12	12	-9	87
Denis Gauthier	72	1	11	12	5	99
Scott Nichol	68	5	5	10	-7	149
Blake Sloan	67	2	8	10	-5	28
Petr Buzek	44	3	5	8	-6	14
Andrew Ference	38	1	7	8	-15	42
Craig Berube	55	2	4	6	-6	100
Chuck Kobasew	23	4	2	6	-3	8

	GP	G	A	PTS	+/-	PIM
Steve Begin	50	3	1	4	-7	51
Blair Betts	9	1	3	4	3	0
Micki Dupont	16	1	2	3	-5	4
Steve Montador	50	1	1	2	-9	114
Ladislav Kohn	3	0	1	1	1	2
Mike Commodore	6	0	1	1	2	19
Rick Mrozik	2	0	0	0	E	0
Mike Mottau	4	0	0	0	-1	0
Robert Dome	1	0	0	0	E	0

GOALIES	GP	W	L	T	GAA
Roman Turek	65	27	29	9	2.57
Jamie McLennan	22	2	11	4	2.99

CAROLINA HURRICANES

	GP	G	A	PTS	+/-	PIM
Jeff O'Neill	82	30	31	61	-21	38
Ron Francis	82	22	35	57	-22	30
Rod Brind'Amour	48	14	23	37	-9	37
Radim Vrbata	76	16	19	35	-7	18
Sean Hill	82	5	24	29	4	141
Erik Cole	53	14	13	27	1	72
Jan Hlavac	52	9	15	24	-9	22
Josef Vasicek	57	10	10	20	-19	33
Craig Adams	81	6	12	18	-11	71
Kevyn Adams	77	9	9	18	-8	57
Bret Hedican	72	3	14	17	-24	75
Jaroslav Svoboda	48	3	11	14	-5	32
Ryan Bayda	25	4	10	14	-5	16
Pavel Brendl	50	5	8	13	5	6
David Tanabe	68	3	10	13	-27	24
Niclas Wallin	77	2	8	10	-19	71
Aaron Ward	77	3	6	9	-23	90
Bruno St. Jacques	18	2	5	7	-3	12
Harold Druken	22	1	4	5	-1	4
Tomas Kurka	14	3	2	5	1	2
Jeff Daniels	59	0	4	4	-9	8

	GP	G	A	PTS	+/-	PIM
Craig MacDonald	35	1	3	4	-3	20
Jesse Boulerice	48	2	1	3	-2	108
Jeff Heerema	10	3	0	3	-2	2
Brad DeFauw	9	3	0	3	-2	2
Mike Zigomanis	19	2	1	3	-4	0
Tomas Malec	41	0	2	2	-5	43
Damian Surma	1	1	0	1	E	0
Steve Halko	6	0	0	0	1	0
Tommy Westlund	3	0	0	0	E	0

GOALIES	GP	W	L	T	GAA
Kevin Weekes	51	14	24	9	2.55
Arturs Irbe	34	7	24	2	3.18
Patrick Desrochers	6	1	4	0	3.62

CHICAGO BLACKHAWKS

	GP	G	A	PTS	+/-	PIM
Steve Sullivan	82	26	35	61	15	42
Alexei Zhamnov	74	15	43	58	E	70
Eric Daze	54	22	22	44	10	14
Kyle Calder	82	15	27	42	-6	40
Tyler Arnason	82	19	20	39	7	20
Theo Fleury	54	12	21	33	-7	77
Mark Bell	82	14	15	29	E	113
Nathan Dempsey	67	5	23	28	-7	26
Andrei Nikolishin	60	6	15	21	-3	26
Chris Simon	61	12	6	18	7	125
Mike Eastwood	70	3	13	16	-5	32
Jon Klemm	70	2	14	16	-9	44
Alexander Karpovtsev	40	4	10	14	-8	12
Steve Poapst	75	2	11	13	14	50
Igor Korolev	48	4	5	9	-1	30
Jason Strudwick	48	2	3	5	-4	87
Steve McCarthey	57	1	4	5	-1	23
Igor Radulov	7	5	0	5	-3	4
Shawn Thornton	13	1	1	2	-4	31
Burke Henry	16	0	2	2	-13	9

	GP	G	A	PTS	+/-	PIM
Todd Gill	5	0	1	1	3	0
Garry Valk	16	0	1	1	E	6
Sami Helenius	15	0	1	1	4	34
Peter White	6	0	1	1	E	0
Louie Debrusk	4	0	0	0	E	7
Brett McLean	2	0	0	0	-1	0
Ryan Vandenbussche	22	0	0	0	E	58

GOALIES	GP	W	L	T	GAA
Jocelyn Thibault	62	26	28	7	2.37
Michael Leighton	8	2	3	2	2.82
Steve Passmore	11	2	5	2	3.70
Craig Andersson	6	0	3	2	4.00

COLORADO AVALANCHE

	GP	G	A	PTS	+/-	PIM
Peter Forsberg	75	29	77	106	52	70
Milan Hejduk	82	50	48	98	52	32
Alex Tanguay	82	26	41	67	34	36
Joe Sakic	58	26	32	58	4	24
Steven Reinprecht	77	18	33	51	-6	18
Derek Morris	75	11	37	48	16	68
Rob Blake	79	17	28	45	20	57
Greg De Vries	82	6	26	32	15	70
Adam Foote	78	11	20	31	30	88
Bates Battaglia	83	6	19	25	-19	100
Martin Skoula	81	4	21	25	11	68
Dean McAmmond	41	10	8	18	1	10
Bryan Marchment	81	2	12	14	2	141
Eric Messier	72	4	10	14	-2	16
Mike Keane	65	5	5	10	0	34
Serge Aubin	66	4	6	10	-2	64
Dan Hinote	60	6	4	10	4	49
Jeff Shantz	74	3	6	9	-12	35
Vaclav Nedorost	42	4	5	9	8	20
Riku Hahl	42	3	4	7	3	12

	GP	G	A	PTS	+/-	PIM
Scott Parker	43	1	3	4	6	82
Brad Larsen	6	0	3	3	3	2
Bryan Muir	32	0	2	2	3	19
Chris McAllister	33	0	1	1	4	47
D.J. Smith	34	1	0	1	2	55
Brian Willsie	12	0	1	1	0	15
Steve Brule	2	0	0	0	0	0
Jeff Paul	2	0	0	0	0	7
Steve Moore	4	0	0	0	0	0
Charlie Stephens	2	0	0	0	0	0

GOALIES	GP	W	L	T	GAA
Patrick Roy	63	35	15	13	2.18
David Aebischer	22	7	12	0	2.43

HOCKEY

COLUMBUS BLUE JACKETS

	GP	G	A	PTS	+/-	PIM
Ray Whitney	81	24	52	76	-26	22
Andrew Cassels	79	20	48	68	-4	30
Geoff Sanderson	82	34	33	67	-4	34
David Vyborny	79	20	26	46	12	16
Jaroslav Spacek	81	9	36	45	-23	70
Mike Sillinger	75	18	25	43	-21	52
Rick Nash	74	17	22	39	-27	78
Tyler Wright	70	19	11	30	-25	113
Lasse Pirjeta	51	11	10	21	-4	12
Derrick Walser	53	4	13	17	-9	34
Rostislav Klesla	72	2	14	16	-22	71
Luke Richardson	82	0	13	13	-16	73
Sean Pronger	78	7	6	13	-26	72
Espen Knutsen	31	5	4	9	-15	20
Hannes Hyvonen	36	4	5	9	-11	22
Matt Davidson	34	4	5	9	-12	18
Duvie Westcott	39	0	7	7	-3	77
David Ling	35	3	2	5	-6	86
Jody Shelley	68	1	4	5	-5	249
Darren Van Impe	14	1	1	2	-6	10

	GP	G	A	PTS	+/-	PIM
Scott Lachance	61	0	1	1	-20	46
Jamie Allison	48	0	1	1	-15	99
Andrej Nedorost	12	0	1	1	-6	4
Jean-Luc Grand-Pierre	41	1	0	1	-6	64
Kevin Dineen	4	0	0	0	0	12
Paul Manning	8	0	0	0	0	2
Mathieu Darche	1	0	0	0	-1	0
Blake Bellefeuille	3	0	0	0	0	0
Darrel Scoville	2	0	0	0	0	4
Kent McDonell	3	0	0	0	-1	0

GOALIES	GP	W	L	T	GAA
Marc Denis	77	27	41	8	3.09
Jean Labbe	11	2	4	0	3.59

DALLAS STARS

	GP	G	A	PTS	+/-	PIM
Mike Modano	79	28	57	85	34	30
Sergei Zubov	82	11	44	55	21	26
Bill Guerin	64	25	25	50	5	113
Jere Lehtinen	80	31	17	48	39	20
Jason Arnott	72	23	24	47	9	51
Brenden Morrow	71	21	22	43	20	134
Pierre Turgeon	65	12	30	42	4	18
Scott Young	79	23	19	42	24	30
Stu Barnes	81	13	26	39	-11	28
Ulf Dahlen	63	17	20	37	11	14
Darryl Sydor	81	5	31	36	22	40
Niko Kapanen	82	5	29	34	25	44
Derian Hatcher	82	8	22	30	37	106
Philippe Boucher	80	7	20	27	28	94
Claude Lemieux	68	8	12	20	-12	44
Rob DiMaio	69	10	9	19	18	76
Lyle Odelein	68	7	4	11	7	82
Stephane Robidas	76	3	7	10	15	35
Manny Malhotra	59	3	7	10	-2	42
Steve Ott	26	3	4	7	6	31

	GP	G	A	PTS	+/-	PIM
Kirk Muller	55	1	5	6	-6	18
Richard Matvichuk	68	1	5	6	1	58
David Oliver	6	0	3	3	1	2
Aaron Downey	43	1	1	2	1	69
John Erskine	16	2	0	2	1	29
Jim Montgomery	1	0	0	0	0	0

GOALIES	GP	W	L	T	GAA
Marty Turco	55	31	10	10	1.72
Ron Tugnutt	31	15	10	5	2.47
Corey Hirsch	2	0	1	0	2.47

DETROIT RED WINGS

	GP	G	A	PTS	+/-	PIM
Sergei Fedorov	80	36	47	83	15	52
Brett Hull	82	37	39	76	11	22
Brendan Shanahan	78	30	38	68	5	103
Nicklas Lidstrom	82	18	44	62	40	38
Pavel Datsyuk	64	12	39	51	20	16
Mathieu Schneider	78	16	34	50	2	73
Henrik Zetterberg	79	22	22	44	6	8
Igor Larionov	74	10	33	43	-7	48
Tomas Holmstrom	74	20	20	40	11	62
Kirk Maltby	82	14	23	37	17	91
Kris Draper	82	14	21	35	6	82
Luc Robitaille	81	11	20	31	4	50
Jason Woolley	76	6	20	26	11	51
Darren McCarty	73	13	9	22	10	138
Mathieu Dandenault	74	4	15	19	25	64
Chris Chelios	66	2	17	19	4	78
Boyd Devereaux	61	3	9	12	4	16
Dmitri Bykov	71	2	10	12	1	43
Steve Yzerman	16	2	6	8	6	8
Patrick Boileau	25	2	6	8	8	14

	GP	G	A	PTS	+/-	PIM
Jason Williams	16	3	3	6	3	2
Jiri Fischer	15	1	5	6	0	16
Jesse Wallin	32	0	1	1	-2	19
Stacy Roest	2	0	0	0	0	0

GOALIES	GP	W	L	T	GAA
Manny Legace	25	14	5	4	2.18
Curtis Joseph	61	34	19	6	2.49

EDMONTON OILERS

	GP	G	A	PTS	+/-	PIM
Ryan Smyth	66	27	34	61	5	67
Todd Marchant	77	20	40	60	13	48
Mike York	71	22	29	51	-8	10
Mike Comrie	69	20	31	51	-18	90
Radek Dvorak	75	10	25	35	-6	30
Shawn Horcoff	78	12	21	33	10	55
Ethan Moreau	78	14	17	31	-7	112
Marty Reasoner	70	11	20	31	19	28
Ales Hemsky	59	6	24	30	5	14
Eric Brewer	80	8	21	29	-11	45
Brad Isbister	66	13	15	28	-9	43
Steve Staios	76	5	21	26	13	96
Jason Chimera	66	14	9	23	-2	36
Daniel Cleary	57	4	13	17	5	31
Georges Laraque	64	6	7	13	-4	110
Fernando Pisani	35	8	5	13	9	10
Jason Smith	68	4	8	12	5	64
Brian Swanson	44	2	10	12	-7	10
Cory Cross	37	2	7	9	16	24
Scott Ferguson	78	3	5	8	11	120

	GP	G	A	PTS	+/-	PIM
Alexei Semenov	46	1	6	7	-7	58
Jiri Dopita	21	1	5	6	-4	11
Jani Rita	12	3	1	4	2	0
Marc-Andre Bergeron	5	1	1	2	2	9
Jarret Stoll	4	0	1	1	-3	0
Bobby Allen	1	0	0	0	0	0
Kari Haakana	13	0	0	0	-2	4

GOALIES	GP	W	L	T	GAA
Jussi Markkanen	22	7	8	3	2.59
Tommy Salo	65	29	27	8	2.71

HOCKEY

FLORIDA PANTHERS

	GP	G	A	PTS	+/-	PIM
Olli Jokinen	81	36	29	65	-17	79
Viktor Kozlov	74	22	34	56	-8	18
Kristian Huselius	78	20	23	43	-6	20
Marcus Nilson	82	15	19	34	2	31
Matt Cullen	80	13	20	33	-8	34
Ivan Novoseltsev	78	10	17	27	-16	30
Jaroslav Bednar	67	5	22	27	1	18
Niklas Hagman	80	8	15	23	-8	20
Stephen Weiss	77	6	15	21	-13	17
Jay Bouwmeester	82	4	12	16	-29	14
Andreas Lilja	73	4	11	15	13	70
Pavel Trnka	46	3	9	12	1	30
Ivan Majesky	82	4	8	12	-18	92
Mathieu Biron	34	1	8	9	-18	14
Stephane Matteau	52	4	4	8	-9	27
Denis Shvidki	23	4	2	6	-7	12
Peter Worrell	63	2	3	5	-14	193
Jeff Toms	8	2	2	4	2	4
Byron Ritchie	30	0	3	3	-4	19
Igor Ulanov	56	1	1	2	7	39

	GP	G	A	PTS	+/-	PIM
Branislav Mezei	11	2	0	2	-2	10
Igor Kravchuk	7	0	1	1	-3	4
Juraj Kolnik	10	0	1	1	1	0
Eric Beaudoin	15	0	1	1	-7	25
Jim Campbell	1	0	0	0	0	0
Jamie Rivers	1	0	0	0	-2	2
Darcy Hordichuk	28	0	0	0	-2	97
Kyle Rossiter	3	0	0	0	-2	0
Pierre Dagenais	9	0	0	0	-1	4

GOALIES	GP	W	L	T	GAA
Roberto Luongo	65	20	34	7	2.71
Jani Hurme	28	4	11	6	2.88

LOS ANGELES KINGS

	GP	G	A	PTS	+/-	PIM
Zigmund Palffy	76	37	48	85	22	47
Jaroslav Modry	82	13	25	38	-13	68
Derek Armstrong	66	12	26	38	5	30
Eric Belanger	62	16	19	35	-5	26
Alexander Frolov	79	14	17	31	12	34
Jason Allison	26	6	22	28	9	22
Lubomir Visnovsky	57	8	16	24	2	28
Ian Laperriere	73	7	12	19	-9	122
Adam Deadmarsh	20	13	4	17	2	21
Mikko Eloranta	75	5	12	17	-15	56
Erik Rasmussen	57	4	12	16	-1	28
Sean Avery	51	6	9	15	7	153
Brad Chartrand	62	8	6	14	-10	33
Steve Heinze	27	5	7	12	-5	12
Joseph Corvo	50	5	7	12	2	14
Craig Johnson	70	3	6	9	-13	22
Michael Cammalleri	28	5	3	8	-4	22
Aaron Miller	49	1	5	6	-7	24
Mattias Norstrom	82	0	6	6	0	49
Brad Norton	53	3	3	6	1	97

	GP	G	A	PTS	+/-	PIM
Steve Kelly	15	2	3	5	-6	0
Jared Aulin	17	2	2	4	-3	0
Maxim Kuznetsov	56	0	3	3	1	54
Jonathan Sim	22	1	2	3	-4	19
Tomas Zizka	10	0	3	3	-4	4
Chris McAlpine	21	0	2	2	-4	24
Chris Schmidt	10	0	2	2	-1	5
Jerred Smithson	22	0	2	2	-5	21
Jason Holland	2	0	1	1	1	0
Ryan Flinn	19	1	0	1	0	28

GOALIES	GP	W	L	T	GAA
Cristobal Huet	12	4	4	1	2.33
Jamie Storr	39	12	19	2	2.55
Felix Potvin	42	17	20	3	2.66

MINNESOTA WILD

	GP	G	A	PTS	+/-	PIM
Marian Gaborik	81	30	35	65	12	46
Cliff Ronning	80	17	31	48	-6	24
Pascal Dupuis	80	20	28	48	17	44
Andrew Brunette	82	18	28	46	-10	30
Sergei Zholtok	78	16	26	42	1	18
Wes Walz	80	13	19	32	11	63
Antti Laaksonen	82	15	16	31	4	26
Filip Kuba	78	8	21	29	0	29
Jim Dowd	78	8	17	25	-1	31
Richard Park	81	14	10	24	-3	16
Pierre-Marc Bouchard	50	7	13	20	1	18
Andrei Zyuzin	67	4	13	17	-8	36
Brad Bombardir	58	1	14	15	15	16
Willie Mitchell	69	2	12	14	13	84
Jeremy Stevenson	32	5	6	11	6	69
Lubomir Sekeras	60	2	9	11	-12	30
Nick Schultz	75	3	7	10	11	23
Matt Johnson	60	3	5	8	-8	201
Bill Muckalt	8	5	3	8	5	6
Darby Hendrickson	28	1	5	6	-3	8

	GP	G	A	PTS	+/-	PIM
Jason Marshall	45	1	5	6	4	69
Stephane Veilleux	38	3	2	5	-6	23
Brad Brown	57	0	1	1	-1	90
Kyle Wanvig	7	1	0	1	0	13
Rickard Wallin	4	1	0	1	1	0
Hnat Domenichelli	1	0	0	0	0	0
Jean-Guy Trudel	1	0	0	0	0	2
Curtis Murphy	1	0	0	0	0	0
Ladislav Benysek	14	0	0	0	-3	8

GOALIES	GP	W	L	T	GAA
Dwayne Roloson	50	23	16	8	2.00
Emmanuel Fernandez	35	19	13	2	2.24
Dieter Kochan	1	0	1	0	5.00

MONTREAL CANADIENS

	GP	G	A	PTS	+/-	PIM
Saku Koivu	82	21	50	71	5	72
Richard Zednik	80	31	19	50	4	79
Yanic Perreault	73	24	22	46	-11	30
Jan Bulis	82	16	24	40	9	30
Andrei Markov	79	13	24	37	13	34
Patrice Brisebois	73	4	25	29	-14	32
Niklas Sundstrom	80	7	19	26	-1	30
Andreas Dackell	73	7	18	25	-5	24
Donald Audette	54	11	12	23	-7	19
Joe Juneau	72	6	16	22	-10	20
Craig Rivet	82	7	15	22	1	71
Randy McKay	75	6	13	19	-14	72
Mike Ribeiro	52	5	12	17	-3	6
Chad Kilger	60	9	7	16	-4	21
Mariusz Czerkawski	43	5	9	14	-7	16
Patrick Traverse	65	0	13	13	-9	24
Marcel Hossa	34	6	7	13	3	14
Stephane Quintal	67	5	5	10	-4	70
Karl Dykhuis	65	1	4	5	-5	34
Jason Ward	8	3	2	5	3	0

	GP	G	A	PTS	+/-	PIM
Francis Bouillon	24	3	1	4	-2	4
Bill Lindsay	19	0	2	2	-1	23
Gordie Dwyer	28	0	1	1	-3	96
Michael Komisarek	21	0	1	1	-6	28
Sylvain Blouin	19	0	0	0	-3	47
Francois Beauchemin	1	0	0	0	-1	0
Ron Hainsey	21	0	0	0	-1	2

GOALIES	GP	W	L	T	GAA
Mathieu Garon	8	3	5	0	1.99
Jose Theodore	57	20	31	6	2.90

HOCKEY

NASHVILLE PREDATORS

	GP	G	A	PTS	+/-	PIM		GP	G	A	PTS	+/-	PIM
David Legwand	64	17	31	48	-2	34	Martin Erat	27	1	7	8	-9	14
Kimmo Timonen	72	6	34	40	-3	46	Bill Houlder	82	2	4	6	-2	46
Andreas Johansson	56	20	17	37	-4	22	Vernon Fiddler	19	4	2	6	2	14
Denis Arkhipov	79	11	24	35	-18	32	Brent Gilchrist	41	1	2	3	-11	14
Andy Delmore	71	18	16	34	-17	28	Reid Simpson	26	0	1	1	-4	56
Scott Hartnell	82	12	22	34	-3	101	Wyatt Smith	11	1	0	1	-1	0
Scott Walker	60	15	18	33	2	58	Scottie Upshall	8	1	0	1	2	0
Vladimir Orszagh	78	16	16	32	-1	38	Domenic Pittis	2	0	0	0	0	2
Rem Murray	85	12	19	31	-2	22	Nathan Perrott	1	0	0	0	0	5
Adam Hall	79	16	12	28	-8	31	Andy Berenzweig	4	0	0	0	0	0
Oleg Petrov	70	9	18	27	-6	18							
Vitali Yachmenev	62	5	15	20	7	12							
Jason York	74	4	15	19	13	52							
Greg Johnson	38	8	9	17	7	22							
Todd Warriner	49	6	10	16	1	32							
Clarke Wilm	82	5	11	16	-11	36	**GOALIES**	GP	W	L	T	GAA	
Karlis Skrastins	82	3	10	13	-18	44	Tomas Vokoun	69	25	31	11	2.20	
Denis Pederson	43	4	6	10	2	39	Jan Lasak	3	0	1	0	3.33	
Mark Eaton	50	2	7	9	1	22	Brian Finley	1	0	0	0	3.83	
Cale Hulse	80	2	6	8	-11	121	Wade Flaherty	1	0	1	0	4.71	

NEW JERSEY DEVILS

	GP	G	A	PTS	+/-	PIM		GP	G	A	PTS	+/-	PIM
Patrik Elias	81	28	29	57	17	22	Ken Daneyko	69	2	7	9	6	33
Jamie Langenbrunner	78	22	33	55	17	65	Christian Berglund	38	4	5	9	3	20
Scott Gomez	80	13	42	55	17	48	Michael Rupp	26	5	3	8	0	21
Jeff Friesen	81	23	28	51	23	26	Tommy Albelin	37	1	6	7	10	6
Joe Nieuwendyk	80	17	28	45	10	56	Stephen Guolla	12	2	0	2	1	2
John Madden	80	19	22	41	13	26	Mike Danton	17	2	0	2	0	35
Brian Rafalski	79	3	37	40	18	14	Craig Darby	3	0	1	1	-1	0
Scott Niedermayer	81	11	28	39	23	62	Raymond Giroux	11	0	1	1	-2	6
Grant Marshall	76	9	23	32	-11	78							
Brian Gionta	58	12	13	25	5	23							
Scott Stevens	81	4	16	20	18	41							
Turner Stevenson	77	7	13	20	7	115							
Sergei Brylin	52	11	8	19	-2	16							
Pascal Rheaume	77	8	10	18	-5	32							
Jay Pandolfo	68	6	11	17	12	23							
Richard Smehlik	55	2	11	13	-5	16							
Oleg Tverdovsky	50	5	8	13	2	22							
Colin White	72	5	8	13	19	98	**GOALIES**	GP	W	L	T	GAA	
Jim McKenzie	76	4	8	12	3	88	Corey Schwab	11	5	3	1	1.47	
Jiri Bicek	44	5	6	11	7	25	Martin Brodeur	73	41	23	9	2.02	

NEW YORK ISLANDERS

	GP	G	A	PTS	+/-	PIM
Alexei Yashin	81	26	39	65	-12	32
Jason Blake	81	25	30	55	16	58
Mark Parrish	81	23	25	48	-11	28
Dave Scatchard	81	27	18	45	9	108
Michael Peca	66	13	29	42	-4	43
Shawn Bates	74	13	29	42	-9	52
Roman Hamrlik	73	9	32	41	21	87
Adrian Aucoin	73	8	27	35	-5	70
Janne Niinimaa	76	5	29	34	-9	80
Arron Asham	78	15	19	34	1	57
Jason Wiemer	81	9	19	28	5	116
Kenny Jonsson	71	8	18	26	-8	24
Oleg Kvasha	69	12	14	26	4	44
Mattias Weinhandl	47	6	17	23	-2	10
Randy Robitaille	51	6	14	20	5	10
Mattias Timander	80	3	13	16	-2	24
Radek Martinek	66	2	11	13	15	26
Justin Papineau	16	3	3	6	0	4
Eric Cairns	60	1	4	5	-7	124
Raffi Torres	17	0	5	5	0	10

	GP	G	A	PTS	+/-	PIM
Sven Butenschon	37	0	4	4	-6	26
Justin Mapletoft	11	2	2	4	-1	2
Trent Hunter	8	0	4	4	5	4
Eric Manlow	8	2	1	3	2	4
Steve Webb	49	1	0	1	-5	75
Brandon Smith	3	0	0	0	-2	0
Tomi Pettinen	2	0	0	0	1	0
Eric Godard	19	0	0	0	-3	48
Alain Nasreddine	3	0	0	0	0	2
Ray Schultz	4	0	0	0	-1	28

GOALIES	GP	W	L	T	GAA
Garth Snow	43	16	17	5	2.31
Rick DiPietro	10	2	5	2	2.97

NEW YORK RANGERS

	GP	G	A	PTS	+/-	PIM
Alexei Kovalev	78	37	40	77	-9	70
Anson Carter	79	26	34	60	-11	26
Petr Nedved	78	27	31	58	-4	64
Eric Lindros	81	19	34	53	5	141
Tom Poti	80	11	37	48	-6	60
Mark Messier	78	18	22	40	-2	30
Matthew Barnaby	79	14	22	36	9	142
Bobby Holik	64	16	19	35	-1	50
Pavel Bure	39	19	11	30	4	16
Brian Leetch	51	12	18	30	-3	20
Jamie Lundmark	55	8	11	19	-3	16
Vladimir Malahhov	71	3	14	17	-7	52
Boris Mironov	56	6	10	16	2	56
Sandy McCarthy	82	6	9	15	-4	81
Ronald Petrovicky	66	5	9	14	-12	77
Darius Kasparaitis	80	3	11	14	5	85
Dale Purinton	58	3	9	12	-2	161
Dan Lacouture	68	3	6	9	-4	72
Ales Pisa	51	1	3	4	12	24
Ted Donato	49	2	1	3	-1	6

	GP	G	A	PTS	+/-	PIM
John Tripp	9	1	2	3	1	2
Sylvain Lefebvre	35	0	2	2	-7	10
Dave Karpa	19	0	2	2	-1	14
Dixon Ward	8	0	0	0	-2	2
Roman Lyashenko	2	0	0	0	-2	0
Billy Tibbetts	11	0	0	0	-2	12
Mike Wilson	1	0	0	0	1	0

GOALIES	GP	W	L	T	GAA
Mike Dunham	58	21	26	7	2.50
Mike Richter	13	5	6	1	2.94
Johan Holmqvist	1	0	1	0	3.08
Dan Blackburn	32	8	16	4	3.17

HOCKEY

OTTAWA SENATORS

	GP	G	A	PTS	+/-	PIM
Marian Hossa	80	45	35	80	8	34
Daniel Alfredsson	78	27	51	78	15	42
Todd White	80	25	35	60	19	28
Martin Havlat	67	24	35	59	20	30
Radek Bonk	70	22	32	54	6	36
Bryan Smolinski	68	21	25	46	0	20
Wade Redden	76	10	35	45	23	70
Zdeno Chara	74	9	30	39	29	116
Mike Fisher	74	18	20	38	13	54
Magnus Arvedson	80	16	21	37	13	48
Shaun Van Allen	78	12	20	32	17	66
Karel Rachunek	58	4	25	29	23	30
Peter Schaefer	75	6	17	23	11	32
Jason Spezza	33	7	14	21	-3	8
Vaclav Varada	55	9	10	19	1	31
Chris Phillips	78	3	16	19	7	71
Petr Schastlivy	33	9	10	19	3	4
Anton Volchenkov	57	3	13	16	-4	40
Jody Hull	70	3	8	11	-3	14
Chris Neil	68	6	4	10	8	147

	GP	G	A	PTS	+/-	PIM
Shane Hnidy	67	0	8	8	-1	130
Curtis Leschyshyn	54	1	6	7	11	18
Brian Pothier	14	2	4	6	11	6
Brad Smyth	12	3	1	4	-2	15
Josh Langfeld	12	0	1	1	2	4
Toni Dahlman	12	1	0	1	-1	0
Rob Ray	46	0	0	0	-5	96
Joey Tetarenko	4	0	0	0	-1	9
Dennis Bonvie	12	0	0	0	-1	29

GOALIES	GP	W	L	T	GAA
Ray Emery	3	1	0	0	1.41
Patrick Lalime	67	39	20	7	2.16
Martin Prusek	18	12	2	1	2.37

PHILADELPHIA FLYERS

	GP	G	A	PTS	+/-	PIM
Jeremy Roenick	79	27	32	59	20	75
Mark Recchi	79	20	32	52	0	35
Tony Amonte	72	20	31	51	0	28
Keith Primeau	80	19	27	46	4	93
Michal Handzus	82	23	21	44	13	46
Kim Johnsson	82	10	29	39	11	38
Eric Desjardins	79	8	24	32	30	35
Sami Kapanen	71	10	21	31	-18	18
John LeClair	35	18	10	28	10	16
Simon Gagne	46	9	18	27	20	16
Marty Murray	76	11	15	26	-1	13
Donald Brashear	80	8	17	25	5	161
Justin Williams	41	8	16	24	15	22
Eric Weinrich	81	2	18	20	16	40
Radovan Somik	60	8	10	18	9	10
Claude Lapointe	80	8	8	16	2	36
Marcus Ragnarsson	68	3	13	16	7	62
Dmitry Yushkevich	83	3	11	14	-9	46
Dennis Seidenberg	58	4	9	13	8	20
Eric Chouinard	28	4	4	8	2	8

	GP	G	A	PTS	+/-	PIM
Chris Therien	67	1	6	7	10	36
Joe Sacco	34	1	5	6	0	20
Tomi Kallio	24	2	4	6	-10	14
Todd Fedoruk	63	1	5	6	1	105
Jamie Wright	23	2	2	4	0	16
Andre Savage	16	2	1	3	2	4
Jim Vandermeer	24	2	1	3	9	27
Mark Greig	5	0	1	1	1	2
Ian MacNeil	2	0	0	0	1	0
Mike Siklenka	1	0	0	0	0	0

GOALIES	GP	W	L	T	GAA
Roman Cechmanek	58	33	15	10	1.83
Robert Esche	30	12	9	3	2.20

PHOENIX COYOTES

	GP	G	A	PTS	+/-	PIM
Mike Johnson	82	23	40	63	9	47
Shane Doan	82	21	37	58	3	86
Ladislav Nagy	80	22	35	57	17	92
Daymond Langkow	82	20	32	52	20	56
Chris Gratton	80	15	30	45	-16	107
Jan Hrdina	61	14	29	43	4	42
Teppo Numminen	78	6	24	30	0	30
Branko Radivojevic	79	12	15	27	-2	63
Paul Mara	73	10	15	25	-7	78
Danny Markov	64	4	16	20	2	36
Deron Quint	51	7	10	17	-5	20
Brian Savage	43	6	10	16	-4	22
Landon Wilson	31	6	8	14	1	26
Kelly Buchberger	79	3	9	12	0	109
Paul Ranheim	68	3	8	11	-8	16
Todd Simpson	66	2	7	9	7	135
Brad Ference	75	2	7	9	-3	146
Radoslav Suchy	77	1	8	9	2	18
Ossi Vaananen	67	2	7	9	1	82
Scott Pellerin	43	1	4	5	-8	16

	GP	G	A	PTS	+/-	PIM
Jeff Taffe	20	3	1	4	-4	4
Drake Berehowsky	7	1	2	3	0	27
Andrei Nazarov	59	3	0	3	-9	135
Frank Banham	5	0	0	0	-1	2
Krystofer Kolanos	2	0	0	0	0	0
Martin Grenier	3	0	0	0	-1	0
Jason Jaspers	2	0	0	0	-1	0

GOALIES	GP	W	L	T	GAA
Sean Burke	22	12	6	2	2.12
Zac Bierk	16	4	9	1	2.17
Brian Boucher	45	15	20	8	3.02
Jean-Marc Pelletier	2	0	2	0	3.03

PITTSBURGH PENGUINS

	GP	G	A	PTS	+/-	PIM
Mario Lemieux	67	28	63	91	-25	43
Martin Straka	60	18	28	46	-18	12
Dick Tarnstrom	61	7	34	41	-11	50
Aleksey Morozov	27	9	16	25	-3	16
Mikael Samuelsson	80	10	14	24	-21	40
Ville Nieminen	75	9	12	21	-25	93
Rico Fata	63	7	12	19	-7	16
Ramzi Abid	33	10	8	18	-4	32
Mathias Johansson	58	5	10	15	-14	16
Joel Bouchard	34	5	8	13	E	14
Milan Kraft	31	7	5	12	-8	10
Tomas Surovy	26	4	7	11	E	10
Steve McKenna	79	9	1	10	-18	128
Michal Rozsival	53	4	6	10	-5	40
Kent Manderville	82	2	5	7	-22	46
Alexandre Daigle	33	4	3	7	-10	8
Eric Meloche	13	5	1	6	-2	4
Richard Lintner	29	4	2	6	-14	10
Michal Sivek	38	3	3	6	-5	14
Guillaume Lefebvre	26	2	4	6	2	4
Hans Jonsson	63	1	4	5	-23	36
Jamie Pushor	76	3	1	4	-28	76
Brian Holzinger	14	1	3	4	-5	8
Shawn Heins	47	1	2	3	-4	42
Dan Focht	22	0	3	3	-9	29

	GP	G	A	PTS	+/-	PIM
Vladimir Vujtek	5	0	1	1	-4	0
Kris Beech	12	0	1	1	-3	6
Tom Kostopoulos	8	0	1	1	-4	0
Josef Melichar	8	0	0	0	-2	2
Ross Lupaschuk	3	0	0	0	-3	4

GOALIES	GP	W	L	T	GAA
Sebastien Caron	24	7	14	2	2.64
Jean-Sebastien Aubin	21	6	13	0	3.13
Johan Hedberg	41	14	22	4	3.14

HOCKEY

SAN JOSE SHARKS

	GP	G	A	PTS	+/-	PIM
Teemu Selanne	82	28	36	64	-6	30
Vincent Damphousse	82	23	38	61	-13	66
Patrick Marleau	82	28	29	57	-10	33
Marco Sturm	82	28	20	48	9	16
Mike Ricci	75	11	23	34	-12	53
Mike Rathje	82	7	22	29	-19	48
Alyn McCauley	80	9	16	25	1	20
Scott Hannan	81	3	19	22	0	61
Scott Thornton	41	9	12	21	-7	41
Jim Fahey	43	1	19	20	-3	33
Todd Harvey	76	3	16	19	5	74
Adam Graves	82	9	9	18	-14	32
Wayne Primeau	77	6	12	18	-28	55
Jonathan Cheechoo	66	9	7	16	-5	39
Mark Smith	75	4	11	15	1	64
Brad Stuart	36	4	10	14	-6	46
Nicholas Dimitrakos	21	6	7	13	-7	8
Kyle McLaren	33	0	8	8	-10	30
Jeff Jillson	26	0	6	6	-7	9
Matt Bradley	46	2	3	5	-1	37

	GP	G	A	PTS	+/-	PIM
Rob Davison	15	1	2	3	4	22
Miroslav Zalesak	10	1	2	3	-2	0
Lynn Loyns	19	3	0	3	-4	19
Ryan Kraft	7	0	1	1	2	0
John Jakopin	12	0	0	0	0	11
Chad Wiseman	4	0	0	0	-2	4
Jesse Fibiger	16	0	0	0	-5	2

GOALIES	GP	W	L	T	GAA
Vesa Toskala	11	4	3	1	2.35
Evgeni Nabokov	55	19	28	8	2.71
Miikka Kiprusoff	22	5	14	0	3.25

ST. LOUIS BLUES

	GP	G	A	PTS	+/-	PIM
Pavol Demitra	78	36	57	93	0	32
Al MacInnis	80	16	52	68	22	61
Doug Weight	70	15	52	67	-6	52
Cory Stillman	79	24	43	67	12	56
Scott Mellanby	80	26	31	57	1	176
Keith Tkachuk	56	31	24	55	1	139
Eric Boguniecki	80	22	27	49	22	38
Petr Cajanek	51	9	29	38	16	20
Alexander Khavanov	81	8	25	33	-1	48
Dallas Drake	80	20	10	30	-7	66
Martin Rucinsky	61	16	14	30	-1	38
Valeri Bure	51	5	23	28	-13	10
Barret Jackman	82	3	16	19	23	190
Steve Martins	42	5	6	11	-5	28
Shjon Podein	68	4	6	10	7	28
Bryce Salvador	71	2	8	10	7	95
Tyson Nash	66	6	3	9	0	114
Christian Laflamme	47	0	9	9	1	45
Jamal Mayers	15	2	5	7	1	8
Ryan Johnson	75	2	5	7	-13	38

	GP	G	A	PTS	+/-	PIM
Steve Dubinsky	28	0	6	6	3	4
Reed Low	79	2	4	6	3	234
Tom Koivisto	22	2	4	6	1	10
Jeff Finley	64	1	3	4	-2	46
Chris Pronger	5	1	3	4	-2	10
Mike Van Ryn	20	0	3	3	3	8
Eric Nickulas	8	0	1	1	-2	6
Matt Walker	16	0	1	1	0	38
Peter Sejna	1	1	0	1	0	0
Daniel Corso	1	0	0	0	-1	0

GOALIES	GP	W	L	T	GAA
Cody Rudkowsky	1	1	0	0	0.00
Reinhard Divis	2	2	0	0	0.72
Curtis Sanford	8	5	1	0	1.96
Brent Johnson	38	16	13	5	2.47
Fred Brathwaite	30	12	9	4	2.75
Chris Osgood	46	21	17	6	2.95
Tom Barrasso	6	1	4	0	3.28

TAMPA BAY LIGHTNING

	GP	G	A	PTS	+/-	PIM
Vaclav Prospal	80	22	57	79	9	53
Vincent LeCavalier	80	33	45	78	0	39
Brad Richards	80	17	57	74	3	24
Martin St. Louis	82	33	37	70	10	32
Dan Boyle	77	13	40	53	9	44
Fredrik Modin	76	17	23	40	7	43
Dave Andreychuk	72	20	14	34	-12	34
Ruslan Fedotenko	76	19	13	32	-7	44
Pavel Kubina	75	3	19	22	-7	78
Ben Clymer	65	6	12	18	-2	57
Andre Roy	62	10	7	17	0	119
Brad Lukowich	70	1	14	15	4	46
Cory Sarich	82	5	9	14	-3	63
Tim Taylor	82	4	8	12	-13	38
Janne Laukkanen	19	2	6	8	-2	8
Nolan Pratt	67	1	7	8	-6	35
Alexander Svitov	63	4	4	8	-4	58
Marc Bergevin	70	2	5	7	-11	36
Sheldon Keefe	37	2	5	7	-1	24
Nikita Alexeev	37	4	2	6	-6	8

	GP	G	A	PTS	+/-	PIM
Stan Neckar	70	1	4	5	-6	43
Jassen Cullimore	28	1	3	4	3	31
Chris Dingman	51	2	1	3	-11	91
Jimmie Olvestad	37	0	3	3	-2	16
Darren Rumble	19	0	0	0	-2	6

GOALIES	GP	W	L	T	GAA
Nikolai Khabibulin	65	30	22	11	2.47
John Grahame	40	17	14	6	2.52
Kevin Hodson	7	0	3	1	2.54
Evgeny Konstantinov	1	0	0	0	3.00

TORONTO MAPLE LEAFS

	GP	G	A	PTS	+/-	PIM
Alexander Mogilny	73	33	46	79	4	12
Mats Sundin	75	37	35	72	1	58
Owen Nolan	75	29	25	54	-3	107
Tomas Kaberle	82	11	36	47	20	30
Robert Svehla	82	7	38	45	13	46
Nik Antropov	72	16	29	45	11	124
Robert Reichel	81	12	30	42	7	26
Darcy Tucker	77	10	26	36	-7	119
Mikael Renberg	67	14	21	35	5	36
Jonas Hoglund	79	13	19	32	2	12
Doug Gilmour	62	11	19	30	-6	36
Tie Domi	79	15	14	29	-1	171
Phil Housley	58	6	23	29	6	26
Travis Green	75	12	12	24	2	67
Bryan McCabe	75	6	18	24	9	135
Tom Fitzgerald	66	4	13	17	10	57
Jyrki Lumme	73	6	11	17	10	46
Shayne Corson	46	7	8	15	-5	49
Glen Wesley	70	1	10	11	-2	44
Aki Berg	78	4	7	11	3	28

	GP	G	A	PTS	+/-	PIM
Paul Healey	44	3	7	10	8	16
Wade Belak	55	3	6	9	-2	196
Gary Roberts	14	5	3	8	-2	10
Karel Pilar	17	3	4	7	-7	12
Alexei Ponikarovsky	13	0	3	3	4	11
Richard Jackman	42	0	2	2	-10	41
Aaron Gavey	5	0	1	1	1	0
Josh Holden	5	1	0	1	-2	2
Carlo Colaiacovo	2	0	1	1	0	0
Matthew Stajan	1	1	0	1	1	0

GOALIES	GP	W	L	T	GAA
Ed Belfour	62	37	20	5	2.26
Mikael Telqvist	3	1	1	0	2.79
Trevor Kidd	19	6	10	2	3.10

VANCOUVER CANUCKS

	GP	G	A	PTS	+/-	PIM
Markus Naslund	82	48	56	104	6	52
Todd Bertuzzi	82	46	51	97	2	144
Brendan Morrison	82	25	46	71	18	36
Ed Jovanovski	67	6	40	46	19	113
Matt Cooke	82	15	27	42	21	82
Trevor Linden	71	19	22	41	-1	30
Henrik Sedin	78	8	31	39	9	38
Brent Sopel	81	7	30	37	-15	23
Daniel Sedin	79	14	17	31	8	34
Sami Salo	79	9	21	30	9	10
Trent Klatt	82	16	13	29	10	8
Mattias Ohlund	59	2	27	29	1	42
Trevor Letowski	78	11	14	25	8	36
Marek Malik	79	7	13	20	20	68
Artem Chubarov	62	7	13	20	4	6
Mats Lindgren	54	5	9	14	-2	18
Bryan Allen	48	5	3	8	8	73
Brad May	23	3	4	7	4	42
Murray Baron	78	2	4	6	13	62
Brandon Reid	7	2	3	5	4	0

	GP	G	A	PTS	+/-	PIM
Jarkko Ruutu	36	2	2	4	-7	66
Nolan Baumgartner	8	1	2	3	4	4
Jason King	8	0	2	2	0	0
Darren Langdon	54	0	1	1	-2	159
Fedor Fedorov	7	0	1	1	0	4
Pat Kavanagh	3	1	0	1	2	2
Bryan Helmer	2	0	0	0	1	0
Zenith Komarniski	1	0	0	0	0	2
Mikko Jokela	1	0	0	0	0	0

GOALIES	GP	W	L	T	GAA
Alexander Auld	7	3	3	0	1.57
Dan Cloutier	57	33	16	7	2.42
Peter Skudra	23	9	5	6	2.72
Tyler Moss	1	0	0	0	2.73

WASHINGTON CAPITALS

	GP	G	A	PTS	+/-	PIM
Jaromir Jagr	75	36	41	77	5	38
Robert Lang	82	22	47	69	12	22
Sergei Gonchar	82	18	49	67	13	52
Michael Nylander	80	17	43	60	3	40
Peter Bondra	76	30	26	56	-3	52
Kip Miller	72	12	38	50	-1	18
Sergei Berezin	75	23	17	40	7	12
Dainius Zubrus	63	13	22	35	15	43
Jeff Halpern	82	13	21	34	6	88
Mike Grier	82	15	17	32	-14	36
Steve Konowalchuk	77	15	15	30	3	71
Ivan Ciernik	47	8	10	18	6	24
Ken Klee	70	1	16	17	22	89
Calle Johansson	82	3	12	15	9	22
Brendan Witt	69	2	9	11	12	106
Brian Sutherby	72	2	9	11	7	93
Jason Doig	55	3	5	8	-3	108
Glen Metropolit	23	2	3	5	4	6
Joel Kwiatkowski	54	0	5	5	3	18
Josh Green	45	1	4	5	-3	21

	GP	G	A	PTS	+/-	PIM
Andreas Salomonsson	32	1	4	5	-1	14
Rick Berry	43	2	1	3	-3	87
Trent Whitfield	14	1	1	2	1	6
Steve Eminger	17	0	2	2	-3	24
Josef Boumedienne	6	1	0	1	-1	0
Stephen Peat	27	1	0	1	-3	57
Jean-Francois Fortin	33	0	1	1	-3	22
Sylvain Cote	1	0	0	0	0	4
Alex Henry	41	0	0	0	-5	80
Michael Farrell	4	0	0	0	1	2

GOALIES	GP	W	L	T	GAA
Olaf Kolzig	66	33	25	6	2.40
Sebastien Charpentier	17	5	7	1	2.79
Craig Billington	5	1	3	1	4.70

Legends

Bobby Orr, defenseman, b. March 20, 1948, Parry Sound, Ontario, Canada. Orr revolutionized the position of defenseman. Before he entered the NHL, in 1966-67, defensemen played a small role in their team's offense. Orr used his blinding speed and sharp puck control to fly past opponents and lead his team's attack. He topped the league in assists five times and in points twice. Orr played the majority of his career with the Boston Bruins, where he won two Stanley Cups (1969-70, 1971-72). He hung up his skates at age 31 in 1979. He was inducted into the Hockey Hall of Fame that same year.

Wayne Gretzky, center, b. January 26, 1961, Brantford, Ontario, Canada. Gretzky is considered the best NHL player to lace up a pair of skates. In his 20-season career (1979-99), "The Great One" won four Stanley Cups and became the game's all-time leading scorer (2,857 points). He holds or shares more than 60 major records, including most goals in a season (92 in 1981-82) and the consecutive scoring streak (51 games with at least one point). Gretzky retired in 1999 and was inducted into the Hockey Hall of Fame later that year. His number 99 is retired by every NHL team.

Terry Sawchuk, goaltender, b. December 28, 1929, Winnipeg, Manitoba, Canada; d. May 31, 1970. Sawchuk is the NHL record-holder for career shutouts (103) and is one of only three goalies to play in more than 900 games (971). His innovative style of crouching low in the goal and attacking the puck changed goaltending. Sawchuck broke into the NHL in 1949-50 with the Detroit Red Wings. He also played for the Boston Bruins, Toronto Maple Leafs, and the Los Angeles Kings before spending his final season (1969-70) with the New York Rangers. Tragically, Sawchuk died a little more than a month after the 1970 playoffs. He won the Stanley Cup four times and the Vezina Trophy as the league's best goalie four times. He was inducted into the Hockey Hall of Fame in 1971.

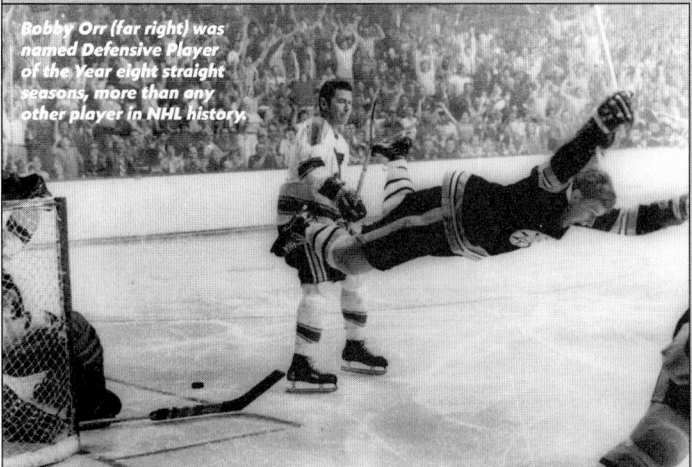

Bobby Orr (far right) was named Defensive Player of the Year eight straight seasons, more than any other player in NHL history.

RAY LUSSIER/BOSTON HERALD AMERICAN/AP

Did You Know?

Before the 1917-18 season, goaltenders received a penalty for dropping to the ice to make a save.

Trivia Challenge

The NHL has 30 teams today. But from 1942 to 1967, the league was made up of six teams. Can you name the "Original Six"?

Boston Bruins, Chicago Blackhawks, Detroit Red Wings, Montreal Canadiens, New York Rangers, Toronto Maple Leafs

The Stanley Cup

Awarded annually to the team that wins the NHL's best-of-seven final-round playoffs. The Stanley Cup is the oldest trophy competed for by professional athletes in North America. It was donated in 1893 by Frederick Arthur, Lord Stanley of Preston.

Season	Champion	Finalist	Games Played in Final
2002–03	New Jersey Devils	Anaheim Mighty Ducks	7
2001–02	Detroit Red Wings	Carolina Hurricanes	5
2000–01	Colorado Avalanche	New Jersey Devils	7
1999–00	New Jersey Devils	Dallas Stars	6
1998–99	Dallas Stars	Buffalo Sabres	6
1997–98	Detroit Red Wings	Washington Capitals	4
1996–97	Detroit Red Wings	Philadelphia Flyers	4
1995–96	Colorado Avalanche	Florida Panthers	4
1994–95	New Jersey Devils	Detroit Red Wings	4
1993–94	New York Rangers	Vancouver Canucks	7
1992–93	Montreal Canadiens	Los Angeles Kings	5
1991–92	Pittsburgh Penguins	Chicago Blackhawks	4
1990–91	Pittsburgh Penguins	Minnesota North Stars	6
1989–90	Edmonton Oilers	Boston Bruins	5
1988–89	Calgary Flames	Montreal Canadiens	6
1987–88	Edmonton Oilers	Boston Bruins	4
1986–87	Edmonton Oilers	Philadelphia Flyers	7
1985–86	Montreal Canadiens	Calgary Flames	5
1984–85	Edmonton Oilers	Philadelphia Flyers	5
1983–84	Edmonton Oilers	New York Islanders	5
1982–83	New York Islanders	Edmonton Oilers	4
1981–82	New York Islanders	Vancouver Canucks	4
1980–81	New York Islanders	Minnesota North Stars	5
1979–80	New York Islanders	Philadelphia Flyers	6
1978–79	Montreal Canadiens	New York Rangers	5
1977–78	Montreal Canadiens	Boston Bruins	6
1976–77	Montreal Canadiens	Boston Bruins	4
1975–76	Montreal Canadiens	Philadelphia Flyers	4
1974–75	Philadelphia Flyers	Buffalo Sabres	6
1973–74	Philadelphia Flyers	Boston Bruins	6
1972–73	Montreal Canadiens	Chicago Blackhawks	6
1971–72	Boston Bruins	New York Rangers	6
1970–71	Montreal Canadiens	Chicago Blackhawks	7
1969–70	Boston Bruins	St. Louis Blues	4
1968–69	Montreal Canadiens	St. Louis Blues	4
1967–68	Montreal Canadiens	St. Louis Blues	4
1966–67	Toronto Maple Leafs	Montreal Canadiens	6
1965–66	Montreal Canadiens	Detroit Red Wings	6
1964–65	Montreal Canadiens	Chicago Blackhawks	7
1963–64	Toronto Maple Leafs	Detroit Red Wings	7
1962–63	Toronto Maple Leafs	Detroit Red Wings	5
1961–62	Toronto Maple Leafs	Chicago Blackhawks	6
1960–61	Chicago Blackhawks	Detroit Red Wings	6
1959–60	Montreal Canadiens	Toronto Maple Leafs	4
1958–59	Montreal Canadiens	Toronto Maple Leafs	5
1957–58	Montreal Canadiens	Boston Bruins	6
1956–57	Montreal Canadiens	Boston Bruins	5
1955–56	Montreal Canadiens	Detroit Red Wings	5
1954–55	Detroit Red Wings	Montreal Canadiens	7
1953–54	Detroit Red Wings	Montreal Canadiens	7
1952–53	Montreal Canadiens	Boston Bruins	5
1951–52	Detroit Red Wings	Montreal Canadiens	4
1950–51	Toronto Maple Leafs	Montreal Canadiens	5
1949–50	Detroit Red Wings	New York Rangers	7
1948–49	Toronto Maple Leafs	Detroit Red Wings	4
1947–48	Toronto Maple Leafs	Detroit Red Wings	4
1946–47	Toronto Maple Leafs	Montreal Canadiens	6
1945–46	Montreal Canadiens	Boston Bruins	5
1944–45	Toronto Maple Leafs	Detroit Red Wings	7
1943–44	Montreal Canadiens	Chicago Blackhawks	4

The Stanley Cup (cont.)

Season	Champion	Finalist	Games Played in Final
1942 – 43	Detroit Red Wings	Boston Bruins	4
1941 – 42	Toronto Maple Leafs	Detroit Red Wings	7
1940 – 41	Boston Bruins	Detroit Red Wings	4
1939 – 40	New York Rangers	Toronto Maple Leafs	6
1938 – 39	Boston Bruins	Toronto Maple Leafs	5
1937 – 38	Chicago Blackhawks	Toronto Maple Leafs	4
1936 – 37	Detroit Red Wings	New York Rangers	5
1935 – 36	Detroit Red Wings	Toronto Maple Leafs	4
1934 – 35	Montreal Maroons	Toronto Maple Leafs	3
1933 – 34	Chicago Blackhawks	Detroit Red Wings	4
1932 – 33	New York Rangers	Toronto Maple Leafs	4
1931 – 32	Toronto Maple Leafs	New York Rangers	3
1930 – 31	Montreal Canadiens	Chicago Blackhawks	5
1929 – 30	Montreal Canadiens	Boston Bruins	2
1928 – 29	Boston Bruins	New York Rangers	2
1927 – 28	New York Rangers	Montreal Maroons	5
1926 – 27	Ottawa Senators	Boston Bruins	4
1925 – 26	Montreal Maroons	Victoria Cougars	4
1924 – 25	Victoria Cougars	Montreal Canadiens	4
1923 – 24	Montreal Canadiens	Vancouver Maroons, Calgary Tigers	2, 2
1922 – 23	Ottawa Senators	Edmonton Eskimos, Vancouver Maroons	2, 4
1921 – 22	Toronto St. Pats	Vancouver Millionaires	5
1920 – 21	Ottawa Senators	Vancouver Millionaires	5
1919 – 20	Ottawa Senators	Seattle Metropolitans	5
1918 – 19	No decision*	No decision*	5
1917 – 18	Toronto Arenas	Vancouver Millionaires	5

*In 1918-19, the Montreal Canadiens traveled to meet Seattle. After five games had been played — the teams were tied at two wins and one tie — the series was called off by the local Department of Health because of the influenza epidemic and the death of Canadien defenseman Joe Hall from influenza.

Today's Stars

In 2002-03, Dany Heatley became the fifth player to score four goals in the NHL All-Star Game..

ROBERT BECK/SPORTS ILLUSTRATED

Dany Heatley, right wing, b. January 21, 1981, Freiburg, Germany. In 2002-03, the Atlanta Thrashers' smart and creative playmaker became the youngest player (age 22) to score four goals in the NHL All-Star Game. Heatley finished the regular season sixth in the NHL in goals (41) and ninth in points (89). He was the NHL Rookie of the Year in 2001-02, leading all first-year players in assists (41) and points (67).

Peter Forsberg, center, b. July 20, 1973, Ornskoldsvik, Sweden. Forsberg is often called hockey's best all-around player. He led the NHL in assists (77) and points (106) in 2002-03. In 2001-02, Forsberg missed the entire regular season with a foot injury but returned to the Colorado Avalanche for the playoffs, where he led all players in assists (18) and points (27) and helped the team reach the Western Conference finals. The Swedish star has won two Stanley Cup championships with the Avs (1995-96, 2000-01) and was the NHL's Rookie of the Year in 1994-95.

Martin Brodeur, goaltender, b. May 6, 1972, Montreal, Quebec, Canada. Brodeur's 41 wins in 2002-03 was tops in the NHL and gave him a league record: most seasons in a career with 40 or more wins (4). He also finished Number 1 in shutouts (9). Brodeur is known for being cool and consistent, especially in big games. In 1994-95, he helped the New Jersey Devils win their first Stanley Cup championship by leading all playoff goalies with a 1.67 goals-against average (GAA). He won his second Cup in 1999-00 and again posted the lowest GAA (1.61). Brodeur was the NHL Rookie of the Year in 1993-94.

HOCKEY

The Stanley Cup (cont.)

Season	Champion	Finalist	Games Played in Final
1916–17	Seattle Metropolitans	—	—
1915–16	Montreal Canadiens	—	—
1914–15	Vancouver Millionaires	—	—
1913–14	Toronto Blueshirts	—	—
1912–13	Quebec Bulldogs	—	—
1911–12	Quebec Bulldogs	—	—
1910–11	Ottawa Senators	—	—
1909–10	Montreal Wanderers	—	—
1908–09	Ottawa Senators	—	—
1907–08	Montreal Wanderers	—	—
1906–07	Montreal Wanderers (Mar.)	—	—
1906–07	Kenora Thistles (Jan.)	—	—
1905–06	Montreal Wanderers (Mar.)	—	—
1905–06	Ottawa Silver Seven (Feb.)	—	—
1904–05	Ottawa Silver Seven	—	—
1903–04	Ottawa Silver Seven	—	—
1902–03	Ottawa Silver Seven (Mar.)	—	—
1902–03	Montreal A.A.A. (Feb.)	—	—
1901–02	Montreal A.A.A. (Mar.)	—	—
1901–02	Winnipeg Victorias (Jan.)	—	—
1900–01	Winnipeg Victorias	—	—
1899–1900	Montreal Shamrocks	—	—
1898–99	Montreal Shamrocks (Mar.)	—	—
1898–99	Montreal Victorias (Feb.)	—	—
1897–98	Montreal Victorias	—	—
1896–97	Montreal Victorias	—	—
1895–96	Montreal Victorias (Dec.)	—	—
1895–96	Winnipeg Victorias (Feb.)	—	—
1894–95	Montreal Victorias	—	—
1893–94	Montreal A.A.A.	—	—
1892–93	Montreal A.A.A.	—	—

> ▷ **Random Fact:** Center Mario Lemieux of the Pittsburgh Penguins is the only player to score a goal in all five possible ways (power-play, short-handed, even-strength, penalty shot, empty-net) in a single game. "Super Mario" accomplished the feat on December 31, 1988, against the New Jersey Devils.

Conn Smythe Trophy (past 20 years)

Awarded to the Most Valuable Player of the Stanley Cup playoffs, as selected by the Professional Hockey Writers Association. The trophy is named after the former coach, general manager, president, and owner of the Toronto Maple Leafs.

Season	Player	Season	Player
2003	Jean-Sebastien Giguere, Anaheim Mighty Ducks	1993	Patrick Roy, Montreal Canadiens
2002	Nicklas Lidstrom, Detroit Red Wings	1992	Mario Lemieux, Pittsburgh Penguins
2001	Patrick Roy, Colorado Avalanche	1991	Mario Lemieux, Pittsburgh Penguins
2000	Scott Stevens, New Jersey Devils	1990	Bill Ranford, Edmonton Oilers
1999	Joe Nieuwendyk, Dallas Stars	1989	Al MacInnis, Calgary Flames
1998	Steve Yzerman, Detroit Red Wings	1988	Wayne Gretzky, Edmonton Oilers
1997	Mike Vernon, Detroit Red Wings	1987	Ron Hextall, Philadelphia Flyers
1996	Joe Sakic, Colorado Avalanche	1986	Patrick Roy, Montreal Canadiens
1995	Claude Lemieux, New Jersey Devils	1985	Wayne Gretzky, Edmonton Oilers
1994	Brian Leetch, New York Rangers	1984	Mark Messier, Edmonton Oilers

Hart Memorial Trophy (past 20 years)

Awarded annually "to the player adjudged to be the most valuable to his team." The original trophy was donated by Dr. David A. Hart, father of Cecil Hart, former manager-coach of the Montreal Canadiens.

Year	Winner	Year	Winner
2003	Peter Forsberg, Colorado Avalanche	2001	Joe Sakic, Colorado Avalanche
2002	Jose Theodore, Montreal Canadiens	2000	Chris Pronger, St. Louis Blues

Hart Memorial Trophy (cont.)

Year	Winner	Year	Winner
1999	Jaromir Jagr, Pittsburgh Penguins	1991	Brett Hull, St. Louis Blues
1998	Dominik Hasek, Buffalo Sabres	1990	Mark Messier, Edmonton Oilers
1997	Dominik Hasek, Buffalo Sabres	1989	Wayne Gretzky, Los Angeles Kings
1996	Mario Lemieux, Pittsburgh Penguins	1988	Mario Lemieux, Pittsburgh Penguins
1995	Eric Lindros, Philadelphia Flyers	1987	Wayne Gretzky, Edmonton Oilers
1994	Sergei Fedorov, Detroit Red Wings	1986	Wayne Gretzky, Edmonton Oilers
1993	Mario Lemieux, Pittsburgh Penguins	1985	Wayne Gretzky, Edmonton Oilers
1992	Mark Messier, New York Rangers	1984	Wayne Gretzky, Edmonton Oilers

Art Ross Trophy (past 20 years)

Awarded annually "to the player who leads the league in scoring points at the end of the regular season." The trophy was presented to the NHL in 1947 by Arthur Howie Ross, former manager-coach of the Boston Bruins. The tie-breakers, in order, are as follows: (1) player with most goals, (2) player with fewer games played, (3) player scoring first goal of the season.

Year	Winner	Points	Year	Winner	Points
2003	Peter Forsberg, Colorado Avalanche	106	1993	Mario Lemieux, Pittsburgh Penguins	160
2002	Jarome Iginla, Calgary Flames	96	1992	Mario Lemieux, Pittsburgh Penguins	131
2001	Jaromir Jagr, Pittsburgh Penguins	121	1991	Wayne Gretzky, Los Angeles Kings	163
2000	Jaromir Jagr, Pittsburgh Penguins	96	1990	Wayne Gretzky, Los Angeles Kings	142
1999	Jaromir Jagr, Pittsburgh Penguins	127	1989	Mario Lemieux, Pittsburgh Penguins	199
1998	Jaromir Jagr, Pittsburgh Penguins	102	1988	Mario Lemieux, Pittsburgh Penguins	168
1997	Mario Lemieux, Pittsburgh Penguins	122	1987	Wayne Gretzky, Edmonton Oilers	183
1996	Mario Lemieux, Pittsburgh Penguins	161	1986	Wayne Gretzky, Edmonton Oilers	215
1995	Jaromir Jagr, Pittsburgh Penguins	70	1985	Wayne Gretzky, Edmonton Oilers	208
1994	Wayne Gretzky, Los Angeles Kings	130	1984	Wayne Gretzky, Edmonton Oilers	205

Lady Byng Memorial Trophy (past 20 years)

Awarded annually "to the player adjudged to have exhibited the best type of sportsmanship and gentlemanly conduct combined with a high standard of playing ability." Lady Byng, who first presented the trophy in 1925, was the wife of Canada's Governor-General. She donated a second trophy in 1936 after the first was given permanently to Frank Boucher of the New York Rangers, who won it seven times in eight seasons.

Year	Winner	Year	Winner
2003	Alexander Mogilny, Toronto Maple Leafs	1993	Pierre Turgeon, New York Islanders
2002	Ron Francis, Carolina Hurricanes	1992	Wayne Gretzky, Los Angeles Kings
2001	Joe Sakic, Colorado Avalanche	1991	Wayne Gretzky, Los Angeles Kings
2000	Pavol Demitra, St. Louis Blues	1990	Brett Hull, St. Louis Blues
1999	Wayne Gretzky, New York Rangers	1989	Joe Mullen, Calgary Flames
1998	Ron Francis, Pittsburgh Penguins	1988	Mats Naslund, Montreal Canadiens
1997	Paul Kariya, Anaheim Mighty Ducks	1987	Joe Mullen, Calgary Flames
1996	Paul Kariya, Anaheim Mighty Ducks	1986	Mike Bossy, New York Islanders
1995	Ron Francis, Pittsburgh Penguins	1985	Jari Kurri, Edmonton Oilers
1994	Wayne Gretzky, Los Angeles Kings	1984	Mike Bossy, New York Islanders

James Norris Memorial Trophy (past 20 years)

Awarded annually "to the defense player who demonstrates throughout the season the greatest all-around ability in the position." James Norris was the former owner-president of the Detroit Red Wings.

Year	Winner	Year	Winner
2003	Nicklas Lidstrom, Detroit Red Wings	1993	Chris Chelios, Chicago Blackhawks
2002	Nicklas Lidstrom, Detroit Red Wings	1992	Brian Leetch, New York Rangers
2001	Nicklas Lidstrom, Detroit Red Wings	1991	Ray Bourque, Boston Bruins
2000	Chris Pronger, St. Louis Blues	1990	Ray Bourque, Boston Bruins
1999	Al MacInnis, St. Louis Blues	1989	Chris Chelios, Montreal Canadiens
1998	Rob Blake, Los Angeles Kings	1988	Ray Bourque, Boston Bruins
1997	Brian Leetch, New York Rangers	1987	Ray Bourque, Boston Bruins
1996	Chris Chelios, Chicago Blackhawks	1986	Paul Coffey, Edmonton Oilers
1995	Paul Coffey, Detroit Red Wings	1985	Paul Coffey, Edmonton Oilers
1994	Ray Bourque, Boston Bruins	1984	Rod Langway, Washington Capitals

Calder Memorial Trophy (past 20 years)

Awarded annually "to the player selected as the most proficient in his first year of competition in the National Hockey League." Frank Calder was a former NHL president. Sergei Makarov, who won the award in 1989–90, was the oldest recipient of the trophy, at 31. Players are no longer eligible for the award if they are 26 or older as of September 15 of the season in question.

Year	Winner	Year	Winner
2003	Barret Jackman, St. Louis Blues	1988	Joe Nieuwendyk, Calgary Flames
2002	Dany Heatley, Atlanta Thrashers	1987	Luc Robitaille, Los Angeles Kings
2001	Evgeni Nabokov, San Jose Sharks	1986	Gary Suter, Calgary Flames
2000	Scott Gomez, New Jersey Devils	1985	Mario Lemieux, Pittsburgh Penguins
1999	Chris Drury, Colorado Avalanche	1984	Tom Barrasso, Buffalo Sabres
1998	Sergei Samsonov, Boston Bruins		
1997	Bryan Berard, New York Islanders		
1996	Daniel Alfredsson, Ottawa Senators		
1995	Peter Forsberg, Quebec Nordiques		
1994	Martin Brodeur, New Jersey Devils		
1993	Teemu Selanne, Winnipeg Jets		
1992	Pavel Bure, Vancouver Canucks		
1991	Ed Belfour, Chicago Blackhawks		
1990	Sergei Makarov, Calgary Flames		
1989	Brian Leetch, New York Rangers		

> ▷**Random Fact**: Gordie Howe, the NHL's record holder for most career games (1,767), played in five decades. The 21-time All-Star spent 1946-71 with the Detroit Red Wings and skated the 1979-80 season with the Hartford Whalers.

Vezina Trophy (past 20 years)

Awarded annually "to the goalkeeper adjudged to be the best at his position." The trophy is named after Georges Vezina, an outstanding goalie for the Montreal Canadiens who collapsed during a game on November 28, 1925, and died four months later of tuberculosis. The general managers of the NHL teams vote on the award.

Year	Winner	Year	Winner
2003	Martin Brodeur, New Jersey Devils	1993	Ed Belfour, Chicago Blackhawks
2002	Jose Theodore, Montreal Canadiens	1992	Patrick Roy, Montreal Canadiens
2001	Dominik Hasek, Buffalo Sabres	1991	Ed Belfour, Chicago Blackhawks
2000	Olaf Kolzig, Washington Capitals	1990	Patrick Roy, Montreal Canadiens
1999	Dominik Hasek, Buffalo Sabres	1989	Patrick Roy, Montreal Canadiens
1998	Dominik Hasek, Buffalo Sabres	1988	Grant Fuhr, Edmonton Oilers
1997	Dominik Hasek, Buffalo Sabres	1987	Ron Hextall, Philadelphia Flyers
1996	Jim Carey, Washington Capitals	1986	John Vanbiesbrouck, New York Rangers
1995	Dominik Hasek, Buffalo Sabres	1985	Pelle Lindbergh, Philadelphia Flyers
1994	Dominik Hasek, Buffalo Sabres	1984	Tom Barrasso, Buffalo Sabres

Selke Trophy (past 20 years)

Awarded annually "to the forward who best excels in the defensive aspects of the game." The trophy is named after Frank J. Selke, the architect of the Montreal Canadiens dynasty that won five consecutive Stanley Cups in the late 1950s. The winner is selected by a vote of the Professional Hockey Writers Association.

Year	Winner	Year	Winner
2003	Jere Lehtinen, Dallas Stars	1990	Rick Meagher, St. Louis Blues
2002	Michael Peca, New York Islanders	1989	Guy Carbonneau, Montreal Canadiens
2001	John Madden, New Jersey Devils	1988	Guy Carbonneau, Montreal Canadiens
2000	Steve Yzerman, Detroit Red Wings	1987	Dave Poulin, Philadelphia Flyers
1999	Jere Lehtinen, Dallas Stars	1986	Troy Murray, Chicago Blackhawks
1998	Jere Lehtinen, Dallas Stars	1985	Craig Ramsay, Buffalo Sabres
1997	Michael Peca, Buffalo Sabres	1984	Doug Jarvis, Washington Capitals
1996	Sergei Fedorov, Detroit Red Wings		
1995	Ron Francis, Pittsburgh Penguins		
1994	Sergei Fedorov, Detroit Red Wings		
1993	Doug Gilmour, Toronto Maple Leafs		
1992	Guy Carbonneau, Montreal Canadiens		
1991	Dirk Graham, Chicago Blackhawks		

Trivia Challenge

Three players won every NHL scoring title from 1980-81 through 2000-01. Who were they?

Wayne Gretzky (1981-87; 1990-91; 1994), Mario Lemieux (1988-89; 1992-93; 1996-97), Jaromir Jagr (1995; 1998-2001).

Career Records

All-time Point Leaders

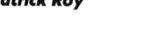

Wayne Gretzky

Player	YRS	GP	G	A	PTS	PTS/GAME
Wayne Gretzky, Edm, LA, StL, NYR	20	1,487	894	1,963	2,857	1.921
Gordie Howe, Det, Hart	26	1,767	801	1,049	1,850	1.047
*Mark Messier, Edm, NYR, Van	24	1,680	676	1,168	1,844	1.098
Marcel Dionne, Det, LA, NYR	18	1,348	731	1,040	1,771	1.314
*Ron Francis, Hart, Pitt, Car	22	1,651	536	1,222	1,758	1.065

All-time Goal-Scoring Leaders

Player	YRS	GP	G	G/GAME
Wayne Gretzky, Edm, LA, StL, NYR	20	1,487	894	.601
Gordie Howe, Det, Hart	26	1,767	801	.453
Marcel Dionne, Det, LA, NYR	18	1,348	731	.542
Phil Esposito, Chi, Bos, NYR	18	1,282	717	.559
*Brett Hull, Cal, StL, Dall, Det	18	1,183	716	.605

All-time Assist Leaders

Player	YRS	GP	A	A/GAME
Wayne Gretzky, Edm, LA, StL, NYR	20	1,487	1,963	1.320
*Ron Francis, Hart, Pitt, Car	22	1,651	1,222	.740
Ray Bourque, Bos, Col	22	1,612	1,169	.725
*Mark Messier, Edm, NYR, Van	24	1,680	1,168	.695
Paul Coffey, eight teams	21	1,409	1,135	.806

GOALTENDING

All-time Win Leaders

Patrick Roy

Goaltender	W	L	T
*Patrick Roy, Mtl, Col	551	315	131
Terry Sawchuk, five teams	447	330	172
Jacques Plante, five teams	435	247	145
Tony Esposito, Mtl, Chi	423	306	151
Glenn Hall, Det, Chi, StL	407	326	163

All-time Shutout Leaders

Goaltender	Team	YRS	GP	SO
Terry Sawchuk	Det, Bos, Tor, LA, NYR	21	971	103
George Hainsworth	Mtl, Tor	11	465	94
Glenn Hall	Det, Chi, StL	18	906	84
Jacques Plante	Mtl, NYR, StL, Tor, Bos	18	837	82
Tiny Thompson	Bos, Det	12	553	81
Alex Connell	Ott, Det, NYA, Mtl M	12	417	81

All-time Goals-Against Average Leaders (Pre-1950)

Goaltender	Team	YRS	GP	GA	GAA
George Hainsworth	Mtl, Tor	11	465	937	1.91
Alex Connell	Ott, Det, NYA, Mtl M	12	417	830	1.91
Chuck Gardiner	Chi	7	316	664	2.02
Lorne Chabot	NYR, Tor, Mtl, Chi, Mtl M, NYA	11	411	861	2.04
Tiny Thompson	Bos, Det	12	553	1,183	2.08

All-time Goals-Against Average Leaders (Post-1950)

Goaltender	Team	YRS	GP	GA	GAA
*Martin Brodeur	NJ	11	665	1,419	2.19
Dominik Hasek	Chi, Buff, Det	12	581	1,254	2.23
Ken Dryden	Mtl	8	397	870	2.24
Jacques Plante	Mtl, NYR, StL, Tor, Bos	18	837	1,965	2.38
*Ed Belfour	Chi, SJ, Dall, Tor	14	797	1,884	2.45

Note: Minimum 350 games played. Goals-against average equals goals against per 60 minutes played.
*Active in 2002-03.

KEY YRS=years; GP=games played; G=goals; A=assists; PTS=points; PTS/GAME=points per game; G/Game=goals per game; A/GAME=assists per game; W=win; L=loss; T=tie; SO=shutout; GA=goals allowed; GAA=goals-against average

PAUL KENNEDY

JACK DEMPSEY/AP

2002-03 TIMELINE

October 9, 2002: The opening of the 86th NHL season brings three big changes: 1. Safety nets are hung at the ends of all 30 NHL rinks to protect fans from flying pucks. 2. A new "hurry-up" face-off rule cuts down on the time teams waste before the puck is dropped. 3. Referees are told by the league to call more obstruction (blocking) penalties to allow skaters to move the puck more freely.

October 26, 2002: Left wing Marian Gaborik of the Minnesota Wild personally pummels the Phoenix Coyotes by scoring two goals and four assists in a 6–1 win. The 20-year-old's six points set a Wild single-game record.

November 15, 2002: Thirty-nine-year-old left wing Dave Andreychuk of the Tampa Bay Lightning sets the NHL career mark for power-play goals (250) when he lights the lamp in the first period against the San Jose Sharks.

February 1, 2003: Hayley Wickenheiser becomes the first woman to record a goal in a men's pro league. Wickenheiser, playing for Kirkkonummi Salamat in Finland, scores in the first period to tie the game 1–1. (She scores her second goal on March 20.)

February 2, 2003: The NHL All-Star Game is one of the most exciting in the 53-year history of the event. The game ends in a shoot-out, with the West beating the East, 6–5. Second-year-star Dany Heatley of the Atlanta Thrashers scores four goals, adds an assist and a shoot-out goal, and is named MVP.

February 9, 2003: Martin Brodeur of the New Jersey Devils becomes the first NHL goalie to win at least 30 games eight seasons in a row when the Devils defeat the Minnesota Wild, 3–2. On March 30, Brodeur shuts out the New York Islanders, 6–0, giving him the NHL record for most 40-win seasons (4).

February 23, 2003: Right wing Jarome Iginla of the Calgary Flames scores a goal in four different ways (power-play, shorthanded, even-strength, empty-net) as the Flames beat the Phoenix Coyotes, 4–2.

March 15, 2003: Right wing Brett Hull of the Detroit Red Wings scores his 709th career goal in a game against the Colorado Avalanche. He moves into fifth place on the all-time goal-scoring list.

March 23, 2003: The Minnesota Wild blank the Detroit Red Wings, 4–0, and clinch their first playoff spot. The Wild is the third NHL expansion team in the past 30 years to advance to the playoffs in its third season in the league.

May 28, 2003: Goalie Patrick Roy of the Colorado Avalanche announces his retirement. After 19 NHL seasons and four Stanley Cup championships, the 37-year-old Roy leaves as the league's leader in victories (551) and games played (1,029).

June 9, 2003: The New Jersey Devils beat the Anaheim Mighty Ducks four games to three to win their third Stanley Cup in nine seasons. Goalie Jean-Sebastien Giguere of the Ducks wins the Conn Smythe trophy as the most valuable player of the playoffs. He becomes just the fifth player from the losing team to win the award.

Visit **www.sikids.com** for the latest sports stats and info.
Site code: slamdunk
AOL keyword: sikids

NHL All-Star Game

First played in 1947, this game was scheduled before the start of the regular season and used to match the defending Stanley Cup Champions against a squad made up of the league All-stars from other teams. In 1966, the games were moved to mid-season, although there was no game that year. The format changed to a conference-versus-conference showdown in 1969.

RESULTS

Year	Site	Score	MVP	Attendance
2003	Sunrise, FL	West 6, East 5	Dany Heatley, Atl (East)	19,250
2002	Los Angeles, CA	World 8, N America 5	Eric Daze, Chi (N America)	18,118
2001	Denver, CO	N America 14, World 12	Bill Guerin, Bos (N America)	18,646
2000	Toronto, ONT	World 9, N America 4	Pavel Bure, Fla (World)	19,300
1999	Tampa Bay, FL	N America 8, World 6	Wayne Gretzky, NYR (N America)	19,758
1998	Vancouver, BC	N America 8, World 7	Teemu Selanne, Ana (World)	18,422
1997	San Jose, CA	East 11, West 7	Mark Recchi, Mtl	17,422
1996	Boston, MA	East 5, West 4	Ray Bourque, Bos	17,565
1994	New York, NY	East 9, West 8	Mike Richter, NYR	18,200
1993	Montreal, QUE	Wales 16, Campbell 6	Mike Gartner, NYR	17,137
1992	Philadelphia, PA	Campbell 10, Wales 6	Brett Hull, StL	17,380
1991	Chicago, IL	Campbell 11, Wales 5	Vince Damphousse, Tor	18,472
1990	Pittsburgh, PA,	Wales 12, Campbell 7	Mario Lemieux, Pitt	16,236
1989	Edmonton, ALB	Campbell 9, Wales 5	Wayne Gretzky, LA	17,503
1988	St. Louis, MO	Wales 6, Campbell 5 (OT)	Mario Lemieux, Pitt	17,878
1986	Hartford, CT	Wales 4, Campbell 3 (OT)	Grant Fuhr, Edm	15,100
1985	Calgary, ALB	Wales 6, Campbell 4	Mario Lemieux, Pitt	16,825
1984	East Rutherford, NJ	Wales 7, Campbell 6	Don Maloney, NYR	18,939
1983	Uniondale, NY	Campbell 9, Wales 3	Wayne Gretzky, Edm	15,230
1982	Washington, DC	Wales 4, Campbell 2	Mike Bossy, NYI	18,130
1981	Los Angeles, CA	Campbell 4, Wales 1	Mike Liut, StL	15,761
1980	Detroit, MI	Wales 6, Campbell 3	Reg Leach, Phil	21,002
1978	Buffalo, NY	Wales 3, Campbell 2 (OT)	Billy Smith, NYI	16,433
1977	Vancouver, BC	Wales 4, Campbell 3	Rick Martin, Buff	15,607
1976	Philadelphia, PA	Wales 7, Campbell 5	Pete Mahovlich, Mtl	16,436
1975	Montreal, QUE	Wales 7, Campbell 1	Syl Apps Jr, Pitt	16,080
1974	Chicago, IL	West 6, East 4	Garry Unger, StL	16,426
1973	New York, NY	East 5, West 4	Greg Polis, Pitt	16,986
1972	Minneapolis, MN	East 3, West 2	Bobby Orr, Bos	15,423
1971	Boston, MA	West 2, East 1	Bobby Hull, Chi	14,790
1970	St. Louis, MO	East 4, West 1	Bobby Hull, Chi	16,587
1969	Montreal, QUE	East 3, West 3	Frank Mahovlich, Det	16,260
1968	Toronto, ONT	Toronto 4, All-Stars 3	Bruce Gamble, Tor	15,753
1967	Montreal, QUE	Montreal 3, All-Stars 0	Henri Richard, Mtl	14,284
1965	Montreal, QUE	All-Stars 5, Montreal 2	Gordie Howe, Det	13,529
1964	Toronto, ONT	All-Stars 3, Toronto 2	Jean Beliveau, Mtl	14,232
1963	Toronto, ONT	All-Stars 3, Toronto 3	Frank Mahovlich, Tor	14,034
1962	Toronto, ONT	Toronto 4, All-Stars 1	Eddie Shack, Tor	14,236
1961	Chicago, IL	All-Stars 3, Chicago 1	None named	14,534
1960	Montreal, QUE	All-Stars 2, Montreal 1	None named	13,949
1959	Montreal, QUE	Montreal 6, All-Stars 1	None named	13,818
1958	Montreal, QUE	Montreal 6, All-Stars 3	None named	13,989
1957	Montreal, QUE	All-Stars 5, Montreal 3	None named	13,003
1956	Montreal, QUE	All-Stars 1, Montreal 1	None named	13,095
1955	Detroit, MI	Detroit 3, All-Stars 1	None named	10,111
1954	Detroit, MI	All-Stars 2, Detroit 2	None named	10,689
1953	Montreal, QUE	All-Stars 3, Montreal 1	None named	14,153
1952	Detroit, MI	1st team 1, 2nd team 1	None named	10,680
1951	Toronto, ONT	1st team 2, 2nd team 2	None named	11,469
1950	Detroit, MI	Detroit 7, All-Stars 1	None named	9,166
1949	Toronto, ONT	All-Stars 3, Toronto 1	None named	13,541
1948	Chicago, IL	All-Stars 3, Toronto 1	None named	12,794
1947	Toronto, ONT	All-Stars 4, Toronto 3	None named	14,169

Note: The Challenge Cup, a series between the NHL All-Stars and the Soviet Union, was played instead of the All-Star Game in 1979. Eight years later, Rendez-Vous '87, a two-game series matching the Soviet Union and the NHL All-Stars, replaced the All-Star Game. The 1995 NHL All-Star Game was canceled due to a labor dispute. The 1998 NHL All-Star Game, billed as a preview to the 1998 Winter Olympics, in Nagano, Japan, matched North Amercian–born All-Stars and All-Stars born elsewhere. Games from 1999-02 also followed this format.

SOCCER

The United States was no longer a soccer doormat in 2002. After finishing dead last in the 1998 World Cup, the U.S. reached the quarterfinals of the 2002 World Cup, in South Korea, its best result since 1930. Exciting young players, including forwards Landon Donovan and Clint Mathis, and midfielder DaMarcus Beasley, breathed new life into the team. The upstarts toppled powerful Portugal, 3–2, tied host South Korea, 1–1, and beat arch rival Mexico, 2–0. Their remarkable run was halted by Germany, which defeated the U.S., 1–0, in a quarterfinal match. The eventual World Cup champion was Brazil, led by superstar forward Ronaldo, the leading scorer of the tournament. It was Brazil's record fifth World Cup title.

In Major League Soccer (MLS), the Los Angeles Galaxy won its first MLS Cup, defeating the New England Revolution in the championship game, 1–0. The Galaxy had been to the MLS Cup finals three times but had come away empty-handed.

Guatemalan forward Carlos Ruiz of the Los Angeles Galaxy led MLS with 24 goals and was named the league's Most Valuable Player. He also netted the lone goal in the Galaxy's MLS Cup victory.

Carlos Ruiz of the Los Angeles Galaxy was named MLS's Most Valuable Player and MVP of the 2002 MLS Cup.

ISAAC MENASHE/DIGITAL SPORTS ARCHIVE

MLS TEAMS

EASTERN CONFERENCE
Chicago Fire
Columbus Crew
D.C. United
MetroStars
New England Revolution

WESTERN CONFERENCE
Colorado Rapids
Dallas Burn
Kansas City Wizards
Los Angeles Galaxy
San Jose Earthquakes

2002 Final Standings

Eastern Conference

TEAM	GP	W	L	T	PTS	GF	GA
†Revolution	28	12	14	2	38	49	49
*Crew	28	11	12	5	38	44	43
*Fire	28	11	13	4	37	43	38
MetroStars	28	11	15	2	35	41	47
D.C. United	28	9	14	5	32	31	40

Western Conference

TEAM	GP	W	L	T	PTS	GF	GA
†Galaxy	28	16	9	3	51	44	33
*Earthquakes	28	14	11	3	45	45	35
*Burn	28	12	9	7	43	44	43
*Rapids	28	13	11	4	43	43	48
*Wizards	28	9	10	9	36	37	45

Note: Three points for a win. One point for a tie. †Conference champion.
*Qualified for playoffs.

 KEY GP=games played; W=win; L=loss; T=tie; PTS=points; GF=goals for; GA=goals against

MLS CUP 2002

Foxboro, Massachusetts, October 20, 2002
Attendance: 61,316

	1st half	2nd half	Overtime	Final
Galaxy	0	0	1	1
Revolution	0	0	0	0

Goal: Ruiz (Marshall, Albright) 113
Galaxy: Hartman, Lalas, Califf, Marshall, Hendrickson, Victorine, Cienfuegos (Vagenas, 61), Elliott, Jones, Moreno (Albright, 67), Ruiz
Revolution: Brown, Llamosa (Pierce, 92), Franchino, Kante, Heaps, Cullen, Kamler (Griffiths, 90), Hernandez, Ralston, Twellman, Harris (Pineda Chacon)

Note: Numbers next to player names indicate time of game.

Brian McBride (left) and his Columbus Crew won the 2002 U.S. Open Cup.

CHRIS PUTNAM/DIGITAL SPORTS ARCHIVE

Trivia Challenge

Who scored the first goal in Major League Soccer history?

Forward Eric Wynalda of the San Jose Clash (now Earthquakes) scored the first goal in MLS history. The Clash defeated D.C. United, 1-0, in the league's first game, on April 6, 1996.

2002 MLS Playoffs

Revolution
Fire
— Revolution (6-3)
— Revolution (5-2)
Earthquakes
Crew
— Crew (6-0)

GALAXY 1-0 (OT)

Galaxy (6-0)

Galaxy (6-3)
Rapids** (4-4)

Galaxy
Wizards
Burn
Rapids

**Won tiebreaking minigame. *Note:* Except for the final, which was a single game, scores in parentheses are points earned (three for a win, one for a tie) in a three-game series. The winner is the first team to accumulate 5 points.

PLAYOFF LEADERS

SCORING	Games	Goals	Assists	Points
Carlos Ruiz, Galaxy	6	8	2	18
Cobi Jones, Galaxy	6	3	4	10
Preki, Wizards	3	3	1	7
Brian Kamler, Revolution	7	2	2	6
Eric Quill, Wizards	3	1	3	5
Freddy Garcia, Crew	5	2	1	5
Edson Buddle, Crew	3	1	2	4
Chris Brown, Wizards	3	1	2	4
Ante Razov, Fire	3	2	0	4
John Spencer, Rapids	5	2	0	4

ASSISTS	Games	Assists
Jeff Cunningham, Crew	5	4
Cobi Jones, Galaxy	6	4
Eric Quill, Wizards	3	3
Edson Buddle, Crew	3	2
Chris Brown, Wizards	3	2
Oscar Pareja, Burn	3	2
Kyle Martino, Crew	4	2
Chris Carrieri, Rapids	5	2
Chris Henderson, Rapids	5	2
Simon Elliott, Galaxy	6	2

GOALS	Games	Goals
Carlos Ruiz, Galaxy	6	8
Preki, Wizards	3	3
Cobi Jones, Galaxy	6	3
Ante Razov, Fire	3	2
John Spencer, Rapids	5	2
Freddy Garcia, Crew	5	2
Brian McBride, Crew	5	2
Taylor Twellman, Revolution	6	2
Brian Kamler, Revolution	7	2
Dario Fabbro, Wizards	2	1

GOALS-AGAINST AVERAGE	Games	GAA
Adin Brown, Revolution	7	.67
Jon Busch, Crew	5	.96
Kevin Hartman, Galaxy	6	1.26
Matt Jordan, Burn	3	1.60
Zach Thornton, Fire	3	1.67
David Kramer, Rapids	5	1.95
Joe Cannon, Earthquakes	2	2.00
Tony Meola, Wizards	3	2.90

Kevin Hartman,
Los Angeles Galaxy

JOE SANTOS/DIGITAL SPORTS ARCHIVE

Today's Stars

DaMarcus Beasley, midfielder, b. May 24, 1982, Fort Wayne, Indiana. At age 16 years and 10 months, Beasley was the youngest player to sign an MLS contract, in 1999. He is a member of the Chicago Fire. He was the youngest member of the 2002 U.S. World Cup team, which reached the quarterfinals for the first time since 1930. He was named the 2001 U.S. Soccer Young Male Athlete of the Year.

Landon Donovan, forward, b. March 4, 1982, Ontario, California. Donovan joined the San Jose Earthquakes in March 2001. His goal in the 2001 MLS Cup championship helped lead the 'Quakes over the Los Angeles Galaxy, 2–1, in overtime. At the 2002 World Cup, Donovan scored two goals for the U.S., tied for first on the team.

DaMarcus Beasley had 3 goals and 4 assists for the Fire in 2002.

Clint Mathis, forward, b. November 25, 1976, Conyers, Georgia. Mathis is a two-time MetroStar scoring champion (2000, 2001). He was one of only two U.S. players to notch both a goal and an assist during the 2002 World Cup.

CHRIS KELLY/DIGITAL SPORTS ARCHIVE

Trivia Challenge

Which two teams were eliminated from Major League Soccer in 2002?

The Miami Fusion and the Tampa Bay Mutiny

TEAM-BY-TEAM STATS

CHICAGO FIRE

PLAYER	GP	MIN	G	A	PTS	SHOTS	SOG
Ante Razov	25	2,120	14	8	36	115	56
Josh Wolff	14	1,223	5	5	15	30	12
Dema Kovalenko	23	2,034	1	8	10	38	12
DaMarcus Beasley	19	1,719	3	4	10	26	12
Peter Nowak	16	1,377	3	4	10	23	9
Jesse Marsch	28	2,557	1	7	9	21	6
Kelly Gray	25	1,780	2	5	9	18	7
Hristo Stoitchkov	16	693	2	3	7	39	18
Carlos Bocanegra	26	2,291	2	3	7	16	9
Jim Curtin	24	2,121	2	0	4	12	6
Amos Magee	5	197	2	0	4	4	2
C.J. Brown	24	2,153	0	3	3	6	3
David Vaudreuil	17	1,280	1	1	3	4	2
Sergi Daniv	8	480	1	0	2	6	3
Jason Moore	10	314	1	0	2	3	2
John Wolyniec	2	180	1	0	2	3	3
Billy Walsh	13	776	0	1	1	3	0
Billy Sleeth	13	799	0	1	1	2	1
Chris Armas	4	347	0	1	1	1	1
Orlando Perez	11	808	0	0	0	3	0
Mike Nugent	4	54	0	0	0	3	1
Craig Capano	4	92	0	0	0	2	0
Johnny Torres	2	73	0	0	0	2	0
Zach Thornton	27	2,483	0	0	0	0	0
Evan Whitfield	2	138	0	0	0	0	0
Henry Ring	1	90	0	0	0	0	0
Aleksey Korol	1	22	0	0	0	0	0
Dipsy Seloolwane	1	1	0	0	0	0	0
FIRE			43	54	136	380	165
OPPONENTS			38	43	119	351	171

INDIVIDUAL GOALKEEPING

GOALKEEPER	GP	MIN	SHOTS	SVS	C/P	GA	GAA
Zach Thornton	27	2,483	164	124	83	34	1.23
Henry Ring	1	90	7	3	0	4	4.00
TOTALS	28	2,573	171	127	83	38	1.33

COLORADO RAPIDS

PLAYER	GP	MIN	G	A	PTS	SHOTS	SOG
Mark Chung	27	2,401	11	10	32	83	33
Chris Henderson	28	2,414	11	7	29	56	28
Chris Carrieri	25	1,830	11	5	27	54	23
Carlos Valderrama	27	2,479	1	16	18	18	8
John Spencer	16	1,149	5	4	14	49	21
Zach Kingsley	15	997	4	2	10	20	17
Raul Palacios	16	836	0	5	5	12	2
Jeff Stewart	23	1,723	0	3	3	6	3
Pablo Mastroeni	15	1,329	0	3	3	4	2
Wes Hart	27	2,063	0	2	2	18	6
Ritchie Kotschau	23	1,757	0	2	2	18	6
Kyle Beckerman	14	477	0	1	1	11	4
Rick Titus	25	2,202	0	1	1	5	3
Robin Fraser	28	2,453	0	1	1	4	0
Marvin Quijano	6	77	0	1	1	2	1
Imad Baba	10	443	0	0	0	5	3
Steven Herdsman	13	858	0	0	0	2	1
Seth Trembly	4	43	0	0	0	1	0
Musa Shannon	1	30	0	0	0	1	0
Scott Garlick	15	1,374	0	0	0	0	0
David Kramer	13	1,195	0	0	0	0	0
Danny Jackson	1	15	0	0	0	0	0
Steve Shak	1	1	0	0	0	0	0
RAPIDS			43	63	149	369	161
OPPONENTS			48	65	161	380	167

INDIVIDUAL GOALKEEPING

GOALKEEPER	GP	MIN	SHOTS	SVS	C/P	GA	GAA
Scott Garlick	15	1,374	92	61	58	24	1.57
David Kramer	13	1,195	75	49	47	24	1.81
TOTALS	28	2,569	167	110	105	48	1.68

KEY GP=games played; MIN=minutes played; G=goals; A=assists; PTS=points; SOG=shots on goal; SVS=saves;C/P=catches/punches; GA=goals allowed; GAA=goals-against average

COLUMBUS CREW

PLAYER	GP	MIN	G	A	PTS	SHOTS	SOG
Jeff Cunningham	27	1,962	16	5	37	78	37
Edson Buddle	21	1,304	9	5	23	51	19
Brian McBride	14	1,239	5	5	15	37	14
Dante Washington	21	1,122	6	2	14	36	19
Brian West	24	1,944	1	8	10	32	11
Kyle Martino	22	1,455	2	5	9	28	11
Brian Maisonneuve	26	2,238	1	6	8	29	9
John Wilmar Perez	20	1,256	1	4	6	21	6
Eric Denton	23	1,875	1	4	6	8	4
Duncan Oughton	20	1,608	0	4	4	15	7
Chad McCarty	18	1,176	1	2	4	5	1
Mike Clark	21	1,599	1	0	2	7	6
Freddy Garcia	5	215	0	2	2	7	2
Robert Warzycha	15	495	0	2	2	6	1
John Harkes	11	739	0	2	2	3	1
Brian Dunseth	27	2,436	0	1	1	7	4
Daniel Torres	25	2,085	0	1	1	3	1
Tom Presthus	15	1,365	0	1	1	0	0
Todd Yeagley	3	74	0	1	1	0	0
Chris Leitch	13	989	0	0	0	2	2
Jon Busch	14	1,236	0	0	0	0	0
Mike Lapper	4	141	0	0	0	0	0
Jeff Matteo	1	14	0	0	0	0	0
CREW			**44**	**60**	**148**	**375**	**155**
OPPONENTS			**43**	**51**	**137**	**399**	**183**

INDIVIDUAL GOALKEEPING

GOALKEEPER	GP	MIN	SHOTS	SVS	C/P	GA	GAA
Jon Busch	14	1,236	80	63	55	15	1.09
Tom Presthus	15	1,365	103	73	39	28	1.85
TOTALS	**29**	**2,601**	**183**	**136**	**94**	**43**	**1.49**

DALLAS BURN

PLAYER	GP	MIN	G	A	PTS	SHOTS	SOG
Jason Kreis	27	2,303	13	4	30	81	38
Bobby Rhine	27	1,686	7	6	20	44	19
Antonio Martinez	26	1,774	4	10	18	24	9
Ronald Cerritos	23	1,209	4	6	14	40	25
Joselito Vaca	25	2,005	1	9	11	44	20
Jorge Rodriguez	22	1,693	4	2	10	30	13
Oscar Pareja	24	2,000	1	6	8	31	15
Chad Deering	27	2,168	1	4	6	24	4
Ronnie O'Brian	11	506	2	2	6	15	10
Steve Morrow	24	2,199	3	0	6	12	6
Edward Johnson	11	326	2	1	5	11	4
Ryan Suarez	24	2,061	1	2	4	19	10
Paul Broome	25	2,315	0	4	4	4	3
Hamisi Amani-Dove	6	101	0	1	1	6	1
Carl Bussey	9	184	0	1	1	3	1
Tenywa Bonseu	27	2,370	0	0	0	6	2
Richard Farrer	8	508	0	0	0	4	1
Percy Olivares	6	251	0	0	0	3	0
Matt Behncke	3	190	0	0	0	1	1
Lee Morrison	3	103	0	0	0	1	0
Matt Jordan	27	2,511	0	0	0	0	0
D.J. Countess	1	100	0	0	0	0	0
Jordan Stone	4	91	0	0	0	0	0
BURN			**44**	**58**	**144**	**403**	**182**
OPPONENTS			**43**	**61**	**147**	**417**	**165**

INDIVIDUAL GOALKEEPING

GOALKEEPER	GP	MIN	SHOTS	SVS	C/P	GA	GAA
D.J. Countess	1	100	7	6	1	1	0.90
Matt Jordan	27	2,511	158	109	93	42	1.51
TOTALS	**28**	**2,611**	**165**	**115**	**94**	**43**	**1.48**

D.C. UNITED

PLAYER	GP	MIN	G	A	PTS	SHOTS	SOG
Marco Etcheverry	24	2,146	3	8	14	26	12
Bobby Convey	26	2,248	5	3	13	39	25
Ali Curtis	20	806	5	1	11	25	12
Ryan Nelsen	20	1,596	4	3	11	15	12
Jaime Moreno	16	1,157	3	4	10	29	13
Santino Quaranta	11	949	3	4	10	24	11
Petter Villegas	18	1,346	2	5	9	30	11
Eliseo Quintanilla	9	726	2	2	6	19	11
Ivan McKinley	23	1,786	1	2	4	20	7
Eddie Pope	17	1,471	1	1	3	11	3
Richie Williams	26	2,307	0	3	3	8	6
Henry Zambrano	5	240	1	0	2	10	4
Milton Reyes	24	2,204	0	2	2	9	3
Abdul Thompson Conteh	5	286	1	0	2	9	4
Jose Alegria	14	900	0	1	1	19	11
Ben Olsen	10	718	0	1	1	12	8
Lazo Alavanja	17	1,001	0	0	0	13	5
Roy Lassiter	12	440	0	0	0	5	2
*Orlando Perez	8	268	0	0	0	4	2
Brandon Prideaux	27	2,389	0	0	0	3	1
Dennis Ludwig	2	30	0	0	0	2	1
Bryan Namoff	11	442	0	0	0	1	0
*Craig Ziadie	1	27	0	0	0	1	0
Nick Rimando	28	2,588	0	0	0	0	0
*Mark Lisi	6	265	0	0	0	0	0
Justin Mapp	3	28	0	0	0	0	0
D.C. UNITED			**31**	**40**	**102**	**334**	**164**
OPPONENTS			**40**	**52**	**132**	**364**	**183**

INDIVIDUAL GOALKEEPING

GOALKEEPER	GP	MIN	SHOTS	SVS	C/P	GA	GAA
Nick Rimando	28	2,588	183	131	85	40	1.39
TOTALS	**28**	**2,588**	**183**	**131**	**85**	**40**	**1.39**

KANSAS CITY WIZARDS

PLAYER	GP	MIN	G	A	PTS	SHOTS	SOG
Preki	25	2,141	7	10	24	84	44
Chris Klein	25	2,171	7	5	19	34	17
Dario Fabbro	16	1,116	6	3	15	35	19
Ior Simutenkov	19	1,480	4	5	13	55	23
Stephen Armstrong	26	1,791	3	6	12	31	14
Chris Brown	28	1,512	4	3	11	35	17
Carey Talley	24	1,902	3	1	7	14	7
Diego Gutierrez	22	1,914	1	3	5	25	4
Francisco Gomez	20	1,249	0	4	4	31	8
Kerry Zavagnin	27	2,484	1	2	4	12	5
Matt McKeon	23	1,146	1	2	4	12	5
Nick Garcia	27	2,499	0	2	2	2	0
Eric Quill	16	992	0	1	1	24	10
Mike Burns	24	1,966	0	1	1	4	1
Tony Meola	17	1,519	0	1	1	0	0
Chris Brunt	5	158	0	0	0	2	1
Davy Arnaud	3	43	0	0	0	2	1
Gary Glasgow	3	174	0	0	0	1	0
Peter Vermes	13	1,181	0	0	0	0	0
Bo Oshoniyi	13	1,096	0	0	0	0	0
*Roy Lassiter	2	61	0	0	0	0	0
WIZARDS			**37**	**49**	**123**	**403**	**176**
OPPONENTS			**45**	**65**	**155**	**392**	**168**

INDIVIDUAL GOALKEEPING

GOALKEEPER	GP	MIN	SHOTS	SVS	C/P	GA	GAA
Tony Meola	17	1,519	88	65	43	21	1.24
Bo Oshoniyi	13	1,096	80	55	45	24	1.97
TOTALS	**30**	**2,615**	**168**	**120**	**88**	**45**	**1.55**

*Played for more than one team. Most recent team listed.

SOCCER MEN'S

LOS ANGELES GALAXY

PLAYER	GP	MIN	G	A	PTS	SHOTS	SOG
Carlos Ruiz	26	2,376	24	1	49	100	56
Cobi Jones	19	1,638	3	13	19	31	21
Simon Elliott	26	2,347	1	10	12	40	11
Mauricio Cienfuegos	23	1,879	2	8	12	26	13
Alexi Lalas	26	2,364	4	4	12	25	16
Ezra Hendrickson	23	2,048	2	8	12	20	9
Sasha Victorine	25	1,985	2	5	9	25	8
Brian Mullan	21	1,019	3	2	8	23	13
Gavin Glinton	22	790	1	4	6	19	10
Tyrone Marshall	24	1,838	0	5	5	9	5
Peter Vegenas	17	1,390	0	3	3	4	1
Danny Califf	25	2,118	1	0	2	15	4
Alejandro Moreno	12	561	0	2	2	14	7
*Winston Griffiths	6	310	1	0	2	6	4
Chris Albright	15	814	0	1	1	24	12
Craig Waibel	12	860	0	1	1	7	3
Jesus Ochoa	9	352	0	1	1	7	2
Adam Frye	20	956	0	0	0	5	2
Alex Bengard	4	26	0	0	0	1	1
Kevin Hartman	18	1,648	0	0	0	0	0
Matt Reis	11	929	0	0	0	0	0
GALAXY			**44**	**68**	**156**	**401**	**198**
OPPONENTS			**33**	**46**	**112**	**352**	**155**

INDIVIDUAL GOALKEEPING

GOALKEEPER	GP	MIN	SHOTS	SVS	C/P	GA	GAA
Kevin Hartman	18	1,648	108	83	49	20	1.09
Matt Reis	11	929	47	33	21	13	1.26
TOTALS	**29**	**2,577**	**155**	**116**	**70**	**33**	**1.15**

METROSTARS

PLAYER	GP	MIN	G	A	PTS	SHOTS	SOG
Rodrigo Faria	28	2,285	12	5	29	90	49
Mamadou Diallo	17	1,135	11	4	26	51	32
Andy Williams	19	1,539	2	13	17	46	15
Brad Davis	24	1,246	4	3	11	22	10
Clint Mathis	14	1,106	4	2	10	40	20
Ross Paule	26	2,207	2	2	6	29	11
*Diego Serna	8	696	1	3	5	22	8
Mark Lisi	17	609	2	1	5	7	5
Ted Chronopoulos	18	1,462	0	4	4	8	3
Tab Ramos	14	926	0	3	3	11	7
*Petter Villegas	7	607	0	3	3	11	3
Steve Jolley	27	2,327	1	1	3	7	3
Jeff Moore	18	1,482	0	3	3	5	2
*Brian Kamler	8	581	1	1	3	4	1
*Daniel Hernandez	9	809	0	2	2	11	0
Joe Addo	15	918	0	1	1	2	1
Tim Howard	27	2,463	0	1	1	0	0
Mike Petke	27	2,398	0	0	0	8	2
Byron Alvarez	8	119	0	0	0	3	1
Craig Ziadie	20	1,610	0	0	0	2	0
Nelson Akwari	7	325	0	0	0	2	0
Sam Forko	9	356	0	0	0	1	1
*Winston Griffiths	3	17	0	0	0	1	0
Birahim Diop	4	228	0	0	0	0	0
*Orlando Perez	2	98	0	0	0	0	0
Paul Grafer	2	91	0	0	0	0	0
Dustin Sheppard	2	64	0	0	0	0	0
Darin Lewis	3	48	0	0	0	0	0
Marcelo Balboa	1	5	0	0	0	0	0
Brian Piesner	1	1	0	0	0	0	0
METROSTARS			**41**	**52**	**132**	**383**	**174**
OPPONENTS			**47**	**66**	**160**	**422**	**202**

INDIVIDUAL GOALKEEPING

GOALKEEPER	GP	MIN	SHOTS	SVS	C/P	GA	GAA
Tim Howard	27	2,463	195	140	115	44	1.61
Paul Grafer	2	91	7	3	3	3	2.97
TOTALS	**29**	**2,554**	**202**	**143**	**118**	**47**	**1.66**

*Played for more than one team. Most recent team listed.

NEW ENGLAND REVOLUTION

PLAYER	GP	MIN	G	A	PTS	SHOTS	SOG
Taylor Twellman	28	2,418	23	6	52	92	58
Steve Ralston	27	2,460	5	19	29	27	13
Jay Heaps	27	2,389	2	6	10	23	13
Brian Kamler	16	1,099	2	5	9	14	4
Wolde Harris	22	1,117	4	0	8	41	24
Daniel Hernandez	19	1,492	3	1	7	23	9
Joe Franchino	23	2,015	1	5	7	16	4
Alex Pineda Chacon	20	1,014	2	2	6	20	9
Leo Cullen	28	2,444	2	2	6	10	6
Jim Rooney	20	1,715	1	2	4	19	5
*Mamadou Diallo	7	488	1	1	3	30	19
Diego Serna	5	248	1	1	3	12	6
Ian Fuller	11	446	0	3	3	5	2
*Andy Williams	5	275	0	2	2	8	3
Winston Griffiths	8	428	0	2	2	7	2
*Ted Chronopoulos	5	415	0	2	2	2	1
Daouda Kante	8	729	1	0	2	1	1
John Wilson	1	16	1	0	2	1	1
Braeden Cloutier	11	608	0	1	1	6	1
Carlos Llamosa	14	1,056	0	1	1	1	0
Carlos Semedo	9	631	0	1	1	1	0
Rusty Pierce	14	1,161	0	0	0	5	0
Shaker Asad	6	140	0	0	0	3	2
Nick Downing	12	667	0	0	0	1	1
Adin Brown	16	1,460	0	0	0	0	0
Juergen Sommer	12	1,090	0	0	0	0	0
REVOLUTION			49	62	160	368	184
OPPONENTS			49	70	168	382	189

INDIVIDUAL GOALKEEPING

GOALKEEPER	GP	MIN	SHOTS	SVS	C/P	GA	GAA
Adin Brown	16	1,460	102	72	54	20	1.23
Juergen Sommer	12	1,090	87	53	38	29	2.39
TOTALS	28	2,550	189	125	92	49	1.73

SAN JOSE EARTHQUAKES

PLAYER	GP	MIN	G	A	PTS	SHOTS	SOG
Ariel Graziani	28	2,289	14	5	33	69	39
Ronnie Ekelund	27	2,347	6	8	20	43	20
Landon Donovan	20	1,681	7	3	17	42	23
Dwayne DeRosario	27	1,637	4	8	16	56	29
Ramiro Corrales	28	2,354	3	9	15	38	16
Manny Lagos	26	1,683	3	4	10	37	16
Richard Mulrooney	26	2,312	1	8	10	22	5
Wade Barrett	28	2,555	1	6	8	9	5
Jimmy Conrad	25	2,248	1	3	5	13	6
Eddie Robinson	19	1,427	2	1	5	11	5
Ian Russell	24	1,348	0	2	2	14	6
Troy Dayak	15	1,235	0	1	1	5	2
Zak Ibsen	17	1,077	0	1	1	4	1
Jeff Agoos	12	839	0	0	0	7	3
Devin Barclay	12	321	0	0	0	2	1
Joe Cannon	26	2,375	0	0	0	0	0
Jon Conway	3	181	0	0	0	0	0
Luchi Gonzalez	8	47	0	0	0	0	0
Chris Roner	4	29	0	0	0	0	0
EARTHQUAKES			45	59	143	372	177
OPPONENTS			35	46	116	329	153

INDIVIDUAL GOALKEEPING

GOALKEEPER	GP	MIN	SHOTS	SVS	C/P	GA	GAA
Joe Cannon	26	2,375	136	100	99	29	1.10
Jon Conway	3	181	17	11	6	6	2.89
TOTALS	29	2,556	153	111	105	35	1.23

*Played for more than one team. Most recent team listed.

TONY QUINN/DIGITAL SPORTS ARCHIVE

Taylor Twellman,
New England Revolution

2002 MLS
Statistical Leaders

SCORING	Games	Goals	Assists	Points
Taylor Twellman, Revolution	28	23	6	52
Carlos Ruiz, Galaxy	26	24	1	49
Jeff Cunningham, Crew	27	16	5	37
Ante Razov, Fire	25	14	8	36
Ariel Graziani, Earthquakes	28	14	5	33
Mark Chung, Rapids	27	11	10	32
Jason Kreis, Burn	27	13	4	30
*Mamadou Diallo, MetroStars	24	12	5	29
Steve Ralston, Revolution	27	5	19	29
Rodrigo Faria, MetroStars	28	12	5	29
Chris Henderson, Crew	28	11	7	29

GOALS	Games	Goals
Carlos Ruiz, Galaxy	26	24
Taylor Twellman, Revolution	28	23
Jeff Cunningham, Crew	27	16
Ante Razov, Fire	25	14
Ariel Graziani, Earthquakes	28	14
Jason Kreis, Burn	27	13
*Mamadou Diallo, MetroStars	24	12
Rodrigo Faria, MetroStars	28	12
Chris Carrieri, Rapids	25	11
Mark Chung, Rapids	27	11
Chris Henderson, Rapids	28	11

ASSISTS	Games	Assists
Steve Ralston, Revolution	27	19
Carlos Valderrama, Rapids	27	16
*Andy Williams, MetroStars	24	15
Cobi Jones, Galaxy	19	13
Preki, Wizards	25	10
Simon Elliott, Galaxy	26	10
Antonio Martinez, Burn	26	10
Mark Chung, Rapids	27	10
Joselito Vaca, Burn	25	9
Ramiro Corrales, Earthquakes	28	9

GOALS-AGAINST AVERAGE	GAA
Kevin Hartman, Galaxy	1.09
Jon Busch, Crew	1.09
Joe Cannon, Earthquakes	1.10
Zach Thornton, Fire	1.23
Adin Brown, Revolution	1.23
Tony Meola, Wizards	1.24
Nick Rimando, D.C. United	1.39
Matt Jordan, Burn	1.51
Scott Garlick, Rapids	1.57
Tim Howard, MetroStars	1.61

*Played for more than one team. Most recent team listed.

A-League

2002 FINAL STANDINGS
Eastern Conference
Northeast Division

Team	GP	W	L	T
Rochester Raging Rhinos	28	17	8	3
Montreal Impact	28	16	9	3
Toronto Lynx	28	10	13	5
Pittsburgh Riverhounds	28	8	15	5

Southeast Division

Team	GP	W	L	T
Charleston Battery	28	19	3	6
Richmond Kickers	28	13	9	6
Atlanta Silverbacks	28	13	13	2
Charlotte Eagles	28	10	14	4
Hampton Roads Mariners	28	6	19	3

Western Conference
Pacific Division

Team	GP	W	L	T
Seattle Sounders	28	23	4	1
Portland Timbers	28	13	12	3
Vancouver Whitecaps	28	11	12	5
El Paso Patriots	28	10	11	7
Calgary Storm	28	4	21	3

Central Division

Team	GP	W	L	T
Milwaukee Rampage	28	16	7	5
Minnesota Thunder	28	14	9	5
Cincinnati Riverhawks	28	8	20	0
Indiana Blast	28	6	18	4

2002 A-LEAGUE PLAYOFFS
First Round
*Montreal Impact 1, Charlotte Eagles 1
Vancouver Whitecaps 2, Portland Timbers 0
Richmond Kickers 3, Atlanta Silverbacks 2
Minnesota Thunder 3, El Paso Patriots 2

Quarterfinals
Rochester Raging Rhinos 1, Montreal Thunder 0
Richmond Kickers 4, Charleston Battery 3
Milwaukee Rampage 2, Minnesota Thunder 1
Vancouver Whitecaps 8, Seattle Sounders 2

Semi-finals
*Richmond Kickers 1, Rochester Raging Rhinos 1
Milwaukee Rampage 2, Vancouver Whitecaps 1

*Advanced on penalties.
  Note: Scores from first round, quarterfinals, and semi-finals
  are two-game totals.

**A-League Championship
  Milwaukee Rampage 2, Richmond Kickers 1 (2 ot)

**One game

2002 U.S. Open Cup Results

The annual U.S. Open Cup is open to all amateur and professional teams in the United States. The tournament is a single-elimination event running at the same time as the MLS season. The winner advances to the CONCACAF (Confederation of North, Central American, and Caribbean Association Football) Cup, a tournament of the top club teams from North and Central America and the Caribbean.

QUARTERFINALS

Kansas City Wizards (MLS) 2, Milwaukee Rampage (A-League) 0

Dallas Burn (MLS) 1, Colorado Rapids (MLS) 0 (2 OT)

Columbus Crew (MLS) 2, MetroStars (MLS) 1

Los Angeles Galaxy (MLS) 1, San Jose Earthquakes (MLS) 0 (OT)

Note: MLS: Major League Soccer (1st division); A-League (2nd division)

SEMI-FINALS

Columbus Crew 3, Kansas City Wizards 2 (2 OT)

Los Angeles Galaxy 4, Dallas Burn 1

2002 LAMAR HUNT
U.S. OPEN CUP FINAL RESULTS
October 24, 2002, Columbus, Ohio

Columbus Crew (MLS) 1, Los Angeles Galaxy (MLS) 0

Scoring summary: Columbus — Freddy Garcia, 30

All-time MLS Cup Results

Year	Champion	Score	Runner-up
2002	Los Angeles Galaxy	1–0 (OT)	New England Revolution
2001	San Jose Earthquakes	2–1 (OT)	Los Angeles Galaxy
2000	Kansas City Wizards	1–0	Chicago Fire
1999	D.C. United	2–0	Los Angeles Galaxy
1998	Chicago Fire	2–0	D.C. United
1997	D.C. United	2–1	Colorado Rapids
1996	D.C. United	3–2 (OT)	Los Angeles Galaxy

▷**Random Fact:** The first MLS All-Star Game was held on July 14, 1996. A capacity crowd of 78,416 was on hand at the Meadowlands Sports Complex, in East Rutherford, New Jersey. At the time, the crowd was the largest ever for a sporting event at the Meadowlands.

MLS All-Star Game Results

Year	Result	Site	Most Valuable Player
2002	MLS 3, USA 2	Washington, D.C.	Marco Etcheverry, D.C. United
2001	East 6, West 6	San Jose, California	Landon Donovan, San Jose Earthquakes
2000	East 9, West 4	Columbus, Ohio	Mamadou Diallo, Tampa Bay Mutiny
1999	West 6, East 4	San Diego, California	Preki, Kansas City Wizards
1998	MLS USA 6, World 1	Orlando, Florida	Brian McBride, Columbus Crew
1997	East 5, West 4	East Rutherford, New Jersey	Carlos Valderrama, Tampa Bay Mutiny
1996	East 3, West 2	East Rutherford, New Jersey	Carlos Valderrama, Tampa Bay Mutiny

Visit *www.sikids.com* for the latest sports stats and info.
Site code: slam dunk   AOL keyword: sikids

MLS Award Winners

Year	MVP	Scoring Champion	Goal of the Year	Coach
2002	Carlos Ruiz, Galaxy	Taylor Twellman, Revolution	Carlos Ruiz, Galaxy	Steve Nicol, Revolution
2001	Alex Pineda Chacon, Fusion	Alex Pineda Chacon, Fusion	Clint Mathis, MetroStars	Frank Yallop, Earthquakes
2000	Tony Meola, Wizards	Mamadou Diallo, Mutiny	Marcelo Balboa, Rapids	Bob Gansler, Wizards
1999	Jason Kreis, Burn	Jason Kreis, Burn	Marco Etcheverry, D.C. United	Sigi Schmid, Galaxy
1998	Marco Etcheverry, D.C. United	Stern John, Crew	Brian McBride, Crew	Bob Bradley, Fire
1997	Preki, Wizards	Preki, Wizards	Marco Etcheverry, D.C. United	Bruce Arena, D.C. United
1996	Carlos Valderrama, Mutiny	Roy Lassiter, Mutiny	Eric Wynalda, Clash	Thomas Rongen, Mutiny

Year	Goalkeeper	Defender	Rookie	Comeback Player
2002	Joe Cannon, Earthquakes	Carlos Bocanegra, Fire	Kyle Martino, Crew	Chris Klein, Wizards
2001	Tim Howard, MetroStars	Jeff Agoos, Earthquakes	Rodrigo Faria, MetroStars	Troy Dayak, Earthquakes
2000	Tony Meola, Wizards	Peter Vermes, Wizards	Carlos Bocanegra, Fire	Tony Meola, Wizards
1999	Kevin Hartman, Galaxy	Robin Fraser, Galaxy	Jay Heaps, Fusion	N/A
1998	Zach Thornton, Fire	Lubos Kubik, Fire	Ben Olsen, D.C. United	N/A
1997	Brad Friedel, Crew	Eddie Pope, D.C. United	Mike Duhaney, Mutiny	N/A
1996	Mark Dodd, Burn	John Doyle, Clash	Steve Ralston, Mutiny	N/A

A-League Results

Year	Champion	Score	Runner-up
2002	Milwaukee Thunder	2–1 (2OT)	Richmond Kickers
2001	Rochester Raging Rhinos	2–0	Vancouver Whitecaps
2000	Rochester Raging Rhinos	3–1	Minnesota Thunder
1999	Minnesota Thunder	2–1	Rochester Raging Rhinos
1998	Rochester Raging Rhinos	3–1	Minnesota Thunder
1997	Milwaukee Rampage	2–1 (SO)	Carolina Dynamo
1996	Seattle Sounders	2–0	Rochester Raging Rhinos
1995	Seattle Sounders	1–2 (SO), 3–0, 2–1 (SO)	Atlanta Ruckus
1994	Montreal Impact	1–0	Colorado Foxes
1993	Colorado Foxes	3–1 (OT)	Los Angeles Salsa
1992	Colorado Foxes	1–0	Tampa Bay Rowdies
1991	San Francisco Bay Blackhawks	1–3, 2–0 (1–0 on PKs)	Albany Capitals

U.S. Open Cup Results

YEAR	CHAMPION	YEAR	CHAMPION
2002	Columbus Crew (MLS)	1957	Kutis SC (St. Louis, MO)
2001	Los Angeles Galaxy (MLS)	1956	Harmarville SC (PA)
2000	Chicago Fire (MLS)	1955	Eintracht Sport Club (New York City)
1999	Rochester Rhinos (A-League)	1954	New York Americans (New York City)
1998	Chicago Fire (MLS)	1953	Falcons SC (Chicago, IL)
1997	Dallas Burn (MLS)	1952	Harmarville SC (PA)
1996	D.C. United (MLS)	1951	German Hungarian SC (New York City)
1995	Richmond Kickers (VA)	1950	Simpkins-Ford SC (St. Louis, MO)
1994	Greek American AC (San Francisco, CA)	1949	Morgan SC (PA)
1993	Club Deportivo Mexico (San Francisco, CA)	1948	Simpkins-Ford SC (St. Louis, MO)
1992	San Jose Oaks (CA)	1947	Ponta Delgada SC (Fall River, MA)
1991	Brooklyn Italians SC (East New York, NY)	1946	Chicago Viking FC (IL)
1990	AAC Eagles (Chicago, IL)	1945	Brookhattan FC (New York City)
1989	HRC Kickers (St. Petersburg, FL)	1944	Brooklyn Hispano SC (New York City)
1988	Busch SC (St. Louis, MO)	1943	Brooklyn Hispano SC (New York City)
1987	Club Espana (Washington, D.C.)	1942	Gallatin SC (PA)
1986	Kutis SC (St. Louis, MO)	1941	Pawtucket FC (RI)
1985	Greek American AC (San Francisco, CA)	1940	No winner
1984	AO Krete (New York City)	1939	St. Mary's Celtic SC (Brooklyn, NY)
1983	NY Pancyprian-Freedoms (New York City)	1938	Sparta A and BA (Chicago, IL)
1982	NY Pancyprian-Freedoms (New York City)	1937	New York American FC (New York City)
1981	Maccabee SC (Los Angeles, CA)	1936	German-Americans (Philadelphia, PA)
1980	NY Pancyprian-Freedoms (New York City)	1935	Central Breweries FC (Chicago, IL)
1979	Brooklyn Dodgers SC (New York City)	1934	Stix, Baer and Fuller FC (St. Louis, MO)
1978	Maccabee SC (Los Angeles, CA)	1933	Stix, Baer and Fuller FC (St. Louis, MO)
1977	Maccabee SC (Los Angeles, CA)	1932	New Bedford FC (MA)
1976	San Francisco AC (CA)	1931	Fall River FC (MA)
1975	Maccabee SC (Los Angeles, CA)	1930	Fall River FC (MA)
1974	Greek American AA (New York City)	1929	Hakoah All Stars SC (New York City)
1973	Maccabee SC (Los Angeles, CA)	1928	New York National FC (NYC)
1972	Elizabeth SC (Union, NJ)	1927	Fall River FC (MA)
1971	Hota SC (New York City)	1926	Bethlehem Steel FC (PA)
1970	Elizabeth SC (Union, NJ)	1925	Shawsheen FC (Andover, MA)
1969	Greek American AA (New York City)	1924	Fall River FC (MA)
1968	Greek American AA (New York City)	1923	Paterson FC (NJ)
1967	Greek American AA (New York City)	1922	Scullin Steel FC (St. Louis, MO)
1966	Ukrainian Nationals (Philadelphia, PA)	1921	Robbins Dry Dock FC (Brooklyn, NY)
1965	New York Hungaria (New York City)	1920	Ben Miller FC (St. Louis, MO)
1964	Los Angeles Kickers (CA)	1919	Bethlehem Steel FC (PA)
1963	Ukrainian Nationals (Philadelphia, PA)	1918	Bethlehem Steel FC (PA)
1962	New York Hungaria (New York City)	1917	Fall River Rovers (MA)
1961	Ukrainian Nationals (Philadelphia, PA)	1916	Bethlehem Steel FC (PA)
1960	Ukrainian Nationals (Philadelphia, PA)	1915	Bethlehem Steel FC (PA)
1959	McIlvaine Canvasbacks (Los Angeles, CA)	1914	Brooklyn Field Club (New York City)
1958	Los Angeles Kickers (CA)		

2002 World Cup Results
Group Play Scores

GROUP A

Senegal 1, France 0
Denmark 2, Uruguay 1
France 0, Uruguay 0
Denmark 1, Senegal 1
Denmark 2, France 0
Senegal 3, Uruguay 3

GROUP B

Paraguay 2, South Africa 2
Spain 3, Slovenia 1
Spain 3, Paraguay 1
South Africa 1, Slovenia 0
Spain 3, South Africa 2
Paraguay 3, Slovenia 1

GROUP C

Brazil 2, Turkey 1
Costa Rica 2, China 0
Brazil 4, China 0
Costa Rica 1, Turkey 1
Brazil 5, Costa Rica 2
Turkey 3, China 0

GROUP D

South Korea 2, Poland 0
U.S. 3, Portugal 2
U.S. 1, South Korea 1
Portugal 4, Poland 0
South Korea 1, Portugal 0
Poland 3, U.S. 1

GROUP E

Ireland 1, Cameroon 1
Germany 8, Saudi Arabia 0
Germany 1, Ireland 1
Cameroon 1, Saudi Arabia 0
Germany 2, Cameroon 0
Ireland 3, Saudi Arabia 0

GROUP F

Sweden 1, England 1
Argentina 1, Nigeria 0
Sweden 2, Nigeria 1
England 1, Argentina 0
Sweden 1, Argentina 1
Nigeria 0, England 0

GROUP G

Mexico 1, Croatia 0
Italy 2, Ecuador 0
Croatia 2, Italy 1
Mexico 2, Ecuador 1
Mexico 1, Italy 1
Ecuador 1, Croatia 0

GROUP H

Japan 2, Belgium 2
Russia 2, Tunisia 0
Japan 1, Russia 0
Tunisia 1, Belgium 1
Japan 2, Tunisia 0
Belgium 3, Russia 2

2002 WORLD CUP FINAL

	1st half	2nd half	Final
BRAZIL	0	2	2
GERMANY	0	0	0

Second-half Scoring: 1, Brazil, Ronaldo (67); 2, Brazil, Ronaldo (79).
Brazil: Marcos, Cafu, Lucio, Roque Jr., Edmilson, Carlos, Silva, Ronaldo (Denilson, 90), Rivaldo, Ronaldinho (Juninho, 85), Kleberson.
Germany: Kahn, Linke, Ramelow, Neuville, Hamann, Klose (Bierhoff, 74), Jeremies (Asamoah, 77), Bode (Ziege, 84), Schneider, Metzelder, Frings.
Referee: Collina (Italy)

2002 World Cup Group Standings

GROUP A

Country	GP	W	L	T	GF	GA	Pts
*Denmark	3	2	0	1	5	2	7
*Senegal	3	1	0	2	5	4	5
Uruguay	3	0	1	2	4	5	2
France	3	0	2	1	0	3	1

GROUP B

Country	GP	W	L	T	GF	GA	Pts
*Spain	3	3	0	0	9	4	9
*Paraguay	3	1	1	1	6	6	4
South Africa	3	1	1	1	5	5	4
Slovenia	3	0	3	0	2	7	0

GROUP C

Country	GP	W	L	T	GF	GA	Pts
*Brazil	3	3	0	0	11	3	9
*Turkey	3	1	1	1	5	3	4
Costa Rica	3	1	1	1	5	6	4
China	3	0	3	0	0	9	0

GROUP D

Country	GP	W	L	T	GF	GA	Pts
*South Korea	3	2	0	1	4	1	7
*U.S.	3	1	1	1	5	6	4
Portugal	3	1	2	0	6	4	3
Poland	3	1	2	0	3	7	3

GROUP E

Country	GP	W	L	T	GF	GA	Pts
*Germany	3	2	0	1	11	1	7
*Ireland	3	1	0	2	5	2	5
Cameroon	3	1	1	1	2	3	4
Saudi Arabia	3	0	3	0	0	12	0

GROUP F

Country	GP	W	L	T	GF	GA	Pts
*Sweden	3	1	0	2	4	3	5
*England	3	1	0	2	2	1	5
Argentina	3	1	1	1	2	2	4
Nigeria	3	0	2	1	1	3	1

GROUP G

Country	GP	W	L	T	GF	GA	Pts
*Mexico	3	2	0	1	4	2	7
*Italy	3	1	1	1	4	3	4
Croatia	3	1	2	0	2	3	3
Ecuador	3	1	2	0	2	4	3

GROUP H

Country	GP	W	L	T	GF	GA	Pts
*Japan	3	2	0	1	5	2	7
*Belgium	3	1	0	2	6	5	5
Russia	3	1	2	0	4	4	3
Tunisia	3	0	2	1	1	5	1

*Advanced to second round.
Note: In group play, teams are awarded three points for a victory, one for a tie. The top two in each group advance to the Round of 16.

Legends

▷**Random Fact**: Pelé is the youngest player to appear and score in a World Cup final. He was 17 years old during the 1958 World Cup.

Pelé, forward, b. October 23, 1940, Tres Coracoes, Brazil. Born Edson Arantes do Nascimento, Pelé played on three World Cup winners (1958, 1962, 1970). He also played for the New York Cosmos of the North American Soccer League from 1975-77, helping to promote soccer in the United States. He scored 1,281 goals in his 22-year career.

Diego Maradona, midfielder/forward, b. October 30, 1960, Buenos Aires, Argentina. Maradona almost single-handedly led Argentina to the 1986 World Cup championship with his famous "Hand of God" goal against England in the quarterfinals. (He punched the ball past goalkeeper Peter Shilton, a violation that was not seen by the officials.) Four years later, he and his team reached the 1990 World Cup Finals again, but lost to Germany, 1–0. Maradona scored 34 goals for Argentina from 1977 to 1994.

Franz Beckenbauer, defender/midfielder, b. September 11, 1945, Munich, Germany. Beckenbauer is the only man to win a World Cup as a player (1974) and as a coach (1990). He played in two other World Cups (1966, second place; and 1970, fourth place). He also played for the New York Cosmos from 1977-80 and again in 1983.

Pelé led Brazil to three World Cup titles.

EMPICS/DIGITAL SPORTS ARCHIVE

2002 World Cup Final Bracket

England
England (3–0)
Denmark
Brazil (2–1)
Brazil
Brazil (2–0)
Belgium
Brazil (1–0)
Sweden
Senegal (2–1) OT
Senegal
Turkey (1–0) OT
Japan
Turkey (1–0)
Turkey

BRAZIL 2 GERMANY 0

Germany (1–0)
Germany (1–0)
Germany
Germany (1–0)
South Korea (0–0)*

Germany (1–0)
Germany
Paraguay
United States (2–0)
Mexico
United States
Spain (1–1)*
Spain
Ireland
South Korea (2–1) OT
South Korea
Italy

*Advanced on penalty kicks

Individual Statistical Leaders

GOALS	Team	Total
Ronaldo	Brazil	8
Miroslav Klose	Germany	5
Rivaldo	Brazil	5
Jon Dahl Tomasson	Denmark	4
Christian Vieri	Italy	4
Nine tied with 3.		

ASSISTS	Team	Total
Michael Ballack	Germany	4
Christian Ziege	Germany	3
David Beckham	England	3
Francisco De Pedro	Spain	3
Bernd Schneider	Germany	3
Ten tied with 2.		

GOALS-AGAINST AVERAGE	Team	Total
Oliver Kahn	Germany	.43
Marcos	Brazil	.57
David Seaman	England	.60
Pablo Cavallero	Argentina	.67
Shay Given	Ireland	.75
Seigo Narazaki	Japan	.75
Lee Woon Jae	South Korea	.86
Rustu Recber	Turkey	.86

SOCCER MEN'S

Did You Know?

Ronaldo is the youngest player to have won the FIFA World Player of the Year award. He was 20 years old in 1996, when he won his first award.

All-time World Cup Results

Year	Champion	Score	Runner-up	Winning coach
2002	Brazil	2–0	Germany	Luis Felipe Scolari
1998	France	3–0	Brazil	Aime Jacquet
1994	Brazil	0–0 (3–2)	Italy	Carlos Alberto Parreira
1990	W. Germany	1–0	Argentina	Franz Beckenbauer
1986	Argentina	3–2	W. Germany	Carlos Bilardo
1982	Italy	3–1	W. Germany	Enzo Bearzot
1978	Argentina	3–1	Netherlands	César Menotti
1974	W. Germany	2–1	Netherlands	Helmut Schoen
1970	Brazil	4–1	Italy	Mario Zagalo
1966	England	4–2	W. Germany	Alf Ramsey
1962	Brazil	3–1	Czechoslovakia	Aymore Moreira
1958	Brazil	5–2	Sweden	Vicente Feola
1954	W. Germany	3–2	Hungary	Sepp Herberger
1950	Uruguay	2–1	Brazil	Juan Lopez
1938	Italy	4–2	Hungary	Vittorio Pozzo
1934	Italy	2–1	Czechoslovakia	Vittorio Pozzo
1930	Uruguay	4–2	Argentina	Alberto Supicci

2002-03 TIMELINE

March 23, 2002: MLS kicks off its seventh season. The Columbus Crew host the Chicago Fire in the season's first game. Chicago wins, 2–0.

April 22, 2002: The U.S. World Cup roster of 23 players is announced. Eleven players are returning members from the 1998 World Cup team.

May 31, 2002: The 2002 World Cup opens in Seoul, Korea. In the first match of the tournament, Senegal stuns 1998 World Cup champion France, 1–0.

June 5, 2002: The United States defeats one of the Cup favorites, Portugal, 3–2. The three goals are equal to the U.S.'s total goals in 1994 and more than they scored in 1990 and 1998.

June 17, 2002: The United States defeats Mexico, 2–0, to advance to the quarter-finals, its best showing since 1930.

June 30, 2002: Brazil defeats Germany, 2–0, to win the World Cup. Star forward Ronaldo scores both goals for Brazil. He wins the Golden Boot award as the tournament's leading scorer (8 goals).

August 3, 2002: The seventh MLS All-Star Game is held at RFK Stadium, in Washington, D.C. MLS players defeat members of the U.S. national team, 3–2. Midfielder Marco Etcheverry of D.C. United is named MVP of the game.

October 18, 2002: Forward Carlos Ruiz of the Los Angeles Galaxy is named the league MVP. He leads MLS in goals (24).

October 20, 2002: The Los Angeles Galaxy defeat the New England Revolution, 1–0, to win their first MLS Cup.

April 3, 2003: Five-time All-Star Marcelo Balboa of the Colorado Rapids retires. He is the first defender in MLS to record more than 20 goals and 20 assists in his career. Two days later, midfielder John Harkes of the Columbus Crew also retires. He won two MLS Cup championships with D.C. United in 1996 and 1997.

April 5, 2003: Defending MLS Cup champion Los Angeles Galaxy ties the Columbus Crew, 1–1, on opening day of MLS's eighth season.

July 1, 2003: Superstar David Beckham of Manchester United signs a four-year deal with Real Madrid in Spain.

Today's Stars

Ronaldo, forward, b. September 22, 1976, Rio de Janeiro, Brazil. Ronaldo proved he is one of the greatest soccer players in the world at the 2002 World Cup. He won the Golden Boot award as the tournament's leading scorer, with eight goals. Two of those goals came against Germany in the final game, which Brazil won, giving the country a record fifth title. Ronaldo has won the FIFA Player of the Year award three times (1996, 1997, 2002). He plays professionally for Real Madrid, in Spain.

Oliver Kahn, goalkeeper, b. June 15, 1969, Karlsruhe, Germany. Kahn won the Golden Ball award as the best player in the 2002 World Cup, the first goalkeeper to win the honor. He was also named the tournament's best goalie. Kahn, a sure-handed shot stopper, led Germany to the World Cup final, where they lost 2–0, to Brazil. Kahn plays professionally for Bayern Munich of the German Bundesliga.

David Beckham, midfielder, b. May 2, 1975, Leytonstone, England. Beckham came back from a broken left foot to lead England to the quarterfinals of the 2002 World Cup, where they were defeated by Brazil. He scored one goal in the tournament and tied for second in assists with three. Beckham is regarded as the best in the world at free kicks. His strike against Colombia in the 1998 World Cup assured England a spot in the second round. He plays for Real Madrid in Spain.

JOHN TODD/DIGITAL SPORTS ARCHIVE

Ronaldo was the leading scorer in the 2002 World Cup (8 goals).

Did You Know?

Forward Geoff Hurst of England is the only player to have scored a hat trick in a World Cup final. He accomplished the feat during the 1966 World Cup. England won the tournament, defeating Germany, 4–2.

All-time World Cup Scoring Leaders

GOALS

Player, Nation	Tournaments	Goals
Gerd Müller, W. Germany	1970, 1974	14
Just Fontaine, France	1958	13
Pelé, Brazil	1958, 1962, 1966, 1970	12
Ronaldo, Brazil	1998, 2002	12
Sandor Kocsis, Hungary	1954	11
Teofilo Cubillas, Peru	1970, 1978	10
Gregorz Lato, Poland	1974, 1978, 1982	10
Helmut Rahn, W. Germany	1954, 1958	10
Gary Lineker, England	1986, 1990	10
Ademir, Brazil	1950	9
Eusebio, Portugal	1966	9
Jairzinho, Brazil	1970, 1974	9
Paolo Rossi, Italy	1982, 1986	9
K.H. Rummenigge, W. Germany	1978, 1982, 1986	9
Uwe Seeler, W. Germany	1958, 1962, 1966, 1970	9
Vava, Brazil	1958, 1962	9

SOCCER *WOMEN'S*

The Women's United Soccer Association (WUSA) ended its second season with an unlikely new champion: the Carolina Courage, who went from worst to first and won the 2002 Founder's Cup championship by defeating the Washington Freedom, 3–2. It was a season in which foreign players and rookies emerged as the league's stars. Forward Katia of Brazil and the San Jose CyberRays was the league's leading scorer and provided the WUSA's goal of the year *(see page 231)*. Forward Marinette Pichon of France added offensive spark to the Philadelphia Charge.

Pichon finished sixth in the league in scoring and was named league MVP. Forward Birgit Prinz of Germany joined the Carolina Courage and immediately made an impact. She finished third in the league in scoring and was named Founder's Cup MVP. Rookie forward Abby Wambach of the Freedom led her team in scoring. She was named MVP of the inaugural WUSA All-Star Game and Rookie of the Year. Defender Danielle Slaton of the Carolina Courage, the Number 1 pick in the 2002 WUSA draft, scored four goals and was named Defensive Player of the Year.

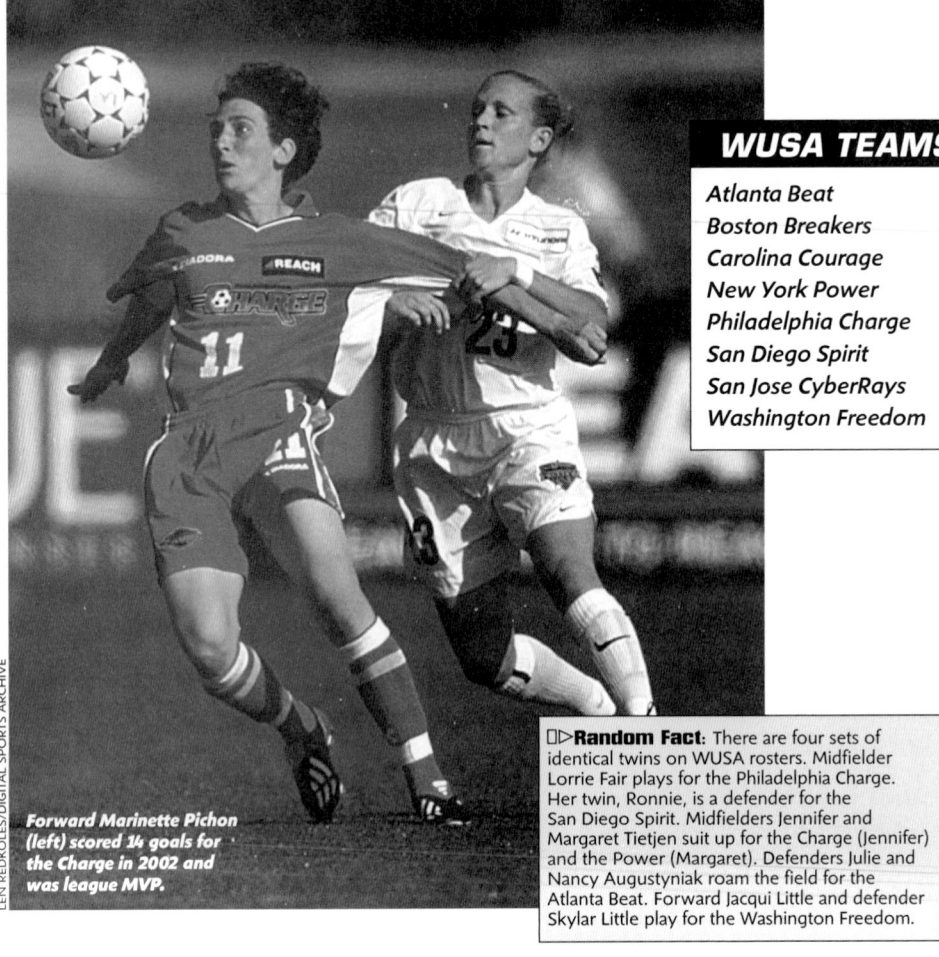

WUSA TEAMS

Atlanta Beat
Boston Breakers
Carolina Courage
New York Power
Philadelphia Charge
San Diego Spirit
San Jose CyberRays
Washington Freedom

Forward Marinette Pichon (left) scored 14 goals for the Charge in 2002 and was league MVP.

LEN REDKOLES/DIGITAL SPORTS ARCHIVE

▯▷**Random Fact:** There are four sets of identical twins on WUSA rosters. Midfielder Lorrie Fair plays for the Philadelphia Charge. Her twin, Ronnie, is a defender for the San Diego Spirit. Midfielders Jennifer and Margaret Tietjen suit up for the Charge (Jennifer) and the Power (Margaret). Defenders Julie and Nancy Augustyniak roam the field for the Atlanta Beat. Forward Jacqui Little and defender Skylar Little play for the Washington Freedom.

2002 WUSA Final Standings

Team	GP	W	L	T	PTS	Home	Road
Carolina Courage	21	12	5	4	40	6–3–1	6–2–3
Philadelphia Charge	21	11	4	6	39	7–1–3	4–3–3
Washington Freedom	21	11	5	5	38	6–2–3	5–3–2
Altanta Beat	21	11	9	1	34	6–3–1	5–6–0
San Jose CyberRays	21	8	8	5	29	7–3–1	1–5–4
Boston Breakers	21	6	8	7	25	5–0–5	1–8–2
San Diego Spirit	21	5	11	5	20	3–4–3	2–7–2
New York Power	21	3	17	1	10	1–10–0	2–7–1

KEY GP=games played; W=win; L=loss; T=tie; PTS=points

2002 PLAYOFFS

Washington Freedom 1
Philadelphia Charge 0

Atlanta Beat 1
Carolina Courage 2 (OT)

2002 FOUNDER'S CUP

Atlanta, Georgia   August 24, 2002

**Washington Freedom 2
Carolina Courage 3**

	1st Half	2nd Half	Final
Freedom	1	1	2
Courage	1	2	3

Scoring Summary:
CAR – Riise (Fotopoulos, Burt) 20
WAS – own goal 31
CAR – Fotopoulos (Prinz, James) 53
CAR – Prinz (unassisted) 58
WAS – Hamm (Wambach) 64

Washington Freedom: Siri Mullinix, Emmy Barr (Tracey Milburn 84), Jennifer Grubb, Skylar Little, Carrie Moore, Ann Cook (Mia Hamm 45), Steffi Jones, Anne Makinen (Jacqui Little 62), Pu Wei, Bai Jie (Monica Gerardo 72), Abby Wambach

Carolina Courage: Kristin Luckenbill, Erin Baxter, Staci Burt, Nel Fettig, Danielle Slaton, Unni Lehn (Staci Wilson 84), Brooke O'Hanley (Venus James 45), Hege Riise, Tiffany Roberts, Danielle Fotopoulos, Birgit Prinz

Note: Numbers next to player names indicate time of game.

Mia Hamm came back from a knee injury to score 8 goals for the Freedom in 2002.

ISAAC MENASHE/DIGITAL SPORTS ARCHIVE

Trivia Challenge

Which U.S. player substituted at goalkeeper in the final six minutes of the 1995 Women's World Cup match against Denmark?

Forward Mia Hamm played goal after U.S. keeper Briana Scurry was elected and the U.S. had used all its substitutes. Mia gave up no goals.

TEAM-BY-TEAM STATS

ATLANTA BEAT

PLAYER	GP	MIN	G	A	PTS	SHOTS	SOG
Charmaine Hooper	19	1,561	11	3	25	40	24
Homare Sawa	21	1,829	7	6	20	46	29
Cindy Parlow	19	1,431	5	4	14	42	20
Nikki Serlenga	21	1,847	3	6	12	29	13
Sun Wen	18	853	4	0	8	23	12
Kylie Bivens	18	1,443	1	4	6	19	9
Liping Wang	14	835	1	2	4	7	2
Emily Burt	14	451	0	4	4	10	4
Kelly Cagle	18	636	1	2	4	11	4
Nancy Augustyniak	19	1,525	0	3	3	3	1
Lisa Krzykowski	13	814	0	2	2	2	1
Julie Augustyniak	20	1,628	0	1	1	8	5
Marci Miller	18	997	0	1	1	6	2
Sharolta Nonen	21	1,876	0	1	1	0	0
Amanda Cromwell	12	740	0	0	0	3	1
Anne Remy	1	1	0	0	0	0	0
Dayna Smith	5	425	0	0	0	0	0
Nicky Thrasher	0	0	0	0	0	0	0
BEAT	**21**	**1,890**	**34**	**39**	**107**	**249**	**127**
OPPONENTS	**21**	**1,890**	**29**	**36**	**94**	**127**	**133**

INDIVIDUAL GOALKEEPING

GOALKEEPER	GP	MIN	SOG	SVS	C/P	GA	GAA
Briana Scurry	18	1,620	115	80	95	24	1.33
Melanie Wilson	3	270	18	13	8	5	1.67
Kristin DePlatchett	0	0	0	0	0	0	0.0
BEAT	**21**	**1,890**	**133**	**104**	**103**	**29**	**1.38**
OPPONENTS	**21**	**1,890**	**127**	**94**	**90**	**34**	**1.62**

BOSTON BREAKERS

PLAYER	GP	MIN	G	A	PTS	SHOTS	SOG
Maren Meinert	21	1,783	7	16	30	52	25
Kristine Lilly	19	1,699	8	13	29	62	33
Dagny Mellgren	20	1,616	11	2	24	53	32
Bettina Wiegmann	20	1,664	2	9	13	24	7
Angela Hucles	19	1,496	3	4	10	23	15
Sarah Yohe	13	469	1	4	6	14	8
Allie Kemp	14	219	2	0	4	6	6
Alexa Borisjuk	13	363	1	1	3	4	3
Jena Kluegel	19	1,677	0	2	2	3	0
Heather Aldama	17	1,354	0	1	1	4	3
Sarah Dacey	16	955	0	1	1	6	4
Monica Gonzalez	12	750	0	1	1	6	2
Ragnhild Gulbrandsen	6	77	0	1	1	3	1
Christine McCann	21	1,879	0	1	1	3	3
Kate Sobrero	16	1,369	0	1	1	1	1
Kalli Kamholz	2	173	0	0	0	1	1
Keri Sanchez	16	1,145	0	0	0	11	5
BREAKERS	**21**	**1,890**	**36**	**57**	**129**	**276**	**149**
OPPONENTS	**21**	**1,890**	**35**	**38**	**108**	**149**	**122**

INDIVIDUAL GOALKEEPING

GOALKEEPER	GP	MIN	SOG	SVS	C/P	GA	GAA
Karina LeBlanc	17	1,530	101	64	67	27	1.59
Tracy Ducar	4	360	21	13	18	8	2.00
Kristin Slater	0	0	0	0	0	0	0.0
BREAKERS	**21**	**1,890**	**122**	**88**	**85**	**35**	**1.67**
OPPONENTS	**21**	**1,890**	**149**	**114**	**78**	**36**	**1.71**

KEY GP=games played; MIN=minutes played; G=goals; A=assists; PTS=points; SOG=shots on goal; SVS=saves; C/P=catches/punches; GA=goals allowed; GAA=goals-against average

TEAM-BY-TEAM STATS

CAROLINA COURAGE

PLAYER	GP	MIN	G	A	PTS	SHOTS	SOG
Birgit Prinz	15	1,350	12	8	32	51	27
Danielle Fotopoulos	21	1,836	11	11	33	90	47
Hege Riise	19	1,701	6	14	26	41	25
Danielle Slaton	18	1,381	4	0	8	18	14
Venus James	20	624	2	2	6	12	6
Unni Lehn	18	1,511	2	3	7	20	8
Tiffany Roberts	19	1,710	1	4	6	8	3
Staci Burt	20	1,800	0	4	4	9	2
Nel Fettig	21	1,785	0	3	3	7	2
Katie Barnes	15	571	0	1	1	8	1
Meghan Anderson	16	489	0	0	0	4	3
Erin Baxter	16	1,148	0	0	0	2	0
Tracy Grose	1	27	0	0	0	0	0
Brooke O'Hanley	18	1,094	0	0	0	3	1
Carla Overbeck	9	424	0	0	0	2	1
Staci Wilson	14	882	0	0	0	0	0
Kim Montgomery	11	495	0	0	0	13	8
Stacy Roeck	0	0	0	0	0	0	0
COURAGE	**21**	**1,890**	**40**	**50**	**130**	**290**	**149**
OPPONENTS	**21**	**1,890**	**30**	**38**	**98**	**149**	**156**

INDIVIDUAL GOALKEEPING

GOALKEEPER	GP	MIN	SOG	SVS	C/P	GA	GAA
Julie Podhrasky	0	0	0	0	0	0	0.0
Kristin Luckenbill	21	1,890	156	114	77	30	1.43
Emily Oleksiuk	0	0	0	0	0	0	0.0
COURAGE	**21**	**1,890**	**156**	**126**	**77**	**30**	**1.43**
OPPONENTS	**21**	**1,890**	**149**	**111**	**81**	**40**	**1.90**

NEW YORK POWER

PLAYER	GP	MIN	G	A	PTS	SHOTS	SOG
Tiffeny Milbrett	19	1,605	10	8	28	62	33
Emily Janss	21	1,336	8	1	17	29	18
Tammy Pearman	20	1,569	4	1	9	19	9
Linda Ormen	14	1,032	2	3	7	20	12
Krista Davey	20	727	2	1	5	10	5
Anita Rapp	19	1,364	2	1	5	20	6
Minna Mustonen	12	505	1	2	4	7	3
Ronnie Fair	21	1,751	0	4	4	3	2
Wynee McIntosh	14	827	1	1	3	5	2
Justi Baumgardt-Yamada	10	548	0	3	3	10	3
Jaclyn Ravela	10	876	1	0	2	4	3
Jennifer Lalor	20	1,457	0	1	1	36	20
Christie Pearce	19	1,699	0	1	1	3	0
Emily Stauffer	15	538	0	1	1	5	1
Katie Tracy	8	368	0	1	1	3	2
Sarah Whalen	10	872	0	1	1	5	3
Kristy Whelchel	20	1,701	0	1	1	8	2
Rachel Hoffman	7	123	0	0	0	1	0
Bonnie Young	0	0	0	0	0	0	0
POWER	**21**	**1,890**	**31**	**31**	**93**	**250**	**124**
OPPONENTS	**21**	**1,890**	**62**	**74**	**198**	**124**	**192**

INDIVIDUAL GOALKEEPING

GOALKEEPER	GP	MIN	SOG	SVS	C/P	GA	GAA
Nicole Williams	4	272	23	15	10	8	2.65
Saskia Webber	14	1,258	132	91	44	40	2.86
Gao Hong	4	360	37	21	11	14	3.50
POWER	**21**	**1,890**	**192**	**132**	**65**	**62**	**2.95**
OPPONENTS	**21**	**1,890**	**124**	**93**	**52**	**31**	**1.48**

SOCCER *WOMEN'S*

TEAM-BY-TEAM STATS

PHILADELPHIA CHARGE

PLAYER	GP	MIN	G	A	PTS	SHOTS	SOG
Marinette Pichon	18	1,394	14	1	29	68	36
Zhao Lihong	17	1,362	2	9	13	19	13
Kelly Smith	7	603	4	3	11	22	14
Mandy Clemens	18	1,046	2	2	6	32	16
Liu Ailing	20	1,235	2	2	6	22	12
Kerry Connors	18	1,212	2	1	5	20	9
Jennifer Tietjen	20	1,800	1	2	4	4	1
Lorrie Fair	19	1,638	0	5	5	17	6
Erica Iverson	19	1,691	2	0	4	7	3
Erin Martin	11	482	2	0	4	10	5
Stacey Tullock	14	1,012	2	0	4	14	4
Mary-Frances Monroe	15	830	1	2	4	14	5
Heather Mitts	16	1,386	0	5	5	1	1
Jenny Benson	19	1,582	0	3	3	14	7
Tara Koleski	6	200	0	1	1	2	1
Andrea Alfiler	5	339	0	0	0	0	0
Michelle Demko	5	132	0	0	0	0	0
Karyn Hall	4	263	0	0	0	1	0
Rebekah McDowell	12	673	0	0	0	4	3
Rakel Karvelsson	0	0	0	0	0	0	0
CHARGE	**21**	**1,890**	**36**	**37**	**109**	**271**	**136**
OPPONENTS	**21**	**1,890**	**22**	**27**	**71**	**136**	**116**

INDIVIDUAL GOALKEEPING

GOALKEEPER	GP	MIN	SOG	SVS	C/P	GA	GAA
Melissa Moore	20	1,800	110	86	54	20	1.00
Maite Zabala	1	90	6	4	5	2	2.00
Janel Schillig	0	0	0	0	0	0	0.00
CHARGE	**21**	**1,890**	**116**	**94**	**59**	**22**	**1.05**
OPPONENTS	**21**	**1,890**	**136**	**100**	**88**	**36**	**1.71**

SAN DIEGO SPIRIT

PLAYER	GP	MIN	G	A	PTS	SHOTS	SOG
Shannon MacMillan	17	1,424	5	8	18	56	27
Julie Foudy	19	1,645	5	4	14	29	18
Zhang Ouying	17	1,352	5	2	12	23	17
Lori Lindsey	20	1,231	2	5	9	22	9
Julie Fleeting	8	641	3	1	7	30	15
Shannon Boxx	20	1,349	2	2	6	27	12
Jen Mascaro	11	665	1	4	6	7	3
Shauna Rohbock	12	481	2	0	4	10	6
Sherrill Kester	21	1,342	1	2	4	16	9
Joy Fawcett	19	1,627	1	1	3	6	4
Mercy Akide	10	470	0	1	1	11	6
Fan Yunjie	17	1,387	0	1	1	2	0
Kim Pickup	15	576	0	1	1	1	1
Amy Sauer	20	1,489	0	1	1	3	1
Anna Kraus	9	746	0	0	0	1	1
Flo Omagbemi	6	241	0	0	0	2	0
Rhiannon Tanaka	18	1,438	0	0	0	0	0
Margaret Tietjen	13	585	0	0	0	5	4
SPIRIT	**21**	**1,890**	**28**	**33**	**89**	**254**	**135**
OPPONENTS	**21**	**1,890**	**42**	**49**	**133**	**135**	**126**

INDIVIDUAL GOALKEEPING

GOALKEEPER	GP	MIN	SOG	SVS	C/P	GA	GAA
Carly Smolak	10	721	40	25	20	14	1.75
Jaime Pagliarulo	15	1,168	86	54	47	28	2.16
Shelley Finger	0	0	0	0	0	0	0.00
CHARGE	**21**	**1,890**	**126**	**85**	**67**	**42**	**2.00**
OPPONENTS	**21**	**1,890**	**135**	**108**	**78**	**28**	**1.33**

TEAM-BY-TEAM STATS

SAN JOSE CYBERRAYS

PLAYER	GP	MIN	G	A	PTS	SHOTS	SOG
Katia	21	1,847	15	6	36	96	54
Tisha Venturini-Hoch	21	1,734	6	3	15	25	16
Brandi Chastain	18	1,561	4	3	11	38	18
Pretinha	21	1,749	4	5	13	42	26
Sissi	21	1,754	1	9	11	47	23
Michelle French	20	1,600	1	6	8	7	5
Kim Clark	15	643	1	4	6	17	6
Maren Hendershot-Brown	9	159	1	0	2	5	2
Lisa Nanez	10	444	1	0	2	4	1
Theresa Wagner	14	354	0	3	3	3	0
Christina Bell	10	371	0	1	1	11	4
Dianne Alagich	17	1,438	0	0	0	3	2
Danielle Borgman	14	862	0	0	0	3	0
Thori Bryan	21	1,890	0	0	0	7	4
Carey Dorn	13	755	0	0	0	3	2
Kelly Lindsey	19	1,649	0	0	0	4	1
Megan Horvath	0	0	0	0	0	0	0
CYBERRAYS	**21**	**1,890**	**34**	**41**	**109**	**316**	**164**
OPPONENTS	**21**	**1,890**	**30**	**39**	**99**	**164**	**108**

INDIVIDUAL GOALKEEPING

KEEPER	GP	MIN	SOG	SVS	C/P	GA	GAA
LaKeysia Beene	20	1,800	104	72	93	27	1.35
Dawn Greathouse	1	90	4	2	2	3	3.00
Linnea Quinones	0	0	0	0	0	0	0.00
Alice Gleason	0	0	0	0	0	0	0.00
CYBERRAYS	**21**	**1,890**	**108**	**79**	**95**	**30**	**1.43**
OPPONENTS	**21**	**1,890**	**164**	**130**	**87**	**34**	**1.62**

WASHINGTON FREEDOM

PLAYER	GP	MIN	G	A	PTS	SHOTS	SOG
Abby Wambach	19	1,689	10	10	30	54	34
Mia Hamm	11	505	8	6	22	26	18
Bai Jie	16	887	6	5	17	28	16
Jacqui Little	20	1,019	3	4	10	21	14
Pu Wei	20	1,667	1	8	10	24	9
Monica Gerardo	19	985	3	1	7	18	9
Emmy Barr	21	1,863	2	4	8	8	6
Anne Makinen	14	824	2	3	7	12	6
Jennifer Grubb	21	1,890	2	0	4	11	7
Skylar Little	20	1,751	1	2	4	2	1
Meredith Beard	5	84	1	0	2	4	1
Steffi Jones	13	1,170	0	3	3	13	6
Ann Cook	18	747	0	1	1	8	4
Tracey Milburn	11	448	0	1	1	5	2
Sarah Kate Noftsinger	5	289	0	1	1	2	0
Carrie Moore	18	1,491	0	0	0	6	2
Stephanie Rigamat	6	92	0	0	0	1	0
Lindsay Stoecker	11	928	0	0	0	16	2
Casey Zimny	15	570	0	0	0	1	1
FREEDOM	**21**	**1,890**	**40**	**50**	**130**	**260**	**138**
OPPONENTS	**21**	**1,890**	**29**	**37**	**95**	**138**	**169**

INDIVIDUAL GOALKEEPING

KEEPER	GP	MIN	SOG	SVS	C/P	GA	GAA
Kathy Hoverman	0	0	0	0	0	0	0.00
Siri Mullinix	14	1,139	104	84	57	15	1.19
Erin Fahey	6	327	35	27	23	6	1.65
FREEDOM	**21**	**1,890**	**169**	**141**	**97**	**29**	**1.38**
OPPONENTS	**21**	**1,890**	**138**	**99**	**94**	**40**	**1.90**

Danielle Fotopoulos, Carolina Courage

2002 WUSA Statistical Leaders

SCORING

SCORING	GP	G	A	PTS
Katia, CyberRays	21	15	6	36
Danielle Fotopoulos, Courage	21	11	11	33
Birgit Prinz, Courage	15	12	8	32
Abby Wambach, Freedom	19	10	10	30
Maren Meinert, Breakers	21	7	16	30
Marinette Pichon, Charge	18	14	1	29
Kristine Lilly, Breakers	19	8	13	29
Tiffeny Millbrett, Power	19	10	8	28
Hege Riise, Courage	19	6	14	26
Charmaine Hooper, Beat	19	11	3	25

GOALS

GOALS	GP	G
Katia, CyberRays	21	15
Marinette Pichon, Charge	18	14
Birgit Prinz, Courage	15	12
Danielle Fotopoulos, Courage	21	11
Charmaine Hooper, Beat	19	11
Dagny Mellgren, Breakers	20	11
Abby Wambach, Freedom	19	10
Tiffeny Millbrett, Power	19	10
Mia Hamm, Freedom	11	8
Kristine Lilly, Breakers	19	8
Emily Janss, Power	21	8

ASSISTS

ASSISTS	GP	A
Maren Meinert, Breakers	21	16
Hege Riise, Courage	19	14
Kristine Lilly, Breakers	19	13
Danielle Fotopoulos, Courage	21	11
Abby Wambach, Freedom	19	10
Sissi, CyberRays	21	9
Bettina Wiegmann, Breakers	20	9
Zhao Lihong, Charge	17	9
Pu Wei, Freedom	20	8
Tiffeny Millbrett, Power	19	8
Shannon MacMillan, Spirit	17	8
Birgit Prinz, Courage	15	8

KEY GP=games played; G=goals; A=assists; PTS=points; GAA=goals-against average; SOG=shots on goal; SVS=saves; GPG=goals per game; GA=goals allowed

GOALS-AGAINST AVERAGE

GOALS-AGAINST AVERAGE	GP	GAA
Melissa Moore, Charge	20	1.00
Siri Mullinix, Freedom	14	1.19
Briana Scurry, Beat	18	1.33
LaKeysia Beene, CyberRays	20	1.35
Kristin Luckenbill, Courage	21	1.43
Karina LeBlanc, Breakers	17	1.59
Erin Fahey, Freedom	6	1.65
Melanie Wilson, Beat	3	1.67
Dawn Greathouse, Freedom	5	1.70
Carly Smolak, Spirit	10	1.75

SHOTS ON GOAL

SHOTS ON GOAL	GP	SOG
Katia, CyberRays	21	54
Danielle Fotopoulos, Courage	21	47
Marinette Pichon, Charge	18	36
Abby Wambach, Freedom	19	34
Tiffeny Millbrett, Power	19	33
Kristine Lilly, Breakers	19	33
Dagny Mellgren, Breakers	20	32
Homare Sawa, Beat	21	29
Shannon MacMillan, Spirit	17	27
Birgit Prinz, Courage	15	27

SAVES

SAVES	GP	SVS
Kristin Luckenbill, Courage	21	114
Saskia Webber, Power	14	91
Melissa Moore, Charge	20	86
Siri Mullinix, Freedom	14	84
Briana Scurry, Beat	18	80
Lakeysia Beene, CyberRays	20	72
Karina LeBlanc, Breakers	17	64
Jamie Pagliarulo, Spirit	15	54
Erin Fahey, Freedom	6	27
Carly Smolak, Spirit	10	25

Kristin Luckenbill, Carolina Courage

TEAM OFFENSE

TEAM OFFENSE	GP	G	GPG
Washington Freedom	21	40	1.9
Carolina Courage	21	40	1.9
Philadelphia Charge	21	36	1.7
Boston Breakers	21	36	1.7
San Jose CyberRays	21	34	1.6
Atlanta Beat	21	34	1.6
New York Power	21	31	1.5
San Diego Spirit	21	28	1.3

TEAM DEFENSE

TEAM DEFENSE	GP	GA	GAA
Philadelphia Charge	21	22	1.0
Washington Freedom	21	29	1.4
Atlanta Beat	21	29	1.4
San Jose CyberRays	21	30	1.4
Carolina Courage	21	30	1.4
Boston Breakers	21	35	1.7
San Diego Spirit	21	42	2.0
New York Power	21	62	3.0

BRAD SMITH/DIGITAL SPORTS ARCHIVE (FOTOPOULOS); HOWARD SMITH/DIGITAL SPORTS ARCHIVE (LUCKENBILL)

WUSA Award Winners

MVP
2002 Marinette Pichon, Philadelphia Charge
2001 Tiffeny Milbrett, New York Power

Offensive Player of the Year
2002 Marinette Pichon, Philadelphia Charge
2001 Tiffeny Milbrett, New York Power

Defensive Player of the Year
2002 Danielle Slaton, Carolina Courage
2001 Doris Fitschen, Philadelphia Charge

Goalkeeper of the Year
2002 Kristin Luckenbill, Carolina Courage
2001 2001 LaKeysia Beene, San Jose CyberRays

Rookie of the Year
2002 Abby Wambach, Washington Freedom

Goal of the Year
2002 Katia, San Jose CyberRays

Katia, San Jose CyberRays

JOHN TODD/DIGITAL SPORTS ARCHIVE

Today's Stars

Tiffeny Milbrett, forward, b. October 23, 1972, Portland, Oregon. Milbrett finished in the Top 10 in points, goals, and assists in 2002. She was the WUSA's leading scorer, MVP, and offensive player of the year in 2001. Milbrett, a member of the United States women's team since 1991, was the leading scorer (3 goals) for the 1999 U.S. World Cup championship team.

Mia Hamm, forward, b. March 17, 1972, Selma, Alabama. Hamm is the most famous women's soccer player in the world. A member of the U.S. women's team since 1987, she broke the all-time international scoring record (for women and for men) by scoring her 108th career goal on May 16, 1999, against Brazil. Hamm is a founding member of the WUSA. She rebounded from a knee injury in 2001 to score eight goals for the Washington Freedom in 2002.

Tiffeny Milbrett led the Power in scoring (10 goals, 8 assists) in 2002.

HOWARD SMITH/DIGITAL SPORTS ARCHIVE

Marinette Pichon, forward, b. November 26, 1975, Var Sur Aube, France. Pichon has been a member of the French national team since 1994. She joined the Philadelphia Charge in 2002 and scored 14 goals, second-most in the league and nearly 40 percent of the Charge's goals. Pichon was the league's 2002 MVP and Offensive Player of the Year.

Trivia Challenge

Who won the first Women's World Cup? Where and when was the Cup held?

The United States won the first Women's World Cup. The event was held in China in 1991.

CHRIS KELLY/DIGITAL SPORTS ARCHIVE

Rookie Abby Wambach was MVP of the first WUSA All-Star Game, in 2002.

2002 ALL-STAR GAME

Portland, Oregon   September 21, 2002

South All-Stars 6
North All-Stars 1
MVP: Abby Wambach

	1st Half	2nd Half	Final
South All-Stars	3	3	6
North All-Stars	1	0	1

Scoring Summary:
North – Pichon (Venturini-Hoch), 12
South – Riise (Hamm) 21
South – Wambach (MacMillan), 24
South – Bivens (Hamm), 39
South – Wambach (Hooper, MacMillan), 60
South – Hooper (Wambach), 66
South – MacMillan (Hooper), 80

South All-Stars (Starters): Kristin Luckenbill, Danielle Slaton, Jennifer Grubb, Joy Fawcett, Tiffany Roberts, Homare Sawa, Julie Foudy, Shannon MacMillan, Hege Riise, Abby Wambach, Mia Hamm
North All-Stars (Starters): Melissa Moore, Jenny Benson, Jennifer Tietjen, Kate Sobrero, Brandi Chastain, Lorrie Fair, Tisha Venturini-Hoch, Sissi, Katia, Marinette Pichon, Tiffeny Milbrett

Legends

CHRIS KELLY/DIGITAL SPORTS ARCHIVE

Michelle Akers scored 12 goals in three World Cup tournaments (1991, 1995, 1999).

Michelle Akers, midfielder, b. February 1, 1966, Santa Clara, California. Akers was named the Federation Internationale de Football Association (FIFA) Co-Player of the Century in 2000, sharing the honor with Sun Wen of China *(see below)*. She is the second all-time scoring leader (105 goals) for the U.S. women's team. Akers is the all-time scoring leader in Women's World Cup history (12 goals). She earned the Bronze Ball as the third-most valuable player at the 1999 Women's World Cup. Akers retired from competition on October 12, 2001.

Sun Wen, forward, b. April 6, 1973, Fujian, China. Sun was named the FIFA Co-Player of the Century in 2000, sharing the honor with Michelle Akers *(see above)*. She was a member of China's 1991, 1995, and 1999 World Cup teams. At the 1999 Cup, she tied for the tournament lead in goals (7) and was awarded the Golden Boot as the tournament's MVP. The Number 1 overall pick in the 2001 WUSA draft, Sun scored 4 goals for the Atlanta Beat in 2002.

April Heinrichs, forward, b. February 27, 1964, Denver, Colorado. Heinrichs was the captain of the U.S. team that won the first Women's World Cup, in 1991. She scored four goals in the tournament. Heinrichs retired after the Cup, finishing her national team career with 38 goals in 47 games. She has been head coach of the U.S. women's team since 2000. She is the third woman to hold a head coaching job in women's international soccer.

2002-03 TIMELINE --

April 13, 2002: WUSA's second season kicks off with all eight teams in action.

June 1, 2002: Goalkeeper Siri Mullinix of the Washington Freedom sets the WUSA record for saves in a game (13) in a scoreless tie with the Boston Breakers, in Foxboro, Massachusetts.

June 9, 2002: Forward Katia of the San Jose CyberRays scores the WUSA Goal of the Year. She takes a pass out of the air and kicks it from a bad angle before it hits the ground. The CyberRays defeat the San Diego Spirit, 3-1.

July 6, 2002: The San Diego Spirit defeat the Boston Breakers, 5-4, at Torero Stadium, in San Diego, California. The nine total goals are the most scored in a single WUSA match.

August 10, 2002: The Boston Breakers defeat the San Jose CyberRays, 1-0, at Nickerson Field, in Boston, Massachusetts, to become the first WUSA team with an undefeated regular-season home record (5-0-5).

August 24, 2002: The Carolina Courage go from worst to first and win the Founder's Cup championship by defeating the Washington Freedom, 3-2. Courage forward Birgit Prinz is named the game's MVP.

September 16, 2002: The Boston Breakers honor U.S. women's team legend Michelle Akers in an exhibition game against the Washington Freedom. Akers, who retired from competition in 2001, suits up for the Breakers and plays the full first half.

September 21, 2002: WUSA holds its first All-Star Game, at PGE Park, in Portland, Oregon. The South All-Stars defeat the North All-Stars, 6-1. Forward Abby Wambach of the Washington Freedom is named game MVP.

November 15, 2002: Marcia McDermott, the head coach of the 2002 WUSA champion Carolina Courage, steps down. She was the only female head coach in the WUSA during its first two seasons. McDermott holds the WUSA record for wins in a season (12) and finished her coaching career 20-17-7. She becomes the team's assistant general manager in January 2003.

April 5, 2003: WUSA's third season begins with a rematch of the 2002 Founder's Cup. This time, the Washington Freedom defeat the Carolina Courage, 2-1.

May 26, 2003: FIFA announces that the 2003 Women's World Cup will move from China to the U.S. because of the health threat of the SARS virus. The Cup is scheduled for September 20-October 12, 2003.

Visit **www.sikids.com** for the latest sports stats and info.
Site code: slamdunk
AOL keyword: sikids

ACTION SPORTS

Travis Pastrana nailed a backflip at the 2002 Gravity Games to win gold in the freestyle motocross event.

PAUL BUCKLEY

The world of freestyle motocross was flipping out at the 2003 Winter X Games. Mike Metzger landed his latest big trick — a backflip no-footer — on the snow and won gold in the big-air event.

Metzger and Travis Pastrana had unveiled the backflip at the 2002 Gravity Games. Metzger became the first rider to lay down the trick in competition, but Pastrana won the gold. At the 2002 Summer X Games, Metzger pushed the trick further when he pulled the backflip no-footer in the big-air event. The push earned him the gold medal.

Ricky Carmichael and James Stewart owned the sport of motocross racing in 2002. Carmichael won his second-straight supercross championship and his third-straight motocross title in the 250cc class. (The term *cc*, or *cubic centimeters*, refers to the size of a motorcycle's engine.) Stewart won eight consecutive races and became the youngest national motocross champion in the 125cc class.

In skateboarding, it was all about PLG, Pierre-Luc Gagnon. Gagnon *[gan-YONH]* won vert best trick and finished third in vert at the 2002 Gravity Games. He followed that by winning both events at the 2002 Summer X Games. Skater Eric Koston also won his third-straight gold medal in street at the 2002 Gravity Games.

Dave Mirra continued his all-terrain BMX dominance by winning gold in street at the 2002 Gravity Games and gold in vert at the 2002 Summer X Games.

Shaun White proved he was ready to sit at the adult table. The 16-year-old snowboarder won gold medals in both slopestyle and superpipe at the 2003 Winter X Games. White improved on his double silver performance at the 2002 Winter X Games.

In the water, Andy Irons and Layne Beachley ruled the surfing world. Irons snagged his first World Championship Tour title in 2002, after winning four events. Beachley won a record fifth-straight women's world title.

Winter X Games Results

Moto X

Year	Event	Gold	Silver	Bronze
2003	Big Air	Mike Metzger, USA	Dane Kinnaird, Australia	Caleb Wyatt, USA
2002	Big Air	Brian Deegan, USA	Mike Jones, USA	Tommy Clowers, USA
2001	Big Air	Mike Jones, USA	Tommy Clowers, USA	Clifford Adoptante, USA

Skiing—Men

Year	Event	Gold	Silver	Bronze
2003	Skier X	Lars Lewen, Sweden	Reggie Crist, USA	Enak Gavaggio, France
2002	Skier X	Reggie Crist, USA	Peter Lind, Sweden	Enak Gavaggio, France
2001	Skier X	Zach Crist, USA	Tomas Andersson, Sweden	Enak Gavaggio, France
2000	Skier X	Shaun Palmer, USA	Bill Hudson, USA	Zach Crist, USA
1999	Skier X	Enak Gavaggio, France	Shane McConkey, USA	Jeremy Nobis, USA
1998	Skier X	Denis Rey, France	Kent Kreitler, USA	Chris Davenport, USA
2003	Slopestyle	Tanner Hall, USA	Pep Fujas, USA	Jon Olsson, Sweden
2002	Slopestyle	Tanner Hall, USA	C.R. Johnson, USA	Jon Olsson, Sweden
2003	Superpipe	Candide Thovex, France	Tanner Hall, USA	Jon Olsson, Sweden
2002	Superpipe	Jon Olsson, Sweden	Philippe Larose, Canada	Philippe Poirier, Canada
2001	Big Air	Tanner Hall, USA	Evan Raps, USA	C.R. Johnson, USA
2000	Big Air	Candide Thovex, France	Skogen Sprang, USA	Evan Raps, USA
1999	Big Air	J.F. Cusson, Canada	Jonny Moseley, USA	Vincent Dorion, Canada

Skiing—Women

Year	Event	Gold	Silver	Bronze
2003	Skier X	Aleisha Cline, Canada	Karin Hutary, Austria	Cecilie Larsen, Norway
2002	Skier X	Aleisha Cline, Canada	Magdalena Jonsson, Sweden	Patti Sherman-Kauf, USA
2001	Skier X	Aleisha Cline, Canada	Magdalena Jonsson, Sweden	Chiara Lawrence, USA
2000	Skier X	Anik Demers, Canada	Chiara Lawrence, USA	Patti Sherman-Kauf, USA
1999	Skier X	Aleisha Cline, Canada	Darian Boyle, USA	Patti Sherman-Kauf, USA

Snowboarding—Men

Year	Event	Gold	Silver	Bronze
2003	Slopestyle	Shaun White, USA	Jussi Oksanen, Finland	Jimi Tomer, USA
2002	Slopestyle	Travis Rice, USA	Shaun White, USA	Todd Richards, USA
2001	Slopestyle	Kevin Jones, USA	Todd Richards, USA	Jussi Oksanen, Finland
2000	Slopestyle	Kevin Jones, USA	Todd Richards, USA	Peter Line, USA
1999	Slopestyle	Peter Line, USA	Kevin Jones, USA	Jimmy Halopoff, USA
1998	Slopestyle	Ross Powers, USA	Kevin Jones, USA	Rob Kingwill, USA
1997	Slopestyle	Daniel Franck, Norway	Jimmy Halopoff, USA	Bryan Iguchi, USA
2003	Snowboarder X	Ueli Kestenholz, Switzerland	Xavier Delerue, France	Michael Rosengren, USA
2002	Snowboarder X	Philippe Conte, Switzerland	Seth Wescott, USA	Berti Denervaud, Switzerland
2001	Snowboarder X	Scott Gaffney, Canada	Mark Schulz, USA	Seth Wescott, USA
2000	Snowboarder X	Drew Neilson, Canada	Scott Gaffney, Canada	Jason Ford, USA
1999	Snowboarder X	Shaun Palmer, USA	Drew Neilson, Canada	Scott Gaffney, Canada
1998`	Snowboarder X	Shaun Palmer, USA	Jason Brown, USA	Seth Wescott, USA
1997	Snowboarder X	Shaun Palmer, USA	Bertrand Denervaud, Switzerland	Mike Basich, USA
2003	Superpipe	Shaun White, USA	Danny Kass, USA	Markku Koski, Finland
2002	Superpipe	J.J. Thomas, USA	Shaun White, USA	Keir Dillon, USA
2001	Superpipe	Danny Kass, USA	Tommy Czeschin, USA	Ross Powers, USA
2000	Superpipe	Todd Richards, USA	Ross Powers, USA	Tommy Czeschin, USA
1999	Halfpipe	Jimi Scott, USA	Mike Michalchuk, Canada	Luke Wynen, USA
1998	Halfpipe	Ross Powers, USA	Guillaume Chastagnol, France	Todd Richards, USA
1997	Halfpipe	Todd Richards, USA	Daniel Franck, Norway	Fabien Rohrer, Switzerland

Tara Dakides is a three-time Winter X Games gold medalist in slopestyle.

IAN RUHTER

▷ **Random Fact:** The first Winter X Games, in 1997, featured events in ice climbing, snow mountain-bike racing, and super-modified shovel racing.

Winter X Games Results (cont.)

Snowboarding—Men

Year	Event	Gold	Silver	Bronze
2001	Big Air	Jussi Oksanen, Finland	Todd Richards, USA	Josh Dirksen, USA
2000	Big Air	Peter Line, USA	Jason Borgstede, USA	Kevin Jones, USA
1999	Big Air	Kevin Sansalone, Canada	Peter Line, USA	Kevin Jones, USA
1998	Big Air	Jason Borgstede, USA	Ryan W. Williams, USA	Kevin Jones, USA
1997	Big Air	Jimmy Halopoff, USA	Steve Adkins, USA	Bjorn Leines, USA

Snowboarding—Women

Year	Event	Gold	Silver	Bronze
2003	Slopestyle	Janna Meyen, USA	Hana Beaman, USA	Lindsey Jacobellis, USA
2002	Slopestyle	Tara Dakides, USA	Janna Meyen, USA	Barrett Christy, USA
2001	Slopestyle	Jaime MacLeod, USA	Shannon Dunn, USA	Marni Yamada, USA
2000	Slopestyle	Tara Dakides, USA	Jaime MacLeod, USA	Barrett Christy, USA
1999	Slopestyle	Tara Dakides, USA	Barrett Christy, USA	Jaime MacLeod, USA
1998	Slopestyle	Jennie Waara, Sweden	Barrett Christy, USA	Aurelie Sayres, USA
1997	Slopestyle	Barrett Christy, USA	Cara-Beth Burnside, USA	Jennie Waara, Sweden
2003	Snowboarder X	Lindsey Jacobellis, USA	Tanja Frieden, Switzerland	Yvonne Mueller, Switzerland
2002	Snowboarder X	Ine Poetzl, Austria	Erin Simmons, Canada	Tanja Frieden, Switzerland
2001	Snowboarder X	Line Oestvold, Norway	Erin Simmons, Canada	Amy Johnson, USA
2000	Snowboarder X	Leslee Olson, USA	Carlee Baker, Canada	Line Oestvold, Norway
1999	Snowboarder X	Maelle Ricker, Canada	Leslee Olson, USA	Candice Drouin, Canada

Snowboarding—Women (cont.)

Year	Event	Gold	Silver	Bronze
1998	Snowboarder X	Tina Dixon, USA	Corrie Rudishauser, USA	Katrina Warnick, USA
1997	Snowboarder X	Jennie Waara, Sweden	Hillary Maybery, USA	Aurelie Sayres, USA
2003	Superpipe	Gretchen Bleiler, USA	Kelly Clark, USA	Hannah Teter, USA
2002	Superpipe	Kelly Clark, USA	Stine Brun Kjeldaas, Norway	Natasza Zurek, Canada
2001	Superpipe	Shannon Dunn, USA	Natasza Zurek, Canada	Fabienne Reuteler, Switzerland
2000	Superpipe	Stine Brun Kjeldaas, Norway	Barrett Christy, USA	Natasza Zurek, Canada
1999	Halfpipe	Michele Taggart, USA	Shannon Dunn, USA	Cara-Beth Burnside, USA
1998	Halfpipe	Cara-Beth Burnside, USA	Michele Taggart, USA	Nicola Thost, Germany
1997	Halfpipe	Shannon Dunn, USA	Jennie Waara, Sweden	Nicole Angelrath, Switzerland
2001	Big Air	Tara Dakides, USA	Barrett Christy, USA	Jenna Murano, USA
2000	Big Air	Tara Dakides, USA	Leah Wagner, Canada	Jessica Dalpiaz, USA
1999	Big Air	Barrett Christy, USA	Tara Dakides, USA	Janet Matthews, Canada
1998	Big Air	Tina Basich, USA	Barrett Christy, USA	Tara Zwink, USA
1997	Big Air	Barrett Christy, USA	Tara Zwink, USA	Tina Basich, USA

Snowmobiling

Year	Event	Gold	Silver	Bronze
2003	SnoCross	Blair Morgan, Canada	D.J. Eckstrom, USA	Tucker Hibbert, USA
2002	SnoCross	Blair Morgan, Canada	Tucker Hibbert, USA	Tomi Ahmasalo, Finland
2001	SnoCross	Blair Morgan, Canada	Kent Ipsen, USA	D.J. Eckstrom, USA
2000	SnoCross	Tucker Hibbert, USA	Blair Morgan, Canada	T.J. Gulla, USA
1999	SnoCross	Chris Vincent, USA	Blair Morgan, Canada	Trevor John, USA
1998	SnoCross	Toni Haikonen, Finland	Dennis Burks, USA	Per Berggren, Sweden
2003	HillCross	T.J. Gulla, USA	Carl Kuster, Canada	Steve Martin, Canada
2002	HillCross	Carl Kuster, Canada	Steve Martin, Canada	Rick Ward, USA
2001	HillCross	Carl Kuster, Canada	Vinny Clark, Canada	Matt Luczynski, USA

Ultracross *

Year	Gold	Silver	Bronze
2003	Xavier Delerue, France	Seth Wescott, USA	Ben Jacobellis, USA
	Kaj Zackrisson, Sweden	Peter Lind, Sweden	Lars Lewen, Sweden
2002	Seth Wescott, USA	Scott Gaffney, Canada	Rob Fagan, Canada
	Peter Lind, Sweden	Eric Archer, USA	Enak Gavaggio, France
2001	Shaun Palmer, USA	Jason Evans, USA	Pontus Staahlkloo, Sweden
	Hiroomi Takizawa, Japan	Isidor Gruener, Austria	Matt Murphy, USA
2000	Travis McLain, USA	Scott Gaffney, Canada	Terry Plum, USA
	Peter Lind, Sweden	Sverre Liliequist, Sweden	Mike Dill, USA

*First athlete listed in each category is a snowboarder; the second athlete is a skier.

U.S. Open Snowboarding Championship Results

Halfpipe—Men

Year	Gold	Silver	Bronze
2003	Ross Powers, USA	Kazuhiro Kokubo, Japan	Daniel Franck, Norway
2002	Danny Kass, USA	Markku Koski, Finland	Keir Dillon, USA
2001	Danny Kass, USA	Abe Teter, USA	Daniel Franck, Norway
2000	Guillaume Morisset, Canada	Ross Powers, USA	Xavier Hoffman, Germany
1999	Ross Powers, USA	Xavier Hoffman, Germany	Tommy Czeschin, USA
1998	Rob Kingwill, USA	Terje Haakonsen, Norway	Todd Richards, USA
1997	Todd Richards, USA	Terje Haakonsen, Norway	Sebu Kuhlberg, Finland
1996	Jimi Scott, USA	Sami Hyry, Finland	Max Ploetzender, Austria
1995	Terje Haakonsen, Norway	Jason Evans, USA	J.J. Collier, USA
1994	Todd Richards, USA	Lael Gregory, USA	Jason Evans, USA

U.S. Open Snowboarding Championship Results (cont.)

Halfpipe—Men (cont.)

Year	Gold	Silver	Bronze
1993	Terje Haakonsen, Norway	Keith Wallace, USA	Sebu Kuhlberg, Finland
1992	Terje Haakonsen, Norway	Jeff Brushie, USA	Todd Richards, USA
1991	Jimi Scott, USA	Craig Kelly, USA	Shaun Palmer, USA
1990	Craig Kelly, USA	Shaun Palmer, USA	Jeff Brushie, USA
1989	Craig Kelly, USA	Bert Lamar, USA	Terry Kidwell, USA
1988	Terry Kidwell, USA	Bert Lamar, USA	Craig Kelly, USA

Halfpipe—Women

Year	Gold	Silver	Bronze
2003	Gretchen Bleiler, USA	Natasza Zurek, Canada	Hannah Teter, USA
2002	Kelly Clark, USA	Tricia Byrnes, USA	Stine Brun Kjeldaas, Norway
2001	Natasza Zurek, Canada	Shannon Dunn, USA	Gretchen Bleiler, USA
2000	Natasza Zurek, Canada	Shannon Dunn, USA	Barrett Christy, USA
1999	Nicola Thost, Germany	Tricia Byrnes, USA	Shannon Dunn, USA
1998	Nicola Thost, Germany	Tricia Byrnes, USA	Tara Teigen, Canada
1997	Barrett Christy, USA	Tricia Byrnes, USA	Michelle Taggert, USA
1996	Satu Jarvela, Finland	Michelle Taggert, USA	Jennie Waara, Sweden
1995	Satu Jarvela, Finland	Nicole Angelrath, Switzerland	Jennie Waara, Sweden
1994	Shannon Dunn, USA	Tina Basich, USA	Sandra Farmand, Germany
1993	Shannon Dunn, USA	Janna Meyen, USA	Tricia Byrnes, USA
1992	Tricia Byrnes, USA	Nicole Angelrath, Switzerland	Tina Basich, USA
1991	Janna Meyen, USA	Tina Basich, USA	Michelle Taggert, USA
1990	Tina Basich, USA	Lisa Vinciguerra, USA	Jean Higgins, USA
1989	Jean Higgins, USA	Tara Eberhard, USA	Ashild Lofthus, Norway
1988	Petra Mussig, Germany	Jean Higgins, USA	Gayle Guerin, USA

Summer X Games Results

Aggressive In-line—Men

Year	Event	Gold	Silver	Bronze
2002	Park	Jaren Grob, USA	Bruno Lowe, Germany	Blake Dennis, Australia
2001	Park	Jaren Grob, USA	Louie Zamora, USA	Franky Morales, USA
2000	Park	Sven Boekhorst, Netherlands	Jaren Grob, USA	Sam Fogarty, Australia
1999	Street	Nicky Adams, Canada	Blake Dennis, Australia	Aaron Feinberg, USA
1998	Street	Jonathan Bergeron, Canada	Marco Hintze, Mexico	Aaron Feinberg, USA
1997	Street	Aaron Feinberg, USA	Tim Ward, Australia	Chris Edwards, USA
1996	Street	Arlo Eisenberg, USA	Matt Mantz, USA	Chris Edwards, USA
1995	Street	Matt Salerno, Australia	Scott Bentley, New Zealand	Ryan Jacklone, USA
2002	Vert	Takeshi Yasutoko, Japan	Eito Yasutoko, Japan	Marc Englehart, USA
2001	Vert	Taig Khris, France	Takeshi Yasutoko, Japan	Shane Yost, Australia
2000	Vert	Eito Yasutoko, Japan	Takeshi Yasutoko, Japan	Cesar Mora, Australia
1999	Vert	Eito Yasutoko, Japan	Cesar Mora, Australia	Matt Salerno, Australia
1998	Vert	Cesar Mora, Australia	Matt Salerno, Australia	Taig Khris, France
1997	Vert	Tim Ward, Australia	Taig Khris, France	Chris Edwards USA
1996	Vert	Rene Hulgreen, Denmark	Tom Fry, Australia	Chris Edwards, USA
1995	Vert	Tom Fry, Australia	Cesar Mora, Australia	Manuel Billiris, Australia
1999	Vert Triples	Sven Boekhorst, Netherlands Javier Bujanda, Spain Taig Khris, France	Mike Budnik, USA Cesar Mora, Australia Matt Salerno, Australia	Maki Komori, Japan Eito Yasutoko, Japan Takeshi Yasutoko, Japan

Summary

X Games Results (cont.)

Aggressive In-line—Men (cont.)

Year	Event	Gold	Silver	Bronze
1998	Vert Triples	Paul Malina, Australia Viorel Popa, USA Sam Fogarty, Australia	Mike Budnik, USA Matt Salerno, Australia Cesar Mora, Australia	Sven Boekhorst, Netherlands Javier Bujanda, Spain Taig Khris, France
1996	Best Trick	Dion Antony, Australia	Ryan Jacklone, USA	Eric Schrijn, USA
1995	Best Trick	B. Hardin, USA	Ryan Jacklone, USA	Brooke Howard-Smith, New Zealand
1995	High Air	Chris Edwards, USA	Manuel Billiris, Australia	Ichi Komori, Japan

Aggressive In-line—Women

Year	Event	Gold	Silver	Bronze
2002	Park	Martina Svobodova, Slovakia	Jenna Downing, Great Britain	Fallon Heffernan, USA
2001	Park	Martina Svobodova, Slovakia	Fallon Heffernan, USA	Anneke Winter, Germany
2000	Park	Fabiola da Silva, Brazil	Martina Svobodova, Slovakia	Kelly Matthews, USA
1999	Street	Sayaka Yabe, Japan	Kelly Matthews, USA	Jenny Curry, USA
1998	Street	Jenny Curry, USA	Salima Sanga, Switzerland	Sayaka Yabe, Japan
1997	Street	Sayaka Yabe, Japan	Katie Brown, USA	True Otis, USA
2001	Vert	Fabiola da Silva, Brazil	Ayumi Kawasaki, Japan	N/A
2000	Vert	Fabiola da Silva, Brazil	Ayumi Kawasaki, Japan	Merce Borrull, Spain
1999	Vert	Ayumi Kawasaki, Japan	Fabiola da Silva, Brazil	Maki Komori, Japan
1998	Vert	Fabiola da Silva, Brazil	Ayumi Kawasaki, Japan	Maki Komori, Japan
1997	Vert	Fabiola da Silva, Brazil	Claudia Trachsel, Switzerland	Ayumi Kawasaki, Japan
1996	Vert	Fabiola da Silva, Brazil	Jodie Tyler, Australia	Tasha Hodgson, Australia
1995	Vert	Tasha Hodgson, Australia	Angie Walton, New Zealand	Laura Connery, USA

Barefoot Jumping

Year	Gold	Silver	Bronze
1998	Peter Fleck, USA	Ron Scarpa, USA	Massimiliano Colosio, Italy
1997	Peter Fleck, USA	Evan Berger, South Africa	Warren Fine, South Africa
1996	Ron Scarpa, USA	Jon Kretchman, USA	Rael Nurick, South Africa
1995	Justin Seers, Australia	Ron Scarpa, USA	Rael Nurick, South Africa

Fabiola da Silva has won more in-line gold medals at the Summer X Games than any other athlete (6).

TONY DONALDSON

Did You Know?
Skateboarder Tony Hawk and BMX rider Mat Hoffman had cameo roles in the 2002 movie *XXX*.

Summer X Games Results (cont.)

Bike Stunt

Year	Event	Gold	Silver	Bronze
2002	Dirt	Allan Cooke, USA	Ryan Nyquist, USA	Chris Doyle, USA
2001	Dirt	Stephen Murray, Great Britain	Ryan Nyquist, USA	T.J. Lavin, USA
2000	Dirt	Ryan Nyquist, USA	Cory Nastazio, USA	T.J. Lavin, USA
1999	Dirt	T.J. Lavin, USA	Brian Foster, USA	Ryan Nyquist, USA
1998	Dirt	Brian Foster, USA	Ryan Nyquist, USA	Joey Garcia, USA
1997	Dirt	T.J. Lavin, USA	Brian Foster, USA	Ryan Nyquist, USA
1996	Dirt	Joey Garcia, USA	T.J. Lavin, USA	Brian Foster, USA
1995	Dirt	Jay Miron, Canada	Taj Mihelich, USA	Joey Garcia, USA
2002	Flatland	Martti Kuoppa, Finland	Michael Steingraeber, Germany	Phil Dolan, Great Britain
2001	Flatland	Martti Kuoppa, Finland	Phil Dolan, Great Britain	Matt Wilhelm, USA
2000	Flatland	Martti Kuoppa, Finland	Michael Steingraeber, Germany	Phil Dolan, Great Britain
1999	Flatland	Trevor Meyer, USA	Phil Dolan, Great Britain	Nathan Penonzek, Canada
1998	Flatland	Trevor Meyer, USA	Andrew Faris, Canada	Martti Kuoppa, Finland
1997	Flatland	Trevor Meyer, USA	Nate Hanson, USA	Andrew Faris, Canada
2002	Park	Ryan Nyquist, USA	Alistair Whitton, Great Britain	Chad Kagy, USA
2001	Park	Bruce Crisman, USA	Alistair Whitton, Great Britain	Jay Miron, Canada
2000	Park	Dave Mirra, USA	Markus Wilke, Germany	Ryan Nyquist, USA
1999	Street	Dave Mirra, USA	Jay Miron, Canada	Chad Kagy, USA
1998	Street	Dave Mirra, USA	Jay Miron, Canada	Dennis McCoy, USA
1997	Street	Dave Mirra, USA	Dennis McCoy, USA	Dave Voelker, USA
1996	Street	Dave Mirra, USA	Jay Miron, Canada	Rob Nolli, USA
2002	Vert	Dave Mirra, USA	Mat Hoffman, USA	Simon Tabron, Great Britain

Dave Mirra has won 14 Summer X Games medals, second-most in the Games.

MARK LOSEY

Trivia Challenge

Which state hosted both the first Summer X Games (1995) and the first Gravity Games (1999)?

Rhode Island

Today's Stars

Shaun White, snowboarder, b. September 3, 1986, San Diego, California. White won gold in the superpipe and slopestyle events at the 2003 Winter X Games. The 16-year-old improved on his 2002 X Games performance, where he finished second in both events. White's skateboard skills were also on display on the final leg of the 2002 Tony Hawk's Gigantic Skatepark Tour, during which he amazed spectators with his 720s in the halfpipe. White began gaining recognition when he won the overall title at the 1998 U.S.A. Snowboard Association national championships, at age 11.

Travis Pastrana, freestyle motocross rider, b. October 8, 1983, Annapolis, Maryland. Through 2002, Pastrana had never lost a freestyle motocross competition in which he entered. During that stretch, the 19-year-old won four gold medals at the Gravity Games and three golds at the Summer X Games. At the 2002 Gravity Games, Pastrana became the second rider ever to land a backflip in competition, performing seven backflips in one run.

Snowboarder Shaun White won four USASA (United States Amateur Snowboard Association) titles from 1995 through 1998.

TOM ZIKAS

James "Bubba" Stewart, motocross racer, b. December 21, 1985, Bartow, Florida. Stewart became the youngest motocross champion (16 years 247 days) when he won the 125cc American Motorcyclist Association (AMA) Motocross Championship in 2002. He won a record eight races in a row and was named Rookie of the Year. Stewart, who began racing motorcycles when he was four years old, entered the pro ranks in 2002 after winning his 11th AMA Amateur National title. He is the all-time winningest AMA amateur rider.

Summer X Games Results (cont.)

Bike Stunt (cont.)

Year	Event	Gold	Silver	Bronze
2001	Vert	Dave Mirra, USA	Jay Miron, Canada	Mat Hoffman, USA
2000	Vert	Jamie Bestwick, Great Britain	Dave Mirra, USA	Mat Hoffman, USA
1999	Vert	Dave Mirra, USA	Jay Miron, Canada	Simon Tabron, Great Britain
1998	Vert	Dave Mirra, USA	Dennis McCoy, USA	Simon Tabron, Great Britain
1997	Vert	Dave Mirra, USA	Dennis McCoy, USA	Mat Hoffman, USA
1996	Vert	Mat Hoffman, USA	Dave Mirra, USA	Jamie Bestwick, Great Britian
1995	Vert	Mat Hoffman, USA	Dave Mirra, USA	Jay Miron, Canada
1998	Vert Doubles	Dave Mirra, USA Dennis McCoy, USA	Jay Miron, Canada Dave Osato, Canada	Jason Davies, Great Britain John Parker, USA

Bungy

Year	Gold	Silver	Bronze
1996	Peter Bihun, Canada	Doug Anderson, Canada	Carolyn Anderson, Canada
1995	Doug Anderson, Canada	Mark Baldwin, USA	Todd Watkins, USA

Summer X Games Results (cont.)

Downhill BMX

Year	Gold	Silver	Bronze
2002	Robbie Miranda, USA	Kyle Bennett, USA	Robert de Wilde, Netherlands
2001	Brandon Meadows, USA	Brian Foster, USA	John Whipperman, USA

Downhill In-line—Men

Year		Gold	Silver	Bronze
1998		Patrick Naylor, USA	Jeremy Anderson, USA	Dane Lewis, USA
1997		Derek Downing, USA	Keith Turner, USA	B.J. Steketee, USA
1996		Dante Muse, USA	Derek Parra, USA	Jim Wiederhold, USA
1995	Combined	Derek Downing, USA	Jim Wiederhold, USA	Jondon Trevena, USA

Downhill In-line—Women

Year	Gold	Silver	Bronze
1998	Julie Brandt, USA	Aimee Sanderson, USA	Theresa Cliff, USA
1997	Gypsy Tidwell, USA	Julie Brandt, USA	Jessica Apgar, USA
1996	Gypsy Tidwell, USA	Jennifer Jones, USA	Desly Hill, Australia

Kiteskiing

Year	Gold	Silver	Bronze
1995	Cory Roessler, USA	Clarin Mustad, Norway	Thomas Jeltsch, Germany

Mountain Biking—Men

Year	Event	Gold	Silver	Bronze
1995	Dual Downhill	Robert Naughton, USA	Jurgen Beneke, Germany	Todd Tanner, USA
1995	Dual Slalom	Jimmy Knight, USA	Myles Rockwell, USA	Mike King, USA
1995	Observed Trials	Libor Karas, Czech Republic	Hans Rey, Germany	Marc Brooks, USA

Mountain Biking—Women

Year	Event	Gold	Silver	Bronze
1995	Dual Downhill	Cheri Elliott, USA	Kim Sonier, USA	Leigh Donovan, USA
1995	Dual Slalom	Leigh Donovan, USA	Cheri Elliott, USA	Giovanna Bonazzi, Italy

Moto X

Year	Event	Gold	Silver	Bronze
2002	Big Air	Mike Metzger, USA	Carey Hart, USA	Brian Deegan, USA
2001	Big Air	Kenny Bartram, USA	Dustin Miller, USA	Brian Deegan, USA
2002	Freestyle	Mike Metzger, USA	Kenny Bartram, USA	Drake McElroy, USA
2001	Freestyle	Travis Pastrana, USA	Clifford Adoptante, USA	Jake Windham, USA
2000	Freestyle	Travis Pastrana, USA	Tommy Clowers, USA	Brian Deegan, USA
1999	Freestyle	Travis Pastrana, USA	Mike Cinqmars, USA	Brian Deegan, USA
2002	Step Up	Tommy Clowers, USA	Mike Metzger, USA	Brian Deegan, USA
2001	Step Up	Tommy Clowers, USA	Travis Pastrana, USA	Colin Morrison, USA (tie) Ronnie Renner, USA Kris Rourke, USA Jeremy Stenberg, USA
2000	Step Up	Tommy Clowers, USA	Kris Rourke, USA	Brian Deegan, USA

Skateboarding

Year	Event	Gold	Silver	Bronze
2002	Park	Rodil de Araujo, Jr., Brazil	Wagner Ramos, Brazil	Eric Koston, USA
2001	Park	Rodil de Araujo, Jr., Brazil	Kerry Getz, USA	Caine Gayle, USA
2000	Park	Eric Koston, USA	Rodil de Araujo, Jr., Brazil	Kerry Getz, USA
2002	Street	Rodil de Araujo, Jr., Brazil	Wagner Ramos, Brazil	Kyle Berard, USA
2001	Street	Kerry Getz, USA	Eric Koston, USA	Chris Senn, USA
1999	Street	Chris Senn, USA	Pat Channita, USA	Chad Fernandez, USA
1998	Street	Rodil de Araujo, Jr., Brazil	Andy Macdonald, USA	Chris Senn, USA
1997	Street	Chris Senn, USA	Andy Macdonald, USA	Brian Patch, USA
1996	Street	Rodil de Araujo, Jr., Brazil	Chris Senn, USA	Brian Patch, USA
1995	Street	Chris Senn, USA	Tony Hawk, USA	Willy Santos, USA
2002	Street Best Trick	Rodil de Araujo, Jr., Brazi	Wagner Ramos, Brazil	Dayne Brummet, USA
2001	Street Best Trick	Rick McCrank, Canada	Kerry Getz, USA	Eric Koston, USA
1996	Street Best Trick	Gershon Mosley, USA	Chris Senn, USA	Brian Patch, USA
1995	Street Best Trick	Jamie Thomas, USA	Gershon Mosley, USA	Kareem Campbell, USA
2002	Vert	Pierre-Luc Gagnon, Canada	Bob Burnquist, Brazil	Rune Glifberg, Denmark
2001	Vert	Bob Burnquist, Brazil	Bucky Lasek, USA	Tas Pappas, Australia
2000	Vert	Bucky Lasek, USA	Pierre-Luc Gagnon, Canada	Colin McKay, Canada
1999	Vert	Bucky Lasek, USA	Andy Macdonald, USA	Tony Hawk, USA
1998	Vert	Andy Macdonald, USA	Giorgio Zattoni, Italy	Tony Hawk, USA
1997	Vert	Tony Hawk, USA	Rune Glifberg, Denmark	Bob Burnquist, Brazil
1996	Vert	Andy Macdonald, USA	Tony Hawk, USA	Tas Pappas, Australia
1995	Vert	Tony Hawk, USA	Neal Hendrix, USA	Rune Glifberg, Denmark
2002	Vert Best Trick	Pierre-Luc Gagnon, Canada	Sandro Dias, Brazil	Tony Hawk, USA
2001	Vert Best Trick	Matt Dove, USA	Tony Hawk, USA	Bob Burnquist, Brazil
2000	Vert Best Trick	Bob Burnquist, Brazil	Colin McKay, Canada	Andy Macdonald, USA
1999	Vert Best Trick	Tony Hawk, USA	Colin McKay, Canada	Bob Burnquist, Brazil
2002	Vert Doubles	Tony Hawk, USA	Bob Burnquist, Brazil	Mike Crum, USA
		Andy Macdonald, USA	Bucky Lasek, USA	Rune Glifberg, Denmark
2001	Vert Doubles	Tony Hawk, USA	Mike Crum, USA	Mike Frazier, USA
		Andy Macdonald, USA	Chris Gentry, USA	Neal Hendrix, USA
2000	Vert Doubles	Tony Hawk, USA	Pierre-Luc Gagnon, Canada	Sandro Dias, Brazil
		Andy Macdonald, USA	Max Dufour, Canada	Cristiano Mateus, Brazil
1999	Vert Doubles	Tony Hawk, USA	Bucky Lasek, USA	Mike Crum, USA
		Andy Macdonald, USA	Brian Patch, USA	Rune Glifberg, Denmark
1998	Vert Doubles	Tony Hawk, USA	Bucky Lasek, USA	Bob Burnquist, Brazil
		Andy Macdonald, USA	Brian Patch, USA	Lincoln Ueda, Brazil
1997	Vert Doubles	Tony Hawk, USA	Mike Frazier, USA	Max Dufour, Canada
		Andy Macdonald, USA	Neal Hendrix, USA	Mathias Ringstrom, Sweden
1995	High Air	Danny Way, USA	Neal Hendrix, USA	Tas Pappas, Australia

Skysurfing

Year	Gold	Silver	Bronze
2000	Stefan Klaus, Switzerland	Clif Burch, USA	Eric Fradet, France
	Brian Rogers, USA	Valery Rozov, Russia	Alessandro Iodice, France
1999	Eric Fradet, France	Stefan Klaus, Switzerland	Oliver Furrer, Switzerland
	Alex Iodice, France	Brian Rogers, USA	Marcus Heggli, Switzerland
1998	Clif Burch, USA	Marcus Heggli, Switzerland	Oliver Furrer, Switzerland
	Valery Rozov, Russia	Viviane Wegrath, Switzerland	Knut Krecker, Germany
1997	Troy Hartman, USA	Oliver Furrer, Switzerland	Eric Fradet, France
	Vic Pappadato, USA	Christian Schmid, Switzerland	Olav Zipser, Germany
1996	Clif Burch, USA	Troy Hartman, USA	Patrick De Gayardon, France
	Bob Greiner, USA	Vic Pappadato, USA	Joe Jennings, USA
1995	Rob Harris, USA	Eric Fradet, France	Clif Burch, USA
	Joe Jennings, USA	Werner Noremberg, France	Bob Greiner, USA

ACTION SPORTS

Summer X Games Results (cont.)

Snowboarding—Men

Year	Event	Gold	Silver	Bronze
1999	Big Air	Peter Line, USA	Ben Hinkley, USA	Chris Engelsman, USA
1998	Big Air	Kevin Jones, USA	Ben Hinkley, USA	Jim Rippey, USA
1997	Big Air	Peter Line, USA	Kevin Jones, USA	Jason Borgstede, USA

Snowboarding—Women

Year	Event	Gold	Silver	Bronze
1999	Big Air	Barrett Christy, USA	Tina Dixon, USA	Janet Matthews, Canada
1998	Big Air	Janet Matthews, Canada	Tina Basich, USA	Tina Dixon, USA
1997	Big Air	Tina Dixon, USA	Hillary Maybery, USA	Shelly Ueckert, USA

Sport Climbing—Men

Year	Event	Gold	Silver	Bronze
2002	Speed	Maxim Stenkovoy, Ukraine	Alexandre Pechekhonov, Russia	Serguei Sinitsyn, Russia
2001	Speed	Maxim Stenkovoy, Ukraine	Vladimir Zakharov, Ukraine	Chris Bloch, USA
2000	Speed	Vladimir Zakharov, Ukraine	Chris Bloch, USA	Tomasz Oleksy, Poland
1999	Speed	Aaron Shamy, USA	Chris Bloch, USA	Vladimir Netsvetaev, Russia
1998	Speed	Vladimir Netsvetaev, Russia	Aaron Shamy, USA	Chris Bloch, USA
1997	Speed	Hans Florine, USA	Chris Bloch, USA	Jason Campbell, USA
1996	Speed	Hans Florine, USA	Chris Bloch, USA	Tim Fairfield, USA
1995	Speed	Hans Florine, USA	Salavat Rakhmetov, Russia	Yuji Hirayama, Japan
1999	Bouldering	Chris Sharma, USA	Francois Petit, France	Stephane Julien, France
1998	Difficulty	Christian Core, Italy	Francois Legrand, France	Vadim Vinokur, USA
1997	Difficulty	Francois Legrand, France	Yuji Hirayama, Japan	Chris Sharma, USA
1996	Difficulty	Arnaud Petit, France	Francois Lombard, France	Cristian Brenna, Italy
1995	Difficulty	Ian Vickers, Great Britain	Arnaud Petit, France	Francois Petit, France

Sport Climbing—Women

Year	Event	Gold	Silver	Bronze
2002	Speed	Tori Allen, USA	Olga Zakharova, Ukraine	Etti Hendrawati, Indonesia
2001	Speed	Elena Repko, Ukraine	Olga Zakharova, Ukraine	Alena Ostapenko, Ukraine
2000	Speed	Etti Hendrawati, Indonesia	Elena Repko, Ukraine	Olga Zakharova, Ukraine
1999	Speed	Renata Piszczek, Poland	Olga Zakharova, Ukraine	Etti Hendrawati, Indonesia
1998	Speed	Elena Ovchinnikova, USA	Yuyun Yuniar, Indonesia	Venera Tchereshneva, Russia
1997	Speed	Elena Ovchinnikova, USA	Abby Watkins, Australia	Mi Sun Go, South Korea
1996	Speed	Cecile Le Flem, France	Elena Choumilova, Russia	Natalie Richer, France
1995	Speed	Elena Ovchinnikova, Russia	Diane Russell, USA	Georgia Phipps-Franklin, USA
1999	Bouldering	Stephanie Bodet, France	Liv Sansoz, France	Elena Choumilova, Russia
1998	Difficulty	Katie Brown, USA	Mi Sun Go, South Korea	Elena Choumilova, Russia
1997	Difficulty	Katie Brown, USA	Liv Sansoz, France	Muriel Sarkany, Belgium
1996	Difficulty	Katie Brown, USA	Laurence Guyon, France	Liv Sansoz, France
1995	Difficulty	Robyn Erbesfield, USA	Elena Ovchinnikova, Russia	Mia Axon, USA

2002-03 TIMELINE --

January 20, 2002: Snowboarder Shaun White finishes second in slopestyle at the Winter X Games one day after taking the silver in superpipe.

May 4, 2002: Motocross racer Ricky Carmichael wins his second straight 250cc Supercross championship. Four months later, he wins his third-straight 250cc Motocross championship.

August 1, 2002: Eric Koston wins the street skateboarding event at the Gravity Games for the third-straight time.

August 3, 2002: Freestyle motocross star Mike Metzger becomes the first rider to land a backflip in competition at the Gravity Games. Travis Pastrana pulls one immediately after Metzger.

August 17, 2002: Skateboarders Tony Hawk and Andy Macdonald win the Summer X Games vert doubles event for the sixth-straight time.

August 18, 2002: In the park event, BMX rider Ryan Nyquist wins his second

career Summer X Games gold medal. It is his eighth career X Games medal.

August 25, 2002: At age 16 years 247 days, motocross racer James "Bubba" Stewart clinches his first national motocross championship (125cc class) and becomes the sport's youngest national champion.

December 3, 2002: U.S. surfer Andy Irons wins the Association of Surfing Professionals (ASP) world championship, in Oahu, Hawaii.

December 15, 2002: Australian surfer Layne Beachley wins a record fifth-straight women's world championship, in Maui, Hawaii.

January 2, 2003: Seven-time supercross champion Jeremy McGrath announces his retirement from motocross racing.

February 2, 2003: At the Winter X Games, snowboarder Shaun White wins the gold medal in slopestyle two days after winning the superpipe event.

Summer X Games Results (cont.)

Street Luge

Year	Event	Gold	Silver	Bronze
2001	Super Mass	Brent DeKeyser, USA	David Rogers, USA	Dave Auld, USA
2000	Super Mass	Bob Pereyra, USA	Lee Dansie, Great Britain	John Rogers, USA
1999	Super Mass	David Rogers, USA	Biker Sherlock, USA	Sean Slate, USA
1998	Super Mass	Rat Sult, USA	Bob Pereyra, USA	Todd Lehr, USA
1997	Super Mass	Chris Ponseti, USA	Biker Sherlock, USA	Rat Sult, USA
2000	Dual	Bob Ozman, USA	Wade Sokol, USA	Bob Pereyra, USA
1999	Dual	Dennis Derammelaere, USA	Lee Dansie, Great Britain	Biker Sherlock, USA
1998	Dual	Biker Sherlock, USA	Stefan Wagner, Germany	Dave Auld, USA
1997	Dual	Biker Sherlock, USA	Dennis Derammelaere, USA	Darren Lott, USA
1996	Dual	Shawn Goulart, USA	Stefan Wagner, Germany	Dennis Derammelaere, USA
1995	Dual	Bob Pereyra, USA	Stefan Wagner, Germany	Shawn Goulart, USA
1998	Mass	Rat Sult, USA	Sean Slate, USA	Steve Fernando, USA

Summer X Games Results (cont.)

Street Luge (cont.)

Year	Event	Gold	Silver	Bronze
1997	Mass	Biker Sherlock, USA	Dennis Derammelaere, USA	Lee Dansie, Great Britain
1996	Mass	Biker Sherlock, USA	Daryl Thompson, USA	Dennis Derammelaere, USA
1995	Mass	Shawn Goulart, USA	Lee Dansie, Great Britain	Stefan Wagner, Germany

Wakeboarding—Men

Year	Gold	Silver	Bronze
2002	Danny Harf, USA	Darin Shapiro, USA	Shaun Murray, USA
2001	Danny Harf, USA	Darin Shapiro, USA	Erik Ruck, USA
2000	Darin Shapiro, USA	Shaun Murray, USA	Shane Bonifay, USA
1999	Parks Bonifay, USA	Darin Shapiro, USA	Brannan Johnson, USA
1998	Darin Shapiro, USA	Shaun Murray, USA	Zane Schwenk, USA
1997	Jeremy Kovak, Canada	Darin Shapiro, USA	Parks Bonifay, USA
1996	Parks Bonifay, USA	Jeremy Kovak, Canada	Scott Byerly, USA

Wakeboarding—Women

Year	Gold	Silver	Bronze
2002	Emily Copeland, USA	Dallas Friday, USA	Leslie Kent, USA
2001	Dallas Friday, USA	Emily Copeland, USA	Tara Hamilton, USA
2000	Tara Hamilton, USA	Dallas Friday, USA	Maeghan Major, USA

Darin Shapiro has won a medal in every Summer X Games since 1997.

JOHN GILLOOLY

Visit **www.sikids.com** for the latest sports stats and info.
Site code: slamdunk
AOL keyword: sikids

Did You Know?

A freestyle motocross motorcycle weighs approximately 225 pounds.

Summer X Games Results (cont.)

Wakeboarding—Women (cont.)

Year	Gold	Silver	Bronze
1999	Maeghan Major, USA	Emily Copeland, USA	Andrea Gaytan, Mexico
1998	Andrea Gaytan, Mexico	Dana Preble, USA	Tara Hamilton, USA
1997	Tara Hamilton, USA	Andrea Gaytan, Mexico	Jaime Necrason, USA

Windsurfing—Men

Year	Gold	Silver	Bronze
1995	Bjorn Dunkerbeck, Spain	Micah Buzianis, USA	Al Aguera, USA

Windsurfing—Women

Year	Gold	Silver	Bronze
1995	Angela Cochran, USA	Jayne Fenner-Benedict, USA	Jutta Mueller, Germany

X Venture Race

Year	Gold	Silver	Bronze
1997	**Team Presidio**	**Team Endeavour**	**Team Red Hot**
	Ian Adamson, Australia	Louise Cooper-Lovelace, USA	Sharyn Davis, Australia
	John Howard, New Zealand	Neil Jones, New Zealand	John Jacoby, Australia
	Andrea Spitzer, Germany	Jeff Mitchell, New Zealand	Tim Smallwood, Australia
1996	**Team Kobeer**	**Team Eco-Internet**	**Team Mirage**
	Angelika Castaneda, USA	Ian Adamson, Australia	Kirk Boylston, USA
	John Howard, New Zealand	Robert Nagle, Ireland	Nancy Bristow, USA
	Keith Murray, New Zealand	Vivienne Prince, USA	Steve Gurney, New Zealand
1995	**Team Thredbo**	**Twin Team**	**Team Eco-Internet**
	Jane Hall, Australia	Angelika Castaneda, USA	Ian Adamson, Australia
	Andrew Hislop, Australia	Adrian Crane, USA	John Howard, New Zealand
	Rod Hislop, Australia	Tom Possert, USA	Keith Murray, New Zealand
	John Jacoby, Australia	Robert Rambach, USA	Robert Nagle, Ireland
	Novak Thompson, Australia	Marchall Ulrich, USA	Cathy Sassin-Smith, USA

Summer Gravity Games Results

Bike

Year	Event	Gold	Silver	Bronze
2002	Street	Dave Mirra, USA	Ryan Nyquist, USA	Tom Haugen, USA
2001	Street	Ryan Nyquist, USA	Dave Osato, Canada	Chad Kagy, USA
2000	Street	Dave Osato, Canada	Ryan Nyquist, USA	Mike Laird, USA
1999	Street	Dave Mirra, USA	Ryan Nyquist, USA	Jay Miron, Canada
2002	Dirt	Stephen Murray, Great Britain	Allan Cooke, USA	Chris Doyle, USA
2001	Dirt	Stephen Murray, Great Britain	Todd Walkowiak, USA	Chris Doyle, USA
2000	Dirt	T.J. Lavin, USA	Chris Doyle, USA	Ryan Jordan, USA
1999	Dirt	Ryan Nyquist, USA	Todd Walkowiak, USA	T.J. Lavin, USA
2002	Vert	Simon Tabron, Great Britain	Dave Mirra, USA	Jay Miron, Canada
2001	Vert	Jamie Bestwick, Great Britain	Kevin Robinson, USA	Simon Tabron, Great Britain
2000	Vert	Dave Mirra, USA	Jamie Bestwick, Great Britain	Jay Miron, Canada
1999	Vert	Jamie Bestwick, Great Britain	Jay Miron, Canada	John Parker, USA

Motocross

Year	Event	Gold	Silver	Bronze
2002	Freestyle	Travis Pastrana, USA	Mike Metzger, USA	Kenny Bartram, USA

Summer Gravity Games Results (cont.)

Motocross (cont.)

Year	Event	Gold	Silver	Bronze
2001	Freestyle	Travis Pastrana, USA	Clifford Adoptante, USA	Tommy Clowers, USA
2000	Freestyle	Brian Deegan, USA	Mike Metzger, USA	Kenny Bartram, USA
1999	Freestyle	Travis Pastrana, USA	Brian Deegan, USA	Carey Hart, USA

Skateboarding

Year	Event	Gold	Silver	Bronze
2002	Vert	Bucky Lasek, USA	Bob Burnquist, Brazil	Pierre-Luc Gagnon, Canada
2001	Vert	Rune Glifberg, Denmark	Bucky Lasek, USA	Andy Macdonald, USA
2000	Vert	Andy Macdonald, USA	Bob Burnquist, Brazil	Pierre-Luc Gagnon, Canada
1999	Vert	Bob Burnquist, Brazil	Bucky Lasek, USA	Andy Macdonald, USA
2002	Downhill, 2-person	Mark Golter, USA	Dane Van Bommel, USA	Alex Wenk, Switzerland
2001	Downhill, 2-person	Dane Van Bommel, USA	Gary Hardwick, USA	Mark Golter, USA
2000	Downhill, 2-person	Dane Van Bommel, USA	John Gwiazdowski, USA	Alex Wenk, Switzerland
1999	Downhill, 2-person	Lee Dansie, Great Britain	Biker Sherlock, USA	Dane Van Bommel, USA
2002	Downhill, 4-person	Darryl Freeman, USA	Mark Golter, USA	Dane Van Bommel, USA
2001	Downhill, 4-person	Dane Van Bommel, USA	Alex Wenk, Switzerland	Lee Dansie, Great Britain
2000	Downhill, 4-person	Dane Van Bommel, USA	John Gwiazdowski, USA	Alex Wenk, Switzerland
1999	Downhill, 4-person	Biker Sherlock, USA	Dane Van Bommel, USA	Emanuel Antuna, France
2002	Street	Eric Koston, USA	Pat Channita, USA	Kerry Getz, USA
2001	Street	Eric Koston, USA	Rick McCrank, Canada	Kyle Berard, USA
2000	Street	Eric Koston, USA	Brian Anderson, USA	Kerry Getz, USA
1999	Street	Brian Anderson, USA	Rodil Araujo, Jr., Brazil	Eric Koston, USA

Aggressive In-Line—Men

Year	Event	Gold	Silver	Bronze
2001	Street	Blake Dennis, Australia	Louie Zamora, USA	Aaron Feinberg, USA
2000	Street	Sven Boekhorst, Netherlands	Blake Dennis, Australia	Wilfried Rossignol, France
1999	Street	Sven Boekhorst, Netherlands	Den Bosch, Netherlands	Louie Zamora, USA
2002	Vert	Marc Englehart, USA	Takeshi Yasutoko, Japan	Shane Yost, Tasmania
2001	Vert	Taig Khris, France	Takeshi Yasutoko, Japan	Matt Lindenmuth, USA
2000	Vert	Matt Salerno, Australia	Taig Khris, France	Eito Yasutoko, Japan
1999	Vert	Taig Khris, France	Shane Yost, Australia	Cesar Mora, Australia

Aggressive In-Line—Women

Year	Event	Gold	Silver	Bronze
2001	Street	Martina Svobodova, Slovakia	Fabiola da Silva, Brazil	Deborah West, USA
2000	Street	Martina Svobodova, Slovakia	Fabiola da Silva, Brazil	Kelly Matthews, USA
1999	Street	Fabiola da Silva, Brazil	Anneke Winter, Germany	Kelly Matthews, USA
2001	Vert	Ayumi Kawasaki, Japan	Fabiola da Silva, Brazil	N/A
2000	Vert	Fabiola da Silva, Brazil	Ayumi Kawasaki, Japan	Merce Borrull, Spain
1999	Vert	Fabiola da Silva, Brazil	Merce Borrull, Spain	Maki Komori, Japan

Wakeboarding—Men

Year	Gold	Silver	Bronze
2002	Mark Kenney, USA	Danny Harf, USA	Darin Shapiro, USA
2001	Darin Shapiro, USA	Parks Bonifay, USA	Daniel Watkins, Australia
2000	Parks Bonifay, USA	Darin Shapiro, USA	Ryan Wynne, USA
1999	Shaun Murray, USA	Parks Bonifay, USA	Rob Struharik, USA

Legends

Tony Hawk, skateboarder, b. May 12, 1968, San Diego, California. Hawk became a pro skateboarder when he was 14 years old. Twenty-one years later, he is responsible for bringing the sport into the mainstream and inventing more than 80 tricks. Perhaps the most famous of those tricks is the 900, which Hawk landed for the first time at the 1999 Summer X Games. No other skater has ever landed the trick. Hawk's career haul from the X Games includes nine gold medals, three silver medals, and three bronze medals.

Tony Hawk has invented more than 80 skateboarding tricks in his 21-year career.

Mat Hoffman, BMX rider, b. January 9, 1972, Oklahoma City, Oklahoma. With the nickname "The Condor," Hoffman has soared to the world record for highest air (26.5 feet) and is constantly pushing the envelope in his sport. He has won 10 BMX world championships and six Summer X Games medals (2 gold, 1 silver, 3 bronze) and shows no signs of slowing down. He did the first 900 on a bike in 1989. Then in 2002, he became the first rider to do a no-handed 900.

Kelly Slater, surfer, b. February 11, 1972, Cocoa Beach, Florida. Slater's six World Championship Tour (WCT) titles are the most of any surfer. He won his first title in 1992, and won five straight from 1994 through 1998. He then stopped competing full-time to focus more on free-surfing. He returned to the tour in 2002 and finished ninth overall. Throughout his pro career, he has racked up 33 contest victories, not to mention a role on the TV series *Baywatch.*

▷**Random Fact:** Skateboarder Tony Hawk has won 15 Summer X Games medals, the most of any athlete.

Summer Gravity Games Results (cont.)

Wakeboarding—Women

Year	Gold	Silver	Bronze
2002	Emily Copeland, USA	Melissa Marquardt, USA	Dallas Friday, USA
2001	Dallas Friday, USA	Tara Hamilton, USA	Christy Smith, USA
2000	Maeghan Major, USA	Tara Hamilton, USA	Lauren Loe, USA
1999	Andrea Gaytan, Mexico	Tara Hamilton, USA	Christy Smith, USA

Street Luge

Year	Event	Gold	Silver	Bronze
2002	4-person	Mike McIntyre, USA	John Rogers, USA	Dave Rogers, USA
2001	4-person	Rat Sult, USA	Biker Sherlock, USA	John Fryer, USA
1999	4-person	Sean Mallard, USA	Biker Sherlock, USA	George Orton, USA
2002	6-person	Dave Rogers, USA	Mike McIntyre, USA	John Rogers, USA
2001	6-person	Rat Sult, USA	Kurtis Head, USA	David Kelly, USA
1999	6-person	Biker Sherlock, USA	Sean Slate, USA	Wade Sokol, USA

Andy Irons won his first pro-surfing title in 2002.

PETE FRIEDEN/SURFING MAGAZINE

Surfing—All-time Results

Association of Surfing Professionals (ASP) World Champions

Year	Men
2002	Andy Irons, USA
2001	C.J. Hobgood, USA
2000	Sunny Garcia, USA
1999	Mark Occhilupo, Australia
1998	Kelly Slater, USA
1997	Kelly Slater, USA
1996	Kelly Slater, USA
1995	Kelly Slater, USA
1994	Kelly Slater, USA
1993	Derek Ho, USA
1992	Kelly Slater, USA
1991	Damien Hardman, Australia
1990	Tom Curren, USA
1989	Martin Potter, Great Britain
1988	Barton Lynch, Australia
1987	Damien Hardman, Australia
1986	Tom Curren, USA
1985	Tom Curren, USA
1984	Tom Carroll, Australia
1983	Tom Carroll, Australia
1982	Mark Richards, Australia
1981	Mark Richards, Australia
1980	Mark Richards, Australia
1979	Mark Richards, Australia
1978	Wayne Bartholomew, Australia
1977	Shaun Tomson, South Africa
1976	Peter Townend, Australia

Year	Women
2002	Layne Beachley, Australia
2001	Layne Beachley, Australia
2000	Layne Beachley, Australia
1999	Layne Beachley, Australia
1998	Layne Beachley, Australia
1997	Lisa Andersen, USA
1996	Lisa Andersen, USA
1995	Lisa Andersen, USA

Year	Women
1994	Lisa Andersen, USA
1993	Pauline Menczer, Australia
1992	Wendy Botha, Australia
1991	Wendy Botha, Australia
1990	Pam Burridge, Australia
1989	Wendy Botha, Australia
1988	Freida Zamba, USA
1987	Wendy Botha, South Africa
1986	Freida Zamba, USA
1985	Freida Zamba, USA
1984	Freida Zamba, USA
1983	Kim Mearig, USA
1982	Debbie Beacham, USA
1981	Margo Oberg, USA
1980	Margo Oberg, USA
1979	Lynne Boyer, USA
1978	Lynne Boyer, USA
1977	Margo Oberg, USA

Year	Longboard
2002	Colin McPhillips, USA
2001	Colin McPhillips, USA
2000	Beau Young, Australia
1999	Colin McPhillips, USA
1998	Joel Tudor, USA
1997	Dino Miranda, USA
1996	Bonga Perkins, USA
1995	Rusty Keaulana, USA
1994	Rusty Keaulana, USA
1993	Rusty Keaulana, USA
1992	Joey Hawkins, USA
1991	Martin McMillan, Australia
1990	Nat Young, Australia
1989	Nat Young, Australia
1988	Nat Young, Australia
1987	Stuart Entwistle, Australia
1986	Nat Young, Australia

Motocross—All-time Results

250cc Supercross

Year	Champion	Hometown
2002	Ricky Carmichael	Havana, Florida
2001	Ricky Carmichael	Havana, Florida
2000	Jeremy McGrath	Menifee, California
1999	Jeremy McGrath	Menifee, California
1998	Jeremy McGrath	Menifee, California
1997	Jeff Emig	Riverside, California
1996	Jeremy McGrath	Menifee, California
1995	Jeremy McGrath	Murietta, California
1994	Jeremy McGrath	Murietta, California
1993	Jeremy McGrath	Murietta, California
1992	Jeff Stanton	Sherwood, Michigan
1991	Jean-Michel Bayle	Manosque, France
1990	Jeff Stanton	Sherwood, Michigan
1989	Jeff Stanton	Sherwood, Michigan
1988	Rick Johnson	El Cajon, California
1987	Jeff Ward	Mission Viejo, California
1986	Rick Johnson	El Cajon, California
1985	Jeff Ward	Mission Viejo, California
1984	Johnny O'Mara	Simi Valley, California

Year	Champion	Hometown
1983	David Bailey	Axton, Virginia
1982	Donnie Hansen	Canyon Country, California
1981	Mark Barnett	Bridgeview, Illinois
1980	Mike Bell	Lakewood, California
1979	Bob Hannah	Carson, Nevada
1978	Bob Hannah	Whittier, California
1977	Bob Hannah	Whittier, California
1976	Jim Weinert	Laguna Beach, California
1975	Jim Ellis	Cobalt, Connecticut
1974	Pierre Karsmakers	Netherlands

250cc Motocross

Year	Champion	Hometown
2002	Ricky Carmichael	Havana, Florida
2001	Ricky Carmichael	Havana, Florida
2000	Ricky Carmichael	Havana, Florida
1999	Greg Albertyn	Johannesburg, South Africa
1998	Doug Henry	Oxford, Connecticut
1997	Jeff Emig	Riverside, California
1996	Jeff Emig	Riverside, California
1995	Jeremy McGrath	Murrieta, California
1994	Mike LaRocco	South Bend, Indiana
1993	Mike Kiedrowski	Acton, California
1992	Jeff Stanton	Sherwood, Michigan
1991	Jean-Michel Bayle	Manosque, France
1990	Jeff Stanton	Sherwood, Michigan
1989	Jeff Stanton	Sherwood, Michigan
1988	Jeff Ward	Mission Viejo, California
1987	Rick Johnson	El Cajon, California
1986	Rick Johnson	El Cajon, California

Year	Champion	Hometown
1985	Jeff Ward	Mission Viejo, California
1984	Rick Johnson	El Cajon, California
1983	David Bailey	Axton, Virginia
1982	Donnie Hansen	Canyon Country, California
1981	Kent Howerton	San Antonio, Texas
1980	Kent Howerton	San Antonio, Texas
1979	Bob Hannah	Carson City, Nevada
1978	Bob Hannah	Whittier, California
1977	Tony DiStefano	Morrisville, Pennsylvania
1976	Tony DiStefano	Morrisville, Pennsylvania
1975	Tony DiStefano	Morrisville, Pennsylvania
1974	Gary Jones	Hacienda Heights, California
1973	Gary Jones	Hacienda Heights, California
1972	Gary Jones	Hacienda Heights, California

125cc Motocross

Year	Champion	Hometown
2002	James Stewart, Jr.	Haines City, Florida
2001	Michael Brown	Piney Flats, Tennessee
2000	Travis Pastrana	Annapolis, Maryland
1999	Ricky Carmichael	Havana, Florida
1998	Ricky Carmichael	Havana, Florida
1997	Ricky Carmichael	Havana, Florida
1996	Steve Lamson	Pollock Pines, California
1995	Steve Lamson	Pollock Pines, California
1994	Doug Henry	Oxford, Connecticut
1993	Doug Henry	Oxford, Connecticut
1992	Jeff Emig	Highland, California
1991	Mike Kiedrowski	Canyon Country, California
1990	Guy Cooper	Stillwater, Oklahoma
1989	Mike Kiedrowski	Canyon Country, California

Year	Champion	Hometown
1988	George Holland	Kerman, California
1987	Micky Dymond	Yorba Linda, California
1986	Micky Dymond	Yorba Linda, California
1985	Ron Lechien	El Cajon, California
1984	Jeff Ward	Mission Viejo, California
1983	Johnny O'Mara	Simi Valley, California
1982	Mark Barnett	Bridgeview, Illinois
1981	Mark Barnett	Bridgeview, Illinois
1980	Mark Barnett	Bridgeview, Illinois
1979	Broc Glover	El Cajon, California
1978	Broc Glover	El Cajon, California
1977	Broc Glover	El Cajon, California
1976	Bob Hannah	Whittier, California
1975	Marty Smith	San Diego, California
1974	Marty Smith	San Diego, California

GOLF

P ast champions rose to the top of the PGA Tour leader board in the first quarter of 2003. Tiger Woods, Davis Love III, and Mike Weir each won three tournaments. Among the victories, Woods won the season's first World Golf Championship event, Love turned out a brilliant final round to win the Players Championship, and Weir prevailed at the Masters. Experienced players may have had great success in early 2003, but 18 pros were first-time winners on the PGA Tour in 2002. But the biggest winner of all was — no surprise — Woods, who further cemented his status as the world's best golfer. He won five events, including the Masters and the U.S. Open.

Annika Sorenstam took on a huge challenge. She became the first woman in 58 years to play in a PGA Tour event when she entered the Colonial Golf Tournament, in May 2003. She shot five over par and missed the cut, but gained a legion of new fans impressed by her gutsy performance. A confident Sorenstam won her next two starts on the LPGA Tour, including the LPGA Championship in a playoff.

In 2002, Sorenstam was even more dominant on the LPGA Tour than Woods was on the PGA Tour. She won 11 tournaments, becoming the first player to do so since Mickey Wright in 1964. Sorenstam ran away with the Player of the Year award.

The spotlight was intense around Sorenstam, but several young up-and-coming LPGA players made their presence known in 2002. Beth Bauer and Natalie Gulbis turned out excellent rookie seasons, with Bauer narrowly winning Rookie of the Year honors. She had six Top 10 finishes and 15 Top 20 finishes. Se Ri Pak continued her successful young career by winning five events, including a major championship.

The most impressive win in early 2003 was 13-year-old Michelle Wie's in the U.S. Women's Amateur Public Links. She is the youngest winner in the event's 27-year history.

ROBERT BECK/SPORTS ILLUSTRATED

Tiger Woods won five events in 2002 and stormed to three victories in early 2003.

▫▷**Random Fact:** Sam Snead won the 1965 Greater Greensboro Open at the age of 52 years, 10 months, making him the oldest winner on the PGA Tour.

Annika Sorenstam won 11 LPGA tournaments in 2002. In May 2003, she became the first woman in 58 years to play in a PGA event.

GARY BOGDON/SPORTS ILLUSTRATED

Did You Know?

Before Babe Didrikson Zaharias won 31 times on the LPGA Tour, she had been an accomplished track-and-field star who broke world records in the 80-meter hurdles, the javelin throw, and the high jump.

All-time Champions—Men

The Masters

Year	Winner	Year	Winner	Year	Winner
		1981	Tom Watson	1957	Doug Ford
		1980	Seve Ballesteros	1956	Jack Burke Jr.
2003	Mike Weir	1979 †	*Fuzzy Zoeller	1955	Cary Middlecoff
2002	Tiger Woods	1978	Gary Player	1954	*Sam Snead
2001	Tiger Woods	1977	Tom Watson	1953	Ben Hogan
2000	Vijay Singh	1976	Ray Floyd	1952	Sam Snead
1999	José María Olazábal	1975	Jack Nicklaus	1951	Ben Hogan
1998	Mark O'Meara	1974	Gary Player	1950	Jimmy Demaret
1997	Tiger Woods	1973	Tommy Aaron	1949	Sam Snead
1996	Nick Faldo	1972	Jack Nicklaus	1948	Claude Harmon
1995	Ben Crenshaw	1971	Charles Coody	1947	Jimmy Demaret
1994	José María Olazábal	1970	*Billy Casper	1946	Herman Keiser
1993	Bernhard Langer	1969	George Archer	1943–45	No tournament
1992	Fred Couples	1968	Bob Goalby	1942	*Byron Nelson
1991	Ian Woosnam	1967	Gay Brewer Jr.	1941	Craig Wood
1990	*Nick Faldo	1966	*Jack Nicklaus	1940	Jimmy Demaret
1989	*Nick Faldo	1965	Jack Nicklaus	1939	Ralph Guldahl
1988	Sandy Lyle	1964	Arnold Palmer	1938	Henry Picard
1987	*Larry Mize	1963	Jack Nicklaus	1937	Byron Nelson
1986	Jack Nicklaus	1962	Arnold Palmer	1936	Horton Smith
1985	Bernhard Langer	1961	Gary Player	1935	*Gene Sarazen
1984	Ben Crenshaw	1960	Arnold Palmer	1934	Horton Smith
1983	Seve Ballesteros	1959	Art Wall Jr.		
1982	*Craig Stadler	1958	Arnold Palmer		

* Winner in playoff.
† Playoff cut from 18 holes to sudden death.
Note: Played at Augusta National Golf Club, Augusta, Georgia.

All-time Champions—Men (cont.)

U.S. Open

Year	Winner	Year	Winner	Year	Winner
		1969	Orville Moody	1930	Bobby Jones
		1968	Lee Trevino	1929	*Bobby Jones
Year	Winner	1967	Jack Nicklaus	1928	*Johnny Farrell
2003	Jim Furyk	1966	*Billy Casper	1927	*Tommy Armour
2002	Tiger Woods	1965	*Gary Player	1926	Bobby Jones
2001	*Retief Goosen	1964	Ken Venturi	1925	*Willie MacFarlane
2000	Tiger Woods	1963	*Julius Boros	1924	Cyril Walker
1999	Payne Stewart	1962	*Jack Nicklaus	1923	*Bobby Jones
1998	Lee Janzen	1961	Gene Littler	1922	Gene Sarazen
1997	Ernie Els	1960	Arnold Palmer	1921	Jim Barnes
1996	Steve Jones	1959	Billy Casper	1920	Edward Ray
1995	Corey Pavin	1958	Tommy Bolt	1919	*Walter Hagen
1994	*Ernie Els	1957	*Dick Mayer	1917–18	No tournament
1993	Lee Janzen	1956	Cary Middlecoff	1916	Chick Evans
1992	Tom Kite	1955	*Jack Fleck	1915	Jerry Travers
1991	*Payne Stewart	1954	Ed Furgol	1914	Walter Hagen
1990	*Hale Irwin	1953	Ben Hogan	1913	*Francis Ouimet
1989	Curtis Strange	1952	Julius Boros	1912	John McDermott
1988	*Curtis Strange	1951	Ben Hogan	1911	*John McDermott
1987	Scott Simpson	1950	*Ben Hogan	1910	*Alex Smith
1986	Ray Floyd	1949	Cary Middlecoff	1909	George Sargent
1985	Andy North	1948	Ben Hogan	1908	*Fred McLeod
1984	*Fuzzy Zoeller	1947	*Lew Worsham	1907	Alex Ross
1983	Larry Nelson	1946	*Lloyd Mangrum	1906	Alex Smith
1982	Tom Watson	1942–45	No tournament	1905	Willie Anderson
1981	David Graham	1941	Craig Wood	1904	Willie Anderson
1980	Jack Nicklaus	1940	*Lawson Little	1903	*Willie Anderson
1979	Hale Irwin	1939	*Byron Nelson	1902	Laurie Auchterlonie
1978	Andy North	1938	Ralph Guldahl	1901	*Willie Anderson
1977	Hubert Green	1937	Ralph Guldahl	1900	Harry Vardon
1976	Jerry Pate	1936	Tony Manero	1899	Willie Smith
1975	*Lou Graham	1935	Sam Parks, Jr.	1898	Fred Herd
1974	Hale Irwin	1934	Olin Dutra	1897 †	Joe Lloyd
1973	Johnny Miller	1933	Johnny Goodman	1896 †	James Foulis
1972	Jack Nicklaus	1932	Gene Sarazen	1895 †	Horace Rawlins
1971	*Lee Trevino	1931	*Billy Burke		
1970	Tony Jacklin				

*Winner in playoff. The 1990 playoff went to one hole of sudden death after an 18-hole playoff. In the 1994 playoff, Montgomerie was eliminated after 18 playoff holes, and Els beat Roberts on the 20th. †Before 1898, 36 holes; from 1898 on, 72 holes.

British Open

Year	Winner	Year	Winner	Year	Winner
2003	Ben Curtis	1984	Seve Ballesteros	1965	Peter Thomson
2002	*Ernie Els	1983	Tom Watson	1964	Tony Lema
2001	David Duval	1982	Tom Watson	1963	*Bob Charles
2000	Tiger Woods	1981	Bill Rogers	1962	Arnold Palmer
1999	*Paul Lawrie	1980	Tom Watson	1961	Arnold Palmer
1998	*Mark O'Meara	1979	Seve Ballesteros	1960	Kel Nagle
1997	Justin Leonard	1978	Jack Nicklaus	1959	Gary Player
1996	Tom Lehman	1977	Tom Watson	1958	*Peter Thomson
1995	*John Daly	1976	Johnny Miller	1957	Bobby Locke
1994	Nick Price	1975	*Tom Watson	1956	Peter Thomson
1993	Greg Norman	1974	Gary Player	1955	Peter Thomson
1992	Nick Faldo	1973	Tom Weiskopf	1954	Peter Thomson
1991	Ian Baker-Finch	1972	Lee Trevino	1953	Ben Hogan
1990	Nick Faldo	1971	Lee Trevino	1952	Bobby Locke
1989 ††	*Mark Calcavecchia	1970	*Jack Nicklaus	1951	Max Faulkner
1988	Seve Ballesteros	1969	Tony Jacklin	1950	Bobby Locke
1987	Nick Faldo	1968	Gary Player	1949	*Bobby Locke
1986	Greg Norman	1967	Robert DeVicenzo	1948	Henry Cotton
1985	Sandy Lyle	1966	Jack Nicklaus	1947	Fred Daly

*Winner in playoff.
††Playoff cut from 18 holes to 4 holes.

British Open (cont.)

Year	Winner
1946	Sam Snead
1940–45	No tournament
1939	Richard Burton
1938	Reginald A. Whitcombe
1937	Henry Cotton
1936	Alfred Padgham
1935	Alfred Perry
1934	Henry Cotton
1933	*Denny Shute
1932	Gene Sarazen
1931	Tommy Armour
1930	Bobby Jones
1929	Walter Hagen
1928	Walter Hagen
1927	Bobby Jones
1926	Bobby Jones
1925	Jim Barnes

* Winner in playoff.
** Championship extended from 36 to 72 holes.

Year	Winner
1924	Walter Hagen
1923	Arthur G. Havers
1922	Walter Hagen
1921	*Jock Hutchison
1920	George Duncan
1915–19	No tournament
1914	Harry Vardon
1913	John H. Taylor
1912	Ted Ray
1911	Harry Vardon
1910	James Braid
1909	John H. Taylor
1908	James Braid
1907	Arnaud Massy
1906	James Braid
1905	James Braid
1904	Jack White
1903	Harry Vardon
1902	Alexander Herd
1901	James Braid

Year	Winner
1900	John H. Taylor
1899	Harry Vardon
1898	Harry Vardon
1897	Harold Hilton
1896	*Harry Vardon
1895	John H. Taylor
1894	John H. Taylor
1893	William Auchterlonie
1892**	Harold Hilton
1891	Hugh Kirkaldy
1890	John Ball
1889	*Willie Park, Jr.
1888	Jack Burns
1887	Willie Park, Jr.
1886	David Brown
1885	Bob Martin
1884	Jack Simpson
1883	*Willie Fernie
1882	Robert Ferguson

Trivia Challenge

What player is tied with Jack Nicklaus for the most PGA Championship victories (5)?

Walter Hagen

Legends

Jack Nicklaus was a five-time PGA Player of the Year.

Jack Nicklaus, b. January 21, 1940, Columbus, Ohio. Nicklaus has been a driving force in golf for more than 40 years, and has long been regarded as the best to ever play. "The Golden Bear" won 71 times on the PGA Tour. At the age of 46, he became the oldest player to win the Masters, his sixth victory at Augusta National. It was also his 18th professional major championship. Since leaving the PGA Tour as a full-time player in 1990, Nicklaus has racked up 10 victories on the Champions Tour, including the U.S. Senior Open in 1991 and 1993. Nicklaus is also one of the world's premier golf-course designers.

Bobby Jones, b. March 17, 1902, Atlanta, Georgia; d. December 18, 1971. As a popular amateur, Jones laid the foundation for professional golf in the United States. From 1923 to 1930, he won 13 of 21 major championships he entered. The climax of that run came in 1930, when he won all four major championships of that era: the British Amateur, the British Open, the U.S. Open, and the U.S. Amateur. It was the first and only single-season Grand Slam in history. Jones shocked the golf world when he retired at the age of 28, but his impact on the game was far from over. He later designed Augusta National, the site of the Masters.

Arnold Palmer, b. September 10, 1929, Latrobe, Pennsylvania. Palmer popularized the game of golf with his exciting style. His success helped dramatically grow the PGA Tour's fan base. Those who followed Palmer earned the nickname "Arnie's Army" for their size and energy. Palmer won 62 times on the Tour, was the first golfer ever to win four Masters titles, and was the first to earn more than $1 million in his career.

FRED VUICH/SPORTS ILLUSTRATED

All-time Champions—Men (cont.)

Year	Winner	Year	Winner	Year	Winner
British Open (cont.)		1875	Willie Park	1866	Willie Park
		1874	Mungo Park	1865	Andrew Strath
Year	**Winner**	1873	Tom Kidd	1864	Tom Morris, Sr.
1881	Robert Ferguson	1872	Tom Morris, Jr.	1863	Willie Park
1880	Robert Ferguson	1871	No tournament	1862	Tom Morris, Sr.
1879	Jamie Anderson	1870	Tom Morris, Jr.	1861 ‡	Tom Morris, Sr.
1878	Jamie Anderson	1869	Tom Morris, Jr.	1860†	Willie Park
1877	Jamie Anderson	1868	Tom Morris, Jr.		
1876	#Bob Martin	1867	Tom Morris, Sr.		

#Tied, but opponent refused playoff. ‡The second annual open was open to amateurs and pros. †The first event was open only to professional golfers.

Today's Stars

Ernie Els, b. October 17, 1969, Johannesburg, South Africa. Els started the 2003 season on fire, winning four out of his first five starts, including the PGA Tour's first two events. In 2002, the smooth swinging Els notched his third major championship with a playoff victory at the British Open. With the British Open win and his two victories at the U.S. Open (1994, 1997), Els has more major titles than any golfer in the Top 10 of the World Golf Rankings, other than Tiger Woods (8).

Tiger Woods, b. December 30, 1975, Cypress, California. Woods missed the first five tournaments of 2003 while recovering from knee surgery. He returned in February, winning three events in five weeks. Woods picked up where he left off in 2002, when he won five times, including victories at the Masters and U.S. Open, his seventh and eighth career major championships. His strong performance that year helped him win his fourth consecutive Player of the Year award. Woods has won the Masters three times (1997, 2000, 2001), the PGA Championship twice (1999, 2000), the U.S. Open twice (2000, 2002), and the British Open once (2000).

Phil Mickelson, b. June 16, 1970, San Diego, California. Despite carrying the reputation as the best player never to have won a major championship, Mickelson still plays some of the world's best golf. He finished in the Top 10 in five events in early 2003, including a third-place finish at the Masters. In 2002, Mickelson won twice on the PGA Tour, giving the lefty multiple wins in a season for the seventh time in 10 years. Mickelson also eclipsed the $20 million career earning mark, becoming one of only four players in history to do so.

In 2003, Ernie Els became the first player since 1989 to win the first two tournaments of the season.

JOHN BIEVER/SPORTS ILLUSTRATED

2002-03 MEN'S TIMELINE

January 6, 2002: Sergio Garcia of Spain kicks off the PGA Tour season with a win at the Mercedes Championship, in Hawaii. It will be his only victory on American soil for the year.

June 16, 2002: After winning the Masters in April, Tiger Woods is victorious at the U.S. Open. He becomes the first golfer since Jack Nicklaus in 1972 to win the season's first two major championships.

July 21, 2002: Ernie Els of South Africa overcomes some shaky play down the stretch to win the British Open in a playoff. Tiger Woods's pursuit of a single-season Grand Slam ends in the third round with an 81, his worst score as a professional.

August 18, 2002: Starting the final round of the PGA Championship three strokes behind leader Justin Leonard of the U.S., Rich Beem, also of the U.S., storms in front before holding off a furious rally by Tiger Woods to win his first major championship.

September 29, 2002: The European squad storms out early on the final day of the 34th Ryder Cup to win by 3 points, taking back the trophy it lost on American soil in 1999.

December 12, 2002: Tiger Woods has surgery on his knee. He takes two months off and returns to play in the Buick Invitational on February 13, 2003. He wins the event.

March 23, 2003: Tiger Woods wins the Bay Hill Invitational by 11 strokes, joining Gene Sarazen and Walter Hagen as the only players to win an event four straight times.

April 13, 2003: Mike Weir becomes the first Canadian and only the second left-handed player to win a major championship when he beats Len Mattiace of the U.S. on the first playoff hole at the Masters. Tiger Woods finishes in a tie for 15th place in his pursuit for three straight Masters titles.

April 27, 2003: Former Masters champion Fred Couples of the U.S. breaks out of a five-year slump to win the Shell Houston Open by four strokes.

July 20, 2003: PGA Tour rookie Ben Curtis pulls an upset victory at the British Open, becoming the first player to win his major championship debut since Francis Ouimet in the 1913 U.S. Open.

All-time Champions—Men (cont.)

PGA Championship

Year	Winner	Year	Winner	Year	Winner
		1987	*Larry Nelson	1972	Gary Player
		1986	Bob Tway	1971	Jack Nicklaus
2002	Rich Beem	1985	Hubert Green	1970	Dave Stockton
2001	David Toms	1984	Lee Trevino	1969	Ray Floyd
2000	*Tiger Woods	1983	Hal Sutton	1968	Julius Boros
1999	Tiger Woods	1982	Raymond Floyd	1967	*Don January
1998	Vijay Singh	1981	Larry Nelson	1966	Al Geiberger
1997	Davis Love III	1980	Jack Nicklaus	1965	Dave Marr
1996	*Mark Brooks	1979	*David Graham	1964	Bobby Nichols
1995	*Steve Elkington	1978	*John Mahaffey	1963	Jack Nicklaus
1994	Nick Price	1977 †	*Lanny Wadkins	1962	Gary Player
1993	*Paul Azinger	1976	Dave Stockton	1961	*Jerry Barber
1992	Nick Price	1975	Jack Nicklaus	1960	Jay Hebert
1991	John Daly	1974	Lee Trevino	1959	Bob Rosburg
1990	Wayne Grady	1973	Jack Nicklaus	1958	Dow Finsterwald
1989	Payne Stewart				
1988	Jeff Sluman				

*Winner in playoff.
†Playoff changed from 18 holes to sudden death.

▷**Random Fact:** Jack Nicklaus holds the PGA Tour record for most career major championships (18) as well as most second-place finishes (19).

 **G OLF**

All-time Champions—Men (cont.)

PGA Championship (cont.)

Year	Winner	Year	Winner	Year	Winner
1957	Lionel Hebert	1945	Byron Nelson	1930	Tommy Armour
1956	Jack Burke	1944	Bob Hamilton	1929	Leo Diegel
1955	Doug Ford	1943	No tournament	1928	Leo Diegel
1954	Chick Harbert	1942	Sam Snead	1927	Walter Hagen
1953	Walter Burkemo	1941	Vic Ghezzi	1926	Walter Hagen
1952	Jim Turnesa	1940	Byron Nelson	1925	Walter Hagen
1951	Sam Snead	1939	Henry Picard	1924	Walter Hagen
1950	Chandler Harper	1938	Paul Runyan	1923	Gene Sarazen
1949	Sam Snead	1937	Denny Shute	1922	Gene Sarazen
1948	Ben Hogan	1936	Denny Shute	1921	Walter Hagen
1947	Jim Ferrier	1935	Johnny Revolta	1920	Jock Hutchison
1946	Ben Hogan	1934	Paul Runyan	1919	Jim Barnes
		1933	Gene Sarazen	1917–18	No tournament
		1932	Olin Dutra	1916	Jim Barnes
		1931	Tom Creavy		

All-time Champions—Women

LPGA Championship

Year	Winner	Year	Winner	Year	Winner
2003	Annika Sorenstam	1988	Sherri Turner	1971	Kathy Whitworth
2002	Se Ri Pak	1987	Jane Geddes	1970	*Shirley Englehorn
2001	Karrie Webb	1986	Pat Bradley	1969	Betsy Rawls
2000	*Juli Inkster	1985	Nancy Lopez	1968	*Sandra Post
1999	Juli Inkster	1984	Patty Sheehan	1967	Kathy Whitworth
1998	Se Ri Pak	1983	Patty Sheehan	1966	Gloria Ehret
1997	*Chris Johnson	1982	Jan Stephenson	1965	Sandra Haynie
1996	Laura Davies	1981	Donna Caponi	1964	Mary Mills
1995	Kelly Robbins	1980	Sally Little	1963	Mickey Wright
1994	Laura Davies	1979	Donna Caponi	1962	Judy Kimball
1993	Patty Sheehan	1978	Nancy Lopez	1961	Mickey Wright
1992	Betsy King	1977	Chako Higuchi	1960	Mickey Wright
1991	Meg Mallon	1976	Betty Burfeindt	1959	Betsy Rawls
1990	Beth Daniel	1975	Kathy Whitworth	1958	Mickey Wright
1989	Nancy Lopez	1974	Sandra Haynie	1957	Louise Suggs
		1973	Mary Mills	1956	*Marlene Hagge
		1972	Kathy Ahern	1955	†Beverly Hanson

* Won in playoff. 1956 and 1997 were sudden death; 1968 and 1970 were 18-hole playoffs. †Won match-play final.

U.S. Women's Open

Year	Winner	Year	Winner	Year	Winner
2003	*Hilary Lunke	1990	Betsy King	1975	Sandra Palmer
2002	Juli Inkster	1989	Betsy King	1974	Sandra Haynie
2001	Karrie Webb	1988	Liselotte Neumann	1973	Susie Berning
2000	Karrie Webb	1987	*Laura Davies	1972	Susie Berning
1999	Juli Inkster	1986	*Jane Geddes	1971	JoAnne Carner
1998	†Se Ri Pak	1985	Kathy Baker	1970	Donna Caponi
1997	Alison Nicholas	1984	Hollis Stacy	1969	Donna Caponi
1996	Annika Sorenstam	1983	Jan Stephenson	1968	Susie Berning
1995	Annika Sorenstam	1982	Janet Anderson	1967	Catherine LaCoste
1994	Patty Sheehan	1981	Pat Bradley	1966	Sandra Spuzich
1993	Lauri Merten	1980	Amy Alcott	1965	Carol Mann
1992	*Patty Sheehan	1979	Jerilyn Britz	1964	*Mickey Wright
1991	Meg Mallon	1978	Hollis Stacy	1963	Mary Mills
		1977	Hollis Stacy	1962	Murle Breer
		1976	*JoAnne Carner	1961	Mickey Wright

* Winner in playoff. †Winner on second hole of sudden death after 18-hole playoff ended in a tie.

U.S. Women's Open (cont.)		Year	Winner	Year	Winner
		1957	Betsy Rawls	1951	Betsy Rawls
		1956	*Kathy Cornelius	1950	Babe Zaharias
Year	Winner	1955	Fay Crocker	1949	Louise Suggs
1960	Betsy Rawls	1954	Babe Zaharias	1948	Babe Zaharias
1959	Mickey Wright	1953	*Betsy Rawls	1947	Betty Jameson
1958	Mickey Wright	1952	Louise Suggs	1946	Patty Berg

* Winner in playoff.

Legends

Nancy Lopez, b. January 6, 1957, Torrance, California. At the age of 12, Lopez won the New Mexico Women's Amateur title. She won the USGA Junior Girls Championship twice (1972, 1974). In 1975, she finished second in the U.S. Women's Open as an amateur. It was a sign of good things to come. During her LPGA rookie campaign in 1978, Lopez recorded nine wins, a rookie record. In all, she won 48 times during her professional career, including three LPGA Championships (1978, 1985, 1989). On July 20, 1987, Lopez became the 11th member of the LPGA Hall of Fame.

Kathy Whitworth, b. September 27, 1939, Monahans, Texas. Whitworth has more official tour victories (88) than any other professional golfer — male or female. She joined the tour in 1958 and won her first event four years later, at the Kelly Girl Open. Her most productive span was 1965-68, when she won 35 times. In 1981, she finished third in the U.S. Women's Open to become the first LPGA player to surpass the $1 million mark in career earnings.

Mickey Wright, b. February 14, 1935, San Diego, California. Wright is one of the greatest players in LPGA history. Her 82 career victories ranks second all-time. The majority of those wins (68) came in the 1960's. In 1961, Wright won three of the four LPGA majors, and in 1963, she won 13 times. She was one of the six inaugural inductees into the LPGA Tour Hall of Fame and was named the Female Golfer of the Century by the *Associated Press*.

Nancy Lopez was the youngest-ever (age 30) inductee into the LPGA Tour Hall of Fame (1987).

DAVID E. KLUTHO/SPORTS ILLUSTRATED

Today's Stars

Se Ri Pak, b. September 28, 1977, Daejeon, Korea. The Number 2-ranked women's player has made a huge impact in five seasons on tour. In 1998, as a rookie, Pak won two major titles (LPGA Championship, U.S. Women's Open) and Rookie of the Year honors. She followed that with major titles in 2001 and 2002. In early 2003, she won two tournaments and had five Top 10-finishes.

Annika Sorenstam, b. October 9, 1970, Stockholm, Sweden. Sorenstam's 2001 and 2002 LPGA tour seasons were two of the best in golf history — men's or women's. She earned 19 official victories during that span, including back-to-back major titles at the Nabisco Championship. After dominating the women's circuit year after year, Sorenstam took on PGA players at the Colonial Golf Tournament, beginning on May 22, in Fort Worth, Texas. She finished at five over par and missed the cut, but won many new fans.

Karrie Webb, b. December 21, 1974, Queensland, Australia. Webb's LPGA career got off to a record-breaking start. She won four times and earned more than $1 million in 1996, making her the second-most-productive rookie in LPGA history (Nancy Lopez won nine times in her rookie season). Webb also became the first rookie on any tour to surpass $1 million in earnings. She has won at least one major championship in four consecutive seasons, entering 2003. Her most dominant performance came at the 2001 U.S. Women's Open, where she won by eight strokes.

In 2002, Se Ri Pak became the youngest player (24 years, 8 months, and 11 days old) to win four major championships.

GARY BOGDON/SPORTS ILLUSTRATED

All-time Champions—Women (cont.)

Nabisco Championship		Year	Winner	Year	Winner
		1993	Helen Alfredsson	1981	Nancy Lopez
Year	**Winner**	1992	*Dottie Mochrie	1980	Donna Caponi
2003	Patricia Meunier-Lebouc	1991	Amy Alcott	1979	Sandra Post
2002	Annika Sorenstam	1990	Betsy King	1978	*Sandra Post
2001	Annika Sorenstam	1989	Juli Inkster	1977	Kathy Whitworth
2000	Karrie Webb	1988	Amy Alcott	1976	Judy Rankin
1999	Dottie Pepper	1987	*Betsy King	1975	Sandra Palmer
1998	Pat Hurst	1986	Pat Bradley	1974	*Jo Ann Prentice
1997	Betsy King	1985	Alice Miller	1973	Mickey Wright
1996	Patti Sheehan	1984	*Juli Inkster	1972	Jane Blalock
1995	Nanci Bowen	1983	Amy Alcott		
1994	Donna Andrews	1982	Sally Little		

* Winner in sudden-death playoff. *Note:* Designated fourth major in 1983; played at Mission Hills Country Club, Rancho Mirage, California.

du Maurier Classic

Year	Winner
2000	Meg Mallon
1999	Karrie Webb
1998	Brandie Burton
1997	Colleen Walker
1996	Laura Davies
1995	Jenny Lidback
1994	Martha Nause
1993	Brandie Burton

Year	Winner
1992	Sherri Steinhauer
1991	Nancy Scranton
1990	Cathy Johnston
1989	Tammie Green
1988	Sally Little
1987	Jody Rosenthal
1986	*Pat Bradley
1985	Pat Bradley
1984	Juli Inkster
1983	Hollis Stacy

Year	Winner
1982	Sandra Haynie
1981	Jan Stephenson
1980	Pat Bradley
1979	Amy Alcott
1978	JoAnne Carner
1977	Judy Rankin
1976	*Donna Caponi
1975	*JoAnne Carner
1974	Carole Jo Callison
1973	*Jocelyne Bourassa

* Winner in sudden-death playoff. *Note:* Designated third major in 1979; discontinued in 2001.

Women's British Open

Year	Winner
2002	Karrie Webb
2001	Se Ri Pak

Note: Designated fourth major in 2001.

Trivia Challenge

Which four women have each won more than 10 professional major championships in their careers?

Mickey Wright, Louise Suggs, Patty Berg, and Babe Didrikson Zaharias

Visit **www.sikids.com** for the latest sports stats and info.
Site code: slamdunk
AOL keyword: sikids

2002-03 WOMEN'S TIMELINE

March 31, 2002: Annika Sorenstam of Sweden wins the season's first major, the Nabisco Championship, by one shot.

June 9, 2002: Se Ri Pak of Korea comes from behind in the final round of the LPGA Championship to defeat Beth Daniel of the U.S. by three strokes. Pak becomes the youngest woman (24 years, 8 months, and 11 days) to win four major titles.

July 7, 2002: Juli Inkster of the U.S. wins the U.S. Women's Open over Annika Sorenstam in thrilling fashion, firing a 66 in the final round. She is the second-oldest player (42 years) to win the event.

August 11, 2002: Karrie Webb of Australia wins the women's British Open, becoming the first LPGA player to win all five major championships.

September 17, 2002: Suzy Whaley, a Connecticut golf-course head pro and former LPGA player, becomes the first woman to qualify for a PGA Tour event, the 2003 Greater Hartford Open. Whaley qualifies by winning a PGA Section Championship.

February 12, 2003: Annika Sorenstam accepts an invitation to play in a men's pro event, the Colonial Golf Tournament, on May 22-25.

March 30, 2003: Michelle Wie, a 13-year-old amateur from Hawaii, finishes in a tie for ninth place at the Nabisco Championship, in Rancho Mirage, California.

May 23, 2003: Annika Sorenstam finishes five over par and misses the cut at the Colonial Golf Tournament, a PGA event.

MOTOR SPORTS

I n February 2003, the Daytona 500, the Super Bowl of NASCAR, was shortened because of rain for only the third time in 45 years. The winner, Michael Waltrip, was leading after Lap 109 when the 200-lap race was called.

Winston Cup races used to be dominated by drivers from southern states, such as North Carolina, Alabama, and Kentucky. But in 2002, young drivers from other parts of the country made their mark on the sport. Matt Kenseth

(Cambridge, Wisconsin) and Kurt Busch (Las Vegas, Nevada) were strong competitors. Kenseth led the circuit with five victories, and Busch, who finished third in the final points standings, was second with four. Ryan Newman (South Bend, Indiana) had one victory and was named Rookie of the Year, just ahead of Jimmie Johnson (El Cajon, California), who had three victories.

The points race for the Cup championship was close

all season. Sterling Marlin led the standings for 25 straight weeks until a neck injury in September ended his season. Tony Stewart emerged as the winner. Stewart's Cup championship was the second in three years for Joe Gibbs Racing.

The rivalry between open-wheel circuits CART and the IRL continued in 2002. CART is the older and more established organization, but the IRL overtook it as America's premier open-wheel circuit. Sam Hornish, Jr., won

Tony Stewart won his first Winston Cup Championship in 2002.

WORTH CANOY/ICON SMI; KEVIN KANE/WIREIMAGE/ICON SMI (INSET)

WORTH CANOV/ICON SMI; NIGEL KINRADE (INSET)

his second-straight IRL championship, but there was controversy over who won the Indianapolis 500 (see "2002-03 Timeline," page 264). Runner-up Paul Tracy protested Helio Castroneves' victory, but IRL officials upheld the win.

Meanwhile, the slow death of CART continued. Legendary team owner Roger Penske moved both his teams, including two-time defending CART champion Gil de Ferran, to the IRL for the 2002 season. The IRL also gained two new engine manufacturers — Honda and Toyota. Both had been

▷**Random Fact:** Jeff Gordon is the only Winston Cup driver to top $10 million in a season. He won $10,879,757 in 2001.

Jeff Gordon finished the 2002 season fourth in the Winston Cup standings.

CART's main engine suppliers. Another blow came before the 2002 CART season ended. Michael Andretti, the circuit's all-time wins leader (42), announced he would move to the IRL full-time in 2003.

Indy Racing League (IRL)

Indianapolis 500 All-time Winners

ROBERT LABERGE/GETTY IMAGES

Year	Driver	Miles per hour (m.p.h.)	Year	Driver	m.p.h.
2003	Gil de Ferran	156.291	1976	Johnny Rutherford (255-Rain*)	148.725
2002	Helio Castroneves	166.499	1975	Bobby Unser (435-Rain*)	149.213
2001	Helio Castroneves	141.574	1974	Johnny Rutherford	158.589
2000	Juan Montoya	167.607	1973	Gordon Johncock (332.5-Rain*)	159.036
1999	Kenny Brack	153.176	1972	Mark Donohue	162.962
1998	Eddie Cheever, Jr.	145.155	1971	Al Unser	157.735
1997	Arie Luyendyk	145.827	1970	Al Unser	155.749
1996	Buddy Lazier	147.956	1969	Mario Andretti	156.867
1995	Jacques Villeneuve	153.616	1968	Bobby Unser	152.882
1994	Al Unser, Jr.	160.872	1967	A.J. Foyt, Jr.	151.207
1993	Emerson Fittipaldi	157.207	1966	Graham Hill	144.317
1992	Al Unser, Jr.	134.477	1965	Jim Clark	150.686
1991	Rick Mears	176.457	1964	A.J. Foyt, Jr.	147.350
1990	Arie Luyendyk	185.981	1963	Parnelli Jones	143.137
1989	Emerson Fittipaldi	167.581	1962	Rodger Ward	140.293
1988	Rick Mears	144.809	1961	A.J. Foyt, Jr.	139.130
1987	Al Unser	162.175	1960	Jim Rathmann	138.767
1986	Bobby Rahal	170.722	1959	Rodger Ward	135.857
1985	Danny Sullivan	152.982	1958	Jimmy Bryan	133.791
1984	Rick Mears	163.612	1957	Sam Hanks	135.601
1983	Tom Sneva	162.117	1956	Pat Flaherty	128.490
1982	Gordon Johncock	162.029	1955	Bob Sweikert	128.213
1981	Bobby Unser	139.084	1954	Bill Vukovich	130.840
1980	Johnny Rutherford	142.862	1953	Bill Vukovich	128.740
1979	Rick Mears	158.899	1952	Troy Ruttman	128.922
1978	Al Unser	161.363	1951	Lee Wallard	126.244
1977	A.J. Foyt, Jr.	161.331	1950	Johnnie Parsons (345-Rain)	124.00

Helio Castroneves

Note: Miles per hour (m.p.h.) denotes average race speed. *Race called because of rain.

Indy Racing League (cont.)

Indianapolis 500 All-time Winners

Year	Driver	Miles per hour (m.p.h.)
1949	Bill Holland	121.327
1948	Mauri Rose	119.814
1947	Mauri Rose	116.338
1946	George Robson	114.820
1942-45	No races held during World War II	
1941	Floyd Davis	115.117
	Mauri Rose	115.117
1940	Wilbur Shaw	114.277
1939	Wilbur Shaw	115.035
1938	Floyd Roberts	117.200
1937	Wilbur Shaw	113.580
1936	Louis Meyer	109.069
1935	Kelly Petillo	106.240
1934	Bill Cummings	104.863
1933	Louis Meyer	104.162
1932	Fred Fame	104.144
1931	Louis Schneider	96.629
1930	Billy Arnold	100.448

Year	Driver	m.p.h.
1929	Ray Keech	97.585
1928	Louis Meyer	99.482
1927	George Souders	97.545
1926	Frank Lockhart (400-Rain)	95.904
1925	Peter DePaolo	101.127
1924	L.L. Corum / Joe Boyer	98.234
1923	Tommy Milton	90.954
1922	Jimmy Murphy	94.484
1921	Tommy Milton	89.621
1920	Gaston Chevrolet	88.618
1919	Howdy Wilcox	88.050
1917-18	No races held during World War I	
1916	Dario Resta (scheduled for 300 miles)	84.001
1915	Ralph DePalma	89.840
1914	Rene Thomas	82.474
1913	Jules Goux	75.933
1912	Joe Dawson	78.719
1911	Ray Harroun	74.602

AP PHOTO

**Sam Hornish, Jr.,
2002 IRL champion**

Did You Know?

A.J. Foyt is the only driver to win the Indianapolis 500, Daytona 500, and the 24 Hours of Le Mans, the most important race in international competition.

All-time IRL Champions

2002	Sam Hornish, Jr.
2001	Sam Hornish, Jr.
2000	Buddy Lazier
1999	Greg Ray
1998	Kenny Brack
1996-97 *	Tony Stewart
1996 (Series' first year)	Buzz Calkins and Scott Sharp (co-champions)

*This season started in 1996 and ended in 1997.

All-time IRL Rookies of the Year

2002	Laurent Redon
2001	Felipe Giaffone
2000	Airton Dare
1999	Scott Harrington
1998	Robby Unser
1996-97	Jim Guthrie
1996 (Series' first year)	N/A

Championship Auto Racing Teams (CART)

All-time CART Championship Series Champions

Year	Driver	Year	Driver	Year	Driver
2002	Cristiano da Matta	1991	Michael Andretti	1980	Johnny Rutherford
2001	Gil de Ferran	1990	Al Unser, Jr.	1979	Rick Mears
2000	Gil de Ferran	1989	Emerson Fittipaldi		
1999	Juan Montoya	1988	Danny Sullivan		
1998	Alex Zanardi	1987	Bobby Rahal		
1997	Alex Zanardi	1986	Bobby Rahal		
1996	Jimmy Vasser	1985	Al Unser		
1995	Jacques Villeneuve	1984	Mario Andretti		
1994	Al Unser, Jr.	1983	Al Unser		
1993	Nigel Mansell	1982	Rick Mears		
1992	Bobby Rahal	1981	Rick Mears		

Today's Stars

Sarah Fisher, b. October 4, 1980, Columbus, Ohio. In 2000, Fisher became only the third woman in history to qualify for the Indianapolis 500. She made her IRL debut in 1999 as a 19-year-old, the youngest driver — male or female — in series history. Fisher won the pole position at the 2002 Belterra Casino Indy 300, making her the first woman to win the pole position for a major-league, open-wheel race in North American motor sports history.

Jeff Gordon, b. August 4, 1971, Vallejo, California. Gordon is a four-time Winston Cup champion (1995, 1997, 1998, 2001), a two-time Daytona 500 winner (1997, 1999), and the winner of the first Brickyard 400 (1994), a race he also won in 1998 and 2001. At the start of the 2003 season, Gordon had 61 career Cup victories, seventh all-time.

Tony Stewart, b. May 20, 1971, Columbus, Indiana. Stewart had three victories in 2002 and won the 2002 Winston Cup championship. At the start of the 2003 season, he had 15 career victories, including a Cup-leading six in 2000. Stewart was the IRL champion in 1996-97 and began racing in Winston Cup full time in 1999.

In 2002, Sarah Fisher became the fastest woman at the Indy 500. She had a four-lap qualifying average of more than 229 miles per hour.

STAN HONDA/AFP PHOTO

Did You Know?

Richard Petty's last Winston Cup race of 1992 (which was also the last race of his career) was the first Cup race of Jeff Gordon's career.

Trivia Challenge

Who holds the record for leading in the Indianapolis 500 for the most laps without ever winning the race?

Michael Andretti (426 laps in seven races)

MOTOR SPORTS

Trivia Challenge

In 2003, which three Winston Cup drivers were nephews of open-wheel racing legends?

Casey Means (Rick Means), John Andretti (Mario Andretti), Christian Fittipaldi (Emerson Fittipaldi).

2002-03 TIMELINE

February 17, 2002: Ward Burton wins his first career Daytona 500. Sterling Marlin was in position to win the race but was penalized for getting out of his car and working on it during a red flag (a time during which the race is stopped and work is not allowed on cars).

April 19, 2002: Roush Racing owner Jack Roush is critically injured in a plane crash. He suffers a shattered left leg, a broken left ankle, and a collapsed right lung. Roush, who owns the Mark Martin, Kurt Busch, Matt Kenseth, Jeff Burton, and Greg Biffle Winston Cup cars, returns to the track at Dover, Delaware, on May 31.

May 23, 2002: In the continuing battle for racing supremacy between the Top 2 open-wheel circuits in America, the IRL scores a major victory over CART. Honda, which had supplied engines for CART, announces that it will supply engines for the IRL, beginning in 2003.

May 26, 2002: Helio Castroneves wins the Indianapolis 500, but not without controversy. On the next-to-last lap, Paul Tracy passed Castroneves, who had slowed down because the yellow caution flag was out, which makes passing illegal. Tracy argues that he passed Castroneves before the yellow flag, and his team files a protest.

July 3, 2002: IRL president and CEO Tony George denies the final appeal of Tracy's team and upholds Castroneves's victory. The victory is his second-straight Indy 500 win.

August 4, 2002: Bill Elliott wins his first Brickyard 400, but Tony Stewart's off-the-track antics grab bigger headlines. Stewart wins the pole but finishes 12th. NASCAR fines him $10,000 and places him on probation for the rest of the season for shoving a photographer after the race.

August 24, 2002: Jeff Gordon breaks his 31-race winless streak by winning the Sharpie 500, at Bristol, Tennessee. He wins the Southern 500, at Darlington, South Carolina, a week later.

September 17, 2002: Michael Andretti announces that he is leaving CART and heading to the IRL for the 2003 season. Andretti owns the cars driven by fellow CART stars Dario Franchitti and Tony Kanaan, who leave with him.

November 3, 2002: Tony Stewart's chances for the 2002 Winston Cup championship improve when his closest rival, Mark Martin, is docked 25 points by NASCAR because his car's left-front springs do not have the minimum number of coils. The penalty leaves Martin 112 points behind Stewart with two races left.

November 17, 2002: Tony Stewart clinches his first career Winston Cup championship at Homestead, Florida, in the season's final race. He collects enough points in the race to keep Mark Martin from passing him in the points standings, finishing 38 points ahead of Martin. Stewart becomes the first driver to win the championship while on probation.

February 16, 2003: Michael Waltrip wins his second Daytona 500 in three years. The race is called after 109 laps because of rain.

June 19, 2003: NASCAR announces that Nextel Communications will become the title sponsor of its premier national series, to be named the NASCAR Nextel Cup Series. R.J. Reynolds had sponsored the NASCAR Winston Cup Series since 1971.

All-time Winston Cup Champions

Year	Driver	Year	Driver	Year	Driver
2002	Tony Stewart	1984	Terry Labonte	1966	David Pearson
2001	Jeff Gordon	1983	Bobby Allison	1965	Ned Jarrett
2000	Bobby Labonte	1982	Darrell Waltrip	1964	Richard Petty
1999	Dale Jarrett	1981	Darrell Waltrip	1963	Joe Weatherly
1998	Jeff Gordon	1980	Dale Earnhardt	1962	Joe Weatherly
1997	Jeff Gordon	1979	Richard Petty	1961	Ned Jarrett
1996	Terry Labonte	1978	Cale Yarborough	1960	Rex White
1995	Jeff Gordon	1977	Cale Yarborough	1959	Lee Petty
1994	Dale Earnhardt	1976	Cale Yarborough	1958	Lee Petty
1993	Dale Earnhardt	1975	Richard Petty	1957	Buck Baker
1992	Alan Kulwicki	1974	Richard Petty	1956	Buck Baker
1991	Dale Earnhardt	1973	Benny Parsons	1955	Tim Flock
1990	Dale Earnhardt	1972	Richard Petty	1954	Lee Petty
1989	Rusty Wallace	1971	Richard Petty	1953	Herb Thomas
1988	Bill Elliott	1970	Bobby Isaac	1952	Tim Flock
1987	Dale Earnhardt	1969	David Pearson	1951	Herb Thomas
1986	Dale Earnhardt	1968	David Pearson	1950	Bill Rexford
1985	Darrell Waltrip	1967	Richard Petty	1949	Red Byron

All-time Winston Cup Wins Leaders

1. Richard Petty (200)
2. David Pearson (105)
3. Bobby Allison (84)
(tie) Darrell Waltrip (84)
5. Cale Yarborough (83)
6. Dale Earnhardt (76)
7. Jeff Gordon (62)
8. Lee Petty (55)
9. Rusty Wallace (54)
10. Ned Jarrett (50)
(tie) Junior Johnson (50)
12. Herb Thomas (48)
13. Buck Baker (46)
14. Bill Elliott (43)
15. Tim Flock (40)
16. Bobby Isaac (37)
17. Mark Martin (33)
18. Fireball Roberts (32)
19. Dale Jarrett (31)
20. Rex White (28)
(tie) Fred Lorenzen (28)

All-time Winston Cup Rookies of the Year

Year	Driver	Year	Driver
2002	Ryan Newman	1979	Dale Earnhardt
2001	Kevin Harvick	1978	Ronnie Thomas
2000	Matt Kenseth	1977	Ricky Rudd
1999	Tony Stewart	1976	Skip Manning
1998	Kenny Irwin	1975	Bruce Hill
1997	Mike Skinner	1974	Earl Ross
1996	Johnny Benson	1973	Lennie Pond
1995	Ricky Craven	1972	Larry Smith
1994	Jeff Burton	1971	Walter Ballard
1993	Jeff Gordon	1970	Bill Dennis
1992	Jimmy Hensley	1969	Dick Brooks
1991	Bobby Hamilton	1968	Pete Hamilton
1990	Rob Moroso	1967	Donnie Allison
1989	Dick Trickle	1966	James Hylton
1988	Ken Bouchard	1965	Sam McQuagg
1987	Davey Allison	1964	Doug Cooper
1986	Alan Kulwicki	1963	Billy Wade
1985	Ken Schrader	1962	Tom Cox
1984	Rusty Wallace	1961	Woodie Wilson
1983	Sterling Marlin	1960	David Pearson
1982	Geoffrey Bodine	1959	Richard Petty
1981	Ron Bouchard	1958	Shorty Rollins
1980	Jody Ridley		

All-time Daytona 500 Champions

Year	Driver	m.p.h.	Year	Driver	m.p.h.	Year	Driver	m.p.h.
2003	Michael Waltrip	133.870	1988	Bobby Allison	137.531	1973	Richard Petty	157.205
2002	Ward Burton	142.971	1987	Bill Elliott	176.263	1972	A.J. Foyt	161.550
2001	Michael Waltrip	161.783	1986	Geoffrey Bodine	148.124	1971	Richard Petty	144.462
2000	Dale Jarrett	155.669	1985	Bill Elliott	172.265	1970	Pete Hamilton	149.601
1999	Jeff Gordon	161.551	1984	Cale Yarborough	150.994	1969	Lee Roy Yarbrough	157.950
1998	Dale Earnhardt	172.712	1983	Cale Yarborough	155.979	1968	Cale Yarborough	143.251
1997	Jeff Gordon	148.295	1982	Bobby Allison	153.991	1967	Mario Andretti	146.926
1996	Dale Jarrett	154.308	1981	Richard Petty	169.651	1966	Richard Petty	160.627
1995	Sterling Marlin	141.710	1980	Buddy Baker	177.602	1965	Fred Lorenzen	141.539
1994	Sterling Marlin	156.931	1979	Richard Petty	143.977	1964	Richard Petty	154.334
1993	Dale Jarrett	154.972	1978	Bobby Allison	159.730	1963	Tiny Lund	151.566
1992	Davey Allison	168.256	1977	Cale Yarborough	153.218	1962	Fireball Roberts	152.529
1991	Ernie Irvan	148.148	1976	David Pearson	152.181	1961	Marvin Panch	149.601
1990	Derrike Cope	165.761	1975	Benny Parsons	153.649	1960	Junior Johnson	124.740
1989	Darrell Waltrip	148.466	1974	Richard Petty	140.894	1959	Lee Petty	135.521

NASCAR (cont.)

All-time Brickyard 400 Winners

Year	Driver	m.p.h.
2002	Bill Elliott	125.033
2001	Jeff Gordon	130.790
2000	Bobby Labonte	155.912
1999	Dale Jarrett	148.194
1998	Jeff Gordon	126.772
1997	Ricky Rudd	130.814
1996	Dale Jarrett	139.508
1995	Dale Earnhardt	155.206
1994	Jeff Gordon	131.977

WORTH CANOY/ICON SMI

▯▷**Random Fact**: Dale Earnhardt is the only NASCAR driver to win the Winston Cup championship (1980) the year after being named the Cup's Rookie of the Year (1979).

All-time Coca-Cola 600 Winners

Year	Driver	m.p.h.
2003	Jimmie Johnson	126.198
2002	Mark Martin	137.729
2001	Jeff Burton	138.107
2000	Matt Kenseth	142.640
1999	Jeff Burton	151.367
1998	Jeff Gordon	136.424
1997	Jeff Gordon	136.745
1996	Dale Jarrett	147.581
1995	Bobby Labonte	151.952
1994	Jeff Gordon	139.445
1993	Dale Earnhardt	145.504
1992	Dale Earnhardt	132.980
1991	Davey Allison	138.951
1990	Rusty Wallace	137.650
1989	Darrell Waltrip	144.077
1988	Darrell Waltrip	124.460
1987	Kyle Petty	131.483
1986	Dale Earnhardt	140.406
1985	Darrell Waltrip	141.807
1984	Bobby Allison	129.233
1983	Neil Bonnett	140.707
1982	Neil Bonnett	130.058

Year	Driver	m.p.h.
1981	Bobby Allison	129.326
1980	Benny Parsons	119.265
1979	Darrell Waltrip	136.674
1978	Darrell Waltrip	138.355
1977	Richard Petty	137.676
1976	David Pearson	137.352
1975	Richard Petty	145.327
1974	David Pearson	135.720
1973	Buddy Baker	134.890
1972	Buddy Baker	142.255
1971	Bobby Allison	140.442
1970	Donnie Allison	129.680
1969	Lee Roy Yarbrough	134.361
1968	Buddy Baker	104.207
1967	Jim Paschal	135.832
1966	Marvin Panch	135.042
1965	Fred Lorenzen	121.772
1964	Jim Paschal	125.772
1963	Fred Lorenzen	132.418
1962	Nelson Stacy	125.552
1961	David Pearson	111.633
1960	Joe Lee Johnson	107.735

KEVIN KANE/WIREIMAGE/ICON SMI

All-time Talladega 500 Winners

Year	Driver	m.p.h.	Year	Driver	m.p.h.	Year	Driver	m.p.h.
2003	Dale Earnhardt, Jr.	144.625	1991	Dale Earnhardt	147.383	1979	Darrell Waltrip	161.229
2002	Dale Earnhardt, Jr.	159.022	1990	Dale Earnhardt	174.430	1978	Lennie Pond	174.700
2001	Bobby Hamilton	184.003	1989	Terry Labonte	157.354	1977	Donnie Allison	162.524
2000	Jeff Gordon	161.157	1988	Ken Schrader	154.505	1976	Dave Marcis	157.547
1999	Dale Earnhardt	163.395	1987	Bill Elliott	171.293	1975	Buddy Baker	130.892
1998	Bobby Labonte	163.439	1986	Bobby Hillin	151.552	1974	Richard Petty	148.637
1997	Terry Labonte	156.601	1985	Cale Yarborough	148.772	1973	Dick Brooks	145.454
1996	Jeff Gordon	133.387	1984	Dale Earnhardt	155.485	1972	James Hylton	148.728
1995	Sterling Marlin	173.188	1983	Dale Earnhardt	170.611	1971	Bobby Allison	145.945
1994	Jimmy Spencer	163.217	1982	Darrell Waltrip	168.157	1970	Pete Hamilton	158.517
1993	Dale Earnhardt	153.858	1981	Ron Bouchard	156.737	1969	Richard Brickhouse	153.778
1992	Ernie Irvan	176.309	1980	Neil Bonnett	166.894			

Note: From 1969 to 1988, the race was known as the Talladega 500. From 1989 to 2001, it was known as the Die Hard 500. In 2001, the name returned to the Talladega 500. In 2002, the race was named the Aaron's 499.

All-time Southern 500 Winners

Year	Driver	m.p.h.	Year	Driver	m.p.h.	Year	Driver	m.p.h.
2002	Jeff Gordon	118.617	1984	Harry Gant	128.270	1966	Darel Dieringer	114.830
2001	Ward Burton	122.773	1983	Bobby Allison	123.343	1965	Ned Jarrett	115.924
2000	Bobby Labonte	108.273	1982	Cale Yarborough	115.224	1964	Buck Baker	117.757
1999	Jeff Burton	107.816	1981	Neil Bonnett	126.410	1963	Fireball Roberts	129.784
1998	Jeff Gordon	139.031	1980	Terry Labonte	115.210	1962	Larry Frank	117.965
1997	Jeff Gordon	121.149	1979	David Pearson	126.259	1961	Nelson Stacy	117.787
1996	Jeff Gordon	135.757	1978	Cale Yarborough	116.828	1960	Buck Baker	105.901
1995	Jeff Gordon	121.231	1977	David Pearson	106.797	1959	Jim Reed	111.840
1994	Bill Elliott	127.952	1976	David Pearson	120.534	1958	Fireball Roberts	102.590
1993	Mark Martin	137.932	1975	Bobby Allison	116.825	1957	Speedy Thompson	100.094
1992	Darrell Waltrip	129.114	1974	Cale Yarborough	111.075	1956	Curtis Turner	95.067
1991	Harry Gant	133.508	1973	Cale Yarborough	134.033	1955	Herb Thomas	93.281
1990	Dale Earnhardt	123.141	1972	Bobby Allison	128.124	1954	Herb Thomas	94.930
1989	Dale Earnhardt	135.462	1971	Bobby Allison	131.398	1953	Buck Baker	92.780
1988	Bill Elliott	128.297	1970	Buddy Baker	128.817	1952	Fonty Flock	74.510
1987	Dale Earnhardt	115.520	1969	Lee Roy Yarbrough	105.612	1951	Herb Thomas	76.900
1986	Tim Richmond	121.068	1968	Cale Yarborough	126.132	1950	Johnny Mantz	76.260
1985	Bill Elliott	121.254	1967	Richard Petty	130.423			

Legends

Dale Earnhardt won his first Daytona 500 in February 1998 on his 20th attempt.

Dale Earnhardt, b. April 29, 1951, Kannapolis, North Carolina; d. February 18, 2001. "The Intimidator" is tied with Richard Petty for most Winston Cup championships (7). Earnhardt's 76 career wins are the sixth-most in Cup history. His 281 career Top 5 finishes are fourth all time, and his 428 Top 10 finishes ranks third-best. He was killed in an accident on the final lap of the 2001 Daytona 500.

Richard Petty, b. July 2, 1937, Level Cross, North Carolina. Petty's 200 career Winston Cup victories are the most all time. He is tied with Dale Earnhardt for the most Cup championships in history (7). Petty holds the Cup record for most victories in a single season (27, in 1967). He won the Daytona 500 a record seven times. "The King" was inducted into the International Motorsports Hall of Fame in 1997.

Mario Andretti, b. February 28, 1940, Montana, Italy. Andretti has a diverse list of racing accomplishments. He is a four-time Champ car national champion (1965, 1966, 1969, 1984), won the Daytona 500 in 1967, and won his only Indianapolis 500 two years later. He was also the Formula One world champion in 1978. Andretti is a three-time winner of the 12 Hours of Sebring, America's oldest sports car endurance race. In 1999, *The Associated Press* named him its "driver of the century."

PETER GREGOIRE/SPORTS ILLUSTRATED

TENNIS

The dominance of Serena Williams grabbed most of the attention during 2002 and early 2003. But Pete Sampras managed to steal some of the spotlight. His comeback victory at the 2002 U.S. Open ranks as one of the most exciting Grand Slam moments in tennis history.

Sampras proved that he still had what it takes to be champion — even at age 31. At the 2002 U.S. Open, he silenced critics who had said his career was finished by winning a record 14th men's Grand Slam singles title. His victory over rival Andre Agassi was his first tournament win since 2000. Agassi proved he wasn't ready for retirement either. At age 32, he won the 2003 Australian Open.

On the women's tour, Serena and her sister Venus left no doubt that they were the Number 1 and Number 2 women's players in the world. In 2002, the siblings met in three Grand Slam finals — the French Open, Wimbledon, and the U.S. Open. Serena defeated Venus in all of them. She finished 2002 with a 56–5 record and began 2003 ranked Number 1 in the world. In January, Serena kept right on rolling, winning the Australian Open and completing the "Serena Slam."

Meanwhile, up-and-comer Kim Clijsters of Belgium rose to Number 3 in the rankings, while five-time Grand Slam champion Martina Hingis announced her retirement, at age 22.

Number 1-ranked Serena Williams defeated her sister Venus in three Grand Slam finals in 2002.

BOB MARTIN/SPORTS ILLUSTRATED

Grand Slam Tournaments: All-Time Male Champions

Australian Championships

Year	Winner	Year	Winner	Year	Winner
		1990	Ivan Lendl	1976	Mark Edmondson
Year	Winner	1989	Ivan Lendl	1975	John Newcombe
2003	Andre Agassi	1988	Mats Wilander	1974	Jimmy Connors
2002	Thomas Johansson	1987	Stefan Edberg	1973	John Newcombe
2001	Andre Agassi	1986	No tournament	1972	Ken Rosewall
2000	Andre Agassi	1985	Stefan Edberg	1971	Ken Rosewall
1999	Yevgeny Kafelnikov	1984	Mats Wilander	1970	Arthur Ashe
1998	Petr Korda	1983	Mats Wilander	* 1969	Rod Laver
1997	Pete Sampras	1982	Johan Kriek	1968	Bill Bowrey
1996	Boris Becker	1981	Johan Kriek	1967	Roy Emerson
1995	Andre Agassi	1980	Brian Teacher	1966	Roy Emerson
1994	Pete Sampras	1979	Guillermo Vilas	1965	Roy Emerson
1993	Jim Courier	1978	Guillermo Vilas	1964	Roy Emerson
1992	Jim Courier	1977 (Jan.)	Roscoe Tanner	1963	Roy Emerson
1991	Boris Becker	1977 (Dec.)	Vitas Gerulaitis	1962	Rod Laver

* Became Open (amateur and professional) in 1969.

Note: Traditionally, the Australian Open was held in January. In 1977, it was moved to December, resulting in two tournaments that year. It returned to January in 1987.

Australian Championships (cont.)

Year	Winner
1961	Roy Emerson
1960	Rod Laver
1959	Alex Olmedo
1958	Ashley Cooper
1957	Ashley Cooper
1956	Lew Hoad
1955	Ken Rosewall
1954	Mervyn Rose
1953	Ken Rosewall
1952	Ken McGregor
1951	Richard Savitt
1950	Frank Sedgman
1949	Frank Sedgman
1948	Adrian Quist
1947	Dinny Pails
1946	John Bromwich
1941-45	No tournament
1940	Adrian Quist
1939	John Bromwich
1938	Don Budge
1937	Vivian B. McGrath
1936	Adrian Quist
1935	Jack Crawford
1934	Fred Perry
1933	Jack Crawford
1932	Jack Crawford
1931	Jack Crawford
1930	Gar Moon
1929	John C. Gregory
1928	Jean Borotra
1927	Gerald Patterson
1926	John Hawkes
1925	James Anderson
1924	James Anderson
1923	Pat O'Hara Wood
1922	James Anderson
1921	Rhys H. Gemmell
1920	Pat O'Hara Wood
1919	A.R.F. Kingscote
1916-18	No tournament
1915	Francis G. Lowe
1914	Arthur Wood
1913	E. F. Parker
1912	J. Cecil Parke
1911	Norman Brookes
1910	Rodney Heath
1909	Tony Wilding
1908	Fred Alexander
1907	Horace M. Rice
1906	Tony Wilding
1905	Rodney Heath

French Championships

Year	Winner
2003	Juan Carlos Ferrero
2002	Albert Costa
2001	Gustavo Kuerten
2000	Gustavo Kuerten
1999	Andre Agassi
1998	Carlos Moya
1997	Gustavo Kuerten
1996	Yevgeny Kafelnikov
1995	Thomas Muster
1994	Sergi Bruguera
1993	Sergi Bruguera

Year	Winner
1992	Jim Courier
1991	Jim Courier
1990	Andres Gomez
1989	Michael Chang
1988	Mats Wilander
1987	Ivan Lendl
1986	Ivan Lendl
1985	Mats Wilander
1984	Ivan Lendl
1983	Yannick Noah
1982	Mats Wilander
1981	Bjorn Borg
1980	Bjorn Borg
1979	Bjorn Borg
1978	Bjorn Borg
1977	Guillermo Vilas
1976	Adriano Panatta
1975	Bjorn Borg
1974	Bjorn Borg
1973	Ilie Nastase
1972	Andres Gimeno
1971	Jan Kodes
1970	Jan Kodes
1969	Rod Laver
* 1968	Ken Rosewall
1967	Roy Emerson
1966	Tony Roche
1965	Fred Stolle
1964	Manuel Santana
1963	Roy Emerson
1962	Rod Laver
1961	Manuel Santana
1960	Nicola Pietrangeli
1959	Nicola Pietrangeli
1958	Mervyn Rose
1957	Sven Davidson
1956	Lew Hoad
1955	Tony Trabert
1954	Tony Trabert
1953	Ken Rosewall
1952	Jaroslav Drobny
1951	Jaroslav Drobny
1950	Budge Patty
1949	Frank Parker
1948	Frank Parker
1947	Joseph Asboth
1946	Marcel Bernard
1940-45	No tournament
1939	Don McNeill
1938	Don Budge
1937	Henner Henkel
1936	Gottfried von Cramm
1935	Fred Perry
1934	Gottfried von Cramm
1933	Jack Crawford
1932	Henri Cochet
1931	Jean Borotra
1930	Henri Cochet
1929	Rene Lacoste
1928	Henri Cochet
1927	Henri Cochet
1926	Henri Cochet
† 1925	Rene Lacoste

Wimbledon Championships

Year	Winner
2003	Roger Federer
2002	Lleyton Hewitt

Year	Winner
2001	Goran Ivanisevic
2000	Pete Sampras
1999	Pete Sampras
1998	Pete Sampras
1997	Pete Sampras
1996	Richard Krajicek
1995	Pete Sampras
1994	Pete Sampras
1993	Pete Sampras
1992	Andre Agassi
1991	Michael Stich
1990	Stefan Edberg
1989	Boris Becker
1988	Stefan Edberg
1987	Pat Cash
1986	Boris Becker
1985	Boris Becker
1984	John McEnroe
1983	John McEnroe
1982	Jimmy Connors
1981	John McEnroe
1980	Bjorn Borg
1979	Bjorn Borg
1978	Bjorn Borg
1977	Bjorn Borg
1976	Bjorn Borg
1975	Arthur Ashe
1974	Jimmy Connors
1973	Jan Kodes
1972	Stan Smith
1971	John Newcombe
1970	John Newcombe
1969	Rod Laver
* 1968	Rod Laver
1967	John Newcombe
1966	Manuel Santana
1965	Roy Emerson
1964	Roy Emerson
1963	Chuck McKinley
1962	Rod Laver
1961	Rod Laver
1960	Neale Fraser
1959	Alex Olmedo
1958	Ashley Cooper
1957	Lew Hoad
1956	Lew Hoad
1955	Tony Trabert
1954	Jaroslav Drobny
1953	Vic Seixas
1952	Frank Sedgman
1951	Dick Savitt
1950	Budge Patty
1949	Fred Schroeder, Jr.
1948	Bob Falkenburg
1947	Jack Kramer
1946	Yvon Petra
1940-45	No tournament
1939	Bobby Riggs
1938	Don Budge
1937	Don Budge
1936	Fred Perry
1935	Fred Perry
1934	Fred Perry
1933	Jack Crawford
1932	Ellsworth Vines
1931	Sidney B. Wood, Jr.
1930	Bill Tilden
1929	Henri Cochet
1928	Rene Lacoste

*Became Open (amateur and professional) in 1968.
†1925 was the first year in which entries were accepted from all countries.

Today's Stars

Andy Roddick, b. August 30, 1982, Omaha, Nebraska. At the start of the 2003 season, Roddick had won five career titles. He made his first Grand Slam semi-final appearance, at the 2003 Australian Open, where he played one of the longest matches in tennis history, defeating Younes El Aynaoui of Morocco in five hours. He unleashed an ATP season-best and personal-best 144-mile-per-hour serve at Wimbledon in 2002. Roddick made his mark on the men's tour in 2001, when he jumped from Number 325 in the world to the Top 20.

Lleyton Hewitt, b. February 24, 1981, Adelaide, Australia. In 2002, Hewitt won five titles, including Wimbledon. He finished the year ranked Number 1 in the world, becoming the seventh player in history to hold the top spot for two straight seasons. Hewitt's career took off in 2001, when he won the U.S. Open. He became the youngest player (20 years 10 months) and the first Australian to finish the year ranked Number 1 in the history of Association of Tennis Professionals (ATP) rankings.

Marat Safin, b. January 27, 1980, Moscow, Russia. Safin was ranked Number 3 in the world at the beginning of 2003. In 2002, he had a 56–26 record and reached the finals of the Australian Open. He won his first Grand Slam title at the 2000 U.S. Open and was named the tour's most improved player that year.

Andy Roddick unleashed a 147-mile-per-hour serve in 2003, the second-fastest of all-time.

SIMON BRUTY/SPORTS ILLUSTRATED

Grand Slam Tournaments: All-Time Male Champions (cont.)

Wimbledon Championships (cont.)

Year	Winner
1927	Henri Cochet
1926	Jean Borotra
1925	Rene Lacoste
1924	Jean Borotra
1923	Bill Johnston
1922	Gerald L. Patterson
1921	Bill Tilden
1920	Bill Tilden
1919	Gerald L. Patterson
1915-18	No tournament
1914	Norman E. Brookes
1913	Anthony F. Wilding
1912	Anthony F. Wilding
1911	Anthony F. Wilding
1910	Anthony F. Wilding
1909	Arthur W. Gore
1908	Arthur W. Gore
1907	Norman E. Brookes
1906	H. Laurie Doherty

Year	Winner
1905	H. Laurie Doherty
1904	H. Laurie Doherty
1903	H. Laurie Doherty
1902	H. Laurie Doherty
1901	Arthur W. Gore
1900	Reggie F. Doherty
1899	Reggie F. Doherty
1898	Reggie F. Doherty
1897	Reggie F. Doherty
1896	Harold S. Mahoney
1895	Wilfred Baddeley
1894	Joshua Pim
1893	Joshua Pim
1892	Wilfred Baddeley
1891	Wilfred Baddeley
1890	William J. Hamilton
1889	William Renshaw
1888	Ernest Renshaw
1887	Herbert F. Lawford
1886	William Renshaw
1885	William Renshaw
1884	William Renshaw

Year	Winner
1883	William Renshaw
1882	William Renshaw
1881	William Renshaw
1880	John T. Harley
1879	John T. Harley
1878	P. Frank Hadow
1877	Spencer W. Gore

United States Championships

Year	Winner
2002	Pete Sampras
2001	Lleyton Hewitt
2000	Marat Safin
1999	Andre Agassi
1998	Patrick Rafter
1997	Patrick Rafter
1996	Pete Sampras
1995	Pete Sampras
1994	Andre Agassi
1993	Pete Sampras

Grand Slam Tournaments: All-Time Male Champions (cont.)

United States Championships (cont.)

Year	Winner	Year	Winner	Year	Winner
1992	Stefan Edberg	1973	John Newcombe	1953	Tony Trabert
1991	Stefan Edberg	1972	Ilie Nastase	1952	Frank Sedgman
1990	Pete Sampras	1971	Stan Smith	1951	Frank Sedgman
1989	Boris Becker	1970	Ken Rosewall	1950	Arthur Larsen
1988	Mats Wilander	** 1969	Stan Smith	1949	Pancho Gonzales
1987	Ivan Lendl	1969	Rod Laver	1948	Pancho Gonzales
1986	Ivan Lendl	* 1968	Arthur Ashe	1947	Jack Kramer
1985	Ivan Lendl	** 1968	Arthur Ashe	1946	Jack Kramer
1984	John McEnroe	1967	John Newcombe	1945	Frank Parker
1983	Jimmy Connors	1966	Fred Stolle	1944	Frank Parker
1982	Jimmy Connors	1965	Manuel Santana	1943	Joseph R. Hunt
1981	John McEnroe	1964	Roy Emerson	1942	Fred R. Schroeder, Jr.
1980	John McEnroe	1963	Rafael Osuna	1941	Bobby Riggs
1979	John McEnroe	1962	Rod Laver	1940	Don McNeill
1978	Jimmy Connors	1961	Roy Emerson	1939	Bobby Riggs
1977	Guillermo Vilas	1960	Neale Fraser	1938	Don Budge
1976	Jimmy Connors	1959	Neale Fraser	1937	Don Budge
1975	Manuel Orantes	1958	Ashley Cooper	1936	Fred Perry
1974	Jimmy Connors	1957	Mal Anderson	1935	Wilmer L. Allison
		1956	Ken Rosewall	1934	Fred Perry
		1955	Tony Trabert	1933	Fred Perry
		1954	Vic Seixas	1932	Ellsworth Vines

* Became Open (amateur and professional) in 1968.
** Amateur event held.

2002-03 MEN'S TIMELINE

January 27, 2002: Thomas Johansson becomes the first Swede since Stefan Edberg (1992 U.S. Open) to win a Grand Slam singles title. He upsets Marat Safin of Russia in the final of the Australian Open.

February 24, 2002: Andy Roddick of the U.S. defeats countryman James Blake in a three-set final at the Kroger St. Jude Tennis Championships, in Memphis, Tennessee. It is Blake's first career ATP final and Roddick's fourth career singles title.

March 10, 2002: Andre Agassi of the U.S. wins his 50th career singles title by defeating Juan Balcells of Spain in straight sets at the Franklin Templeton Classic, in Scottsdale, Arizona.

April 28, 2002: Andy Roddick beats countryman Pete Sampras in the final of the U.S. Clay Court Championships, in Houston, Texas. Roddick also wins the doubles title, making him the lone double winner on the ATP circuit for the season.

June 9, 2002: Albert Costa of Spain defeats countryman Juan Carlos Ferrero in the French Open championship. The victory is Costa's first Grand Slam title.

July 7, 2002: Lleyton Hewitt becomes the first Australian to win the Wimbledon singles title since Pat Cash won it in 1987.

August 18, 2002: James Blake of the U.S. defeats Paradorn Srichaphan of Thailand in the Legg Mason Tennis Classic to become only the fourth African American to win an ATP title in the Open era (since 1968).

September 8, 2002: Pete Sampras fires 33 aces and beats long-time rival Andre Agassi at the 2002 U.S. Open to win his 14th Grand Slam title.

November 17, 2002: Lleyton Hewitt of Australia defends his Tennis Masters Cup title in Shanghai, China, and finishes the season ranked Number 1 for the second time in a row.

January 26, 2003: At age 32, Andre Agassi defeats Ranier Schuettler of Germany in straight sets to win the Australian Open. The victory is Agassi's eighth Grand Slam title.

Grand Slam Tournaments: All-Time Male Champions (cont.)

United States Championships (cont.)		Year	Winner	Year	Winner
Year	**Winner**	1913	Maurice E. McLoughlin	1892	Oliver S. Campbell
1931	Ellsworth Vines	1912	Maurice E. McLoughlin	1891	Oliver S. Campbell
1930	John H. Doeg	1911	William A. Larned	1890	Oliver S. Campbell
1929	Bill Tilden	1910	William A. Larned	1889	H. W. Slocum, Jr.
1928	Henri Cochet	1909	William A. Larned	1888	H. W. Slocum, Jr.
1927	Rene Lacoste	1908	William A. Larned	1887	Richard D. Sears
1926	Rene Lacoste	1907	William A. Larned	1886	Richard D. Sears
1925	Bill Tilden	1906	William J. Clothier	1885	Richard D. Sears
1924	Bill Tilden	1905	Beals C. Wright	1884	Richard D. Sears
1923	Bill Tilden	1904	Holcombe Ward	1883	Richard D. Sears
1922	Bill Tilden	1903	H. Laurie Doherty	1882	Richard D. Sears
1921	Bill Tilden	1902	William A. Larned	1881	Richard D. Sears
1920	Bill Tilden	1901	William A. Larned		
1919	Bill Johnston	1900	Malcolm D. Whitman		
1918	R.L. Murray	1899	Malcolm D. Whitman		
1917	R.L. Murray	1898	Malcolm D. Whitman		
1916	Richard N. Williams	1897	Robert D. Wrenn		
1915	Bill Johnston	1896	Robert D. Wrenn		
1914	Richard N. Williams	1895	Frederick H. Hovey		
		1894	Robert D. Wrenn		
		1893	Robert D. Wrenn		

Did You Know?

The two oldest players to compete in a Grand Slam final were Ken Rosewall (age 37) and Mal Anderson (36). Rosewall defeated Anderson at the 1972 Australian Open.

Legends

Arthur Ashe, b. July 10, 1943, Richmond, Virginia; d. February 6, 1993. Ashe was a great tennis player and an even greater role model. He was the first black tennis player ranked Number 1 in the world and became the first African-American man to win the U.S. Open (1968), the Australian Open (1970), and Wimbledon (1975). Ashe was involved with many charities and was an outspoken opponent of discrimination. On April 8, 1992, he announced that he had AIDS, which he contracted from a blood transfusion in 1983. He spent the rest of his life raising funds to fight the disease and raising people's awareness about it.

Arthur Ashe is the only African-American man to win the U.S. Open, the Australian Open, and Wimbledon.

AP

Jimmy Connors, b. September 2, 1952, Belleville, Illinois. Connors is the all-time leader in men's tennis in pro singles titles (109). He won the U.S. Open championship five times (1974, 1976, 1978, 1982, 1983), Wimbledon twice (1974, 1982), and the Australian Open title (1974). He was inducted into the International Tennis Hall of Fame in 1998.

Rod Laver, b. August 9, 1938, Rockhampton, Queensland, Australia. Laver is the only player in the history of the sport to twice win all four Grand Slam titles in the same year (1962, 1969). Laver won a total of 11 Grand Slam titles and became the first tennis player to earn more than $1 million in prize money.

Australian Championships

Year	Winner
2003	Serena Williams
2002	Jennifer Capriati
2001	Jennifer Capriati
2000	Lindsay Davenport
1999	Martina Hingis
1998	Martina Hingis
1997	Martina Hingis
1996	Monica Seles
1995	Mary Pierce
1994	Steffi Graf
1993	Monica Seles
1992	Monica Seles
1991	Monica Seles
1990	Steffi Graf
1989	Steffi Graf
1988	Steffi Graf
1987 (Jan.)	Hana Mandlikova
1985 (Dec.)	Martina Navratilova
1984	Chris Evert Lloyd
1983	Martina Navratilova
1982	Chris Evert Lloyd
1981	Martina Navratilova
1980	Hana Mandlikova
1979	Barbara Jordan
1978	Chris O'Neil
1977 (Dec.)	Evonne Goolagong Cawley
1977 (Jan.)	Kerry Melville Reid
1976	Evonne Goolagong Cawley
1975	Evonne Goolagong
1974	Evonne Goolagong
1973	Margaret Smith Court
1972	Virginia Wade
1971	Margaret Smith Court
1970	Margaret Smith Court
*1969	Margaret Smith Court
1968	Billie Jean King
1967	Nancy Richey
1966	Margaret Smith
1965	Margaret Smith
1964	Margaret Smith
1963	Margaret Smith
1962	Margaret Smith
1961	Margaret Smith
1960	Margaret Smith
1959	Mary Carter-Reitano
1958	Angela Mortimer
1957	Shirley Fry
1956	Mary Carter
1955	Beryl Penrose
1954	Thelma Long
1953	Maureen Connolly
1952	Thelma Long
1951	Nancye Wynne Bolton
1950	Louise Brough
1949	Doris Hart
1948	Nancye Wynne Bolton
1947	Nancye Wynne Bolton
1946	Nancye Wynne Bolton
1941-45	No tournament
1940	Nancye Wynne Bolton
1939	Emily Westacott
1938	Dorothy Bundy
1937	Nancye Wynne Bolton
1936	Joan Hartigan
1935	Dorothy Round
1934	Joan Hartigan
1933	Joan Hartigan
1932	Coral Buttsworth
1931	Coral Buttsworth
1930	Daphne Akhurst
1929	Daphne Akhurst
1928	Daphne Akhurst
1927	Esna Boyd
1926	Daphne Akhurst
1925	Daphne Akhurst
1924	Sylvia Lance
1923	Margaret Molesworth
1922	Margaret Molesworth

French Championships

Year	Winner
2003	Justine Henin-Hardenne
2002	Serena Williams
2001	Jennifer Capriati
2000	Mary Pierce
1999	Steffi Graf
1998	Arantxa Sánchez-Vicario
1997	Iva Majoli
1996	Steffi Graf
1995	Steffi Graf
1994	Arantxa Sánchez-Vicario
1993	Steffi Graf
1992	Monica Seles
1991	Monica Seles
1990	Monica Seles
1989	Arantxa Sánchez-Vicario
1988	Steffi Graf
1987	Steffi Graf
1986	Chris Evert Lloyd
1985	Chris Evert Lloyd
1984	Martina Navratilova
1983	Chris Evert Lloyd
1982	Martina Navratilova
1981	Hana Mandlikova
1980	Chris Evert Lloyd
1979	Chris Evert Lloyd
1978	Virginia Ruzici
1977	Mima Jausovec
1976	Sue Barker
1975	Chris Evert
1974	Chris Evert
1973	Margaret Smith Court
1972	Billie Jean King
1971	Evonne Goolagong
1970	Margaret Smith Court
1969	Margaret Smith Court
**1968	Nancy Richey
1967	Francoise Durr
1966	Ann Jones
1965	Lesley Turner
1964	Margaret Smith
1963	Lesley Turner
1962	Margaret Smith
1961	Ann Haydon
1960	Darlene Hard
1959	Christine Truman
1958	Zsuzsi Kormoczy
1957	Shirley Bloomer
1956	Althea Gibson
1955	Angela Mortimer
1954	Maureen Connolly
1953	Maureen Connolly
1952	Doris Hart
1951	Shirley Fry
1950	Doris Hart
1949	Margaret Osborne duPont
1948	Nelly Landry
1947	Patricia Todd
1946	Margaret Osborne
1940-45	No tournament
1939	Simone Mathieu
1938	Simone Mathieu
1937	Hilde Sperling
1936	Hilde Sperling
1935	Hilde Sperling
1934	Margaret Scriven
1933	Margaret Scriven
1932	Helen Wills Moody
1931	Cilly Aussem
1930	Helen Wills Moody
1929	Helen Wills
1928	Helen Wills
1927	Kea Bouman
1926	Suzanne Lenglen
†1925	Suzanne Lenglen

Wimbledon Championships

Year	Winner
2003	Serena Williams
2002	Serena Williams
2001	Venus Williams
2000	Venus Williams
1999	Lindsay Davenport
1998	Jana Novotna
1997	Martina Hingis
1996	Steffi Graf
1995	Steffi Graf
1994	Conchita Martinez
1993	Steffi Graf
1992	Steffi Graf
1991	Steffi Graf
1990	Martina Navratilova
1989	Steffi Graf
1988	Steffi Graf
1987	Martina Navratilova
1986	Martina Navratilova
1985	Martina Navratilova
1984	Martina Navratilova
1983	Martina Navratilova
1982	Martina Navratilova
1981	Chris Evert Lloyd
1980	Evonne Goolagong Cawley
1979	Martina Navratilova
1978	Martina Navratilova
1977	Virginia Wade
1976	Chris Evert
1975	Billie Jean King
1974	Chris Evert
1973	Billie Jean King
1972	Billie Jean King
1971	Evonne Goolagong
1970	Margaret Smith Court
1969	Ann Haydon Jones
**1968	Billie Jean King
1967	Billie Jean King
1966	Billie Jean King
1965	Margaret Smith
1964	Maria Bueno

* Became Open (amateur and professional) in 1969.
** Became Open (amateur and professional) in 1968.
† 1925 was the first year in which entries were accepted from all countries.

Today's Stars

Venus Williams, b. June 17, 1980, Lynwood, California. Williams began the 2003 season ranked Number 2 in the world. She reached the finals of four straight Grand Slams in 2002 and early 2003 (2003 Australian Open, 2002 U.S. Open, 2002 Wimbledon, 2002 French Open). Williams has won four Grand Slam singles championships. Her first Slam title came in 2000, at Wimbledon, where she became the second African-American woman to win the tournament. (Althea Gibson won it in 1957 and 1958.)

Kim Clijsters, b. June 8, 1983, Bilzen, Belgium. Clijsters began the 2003 season with a win at the Adidas International, in Sydney, Australia, her fourth title in five tournaments. She also reached the semi-finals of the Australian Open for the second year in a row. In 2002, Clijsters won the season-ending Women's Tennis Association (WTA) Championships for the first time, defeating Venus and Serena Williams along the way. She was the only player in 2002 to defeat both Williams sisters.

Daniela Hantuchova, b. April 23, 1983, Poprad, Slovakia. Hantuchova surged from the Top 100 in 2001 to Number 5 in the world at the start of 2003. She won her first pro title in 2002, at the Pacific Life Open, in Indian Wells, California. She is a two-time Grand Slam Mixed Doubles champion (2002 Australian Open and 2001 Wimbledon) and reached the quarterfinals of three straight Grand Slam Tournaments (2002 Wimbledon, 2002 U.S. Open, 2003 Australian Open).

> ▷**Random Fact:**
> Venus and Serena Williams are the first duo to reach four consecutive Grand Slam finals and the only sisters in tennis history to have each won a Grand Slam singles title.

Venus Williams finshed 2002 with a 62–9 record and the world' Number 2 ranking.

HEINZ KLUETMEIER/SPORTS ILLUSTRATED

Grand Slam Tournaments: All-Time Female Champions (cont.)

Wimbledon Championships (cont.)		Year	Winner	Year	Winner
Year	**Winner**	1938	Helen Wills Moody	1914	Dorothea Lambert Chambers
1963	Margaret Smith	1937	Dorothy Round		
1962	Karen Hantze Susman	1936	Helen Jacobs	1913	Dorothea Lambert Chambers
1961	Angela Mortimer	1935	Helen Wills Moody		
1960	Maria Bueno	1934	Dorothy Round	1912	Ethel Larcombe
1959	Maria Bueno	1933	Helen Wills Moody	1911	Dorothea Lambert Chambers
1958	Althea Gibson	1932	Helen Wills Moody		
1957	Althea Gibson	1931	Cilly Aussem	1910	Dorothea Lambert Chambers
1956	Shirley Fry	1930	Helen Wills Moody		
1955	Louise Brough	1929	Helen Wills	1909	Dora Boothby
1954	Maureen Connolly	1928	Helen Wills	1908	Charlotte Cooper Sterry
1953	Maureen Connolly	1927	Helen Wills		
1952	Maureen Connolly	1926	Kathleen McKane Godfree	1907	May Sutton
1951	Doris Hart			1906	Dorothea Douglass
1950	Louise Brough	1925	Suzanne Lenglen	1905	May Sutton
1949	Louise Brough	1924	Kathleen McKane	1904	Dorothea Douglass
1948	Louise Brough	1923	Suzanne Lenglen	1903	Dorothea Douglass
1947	Margaret Osborne	1922	Suzanne Lenglen	1902	Muriel Robb
1946	Pauline Betz	1921	Suzanne Lenglen	1901	Charlotte Cooper Sterry
1940-45	No tournament	1920	Suzanne Lenglen		
1939	Alice Marble	1919	Suzanne Lenglen	1900	Blanche Bingley Hillyard
		1915-18	No tournament		

Wimbledon Championships (cont.)

Year	Winner
1899	Blanche Bingley Hillyard
1898	Charlotte Cooper
1897	Blanche Bingley Hillyard
1896	Charlotte Cooper
1895	Charlotte Cooper
1894	Blanche Bingley Hillyard
1893	Charlotte Dod
1892	Charlotte Dod
1891	Charlotte Dod
1890	Lena Rice
1889	Blanche Bingley Hillyard
1888	Charlotte Dod
1887	Charlotte Dod
1886	Blanche Bingley
1885	Maud Watson
1884	Maud Watson

United States Championships

Year	Winner
2002	Serena Williams
2001	Venus Williams
2000	Venus Williams
1999	Serena Williams
1998	Lindsay Davenport
1997	Martina Hingis

Year	Winner
1996	Steffi Graf
1995	Steffi Graf
1994	Arantxa Sánchez-Vicario
1993	Steffi Graf
1992	Monica Seles
1991	Monica Seles
1990	Gabriela Sabatini
1989	Steffi Graf
1988	Steffi Graf
1987	Martina Navratilova
1986	Martina Navratilova
1985	Hana Mandlikova
1984	Martina Navratilova
1983	Martina Navratilova
1982	Chris Evert Lloyd
1981	Tracy Austin
1980	Chris Evert Lloyd
1979	Tracy Austin
1978	Chris Evert
1977	Chris Evert
1976	Chris Evert
1975	Chris Evert
1974	Billie Jean King
1973	Margaret Smith Court
1972	Billie Jean King
1971	Billie Jean King
1970	Margaret Smith Court
1969	Margaret Smith Court
* 1968	Virginia Wade
1967	Billie Jean King
1966	Maria Bueno
1965	Margaret Smith
1964	Maria Bueno

Year	Winner
1963	Maria Bueno
1962	Margaret Smith
1961	Darlene Hard
1960	Darlene Hard
1959	Maria Bueno
1958	Althea Gibson
1957	Althea Gibson
1956	Shirley Fry
1955	Doris Hart
1954	Doris Hart
1953	Maureen Connolly
1952	Maureen Connolly
1951	Maureen Connolly
1950	Margaret Osborne duPont
1949	Margaret Osborne duPont
1948	Margaret Osborne duPont
1947	Louise Brough
1946	Pauline Betz
1945	Sarah Palfrey Cooke
1944	Pauline Betz
1943	Pauline Betz
1942	Pauline Betz
1941	Sarah Palfrey Cooke
1940	Alice Marble
1939	Alice Marble
1938	Alice Marble
1937	Anita Lizane
1936	Alice Marble
1935	Helen Jacobs
1934	Helen Jacobs
1933	Helen Jacobs

*Became Open (amateur and professional) in 1968.

2002-03 WOMEN'S TIMELINE

January 26, 2002: Jennifer Capriati of the U.S. wins the Australian Open over Martina Hingis of Switzerland (4–6, 7–6 (9–7), 6–2).

June 8, 2002: Serena Williams of the U.S. wins her first French Open over her sister Venus (7–5, 6–3). It is the first time in French Open history that two sisters meet in a singles final.

July 6, 2002: Serena Williams defeats Venus in the final at Wimbledon, 7–6 (7–4), 6–3. It is the first all-sisters singles final at Wimbledon since 1884.

July 8, 2002: Serena Williams becomes the 11th female player in history to hold the Number 1 spot in the WTA rankings.

August 26, 2002: Corina Morariu of the U.S. returns to the WTA tour after battling leukemia (cancer of the blood) for more than a year. She loses to Serena Williams in the first round of the U.S. Open.

September 7, 2002: Serena Williams wins her second U.S. Open by defeating her sister Venus. It is also her third consecutive Grand Slam title of 2002.

November 11, 2002: Kim Clijsters of Belgium wins the season-ending WTA championships, defeating Serena Williams in the final. Clijsters snaps Williams' 18-match win streak.

January 25, 2003: Serena Williams defeats her sister Venus, 7-6 (7-4), 3-6, 6-4, to win the Australian Open, her fourth straight Grand Slam victory.

February 22, 2003: At the Dubai Open, Martina Navratilova of the U.S. wins her 168th doubles title, the most won by any player, male or female.

Did You Know?

In 1990, Jennifer Capriati became the youngest player in history to reach a pro final (13 years and 11 months).

Grand Slam Tournaments: All-Time Female Champions (cont.)

United States Championships (cont.)		Year	Winner	Year	Winner
		1919	Hazel Hotchkiss Wightman	1903	Elisabeth Moore
Year	**Winner**	1918	Molla Bjurstedt	**1902	Marion Jones
1932	Helen Jacobs	1917	Molla Bjurstedt	1901	Elisabeth Moore
1931	Helen Wills Moody	1916	Molla Bjurstedt	1900	Myrtle McAteer
1930	Betty Nuthall	1915	Molla Bjurstedt	1899	Marion Jones
1929	Helen Wills	1914	Mary K. Browne	1898	Juliette Atkinson
1928	Helen Wills	1913	Mary K. Browne	1897	Juliette Atkinson
1927	Helen Wills	1912	Mary K. Browne	1896	Elisabeth Moore
1926	Molla Bjurstedt Mallory	1911	Hazel Hotchkiss	1895	Juliette Atkinson
1925	Helen Wills	1910	Hazel Hotchkiss	1894	Helen Hellwig
1924	Helen Wills	1909	Hazel Hotchkiss	1893	Aline Terry
1923	Helen Wills	1908	Maud Barger–Wallach	1892	Mabel Cahill
1922	Molla Bjurstedt Mallory	1907	Evelyn Sears	1891	Mabel Cahill
1921	Molla Bjurstedt Mallory	1906	Helen Homans	1890	Ellen C. Roosevelt
1920	Molla Bjurstedt Mallory	1905	Elisabeth Moore	1889	Bertha L. Townsend
		1904	May Sutton	1888	Bertha L. Townsend
				1887	Ellen Hansell

**Five-set final abolished.

Legends

Martina Navratilova, b. October 18, 1956, Prague, Czech Republic. Navratilova is one of the greatest players in the history of the sport. She holds more singles titles than any man or woman (167). She is fourth all-time on the women's list for most Grand Slam singles titles (18). In July 2003, she won the mixed doubles event at Wimbledon. Navratilova is now tied with Billy Jean King for the most Wimbledon titles (20).

Billie Jean King, b. November 22, 1943, Long Beach, California. King has been a pioneer in women's sports. She owns 39 total Grand Slam titles, third on the all-time list. She won 20 Wimbledon titles in singles, doubles, and mixed doubles. King founded the Women's Tennis Association (1973) and the Women's Sports Foundation (1974) to increase opportunities for women in sports. On September 20, 1973, she won a "Battle of the Sexes" tennis match against Bobby Riggs before a televised audience of 90-million viewers.

Martina Navratilova holds 18 Grand Slam singles titles, fourth on the all-time list.

GERRY PENNY/AFP

▷**Random Fact:**
Martina Navratilova is the oldest Grand Slam champion. She paired with Leander Paes of India to win the mixed doubles title at the 2003 Australian Open. She was 46 years and three months old. Navratilova and Paes defeated Todd Woodbridge and Eleni Daniilidou, 6–4, 7–5, in the final.

Steffi Graf, b. June 14, 1969, Bruhl, Germany. Graf was one of the most dominant players in the history of women's tennis. She is one of only five players (male or female) to complete the Grand Slam and the first player (male or female) to complete the "Golden Slam," winning the four Grand Slams and an Olympic gold medal in the same season (1988). She is second all-time in Grand Slam singles titles (22) and holds the record for most weeks at Number 1 (377). She retired on August 13, 1999.

HEINZ KLUETMEIER/SPORTS ILLUSTRATED

Pete Sampras won the 2002 U.S. Open, his record 14th Grand Slam victory.

All-time Grand Slam Singles Champions

MEN

Player	Aus.	French	Wim.	U.S.	Total
*Pete Sampras	2	0	7	5	14
Roy Emerson	6	2	2	2	12
Bjorn Borg	0	6	5	0	11
Rod Laver	3	2	4	2	11
Bill Tilden	†	0	3	7	10
Jimmy Connors	1	0	2	5	8
Ivan Lendl	2	3	0	3	8
Fred Perry	1	1	3	3	8
Ken Rosewall	4	2	0	2	8
*Andre Agassi	4	1	1	2	8
Henri Cochet	†	4	2	1	7
Rene Lacoste	†	3	2	2	7
Bill Larned	†	†	0	7	7
John McEnroe	0	0	3	4	7
John Newcombe	2	0	3	2	7
Willie Renshaw	†	†	7	†	7
Dick Sears	†	†	0	7	7

*Active player. †Did not compete.

WOMEN

Player	Aus.	French	Wim.	U.S.	Total
Margaret Smith Court	11	5	3	5	24
Steffi Graf	4	6	7	5	22
Helen Wills Moody	†	4	8	7	19
Chris Evert	2	7	3	6	18
Martina Navratilova	3	2	9	4	18
Billie Jean King	1	1	6	4	12
Maureen Connolly	1	2	3	3	9
*Monica Seles	4	3	0	2	9
Suzanne Lenglen	†	#2	6	0	8
Molla Bjurstedt Mallory	†	†	0	8	8
Maria Bueno	0	0	3	4	7
Evonne Goolagong	4	1	2	0	7
Dorothea D.L. Chambers	†	†	7	0	7
Nancye Wynne Bolton	6	0	0	0	6
Louise Brough	1	0	4	1	6
Margaret Osborne duPont	†	2	1	3	6
Doris Hart	1	2	1	2	6
Blanche Bingley Hillyard	†	†	6	†	6

*Active player. †Did not compete.
#Suzanne Lenglen also won four singles titles at the French Championships before 1925, when competition was first opened to entries from all nations.

Trivia Challenge

Name the only two male players who have won the Grand Slam (all four Grand Slam singles titles in one season).

Don Budge (1938) and Rod Laver (1962, 1969).

Visit *www.sikids.com* for the latest sports stats and info.
Site code: slamdunk
AOL keyword: sikids

WIMMING

World records didn't stand a chance in 2002 and early 2003, especially when Ian Thorpe, Natalie Coughlin, and Michael Phelps dove into the pool. At the 2002 Commonwealth Games, Thorpe won six gold medals and broke the world record in the 400-meter freestyle. He won six medals, five of them gold, at the 2002 Pan Pacific Championships. At 19, Coughlin became the first woman to swim the 100-meter backstroke in less than one minute. She set that world record at the 2002 U.S. summer nationals, where she won four other events, becoming the first swimmer since 1978 to win five national titles. Seventeen-year-old Michael Phelps continued on his course of record-breaking swims, with two world records in 2002. The first came in the 400-meter individual medley (IM) at the U.S. summer nationals. Then, at the Pan Pacs, he led the U.S. medley relay team to a new world record. In April 2003, Phelps broke his own world record in the 400-meter IM at the U.S. spring nationals. In July, he broke five world records at the world championships, in Barcelona, Spain. Expect to see these three swimmers on the starting blocks when the Summer Olympics begin on August 13, 2004, in Athens, Greece — and watch the records fall.

Natalie Coughlin of the U.S. broke the 100-meter backstroke world record in 2002.

VINCENT LAFORET/GETTY IMAGES

Ian Thorpe of Australia won six gold medals at the 2002 Commonwealth Games.

KAZUHIRO NOGI/AFP PHOTO

2002-03 Major Competitions—Men

U.S. National Championships (Spring)

INDIANAPOLIS, INDIANA, APRIL 1–5, 2003

Event	Swimmer, team	Time
50-meter freestyle	Neil Walker, Circle C Swimming	22.37
100-meter freestyle	Scott Tucker, Novaquatics	49.43
200-meter freestyle	Michael Phelps, N. Baltimore	1:47.37
400-meter freestyle	Klete Keller, Club Wolverine	3:48.15
800-meter freestyle	Larsen Jensen, Mission Viejo	7:54.86
1,500-meter freestyle	Christopher Thompson, Club Wolverine	15:15.00
100-meter backstroke	Lenny Krayzelburg, Trojan SC	54.26
200-meter backstroke	Michael Phelps, N. Baltimore	1:57.04
100-meter breaststroke	Ed Moses, Curl-Burke	1:00.21 (A)
200-meter breaststroke	Ed Moses, Curl-Burke	2:11.22
100-meter butterfly	Michael Phelps, N. Baltimore	51.89
200-meter butterfly	Takashi Yamamoto, Region of Waterloo	1:58.18
200-meter individual medley	Tom Wilkens, Santa Clara SC	2:01.43
400-meter individual medley	Tom Wilkens, Santa Clara SC	4:16.75
400-meter medley relay	UBC Dolphins A	3:45.20
400-meter freestyle relay	Circle C Swimming	3:20.03
800-meter freestyle relay	UBC Dolphins A	7:19.46

Pan Pacific Championships

YOKOHAMA, JAPAN, AUGUST 24–29, 2002

Event	Swimmer, team	Time
50-meter freestyle	Jason Lezak, United States	22.22
100-meter freestyle	Ian Thorpe, Australia	48.84
200-meter freestyle	Ian Thorpe, Australia	1:44.75
400-meter freestyle	Ian Thorpe, Australia	3:45.28
800-meter freestyle	Grant Hackett, Australia	7:44.78
1,500-meter freestyle	Grant Hackett, Australia	14:41.65
100-meter backstroke	Aaron Peirsol, United States	54.22
200-meter backstroke	Aaron Peirsol, United States	1:56.88
100-meter breaststroke	Kosuke Kitajima, Japan	1:00.36
200-meter breaststroke	Brendan Hansen, United States	2:11.80
100-meter butterfly	Ian Crocker, United States	52.45
200-meter butterfly	Tom Malchow, United States	1:55.21
200-meter individual medley	Michael Phelps, United States	1:59.70
400-meter individual medley	Michael Phelps, United States	4:12.48
400-meter medley relay	United States	3:33.48 (WR)
400-meter freestyle relay	Australia	3:15.15
800-meter freestyle relay	Australia	7:09.00

2002-03 Major Competitions—Women

U.S. National Championships (Spring)

INDIANAPOLIS, INDIANA, APRIL 1–5, 2003

Event	Swimmer, team	Time
50-meter freestyle	Jenny Thompson, Badger SC	25.02
100-meter freestyle	Rhiannon Jeffrey, Aqua Crest SC	55.21
200-meter freestyle	Lindsay Benko, Trojan SC	2:00.58
400-meter freestyle	Lindsay Benko, Trojan SC	4:11.34
800-meter freestyle	Diana Munz, Lake Erie Silver Dolphins	8:32.17
1,500-meter freestyle	Flavia Rigamonti, SMU	16:08.30
100-meter backstroke	Haley Cope, California Aquatics	1:01.37
200-meter backstroke	Jennifer Fratesi, Region of Waterloo	2:12.53
100-meter breaststroke	Tara Kirk, Stanford University	1:08.56
200-meter breaststroke	Agnes Kovacs, Arizona State University	2:29.48
100-meter butterfly	Misty Hyman, Desert Fox	59.74
200-meter butterfly	Georgina Lee, SMU	2:09.48
200-meter individual medley	Amanda Beard, Tucson Ford	2:14.41
400-meter individual medley	Kaitlin Sandeno, USC	4:45.48
400-meter medley relay	Circle C Swimming	4:11.57
400-meter freestyle relay	SMU	3:48.86
800-meter freestyle relay	Sun Devil Aquatics	8:13.86

KEY (A)=American record; (WR)=World Record

SWIMMING

⊡▷**Random Fact**: Michael Phelps (15 years old) was the youngest member of the 2000 U.S. Olympic team and the youngest U.S. male Olympian since 1932.

Pan Pacific Championships

YOKOHAMA, JAPAN, AUGUST 24–29, 2002

Event	Swimmer, team	Time
50-meter freestyle	Jenny Thompson, United States	25.13
100-meter freestyle	Natalie Coughlin, United States	53.99
200-meter freestyle	Lindsay Benko, United States	1:58.74
400-meter freestyle	Diana Munz, United States	4:09.50
800-meter freestyle	Diana Munz, United States	8:30.45
1,500-meter freestyle	Diana Munz, United States	16:07.86
100-meter backstroke	Natalie Coughlin, United States	59.72
200-meter backstroke	Margaret Hoelzer, United States	2:11.00
100-meter breaststroke	Amanda Beard, United States	1:08.22
200-meter breaststroke	Amanda Beard, United States	2:26.31
100-meter butterfly	Natalie Coughlin, United States	57.88
200-meter butterfly	Petria Thomas, Australia	2:08.31
200-meter individual medley	Tomoko Hagiwara, Japan	2:13.42
400-meter individual medley	Jennifer Reilly, Australia	4:40.84
400-meter medley relay	Australia	4:00.50
400-meter freestyle relay	Australia	3:39.78
800-meter freestyle relay	United States	7:56.96

2002-03 TIMELINE

April 7, 2002: The United States wins 26 medals, including eight golds, at the FINA Short Course World Championships, in Moscow. Americans set three world records and six American records.

August 4, 2002: Nineteen-year-old Ian Thorpe of Australia wins his sixth gold medal of the Commonwealth Games, in Manchester, England, anchoring the winning 400-meter relay team.

August 13, 2002: Natalie Coughlin of the U.S. becomes the first woman to swim the 100-meter backstroke in less than one minute. She clocks 59.58 seconds at the U.S. nationals, in Fort Lauderdale, Florida. She goes on to win five gold medals and becomes the first swimmer since Tracy Caulkins, in 1978, to win five titles at one nationals meet.

August 15, 2002: Seventeen-year-old Michael Phelps of the U.S. breaks the world record in the 400-meter individual medley at the U.S. nationals. His time of 4:11.09 breaks the mark of 4:11.76, set by Tom Dolan of the U.S. at the 2000 Summer Olympics.

August 29, 2002: U.S. swimmers dominate the Pan Pacific championships, in Yokohama, Japan. The U.S. wins 52 medals, 21 of them gold. Australia wins 11 gold medals.

December 16, 2002: Tom Dolan, king of the 400-meter individual medley (IM), retires at age 27. Dolan held the 400 IM record from September 1994 to August 2002, longer than anyone else. He won gold medals in the event at the 1996 and 2000 Summer Olympic Games and at the 1994 and 1998 world championships.

January 26, 2003: Lindsay Benko of the U.S. becomes the first woman to swim the short-course 400-meter freestyle in less than four minutes. Her world-record time of 3:59:53 betters the six-year-old mark of 4:00:03 held by Claudia Poll of Costa Rica.

April 1, 2003: Diana Munz wins the 800-meter freestyle event at the 2003 spring nationals for her 21st national title, second only to Jenny Thompson of the U.S., who holds 26 national titles.

April 6, 2003: The United States defeats Australia, 196–74, in the "Duel in the Pool" head-to-head event in Indianapolis, Indiana. The Americans win 21 of the 26 events. Michael Phelps of the U.S. wins four events and sets a world record in the 400-meter IM and an American record in the 100-meter butterfly.

Freestyle

Event	Mark	Record Holder	Date	Site
50 meters	21.64	Alexander Popov, Russia (WR)	6-16-00	Moscow, Russia
	21.76	Gary Hall (A)	8-15-00	Indianapolis, Indiana
100 meters	47.84	Pieter van den Hoogenband, Netherlands (WR)	9-19-00	Sydney, Australia
	48.33	Anthony Ervin (A)	7-27-01	Fukuoka, Japan
200 meters	1:44.06	Ian Thorpe, Australia (WR)	7-25-01	Fukuoka, Japan
	1:45.99	Michael Phelps	8-7-03	College Park, Maryland
400 meters	3:40.08	Ian Thorpe, Australia (WR)	7-30-02	Manchester, England
	3:47.00	Klete Keller (A)	9-16-00	Sydney, Australia
800 meters	7:39.16	Ian Thorpe, Australia (WR)	7-24-01	Fukuoka, Japan
	7:52.05	Larsen Jensen (A)	8-25-02	Yokohama, Japan
1,500 meters	14:34.56	Grant Hackett, Australia (WR)	7-30-01	Fukuoka, Japan
	14:56.81	Chris Thompson (A)	9-23-00	Sydney, Australia

Backstroke

Event	Mark	Record Holder	Date	Site
50 meters	24.80	Thomas Rupprath, Germany (WR)	7-27-03	Barcelona, Spain
	24.99	Lenny Krayzelburg (A)	8-28-99	Sydney, Australia
100 meters	53.60	Lenny Krayzelburg (WR, A)	8-24-99	Sydney, Australia
200 meters	1:55.15	Aaron Peirsol (WR, A)	3-20-02	Minneapolis, Minnesota

Lenny Krayzelburg, United States

GREG WOOD/AFP PHOTO

Breaststroke

Event	Mark	Record Holder	Date	Site
50 meters	27.18	Oleg Lisogor, Ukraine (WR)	8-2-02	Berlin, Germany
	27.39	Ed Moses (A)	3-31-01	Austin, Texas
100 meters	59.78	Kosuke Kitajima, Japan (WR)	7-21-03	Barcelona, Spain
	1:00.21	Ed Moses (A)	4-4-03	Indianapolis, Indiana
200 meters	2:09.42	Kosuke Kitajima, Japan (WR)	7-24-03	Barcelona, Spain
	2:10.16	Mike Barrowman (A)	7-29-92	Barcelona, Spain

Butterfly

Event	Time	Record Holder	Date	Site
50 meters	23.43	Matt Welsh, Australia (WR)	7-21-03	Barcelona, Spain
	23.85	Ian Crocker (A)	7-27-01	Fukuoka, Japan
		Bryan Jones (A)	3-29-01	Austin, Texas
100 meters	50.98	Ian Crocker (WR, A)	7-26-03	Barcelona, Spain
200 meters	1:53.93	Michael Phelps (WR, A)	7-22-03	Barcelona, Spain

Individual Medley

Event	Time	Record Holder	Date	Site
200 meters	1:56.04	Michael Phelps (WR, A)	7-25-03	Barcelona, Spain
400 meters	4:09.09	Michael Phelps (WR, A)	7-27-03	Barcelona, Spain

Relays

Event	Time	Record Holder	Date	Site
400-meter medley	3:31.54	United States (WR, A) (Aaron Peirsol, Brendan Hansen, Ian Crocker, Jason Lezak)	7-27-03	Barcelona, Spain
400-meter freestyle	3:13.67	Australia (WR) (Ian Thorpe, Michael Klim, Ashley Callus, Chris Fydler)	9-16-00	Sydney, Australia
	3:13.86	United States (A) (Anthony Ervin, Neil Walker, Jason Lezak, Gary Hall)	9-16-00	Sydney, Australia
800-meter freestyle	7:04.66	Australia (WR) (Ian Thorpe, Michael Klim, Bill Kirby, Grant Hackett)	7-27-01	Fukuoka, Japan
	7:11.81	United States (A) (Nate Dusing, Klete Keller, Michael Phelps, Chad Carvin)	8-26-02	Yokohama, Japan

KEY (A)=American record; (WR)=World Record

SWIMMING

NICK WILSON/GETTY IMAGES

World and American Records—Women

Freestyle

Event	Time	Record Holder	Date	Site
50 meters	24.13	Inge de Bruijn, Netherlands (WR)	9-22-00	Sydney, Australia
	24.63	Dara Torres (A)	9-23-00	Sydney, Australia
100 meters	53.77	Inge de Bruijn, Netherlands (WR)	9-20-00	Sydney, Australia
	53.99	Natalie Coughlin (A)	8-29-02	Yokohama, Japan
200 meters	1:56.64	Franziska van Almsick, Germany (WR)	8-3-02	Berlin, Germany
	1:57.90	Nicole Haislett (A)	7-27-92	Barcelona, Spain
400 meters	4:03.85	Janet Evans (WR, A)	9-22-88	Seoul, Korea
800 meters	8:16.22	Janet Evans (WR, A)	8-20-89	Tokyo, Japan
1,500 meters	15:52.10	Janet Evans (WR, A)	3-26-88	Orlando, Florida

Inge de Bruijn, Netherlands

Backstroke

Event	Time	Record Holder	Date	Site
50 meters	28.25	Sandra Volker, Germany (WR)	6-17-00	Berlin, Germany
	28.49	Natalie Coughlin (A)	7-23-01	Fukuoka, Japan
100 meters	59.58	Natalie Coughlin (WR, A)	8-13-02	Fort Lauderdale, Florida
200 meters	2:06.62	Krisztina Egerszegi, Hungary (WR)	8-25-91	Athens, Greece
	2:08.53	Natalie Coughlin (A)	8-16-02	Fort Lauderdale, Florida

Breaststroke

Event	Time	Record Holder	Date	Site
50 meters	30.57	Zoe Baker, Great Britain (WR)	7-30-02	Manchester, England
	31.34	Megan Quann (A)	8-11-00	Indianapolis, Indiana
100 meters	1:06.37	Leisel Jones, Australia (WR)	7-21-03	Barcelona, Spain
	1:07.05	Megan Quann (A)	9-18-00	Sydney, Australia
200 meters	2:22.99	Hui Qi, China (WR)	4-13-01	Hangzhou, China
	2:22.99	Amanda Beard, United States (WR, A)	7-25-03	Barcelona, Spain

Butterfly

Event	Time	Record Holder	Date	Site
50 meters	25.57	Anna-Karin Kammerling, Sweden (WR)	7-30-02	Berlin, Germany
	26.50	Dara Torres (A)	8-9-00	Indianapolis, Indiana
100 meters	56.61	Inge de Bruijn, Netherlands (WR)	9-17-00	Sydney, Australia
	57.58	Dara Torres (A)	8-9-00	Indianapolis, Indiana
200 meters	2:05.78	Otylia Jedrejczak, Poland (WR)	8-4-02	Berlin, Germany
	2:05.88	Misty Hyman (A)	9-20-00	Sydney, Australia

Individual Medley

Event	Time	Record Holder	Date	Site
200 meters	2:09.72	Yanyan Wu, China (WR)	10-17-97	Shanghai, China
	2:11.91	Summer Sanders (A)	7-30-92	Barcelona, Spain
400 meters	4:33.59	Yana Klochkova, Ukraine (WR)	9-16-00	Sydney, Australia
	4:37.58	Summer Sanders (A)	7-26-92	Barcelona, Spain

Relays

Event	Time	Record Holder	Date	Site
400-meter medley	3:58.30	United States (WR, A) (B.J. Bedford, Megan Quann, Jenny Thompson, Dara Torres)	9-23-00	Sydney, Australia
400-meter freestyle	3:36.00	Germany (WR) (Kathrin Meissner, Petra Dallman, Sandra Volker, Franziska van Almsick)	7-29-02	Berlin, Germany
	3:36.61	United States (A) (Jenny Thompson, Courtney Shealy, Dara Torres, Amy Van Dyken)	9-16-00	Sydney, Australia
800-meter freestyle	7:55.47	East Germany (WR) (Manuela Stellmach, Astrid Strauss, Anke Mohring, Heike Friedrich)	8-18-87	Strasbourg, France
	7:56.53	United States (A) (Natalie Coughlin, Cristina Teuscher, Julie Hardt, Diana Munz)	7-25-01	Fukuoka, Japan

Legends

Mark Spitz, b. February 10, 1950, Modesto, California. Spitz won a record seven gold medals (100-meter free, 200-meter free, 100-meter butterfly, 200-meter butterfly, 400-meter free relay, 800-meter free relay, 400-meter medley relay) at the 1972 Summer Olympics, in Munich, Germany. He set a world record in each event. Spitz also won two gold medals, one silver medal, and one bronze medal at the 1968 Summer Games.

Mark Spitz won a total of 11 Olympic medals (nine gold) in two Olympics (1968, 1972).

JOHN G. ZIMMERMAN

Tracy Caulkins, b. January 11, 1963, Winona, Minnesota. Caulkins is the only swimmer, male or female, to hold American records in every stroke. From 1978 to 1984, she won 48 national titles, more than any other swimmer. Caulkins won three gold medals (200-meter individual medley, 400-meter IM, and 400-meter medley relay) at the 1984 Summer Olympics, in Los Angeles, California..

Janet Evans, b. August 28, 1971, Placentia, California. Evans is the greatest female distance swimmer of all time. She won three gold medals at the 1988 Summer Olympics in the 400-meter freestyle, the 800-meter freestyle, and the 400-meter individual medley. She won a gold medal in the 800-meter free at the 1992 Summer Games, and competed at the 1996 Summer Olympics. Evans set world records in the 400-meter free (1988), the 800-meter free (1989), and the 1,500-meter free (1988).

World Championship Results—Men

50-meter freestyle

1973-82	Event not held	
1986	Tom Jager, United States	22.49
1991	Tom Jager, United States	22.16
1994	Alexander Popov, Russia	22.17
1998	Bill Pilczuk, United States	22.29
2001	Anthony Ervin, United States	22.09

100-meter freestyle

1973	Jim Montgomery, United States	51.70
1975	Andy Coan, United States	51.25
1978	David McCagg, United States	50.24
1982	Jorg Woithe, East Germany	50.18
1986	Matt Biondi, United States	48.94
1991	Matt Biondi, United States	49.18
1994	Alexander Popov, Russia	49.12
1998	Alexander Popov, Russia	48.93
2001	Anthony Ervin, United States	48.33

200-meter freestyle

1973	Jim Montgomery, United States	1:53.02
1975	Tim Shaw, United States	1:51.04
1978	Billy Forrester, United States	1:51.02
1982	Michael Gross, West Germany	1:49.84
1986	Michael Gross, West Germany	1:47.92
1991	Giorgio Lamberti, Italy	1:47.27
1994	Antti Kasvio, Finland	1:47.32
1998	Michael Klim, Australia	1:47.41
2001	Ian Thorpe, Australia	1:44.06

400-meter freestyle

1973	Rick DeMont, United States	3:58.18
1975	Tim Shaw, United States	3:54.88
1978	Vladimir Salnikov, USSR	3:51.94
1982	Vladimir Salnikov, USSR	3:51.30
1986	Rainer Henkel, West Germany	3:50.05
1991	Joerg Hoffman, Germany	3:48.04
1994	Kieran Perkins, Australia	3:43.80
1998	Ian Thorpe, Australia	3:46.29
2001	Ian Thorpe, Australia	3:40.17

1,500-meter freestyle

1973	Stephen Holland, Australia	15:31.85
1975	Tim Shaw, United States	15:28.92
1978	Vladimir Salnikov, USSR	15:03.99
1982	Vladimir Salnikov, USSR	15:01.77
1986	Rainer Henkel, West Germany	15:05.31
1991	Joerg Hoffman, Germany	14:50.36
1994	Kieran Perkins, Australia	14:50.52
1998	Grant Hackett, Australia	14:51.70
2001	Grant Hackett, Australia	14:34.56

World Championship Results—Men (cont.)

50-meter backstroke

1973-98 Event not held
2001   Randall Ball, United States   25.34

100-meter backstroke

1973	Roland Matthes, East Germany	57.47
1975	Roland Matthes, East Germany	58.15
1978	Bob Jackson, United States	56.36
1982	Dirk Richter, East Germany	55.95
1986	Igor Polianski, USSR	55.58
1991	Jeff Rouse, United States	55.23
1994	Martin Zubero, Spain	55.17
1998	Lenny Krayzelburg, United States	55.00
2001	Matt Welsh, Australia	54.31

200-meter backstroke

1973	Roland Matthes, East Germany	2:01.87
1975	Zoltan Varraszto, Hungary	2:05.05
1978	Jesse Vassallo, United States	2:02.16
1982	Rick Carey, United States	2:00.82
1986	Igor Polianski, USSR	1:58.78
1991	Martin Zubero, Spain	1:59.52
1994	Vladimir Selkov, Russia	1:57.42
1998	Lenny Krayzelburg, United States	1:58.84
2001	Aaron Peirsol, United States	1:57.13

50-meter breaststroke

1973-98 Event not held
2001   Oleg Lisogor, Ukraine   27.52

100-meter breaststroke

1973	John Hencken, United States	1:04.02
1975	David Wilkie, Great Britain	1:04.26
1978	Walter Kusch, West Germany	1:03.56
1982	Steve Lundquist, United States	1:02.75
1986	Victor Davis, Canada	1:02.71
1991	Norbert Rozsa, Hungary	1:01.45
1994	Norbert Rozsa, Hungary	1:01.24
1998	Frederik Deburghgraeve, Belgium	1:01.34
2001	Roman Sloudnov, Russia	1:00.16

200-meter breaststroke

1973	David Wilkie, Great Britain	2:19.28
1975	David Wilkie, Great Britain	2:18.23
1978	Nick Nevid, United States	2:18.37
1982	Victor Davis, Canada	2:14.77
1986	Jozsef Szabo, Hungary	2:14.27
1991	Mike Barrowman, United States	2:11.23
1994	Norbert Rozsa, Hungary	2:12.81
1998	Kurt Grote, United States	2:13.40
2001	Brendan Hansen, United States	2:10.69

50-meter butterfly

1973-98 Event not held
2001   Geoff Huegill, Australia   23.50

100-meter butterfly

1973	Bruce Robertson, Canada	55.69
1975	Greg Jagenburg, United States	55.63
1978	Joe Bottom, United States	54.30
1982	Matt Gribble, United States	53.88
1986	Pablo Morales, United States	53.54
1991	Anthony Nesty, Suriname	53.29
1994	Rafal Szukala, Poland	53.51
1998	Michael Klim, Australia	52.25
2001	Lars Frolander, Sweden	52.10

200-meter butterfly

1973	Robin Backhaus, United States	2:03.32
1975	Bill Forrester, United States	2:01.95
1978	Mike Bruner, United States	1:59.38
1982	Michael Gross, West Germany	1:58.85
1986	Michael Gross, West Germany	1:56.53
1991	Melvin Stewart, United States	1:55.69
1994	Denis Pankratov, Russia	1:56.54
1998	Denys Sylantyev, Ukraine	1:56.61
2001	Michael Phelps, United States	1:54.58

200-meter individual medley

1973	Gunnar Larsson, Sweden	2:08.36
1975	Andras Hargitay, Hungary	2:07.72
1978	Graham Smith, Canada	2:03.65
1982	Aleksandr Sidorenko, USSR	2:03.30
1986	Tamás Darnyi, Hungary	2:01.57
1991	Tamás Darnyi, Hungary	1:59.36
1994	Jani Sievin, Finland	1:58.16
1998	Marcel Wouda, Netherlands	2:01.18
2001	Massimiliano Rosolino, Italy	1:59.71

400-meter individual medley

1973	Andras Hargitay, Hungary	4:31.11
1975	Andras Hargitay, Hungary	4:32.57
1978	Jesse Vassallo, United States	4:20.05
1982	Ricardo Prado, Brazil	4:19.78
1986	Tamás Darnyi, Hungary	4:18.98
1991	Tamás Darnyi, Hungary	4:12.36
1994	Tom Dolan, United States	4:12.30
1998	Tom Dolan, United States	4:14.95
2001	Alessio Boggiatto, Italy	4:13.15

400-meter medley relay

1973	United States (Mike Stamm, John Hencken, Joe Bottom, Jim Montgomery)	3:49.49
1975	United States (John Murphy, Rick Colella, Greg Jagenburg, Andy Coan)	3:49.00
1978	United States (Robert Jackson, Nick Nevid, Joe Bottom, David McCagg)	3:44.63
1982	United States (Rick Carey, Steve Lundquist, Matt Gribble, Rowdy Gaines)	3:40.84
1986	United States (Dan Veatch, David Lundberg, Pablo Morales, Matt Biondi)	3:41.25

Did You Know?

The water temperature in an Olympic pool must be between 77 and 82 degrees Fahrenheit.

400-meter medley relay (cont.)

1991	United States (Jeff Rouse, Eric Wunderlich, Mark Henderson, Matt Biondi)	3:39.66
1994	United States (Jeff Rouse, Eric Wunderlich, Mark Henderson, Gary Hall)	3:37.74
1998	Australia (Matt Welsh, Phil Rogers, Michael Klim, Chris Fydler)	3:37.98
2001	Australia (Matt Welsh, Ian Thorpe, Geoff Huegill, Regan Harrison)	3:35.35

400-meter freestyle relay

1973	United States (Mel Nash, Joe Bottom, Jim Montgomery, John Murphy)	3:27.18
1975	United States (Bruce Furniss, Jim Montgomery, Andy Coan, John Murphy)	3:24.85
1978	United States (Jack Babashoff, Rowdy Gaines, Jim Montgomery, David McCagg)	3:19.74
1982	United States (Chris Cavanaugh, Robin Leamy, David McCagg, Rowdy Gaines)	3:19.26
1986	United States (Tom Jager, Mike Heath, Paul Wallace, Matt Biondi)	3:19.59
1991	United States (Tom Jager, Brent Lang, Doug Gjertsen, Matt Biondi)	3:17.15
1994	United States (Jon Olsen, Josh Davis, Ugur Taner, Gary Hall)	3:16.90
1998	United States (Scott Tucker, Jon Olsen, Neil Walker, Gary Hall)	3:16.69
2001	Australia (Michael Klim, Ian Thorpe, Todd Pearson, Ashley Callus)	3:14.10

800-meter freestyle relay

1973	United States (Kurt Krumpholz, Robin Backhaus, Rick Klatt, Jim Montgomery)	7:33.22
1975	West Germany (Klaus Steinbach, Werner Lampe, Hans Joachim Geisler, Peter Nocke)	7:39.44
1978	United States (Bruce Furniss, Billy Forrester, Bobby Hackett, Rowdy Gaines)	7:20.82
1982	United States (Rich Saeger, Jeff Float, Kyle Miller, Rowdy Gaines)	7:21.09
1986	East Germany (Lars Hinneburg, Thomas Flemming, Dirk Richter, Sven Lodziewski)	7:15.91
1991	Germany (Peter Sitt, Steffan, Zesner, Stefan Pfeiffer, Michael Gross)	7:13.50
1994	Sweden (Christer Waller, Tommy Werner, Lars Frolander, Anders Holmertz)	7:17.74
1998	Australia (Daniel Kowalski, Grant Hackett, Ian Thorpe, Michael Klim)	7:12.48
2001	Australia (Michael Klim, Ian Thorpe, William Kirby, Grant Hackett)	7:04.66

Trivia Challenge

What U.S. swimmer starred in 12 Tarzan movies from 1932 to 1948?

Johnny Weissmuller, who became the first man to swim the 100 meters in less than one minute, just before the 1924 Summer Olympics, in Paris, France. He held 52 U.S. titles and 28 world records.

Today's Stars

Michael Phelps, b. June 30, 1985, Baltimore, Maryland. Phelps breaks records practically every time he enters the pool. He broke five world records at the 2003 world championships, in Barcelona, Spain. He broke his own world record in the 400-meter individual medley at the 2003 U.S. spring nationals. He also broke the world record in the 200-meter individual medley in June. At the 2002 Pan Pacific Championships, Phelps led the U.S. 400-medley relay team to a gold medal and a world record. He also won the 200-meter and 400-meter individual medley races. Phelps won four events at the 2002 summer nationals, including the 400 IM, which he finished in world-record time.

At age 17, Michael Phelps held three world records.

ERIKO SUGITA/REUTERS

Ian Thorpe, b. October 13, 1982, Sydney, Australia. Thorpe made a name for himself at the 2000 Summer Olympics, held in his home country of Australia. He won three gold medals and two silver medals. In 2002, Thorpe added more medals to his already growing collection. At the 2002 Commonwealth Games, he won six gold medals and one silver. One month later, he won five gold medals and one silver at the Pan Pacific Championships. Thorpe holds world records in the following events: 200-meter free, 400-meter free, 800-meter free, 400-meter relay, and 800-meter relay.

Natalie Coughlin, b. August 23, 1982, Concord, California. At the 2002 U.S. summer nationals, Coughlin became the first female to swim the 100-meter backstroke in less than one minute. It was one of five events she won. She won six medals at the 2002 Pan Pacs, including gold in the 100-meter freestyle, setting an American record. Coughlin won the Honda Award as the best swimmer in college, for the second year in a row.

World Championship Results—Women

50-meter freestyle

1973-82 Event not held
1986   Tamara Costache, Romania   25.28
1991   Zhuang Yong, China   25.47
1994   Le Jingyi, China   24.51
1998   Amy Van Dyken, United States   25.15
2001   Inge de Bruijn, Netherlands   24.47

100-meter freestyle

1973   Kornelia Ender, East Germany   57.54
1975   Kornelia Ender, East Germany   56.50
1978   Barbara Krause, East Germany   55.68
1982   Birgit Meineke, East Germany   55.79
1986   Kristin Otto, East Germany   55.05
1991   Nicole Haislett, United States   55.17
1994   Le Jingyi, China   54.01
1998   Jenny Thompson, United States   54.95
2001   Inge de Bruijn, Netherlands   54.18

200-meter freestyle

1973   Keena Rothhammer, United States   2:04.99
1975   Shirley Babashoff, United States   2:02.50
1978   Cynthia Woodhead, United States   1:58.53
1982   Annemarie Verstappen, Netherlands   1:59.53
1986   Heike Friedrich, East Germany   1:58.26
1991   Hayley Lewis, Australia   2:00.48
1994   Franziska Van Almsick, Germany   1:56.78
1998   Claudia Poll, Costa Rica   1:58.90
2001   Giaan Rooney, Australia   1:58.57

400-meter freestyle

1973   Heather Greenwood, United States   4:20.28
1975   Shirley Babashoff, United States   4:16.87
1978   Tracey Wickham, Australia   4:06.28
1982   Carmela Schmidt, East Germany   4:08.98
1986   Heike Friedrich, East Germany   4:07.45
1991   Janet Evans, United States   4:08.63
1994   Yang Aihua, China   4:09.64
1998   Chen Yan, China   4:06.72
2001   Yana Klochkova, Ukraine   4:07.30

800-meter freestyle

1973   Novella Calligaris, Italy   8:52.97
1975   Jenny Turrall, Australia   8:44.75
1978   Tracey Wickham, Australia   8:24.94
1982   Kim Linehan, United States   8:27.48
1986   Astrid Strauss, East Germany   8:28.24
1991   Janet Evans, United States   8:24.05
1994   Janet Evans, United States   8:29.85
1998   Brooke Bennett, United States   8:28.71
2001   Hannah Stockbauer, Germany   8:24.66

1,500-meter freestyle

1973-98 Event not held
2001   Hannah Stockbauer, Germany   16:01.02

50-meter backstroke

1973-98 Event not held
2001   Haley Cope, United States   28.51

100-meter backstroke

1973   Ulrike Richter, East Germany   1:05.42
1975   Ulrike Richter, East Germany   1:03.30
1978   Linda Jezek, United States   1:02.55
1982   Kristin Otto, East Germany   1:01.30
1986   Betsy Mitchell, United States   1:01.74
1991   Krisztina Egerszegi, Hungary   1:01.78
1994   He Cihong, China   1:00.57
1998   Lea Maurer, United States   1:01.16
2001   Natalie Coughlin, United States   1:00.37

200-meter backstroke

1973   Melissa Belote, United States   2:20.52
1975   Birgit Treiber, East Germany   2:15.46
1978   Linda Jezek, United States   2:11.93
1982   Cornelia Sirch, East Germany   2:09.91
1986   Cornelia Sirch, East Germany   2:11.37
1991   Krisztina Egerszegi, Hungary   2:09.15
1994   He Cihong, China   2:07.40
1998   Roxanna Maracineanu, France   2:11.26
2001   Diana Mocanu, Romania   2:09.94

50-meter breaststroke

1973-98 Event not held
2001   Xuejuan Luo, China   30.84

100-meter breaststroke

1973   Renate Vogel, East Germany   1:13.74
1975   Hannalore Anke, East Germany   1:12.72
1978   Julia Bogdanova, USSR   1:10.31
1982   Ute Geweniger, East Germany   1:09.14
1986   Sylvia Gerasch, East Germany   1:08.11
1991   Linley Frame, Australia   1:08.81
1994   Samantha Riley, Australia   1:07.96
1998   Kristy Kowal, United States   1:08.42
2001   Xuejuan Luo, China   1:07.18

200-meter breaststroke

1973   Renate Vogel, East Germany   2:40.01
1975   Hannalore Anke, East Germany   2:37.25
1978   Lina Kachushite, USSR   2:31.42
1982   Svetlana Varganova, USSR   2:28.82
1986   Silke Hoerner, East Germany   2:27.40
1991   Elena Volkova, USSR   2:29.53
1994   Samantha Riley, Australia   2:26.87
1998   Agnes Kovacs, Hungary   2:25.45
2001   Agnes Kovacs, Hungary   2:24.90

50-meter butterfly

1973-98 Event not held
2001   Inge de Bruijn, Netherlands   25.90

100-meter butterfly

1973	Kornelia Ender, East Germany	1:02.53
1975	Kornelia Ender, East Germany	1:01.24
1978	Joan Pennington, United States	1:00.20
1982	Mary T. Meagher, United States	59.41
1986	Kornelia Gressler, East Germany	59.51
1991	Qian Hong, China	59.68
1994	Liu Limin, China	58.98
1998	Jenny Thompson, United States	58.46
2001	Petria Thomas, Australia	58.27

200-meter butterfly

1973	Rosemarie Kother, East Germany	2:13.76
1975	Rosemarie Kother, East Germany	2:13.82
1978	Tracy Caulkins, United States	2:09.87
1982	Ines Geissler, East Germany	2:08.66
1986	Mary T. Meagher, United States	2:08.41
1991	Summer Sanders, United States	2:09.24
1994	Liu Limin, China	2:07.25
1998	Susie O'Neill, Australia	2:07.93
2001	Petria Thomas, Australia	2:06.73

200-meter individual medley

1973	Andrea Huebner, East Germany	2:20.51
1975	Kathy Heddy, United States	2:19.80
1978	Tracy Caulkins, United States	2:14.07
1982	Petra Schneider, East Germany	2:11.79
1986	Kristin Otto, East Germany	2:15.56
1991	Li Lin, China	2:13.40
1994	Lu Bin, China	2:12.34
1998	Wu Yanyan, China	2:10.88
2001	Martha Bowen, United States	2:11.93

400-meter individual medley

1973	Gudrun Wegner, East Germany	4:57.71
1975	Ulrike Tauber, East Germany	4:52.76
1978	Tracy Caulkins, United States	4:40.83
1982	Petra Schneider, East Germany	4:36.10
1986	Kathleen Nord, East Germany	4:43.75
1991	Lin Li, China	4:41.45
1994	Dai Guohong, China	4:39.14
1998	Chen Yan, China	4:36.66
2001	Yana Klochkova, Ukraine	4:36.98

400-meter medley relay

1973	East Germany (Ulrike Richter, Renate Vogel, Rosemarie Kother, Kornelia Ender)	4:16.84
1975	East Germany (Ulrike Richter, Hannelore Anke, Rosemarie Kother, Kornelia Ender)	4:14.74
1978	United States (Linda Jezek, Tracy Caulkins, Joan Pennington, Cynthia Woodhead)	4:08.21
1982	East Germany (Kristin Otto, Ute Geweniger, Ines Geissler, Birgit Meineke)	4:05.80
1986	East Germany (Kathrin Zimmermann, Sylvia Gerasch, Kornelia Gressler, Kristin Otto)	4:04.82
1991	United States (Janie Wagstaff, Tracey McFarlane, Crissy Ahmann-Leighton, Nicole Haislett)	4:06.51

1994	China (He Cihong, Dai Guohong, Liu Limin, Lu Bin)	4:01.67
1998	United States (Kristy Kowal, Lea Maurer, Jenny Thompson, Amy Van Dyken)	4:01.93
2001	Australia (Dyana Calub, Sarah Ryan, Petria Thomas, Leisel Jones)	4:01.50

400-meter freestyle relay

1973	East Germany (Kornelia Ender, Andrea Eife, Andrea Huebner, Sylvia Eichner)	3:52.45
1975	East Germany (Kornelia Ender, Barbara Krause, Claudia Hempel, Ute Bruckner)	3:49.37
1978	United States (Tracy Caulkins, Stephanie Elkins, Jill Sterkel, Cynthia Woodhead)	3:43.43
1982	East Germany (Birgit Meineke, Susanne Link, Kristin Otto, Caren Metschuk)	3:43.97
1986	East Germany (Kristin Otto, Manuela Stellmach, Sabine Schulze, Heike Friedrich)	3:40.57
1991	United States (Nicole Haislett, Julie Cooper, Whitney Hedgepeth, Jenny Thompson)	3:43.26
1994	China (Le Jingyi, Ying Shan, Le Ying, Lu Bin)	3:37.91
1998	United States (Catherine Fox, Lindsey Farella, Melanie Valerio, B.J. Bedford)	3:42.11
2001	Germany (Petra Dallman, Antje Buschschulter, Katrin Meissner, Sandra Volker)	3:39.58

800-meter freestyle relay

1973-82	Event not held	
1986	East Germany (Manuela Stellmach, Astrid Strauss, Nadja Bergknecht, Heike Friedrich)	7:59.33
1991	Germany (Kerstin Kielgass, Manuela Stellmach, Dagmar Hase, Stephanie Ortwig)	8:02.56
1994	China (Le Ying, Yang Alhua, Zhou Guabin, Lu Bin)	7:57.96
1998	Germany (Silvia Szalai, Antje Buschschulte, Janina Goetz, Franziska Van Almsick)	8:01.46
2001	Great Britain (Nicola Jackson, Janine Belton, Karen Legg, Karen Pickering)/United States (Natalie Coughlin, Cristina Teuscher, Julie Hardt, Diana Munz)*	7:56.53

Did You Know?

Lynne Cox, a cold-water swimmer, swam the icy waters of Antarctica in December 2002. She swam 1.22 miles in 25 minutes in 32° F water. Cox has also swum the waters of the English Channel, between England and France; the Bering Strait, between Alaska and Russia; and the Strait of Magellan, off Chile.

---

*Due to timing malfunctions and an overturned disqualification of the U.S., duplicate gold medals were awarded to Great Britain and the U.S.

TRACK AND FIELD

Records fell hard — and often — during the 2002-03 track-and-field season. Tim Montgomery of the U.S. became the world's fastest man on September 14, 2002, when he ran the 100-meter sprint in 9.78 seconds in the finals at the Grand Prix in Paris, France. He broke fellow U.S. runner Maurice Greene's record (9.79), which was set in 1999.

While Montgomery was pushing the speed limit, female pole-vaulters were raising the roof. Svetlana Feofanova of Russia set the women's indoor world record at the World Indoor Championships, on March 16, 2003. Her 15' 9" vault broke the 15' 8¼" mark set at the U.S. Indoor Championships three weeks earlier by U.S. vaulter Stacy Dragila.

Middle-distance runner Regina Jacobs of the U.S. became the first woman to run an indoor 1,500-meter race in under four minutes. The 39-year-old's time of 3:59.98 at the adidas Boston Indoor Games broke the world record of 4:00.27, set in 1990.

Heading outdoors, both men's and women's marathon records tumbled. At the London Marathon, on April 14, 2002, Khalid Khannouchi of the U.S. sliced four seconds off his previous world record, finishing in 2:05:38. At the same race a year later, England's Paula Radcliffe smashed the women's world record she had set in 2002 by

Tim Montgomery of the U.S. broke the 100-meter world record in 2002.

JACK GUEZ/AFP PHOTO

more than a minute, finishing her third career marathon in 2:15.25. The gap between the men's and the women's records (9 minutes 47 seconds) became the smallest it has ever been. In the past, women were not allowed to run the marathon. It was believed they were too fragile to cover the distance. The first woman officially timed in a marathon run was Violet Piercy of Great Britain, who ran 3:40.22 on October 3, 1926. It wasn't until 1984 that women were allowed to compete in the marathon at the Olympics.

In 2002, Regina Jacobs of the U.S. ran the fastest-ever women's indoor 1,500 meters.

JESSICA RINALDI/AFP

▱▷**Random Fact:** Legend Jesse Owens is the only track-and-field athlete to set three world records and tie a fourth on one day. At a meet on May 25, 1935, he set the world marks in the 220 yards, 220-yard hurdles, and long jump. He tied the 100-meter mark.

2003 World Indoor Championships

MARCH 14–16, 2003, BIRMINGHAM, ENGLAND

Men's 60 Meters

Athlete	Country	Mark
Justin Gatlin	USA	6.46
Kim Collins	St. Kitts	6.53
Jason Gardener	Great Britain	6.55

Women's 60 Meters

Athlete	Country	Mark
Zhanna Block	Ukraine	7.04
Angela Williams	USA	7.16
Torri Edwards	USA	7.17

Men's 200 Meters

Athlete	Country	Mark
Marlon Devonish	Great Britain	20.62
Joseph Batangdon	Cameroon	20.76
Dominic Demeritte	Bahamas	20.92

Women's 200 Meters

Athlete	Country	Mark
Michelle Collins	USA	22.18
Muriel Hurtis	France	22.54
Anastasiya Kapachinskaya	Russia	22.80

Men's 400 Meters

Athlete	Country	Mark
Tyree Washington	USA	45.34
Daniel Caines	Great Britain	45.43
Paul McKee	Ireland	45.99

Women's 400 Meters

Athlete	Country	Mark
Natalya Nazarova	Russia	50.83
Christine Amertil	Bahamas	51.11
Grit Breuer	Germany	51.13

Men's 800 Meters

Athlete	Country	Mark
David Krummenacker	USA	1:45.69
Wilson Kipketer	Denmark	1:45.87
Wilfred Bungei	Kenya	1:46.54

Women's 800 Meters

Athlete	Country	Mark
Maria Mutola	Mozambique	1:58.94
Stephanie Graf	Austria	1:59.39
Mayte Martínez	Spain	1:59.53

Men's 1,500 Meters

Athlete	Country	Mark
Driss Maazouzi	France	3:42.59
Bernard Lagat	Kenya	3:42.62
Abdelkader Hachlaf	Morocco	3:42.71

Women's 1,500 Meters

Athlete	Country	Mark
Regina Jacobs	USA	4:01.67
Kelly Holmes	Great Britain	4:02.66
Yekaterina Rozenberg	Russia	4:02.80

Men's 3,000 Meters

Athlete	Country	Mark
Haile Gebrselassie	Ethiopia	7:40.97
Alberto García	Spain	7:42.08
Luke Kipkosgei	Kenya	7:42.56

Women's 3,000 Meters

Athlete	Country	Mark
Berhane Adere	Ethiopia	8:40.25
Marta Domínguez	Spain	8:42.17
Meseret Defar	Ethiopia	8:42.58

2003 World Indoor Championships (cont.)

MIKE POWELL/GETTY IMAGES

Men's 60-Meter Hurdles

Athlete	Country	Mark
Allen Johnson	USA	7.47
Anier García	Cuba	7.49
Liu Xiang	China	7.52

Women's 60-Meter Hurdles

Athlete	Country	Mark
Gail Devers	USA	7.81
Glory Alozie	Spain	7.90
Melissa Morrison	USA	7.92

Men's High Jump

Athlete	Country	Mark
Stefan Holm	Sweden	2.35
Yaroslav Rybakov	Russia	2.33
Gennadiy Moroz	Belarus	2.30

Women's High Jump

Athlete	Country	Mark
Kajsa Bergqvist	Sweden	2.01
Yelena Yelesina	Russia	1.99
Anna Chicherova	Russia	1.99

Men's Pole Vault

Athlete	Country	Mark
Tim Lobinger	Germany	5.80
Michael Stolle	Germany	5.75
Rens Blom	Netherlands	5.75

Women's Pole Vault

Athlete	Country	Mark
Svetlana Feofanova	Russia	4.80
Yelena Isinbayeva	Russia	4.60
Monika Pyrek	Poland	4.45

Men's Long Jump

Athlete	Country	Mark
Dwight Phillips	USA	8.29
Yago Lamela	Spain	8.28
Miguel Pate	USA	8.21

Women's Long Jump

Athlete	Country	Mark
Tatyana Kotova	Russia	6.84
Inessa Kravets	Ukraine	6.72
Maurren Higa Maggi	Brazil	6.70

Men's Triple Jump

Athlete	Country	Mark
Christian Olsson	Sweden	17.70
Walter Davis	USA	17.35
Yoelbi Quesada	Cuba	17.27

Women's Triple Jump

Athlete	Country	Mark
Ashia Hansen	Great Britain	15.01
Françoise Mbango Etone	Cameroon	14.88
Kéné Ndoye	Senegal	14.72

John Godina,
United States

Men's Shot Put

Athlete	Country	Mark
Manuel Martínez	Spain	21.24
John Godina	USA	21.23
Yuriy Bilonog	Ukraine	21.13

Women's Shot Put

Athlete	Country	Mark
Irina Korzhanenko	Russia	20.55
Nadezhda Ostapchuk	Belarus	20.31
Astrid Kumbernuss	Germany	19.86

Men's 4x400 Meters

Athlete	Country	Mark
James Davis, Jerome Young, Milton Campbell, Tyree Washington	USA	3:04.09
Leroy Colquhoun, Danny McFarlane, Michael Blackwood, Davian Clarke	Jamaica	3:04.21
Jamie Baulch, Timothy Benjamin, Cori Henry, Daniel Caines	Great Britain and Northern Ireland	3:06.12

Women's 4x400 Meters

Athlete	Country	Mark
Natalya Antyukh, Yuliya Pechonkina, Olesya Zykina, Natalya Nazarova	Russia	3:28.45
Ronetta Smith, Catherine Scott, Sheryl Morgan, Sandie Richards	Jamaica	3:31.23
Monique Hennagan, Meghan Addy, Brenda Taylor, Mary Danner	USA	3:31.69

Men's Heptathlon

Athlete	Country	Points
Tom Pappas	USA	6,361
Lev Lobodin	Russia	6,297
Roman Sebrle	Czech Republic	6,196

Women's Pentathlon

Athlete	Country	Points
Carolina Kluft	Sweden	4,933
Natalya Sazanovich	Belarus	4,715
Marie Collonville	France	4,644

Legends

Jesse Owens, sprinter, b. September 13, 1913, Oakville, Alabama; d. March 31, 1980, Tucson, Arizona. Owens was the first black track-and-field star from the United States and became a hero at the 1936 Summer Olympics, in Berlin, Germany. Adolf Hitler, Germany's Nazi dictator, believed that white people were superior to all other races. But Owens proved to the world just how wrong Hitler was by winning four gold medals (100 meters, 200 meters, long jump, 4x100-meter relay).

Jackie Joyner-Kersee, long jumper and heptathlete, b. March 3, 1962, East St. Louis, Illinois. JJK has been called the world's greatest female athlete — and for good reason. In the 1980's and early 1990's, she dominated the seven-event heptathlon (100-meter hurdles, high jump, shot put, 200 meters, long jump, javelin, and 800 meters). Kersee owns the world record in the heptathlon (7,291 points) and holds the next five highest scores. She competed at the Olympics four times (1984, 1988, 1992, 1996) and won six medals: two gold medals and a silver medal in the heptathlon, and a gold medal and two bronze medals in the long jump.

Carl Lewis, sprinter and long jumper, b. July 1, 1961, Birmingham, Alabama. Lewis may be the most dominant athlete in track-and-field history. The four-time Olympian (1984, 1988, 1992, 1996) won nine gold medals and one silver medal. Only three other athletes in sports have won nine Olympic gold medals, and only one other has won the same event at four Games. (Al Oerter of the U.S. won the discus event in 1956, 1960, 1964, and 1968. Lewis was a four-time winner in the long jump.) In 1984, Lewis won gold in the 100 meters, 200 meters, long jump, and 4x100-meter relay. The only other athlete to win all four events at one Olympics was Lewis's hero, Jesse Owens.

Jesse Owens was the first American to win four gold medals in a single Olympic Games.

AP PHOTO

TRACK AND FIELD

World Cross-Country Championships

MARCH 29–30, 2003, LAUSANNE, SWITZERLAND

Men

Athlete	Country	Mark
Kenenisa Bekele	Ethiopia	35:56
Patrick Ivuti	Kenya	36:09
Gebre-egziabher Gebremariam	Ethiopia	36:17

Women

Athlete	Country	Mark
Werknesh Kidane	Ethiopia	25:53
Deena Drossin	USA	26:02
Merima Denboba	Ethiopia	26:28

2003 USA Indoor Track and Field Championships

FEBRUARY 28–MARCH 2, 2003, BOSTON, MA

Women's 60 meters

Athlete	Team	Mark
Angela Williams	Nike	7.16
Chryste Gaines	Nike	7.18
Torri Edwards	adidas	7.21

Men's 60 meters

Athlete	Team	Mark
Justin Gatlin	Nike	6.45
Terrence Trammell	Mizuno Track	6.48
John Capel	adidas	6.49

Men's 200 meters

Athlete	Team	Mark
John Capel	adidas	20.69
Shawn Crawford	Mizuno Track	20.77
Bobby Williams	Unattached	20.85

Women's 200 meters

Athlete	Team	Mark
Michelle Collins	Nike	22.84
Allyson Felix	Unattached	23.14
Kelli White	Nike	23.21

Men's 400 meters

Athlete	Team	Mark
Tyree Washington	Unattached	46.43
Corey Nelson	Bronco Track Club	46.53
Milton Campbell	Holyfield International	46.55

Women's 400 meters

Athlete	Team	Mark
Monique Hennagan	adidas	52.54
Megan Addy	Nike	53.88
Tiffany Barnes	Delaware State	54.01

Men's 800 meters

Athlete	Team	Mark
David Krummenacker	adidas	1:50.59
Khadevis Robinson	Nike	1:50.69
Bryan Woodward	Nike Farm Team	1:51.60

Women's 800 meters

Athlete	Team	Mark
Nicole Teter	Nike	2:00.09
Sasha Spencer	Nike	2:03.20
Chantee Earl	Nike Farm Team	2:05.13

Men's 1,500 meters

Athlete	Team	Mark
Jason Lunn	Nike	3:42.23
Michael Stember	Nike Farm Team	3:42.73
Charlie Gruber	Unattached	3:43.35

Women's 1,500 meters

Athlete	Team	Mark
Regina Jacobs	Nike	4:15.81
Sarah Schwald	Nike	4:17.23
Jenelle Deatherage	Wisconsin Runner	4:17.56

Men's 3,000 meters

Athlete	Team	Mark
Jonathon Riley	Nike	7:49.79
Bolota Asmerom	Nike	7:51.85
Daniel Wilson	Asics	7:55.08

Women's 3,000 meters

Athlete	Team	Mark
Regina Jacobs	Nike	8:52.57
Shayne Culpepper	adidas	8:56.26
Amy Rudolph	adidas	8:57.44

Men's 60-meter hurdles

Athlete	Team	Mark
Allen Johnson	Nike	7.39
Terrence Trammell	Mizuno Track	7.43
Larry Wade	Nike	7.61

Women's 60-meter hurdles

Athlete	Team	Mark
Gail Devers	Nike	7.85
Melissa Morrison	adidas	7.88
Damu Cherry	adidas	7.90

Men's 5,000-meter Race Walk

Athlete	Team	Mark
Tim Seaman	New York Athletic Club	19:21.56
John Nunn	U.S. Army	19:26.43
Curt Clausen	New York Athletic Club	20:38.34

Women's 3,000-meter Race Walk

Athlete	Team	Mark
Joanne Dow	New England Walkers	13:07.6
Michelle Rohl	Moving Comfort	13:21.1
Sam Cohen	Parkside Athletic Club	13:50.8

Men's High Jump

Athlete	Team	Mark
Charles Austin	Unattached	2.30 meters
Tora Harris	Shore Athletic Club	2.30 meters
Charles Clinger	Nike	2.30 meters

Women's High Jump

Athlete	Team	Mark
Tisha Waller	Nike	1.97 meters
Amy Acuff	Asics	1.94 meters
Ifoma Jones	Unattached	1.91 meters

Men's Pole Vault

Athlete	Team	Mark
Derek Miles	Nike	5.75 meters
Jeremy Scott	Allegheny College	5.70 meters
Timothy Mack	Nike	5.70 meters

Women's Pole Vault

Athlete	Team	Mark
Stacy Dragila	Nike	4.78 meters (WR)
Kellie Suttle	Nike	4.35 meters
Melissa Mueller	Nike	4.30 meters

Men's Long Jump

Athlete	Team	Mark
Miguel Pate	Nike	8.25 meters
Dwight Phillips	Nike	8.21 meters
Savante Stringfellow	Nike	8.03 meters

(WR)=world record

Women's Long Jump

Athlete	Team	Mark
Kiamesha Otey	Virginia	6.33 meters
Adrien Sawyer	Unattached	6.23 meters
Pamela Simpson	U.S. Army	6.21 meters

Men's Triple Jump

Athlete	Team	Mark
Tim Rusan	Nike	17.45 meters
Walter Davis	Nike	17.23 meters
Kenta Bell	Nike	17.06 meters

Women's Triple Jump

Athlete	Team	Mark
Vanitta Kinard	Nike	13.72 meters
Teresa Bundy	Unattached	13.70 meters
Yuliana Perez	Unattached	13.63 meters

Men's Shot Put

Athlete	Team	Mark
Kevin Toth	Nike	21.30 meters
John Godina	adidas	20.86 meters
Adam Nelson	Nike	20.63 meters

Women's Shot Put

Athlete	Team	Mark
Kristin Heaston	Unattached	18.03 meters
Seilala Sua	Nike	17.83 meters
Laura Gerraughty	North Carolina	17.50 meters

Men's Weight Throw

Athlete	Team	Mark
A.G. Kruger	Unattached	22.25 meters
John McEwen	New York Athletic Club	21.86 meters
Thomas Freeman	Unattached	21.59 meters

Women's Weight Throw

Athlete	Team	Mark
Anna Mahon	Nike	22.85 meters
Jamine Moton	Unattached	21.48 meters
Dawn Ellerbe	New York Athletic Club	21.47 meters

▯▷**Random Fact**: U.S. middle-distance runner Marla Runyan became the first legally blind athlete to compete at the Summer Olympics. She finished in eighth place in the 1,500 meters at the 2000 Games.

Trivia Challenge

Who is the only athlete in Olympic history to win both the 200 meters and 400 meters at the same Olympics?

Michael Johnson of the U.S. won both events at the 1996 Summer Games.

2002–2003 Marathons

Chicago Marathon
OCTOBER 12, 2002

Men	Country	Time
Khalid Khannouchi	USA	2:05:56
Daniel Njenga	Japan	2:06:16
Toshinari Takaoka	Japan	2:06:16

Women	Country	Time
Paula Radcliffe	Great Britain	2:17:18
Catherine Ndereba	Kenya	2:19:26
Yoko Shibui	Japan	2:21:22

Paula Radcliffe, Great Britain

New York City Marathon
NOVEMBER 3, 2002

Men	Country	Time
Rodgers Rop	Kenya	2:08:07
Christopher Cheboiboch	Kenya	2:08:17
Laban Kipkemboi	Kenya	2:08:39

Women	Country	Time
Joyce Chepchumba	Kenya	2:25:56
Lyubov Denisova	Russia	2:26:17
Esther Kiplagat	Kenya	2:27:00

Tokyo International Marathon
WOMEN (NOVEMBER 17, 2002)

Women	Country	Time
Banuelia Mrashani	Tanzania	2:24:59
Rie Matsuoka	Japan	2:25:02
Irina Timofeyeva	Russia	2:26:45

Tokyo International Marathon
MEN (FEBRUARY 9, 2003)

Men	Country	Time
Zebedayo Bayo	Tanzania	2:09:07
Shigeru Aburaya	Japan	2:09:30
Noriaki Igarashi	Japan	2:10:11

Paris Marathon
APRIL 6, 2003

Men	Country	Time
Mike Rotich	Kenya	2:06:33
Benoit Zwierzchiewski	France	2:06:36
Wilson Onsare	Kenya	2:06:47

Women	Country	Time
Beatrice Omwanza	Kenya	2:27:44
Rosaria Console	Italy	2:27:48
Banuela Mrashani	Tanzania	2:29:13

London Marathon
APRIL 13, 2003

Men	Country	Time
Gezahegne Abera	Ethiopia	2:07:56
Stefano Baldini	Italy	2:07:56
Joseph Ngolepus	Kenya	2:07:57

Women	Country	Time
Paula Radcliffe	Great Britain	2:15:25 (WR)
Catherine Ndereba	Kenya	2:19:55
Deena Drossin	USA	2:21:16

Boston Marathon
APRIL 21, 2003

Men	Country	Time
Robert Cheruiyot	Kenya	2:10:10
Benjamin Kimutai	Kenya	2:10:34
Martin Lel	Kenya	2:11:11

Women	Country	Time
Svetlana Zakharova	Russia	2:25:20
Lyubov Denisova	Russia	2:26:51
Joyce Chepchumba	Kenya	2:27:20

World Records—Men

Event	Mark	Record Holder	Date	Site
100 meters	9.78	Tim Montgomery, United States	9-14-02	Paris, France
200 meters	19.32	Michael Johnson, United States	8-1-96	Atlanta, Georgia
400 meters	43.18	Michael Johnson, United States	8-26-99	Seville, Spain
800 meters	1:41.11	Wilson Kipketer, Denmark	8-24-97	Cologne, Germany
1,000 meters	2:11.96	Noah Ngeny, Kenya	9-5-99	Rieti, Italy
1,500 meters	3:26.00	Hicham El Guerrouj, Morocco	7-14-98	Rome, Italy
Mile	3:43.13	Hicham El Guerrouj, Morocco	7-7-99	Rome, Italy
2,000 meters	4:44.79	Hicham El Guerrouj, Morocco	9-7-99	Berlin, Germany
3,000 meters	7:20.67	Daniel Komen, Kenya	9-1-96	Rieti, Italy
Steeplechase	7:53.17	Brahim Boulami, Morocco	8-16-02	Zurich, Switzerland
5,000 meters	12:39.36	Haile Gebrselassie, Ethiopia	6-13-98	Helsinki, Finland
10,000 meters	26:22.75	Haile Gebrselassie, Ethiopia	6-1-98	Hengelo, Netherlands

JONATHAN DANIEL/GETTY IMAGES

World Records—Men (cont.)

AP PHOTO

Event	Mark	Record Holder	Date	Site
20,000 meters	56:55.6	Arturo Barrios, Mexico	3-30-91	La Flache, France
Hour	21,101 meters	Arturo Barrios, Mexico	3-30-91	La Flache, France
25,000 meters	1:13:55.8	Toshihiko Seko, Japan	3-22-81	Christchurch, New Zealand
30,000 meters	1:29:18.8	Toshihiko Seko, Japan	3-22-81	Christchurch, New Zealand
Marathon	2:05:38	Khalid Khannouchi, United States	4-14-02	London, England
110-meter hurdles	12.91	Colin Jackson, Great Britain	8-20-93	Stuttgart, Germany
400-meter hurdles	46.78	Kevin Young, United States	8-6-92	Barcelona, Spain
20-kilometer walk	1:17:22	Javier Fernandez, Spain	4-28-02	Turku, Finland
30-kilometer walk	2:01:44.1	Maurizio Damilano, Italy	10-3-92	Cuneo, Italy
50-kilometer walk	3:40:57.9	Thierry Toutain, France	9-29-96	Héricourt, France
4x100-meter relay	37.40*	United States (Mike Marsh, Leroy Burrell, Dennis Mitchell, Carl Lewis)	8-8-92	Barcelona, Spain
		United States (Jon Drummond, Andre Cason, Dennis Mitchell, Leroy Burrell)	8-21-93	Stuttgart, Germany
4x200-meter relay	1:18.68	Santa Monica TC (Mike Marsh, Leroy Burrell, Floyd Heard, Carl Lewis)	4-17-94	Walnut, California
4x400-meter relay	2:54.20	United States (Jerome Young, Antonio Pettigrew, Tyree Washington, Michael Johnson)	7-22-98	New York, New York

Carl Lewis, United States

*Shared record

Today's Stars

STEVE HOLLAND/AP PHOTO

Stacy Dragila is a four-time U.S. outdoor pole-vault champion and a six-time U.S. indoor champion.

Stacy Dragila, pole-vaulter, b. March 25, 1971, Auburn, California. Dragila is the first lady of pole vault. She is the former world outdoor record holder (15' 9¼") and is the first female world champion (1999) and Olympic champion (2000). In 2003, she set the women's indoor world record of 15' 8¼" at the U.S. championships. (The record was broken a little over two weeks later.) Dragila's next goal? To become the first woman to clear 16 feet.

Marion Jones, sprinter, b. October 12, 1975, Los Angeles, California. Simply put, MJ is the fastest woman in the world, and she has the stats to prove it. She finished 2002 undefeated in the 100 meters (16 wins), 200 meters (4), and 400 meters (1). At the 2000 Summer Olympics, she became the first female track-and-field athlete to win five medals at the same Games. Jones is taking 2003 off to have a child. She expects to return to the track in time for the 2004 Summer Olympics.

Hicham El Guerrouj, middle-distance runner, b. September 14, 1974, Berkane, Morocco. This middle-distance master holds the men's world records in the mile (3:43.13) and 1,500 meters (3:26). He ran 11 races in 2002 and won all of them. The only award missing from his trophy case: an Olympic gold medal. At the 1996 Summer Olympics, El Guerrouj tripped and finished in last place in the 1,500 meters. He won the silver medal in the 1,500 at the 2000 Games.

World Records—Men (cont.)

Event	Mark	Record Holder	Date	Site
4x800-meter relay	7:03.89	Great Britain (Peter Elliott, Garry Cook, Steve Cram, Sebastian Coe)	8-30-82	London, England
4x1,500-meter relay	14:38.8	West Germany (Thomas Wessinghage, Harald Hudak, Michael Lederer, Karl Fleschen)	8-17-77	Cologne, Germany
High jump	8 ft ½ in	Javier Sotomayor, Cuba	7-27-93	Salamanca, Spain
Pole vault	20 ft 1¾ in	Sergei Bubka, Ukraine	7-31-94	Sestriere, Italy
Long jump	29 ft 4½ in	Mike Powell, United States	8-30-91	Tokyo, Japan
Triple jump	60 ft ¼ in	Jonathan Edwards, Great Britain	8-7-95	Goteborg, Sweden
Shot put	75 ft 10¼ in	Randy Barnes, United States	5-20-90	Westwood, California
Discus throw	243 ft	Jürgen Schult, East Germany	6-6-86	Neubrandenburg, Germany
Hammer throw	284 ft 7 in	Yuri Syedikh, USSR	8-30-86	Stuttgart, Germany
Javelin throw	323 ft 1 in	Jan Zelezny, Czech Republic	5-25-96	Jena, Germany
Decathlon	9,026 pts	Roman Sebrle, Czech Republic	5-27-01	Gotzis, Austria

Note: The decathlon consists of 10 events: the 100 meters, long jump, shot put, high jump, and 400 meters on the first day; the 110-meter hurdles, discus, pole vault, javelin, and 1,500 meters on the second day.

World Records—Women

Event	Mark	Record Holder	Date	Site
100 meters	10.49	Florence Griffith Joyner, United States	7-16-88	Indianapolis, Indiana
200 meters	21.34	Florence Griffith Joyner, United States	9-29-88	Seoul, Korea
400 meters	47.60	Marita Koch, East Germany	10-6-85	Canberra, Australia
800 meters	1:53.28	Jarmila Kratochvílová, Czechoslovakia	7-26-83	Munich, Germany
1,000 meters	2:28.98	Svetlana Masterkova, Russia	8-23-96	Brussels, Belgium
1,500 meters	3:50.46	Qu Yunxia, China	9-11-93	Beijing, China
Mile	4:12.56	Svetlana Masterkova, Russia	8-14-96	Zurich, Switzerland
2,000 meters	5:25.36	Sonia O'Sullivan, Ireland	7-8-94	Edinburgh, Scotland
3,000 meters	8:06.11	Wang Junxia, China	9-13-93	Beijing, China
Steeplechase	9:16.51	Alesya Turova, Belarus	7-27-02	Gdańsk, Poland
5,000 meters	14:28.09	Jiang Bo, China	10-23-97	Shanghai, China
10,000 meters	29:31.78	Wang Junxia, China	9-8-93	Beijing, China
Hour	18,340 meters	Tegla Loroupe, Kenya	8-8-98	Borgholzhausen, Germany
20,000 meters	1:05:26.6	Tegla Loroupe, Kenya	9-3-00	Borgholzhausen, Germany
25,000 meters	1:27:05.9	Tegla Loroupe, Kenya	9-21-02	Mengerskirchen, Germany
30,000 meters	1:47:05.6	Karolina Szabó, Hungary	9-21-02	Mengerskirchen, Germany
Marathon	2:15:25	Paula Radclifffe, Great Britain	4-13-03	London, England
100-meter hurdles	12.21	Yordanka Donkova, Bulgaria	8-20-88	Stara Zagora, Bulgaria
400-meter hurdles	52.61	Kim Batten, United States	8-11-95	Goteborg, Sweden
5-kilometer walk	20:02.60	Gillian O'Sullivan, Ireland	7-13-02	Dublin, Ireland
10-kilometer walk	41:56.23	Nadezhda Ryashkina, Russia	7-24-90	Seattle, Washington
4x100-meter relay	41.37	East Germany (Silke Gladisch, Sabine Reiger, Ingrid Auerswald, Marlies Gohr)	10-6-85	Canberra, Australia
4x200-meter relay	1:27.46	United States (LaTasha Jenkins, LaTasha Colander-Richardson, Nanceen Perry, Marion Jones)	4-29-00	Philadelphia, Pennsylvania

PAUL HANNA/REUTERS

Marion Jones,
United States

Did You Know?

Runners from the African countries of Kenya and Ethiopia won every long-distance event (3,000-meter steeplechase, 5,000 meters, 10,000 meters, and marathon) at the 2000 Summer Olympics.

World Records—Women (cont.)

Event	Mark	Record Holder	Date	Site
4x400-meter relay	3:15.17	USSR (Tatyana Ledovskaya, Olga Nazarova, Maria Pinigina, Olga Bryzgina)	10-1-88	Seoul, Korea
4x800-meter relay	7:50.17	USSR (Nadezhda Olizarenko, Lyubov Gurina, Lyudmila Borisova, Irina Podyalovskaya)	8-5-84	Moscow, Russia
High jump	6 ft 10 ¼ in	Stefka Kostadinova, Bulgaria	8-30-87	Rome, Italy
Pole vault	15 ft 9 ¾ in	Yelena Isinbayeva, Russia	7-13-03	Gateshead, England
Long jump	24 ft 8 ¼ in	Galina Chistyakova, USSR	6-11-88	Leningrad, Russia
Triple jump	50 ft 10 ¼ in	Inessa Kravets, Ukraine	8-10-95	Goteborg, Sweden
Shot put	74 ft 3 in	Natalya Lisovskaya, USSR	6-7-87	Moscow, Russia
Discus throw	252 ft	Gabriele Reinsch, E Germany	7-9-88	Neubrandenburg, Germany
Hammer throw	247 ft 3 in	Mihaela Melinte, Romania	8-29-99	Rudlingen, Switzerland
Javelin throw	234 ft 8 in	Osleidys Menéndez, Cuba	7-1-01	Réthymno, Greece
Heptathlon	7,291 pts	Jackie Joyner-Kersee, United States	9-23-88/9-24-88	Seoul, Korea

TONY DUFFY/GETTY IMAGES

Jackie Joyner-Kersee, United States

Note: The heptathlon consists of 7 events: the 100-meter hurdles, high jump, shot put, and 200 meters on the first day; the long jump, javelin, and 800 meters on the second.

Did You Know?
The men's shot put weighs 16 pounds. The women's shot put weighs 8 pounds, 13 ounces.

2002-03 TIMELINE

April 14, 2002: Khalid Khannouchi of the U.S. sets the world record in the marathon, in London, England (2:05:38).

September 14, 2002: Sprinter Tim Montgomery of the U.S. sets the world record in the 100 meters (9.78) at the Grand Prix Final, in Paris, France.

February 1, 2003: Middle-distance runner Regina Jacobs of the U.S. becomes the first woman to run an indoor 1,500-meter race in under four minutes. She finishes in 3:59.98, at the adidas Boston Indoor Games.

February 15, 2003: Alan Webb, the fastest high school miler in history, makes his pro debut. He finishes third in the New York Runners Challenge Cup mile.

March 3, 2003: Svetlana Feofanova of Russia sets the women's indoor pole vault world record, clearing 15' 9" at the world indoor championships, in Birmingham, England.

April 13, 2003: Paula Radcliffe of England smashes her own women's marathon world record (2:17.18) by winning the London Marathon in 2:15.25.

April 21, 2003: Legally blind runner Marla Runyan of the U.S. finishes fifth in the Boston Marathon (2:30.28), her second career marathon. Her finish is the best by an U.S. woman in the Boston Marathon since 1993.

August 22-31, 2003: The World Outdoor Track and Field Championships are held in Paris, France.

WINTER OLYMPICS

O n February 8, 2002, the XIX Winter
Olympic Games kicked off in Salt Lake
City, Utah, with great expectations and
tremendous fanfare. It was the fourth time the
United States has been the host nation (the
other times were in 1932, 1960, and 1980).

The Salt Lake City Games were the largest
Winter Olympics ever, with 2,399 athletes from
77 countries competing. Security was at an
all-time high due to the terrorist attacks in the
United States on September 11, 2001. There
was concern over whether the U.S. could
conduct such a large event without incident.
All worries were put to rest when the Games
successfully, and safely, closed 17 days later,
on February 24. In between, there were historic
firsts, dramatic finishes, and some startling
controversies. As always, the Winter Olympics
were exciting and uplifting.

The 2002 Winter
Games begin.

DAVID E. KLUTHO/SPORTS ILLUSTRATED

Salt Lake City 2002 Medal Count (by nation)

		GOLD	SILVER	BRONZE	TOTAL
1.	GERMANY	12	16	7	35
2.	NORWAY	11	7	6	24
3.	UNITED STATES OF AMERICA	10	13	11	34
4.	RUSSIAN FEDERATION	6	6	4	16
5.	CANADA	6	3	8	17
6.	FRANCE	4	5	2	11
7.	ITALY	4	4	4	12
8.	FINLAND	4	2	1	7
9.	NETHERLANDS	3	5	0	8
10.	SWITZERLAND	3	2	6	11
11.	CROATIA	3	1	0	4
12.	AUSTRIA	2	4	10	16
13.	PEOPLE'S REPUBLIC OF CHINA	2	2	4	8
14.	KOREA	2	2	0	4
15.	AUSTRALIA	2	0	0	2
16.	SPAIN	2	0	0	2
17.	ESTONIA	1	1	1	3
18.	GREAT BRITAIN	1	0	2	3
19.	CZECH REPUBLIC	1	0	1	2
20.	SWEDEN	0	2	4	6
21.	BULGARIA	0	1	2	3
22.	JAPAN	0	1	1	2
23.	POLAND	0	1	1	2
24.	SLOVENIA	0	0	1	1
25.	BELARUS	0	0	1	1

2002 Sport-by-Sport Results

Men's Alpine Skiing

■ COMBINED
GOLD – Kjetil Andre Aamodt, Norway
SILVER – Bode Miller, USA
BRONZE – Benjamin Raich, Austria

■ DOWNHILL
GOLD – Fritz Strobl, Austria
SILVER – Lasse Kjus, Norway
BRONZE – Stephan Eberharter, Austria

Bode Miller

■ GIANT SLALOM
GOLD – Stephan Eberharter, Austria
SILVER – Bode Miller, USA
BRONZE – Lasse Kjus, Norway

■ SLALOM
GOLD – Jean-Pierre Vidal, France
SILVER – Sebastien Amiez, France
BRONZE – Alain Baxter, Great Britain

■ SUPER-G
GOLD – Kjetil Andre Aamodt, Norway
SILVER – Stephan Eberharter, Austria
BRONZE – Andreas Schifferer, Austria

Women's Alpine Skiing

■ COMBINED
GOLD – Janica Kostelic, Croatia
SILVER – Renate Goetschl, Austria
BRONZE – Marina Ertl, Germany

■ DOWNHILL
GOLD – Carole Montillet, France
SILVER – Isolde Kostner, Italy
BRONZE – Renate Goetschl, Austria

Janica Kostelic

■ GIANT SLALOM
GOLD – Janica Kostelic, Croatia
SILVER – Anja Paerson, Sweden
BRONZE – Sonja Nef, Switzerland

■ SLALOM
GOLD – Janica Kostelic, Croatia
SILVER – Laure Pequegnot, France
BRONZE – Anja Paerson, Sweden

■ SUPER-G
GOLD – Daniela Ceccarelli, Italy
SILVER – Janica Kostelic, Croatia
BRONZE – Karen Putzer, Italy

Men's Biathlon

■ 10 KM
GOLD – Ole Einar Bjoerndalen, Norway
SILVER – Sven Fischer, Germany
BRONZE – Wolfgang Perner, Austria

■ 12.5 KM PURSUIT
GOLD – Ole Einar Bjoerndalen, Norway
SILVER – Raphael Poiree, France
BRONZE – Ricco Gross, Germany

■ 20 KM
GOLD – Ole Einar Bjoerndalen, Norway
SILVER – Frank Luck, Germany
BRONZE – Victor Maigourov, Russia

■ 4X7.5 KM RELAY
GOLD – Norway
SILVER – Germany
BRONZE – France

Women's Biathlon

■ 7.5 KM
GOLD – Kati Wilhelm, Germany
SILVER – Uschi Disl, Germany
BRONZE – Magdalena Forsberg, Sweden

■ 10 KM PURSUIT
GOLD – Olga Pyleva, Russia
SILVER – Kati Wilhelm, Germany
BRONZE – Irina Nikoultchina, Bulgaria

■ 15 KM
GOLD – Andrea Henkel, Germany
SILVER – Liv Grete Poiree, Norway
BRONZE – Magdalena Forsberg, Sweden

■ 4X7.5 KM RELAY
GOLD – Germany
SILVER – Norway
BRONZE – Russia

Men's Bobsled

■ 4-MAN
GOLD – Germany
SILVER – USA
BRONZE – USA

■ 2-MAN
GOLD – Germany
SILVER – Switzerland
BRONZE – Switzerland

Women's Bobsled

■ 2-PERSON
GOLD – USA
SILVER – Germany
BRONZE – Germany

> **▷Random Fact:** Eddie Eagan is the only person in Olympic history to earn gold medals in both Summer and Winter sports. He won a gold medal in boxing at the 1920 Summer Games, in Antwerp, Belgium. He also was a member of the gold-medal-winning 4-man bobsled team at the 1932 Winter Games, in Lake Placid, New York.

BOB MARTIN/SPORTS ILLUSTRATED (2)

2002 Sport-by-Sport Results

Men's Cross-country Skiing

1.5 KM SPRINT
GOLD – Tor Arne Hetland, Norway
SILVER – Peter Schlickenrieder, Germany
BRONZE – Cristian Zorzi, Italy

10 KM PURSUIT
GOLD – Johann Muehlegg, Spain
SILVER – Frode Estil, Norway
SILVER – Thomas Alsgaard, Norway

15 KM
GOLD – Andrus Veerpalu, Estonia
SILVER – Frode Estil, Norway
BRONZE – Jaak Mae, Estonia

30 KM MASS START
GOLD – Johann Muehlegg, Spain
SILVER – Christian Hoffman, Austria
BRONZE – Mikhail Botvinov, Austria

50 KM
GOLD – Mikhail Ivanov, Russia
SILVER – Andrus Veerpalu, Estonia
BRONZE – Odd-Bjoern Hjelmeset, Norway

4X10 KM RELAY
GOLD – Norway
SILVER – Italy
BRONZE – Germany

Women's Cross-country Skiing

1.5 KM SPRINT
GOLD – Julija Tchepalova, Russia
SILVER – Evi Sachenbacher, Germany
BRONZE – Anita Moen, Norway

5 KM PURSUIT
GOLD – Olga Danilova, Russia
SILVER – Larissa Lazutina, Russia
BRONZE – Beckie Scott, Canada

10 KM
GOLD – Bente Skari, Norway
SILVER – Olga Danilova, Russia
BRONZE – Julija Tchepalova, Russia

15 KM MASS START
GOLD – Stefania Belmondo, Italy
SILVER – Larissa Lazutina, Russia
BRONZE – Katerina Neumannova, Czech Republic

30 KM
GOLD – Gabriella Paruzzi, Italy
SILVER – Stefania Belmondo, Italy
BRONZE – Bente Skari, Norway

4X5 KM RELAY
GOLD – Germany
SILVER – Norway
BRONZE – Switzerland

Men's Curling
GOLD – Norway
SILVER – Canada
BRONZE – Switzerland

Women's Curling
GOLD – Great Britain
SILVER – Switzerland
BRONZE – Canada

Men's Figure Skating
GOLD – Alexei Yagudin, Russia
SILVER – Evgeni Plushenko, Russia
BRONZE – Timothy Goebel, USA

Women's Figure Skating
GOLD – Sarah Hughes, USA
SILVER – Irina Slutskaya, Russia
BRONZE – Michelle Kwan, USA

Pairs Figure Skating
GOLD – Anton Sikharulidze
and Elena Berezhnaya,
Russia
GOLD – David Pelletier
and Jamie Salé, Canada
BRONZE – Xue Shen and
Hongbo Zhao, China

Pelletier and Salé

Ice Dancing
GOLD – Marina Anissina and
Gwendal Peizerat, France
SILVER – Irina Lobacheva and
Ilia Averbukh, Russia
BRONZE – Barbara Fusa Poli and
Maurizio Margaglio, Italy

Men's Freestyle Skiing

AERIALS
GOLD – Ales Valenta,
Czech Republic
SILVER – Joe Pack, USA
BRONZE – Alexei Grichin, Belarus

MOGULS
GOLD – Janne Lahtela, Finland
SILVER – Travis Mayer, USA
BRONZE – Richard Gay, France

HEINZ KLUETMEIER/SPORTS ILLUSTRATED

2002 Sport-by-Sport Results

Women's Freestyle Skiing

■ **AERIALS**
GOLD – Alisa Camplin, Australia
SILVER – Veronica Brenner, Canada
BRONZE – Deidra Dionne, Canada

■ **MOGULS**
GOLD – Kari Traa, Norway
SILVER – Shannon Bahrke, USA
BRONZE – Tae Satoya, Japan

Men's Ice Hockey
GOLD – Canada
SILVER – USA
BRONZE – Russia

Women's Ice Hockey
GOLD – Canada
SILVER – USA
BRONZE – Sweden

> **⫸Random Fact:**
> The U.S. swept the snowboarding halfpipe event at the 2002 Winter Olympics. The last time Americans swept a Winter event was at the 1956 Winter Games, in Cortina d'Ampezzo, Italy, when the U.S. took the top three spots in men's figure skating.

Men's Luge

■ **SINGLES**
GOLD – Armin Zoeggeler, Italy
SILVER – Georg Hackl, Germany
BRONZE – Markus Prock, Austria

■ **DOUBLES**
GOLD – Alexander Resch and Patric-Fritz Leitner, Germany
SILVER – Mark Grimmette and Brian Martin, USA
BRONZE – Chris Thorpe and Clay Ives, USA

Women's Luge

■ **SINGLES**
GOLD – Sylke Otto, Germany
SILVER – Barbara Niedernhuber, Germany
BRONZE – Silke Kraushaar, Germany

Legends

Jean-Claude Killy, Alpine skier b. August 30, 1943, Paris, France. Killy won gold medals in all three Alpine skiing events (downhill, slalom, and giant slalom) at the 1968 Winter Olympics, in Grenoble, France. He became a national hero in France, where the Games were known as the "Killympics." He was also the World Cup overall champion for two consecutive years (1967, 1968).

Sonja Henie, figure skater b. April 8, 1912, Oslo, Norway; d. October 12, 1969. After finishing last at the 1924 Winter Games when she was just 11 years old, Henie won gold medals at the 1928, 1932, and 1936 Winter Olympics. No other woman has won the singles title at three consecutive Olympics. She was also the world champion 10 years in a row (1927-36).

Eric Heiden, speed skater b. June 14, 1958, Madison, Wisconsin. Heiden won all five speed-skating gold medals (500; 1,000; 1,500; 5,000; and 10,000 meters) at the 1980 Winter Olympics, in Lake Placid, New York. He is the only speed skater ever to accomplish the feat. He was also a three-time world champion (1977-79).

Jean-Claude Killy of France won three gold medals at the 1968 Winter Games.

ERIC SCHWEIKARDT/SPORTS ILLUSTRATED

2002 Sport-by-Sport Results

Nordic Combined

■ INDIVIDUAL
GOLD – Samppa Lajunen, Finland
SILVER – Jaakko Tallus, Finland
BRONZE – Felix Gottwald, Austria

■ SPRINT
GOLD – Samppa Lajunen, Finland
SILVER – Ronny Ackermann, Germany
BRONZE – Felix Gottwald, Austria

■ TEAM
GOLD – Finland
SILVER – Germany
BRONZE – Austria

Men's Skeleton

GOLD – Jim Shea, USA
SILVER – Martin Rettl, Austria
BRONZE – Gregor Staehli, Switzerland

Jim Shea

Women's Skeleton

GOLD – Tristan Gale, USA
SILVER – Lea Ann Parsley, USA
BRONZE – Alex Coomber, Great Britain

Ski Jumping

■ K90 INDIVIDUAL
GOLD – Simon Ammann, Switzerland
SILVER – Sven Hannawald, Germany
BRONZE – Adam Malysz, Poland

■ K120 INDIVIDUAL
GOLD – Simon Ammann, Switzerland
SILVER – Adam Malysz, Poland
BRONZE – Matti Hautamaeki, Finland

■ K120 TEAM
GOLD – Germany
SILVER – Finland
BRONZE – Slovenia

Men's Snowboarding

■ GIANT PARALLEL SLALOM
GOLD – Philipp Schoch, Switzerland
SILVER – Richard Richardsson, Sweden
BRONZE – Chris Klug, USA

Kass, Powers, Thomas

■ HALFPIPE
GOLD – Ross Powers, USA
SILVER – Danny Kass, USA
BRONZE – Jarret Thomas, USA

Women's Snowboarding

■ GIANT PARALLEL SLALOM
GOLD – Isabelle Blanc, France
SILVER – Karine Ruby, France
BRONZE – Lidia Trettell, Italy

■ HALFPIPE
GOLD – Kelly Clark, USA
SILVER – Doriane Vidal, France
BRONZE – Fabienne Reuteler, Switzerland

Men's Long-Track Speed Skating

■ 500 M
GOLD – Casey FitzRandolph, USA
SILVER – Hiroyasu Shimizu, Japan
BRONZE – Kip Carpenter, USA

■ 1,000 M
GOLD – Gerard Van Velde, Netherlands
SILVER – Jan Bos, Netherlands
BRONZE – Joey Cheek, USA

■ 1,500 M
GOLD – Derek Parra, USA
SILVER – Jochem Uytdehaage, Netherlands
BRONZE – Andre Sondral, Norway

■ 5,000 M
GOLD – Jochem Uytdehaage, Netherlands
SILVER – Derek Parra, USA
BRONZE – Jens Boden, Germany

Jochem Uytdehaage

■ 10,000 M
GOLD – Jochem Uytdehaage, Netherlands
SILVER – Gianni Romme, Netherlands
BRONZE – Lasse Saetre, Norway

Women's Long-Track Speed Skating

■ 500 M
GOLD – Catriona Lemay Doan, Canada
SILVER – Monique Garbrecht-Enfeldt, Germany
BRONZE – Sabine Voelker, Germany

■ 1,000 M
GOLD – Chris Witty, USA
SILVER – Sabine Voelker, Germany
BRONZE – Jennifer Rodriguez, USA

Trivia Challenge

Who is the youngest individual to win a gold medal in any sport in the history of the Winter Olympics?

Figure skater Tara Lipinski of the United States. She was 15 years old when she won the women's singles title in 1998, in Nagano, Japan.

JOHN BIEVER/SPORTS ILLUSTRATED

DARRON CUMMINGS/AP

DUSAN VRANIC/AP

Today's Stars

Sarah Hughes of the U.S. leaped from fourth to first.

Sarah Hughes, figure skater b. May 2, 1985, Great Neck, New York. Hughes won the gold medal in women's singles. She became the first person to rebound from fourth place after the short program to win an Olympic gold medal since the current scoring system was introduced in 1992. At age 16, she was the fourth-youngest Olympic female figure-skating champion of all time.

Janica Kostelic, Alpine skier b. May 1, 1982, Zagreb, Croatia. "The Croation Sensation" made history by becoming the first woman skier to win four medals. Kostelic won gold in the combined, the slalom, and the giant slalom events. She won a silver medal in the Super-G event.

Apolo Anton Ohno, short-track speed skater b. May 22, 1982, Seattle, Washington. Ohno won a gold medal in the 1,500 meters and a silver medal in the 1,000 meters. He was the 2001 World Cup overall champion and is a four-time U.S. champion.

HEINZ KLUETMEIER/SPORTS ILLUSTRATED

2002 Sport-by-Sport Results

■ 1,500 M
GOLD – Anni Friesinger, Germany
SILVER – Sabine Voelker, Germany
BRONZE – Jennifer Rodriguez, USA

■ 3,000 M
GOLD – Claudia Pechstein, Germany
SILVER – Renate Groenewold, Netherlands
BRONZE – Cindy Klassen, Canada

■ 5,000 M
GOLD – Claudia Pechstein, Germany
SILVER – Gretha Smit, Netherlands
BRONZE – Clara Hughes, Canada

Men's Short-Track Speed Skating

■ 500 M
GOLD – Marc Gagnon, Canada
SILVER – Jonathan Guilmette, Canada
BRONZE – Rusty Smith, USA

■ 1,000 M
GOLD – Steven Bradbury, Australia
SILVER – Apolo Anton Ohno, USA
BRONZE – Mathieu Turcotte, Canada

■ 1,500 M
GOLD – Apolo Anton Ohno, USA
SILVER – Jiajun Li, China
BRONZE – Marc Gagnon, Canada

2002 Sport-by-Sport Results

■ **5,000 M RELAY**
GOLD – Canada
SILVER – Italy
BRONZE – China

Women's Short-Track Speed Skating

■ **500 M**
GOLD – Yang Yang (A), China*
SILVER – Evgenia Radanova, Bulgaria
BRONZE – Chunlu Wang, China

■ **1,000 M**
GOLD – Yang Yang (A), China
SILVER – Gi-Hyun Ko, Korea

Yang Yang (A)

BRONZE – Yang Yang (S), China

■ **1,500 M**
GOLD – Gi-Hyun Ko, Korea
SILVER – Eun-Kyung Choi, Korea
BRONZE – Evgenia Radanova, Bulgaria

■ **3,000 M RELAY**
GOLD – Korea
SILVER – China
BRONZE – Canada

*The letters "A" and "S" are used to differentiate between two Chinese skaters named Yang Yang.

AMY SANCETTA/AP

Past Winter Olympic Hosts

					COMPETITORS		
					MEN	WOMEN	NATIONS
XIX	2002	SALT LAKE CITY, UT, USA		February 8-24	1,513	886	77
XVIII	1998	NAGANO, JAPAN		February 7-22	1,488	814	72
XVII	1994	LILLEHAMMER, NORWAY		February 12-27	1,217	522	67
XVI	1992	ALBERTVILLE, FRANCE		February 8-23	1,313	488	64
XV	1988	CALGARY, CANADA		February 13-28	1,110	313	57
XIV	1984	SARAJEVO, YUGOSLAVIA		February 8-19	1,100	274	49
XIII	1980	LAKE PLACID, NY, USA		February 13-24	839	233	37
XII	1976	INNSBRUCK, AUSTRIA		February 4-15	892	231	37
XI	1972	SAPPORO, JAPAN		February 3-13	800	206	35
X	1968	GRENOBLE, FRANCE		February 6-18	947	211	37
IX	1964	INNSBRUCK, AUSTRIA		January 29-February 9	891	200	36
VIII	1960	SQUAW VALLEY, CA, USA		February 18-28	522	143	30
VII	1956	CORTINA d'AMPEZZO, ITALY		January 26-February 5	688	132	32
VI	1952	OSLO, NORWAY		February 14-25	585	109	30
V	1948	ST. MORITZ, SWITZERLAND		January 30-February 8	592	77	28
--	1944	CORTINA d'AMPEZZO, ITALY		Canceled due to war			
--	1940	GARMISCH-PARTENKIRCHEN, GERMANY		Canceled due to war			
IV	1936	GARMISCH-PARTENKIRCHEN, GERMANY		February 6-16	588	80	28
III	1932	LAKE PLACID, NY, USA		February 4-13	231	21	17
II	1928	ST. MORITZ, SWITZERLAND		February 11-19	438	26	25
I	1924	CHAMONIX, FRANCE		January 25-February 4	245	13	16

All-time Winter Olympic Medal Winners

NATIONS — OVERALL

Nation	GOLD	SILVER	BRONZE	TOTAL
NORWAY	94	93	73	260
SOVIET UNION (1956-88)	78	56	59	193
UNITED STATES	70	70	51	191
AUSTRIA	41	57	65	163
GERMANY	54	51	37	142
FINLAND	41	51	49	141
EAST GERMANY (1956-88)	39	37	35	111
SWEDEN	36	28	38	102
SWITZERLAND	32	33	36	101
CANADA	30	28	37	95

INDIVIDUALS — OVERALL — MEN

ATHLETE, Nation	SPORT	GOLD	SILVER	BRONZE	TOTAL
BJORN DAEHLIE, Norway	Nordic Skiing	8	4	0	12
SIXTEN JERNBERG, Sweden	Nordic Skiing	4	3	2	9
Seven tied with 7.					

INDIVIDUALS — OVERALL — WOMEN

ATHLETE, Nation	SPORT	GOLD	SILVER	BRONZE	TOTAL
RAISA SMETANINA, USSR/United Team	Nordic Skiing	4	5	1	10
LYUBOV EGOROVA, United Team/Russia	Nordic Skiing	6	3	0	9
LARISSA LAZUTINA, United Team/Russia	Nordic Skiing	5	3	1	9
STEFANIA BELMONDO, Italy	Nordic Skiing	2	3	4	9
Four tied with 8.					

INDIVIDUALS — GOLD

MEN		WOMEN	
BJORN DAEHLIE, Norway	8	LYUBOV EGOROVA, United Team/Russia	6
OLE EINAR BJOERNDALEN, Norway	5	LYDIA SKOBILKOVA, USSR	6
ERIC HEIDEN, United States	5	BONNIE BLAIR, United States	5
A. CLAS THUNBERG, Finland	5	LARISSA LAZUTINA, United Team/Russia	5
Nine tied with 4.		Four tied with 4.	

2002 TIMELINE

February 8, 2002: The XIX Winter Olympic Games are officially opened before 52,000 spectators, the largest crowd ever at an Olympic Winter Games opening ceremony. The Olympic flame is lit by members of the 1980 gold-medal-winning U.S. hockey team.

February 9, 2002: Stefania Belmondo of Italy wins gold in the first medal event of the 2002 Winter Games, the 15-kilometer freestyle race in cross-country skiing.

February 10, 2002: Twenty-year-old Simon Ammann of Switzerland stuns the ski-jumping world by winning the gold medal in the K90 event. Three days later, he wins his second gold medal of the Games, in the K120 event, becoming just the second jumper to win two gold medals in ski jumping.

February 11, 2002: Pairs figure skaters Jamie Salé and David Pelletier of Canada are awarded the silver medal amid much controversy over an alleged judging fix. The International Olympic Committee solves the problem by declaring the competition a tie and awarding Salé and Pelletier duplicate gold medals four days later.

February 12, 2002: U.S. mogul skier Jonny Moseley wows the crowd but not the judges with his Dinner Roll move. He leaves the competition without a medal. Janne Lahtela of Finland wins the gold, Travis Mayer of the U.S wins the silver, and Richard Gay of France wins the bronze.

February 13, 2002: Skier Kjetil Andre Aamodt of Norway wins the gold medal in the combined event (which includes the downhill and slalom), his sixth Olympic medal, a record for an Alpine skier. (Three days later he wins his seventh medal, a gold in the Super-G.)

February 14, 2002: Alpine skier Janica Kostelic of Croatia wins the women's combined event, her country's first-ever medal at a Winter Olympic Games.

February 15, 2002: Snowboarder Chris Klug of the U.S., who received a liver transplant in 2000, wins the bronze medal in the slalom event.

February 16, 2002: Yang Yang (A) of China wins the gold medal in the 500-meter short-track speed-skating event. It is her country's first gold medal in 10 years of Winter Olympic participation.

February 17, 2002: Long-track speed-skater Chris Witty of the U.S. wins the 1,000-meter race in world-record time, despite having been ill the month before with mononucleosis (a virus that causes extreme fatigue).

February 18, 2002: Aerial skier Alisa Camplin of Australia wins her country's second-ever Winter Olympic gold medal by landing a triple-twisting double backflip.

February 19, 2002: Vonetta Flowers and Jill Bakken of the U.S. win the gold medal in women's bobsled, a first-time Olympic event. Flowers becomes the first African-American athlete to win Winter gold.

February 20, 2002: Jim Shea of the U.S., the first third-generation Winter Olympian, wins the gold medal in skeleton. His grandfather, Jack Shea, won two gold medals as a speed skater at the 1932 Winter Games, in Lake Placid, New York. His father, Jim, Sr., competed in three cross-country skiing events at the 1964 Winter Games, in Innsbruck, Austria.

2002 TIMELINE (cont.) --

February 21, 2002: Figure skater Sarah Hughes of the U.S. pulls off a stunning upset in the women's singles. In fourth place after the short program, she lands two triple-combination jumps in the free skate and vaults to first place, overtaking favorite Michelle Kwan of the U.S. and Irina Slutskaya of Russia.

February 22, 2002: Long-track speed-skater Jochem Uytdehaage of the Netherlands wins the gold medal in the 10,000 meters in world-record time. It is his second gold medal and second world record at the Games. He won gold in the 5,000 meters 13 days earlier.

February 23, 2002: Not since 1956 has the U.S. won a medal in the four-man bobsled. Today they win two. Driver Todd Hays and his USA 1 team win the silver medal, and driver Brian Shimer and his USA 2 crew win bronze. Hays's sled includes Randy Jones and Garrett Hines, the first African-American men to win medals in the Olympic Winter Games.

February 24, 2002: In the final competition of the Salt Lake City Games, the Canadian men's ice hockey team, led by first-time Olympian Mario Lemieux, wins the gold medal. It had been 50 years since Canada won an Olympic gold medal in hockey.

Did You Know?

Georg Hackl of Germany became the first Olympic athlete to win five medals in the same individual event (luge). He accomplished the feat in five consecutive Olympic Games (1988-2002). He won silver in 1988, gold in 1992, 1994, and 1998, and silver in 2002.

SUMMER OLYMPICS PREVIEW

The 28th Summer Olympics will take place in Greece, the country in which they began, from August 13-29, 2004. Historic records date thefirst Olympic Games at 776 BC, in Olympia, Greece. The Games were held every four years until they were banned by Emperor Theodosius in AD 393 for being "too pagan." In 1896, Baron Pierre de Coubertin of France came up with the idea of a modern Olympic Games. Interest in the Games was strongest in Greece, so the first modern Olympic Games were held in Athens. Now, more than 100 years later, the Games return to that city.

More than 10,000 athletes from 199 countries will compete in 28 sports at 37 venues. Some of the most popular sports will be swimming, gymnastics, track and field, and basketball, and women's wrestling will make its Olympic debut. Among the stars to watch: swimmers Ian Thorpe of Australia, Michael Phelps and Natalie Coughlin of the U.S. *(see Swimming, page 278)*, sprinter Marion Jones of the U.S., and pro basketball players Tracy McGrady and Jason Kidd of the U.S., Dirk Nowitzki of Germany, and Yao Ming of China.

Jason Kidd will lead a star-studded Team USA at the 2004 Summer Games.

JOHN BIEVER/SPORTS ILLUSTRATED

Did You Know?
David Robinson is the only American man to play basketball at three different Olympics. He was a member of the U.S. teams that won a bronze medal in 1988 and gold medals in 1992 and 1996.

Aaron Peirsol of the U.S. holds the world record in the men's 200-meter backstroke.

JOHN BIEVER/SPORTS ILLUSTRATED

2004 Summer Olympics Schedule of Events*

DARYL STONE/USA TODAY

Friday, August 13
Opening Ceremony

Saturday, August 14

Cycling	■ Road Race (M)
Diving	■ Synchronized 3-meter Springboard (W) ■ Synchronized 10-meter Platform (M)
Fencing	■ Individual Sabre (M)
Judo	■ 48 kg (W) ■ 60 kg (M)
Shooting	■ 10-meter Air Rifle (W) ■ 10-meter Air Pistol (M)
Swimming	■ 400-meter Individual Medley (W, M) ■ 400-meter Freestyle (M) ■ 400-meter Freestyle Relay (W)
Weightlifting	■ 48 kg (W)

Keeth Smart, United States

Sunday, August 15

Cycling	■ Road Race (W)
Fencing	■ Individual Épée (W)
Judo	■ 52 kg (W) ■ 66 kg (M)
Shooting	■ 10-meter Air Pistol (W) ■ Trap (M)
Swimming	■ 100-meter Butterfly (W) ■ 100-meter Breaststroke (M) ■ 400-meter Freestyle (W) ■ 400-meter Freestyle Relay (M)
Weightlifting	■ 53 kg (W) ■ 56 kg (M)

Monday, August 16

Diving	■ Synchronized 10-meter Platform (W) ■ Synchronized 3-meter Springboard (M)
Fencing	■ Individual Foil (M)
Gymnastics	■ Team (M)
Judo	■ 57 kg (W) ■ 73 kg (M)
Shooting	■ Trap (W) ■ 10-meter Air Rifle (M)
Swimming	■ 200-meter Freestyle (M) ■ 100-meter Backstroke (W, M) ■ 100-meter Breaststroke (W)
Weightlifting	■ 58 kg (W) ■ 62 kg (M)

Tuesday, August 17

Fencing	■ Individual Épée (M) ■ Individual Sabre (W)
Gymnastics	■ Team (W)
Judo	■ 63 kg (W) ■ 81 kg (M)
Shooting	■ 50-meter Pistol (M) ■ Double Trap (M)
Swimming	■ 200-meter Freestyle (W) ■ 200-meter Butterfly (M) ■ 200-meter Individual Medley (W) ■ 800-meter Freestyle Relay (M)

Wednesday, August 18

Archery	■ Individual (W)
Canoe/Kayak Slalom Racing	■ C1 Canoe Single (M) ■ K1 Kayak Single (W)
Cycling	■ Individual Time Trial (W) ■ Individual Time Trial (M)

BOB MARTIN/SPORTS ILLUSTRATED

*Finals listed

Lance Armstrong, United States

2004 Summer Olympics Schedule of Events (cont.)

Wednesday, August 18 (cont.)

Equestrian	Team Eventing
	Individual Eventing
Fencing	Individual Foil (W)
Gymnastics	Individual All-Around (M)
Judo	70 kg (W)
	90 kg (M)
Shooting	Double Trap (W)
	25-meter Pistol (W)
Swimming	200-meter Breaststroke (M)
	200-meter Butterfly (W)
	100-meter Freestyle (W)
	800-meter Freestyle Relay (W)
Weightlifting	63 kg (W)
	69 kg (M)

Thursday, August 19

Archery	Individual (M)
Badminton	Singles (W)
	Mixed Doubles
Fencing	Team Sabre (M)
Gymnastics	Individual All-Around (W)
Judo	78 kg (W)
	100 kg (M)
Shooting	10-meter Running Target (M)
	Skeet (W)
Swimming	200-meter Breaststroke (W)
	200-meter Backstroke (M)
	200-meter Individual Medley (M)
	100-meter Freestyle (W)
Weightlifting	69 kg (W)
	77 kg (M)

Friday, August 20

Archery	Team (W)
Badminton	Doubles (M)
Canoe/Kayak Slalom Racing	
	C2 Canoe Double (M)
	K1 Kayak Single (M)
Cycling (Track)	500-meter Time Trial (W)
	1-kilometer Time Trial (M)
Fencing	Team Épée (W)
Gymnastics	Trampoline (W)
Judo	+78 kg (W)
	+100 kg (M)
Shooting	50-meter Rifle 3 Position (W)
	50-meter Rifle Prone (M)
Swimming	200-meter Backstroke (W)
	100-meter Butterfly (M)
	800-meter Freestyle (W)
	50-meter Freestyle (M)
Table Tennis	Doubles (W)
Track and Field	20-kilometer Walk (W)
	Shot Put (M)
	10,000 meters (M)
Weightlifting	75 kg (W)

Saturday, August 21

Archery	Team (M)
Badminton	Doubles (W)
	Singles (M)
Cycling (Track)	4,000-meter Individual Pursuit (M)
	Team Sprint (M)
Equestrian	Team Dressage
Fencing	Team Foil (M)
Gymnastics	Trampoline (M)
Rowing	Single Sculls (W, M)
	Pairs (W, M)
	Double Sculls (W, M)
	Four (M)
Sailing	Keelboat: Yngling Class (W)
	Double-handed Dinghy: 470 Class (W, M)
	Single-handed Dinghy: Finn Class (M)
Shooting	25-meter Rapid-fire Pistol (M)
Swimming	50-meter Freestyle (W)
	1,500-meter Freestyle (M)
	400-meter Medley Relay (W, M)
Table Tennis	Doubles (M)
Tennis	Singles (W)
	Doubles (M)
Track and Field	Discus Throw (W)
	100 meters (W)
	Heptathlon (W)
Weightlifting	+75 kg (W)
	85 kg (M)

Cheryl Haworth, United States

DAVID GUTTENFELDER/AP

Sunday, August 22

Cycling (Track)	3,000-meter Individual Pursuit (W)
Diving	10-meter Platform (W)
Fencing	Team Épée (M)
Gymnastics	Floor Exercise (M)
	Vault (W)
	Pommel Horse (M)
	Uneven Bars (W)
	Rings (M)
Rowing	Lightweight Double Sculls (W, M)
	Lightweight Four (M)
	Quadruple Sculls (W, M)
	Eight (W, M)
Sailing	Open Single-handed Dinghy: Laser Class
	Single-handed Dinghy: Europe Class (W)
Shooting	50-meter Rifle 3 Position (M)
	Skeet (M)
Table Tennis	Singles (W)
Tennis	Singles (M)
	Doubles (W)
Track and Field	Hammer Throw (M)
	High Jump (M)
	Triple Jump (M)
	100 meters (M)
	Wheelchair 1,500 meters (M)
	Marathon (W)
	Wheelchair 800 meters (W)

Legends

Greg Louganis, diver, b. January 29, 1960, San Diego, California. Louganis is the greatest male diver in Olympic history. He is the only man — and second person — to win the platform and springboard events at two Olympics (1984, 1988). At the 1988 Games, Louganis won the springboard gold medal after hitting his head on the board in the preliminaries. He also won a silver medal in the platform at the 1976 Olympics.

Nadia Comaneci, gymnast, b. November 12, 1961, Onesti, Romania. At the 1976 Summer Olympics, Comaneci scored the first perfect 10 in Olympic gymnastics, on the uneven bars. She was 14 years old. The 5' 4" Romanian won three gold medals, a silver medal, and a bronze. Comaneci won two gold medals at the 1980 Olympics.

Michael Johnson, sprinter, b. September 13, 1967, Dallas, Texas. Johnson is the only man to win the 200 meters and 400 meters at the same Olympics (1996). He set the world record in the 200 (19.32)

Greg Louganis won the platform and springboard events at the 1984 and 1988 Olympics.

ANDY HAYT/SPORTS ILLUSTRATED

at the 1996 Summer Games. Johnson defended his 400-meter Olympic title at the 2000 Games, becoming the first man to defend an Olympic title in the 400 meters. He holds the world record in that event, too (43.18, set in 1999).

2004 Summer Olympics Schedule of Events (cont.)

Monday, August 23

Cycling (Track)	▪ 4,000-meter Team Pursuit (M)
Gymnastics	▪ Vault (M)
	▪ Balance Beam (W)
	▪ Parallel Bars (M)
	▪ Floor Exercise (W)
	▪ Horizontal Bar (M)
Softball	▪ (W)
Table Tennis	▪ Singles (M)
Track and Field	▪ Discus Throw (M)
	▪ 400 meters (M)
	▪ 20-kilometer Walk (W)
	▪ Triple Jump (W)
	▪ 800 meters (W)
	▪ 5,000 meters (W)
Weightlifting	▪ 94 kg (M)
Wrestling (Freestyle)	
	▪ 48 kg (W)
	▪ 55 kg (W)
	▪ 63 kg (W)
	▪ 72 kg (W)

Tuesday, August 24

Beach Volleyball	▪ (W)
Cycling (Track)	▪ Points Race (M)
	▪ Sprint (W, M)
Diving	▪ 3-meter Springboard (M)
Equestrian	▪ Team Jumping
Track and Field	▪ 3,000-meter Steeplechase (M)
	▪ 1,500 meters (M)
	▪ Decathlon (M)
	▪ Pole Vault (W)
	▪ Shot Put (W)
	▪ 100-meter Hurdles (W)
	▪ 400 meters (W)
Weightlifting	▪ 105 kg (M)

Wednesday, August 25

Baseball	
Beach Volleyball	▪ (M)
Cycling (Track)	▪ Points Race (W)
	▪ Madison (M)
	▪ Keirin (M)

2004 Summer Olympics Schedule of Events (cont.)

Wednesday, August 25 (cont.)

Equestrian	Individual Dressage
Sailing	Windsurfing (W, M)
Synchronized Swimming	Duet
Track and Field	400-meter Hurdles (W)
	Hammer Throw (W)
	200 meters (W)
Triathlon	(W)
Weightlifting	+105 kg (M)
Wrestling (Greco-Roman)	
	55 kg (M)
	66 kg (M)
	84 kg (M)
	120 kg (M)

Thursday, August 26

Diving	3-meter Springboard (W)
Field Hockey	(W)
Modern Pentathlon	
	(M)
Sailing	Open Double-handed Dinghy: 49er Class
Taekwondo	Under 49 kg (W)
	Under 58 kg (M)
Track and Field	Long Jump (M)
	400-meter Hurdles (M)
	200 meters (M)
Triathlon	(M)
Water Polo	(W)
Wrestling (Greco-Roman)	
	60 kg (M)
	74 kg (M)
	96 kg (M)

Friday, August 27

Canoe/Kayak Flatwater Racing	
	K1 1,000 meters (M)
	C1 1,000 meters (M)
	K4 500 meters (W)
	K2 1,000 meters (M)
	C2 1,000 meters (M)
	K4 1,000 meters (M)
Cycling	Mountain Bike (W)
Equestrian	Individual Jumping
Field Hockey	(M)
Modern Pentathlon	
	(W)
Synchronized Swimming	
	Team
Taekwondo	Under 57 kg (W)
	Under 68 kg (M)
Track and Field	50-kilometer Walk (M)
	Pole Vault (M)
	110-meter Hurdles (M)
	Long Jump (W)
	Javelin Throw (W)
	10,000 meters (W)
	4x100-meter Relay (W)

Saturday, August 28

Basketball	(W, M)
Boxing	Flyweight
	Featherweight
	Light Welterweight
	Middleweight
	Heavyweight
Canoe/Kayak Flatwater Racing	
	K1 500 meters (M)
	C1 500 meters (M)
	K1 500 meters (W)
	K2 500 meters (M)
	C2 500 meters (M)
	K2 500 meters (W)
Cycling	Mountain Bike (M)
Diving	10-meter Platform (M)
Rhythmic Gymnastics	
	Group All-Around
Sailing	Open Multihull: Tornado Class
	Keelboat: Star Class (M)
Soccer	(M)
Taekwondo	Under 67 kg (W)
	Under 80 kg (M)
Track and Field	Javelin Throw (M)
	800 meters (M)
	1,500 meters (W)
	5,000 meters (M)
	4x100-meter Relay (M)
	4x400-meter Relay (M)
	4x400-meter Relay (W)
	High Jump (W)
Volleyball	(W)
Wrestling (Freestyle)	
	55 kg (M)
	66 kg (M)
	84 kg (M)
	120 kg (M)

Sunday, August 29

Boxing	Light Flyweight
	Bantamweight
	Lightweight
	Welterweight
	Light Heavyweight
	Super Heavyweight
Handball	(W, M)
Rhythmic Gymnastics	
	Individual All-Around
Soccer	(W)
Taekwondo	Over 67 kg (W)
	Over 80 kg (M)
Track and Field	Marathon (M)
Volleyball	(M)
Water Polo	(M)
Wrestling (Freestyle)	
	60 kg (M)
	74 kg (M)
	96 kg (M)
Closing Ceremony	

Cael Sanderson, United States

SIMON BRUTY/SPORTS ILLUSTRATED

Today's Stars

Tasha Schwikert, gymnast, b. November 21, 1984, Las Vegas, Nevada. Schwikert was the 2002 U.S. champion in the all-around, uneven bars, and floor exercise. She was a member of the U.S. team that earned a bronze medal at the 2001 world championships and a member of the U.S. team that placed fourth at the 2000 Summer Olympics.

Keeth Smart, fencer, b. July 29, 1978, Brooklyn, New York. Smart is the first U.S. fencer to be ranked Number 1 in the world. He competes in the sabre event. Smart has been a member of five world championship teams. He was a three-time NCAA Division I champion and four-time All-America at St. John's University, and graduated in 2001.

Lance Armstrong, cyclist, b. September 18, 1971, Plano, Texas. Armstrong, a three-time Olympian (1992, 1996, 2000), won a bronze medal in the individual time trial at the 2000 Games. Armstrong was the world's top-ranked cyclist when he was diagnosed with cancer in 1996. His return to racing in 1998 is one of the greatest comeback stories in sports. He won his first Tour de France in 1999. He went on to win the race in 2000, 2001, and 2002, one of only five riders to win the Tour four times.

RON SCHWANE/AP

Tasha Schwikert is a two-time U.S. all-around champion (2001, 2002).

▷**Random Fact:** U.S. gymnasts Paul and Morgan Hamm are the first twins to compete in the same Olympic gymnastics competition. They were members of the 2000 U.S. Olympic gymnastics team.

Trivia Challenge

Which of these sports were once Olympic events: tug-of-war, golf, rugby, polo or lacrosse?

All of them. Tug-of-war (1900, 1904, 1906, 1908, 1912, 1920); golf (1900, 1904); rugby (1900, 1908, 1920, 1924); polo (1900, 1908, 1920, 1924, 1936); lacrosse (1904, 1908).

SPORTS DIRECTORY

Major League Baseball
245 Park Avenue
New York, NY 10167
(212) 931-7800

Anaheim Angels
2000 Gene Autry Way
Anaheim, CA 92806
(714) 940-2000

Arizona Diamondbacks
401 East Jefferson Street
Phoenix, AZ 85004
(602) 462-6500

Atlanta Braves
P.O. Box 4064
Atlanta, GA 30302
(404) 522-7630

Baltimore Orioles
Oriole Park at Camden Yards
333 W. Camden Street
Baltimore, MD 21201
(410) 685-9800

Boston Red Sox
4 Yawkey Way
Fenway Park
Boston, MA 02215
(617) 267-9440

Chicago Cubs
Wrigley Field
1060 West Addison
Chicago, IL 60613
(773) 404-2827

Chicago White Sox
Comiskey Park
333 West 35th Street
Chicago, IL 60616
(312) 674-1000

Cincinnati Reds
100 Main Street
Cincinnati, OH 45202
(513) 765-7000

Cleveland Indians
Jacobs Field
2401 Ontario Street
Cleveland, OH 44115-4003
(216) 420-4200

Colorado Rockies
2001 Blake Street
Denver, CO 80205
(303) 292-0200

Detroit Tigers
Comerica Park
2100 Woodward Avenue
Detroit, MI 48201
(313) 962-4000

Florida Marlins
2267 Dan Marino Boulevard
Miami, FL 33056
(305) 626-7400

Houston Astros
P.O. Box 288
Houston, TX 77001
(713) 259-8000

Kansas City Royals
1 Royal Way
Kansas City, MO 64141
(816) 921-8000

Los Angeles Dodgers
1000 Elysian Park Avenue
Los Angeles, CA 90012-1199
(323) 224-1500

Milwaukee Brewers
One Brewers Way
Milwaukee, WI 53214
(414) 902-4400

Minnesota Twins
34 Kirby Puckett Place
Minneapolis, MN 55415
(612) 375-1366

Montreal Expos
P.O Box 500 Station M
Montreal, Quebec H1V 3P2
Canada
(514) 253-3434

New York Mets
Shea Stadium
123-01 Roosevelt Avenue
Flushing, NY 11368
(718) 507-6387

New York Yankees
Yankee Stadium
Bronx, NY 10451
(718) 293-4300

Oakland Athletics
7000 Coliseum Way
Oakland, CA 94621
(510) 638-4900

Philadelphia Phillies
P.O. Box 7575
Philadelphia, PA 19101-7575
(215) 463-6000

Pittsburgh Pirates
115 Federal Street
Pittsburgh, PA 15212
(412) 323-5000

San Diego Padres
P.O. Box 122000
San Diego, CA 92112
(619) 283-4494

San Francisco Giants
24 Willie Mays Plaza
San Francisco, CA 94107
(415) 972-2000

Seattle Mariners
P.O. Box 4100
Seattle, WA 98104
(206) 346-4000

St. Louis Cardinals
Busch Stadium
250 Stadium Plaza
St. Louis, MO 63102
(314) 421-3060

Tampa Bay Devil Rays
One Tropicana Drive
St. Petersburg, FL 33705
(727) 825-3137

Texas Rangers
1000 Ballpark Way, #400
Arlington, TX 76011
(817) 273-5222

Toronto Blue Jays
SkyDome
1 Blue Jays Way, Suite 3200
Toronto, Ontario M5V 1J1
Canada
(416) 341-1000

PRO FOOTBALL

National Football League
280 Park Avenue
New York, NY 10017
(212) 450-2000

Arizona Cardinals
P.O. Box 888
Phoenix, AZ 85001
(602) 379-0101

Atlanta Falcons
4400 Falcon Parkway
Flowery Branch, GA 30542
(770) 965-3115

Baltimore Ravens
11001 Owings Mills Blvd.
Owings Mills, MD 21117
(410) 654-6200

Buffalo Bills
One Bills Drive
Orchard Park, NY 14127
(716) 648-1800

Carolina Panthers
Ericsson Stadium
800 South Mint Street
Charlotte, NC 28202
(704) 358-7000

Chicago Bears
1000 Football Drive
Lake Forest, IL 60045
(847) 295-6600

Cincinnati Bengals
One Paul Brown Stadium
Cincinnati, OH 45202
(513) 621-3550

Cleveland Browns
76 Lou Groza Boulevard
Berea, OH 44017
(440) 891-5000

Dallas Cowboys
One Cowboys Parkway
Irving, TX 75063
(972) 556-9900

Denver Broncos
13655 Broncos Parkway
Englewood, CO 80112
(303) 649-9000

Detroit Lions
222 Republic Drive
Allen Park, MI 48101
(313) 216-4000

Green Bay Packers
1265 Lombardi Avenue
Green Bay, WI 54304
(920) 496-5700

Houston Texans
Two Reliant Park
Houston, TX 77054
(832) 667-2000

Indianapolis Colts
P.O. Box 535000
Indianapolis, IN 46253
(317) 297-2658

Jacksonville Jaguars
One Alltel Stadium Place
Jacksonville, FL 32202
(904) 633-6000

Kansas City Chiefs
One Arrowhead Drive
Kansas City, MO 64129
(816) 920-9300

Miami Dolphins
7500 S.W. 30th Street
Davie, FL 33314
(954) 452-7000

Minnesota Vikings
9520 Viking Drive
Eden Prairie, MN 55344
(952) 828-6500

New England Patriots
Gillette Stadium
1 Patriot Place
Foxboro, MA 02035
(508) 543-8200

New Orleans Saints
5800 Airline Highway
Metairie, LA 70003
(504) 733-0255

New York Giants
Giants Stadium
East Rutherford, NJ 07073
(201) 935-8111

New York Jets
1000 Fulton Avenue
Hempstead, NY 11550
(516) 560-8100

Oakland Raiders
1220 Harbor Bay Parkway
Alameda, CA 94502
(510) 864-5000

Philadelphia Eagles
NovaCare Complex
One NovaCare Way
Philadelphia, PA 19145
(215) 463-2500

Pittsburgh Steelers
3400 South Water Street
Pittsburgh, PA 15203
(412) 432-7800

San Diego Chargers
Qualcomm Stadium
4020 Murphy Canyon Road
San Diego, CA 92123
(858) 874-4500

San Francisco 49ers
4949 Centennial Boulevard
Santa Clara, CA 95054
(408) 562-4949

Seattle Seahawks
11220 N.E. 53rd Street
Kirkland, WA 98033
(425) 827-9777

St. Louis Rams
One Rams Way
St. Louis, MO 63045
(314) 982-7267

Tampa Bay Buccaneers
One Buccaneer Place
Tampa, FL 33607
(813) 870-2700

Tennessee Titans
460 Great Circle Road
Nashville, TN 37228
(615) 565-4000

Washington Redskins
21300 Redskins Park Drive
Ashburn, VA 20147
(703) 726-7000

OTHER LEAGUES

Canadian Football League
50 Wellington Street East
3rd floor
Toronto, Ontario M5E1C8
Canada
(416) 322-9650

NFL Europe
280 Park Avenue
New York, NY 10017
(212) 450-2000

PRO BASKETBALL

National Basketball Association
645 Fifth Avenue
New York, NY 10022
(212) 826-7000

Atlanta Hawks
One CNN Center
Atlanta, GA 30303
(404) 827-3800

Boston Celtics
151 Merrimac Street
Boston, MA 02114
(617) 523-6050

Chicago Bulls
1901 W. Madison Street
Chicago, IL 60612
(312) 455-4000

Cleveland Cavaliers
One Center Court
Cleveland, OH 44115
(216) 420-2000

Dallas Mavericks
2500 Victory Avenue
Dallas, TX 75219
(214) 665-4660

Denver Nuggets
Pepsi Center
1000 Chopper Circle
Denver, CO 80204
(303) 405-1100

Detroit Pistons
The Palace of Auburn Hills
Two Championship Drive
Auburn Hills, MI 48326
(248) 377-0100

Golden State Warriors
1011 Broadway
Oakland, CA 94607-4019
(510) 986-2200

Houston Rockets
Two Greenway Plaza
Suite 400
Houston, TX 77046
(713) 627-3865

Indiana Pacers
125 S. Pennsylvania Street
Indianapolis, IN 46204
(317) 917-2500

Los Angeles Clippers
STAPLES Center
1111 S. Figueroa Street
Suite 1100
Los Angeles, CA 90015
(213) 742-7500

Los Angeles Lakers
555 North Nash Street
El Segundo, CA 90245
(310) 426-6000

Memphis Grizzlies
175 Toyota Plaza
Suite 150
Memphis, TN 38103
(901) 888-4667

Miami Heat
AmericanAirlines Arena
601 Biscayne Boulevard
Miami, FL 33132
(786) 777-4328

Milwaukee Bucks
Bradley Center
1001 N. Fourth Street
Milwaukee, WI 53203
(414) 227-0500

Minnesota Timberwolves
600 First Avenue North
Minneapolis, MN 55403
(612) 673-1600

New Jersey Nets
390 Murray Hill Parkway
East Rutherford, NJ 07073
(201) 935-8888

New Orleans Hornets
1501 Girod Street
New Orleans, LA 70113
(504) 301-4000

New York Knicks
Madison Square Garden
Two Pennsylvania Plaza
New York, NY 10121
(212) 465-5867

Orlando Magic
8701 Maitland Summit Blvd.
Orlando, FL 32810
(407) 916-2400

Philadelphia 76ers
First Union Center
3601 South Broad Street
Philadelphia, PA 19148
(215) 339-7600

Phoenix Suns
201 East Jefferson Street
Phoenix, AZ 85004
(602) 379-7900

Portland Trail Blazers
One Center Court
Suite 200
Portland, OR 97227
(503) 234-9291

Sacramento Kings
One Sports Parkway
Sacramento, CA 95834
(916) 928-0000

San Antonio Spurs
One SBC Center
San Antonio, TX 78203
(210) 554-7787

Seattle SuperSonics
351 Elliott Avenue West
Suite 500
Seattle, WA 98119
(206) 281-5847

Toronto Raptors
40 Bay Street, Suite 400
Toronto, Ontario M5J 2X2
Canada
(416) 815-5600

Utah Jazz
301 West South Temple
Salt Lake City, UT 84101
(801) 325-2500

Washington Wizards
601 F Street, NW
Washington, D.C. 20004
(202) 661-5000

WNBA
645 Fifth Avenue
New York, NY 10022
(212) 688-9622

Charlotte Sting
100 Hive Drive
Charlotte, NC 29217
(704) 357-0252

Cleveland Rockers
Gund Arena
One Center Court
Cleveland, OH 44115
(216) 420-2000

Connecticut Sun
1 Mohegan Sun Boulevard
Uncasville, CT 06382
(888) 226-7711

Detroit Shock
Two Championship Drive
Auburn Hills, MI 48326
(248) 377-0100

Houston Comets
Two Greenway Plaza
Suite 400
Houston, TX 77046-3865
(713) 627-9622

Indiana Fever
125 S. Pennsylvania Street
Indianapolis, IN 46204
(317) 917-2500

Los Angeles Sparks
555 North Nash Street
El Segundo, CA 90245
(310) 330-2434

Minnesota Lynx
Target Center
600 First Avenue North
Minneapolis, MN 55403
(612) 673-8400

New York Liberty
Two Pennsylvania Plaza
New York, NY 10121
(212) 564-WNBA

Phoenix Mercury
201 East Jefferson Street
Phoenix, AZ 85004
(602) 514-8333

Sacramento Monarchs
One Sports Parkway
Sacramento, CA 95834
(916) 455-4647

San Antonio Silver Stars
One SBC Center
San Antonio, TX 78219
(210) 444-5697

Seattle Storm
351 Elliott Avenue West
Suite 500
Seattle, WA 98119
(206) 281-5800

Washington Mystics
MCI Center
601 F Street, NW
Washington, D.C. 20004
(202) 661-5000

National Hockey League
1251 Avenue of the Americas
47th Floor
New York, NY 10020-1198
(212) 789-2000

Mighty Ducks of Anaheim
Arrowhead Pond of Anaheim
2695 Katella Avenue
Anaheim, CA 92806
(714) 940-2900

Atlanta Thrashers
One CNN Center
Atlanta, GA 30303
(404) 827-5300

Boston Bruins
One FleetCenter Place
Suite 250
Boston, MA 02114-1303
(617) 624-1900

Buffalo Sabres
HSBC Arena
One Seymour H. Knox III
Plaza
Buffalo, NY 14203
(716) 855-4100

Calgary Flames
Pengrowth Saddledome
P.O. Box 1540
Station M
Calgary, Alberta T2P 3B9
Canada
(403) 777-2177

Carolina Hurricanes
1400 Edwards Mill Road
Raleigh, NC 27607
(919) 467-7825

Chicago Blackhawks
United Center
1901 W. Madison Street
Chicago, IL 60612
(312) 455-7000

Colorado Avalanche
Pepsi Center
1000 Chopper Circle
Denver, CO 80204
(303) 405-1100

Columbus Blue Jackets
200 West Nationwide
Boulevard
Columbus, OH 43215
(614) 246-4625

Dallas Stars
211 Cowboys Parkway
Irving, TX 75063
(972) 831-2401

Detroit Red Wings
Joe Louis Arena
600 Civic Center Drive
Detroit, MI 48226
(313) 396-7444

Edmonton Oilers
11230 110th Street
Edmonton, Alberta T5G 3H7
Canada
(780) 414-4000

Florida Panthers
One Panther Parkway
Sunrise, FL 33323
(954) 835-7000

SPORTS DIRECTORY

Los Angeles Kings
STAPLES Center
1111 South Figueroa Street
Los Angeles, CA 90015
(213) 742-7100

Minnesota Wild
317 Washington Street
St. Paul, MN 55102
(651) 602-6000

Montreal Canadiens
Bell Centre
1260 de la Gauchetiere West
Montreal, Quebec H3B 5E8
Canada
(514) 932-2582

Nashville Predators
Gaylord Entertainment Center
501 Broadway
Nashville, TN 37203
(615) 770-2300

New Jersey Devils
Continental Airlines Arena
P.O. Box 504
East Rutherford, NJ 07073
(201) 935-6050

New York Islanders
1535 Old Country Road
Plainview, NY 11803
(516) 501-6700

New York Rangers
Madison Square Garden
Two Pennsylvania Plaza
New York, NY 10121
(212) 465-6000

Ottawa Senators
Corel Centre
1000 Palladium Drive
Ottawa, Ontario K2V 1A5
Canada
(613) 599-0250

Philadelphia Flyers
First Union Center
3601 South Broad Street
Philadelphia, PA 19148
(215) 465-4500

Phoenix Coyotes
ALLTEL Ice Den
9375 East Bell Road
Scottsdale, AZ 85260
(480) 473-5600

Pittsburgh Penguins
Mellon Arena
66 Mario Lemieux Place
Pittsburgh, PA 15219
(412) 642-1300

San Jose Sharks
HP Pavilion at San Jose
525 West Santa Clara Street
San Jose, CA 95113
(408) 287-7070

St. Louis Blues
Savvis Center
1401 Clark Avenue
St. Louis, MO 63103
(314) 622-2500

Tampa Bay Lightning
401 Channelside Drive
Tampa, FL 33602
(813) 301-6600

Toronto Maple Leafs
Air Canada Centre
40 Bay Street, Suite 400
Toronto, Ontario M5J 2X2
Canada
(416) 815-5500

Vancouver Canucks
General Motors Place
800 Griffiths Way
Vancouver, British Columbia
V6B 6G1
(604) 899-4600

Washington Capitals
401 Ninth Street, NW
Suite 750
Washington, D.C. 20004
(202) 266-2200

COLLEGE SPORTS

National Collegiate Athletic Association (NCAA)
700 W. Washington Street
P.O. Box 6222
Indianapolis, IN 46206-6222
(317) 917-6222

Atlantic Coast Conference
P.O. Drawer ACC
Greensboro, NC 27417-6724
(336) 854-8787

Big East Conference
222 Richmond Street
Suite 110
Providence, RI 02903
(401) 272-9108

Big Ten Conference
1500 West Higgins Road
Park Ridge, IL 60068-6300
(847) 696-1010

Big 12 Conference
2201 Stemmons Freeway
28th Floor
Dallas, TX 75207
(214) 742-1212

Big West Conference
2 Corporate Park
Irvine, CA 92606
(949) 261-2525

Conference USA
35 East Wacker Drive
Suite 650
Chicago, IL 60601
(312) 553-0483

Ivy League
330 Alexander Street
Princeton, NJ 08544
(609) 258-6426

Mid-American Conference
24 Public Square, 15th floor
Cleveland, OH 44113
(216) 566-4622

Pacific-10 Conference
800 S. Broadway, Suite 400
Walnut Creek, CA 94596
(925) 932-4411

Southeastern Conference
2201 Richard Arrington Blvd.
North
Birmingham, AL 35203
(205) 458-3000

Western Athletic Conference
9250 East Costilla Avenue
Suite 300
Englewood, CO 80112
(303) 799-9221

MISCELLANEOUS SPORTS

Association of Tennis Professionals Tour (ATP)
201 ATP Tour Boulevard
Ponte Vedra Beach, FL 32082
(904) 285-8000

Championship Auto Racing Teams (CART)
5350 Lakeview Parkway
South Drive
Building 36
Inner Park/Park 100
Indianapolis, IN 46268
(317) 715-4100

Indy Racing League
4565 West 16th Street
Indianapolis, IN 46222
(317) 484-6526

Ladies Professional Golf Association (LPGA)
100 International Golf Drive
Daytona Beach, FL 32124
(386) 274-6200

Major League Soccer
110 East 42nd Street
Suite 1000
New York, NY 10017
(212) 687-1400

National Association for Stock Car Auto Racing (NASCAR)
1801 W. International Speedway Blvd.
Daytona Beach, FL 32114-1243
(386) 253-0611

PGA Tour
112 PGA Tour Boulevard
Ponte Vedra Beach, FL 32082
(904) 285-3700

United Soccer Leagues
14497 North Dale Mabry Highway
Suite 201
Tampa, FL 33618
(813) 963-3909

United States Olympic Committee
Olympic House
1 Olympic Plaza
Colorado Springs, CO 80909
(719) 632-5551

USA Basketball
5465 Mark Dabling Blvd.
Colorado Springs, CO 80918
(719) 590-4800

USA Cycling
1 Olympic Plaza
Colorado Springs, CO 80909
(719) 866-4581

USA Hockey
1775 Bob Johnson Drive
Colorado Springs, CO 80906
(719) 576-8724

USA Track & Field
1 RCA Dome, Suite 140
Indianapolis, IN 46225
(317) 261-0500

U.S. Bobsled and Skeleton Federation
P.O. Box 828
Lake Placid, NY 12946
(518) 523-1842

U.S. Figure Skating Association
20 First Street
Colorado Springs, CO 80906
(719) 635-5200

U.S. Luge Association
35 Church Street
Lake Placid, NY 12946
(518) 523-2071

U.S. Ski and Snowboard Association
P.O. Box 100
Park City, UT 84060
(435) 649-9090

U.S. Soccer Federation
1801-1811 South Prairie Avenue
Chicago, IL 60616
(312) 808-1300

U.S. Speed Skating
P.O. Box 450639
Westlake, OH 44145
(440) 899-0128

U.S. Swimming, Inc.
1 Olympic Plaza
Colorado Springs, CO 80909
(719) 866-4578

Women's United Soccer Association
6205 Peachtree Dunwoody Road
Atlanta, GA 30328
(678) 645-0800

WTA Tour (Women's Tennis)
133 First Street, N.E.
St. Petersburg, FL 33701
(727) 895-5000

A special Scholastic offer just for you!

Get **2 Free** preview issues of

And receive a **great discount** on the regular subscription rate

Sports Illustrated For Kids keeps children entertained, gets them reading, and explores many exciting sports and their stars. Edited for children ages 8 & up, the magazine features stories on professional athletes, as well as outstanding kid athletes. Each issue also contains sports tips, video game reviews, posters, sports cards and puzzles.

Sign up today to get 2 Free trial issues of the #1 sports magazine for kids ages 8 & up without being billed a penny! After receiving the 2 Free trial issues you'll get 11 additional issues or 13 issues at just $19.95—**that's a savings of 28%** off the cover price.

If you're not 100% satisfied with *Sports Illustrated For Kids*, you may cancel anytime within 90 days of placing your order, and you will receive a full refund. Allow 4-6 weeks for delivery. *Sports Illustrated For Kids* is published monthly, except for 2 issues combined periodically into one and occasional extra, expanded, or premium issues.

To receive your **2 FREE issues** and the **$19.95** discounted rate on the regular subscription, complete this entry form and send to: *Sports Illustrated For Kids* Scholastic Discount Offer PO Box 60001, Tampa, FL 33660-0001. Offer ends 6/1/04.

Please send me 2 FREE trial issues and sign me up for the discounted subscription rate of $19.95* for the *Sports Illustrated For Kids* Scholastic Discount Offer.

*Price is $39.95 plus GST & QST in Canada.

SKAT7L4

First Name (Please Print):_____

Last Name (Please Print):_____

Address:_____

City:_____ **State:**_____ **Zip:**_____

Home Phone:_____

◪◪ S C H O L A S T I C

SIYS